CONVERSION FACTORS

To change:	Into:	Multiply by:
inches	millimetres	25.4
inches	centimetres	2.54
feet	metres	0.305
yards	metres	0.914
square inches	square centimetres	6.45
square feet	square metres	0.093
square yards	square metres	0.836
cubic inches	cubic centimetres	16.4
cubic feet	cubic metres	0.028
cubic yards	cubic metres	0.765
pints (imperial)	litres	0.568
quarts (imperial)	litres	1.136
gallons (imperial)	litres	4.546
gallons (U.S.)	litres	3.79
ounces	grams	28.35
pounds	kilograms	0.454

LIQUIDS

$1/4$ cup	60 ml
$1/3$ cup	80 ml
$1/2$ cup	125 ml
$2/3$ cup	160 ml
$3/4$ cup	180 ml
1 cup	250 ml
$1 1/2$ cups	375 ml
2 cups	500 ml
3 cups	750 ml
4 cups	1 litre

SPOON MEASURES

$1/4$ tsp	1.25 ml
$1/2$ tsp	2.5 ml
1 tsp	5 ml
1 tbsp	15 ml
2 tbsp	30 ml

LUMBER WIDTHS AND THICKNESSES

Lumber is ordered by thickness, width, and length. When you order in imperial measurements (2 inches x 4 inches x 8 feet, for example), the thickness and width figures (in this instance 2 x 4) refer to nominal size—the dimensions of the piece as it left the saw. But what you get is the smaller, actual size remaining when the piece has been planed smooth; in actual fact, a piece $1 1/2$ inches x $3 1/2$ inches x 8 feet. (Length is not reduced by the processing.)

Metric measurements on the other hand always describe the actual dimensions of the processed piece.

Imperial (in.) nominal size (actual size)		Metric (mm) actual size
2 x 2	($1 1/2$ x $1 1/2$)	38 x 38
2 x 4	($1 1/2$ x $3 1/2$)	38 x 89
2 x 6	($1 1/2$ x $5 1/2$)	38 x 140
2 x 8	($1 1/2$ x $7 1/4$)	38 x 184
2 x 10	($1 1/2$ x $9 1/4$)	38 x 235
4 x 4	($3 1/2$ x $3 1/2$)	89 x 89
4 x 6	($3 1/2$ x $5 1/2$)	89 x 140

TEMPERATURES

To change from degrees Fahrenheit to degrees Celsius, subtract 32, then multiply by $5/9$.

FASTENERS

Nails are sold by penny size or penny weight (expressed by the letter d). Length is designated by the penny size. Some common lengths are:

2d (25 mm / 1 in.)	20d (102 mm / 4 in.)
6d (51 mm / 2 in.)	40d (127 mm / 5 in.)
10d (76 mm / 3 in.)	60d (152 mm / 6 in.)

Below are metric and imperial equivalents of some common bolts:

10 mm	$3/8$ in.	25 mm	1 in.
12 mm	$1/2$ in.	50 mm	2 in.
16 mm	$5/8$ in.	65 mm	$2 1/2$ in.
20 mm	$3/4$ in.	70 mm	$2 3/4$ in.

HOUSEHOLDER'S SURVIVAL MANUAL

HOUSEHOLDER'S SURVIVAL MANUAL

Reader's Digest

The Reader's Digest Association, Inc., Pleasantville, New York/Montreal

The acknowledgments that appear on page 384 are hereby made a part of this copyright page.

Copyright © 1999 The Reader's Digest Association, Inc.
Copyright © 1999 The Reader's Digest Association (Canada) Ltd.
Copyright © 1999 Reader's Digest Association Far East Ltd.
Philippine Copyright 1999 Reader's Digest Association Far East Ltd.

Canadian Cataloguing in Publication Data

Main entry under title:
    Householder's Survival Manual

Includes index.
ISBN 0-88850-675-9
    1. Dwellings—Maintenance and repair. 2. Housekeeping.

TH4817.H66 1999   640   C99–900035-7

Reader's Digest and the Pegasus logo are registered trademarks of The Reader's Digest Association, Inc.

Printed in the United States of America
99 00 01 / 5 4 3 2 1

Address any comments about HOUSEHOLDER'S SURVIVAL MANUAL to Editor, Books and Home Entertainment, c/o Customer Service, Reader's Digest, 1125 Stanley Street, Montreal, Quebec H3B 5H5.

For information on this and other Reader's Digest products or to request a catalogue, please call our 24-hour Customer Service hotline at 1-800-465-0780.

You can also visit us on the World Wide Web at **http://www.readersdigest.ca**

Householder's Survival Manual

Canadian Staff

Senior Editor
Andrew R. Byers

Designer
Andrée Payette

Associate Editor
Anita Winterberg

Copy Editor
Gilles Humbert

Production Manager
Holger Lorenzen

Production Coordinator
Susan Wong

Books and Home Entertainment

Vice President
Deirdre Gilbert

Managing Editor
Philomena Rutherford

Art Director
John McGuffie

U.S. Staff

Senior Editor
Nancy Shuker

Designer
Eleanor Kostyk

Associate Editor
Linda Ingroia

Associate Designers
Bruce R. McKillip
Wendy Wong

Administrative Assistant
Andrea Stein

Contributing Editors
Linda Hetzer
Zuelia Ann Hurt
Wendy Murphy

Photographer
David Hautzig

Production artist
William McGuire

Special Thanks
Carolyn T. Chubet
Don Earnest

Acknowledgments
Perri DeFino
Lee Fowler
Nancy Mace
Audrey Peterson
David Schiff
Joe Hurst-Wajszczuk

Contributors

Project Manager
David W. Toht

Editors
Steve Cory
Sarah Hoban
Liz Poppens

Editorial Art Director
Jean DeVaty

Designers
Melanie Lawson
Brad Cathey

Photographer
Dan Stultz

Editorial Assistants
Rebecca JonMichaels
Betony Toht

Photography Assistants
Susan Craig
Joseph DeVaty
Jeanine Jankovsky
Sue McCracken

Illustrators
Kirsten Soderlind
Steve Fuller

Writers
Jeff Beneke
Linda Eggerss
Veronica Lorson Fowler
Ann Hinga Klein
Heather J. Paper
Steve Slack
Liz Seymour

Copy Editors
Sue Reck
Barbara Webb
Lori Davis
Linda Washington

Indexer
Felice Levy

U.S. Consultants
Don Dybowski
Gordon Ehorn
Cliff Hughes
Denise Key
Gary McClure
Dave Wallace
John Dunlevy

Canadian Consultants
Trevor Cole
Jon Eakes
Robert A. Nelson

Canadian Researcher
Martha Plaine

Special Thanks
Dorothy DeVaty
Beth Edgar
Debbie Gehman
Joe Hansa
Robert Klausmeier
Christine Opitz

ABOUT THIS BOOK

A home should be a haven, where you and your family feel comfortable and at ease, able to relax and pursue hobbies and favorite pastimes in pleasant surroundings. Running such a household takes some doing, but it needn't be onerous. And that is what *Householder's Survival Manual* is all about. Here, you can find answers to all the vexing questions that come up—from how to keep your prized wood floors shining to checking on the boiler before the first cold day of autumn.

Products and care instructions change; we have tried to alert you to improvements that will make your life easier. New stain-resistant fibers, for example, makes it possible for you to use lighter, brighter carpeting colors in living areas than ever before. Modern wrinkle-free fabrics redefine how you use the dryer, but lessen your weekly ironing. Sewing on a button hasn't changed, but fusion tape may put an end to the sewing of hems.

No household keeps going without glitches. Toilets get clogged up, basements spring leaks, and circuit breakers get tripped. That's another area where this book can be useful; it tells you when you can safely solve a problem yourself and how to do it. It also tells you when a repair needs the expertise or special equipment that only a professional can supply.

—The Editors

Contents

1

Floors

Walls

Windows

Doors

FLOORS AND FLOORING

Beautiful floors are literally the foundation of any home decorating scheme. Installing new floors is satisfying but expensive; often, with a small investment and a little elbow grease, you can give renewed life to old floors.

The choices available in home flooring today are wide and wonderful. They range from a sizable selection of wood-planked flooring and various parquet inlays to resilient flooring, various kinds of tile, and carpeting. But a word to the wise: Before you decide on a total makeover, take a second look at what you already have. Sometimes under several layers of resilient flooring or carpeting, there's buried treasure in the form of hardwood floors. By cleaning, refinishing, and patching these tired and neglected surfaces (see pages 25–28), you can often accomplish small miracles.

WOOD FLOORING

Of all the flooring surfaces, wood remains a favorite, as it has been for centuries. Prized for its beauty, resilience, and warmth of color, wood is often regarded as a high-maintenance choice, particularly high-gloss hardwoods. But attitudes are changing as new finishes have been developed to make wood a more care-free option.

Today's wood flooring is available in a number of sizes and makeups, each offering unique advantages. Most often, the flooring is produced from the

class of dense-grained woods known as hardwood (above). Among the family of hardwoods, oak is the most commonly selected species because it is widely available, very receptive to staining, and extremely durable. If well cared for, it will last over many lifetimes. Other, less commonly used, hardwoods for flooring include maple, walnut, beech, birch, aspen, and ash. Softwoods, as the name implies, present a floor surface that is more readily scarred and dented than hardwoods. Of the softwoods, pine (facing page) is the primary choice for flooring.

Grading and type

Every type of wood is graded and priced according to industry-wide standards. Oak and ash have four grades. The highest—"Clear"—indicates wood with uniform grain patterns and no blemishes to mar a formal floor. The higher the grade, the more variation and depth of color. Following in descending order of quality and color are "Select," "No. 1 common," and "No. 2 common." The last, with many irregularities, is still handsome in a rustic setting, if finished well. Hard maple, beech, and birch, are sold in just three grades: "First," "Second," and "Third."

Each type of wood flooring comes in a set of standard dimensions and is laid in a different manner. Because flooring is a major investment, manufacturers recommend that a newly laid floor be professionally sanded and finished.

◆ **Solid-wood flooring** is produced in strips, planks, and parquet, and in unfinished and prefinished versions. The strips are milled in thicknesses of ⅜- to ¾-inch and in widths from 1¼ up to 3¼ inches; the planks, in similar thicknesses and widths of 3 to 7 inches.

◆ **Laminated-wood flooring** (above right) is produced by bonding a thin hardwood veneer over rigid plywood. It is less costly than hardwood flooring, and it has the advantage of being more

stable dimensionally in high-humidity installations, such as below-grade basement rooms, because of its engineered construction. Another plus is the fact that it can be installed (floated) over a foam underlayment without nailing. Or it can be glued down to a concrete slab. Due to the thinness of the veneer, however, laminated wood flooring has a short life span, and does not lend itself to repeated sanding and refinishing. Like solid-wood flooring, it comes both unfinished and factory-finished and in several grades and sizes.

◆ **Acrylic-impregnated wood flooring** is a relatively new wood flooring product. Prefinished in the factory, acrylic and color are driven deep into the grain under high pressure, creating an extremely hard finish that is highly resistant to abrasion and moisture.

◆ **Parquet is a specialty product** favored for somewhat more formal floors. Once an extravagance of the very rich, it involves dozens if not hundreds of small wood slats or tiles, often of many-hued dark and light tones.

In earlier times, the intricate geometric patterns of parquet had to be pain-

stakingly cut and installed by skilled specialists. Today, similar patterns can be found in factory-cut and prefinished versions. Use them to cover an entire floor or to create a decorative border around an otherwise plain hardwood floor. While the more elaborate and expensive parquets should be installed by a professional, do-it-yourselfers can lay, tile-fashion, the less expensive (and less durable) adhesive-backed squares. Precut and prefinished blocks, sometimes referred to as "finger" parquet (above), are another option.

RESILIENT FLOORING
This type of flooring is so named because it is made from flexible synthetic materials. It is manufactured in rolled sheets as well as in several tile sizes. Resilient flooring is relatively inexpensive and easy to maintain.

Vinyl, the most commonly-used material, has the virtue of being resistant to scuffs, scratches, and water. These features also make it a good choice for large spaces and high-traffic areas such as hallways, kitchens, and bathrooms. Many resilient floorings come with a semi-gloss no-wax finish.

Sheet vinyl

Sheet vinyl comes in 6-foot and 12-foot widths, making it awkward to handle and to lay. Even a small error in cutting, preparing the subfloor, applying adhesive, or aligning edges can ruin a whole sheet of flooring. It is generally advisable to hire a professional to install it. Sheet vinyl comes in two grades:

◆ **Inlaid vinyl** (above) consists of layers of colored vinyl granules that are fused under heat and pressure; it is considered tops in durability and price. The patterns go all the way through to the back, so nicks and gouges from normal use are rarely noticeable. The one disadvantage of inlaid sheet vinyl is that it comes in only the 6-foot width, requiring one or more seams for most installations.

◆ **Printed vinyl,** or rotovinyl, is less expensive than inlaid vinyl, in part because the pattern is printed on the surface only. Factory-applied clear vinyl or polyurethane is added to protect the surface, with the thickness of the coating affecting the sturdiness and price of the sheeting. Nonetheless, printed vinyl is bound to show wear and tear sooner, and nicks will be more prominent than on inlaid vinyl. On the positive side, this category of resilient flooring comes in widths up to 12 feet, making seamless installation possible in most rooms. Pattern choices are also extensive. Using a photography-and-print process, manufacturers can mimic other materials, such as marble and tile.

Vinyl tiles

For do-it-yourself projects, vinyl tiles are a particularly good choice. They are commonly available in 9- and 12-inch squares. And because they are tiles, you can mix two or more colors to create custom borders and patterns. Many tiles have peel-and-stick adhesive backing. If the underfloor is clean and smooth, you can lay tiles directly on it. Always buy extras as replacements for tiles that become damaged later. Tiles come in the same grades and with many of the advantages and disadvantages as sheet vinyl.

◆ **Inlaid tiles** are the most durable and expensive offerings in this group. Like inlaid sheets, they are colored through.

◆ **Printed vinyl** is less expensive and less durable, but with a wide range of photographic colors and patterns.

◆ **Composition tiles** are a mixture of vinyl and other materials, making them the least expensive of vinyl tiles.

LAMINATE FLOORING

The same technology used to produce laminate countertop material is also used for flooring. The surface, which can be made to resemble almost any

kind of natural material—from marble to wood to verdigris copper (above)—is bonded to a fiberboard core. It installs with tongue-and-groove fit to "float" on the subfloor. Generally easy to care for, it will eventually show abrasion marks if grit is allowed to grind in.

BRICK, CERAMIC, AND QUARRY TILES

These semi- and nonporous materials offer a wide range of colors, textures, and patterns. They can last indefinitely, but their weight demands appropriate subflooring and installation.

Brick

In addition to being a durable, nonslip, waterproof material, brick (below) has interesting color and texture. Glazed

brick is as easy to maintain as tile. Unglazed brick can be enhanced with a sealer, but it needs an occasional waxing. In choosing brick, or any other nonresilient material, it's important to make sure that it is recommended for use on floors. If you're adding a brick floor, unless you use half-brick tiles, it is very likely your subfloor will need to be reinforced.

Ceramic tile

Made of clay and fired at high temperature, ceramic tiles (above) may be made by hand or by machine, with glazed shiny, matte, or textured finishes, or an unglazed finish with reddish earth tones throughout. Ceramic tile sizes and thicknesses vary. Although squares are the most common shape offered, rectangles and hexagons are also available.

Tiles can be laid on any smooth and stable subfloor, using tile cement to hold them firmly, and colored grout as decorative space fillers between. Ceramic tile is tough, waterproof, and impervious to most household liquids, but it can be cold, hard, and noisy underfoot.

Quarry tile

This broad category of nonresilient flooring (above) includes marble, limestone, granite, sandstone, slate, and travertine. These materials are very durable and also beautiful, but they are typically very expensive to buy and require professional installation. Smooth-surfaced materials have a tendency to become dangerously slippery under wet feet. And the more porous varieties, like limestone and sandstone, will absorb stains unless sealed.

WALL-TO-WALL CARPETING

Soft and forgiving, wall-to-wall carpeting (below) has many virtues. Not only does it absorb sound, but it also creates visual warmth with its texture as well as real warmth with its insulative prop-

erties. In addition, carpeting can hide a multitude of flaws in the floor beneath. Carpeting can even be permanently installed directly on plywood subfloors. With the right fiber and weave, and with consistent maintenance, carpeting can last for decades.

Choosing carpet

Buy the best carpeting you can afford for the particular use. Have it installed by a professional who can estimate the amount required and suggest suitable padding. Keep these factors in mind.

◆ **Construction**—how the yarn is "tufted" or locked into its backing—determines to a large extent its texture and appearance. Tufting may be *level*, with uniform-height loops; *multilevel*, with two or more levels to create patterns; or *cut pile*, in which the tops of loops are sheared, leaving individual yarn tufts. Cut piles—including velvets, plushes, and textures—are the most popular constructions sold today.

◆ **Fiber content** describes the origin—natural or synthetic—of the carpet. Today, roughly 97 percent of all carpet produced uses synthetic fibers.

◆ **The "look"** of carpeting is further defined by color and pattern. Dark colors impart coziness. Light colors make rooms seem larger; with new stain- and soil-resistant finishes, they're more practical than they once were.

◆ **Performance** is a qualitative measure based on yarn density, twist, and the process by which the twist was "set," or finished. Density refers to closeness of the tufts: The denser the

SELECTING CARPET STYLE

Level-loop, textured, cut-and-loop, and plush (also known as saxony) are the predominant styles of carpeting. Any style can be used in high-traffic areas if the fiber is very durable (see below) and if the density (number of tufts per square inch) is high.

level-loop

textured

cut-and-loop

plush (saxony)

SELECTING CARPET FIBER

Fiber	Characteristics	Advantages/Disadvantages
Acrylic	Among man-made fibers, acrylics are the nearest in appearance and feel to wool, but at lesser cost. Commonly used in velvet and level-loop constructions.	Moderately durable, this synthetic resists water-soluble stains but not oily stains. It resists moisture and mildew and has a low static level. It is not very fire-resistant.
Cotton	Used in the foundation of some woven carpets, and occasionally in some cheaper pile carpets, cotton is definitely a low-end choice.	Known for its soft "hand," or feel, this natural fiber tends to soil easily and to compress.
Nylon	Considered to be the strongest carpet fiber, nylon represents more than 65 percent of the pile fibers currently used. It is available in a wide price range, reflecting the quality and density of the particular fiber.	Nylon is wear-resistant, resilient, and withstands heavy use. It resists water-soluble stains, mildew, and shedding. It needs static control. Generally good for all traffic areas.
Olefin	Made of polypropylene, this fiber is remarkably colorfast because color is integral to the fiber's manufacture.	Very durable, it resists soil, stains, moisture, and mildew, making it good indoor/outdoor carpeting. It also resists static electricity.
Polyester	Noted for its lustrous, luxurious "hand" in thick, cut pile, polyester fiber is relatively inexpensive.	Moderately durable, it has excellent color clarity and is resistant to water-soluble stains.
Wool	Soft, with high bulk, and available in many colors, it is used either alone or in mixtures, especially with nylon.	Somewhat more expensive than synthetics, wool is noted for its performance and fire resistance.

better. Twist describes how the yarn is wound around itself: The tighter the twist, the more resilience and durability. The yarn may be set by steam or heat-set; heat-set is more durable.

The importance of padding

All carpets, except those with a cushion backing attached, should be laid over a separate layer of padding. Padding reduces the matting and crushing that comes from furniture and foot traffic. It also prevents slippage and adds to the carpet's insulating and sound-absorption properties.

Carpet padding comes in a variety of densities, weights, and thicknesses. In high-traffic areas, choose a firmer grade. Never buy one more than $7/16$ inch thick: Padding that is too thick leaves the tufting unsupported. Below are the basic types of underlayment and their features.

◆ **Hair or felt padding** wears well and gives good support, but it may stretch and shed over time. It is susceptible to mildew in humid climates and may aggravate some allergies.

◆ **Rubberized felt padding** also wears well and gives good support, but it is less likely to stretch.

◆ **Sponge or foam-rubber padding** is made in flat or waffled sheets that are resilient and resistant to mildew. Foam rubber is nonallergenic.

◆ **Urethane foam padding** is made in a continuous, flat sheet. Strong and durable, it resists moisture. A good quality urethane foam pad will retain half its thickness when you squeeze it.

TOOLS FOR KEEPING FLOORS CLEAN

Having the right tools for the task not only produces better results faster, but it can also make the doing more enjoyable.

To keep your floors in tip-top condition, you need to know which cleaning regimen is best suited to your particular floor materials and finishes. Just as important is the regularity with which you do the job.

REGULAR MAINTENANCE

Depending on the amount of traffic that your floors receive, you may need to dust mop, sweep, or vacuum only once or twice a week, or as frequently as twice a day. Whatever the final tally, faithful upkeep will yield long-term benefits. Not only will you lengthen the time between time-consuming heavy cleanings, but you'll also extend the life of your flooring.

To dust or sweep?

With either vinyl or smooth-wood surfaces, a dust mop or a broom is the usual tool for everyday cleaning up of grit before it is ground into the floor. If the air is very dry, you can hold the dust down by giving the mop head or broom a light spritz of water.

Dust mops are typically more efficient in gathering lightweight "dust bunnies," pet fur, and lint. But they

are not appropriate for rough-finished floors or carpeting. When choosing a dust mop, keep in mind the size of your room and the amount of clutter on the floor. Standard-sized dust mops are best for working around average spaces with an ordinary amount of furniture. Consider using an 18-inch-wide commercial dust mop for oversized, sparsely furnished areas. You'll find the larger size at janitorial supply stores.

Brooms come in several designs and materials and are better for certain tasks than dry mops. The most common type of household broom is the

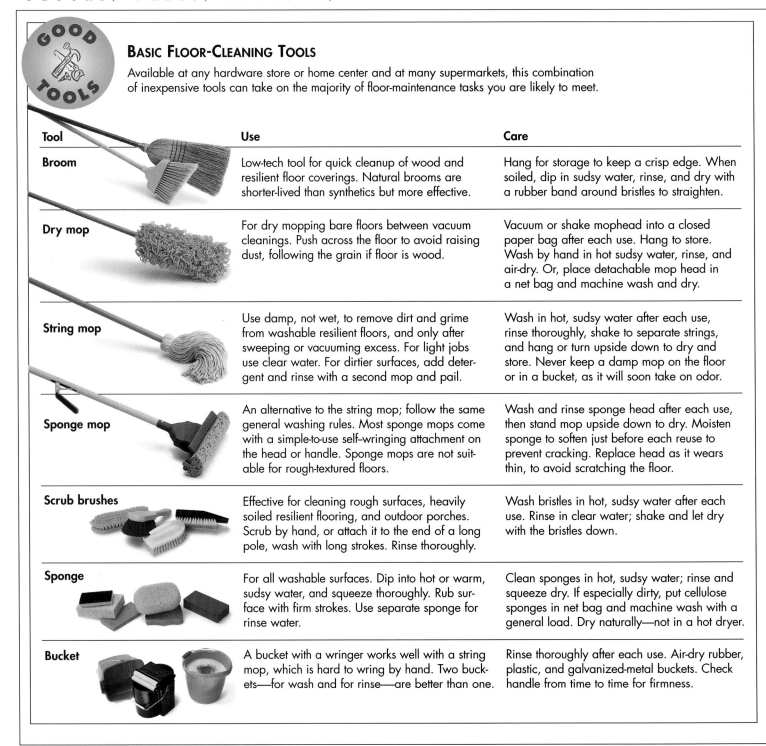

BASIC FLOOR-CLEANING TOOLS

Available at any hardware store or home center and at many supermarkets, this combination of inexpensive tools can take on the majority of floor-maintenance tasks you are likely to meet.

Tool	Use	Care
Broom	Low-tech tool for quick cleanup of wood and resilient floor coverings. Natural brooms are shorter-lived than synthetics but more effective.	Hang for storage to keep a crisp edge. When soiled, dip in sudsy water, rinse, and dry with a rubber band around bristles to straighten.
Dry mop	For dry mopping bare floors between vacuum cleanings. Push across the floor to avoid raising dust, following the grain if floor is wood.	Vacuum or shake mophead into a closed paper bag after each use. Hang to store. Wash by hand in hot sudsy water, rinse, and air-dry. Or, place detachable mop head in a net bag and machine wash and dry.
String mop	Use damp, not wet, to remove dirt and grime from washable resilient floors, and only after sweeping or vacuuming excess. For light jobs use clear water. For dirtier surfaces, add detergent and rinse with a second mop and pail.	Wash in hot, sudsy water after each use, rinse thoroughly, shake to separate strings, and hang or turn upside down to dry and store. Never keep a damp mop on the floor or in a bucket, as it will soon take on odor.
Sponge mop	An alternative to the string mop; follow the same general washing rules. Most sponge mops come with a simple-to-use self-wringing attachment on the head or handle. Sponge mops are not suitable for rough-textured floors.	Wash and rinse sponge head after each use, then stand mop upside down to dry. Moisten sponge to soften just before each reuse to prevent cracking. Replace head as it wears thin, to avoid scratching the floor.
Scrub brushes	Effective for cleaning rough surfaces, heavily soiled resilient flooring, and outdoor porches. Scrub by hand, or attach it to the end of a long pole, wash with long strokes. Rinse thoroughly.	Wash bristles in hot, sudsy water after each use. Rinse in clear water; shake and let dry with the bristles down.
Sponge	For all washable surfaces. Dip into hot or warm, sudsy water, and squeeze thoroughly. Rub surface with firm strokes. Use separate sponge for rinse water.	Clean sponges in hot, sudsy water; rinse and squeeze dry. If especially dirty, put cellulose sponges in net bag and machine wash with a general load. Dry naturally—not in a hot dryer.
Bucket	A bucket with a wringer works well with a string mop, which is hard to wring by hand. Two buckets—for wash and for rinse—are better than one.	Rinse thoroughly after each use. Air-dry rubber, plastic, and galvanized-metal buckets. Check handle from time to time for firmness.

natural-fiber broom. Made of broom-corn (sorghum), this straight-edged sweeper provides a pleasing stiffness to sweeping that traditionalists like. But you will also find more durable, softer polypropylene brooms for sweeping. They come in straight-edged designs as well as in angled designs.

Soft-bristled push brooms, as the name implies, are best for pushing dirt rather than brisk sweeping. Deck or garage brooms should stay outside; their harder bristles can damage indoor floors. Virtually all brooms must be used with a dustpan. Look for pans with a slim, soft leading edge. Plastic-edged pans can scratch floors and tend to chip with use.

Defensive moves

One way to reduce the cleaning needed in a house is to prevent dirt from entering the house in the first place. Carpet and rug manufacturers say that most dirt in the home is tracked in on shoes. Halt the influx by placing sturdy mats with non-slip backing just inside all exterior doors. Each should be long enough to accommodate four steps—about 3 to 5 feet. Also provide good exterior doormats for wiping off the heaviest street mud and dirt. The combination can save you an estimated 200 hours of cleaning time each year.

WASHING FLOORS

Most non-wood floors can be kept clean by damp-mopping with clear water. First sweep or vacuum the loose dirt. Then dip a string mop or sponge mop in clear water, squeezing it out so

MAKE A CORNER CLEANER

Corner dirt can be elusive. But an old whisk broom can be shaped into a custom tool that tackles corner dirt in a snap.

◆ **Starting just below** the stitching on one side of the whisk broom, run duct tape around the bristles at a 45-degree angle toward the opposite corner.

◆ **Using the tape as a guide,** cut the bristles with a utility knife and straightedge or a

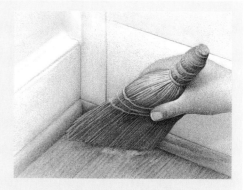

pair of heavy-duty scissors, making sure that the new angled bottom edge is even. Your new whisk broom can now reach into the deepest corners.

that the mop is merely damp. Excess water can damage resilient floors, penetrating the seams of vinyl sheet flooring or tiles, causing the edges to lift and/or curl up. Too much water is even more troublesome where wood floors are concerned, for it can dissolve the protective coatings, alter the color, and even raise the grain to roughen the surface. So always wring out your mop until it's almost dry.

Reserve a mop for rinsing

To thoroughly clean any floor, it's important to have two buckets—one for the washing solution and another for the rinse water. If having two buckets seems like too much equipment to store between washings, consider using a plastic wastebasket as the rinse bucket. Wash the wastebasket before and after using it as a bucket.

If you use two buckets, you should also work with two mops—one for

cleaning, one for rinsing. Not only will the two-mop approach result in a cleaner floor, but it will also save you time, because you won't have to stop to get the dirty water out with each pass of the mop.

VACUUM-CLEANER BASICS

From battery-powered crumb vacuums to wet/dry vacuums for the basement, it is difficult to know which vacuum—or vacuums—you really need.

Choosing a vacuum cleaner

There are two basic types of portable vacuum cleaners: upright and canister/tank. Uprights are designed primarily for deep cleaning carpets, and no other style does this job better. But uprights do a less-satisfactory job on uncarpeted floors and may scratch wood floors if used carelessly. Canister/tank vacuums, on the other hand, because of their attachments, are

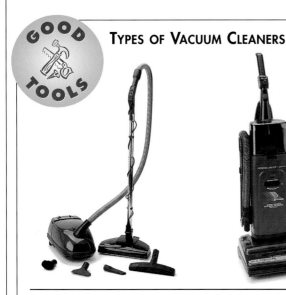

TYPES OF VACUUM CLEANERS

Canister/Tank

A motor-driven fan sucks air through the hose, creating an airstream that carries picked-up dirt to its destination in the bag. An excellent multipurpose tool for a mix of wood floors, rugs, and above-floor tasks. The best include a power nozzle accessory plus specialty attachments.

Upright

A more powerful vacuum mechanism together with a revolving brush agitator offers superior deep cleaning of large carpeted areas. Adjusts to different carpet piles. Often includes an array of attachments for above-floor cleaning. An upright can be awkward in tight spaces.

Central System

With the motor and dirt collector located in a utility room or basement, the central vacuum is quiet, convenient (you carry only the hose and accessories), and easy (it needs emptying less often than other vacuums). The principal drawback is its initial installation cost.

Wet/Dry

Though often described as an all-purpose vacuum, this heavy-duty machine works best in high-soil areas such as basements, workshops, and garages. The unit is designed to suck up wet dirt, including spills. Also good around remodeling and construction sites.

VACUUM CLEANER ATTACHMENTS

Rug-Cleaning Tool

Use on low-pile or worn carpets. Use one that swivels to reach underneath low-slung furniture.

Bare-Floor Brush

For wood floors, tile, stone. Replace when bristles become worn to prevent scratches.

Upholstery Tool

Cleans upholstered furniture, draperies, mattresses, auto interiors, carpeted stairs, fabric-covered walls.

Dusting Brush

Use to clean furniture, light fixtures, blinds, and shutters. Cover with soft cloth for delicate surfaces.

Crevice Tool

For radiator fins, carpet edges, upholstery crevices, refrigerator grilles, registers, and baseboards.

Power Nozzle

Motorized brush for carpets and sturdy rugs. Brush should extend to both edges of the power roller.

well suited to cleaning households with a variety of floors and floor coverings. Look for models that include a power-head attachment, which offers agitator action for cleaning carpet.

Another type, the central vacuum, is not portable but is actually built into the house. It consists of a powerful collection unit in the basement, attic, or utility room; vacuum tubing that snakes through the walls; and outlets in all the principal rooms.

Also described as vacuum cleaners are several special-purpose machines. The "electric broom" or "stick broom" —a mini-upright without a brush roller—and the even smaller hand vacuum are two types best reserved for small jobs. The wet/dry or shop vacuum is, by contrast, often quite powerful and is best used in really dirty or wet situations.

SAFETY SMART

VACUUMS AND DUST CONTROL

Some vacuums are equipped with HEPA (High-Efficiency Particulate Air Emission) filters. These remove some of the irritants associated with some allergies as air moves through the machine. However, if such allergies plague your household, a HEPA filter alone may not fully solve the problem. Use it as one component in a defense that includes high-efficiency furnace filters, annual cleaning of air ducts, and minimal carpeting. Consult an allergy specialist for other strategies.

Shoppers will find the differences in similar-style machines often subtle, and manufacturers' claims confusing. For example, higher motor amperage does not necessarily mean the machine is more effective. Nor is the presence of a high-efficiency filter necessarily an advantage—if not designed properly, it can actually reduce a machine's effectiveness. Features that should affect choice are: kinds of attachments included, weight of the machine, length of the cord, ease of controls, and ease of changing the dirt-gathering bag and drive belt.

Consult the latest consumer buying guides in selecting a machine that fits your needs and budget. Or deal with experienced and reputable dealers who can back up their recommendation.

Using a vacuum cleaner

Prepare the area before you begin to vacuum. Start by picking up any small, hard objects—pins, buttons, coins, toys, and the like—since such items can be sucked into the vacuum and damage the machine. Once inside, they can clog the filter and damage the fan. Or if a small object becomes lodged in the hose, it can cause the motor to overheat and burn out.

Also, give yourself maximum freedom to vacuum in corners and around furniture by putting chairs, wastebaskets, and other small furnishings out of the room or atop larger pieces.

◆ **Use the right attachment**—the wrong one can do more harm than good. For low-pile carpets and woven or braided rugs, for example, use the bare-floor brush or rug-cleaning tool; the harsh, rotating brushes of a power nozzle could damage them.

◆ **Clear lint, hair, or thread** collected on a vacuum's dusting brush (below) with an old coarse-toothed comb. Cut away more-persistent tangles with a knife, since clogged bristles reduce cleaning action.

dusting brush attachment

◆ **Use the roller brush adjustment** on an upright vacuum so that the brush always rides in proper contact with the carpet's pile. If set too low, the vacuum will be hard to push. If set too high, the sucking effect is diminished and the vacuum cleaner will not gather all the dirt, especially when it is running over debris embedded deep in carpet pile.

◆ **Make repeated passes,** going over your carpet three times for a light cleaning, up to seven times for a heavy cleaning. And don't hurry. Move the vacuum slowly, and make overlapping, parallel strokes. Pay special attention to doorways and to areas in front of sofas and chairs. People tend to shift their feet as they sit, loosening dirt from their shoes and grinding it into the carpet Switch to a different attachment when

TROUBLE SHOOTER

VACUUM CLEANER PROBLEMS

Problem	Possible Cause	Solution
Motor doesn't run	Plug not secure	Reinsert plug firmly into outlet
	Power off at outlet	Check household service panel (see page 93)
	On-Off switch broken	Replace switch
	Power cord broken	Replace power cord
	Handle wiring (from switch to motor) broken	Have wiring replaced
Motor runs but suction is poor	Dust bag filled	Replace or empty dust bag
	Filter dirty	Clean or replace filter
	Slipped, worn, or broken roller brush belt	Reattach or replace belt (see facing page)
	Hose improperly mounted on vacuum	Reattach hose to cleaner
	Hose or attachment obstructed	Remove the obstruction (see facing page)
	Leak in hose, wand, or attachment	Repair leak with duct tape or replace part
	Fan obstructed	Remove debris, caked dirt, and other obstructions
Vacuum blows fuses	Too many appliances on circuit	Turn off other appliances on circuit
	Short circuit in power cord or plug	Replace power cord
	Short circuit in handle cord	Replace handle cord
Vacuum makes excessive noise	Power-brush belt loose or obstructed	Adjust or replace belt
	Defective fan	Replace fan
Vacuum shocks user	Power cord frayed	Replace power cord

Upright

access to dust bag

access to roller belt

Upright with Front Panel

dust bag

front panel

access to roller belt

Cannister/Tank

access to roller belt

dust bag

filter

Upright Bypass

dust bag

access to roller belt

the tool you are using fails to do a thorough job. The work will seem twice as hard, however, if your hose attachments tend to stick when you're pulling them apart. To make the change easier, rub the joints periodically with waxed paper.

Testing your vacuum cleaner

To test how well your vacuum cleaner is working, see how well it picks up a granular substance, such as sand or salt, from your carpet. Sprinkle sand or salt in a small area and vacuum as usual. Then check your work carefully; even a poorly functioning vacuum may leave neat groom marks on the carpet. Make sure the granules have been picked up and have not been pushed farther down into the pile. The cleaner the test area, the more efficiently your vacuum cleaner is working.

Vacuum maintenance

If your vacuum cleaner is running smoothly but still isn't picking up dirt as well as it used to, unplug the machine and check the following.

◆ **A full dust bag** will drastically reduce a vacuum cleaner's suction power. Change or empty the bag when debris hits the "full" line.

◆ **Some vacuums have filters** that are designed to keep fine dust from getting into the motor and damaging it. To work properly, they need regular cleaning or replacement. Keep extra filters on hand.

◆ **A blocked hose or wand** could be the hang-up. Attach the hose to the exhaust and the nozzle to the intake, sealing the space around with a rag to create pressure. If the exhaust does not propel the blockage into the dust

bag, disconnect the hose again and carefully feed a garden hose or a broom handle through to the obstruction. Push gently to dislodge it, taking care not to tear the hose.

◆ **A brush roller belt** that is not functioning well can drastically reduce cleaning power. If you find yourself making repeated passes to pick up a piece of lint, or if you smell burning rubber, your problem might be a detached or slipping roller belt. Most belts are relatively easy to change (below). To buy replacement belts, you'll need the machine's model number, which appears on the underside or back of the unit.

◆ **A professional tune-up** will keep top-of-the-line machines running for many years, but it may not make financial sense for cheaper machines.

REPLACING A BRUSH ROLLER BELT

1. Unplug the vacuum. Remove the screws or release the catches to take off the bottom panel on the power nozzle or upright base. (On some machines, also remove the top panel.) Gently pry the brush roller out of the sockets at each end of the holder.

2. Use a utility knife to cut any hair or thread wound around the roller. Take particular care to clear the ends of the roller without damaging the shafts. If the bearings are removable, pop them off and clean them.

3. Loop one end of the belt to the motor shaft and the other around the roller brush. Stretch the belt until the roller ends snap into their sockets. (Lever with a screwdriver if needed.) Reattach the bottom panel.

TAKING CARE OF FLOORS

Regular maintenance and timely repairs keep household flooring looking beautiful and postpone costly refinishing or replacement.

Different types of flooring require different kinds of care; give them the wrong care, and they could be permanently damaged. Begin by identifying your types of flooring (see pages 12–16), then consult this section for the tools, supplies, and methods required for their care.

WOOD FLOORS

All wood floors are stained for color immediately after they are sanded, then coated with a sealer to protect the wood from superficial scratching, spills, and water damage. One or more finishing coats of wax or polyurethane is then applied for even more protection. If your floors are over 20 years old, then varnish or shellac, rather than polyurethane, may have been applied.

To identify the finish, rub your finger across the surface of the floor. If you've left a smudge, the floor has a wax finish. Or close your eyes and run your hand across a floorboard. If you can feel the grain of the wood, the floor has been waxed or treated with a penetrating oil. A floor finished with polyurethane (whether alkyd or water-based), shellac, or varnish feels smooth and will "lift" if you place a small amount of paint remover on it. (Do so in an inconspicuous corner, as this spot will be permanently altered.) To further isolate the finish, check the color. Shellac reddens as it ages. Varnish develops a rich patina. Polyurethane yellows slightly with age but remains characteristically light in color.

Keeping floors grit-free

Cleanliness is just one reason to keep wood floors clean. Sand and grit, ground underfoot and scuffed on the wood finish by ordinary use, can damage the finish. Here are some options for preventive maintenance.

◆ **Every few days use a broom** to sweep high-traffic areas like exterior doorways and stair landings, and, if your kitchen has a wood floor, in front of the sink, refrigerator, and stove. Also pay special attention to the corners, where dirt, grime, and grit collect.

◆ **Vacuum wood floors** by using a bare-floor brush attachment. (Don't use an upright vacuum or a canister vacuum equipped with a roller brush—both can damage your floor.) Pull the bare-floor brush toward you. Keep the handle raised slightly so that the leading edge (the edge nearest you) will not scratch the floor. Or lift the brush and put it down in a new spot. You need to vacuum only once a week to pick up the fine dust and particles that you can't catch with a broom. Concentrate on high-traffic areas.

◆ **Never use water** to clean a wood floor; not only can it cause warping, but in excess it can even cause wood to rot. Instead, wrap the head of a sponge mop with a damp, soft cloth that's been thoroughly wrung out. Go over a small area of floor at a time, wiping dry with a second cloth before you move on.

Restoring shine to polyurethane

To bring back the shine and remove greasy film and dirt on polyurethane, go over floors with a damp mop. Use ammonia diluted with warm water—about 1 part ammonia to 20 parts water—as a dampening agent. Or use a mix of 1 cup white vinegar to 1 gallon warm water. Both solutions are non-abrasive and do not leave streaks. Remember to wring out the mop until it's half-dry. Mop up any puddles immediately, or you'll end up with water-damaged floors, which may require costly refinishing. Avoid oil-based soaps—they build up and dull the finish.

Some polyurethane manufacturers recommend a neutral-pH cleaner, available at hardware stores. However, if you use a pH cleaner, be prepared to do a two-step process, using two buckets. Fill one with the cleaning solution,

mixed according to the manufacturer's directions, the other with water. Wet a sponge mop with the cleaner, wring until half-dry, then run it over the floor. Dip a second mop into the clean water, wring it well, and mop again.

Buffing up varnish and shellac

Unfortunately, you can't damp-mop older finishes such as varnish and shellac; doing so will remove any remaining shine. Instead, clean them with a wood floor cleaner intended for use on unwaxed varnish or shellac surfaces. If cleaning does not restore the shine, you have two other options: wax over the old finish and then care for it as you would any waxed floor; or start anew and have the floors sanded, stained, and polyurethaned.

Waxing a wood floor

Before waxing a hardwood floor, it's important to remove all of the old dirt and wax. The cleaning solution is simple—mix 1 cup ammonia with 1 gallon water. Evenly apply the ammonia-and-water solution with a damp mop. Once the floor is completely dry, apply floor wax according to the manufacturer's instructions. (Note that waxes for wood floors are formulated with a petroleum solvent, as distinguished from water-based waxes for resilient floors. Because of the solvents, you need good ventilation while applying the wax.)

Your choices in wood floor waxes are several, starting with a liquid paste wax or a solid paste wax. Liquid paste waxes are easier to apply, but solid

QUICK FIX

TO REPAIR A SCRATCH IN WAXED FLOORS:

◆ **Rub the scratch** with steel wool, following the grain of the wood.

◆ **Mix floor wax** with a little brown shoe polish. Using a buffer or a cloth-covered broom, blend it in well.

paste waxes are generally more durable. Do not under any circumstance use one of the liquid self-polishing acrylic waxes on wood. Here are some other maintenance tips.

◆ **Self-polishing liquid paste wax** is easy to apply. Simply pour out a small amount on a section of the prepared floor and spread it evenly with a long-handled wax applicator. Quick to dry, and consequently ready to be walked on in 10 minutes, this quick-drying convenience brings with it a caveat. Because this floor dressing hardens so quickly, it can become permanently affixed to the applicator, so wash the soft pad immediately after each use in a detergent solution. Liquid paste waxes are self-polishing, providing a lustrous rather than high-gloss finish, and they are less slippery than most solid paste waxes. Since the finish is less durable, apply a fresh coat of wax several times a year. If the new coat of fresh liquid paste wax does not yield satisfactory results, you may need to use a commercial stripping solution to remove the old wax before applying new wax.

◆ **Solid paste wax** is a bit more expensive and harder to apply than liquid paste wax. You can do the job by hand with a soft cloth and elbow grease, or apply it yourself with a rented home floor waxing/buffing machine. (If you are maintaining many wood floors, and you want them to look good all the time, it makes sense to own rather than rent an electric waxer/buffer.) Alternatively, you can have a pro do the job from time to time.

Solid paste wax is initially more time-consuming to apply, but it saves labor in the long run. First of all, you need to rewax less often than with the liquid paste products. And secondly, when you do rewax, you'll rarely need to strip away the old, because the paste wax wears off in the process of being walked on.

◆ **Do not overwax a floor.** In between waxings, it is often possible to restore somewhat-dulled solid paste wax to its original shine with the buffer brush on the floor-waxing machine, removing dirt in the process. With such occasional treatments, you may need only paste-wax the entire floor annually.

◆ **Avoid wax buildup.** Apply wax in those areas that do not receive a lot of wear—around furniture legs and in corners—only every other time you wax. To avoid waxing these places, put newspapers on the floor where the furniture is positioned, and wax around the newspapers. Similarly, wax only to within 6 inches of the wall.

◆ **Protect high-traffic areas** with an extra coat of wax. Every house has certain spots—in doorways or at the bottom of stairways—that get extra wear and tear. Once or twice a month, protect worn spots with a thin coat of paste wax applied with a piece of cheesecloth. Allow the area to dry for 15 minutes, then polish to a high sheen with a clean, folded cloth. Repeat the procedure an hour or two later.

◆ **For a quick pickup,** dust mop the room thoroughly, making sure to remove all dirt particles. Place waxed paper under a sponge mop, and work your way around the room, changing the paper as often as necessary.

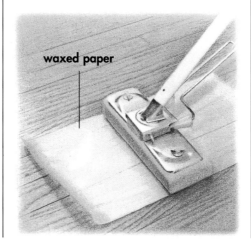

waxed paper

Restaining floors

Unlike laminated wood, solid wood can be sanded and refinished many times. You can even change its color by sanding it down to its natural state and restaining the floor with a different color stain.

Some homeowners choose to do this job themselves with rented machinery, but sanding floors is hard, dusty work, requiring a certain amount of expertise and finesse. If you linger too long in any single spot with a heavy-duty sander, for example, you can permanently damage the floor. Ask friends and neighbors for recommendations for experienced floor refinishers.

If you decide to hire professionals, you can cut some of the cost by getting the rooms ready yourself. First, move all the furniture and furnishings out of the rooms in which the work is to be done. (The amount of dust raised will be harmful to draperies, pictures, and books, as well as the furniture.) Then gently pry off the baseboard shoe (bottom) molding in those rooms.

Sanding, restaining, sealing, and finishing a floor can take as long as a week, depending on the size of the floor and the humidity (which affects how long it takes the different finishes to dry). Foot traffic should be kept to a minimum during sanding. While the floor is being stained and given its two or more coats of resurfacing, it should not be walked on at all.

Removing mars and stains

Accidents happen, and even a small scratch or stain can leave a waxed floor open to further damage or deep soiling. Rules of thumb: The sooner you treat stains, the better; and always work from the outside to the center.

♦ **To remove shallow scratches** from a waxed wood floor, buff the area lightly with a piece of super-fine (#0000) steel wool, rubbing with the grain of the wood. Once the scratches have been sanded out, apply two coats of paste wax, buffing each coat with a soft, clean cloth. Or try applying a commercial touch-up stain.

♦ **To remove an alcohol stain** from a waxed hardwood floor, rub it with silver polish or an ammonia-dampened cloth. Wipe away the residue, allow the area to dry thoroughly, then rewax.

♦ **Moisten dried food or milk** spills with a damp cloth. Let the moisture soak in to soften the caked-on material,

then gently wipe the stain away with a clean, damp cloth. Rub dry, and, if the cleaned area looks dull, rewax and polish to match the rest of the floor.

♦ **Remove white spots or water stains** by putting a little paste wax on them. Rub the area with a piece of #0000 steel wool, following the grain, and buff to a shine. If this fails to restore the surface, sand very lightly, clean with #00 steel wool and mineral spirits, and let dry. Finally, stain the bare area to match, apply wax, and buff the spot to its original finish.

♦ **To remove black heel marks,** start with a piece of steel wool that's been dipped in wood floor cleaner for that finish. Gently rub the heel mark, always working with the grain of the wood. Finally, let the floor dry completely and, if necessary, rewax and hand-buff the area to a shine.

WORK SAVERS

PREVENTIVE MEASURES

♦ **Wipe up spills immediately** because moisture warps wood. Be particularly wary of alcohol, which eats through protective wax quickly.

♦ **Place rubber or plastic casters** under the narrow legs of furniture to prevent gouging. Or use stick-on fabric protectors, available in different sizes.

♦ **Protect against midday sun,** which can discolor and fade floors, by closing curtains and blinds or hanging sheer drapes.

♦ **Use glazed ceramic or plastic coasters** under planters; water can soak through terra cotta coasters and ruin the wood underneath. Move planters periodically to be sure there are no rings.

SILENCING SQUEAKS

1. Use your ears to locate the squeak. Apply powdered graphite or talcum powder to the joints between the noisy floor boards. If this method fails, nail down the loose or warped board. Drill pilot holes with a 3/32-inch drill bit so that the wood doesn't split.

2. Drill holes on both ends of the board to anchor it more securely to the subfloor. Pound the nails nearly home. Then, to avoid leaving hammer marks on the floor, use a nailset (above) to countersink the nail heads 1/8 inch below the surface of the board.

3. Fill the nail holes with wood putty. Use a color that matches the floor and apply it with a putty knife. Wipe away any excess putty before it dries. When the putty is dry, apply paste wax to the area around the repairs and buff it to a shine.

◆ **Burns on wood floors** may not be as bad as they look. Most floors have a fairly tough protective finish, so the burn is often only on the surface and can be rubbed away with a damp sponge or cloth or very fine steel wool. However, if the burn has etched deeply into the wood, moisten a piece of fine steel wool in a mild solution of soap and water; using a circular motion, rub the burned area until the charred wood fibers are removed. Then rub the area with fine sandpaper. Apply some matching touch-up stain, wax, and hand-buff with a clean cloth.

RESILIENT FLOORING

Practicing a program of regular maintenance and timely repair will extend the life of resilient flooring for many years, whether it is in sheet or tile form. (See page 19 for other tips on washing.)

No-wax vinyl

For the so-called no-wax vinyl-surfaced flooring materials, any kind of wax is going to be superfluous in the beginning months—and even years—of the floor's existence. That's because a thin film of vinyl or polyurethane has been applied to the surface to maintain a shine without waxing. Keeping a no-wax surface clean is the key to keeping it shiny. However, if you use a one-step "clean and wax" product, you must be sure to rinse it off thoroughly, or it can leave a dulling finish.

After a while, tiny scratches will inevitably begin to accumulate even on the no-wax surface. Renew it by applying a water-based self-polishing

wax or one of the specially formulated vinyl finishes. (Most flooring manufacturers produce such dressings, which are sold at flooring retailers and home centers.) Apply the dressing only on a well-vacuumed and washed surface.

Standard vinyl floor coverings

Use the mildest method you can to keep the floor clean, including regular vacuuming and sweeping before dirt gets ground in. When the dirt will not come off with a broom or a vacuum, mop with a damp mop that has been dipped in lukewarm water and squeezed half-dry. Rub only enough to get the dirt up.

For more resistant dirt, prepare a solution of warm water and detergent, apply a small amount to the surface, and wipe away quickly. Rinse with a mop dipped in clean water, making sure to remove all detergent or soap, even if the label doesn't require it.

◆ **Wax only when washing fails** to restore the shine. Wash the floor thoroughly and, when dry, apply a thin coat of self-polishing wax. Regular wax is more protective than one-step wax-and-clean products, but it will build up eventually and need to be stripped. Solvent-based polishing wax will not build up, but it does need to be buffed with an electric polisher.

◆ **To keep liquid wax from collecting** in any depressed areas, do not pour it directly onto the floor. Instead, apply it from a shallow pan (an old 8½ × 11-inch cake pan works well), using a clean half-dry sponge mop.

◆ **Remove old wax once a year.** Start by soaking and scrubbing your floor with a detergent or wax remover. (Take care not to get your floor too wet.) Then use a squeegee to strip away the old wax. Make sure that you buy a squeegee that is made specifically for floor use and not one intended for windows. Push the dirty residue into an uncleaned area, and immediately scoop it into a dustpan or some other picker-upper and discard. Finish by damp mopping with clear water, again being careful not to overwet.

squeegee

old wax

◆ **Light scratches** in vinyl can result when you drop a utensil or pull out a chair. While shallow scratches can't be removed, they can be concealed. Start by rubbing the area with a soft cloth moistened with floor wax; continue the process until the scratches all but disappear and the area has the same shine as the rest of the floor.

REPLACING A VINYL FLOOR TILE

1. Warm the damaged tile with a steam iron, using a folded dish towel between the iron and the vinyl. Pry out the damaged tile with a putty knife, taking care not to lift or damage adjoining tiles. Scrape and vacuum up the old adhesive dust.

2. Before spreading fresh adhesive on the floor, check the fit of the replacement tile. If it needs trimming, cut the tile down to size with a sharp utility knife, using a metal straightedge as a guide. Sand the edge lightly with a sanding block if the fit is tight.

3. Spread fresh adhesive lightly on the floor. Warm the replacement tile, protected by a dish towel, with an iron until it is flexible. Set the tile in place, wipe away any adhesive residue, and weigh the tile down with books until the adhesive sets.

Difficult stains

Some spots and spills on resilient flooring resist routine cleaning. Handle such problems as follows.

◆ **To remove stubborn stains** and ground-in soil, use a 1 to 10 solution of ammonia and water, and scrub the area lightly with a plastic scouring pad. Go over stubborn stains again with extra-fine (#0000) steel wool. Wax or polish to bring the floor back to its shine.

◆ **To remove black heel marks** from resilient floors, rub the marks with silver polish until they've completely disappeared. An alternative is to use white appliance wax (appliance retailers sell this). Remove any excess silver polish or appliance wax by rubbing the area with a soft, clean cloth.

◆ **To remove chewing gum,** put some crushed ice in a small, sealable plastic bag and place the ice directly on top of the gum for a few minutes. Once the gum is brittle, remove the ice and gently pry the gum free with a dull knife.

◆ **Spilled nail polish** can be peeled off, if you first let it dry until tacky. Remove the remaining residue with nail-polish remover. However, if you use nail-polish remover, which is a solvent, the area will probably be dulled slightly. Brighten it with floor wax or polish.

Flattening curled tiles

To flatten the occasional tile that curls slightly at the corners, warm the problem area with a steam iron set on low and placed on a doubled cotton dish towel or rag. Move the iron back and forth long enough to soften the adhesive underneath. Carefully apply fresh adhesive under the curled-up areas—or under the entire tile, if needed. Wipe away excess adhesive, and weigh the tile corners down until the adhesive dries and sets. Heavy books make good weights.

doubled cotton cloth

29

TILE, STONE, OR BRICK FLOORS

These long-wearing, beautiful materials need specialized care and occasional repairs. Typically, the problem will lie not with the flooring material itself but with the grout, mortar, or cement in the joints. More rarely, a cracked tile, stone, or brick will need replacement, a job you may want to leave to a flooring specialist. Here's how to keep these floors looking their best.

Cleaning and sealing

Unglazed tiles and the grout that fills the spaces between should be sealed with a silicone sealer designed for this purpose; otherwise both tiles and grout can become soiled. With glazed tiles, only the grout must be sealed. Do this after installation, and repeat as needed.

◆ **The easiest way to keep ceramic** tiles clean is to scrub them with an electric floor washer and a solution of

WORK SAVERS

SCRUBBING BRICK SURFACES

To remove paint specks and mortar smudges from brick, find a piece of broken brick that's the same color as the brick you're cleaning. Scrub the brick surface with the broken piece. (Don't use the face of the brick; it's harder and can cause scratches.) Sweep away the pieces of brick

that have been left behind. This transfer technique also works for other masonry surfaces, such as stone and concrete block.

¼ cup low-sudsing detergent, or 1 to 2 tablespoons of washing soda (borax), or a commercial cleaning powder in a gallon of water. Rinse well and wipe dry.

◆ **To clean heavily stained grout,** mix a solution of 2 tablespoons liquid chlorine bleach and 1 quart water. Apply to the grout using an old toothbrush, and let stand for 20 minutes.

Mop the floor, rinse, and wipe dry. Then brush on an acrylic sealer. As an alternative sealer, apply three coats of lemon oil, allowing an hour drying time between coats.

◆ **Stubborn stains on ceramic tile,** while uncommon, can happen. Treat them with a paste made of scouring powder and water. Apply it to the stain

REPLACING DAMAGED MORTAR

1. Wearing safety goggles to protect your eyes, use a small masonry chisel to remove all the damaged mortar. Brush and vacuum the mortar lines completely.

2. Mix the mortar, and add latex binder according to the manufacturer's instructions. Dampen, but don't soak, the mortar lines; add the mortar mix with a small trowel.

3. "Strike" or groove the mortar line to match the rest of the floor. Wipe off excess mortar repeatedly with a sponge, until the area around the repair is completely clean.

and let it sit for five minutes. Scrub the area with a nonscratch nylon pad, then rinse with water and wipe dry. If necessary, repeat the procedure.

◆ **A sealed brick floor** can be kept clean with regular vacuuming and only occasional damp-mopping with plain water to remove soil and dirt. For heavier soil, or for unsealed, more porous brick surfaces, wash with a mild detergent, rinse, and wipe dry.

◆ **Use a rag mop** to clean brick or stone floors. A sponge mop will snag and break apart on these irregular surfaces. Because dried-on cleaner can cause stone surfaces to chip, it's important to keep the floor wet during the cleaning process. Thoroughly wet the floor with water before applying any kind of cleaning product. Once the floor is clean, rinse the area well.

◆ **Some oil and grease stains** in brick and stone can be removed or lightened by immediately spreading a layer of cat litter or powdered cement on the stain. Allow the material to soak up the stain, then sweep clean. If necessary, repeat.

Repairing hard flooring

Replacing an individual cracked floor tile is an isolated problem that is not difficult to fix if you have new tiles to match the old. (If you are new to the house, check the basement or utility room on the chance that the previous owner tucked a few spares away.) If not, look for tiles you can "borrow" from under a cabinet or in a closet—where their loss won't show. It takes finesse to remove an old tile in one piece and reset it. Consider hiring a professional to do this job.

A series of cracked tiles, bricks, or stones suggests that you have a bigger problem: the floor's foundation—the underlayment material and joists that support the floor—is inadequate. Shoring up the foundation may require reworking the entire floor, a costly and disruptive task. If the cracking is not too widespread, however, you may be able to fix the problem adequately by regrouting, this time with a more flexible grouting mix that includes a latex binder (facing page).

CARPETING

Most carpet available today has been manufactured with a stain-resistant treatment, which holds the stain on the surface. If immediate action is taken, many spills can be successfully sopped up. Other kinds of problems require special measures. The principal care of

---

REPAIRING DAMAGED CARPETING

1. Using a utility knife and a metal straightedge, cut a rectangle of scrap carpeting slightly larger than the damaged area. (If you don't have a matching scrap, cut a piece from the back of a carpeted closet.)

2. Use the cut piece as a template for cutting out the damaged area. Test the fit of the patch, and match its weave direction in the intended location. Carefully trim it for a snug fit, if necessary, with a pair of scissors.

3. Apply double-sided tape to the margins of the hole. Dab glue around the edges of the replacement plug, align its fibers to make it look like its surroundings, and carefully press the carpet patch in place.

TROUBLE SHOOTER

CARPET STAIN REMOVAL

When anything spills on a rug, the first step is to get it up quickly. For a liquid like juice, blotting is the best bet; for a thicker substance, use a spoon to lift off as much as you can, working from the outside to the middle. To remove the remaining stain, work in the appropriate cleaner with a clean, white, absorbent cloth. (Pretest on an inconspicuous spot first to make sure the solution won't damage fibers or dyes.) Blot and repeat until the spot no longer transfers to the cloth. Then use clean water to remove any remaining residue. Absorb any moisture with paper towels. Let the area dry, and then vacuum.

Stain	Method
Alcoholic beverage	Use a detergent solution, mixing $1/4$ teaspoon liquid dishwashing detergent with 1 cup lukewarm water. (Never use a stronger concentration, nor an automatic dishwashing detergent, nor a laundry detergent, which may contain such additives as optical brighteners and bleaches.)
Blood	Use an ammonia solution, mixing 2 tablespoons household ammonia with 1 cup water.
Candle wax	Chip off surface wax. Place several layers of paper towel over remaining wax, then apply warm iron and draw wax into the towel. Or use an acetone-based nail polish remover or a spot dry-cleaning solution with acetone.
Chocolate	Use a gentle oil solvent, such as a spot dry-cleaning solution with acetone.
Cosmetics	Use a gentle oil solvent, such as a spot dry-cleaning solution with acetone or acetone-based nail polish remover.
Fruit juice	Use a liquid detergent solution, mixing 1 teaspoon liquid dishwashing detergent with 1 cup lukewarm water. Dab with white vinegar.
Grease/oil	Use a gentle oil solvent, such as a spot dry-cleaning solution with acetone. Follow up with 1 teaspoon liquid dishwashing detergent mixed in 1 cup lukewarm water.
Ink/ballpoint pen	Use a gentle dry-cleaning solvent. Follow with 1 teaspoon liquid dishwashing detergent mixed in 1 cup lukewarm water.

Stain	Method
Mildew	Use a liquid chlorine bleach solution, mixing 1 teaspoon bleach to 1 cup water. Follow up with a liquid detergent solution, mixing 1 teaspoon liquid dishwashing detergent with 1 cup lukewarm water.
Milk	Use a liquid detergent solution, mixing 1 teaspoon liquid dishwashing detergent with 1 cup lukewarm water. Follow up with 1 tablespoon household ammonia in $1/2$ cup water.
Mud	Follow directions for milk.
Mustard/ketchup	Follow directions for milk.
Paint	For oil-based paints, follow directions for grease and oil. For latex paints, follow directions for milk stain removal.
Rust	Use a commercial rust remover or a solution of $1/2$ cup white vinegar and 1 cup water.
Shoe polish	Follow directions for grease and oil.
Soft drinks	Use a liquid detergent solution, mixing 1 teaspoon liquid dishwashing detergent with 1 cup lukewarm water. Follow up with 1 tablespoon household ammonia in $1/2$ cup water.
Toothpaste	Use a liquid detergent solution, mixing 1 teaspoon liquid dishwashing detergent with 1 cup lukewarm water. Follow up with 1 tablespoon household ammonia in $1/2$ cup water.
Urine	Use a commercial enzyme cleaner (facing page).

carpeting is regular vacuuming (see pages 19–23). Here's how to handle nonroutine carpet care.

Reviving indentations

If your carpet becomes indented from the pressure of furniture legs, you can remove the depressions by holding a steam iron 6 inches above each spot until the carpet is moist. (Don't touch the iron to the fibers.) Then work the fibers back and forth with a coin until they rise.

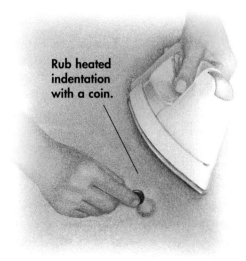

Rub heated indentation with a coin.

If the indentations are particularly deep, lay a damp bath towel over the depression and press the area lightly with an iron, using the wool or cotton heat setting. Leave the towel in place until dry. If this doesn't work the first time, repeat the process.

Eliminating static

Static electricity is a common problem for carpets, especially during the drier winter months. For an anti-static agent, prepare a solution made up of 1 part liquid fabric softener and 5 parts water; apply this with a spray bottle. Because static electricity pulls dust particles from the air, any measures that reduce static help to keep the carpet cleaner.

Removing pet stains and odors

The most effective means of removing pet stains is to use a protein-digester enzyme treatment. Sold in pet supply stores, this product uses enzymes to turn urine and other organic matter into a liquid that can be blotted up. Pet stains can also leave a lasting odor. The solution: Liberally apply baking soda to the carpet and let stand for at least 15 minutes. (Wait overnight for particularly strong odors.) Once the baking soda has had a chance to work, vacuum the carpet.

Deep-cleaning methods

Dry cleaning carpeting requires no special equipment, so it is the easiest deep cleaning method to use. Begin by sprinkling an absorbent cleaning compound on the carpet, and brush it well into the carpet fibers. Wait an hour, then vacuum thoroughly, using an attachment that provides maximum suction.

When a deeper cleaning is needed, rent a carpet cleaner from your local home center or rental store, and purchase the appropriate cleaning compound. Vacuum the carpet before you use the carpet cleaner.

◆ **With a rotary shampoo machine,** move the unit continuously while releasing the shampoo into the carpet—the rotary brushes can damage fibers if left in one place too long. Don't over-wet the carpet, since this can cause shrinkage or discoloration. Place cups under furniture legs to prevent staining. Allow the carpet to dry completely. Then vacuum to remove the released soil and the shampoo residue.

◆ **To use a steam cleaner,** move the unit continuously in a W pattern. Release steam on push strokes and remove the moisture on pull strokes. For badly soiled areas, repeat the steps in the opposite direction. Steam is most effective on wool, shag, and heavily soiled carpets, but water over 150°F can shrink wool fibers. Be careful to control how much moisture you use; overwetting carpet damages the flooring underneath and promotes mildew.

steam cleaner

MAINTAINING WALLS AND CEILINGS

Washing, removing stains, and completing small repairs are the first steps in shaping up surfaces that are past their prime. Painting and wallpapering take you to the finish line in high style.

Walls and ceilings often are treated as mere background to a home's decor, but that doesn't mean they should be ignored or neglected. Keeping them at their best will make everything else in the room look better. It also will make any decorating you do a snap.

PREPARING THE SURFACE

Before redecorating any surface, make it clean and smooth. Painted drywall and plaster in good condition require little more than dusting. First, remove all items hanging on the wall. Next, go after the cobwebs with a feather duster or the dusting brush accessory of your vacuum cleaner. Dust the ceiling and wall with a broom-end covered with a flannel (or other soft cloth) pillowcase. The pillowcase makes a handy cover, and the flannel is textured just enough to grab dirt well. Secure the pillowcase at the open end with a piece of string or large rubber band. Change the case or turn it inside out whenever it gets dirty. Finally, dust or vacuum baseboards and windowsills.

Washing painted walls

Walls and ceilings that are in heavily trafficked areas, near the kitchen, or subject to pollutants from a fireplace or furnace will likely have a uniform film of grease on them and will need to be washed thoroughly. Washing walls takes a lot of preparation time and hard work, but it is essential if the old wall is dirty and the new paint or paper you are about to apply is to adhere properly. (If you don't have the time or inclination to wash walls and ceilings yourself, hire someone. The cost typically runs to about a third of what a professional paint job costs.) To check whether you need to wash a wall, spot-clean an inconspicuous area. If you see a big difference between dirty and clean, washing is in order. Here are some tips for doing the job efficiently:

◆ **Use an abrasive cleaner** for run-of-the-mill soiling, and a touch of mineral spirits on a rag to clean oily spots.

◆ **Use a sponge mop** to wash the walls a section at a time, and work from bottom to top, making sure to squeeze

WORK ORDER

When washing a room, start with the ceiling. Then go to the walls, beginning at the bottom and working your way up. (If you start at the top, some of the wash water will drip onto the dry, unwashed walls and cause permanent stains.) Work rapidly in small areas.

1. Wash walls, working bottom to top.

2. Wash windows (page 51) and doors.

3. Wash the baseboards.

the mop frequently to help prevent drips. When you're using a sponge, water is likely to run down onto your arm; so tie a washcloth around your wrist for protection.

◆ **Use a two-bucket technique** to make your cleaning solution go further and give cleaner results. Fill one bucket with cleaning solution and the other with clean rinse water. Use a sponge mop or rag dipped in cleaning solution to wash walls. Then rinse away the dirt

from the cleaning sponge or rag repeatedly in the bucket of clear water before dipping it back into the bucket of cleaning solution.

◆ **If you prefer using cloths** for washing walls, use only white or off-white ones because the cleaning solution can cause some dyes to bleed.

◆ **Don't strain your back** to clean walls and ceilings; use tools that will do the reaching for you. Choose long-handled sponge mops or other tools that are threaded to accommodate an extension pole (see page 42).

◆ **Be safety-conscious.** Keep water and wet cleaning cloths away from electrical receptacles. Keep all mops, brooms, buckets, and ladders close to the wall so no one will trip over them.

Drying

Drying is just as important as washing. After you wash a wall, dry it from floor to ceiling with a clean towel to prevent streaking. Use terry towels with a high cotton content for maximum absorption. Once you have completed the dusting and washing, you may be pleasantly surprised to find that the walls and ceiling are in better shape than you imagined. You may want to reconsider painting or repapering. High-quality gloss and semi-gloss paints hold up well and look almost new again after washing. This is, incidentally, a good reason to use higher-quality paints. But the same does not hold for flat paints. Whatever the quality, once flat paints are soiled, they don't tolerate washing very well.

WASHING WOODWORK

Moldings are typically painted with gloss or semi-gloss paint. Even though these formulas are generally tougher, smoother, and less likely to show soiling than flat paint, their surfaces gather plenty of dust and dirt. And where moldings serve as baseboards and framing for doors and windows, they are likely to have extra smudging from hands and feet. Start cleaning with the dusting brush attachment of your vacuum to remove surface grime.

To wash the moldings, fill a spray bottle with an all-purpose cleaning solution. If the moldings are fancy millwork with narrow grooves, squirt the cleaner into the indentations and scrub with an old toothbrush (above). Wipe the molding with a sponge, and dry thoroughly with a terrycloth towel.

Be careful not to spray or drip the cleaning solution onto adjacent wall covering or onto painted walls where the liquid could lift seams, cause discoloration, or otherwise do permanent damage. To prevent this, protect the

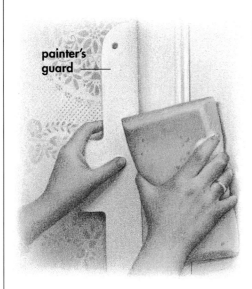

painter's guard

adjacent surface with a flat-edged tool known as a painter's guard (above) as you wash.

CLEANING WALL COVERINGS

The term "wall covering" has many applications but most narrowly refers to wallpapers (solid papers, vinyl-coated papers, foils, flocked papers, or murals); vinyl fabric coverings (fabric- or paper-backed); and textile wall coverings (silk, linen, cotton toile, or grass cloth). Like ordinary walls and woodwork, wall coverings need to be cleaned periodically, too, though their general griminess may not be readily apparent (their patterns and colors tend to hide dirt). A quick dusting a couple of times a year may be all you need to do to prolong the life of most wall coverings and maintain much of their original brilliance. To dust, follow the same procedure recommended for dusting painted walls. Other steps to

revive the appearance of wall coverings depend largely on the kind of wallcovering you have and the type of stains you want to remove.

Wallpapers

Most modern wallpapers are washable, thanks to a transparent vinyl coating applied by manufacturers. The coating makes the wallpaper somewhat water- and stain-repellent, making it relatively easy to remove simple dirt and grime.

To wash such wallpaper, use a mild cleaner and rub gently with a sponge. For a dry technique, try using commercial wallpaper dough, which is available at paint and wallpaper stores. Simply knead the dough and roll it into a ball, then roll the ball along the soiled area (below). Once the dough becomes dirty, roll the soiled part into the center of the ball, reshape it, and continue the cleaning process.

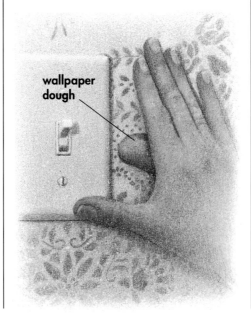

wallpaper dough

Delicate hand-printed wallpapers remain "nonwashable." The delicate dyes involved in the screening process cannot withstand being wetted. If your nonwashable wallpaper is badly soiled, you might try cleaning it with commercial wallpaper dough.

Even when the wallpaper is generally clean, you may find isolated areas that need spot-cleaning. The most common stains on wallpaper are fingerprints and smudges. Wipe them off using a dry sponge. What doesn't come off by this method will probably yield to a common artist's eraser. Try the following methods to remove difficult spots and stains:

◆ **To remove ink spots** from washable wallpaper, liquid chlorine bleach can be very effective. But be careful: The strength of the bleach can sometimes wipe away the color of the wallpaper along with the ink spot. To be safe, test the method in an inconspicuous area. Dab the ink spot with a clean cloth or a cotton swab dampened with the bleach, then quickly rinse the area with a cloth or sponge dipped in clear water to neutralize the bleaching action.

◆ **To remove an old grease spot** from wallpaper, use a commercial stain remover, available at stores that sell wall coverings. If, on the other hand, the spot is fresh and the paper is washable, blot it with a clean paper towel. Holding the towel against the stain, press the area with a warm—not hot—iron. Change the blotter paper each time it becomes greasy. Continue until the spot is gone.

To remove heavy crayon marks, scrape off as much of the wax as possible from the surface with a table knife. Hold several layers of white paper towels over the mark, and press with a warm iron until the wax melts and is absorbed into the paper. Sponge away any residue after lifting the wax.

For lighter crayon marks on conventional wallpaper, clean the area with a sponge soaked in dry-cleaning solvent, available at hardware, paint, and wallpaper stores. If the crayon color remains on the wall, mix 1 teaspoon liquid chlorine bleach in 1 cup water, and apply the solution to the stain. (Test the solution in an inconspicuous area to make sure that it won't damage the pattern or the paper.)

For stubborn stains of any description, consult a wallpaper dealer for suggestions and suitable cleaners. Or cut out the stain and patch the area with a matching piece of wallpaper, if you have it.

Vinyl wallpapers

Scrubbable wall coverings and vinyl-impregnated wallpapers are tougher than either conventional or washable wallpapers. But they are still subject to scratching. Your local paint and wallpaper store may have a cleaner formulated especially for cleaning such materials, or you may get equally good results by wiping with a damp sponge and mild soap. Do not use an abrasive cleanser, scouring pad, or brush. To remove crayon marks from a vinyl wall covering, use silver polish applied

WORK SAVERS

PROTECTING WALLPAPER AROUND A CRIB

A sheet of clear, shatterproof acrylic can protect the wallpaper around a baby's crib from flying food, tossed toys, and the smudge marks of tiny hands. You can mount the acrylic securely with corner brackets, available at any hardware store. Clean it with a wet sponge.

with a clean cloth. Concentrated dishwashing detergent works well, too. Rinse well afterward.

Fabric wall coverings

In cleaning fabric wall coverings— including grass cloth and other porous surfaces—avoid soap and water. They can leave permanent stains on your material and damage the textured surface. As a rule, you should clean fabric wall coverings with a hand-held vacuum only. Delicate fabrics, such as fabric-backed woven silk wall coverings and grass cloth, need professional attention if they are soiled.

CLEANING TILE AND PANELED WALLS

Permeable materials like unglazed tile, tile grout, brick, and some wood paneling are a special challenge because they readily absorb stains that lodge deep below the surface. Glazed tile, on the other hand, won't stain, but its shiny surface can become dulled over time. Here's how to clean these materials.

Tile and brick

To get rid of soapy film on ceramic tile walls, wipe with an ordinary non-abrasive liquid household cleaner (either diluted or full-strength). As an alternative, use a mix of 1 part vinegar to 4 parts water. For the toughest jobs, a mix of 1 cup ammonia, ½ cup vinegar, and ¼ cup baking soda in a gallon of warm water may be even better. Once the tile has been cleaned thoroughly, rinse with water to remove all traces of cleanser. To bring the tile back to its original shine, buff with a soft, clean cloth. Here are additional tips on how to handle special problems.

Stained or mildewed grout in high-moisture areas, such as shower enclosures and backsplashes, takes on an unattractive, blotchy appearance. To make grout look as good as new, mix a bleach solution consisting of ¾ cup liquid chlorine bleach and 1 gallon of water. Apply the mixture liberally with a cloth or sponge. Scrub stubborn stains with an old toothbrush. Rinse the stained spots thoroughly and, if necessary, repeat the procedure.

To remove oil and grease stains from a vertical brick wall, such as a chimney face, use this special blotting technique: Cut a piece of plastic half again as large as the stain. Using duct tape, attach the side and bottom edges to the brick to form a pouch. Fill the pouch with absorbent cement powder or cat litter, then close the top edge. Leave the pouch in place for several days, opening it just enough to stir the granules from time to time so that fresh absorbent material is in contact with the stained brick at all times. Remove when the stain is gone.

Wood paneling

Most paneling—both real wood and simulated wood grain—come from the manufacturer with a pre-applied finish. They can usually be cleaned with nothing more than a damp cloth to remove normal household stains and finger marks. Alternatively, brighten surfaces with any liquid wax cleaner, applied lightly. Wipe away the wax until you no longer see smudge marks when you rub the panel with a clean, dry finger.

◆ **For heavy soil problems,** use a mild soap or detergent. Avoid cleansers with coarse abrasives or solvents, which could damage the protective surface. Textured paneling is best cleaned with a vacuum cleaner's dusting brush.

◆ **To eliminate light scratches** that go no deeper than the finish, apply a coat of clear wax with a damp cloth. Always rub with the grain. Deeper scratches that reach through to the wood, particularly when the panel is stained a dark tone, may require filling. Use a color-matched putty stick, available in most home centers. Finish by waxing and buffing for uniform appearance.

PATCHING A WALL

Plaster walls can take a beating from repeated contact with chairs, door-knobs, and the general mishaps of daily life. Plaster ceilings are prone to small cracks, the result of vibrations from the floor above or from the house settling. If you are planning to paint or to hang

wallpaper, now is the time to examine your walls and ceilings, determine what they are made of, and undertake the appropriate repairs.

Walls and ceilings built after the 1940s are likely to be made of wallboard, also known as gypsum board or plasterboard. Such walls are put together from rigid factory-made sandwich panels that are nailed to interior framing. Typically 4 feet wide, their seams and the nail heads holding them in place are covered (and disguised) with special tape and a plasterlike mixture known as joint compound.

Older, solid-plaster walls consist of several layers of true plaster applied wet on-site over a backing of wire mesh or wooden laths. Before you set out to repair problem walls or ceilings, know your limitations. Minor cracks and holes left by picture-hanging nails are easy to handle for someone new to do-it-yourself repairs. But anything larger takes more preparation and a more practiced hand. For tiny cracks and holes in plasterboard walls or ceilings (½ inch or smaller), clean out the opening, apply spackling compound with a joint knife, allow to dry, and sand smooth. For larger cracks and holes, see the facing page.

Retaping a drywall seam

Sometimes a wall itself may be in fine shape but a section of drywall joint tape used to cover joint seams is peeling away. Repairs to this are easy:

◆ **Cut away** the loose tape and brush clean the area. Cover the open seam with fiberglass mesh tape cut precisely

to fit. Smooth the tape as you go to make a perfectly flat seam. Press the tape to the wall so it adheres.

◆ **Apply a thin, even layer** of joint compound with a 5-inch flexible joint knife to cover the fiberglass mesh tape. Allow to dry. Sand lightly.

◆ **Use an 8-inch joint knife** to apply a second thin coat of compound over the first. Feather the edges of the joint compound outward, decreasing the thickness of the application as you go, so that the tape margins merge smoothly and invisibly into the surroundings. Allow to dry. Sand lightly.

◆ **Repeat with a wider 10-inch joint knife** to add a third coat, feathering the edges as before. Allow to dry. Smooth the final coat with a dampened sponge.

Patching plaster walls

Solid-plaster walls require different repair materials and a different patching technique. Patch holes up to 6 inches across with patching plaster (in powdered or pre-mix form and different in composition from Spackle or drywall compound). For larger areas of damage, hire a professional.

◆ **Begin by cleaning loose plaster** from the cavity, including between lath strips at the back of the hole. Staple a piece of hardware cloth (coarse screen) to the lath for better surface grip.

◆ **Dampen the area**, and use a joint knife narrower than the hole to apply the patching plaster in three shallow coats. Let each coat dry before applying the next.

◆ **Apply wallboard joint compound** for the final coat. This time, use a joint knife wider than the patch, and feather a final, very thin layer of compound. Let dry. Sand until smooth.

Flaking paint

For reasons ranging from roof, window, or radiator leaks to incompatible paints, painted walls can develop chipped or peeling areas. Before dealing with the flaking, make sure to fix whatever caused the problem. Then patch the area before you repaint or paper. Use a wire brush to remove light flaking, or a broad joint knife for larger areas—taking care not to gouge the plaster surface beneath, which will require a coat of spackling compound to repair the damage. Sand the scraped area, particularly the remaining paint edges, until perfectly smooth.

SELECTING PAINT

Most professional painters favor flat latex paints these days for most walls and ceiling jobs; they usually choose latex semi-gloss or gloss paints to paint woodwork. Latex has a number of advantages over the older, natural oil-based and synthetic alkyd paints, which contain solvents that cause pollution. Latex is water-based, meaning it rarely has to be thinned; brushes and any paint drips clean up easily with soap and water; it emits almost no fumes or vapors when applied; and it dries fast.

Latex paint finishes

The choice of finishes available has expanded considerably in recent years.

PATCHING LARGE HOLES IN DRYWALL

A medium to large hole in plasterboard can look formidable, but resist the temptation to simply cover with a picture and forget about it. A professional-looking repair is not very difficult.

1. Draw a rectangle around the damage. Drill ½-inch starter holes in corners, insert a keyhole saw, and cut out the rectangle. Insert oversized backup strips of wood on opposite sides of the hole so that part is hidden behind drywall and part shows through the hole. Fix the strips with drywall screws.

2. Using drywall material that is the same thickness as that used in the wall (typically ½-inch), cut a new rectangular plug. For optimum fit, the plug should be about ⅛ inch smaller than the hole in both dimensions. Seat the plug in the hole and attach to backup wood strips with drywall screws.

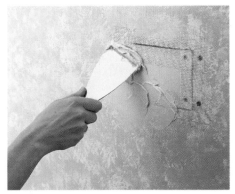

3. Cover the seams with fiberglass mesh; but for the smoothest application, don't overlap tape at the corners. Use a 4-inch joint knife to cover the tape with the first—and thickest—coat of joint compound. Smooth and feather the edges. Let dry.

4. Using progressively wider joint knives, apply three to four light coats of joint compound. Smooth each coat, feathering an ever larger area to disguise the patch. Sand the final coat lightly. Prime the patch before applying finish paint or wallpaper.

Flat paint is an all-purpose paint with a soft, glare-free finish that hides minor surface irregularities to produce the greatest uniformity of appearance. It is the usual choice for ceilings, and for walls in low-traffic areas.

Eggshell paint is very versatile, in that it combines the soft finish of flat with the washability of semi-gloss. Use it wherever you want lustrous surface without the shiny look of gloss paints.

Medium- or semi-gloss paint is highly washable. It works well on windows, doors, and architectural trim, as well as on walls in kitchens and baths, where you want moisture resistance and a greater degree of washability. And semi-gloss applies with nearly the same ease as flat and eggshell paints.

High-gloss paint has the highest luster, has a highly reflective surface, and resists grease and mildew. It takes a lot of abuse and can be washed repeatedly without losing shine. Its disadvantage is a tendency to show flaws and streaks; so be extra careful in preparing the surface and in applying the paint.

Primer paint

Primer is a specialty paint designed to make the topcoat look better, go further, and adhere better. New, unpainted drywall must always be primed. Dark colors, heavily patched walls, and walls that have previously been painted in oil-based paint, also need a primer for the topcoat to cover successfully.

Primer is manufactured in white only but can be tinted to approximate

TIME SAVERS

PAINT BY NUMBERS

How much paint you need depends on the size of the room, the condition of the wall surface, and the paint's spreading rate, which is given on the manufacturer's label. For a rough estimate of how much paint you'll need to cover the walls, measure the total footage around the perimeter and multiply by the wall height in feet. From this subtract 20 square feet for each door and 14 square feet for each window. Divide by the spreading rate (usually 300 to 400 feet per gallon). That's the number of gallons you'll need. Do a similar calculation for the ceiling by measuring the square footage and dividing by the spread rate.

To estimate how much paint needed for the trim in a room, the rule of thumb is about one-fourth of what is required for the walls. It will be more or less, depending on the number of windows and doors and the amount of detail trim.

the color of the finish coat that will follow. If you don't know whether you need a primer, try the topcoat in a well-lighted area. Allow the paint to dry, and observe how well the finish covers and whether any streaks show through. If it doesn't cover well, apply a primer coat.

Other specialty paints

Ceiling paint is a specialty paint that's ultra-flat and formulated to be thicker than standard paint, in order to reduce

drips and spatters. Acoustical ceiling paint is a porous paint best used on acoustical tile ceilings. Textured paint disguises a wall's existing irregularities by adding texture of its own. Mildew-resistant paint is formulated for kitchens and baths; scrubbable paints are available for children's rooms.

Choosing a brush

As a rule, buy the best brushes you can afford. They will do a better job and, with care, can be reused many times. Quality paintbrushes have hardwood handles and flagged or split-bristle tips that hold more paint. Their bristles are anchored at the top with metal or plastic spacers inside a metal ferule. They are tapered at the bottom to deliver a sharp paint edge.

Less-expensive brushes may have plastic handles, unflagged bristles, and blunt ends. Their bristles may be anchored or spaced less securely and be coarser and stiffer-textured, producing more-noticeable brush-stroke marks.

The choice between synthetic and natural bristles should depend on the type of paint you are using. Synthetic or nylon brushes are best suited to water-based paints because they do not absorb water and they maintain consistent stiffness throughout.

Natural-bristle brushes are recommended only for oil-based paints—they absorb the water from latex paints and turn limp, making it difficult to load a brush with paint or keep an edge. For general home painting or decorating, you will need at minimum a sash brush, a trim brush, and a broader wall brush.

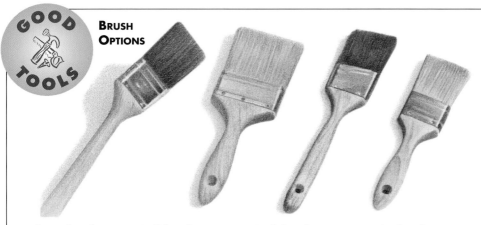

BRUSH OPTIONS

Radiator brush

Reach into crevices, such as radiator fins, with this brush, distinguished by its angled design and longer handle.

Wall brush

Use a 3- to 4-inch flat brush as an alternative to a roller when painting large interior wall spaces.

Sash brush

Use a long-handled, angled–bristle brush to do sashes and other areas where you want tight control.

Trim brush

Use 3-inch straight-edge brushes for doors, wainscoting, window frames, and cutting in along edges.

Rollers

While traditionalists may be happy to do all their painting with brushes, rollers can reduce by half the time required for painting large spaces. The main elements needed for roller painting are a metal roller frame with handle, a disposable textured roller cover or sleeve, and a paint tray that hooks onto the shelf of a stepladder. Roller covers come in various materials, from lamb's wool to synthetics, and in ¼-inch- to 1-inch-deep naps. For latex paints and a smooth finish, a nylon sleeve with a ½-inch nap is a good all-round choice.

Specialty rollers include a 3-inch-wide trim tool, and doughnut or cone-shaped rollers for cutting in right-angle corners and deeply indented moldings.

GETTING ORGANIZED

Once you begin painting, it's most efficient to keep going as the job progresses. So clear the work area of furniture, cover what you can't take out, and mask any hardware that you haven't removed. Here are some tips on getting started.

◆ **Keep a "painter's outfit"** of old clothes for paint days. A long-sleeved shirt, trousers, work gloves, and shoes should suffice. Add an old hat, or a painter's hat, if you're painting ceilings.

◆ **Cover up your work area** with heavy canvas drop cloths rather than spreading newspaper. With drop cloths, paint spatters are absorbed and won't flake off when dry, which means less to clean up later. Canvas drop cloths are

also relatively skid-proof, a feature that you will appreciate when high up on a ladder. And they don't tear easily.

If you are painting the ceiling, protect any ceiling lighting fixtures from splatters: Bag them in garbage bags tied snugly at the top. Remove all switch and receptacle plates or cover with masking tape or painter's tape.

◆ **Pry open a new paint can** with the wide tip of an old screwdriver, working evenly around the lid's edges so as not to bend or deform it. When it pops open, stir thoroughly. Then pour enough paint into a pail for immediate use. Cover the rest to keep it from drying out. To avoid paint accumulating in the rim and dripping down the sides of the paint can, puncture the rim with a nail. The excess will then run back into the can.

Paint odors

With oil paints, good ventilation is a must in all weather. Latex paints have relatively little odor when wet because they don't contain many solvents. Open doors and windows during painting anyway, since it will speed drying.

PAINTING TECHNIQUES

Try to be systematic when painting. Start with the ceiling. Any paint that splatters on walls or drips onto woodwork can be washed off later. Then move to the walls, starting with the wall that has the most open space and the least trim. Paint the wall from top to bottom, beginning at one end.

Start by "cutting in" along the juncture of the wall and ceiling. If

Cut in along ceiling molding.

you choose to use a trim brush, load a controlled amount of paint. Dip no more than a third of the tip in the paint, and tap off any excess. Hold the brush at an angle (above) and work away from the edge, using long, deliberate strokes. Apply just enough pressure to bend the bristles as you draw the brush away; this will force a bead of paint into the angle and make an even edge.

Cut in an area approximately 3 feet long and 6 inches deep. Move the ladder often to avoid stretching. Then, before the cut-in strip dries to create lap marks, use a roller to lay paint on the open expanses of wall beneath.

Roller technique
To ensure that you're rolling out an even coat, paint in zigzags. Work one 3-foot section at a time. On the ceiling make the first diagonals in a W pattern. Fill the spaces with uniform crosswise horizontal and vertical strokes that produce even coverage throughout.

Follow the same principle on walls,

using an inverted W and filling in between. Reload the roller with paint whenever it begins to paint unevenly.

When you reach door trim, window trim, and baseboard trim, use your brush or doughnut roller to cut in again. Then resume work with the full-sized roller. Save the most difficult wall—the one with the most doors and windows—until last. If, however, you know you won't be able to finish in one session, work on walls that you can finish. You don't want to stop midway on a wall, since there's a strong chance the interruption will show permanently.

An extension pole (below) for a paint roller is one of the best labor-saving painting tools you can buy. The pole makes it easy to reach high areas—especially ceilings—without a ladder, which has to be moved every

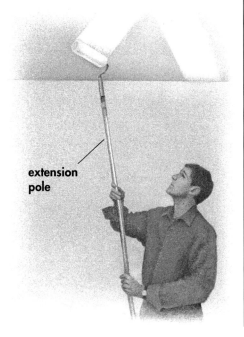

extension pole

few feet. Extensions screw into the threaded handle of most rollers. Make sure that the connection is tight and secure before beginning to apply paint.

TRIM PAINTING
Save trim painting for last, but do the preparation work before you do the wall and ceiling, since the preparation is bound to create dust. Chances are the previously painted woodwork has a semi- or high-gloss finish; so to ensure that the next coat will adhere properly to the old, give it a light sanding.

You should strip woodwork that is in bad condition—if it's chipped or if it has excessive layers of paint obscuring fine detail. You can use a nontoxic paste chemical stripper, available in hardware stores and home centers; you apply this with a brush, and then scrape it off with a joint knife when the paint has softened. A heat gun is a faster way to remove old paint, but it must be used carefully. There is the danger of starting a fire, scarring the wood, or burning yourself. Work in a room with a fire extinguisher, and have a fireproof holder where you can set the hot gun down. Wear heavy work gloves. Holding the gun 6 inches from the paint, move it back and forth over a small area at a time. Scrape off loose paint as it bubbles up. However you strip it, sand the woodwork smooth and dust it before you paint it.

Special trim techniques
If you have patience, a steady hand, and a good chisel-edged trim brush, try painting trim freehand. Otherwise, tape

Mask around the glass panes.

Tape around the window frame.

Canvas drop cloth has edge taped over baseboard.

areas to be protected with masking tape or painter's tape. Apply tape carefully, since it will define the crispness of your edge. If the tape is to protect a wall or ceiling, use the lightly adhesive paper tape made for masking painted surfaces, applying it only on dry paint.

◆ **To paint double-hung windows,** lift them out, if possible, and lay them on a flat surface. If not, paint them in sections, raising and lowering sashes to reach all parts. Begin with sashes just slightly open to get the very top

and bottom and to avoid painting them shut. While these are drying, paint as much of the muntins (pane dividers) as you can reach, then do the rest of the sashes, casing, sill, and apron. Raise the lower sash all the way to do the lower jambs; then lower the upper sash to reach upper jambs. Last, with the window closed, paint any missed areas.

◆ **Use painter's tape** between muntins and window glass (left) to minimize the time spent scraping paint off the glass later. Butt the tape as close as possible to the muntins. Alternatively, remove paint on glass with a straight-edged razor blade or a razor blade in a holder.

◆ **Before you paint a door**, remove the knob and check to see that the door opens and closes freely, with room for the thickness of another coat of paint. Close the door and slide a piece of cardboard between the door and the jamb all the way around. If you discover spots where you cannot slide the cardboard, sand them down before painting. Mask door hinges with tape. Any paint can make hinges stiff; water-based paints can cause them to rust.

FINISHING THE JOB
Remove wet paint spatters from painted woodwork by wiping them away with a damp sponge or rag. Dried spatters can be cleaned up with a light rubbing of very fine (#00) steel wool.

Brush and roller care
If you need to take a few hours' break from painting, or if you're not able to finish in one day, wrap and seal wet brushes or rollers in plastic wrap or

TIME-SAVING PAINT APPLICATORS

◆ **Small foam** brushes are ideal for making quick touchups to cover mars and small repairs. Dip one into the paint can, apply the paint, and discard the brush when you are finished.

◆ **Doughnut rollers** do a fast job of cutting in along the corners of walls. Also use this V-shaped handy tool where the ceiling and wall meet, if they are painted in the same color and finish.

aluminum foil and store in a cool place. When you resume, soften them in water (if using latex paint) or mineral spirits (if using oil-based paint).

For longer storage, take the time to clean quality brushes and rollers thoroughly. Wash latex brushes under a steady stream of warm water, or let them soak flat in a tray of warm water. Use a small comb to rake paint flakes out of bristles. Towel away the excess water in the brushes, and hang them up to dry by the handle hole.

Clean brushes used with oil paint in paint thinner, and hang them in a bucket of thinner. To keep bristle tips above the bottom of the can, so they won't bend while soaking, suspend them from a length of wire coat hanger set across the top of the open can. After a few days, remove the brushes, blot away the thinner with paper towels, wrap, and store by hanging them.

To clean a reusable roller of latex paint, wipe it repeatedly on a sheet of cardboard or newspaper until it appears nearly dry. Slide the roller cover off and hold it under running water until the water runs clear. Wash with soap and warm water, rinse, squeeze, and blot lightly with a clean, dry cloth. Stand the sleeve on end to dry. Wash the roller frame in soap and water, too. It is also possible to clean a roller sleeve of oil-based paint by using mineral spirits, but it may be more trouble than it's worth.

Small touch-ups

For small nicks and scratches, a cotton swab makes a simple, disposable applicator. Pour a small amount of paint in a paper cup. Dip the cotton end of the swab, and use dabbing motions until you've covered the scratch.

GOOD SOLUTIONS

KEEP A PAINT RECORD

To document the paint you have used in redoing a room, write down the brand, color, and finish of the wall, trim, and ceiling paints on a piece of painter's tape. Stick the tape to the underside of the switch plate before you reattach it at the end of the job. Then, when you need to do touch-ups or you want to repaint the room the same colors, you'll know exactly where to find this important information.

Paint storage

Clear glass jars and plastic milk jugs (above) with lids make convenient containers for leftover latex paints. You can see what paint colors you have and how much is left. Use a funnel to fill the container. Drop a few marbles in so you can stir paint just by shaking it when needed.

WALLPAPERING BASICS

No material can transform a room as quickly as fresh wallpaper. And with practice, the proper tools, and the right selection of papers, even a novice can master the basic techniques needed to do a good job. Choose a smaller room, out of the public eye—a bedroom, for example—for your first project. And start on a wall with a minimum of windows and doors because the measuring, hanging, and fitting will be easiest there. Many do-it-yourselfers also find that working with a helper makes everything go more smoothly.

Preparing papered walls

If your walls are already papered, it's advisable to strip the existing paper even if the old paper is holding well, because moisture in the new paste may cause the foundation layer to soften. (However, if there's just one layer of old paper in place, you can experiment by applying a single panel and waiting a day to check results.)

Many wallpapers are "strippable," which means they can be removed with very little trouble. To see if the paper you want to remove is strippable, start at the top and pry up a seam edge with a utility knife. Tug gently and slowly on the lifted corner, pulling down at an angle, keeping both hands close to the lifting edge. If it comes off easily, peels in a long sheet, and leaves no adhesive residue, then removing the old paper will be a simple one-step operation.

Older papers, and the newer ones applied with standard wallpaper adhesive, will probably have to be soaked to soften the paste. Protect the floor with drop cloths before you start.

◆ **Use a special wallpaperer's tool** or a utility knife to "score" or rip the wallpaper so that water can get behind the paper more easily. (An old dinner fork works nearly as well.) Then soak the paper thoroughly a few feet at a

time, using a sponge or a water-soaked paint roller dipped in hot water. For stubborn paper, however, you may want to add a professional liquid paper-remover to the hot water.

◆ **When the old paste** becomes soft and the paper begins to wrinkle—about 10 minutes—scrape it off with a broad wallpaper or joint knife. (To keep the job going, have the next area soaking while you scrape.) Scrape as much adhesive residue off the wall as you can. Go back later with a brush or sponge and warm water to remove any remaining paste. New paper will adhere much better to a clean wall.

◆ **If you are going to remove** several layers of paper, then consider renting a portable, electric wallpaper steamer from a hardware or paint store to make the job go faster. Follow instructions carefully and keep moving, especially on wallboard. Directed too long at any one spot, the steamer can cause wallboard to blister.

◆ **Once the walls are stripped**, go over them for defects that might show through, and make repairs. Paint the ceiling and trim before papering; it's easier to remove paste from painted trim than paint from wallpaper.

Cleaning painted walls

Clean and repair previously painted walls (pages 34–35 and 38–39) before applying wallpaper, to ensure that the paper adheres properly. If a glossy paint has been used (as in a kitchen or bathroom), the surface must also be deglossed with a light sanding. Apply a primer-sealer coat specifically designed as an undercoat (or "sizer") for wall coverings.

Choosing Wallpaper

If you are new to paperhanging, keep your first project as easy as possible. Choose a paper designed with the do-it-yourselfer in mind. Here are some characteristics to look for:

◆ **High-quality, machine-printed**, pretrimmed papers tend to be the most problem-free. Flocked and foil papers or wallpapers with selvage edges that must be trimmed on the job are challenges better left to professionals your first time around.

◆ **Patterns that are "straight"** are easier to hang than "dropped" patterns. Straight patterns are so called because neighboring panels meet in a straight line, so they require little extra figuring when you cut and hang them. Dropped patterns have design repeats that are meant to be matched panel to panel, a somewhat more difficult calculation to measure. Dropped patterns also require more paper to compensate for the matching.

◆ **Small-scaled overall patterns** tend to camouflage uneven surfaces. But striped, shiny, and solid wallcoverings are best reserved for very smooth, perfectly plumb walls.

◆ **Matching pattern scale** to room size is also critical. Too large a pattern in a small room can be oppressive; too small a pattern will be lost in a large room. Bring home samples of wallpaper or wallpaper books to see what patterns work best for your purposes. View them in both natural and artificial light.

Estimating wallpaper quantity

Buy all the paper you need at one time because color can vary from print run to print run. To determine how many rolls a room will need, add together the width of walls in feet, and multiply by height. Divide by 30—the average usable square feet in a standard wall-paper roll—or by 25, if you are using a European-made paper. Subtract a half roll for each normal-sized window and door. You now have a working total; add one roll for good measure (and future patches)—a little more if your pattern has large repeats to match.

If you are uncertain of your calculations, draw a picture of each wall, including measurements and the position and size of all the windows and doors. Take the sketch to your wallpaper supplier. An experienced salesperson can offer advice on how many rolls you need to purchase.

When you place your wallpaper order, also buy compatible paste and a paste brush for standard papers, or a water box for prepasted papers.

Preparing to work

Before you begin wallpapering, remove as much furniture as possible. Spread a drop cloth on the floor, and cover remaining furniture. Plug work lights into an outlet in an adjoining room, and shut off electrical power to circuits in the room to be papered. Remove all mounted light fixtures, register covers, and light-switch and electrical-outlet cover plates. Finally, lay out all of the tools you will need: tape measure, plumb line or chalk line, pencil, utility knife and blades, broad knife, smoothing brush, smoother blade, seam roller, bucket, sponge, rag, step stool or ladder, and worktable.

APPLYING WALLPAPER

Your starting point will also be where you finish. Because it is almost impossible to have the pattern of your first and last panel line up perfectly, you want this joining place to be where it is least likely to be noticed—along the edge of a door or a built-in cabinet, or at an inconspicuous corner. (An excep-

tion is the mural-type scenic paper, which should be centered over a fireplace, behind the sofa, or between matched windows.)

Wherever you begin, push a tack into the wall 1½ inches below the ceiling and tie a plumb line to the tack, letting the bob swing (above). When it comes to rest at true vertical, place a mark on the wall 2 inches above the baseboard. If your plumb line is self-chalking, hold the string to the mark with one hand and pull back with the other; let it snap, leaving a chalk line on the wall. Similarly, rub colored chalk along the string of a plain plumb bob before snapping.

Now check to see where the pattern will best break at the ceiling line. Generally, with individual design elements, it's most visually pleasing to start with a full element at top; with stripes, start at any point. Move the paper up and down until it's positioned where you want the panel to begin at the ceiling and where it will end at the baseline. Lightly mark the locations with a pencil. Add 2 inches to the top and bottom to make adjustments. Cut the panel.

Pasting and booking

For unpasted paper, place measured panels face down on a worktable, one strip at a time. Using a roller or pasting brush, apply paste to the back. Work from the center outward, and cover the upper two-thirds, including edges. Fold the pasted section on itself ("booking") for ease in handling; but don't crease the fold. Similarly, paste the bottom third of the strip and book toward the middle. Wait five minutes.

Prepasted wall coverings require no additional pasting. Measure and cut the strip. Immerse pattern-side down in a tray of warm water, positioned on the floor at the foot of the worktable, for 10 to 15 seconds. Holding the edges nearest the table, slowly pull the strip onto the table, letting water fall back into the tray. Book the panel as before.

Hanging the first panel

Unfold the top section; place the pasted side on the wall with 2 inches overlapping the ceiling. Align one vertical edge with the plumb line, and gently smooth the upper section with a brush (below). Working from the center to the edges, brush smooth about 3 feet of paper at

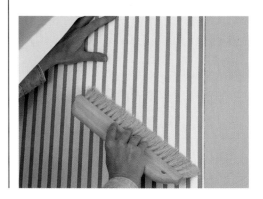

a time, using downward strokes. Continue to check alignment with your plumbed chalk line. Peel up portions of paper to reposition. Unfold the bottom section of the paper strip against the wall and smooth from the center out and down to the baseboard, holding the adjacent edge to the plumb line. Don't force wrinkles out; pull paper from the wall and reposition it.

Trimming and rolling

Using a joint knife or straightedge, press the top of the paper panel against the ceiling. When it is snug, take a

sharp utility knife or single-edged razor knife and, with the edging tool to protect the paper, trim the overlap (above). Repeat the procedure at the baseboard. Change blades often to avoid tearing the paper. Rinse the molding and wall covering with a sponge dipped in warm water to remove excess paste. With each swipe, rinse the sponge. Run a seam roller (above right) along the edge that will not abut the second strip.

Papering the remainder

Match and cut the second strip. Hang it as you did the first, using the edge

of the first strip as your vertical guide. Butt the two edges together, but do not overlap. (The slight ridge at the butt joint will flatten when the paper dries and shrinks.) Continue around the room, repeating each step in hanging. Wait 15 minutes, then firmly press fresh seams against the wall with the seam roller tool. Use a sponge and clean water to remove any paste that squeezes from the seams.

Papering around windows and doors

Where casing partially intersects with a panel, paste the strip over the trim. Make a diagonal relief cut at the outside corner of the trim so that excess paper can be laid back (below). Position the strip so that the adhesive on the back contacts the wall, cut conserv-

atively, and then reposition the paper until it fits. Tap it in place with the brush bristles. Trim the wallpaper with a razor blade and straightedge as you did at the ceiling and the baseboard.

Turning a corner

To paper an inside corner, measure from the last whole strip to the corner at three locations along the vertical edge. Cut and prepare a strip ⅛ inch wider than the widest measurement so that it will actually wrap the corner slightly when hung. Hang the strip.

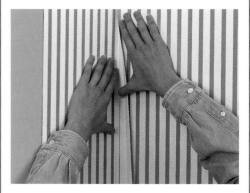

It's safe to assume that the corner is not perfectly perpendicular, so you want to establish a new guideline for hanging the next sequence of panels on the far side of the corner. Drop a plumb line and hang the first panel on this next wall as you did the original panel on the previous wall. Align the panel edge vertically along the freshly marked plumb line. Overlap the previous panel's corner-turned edge (above). If the wall covering has a vinyl-coated surface, run a bead of vinyl-to-vinyl adhesive under the top seam, and roll it firm to ensure that the seam is secure.

WINDOWS AND DOORS

Much is demanded of windows and doors in terms of comfort and serviceability. To perform their tasks well, they need timely repair and maintenance.

As your first defense against the elements, windows and doors deserve your attention more than once or twice a year. Poorly maintained windows will stick, rattle, and leak. Neglected doors will do the same and worse. Neglect can cause structural damage and higher utility bills, not to mention discomfort from cold drafts leaking through the cracks. Windows and doors are expensive to replace, but they are not difficult to maintain if you do so regularly. Inspect them often, and make repairs promptly. Keep them clean, painted, and maintained, and they'll last a lifetime.

WINDOW BASICS

Whether installing a new window or repairing an old one, it helps to understand its structural components. There are two basic types of window—operable and fixed. Fixed windows have the same stationary elements as operable ones but no moving parts. Operable windows have the following elements:

◆ **The jambs** are the pieces that form the sides and top of the window opening itself.

◆ **The stool and apron** comprise the inside windowsill (the actual windowsill sits outside).

◆ **The sash** is the frame into which one or more panes of glass are set. Double-hung windows have upper and lower sashes, for example.

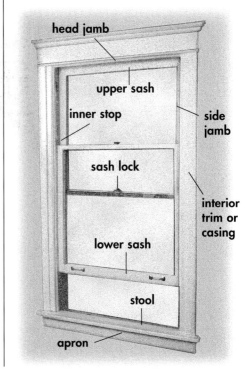

WHAT KIND OF WINDOW IS IT?

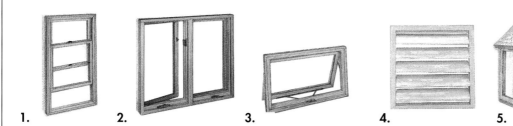

1.   2.   3.   4.   5.   6.

When repairing or replacing a window, it helps to know how it operates. Here are some of the most common configurations.

1. Double-hung: The sashes of these windows slide up and down to open. Older double-hung windows operate with a weighted sash-and-cord arrangement concealed in the sides of the frames, but later designs have less-cumbersome spring counterbalances. The sashes of new double-hung windows come out of their frames for convenient and safe cleaning.

2. Casement: A crank or lever on the stool operates these hinged windows, which swing out to open and have interior screens. Some older homes have casement windows that open inward manually.

3. Awning: An interior crank opens these windows on a horizontal axis. Awning windows are often used in basements or under eaves.

4. Jalousie: When cranked open, a jalousie's linked horizontal glass panes swing out and up. Because of poor energy performance, it is rarely a primary window in homes. But it is ideal for an enclosed porch because it allows maximum ventilation.

5. Bay: The angular bay window and its cousin, the rounded bow window, extend out from an exterior wall, often with a stationary middle pane flanked by two narrow casement windows.

6. Sliding: The sashes of these windows slide sideways to open and close. In some models, one sash is fixed in place.

◆ **The stops** are vertical channels in which the sashes slide up and down. In some windows, they detach so that the sashes may be removed.

◆ **The trim,** or casing, is the interior molding that surrounds the window; it is often decorative.

Easing sticky windows

Sometimes windows don't slide easily. Lubrication may help: Rub household bar soap or paraffin along the channels. If that doesn't work, there are several other possible explanations, generally requiring a more substantial fix. In a new house, for example, it may be excess insulation in the wall that's causing the channels to buckle and pinch the window. In an older house, a window may stick because it's out of square due to poor installation or the natural settling of the house. Test with a square, or look where the sashes meet the jamb; if the lines are not parallel, the window is crooked. Call a professional for repairs or for reinstallation.

Years of accumulated paint also can cause a window to be too tight. Paint may even seal it shut altogether. First, check to make sure that the previous owner hasn't nailed or screwed the window shut. If not, cut around the sash with a utility knife to break the paint seal evenly. Then carefully tap the sash (but not the glass) with a rubber mallet to loosen it.

Eliminating drafts

For a seasonal solution, add removable rope-type caulking (below) in the fall and remove it in the spring. Or, affix plastic sheets to the inside window frame, using one of many kits available at hardware stores and home centers. For a more permanent solution, you can tighten drafty old double-hung windows with weather-stripping.

rope caulk

Tubular, vinyl weather-stripping is best for sealing gaps in older windows. Install it along the horizontal seams and in the tracks where the sashes slide. Self-adhesive varieties are easiest to install. Work carefully, and check continually that the sashes can slide freely.

Choosing replacement units

Sometimes windows are beyond repair and must be replaced. Replacing a window is a major do-it-yourself project. A window-replacement company may not charge very much for installation if you buy the windows from them. Before you shop for new windows, it pays to understand basic window terms:

◆ **Cladding** is a protective material, usually vinyl or aluminum, that encases exterior wood frames to prevent decay and the need for painting.

◆ **Muntins (or mullions)** are the wooden horizontal and vertical trim pieces that divide the sash into small sections, called lights. In older windows, and in many of the more expensive modern replacement windows, the lights are separate panes and the muntins that hold them project on the inside and outside of the sash. In newer moderate-priced windows, faux muntins are a one-piece snap-in cosmetic feature, often plastic, installed only on the inside sash over a single large pane.

◆ **Double- and triple-thickness** windows are separated by slim, hollow spaces filled with inert gases. The gases reduce heat flow, an important advantage in maintaining stable temperatures in the house and boosting energy efficiency. Double-glazed windows with two layers of glass are the minimum recommended for Canada's climate.

REPLACING A SASH CORD

Sash weight access panel

1. Pry along the length of the inner stops with a putty knife. Remove any nails and lift off the stops. Take out the lower sash, removing the cord knots secured to either side. Find and remove the sash weight access panel on either side of the casing.

2. Discard old cords. Find the pulleys at the top of the side jambs for the upper and lower sashes. Thread new cord (measured to match the old one in length) up each sash-weight channel and through the pulley for the lower sash.

3. Tie one end of the new cord to the weight, as shown, and tie the other end around a nail until you put new cord on the other side of the window. When both new cords are ready, place the sash on the window stool while you attach the new cords.

4. Stick each cord through a slot in the sash and knot it. Drive a small nail to secure it. Replace the sash weight access panels. Set the sash back in place. Test it for smooth operation, and reinstall the stops. Repeat the process for the upper sash cords.

◆ **Low-E glazing** is a term used to describe the ability of glass to block ultraviolet radiation as emitted in the form of sunlight. The low emissivity of some modern window glass is achieved by the addition of an invisible metallic coating, either on the glass itself or on plastic film in the sealed air space between double-glazed windows.

◆ **R-values** rate an insulating material's capacity to resist heat flow. Windows are rated on a scale of R-1 to R-5; the higher the number, the better the insulation. But R-values refer to glass only. Window frames, spaces and air infiltration are not taken into account. For this reason, the Canadian Standards Association and Canadian window and door manufacturers have adopted the Canadian Energy Rating (ER) system. It assesses windows on their ability to capture the sun's heat, insulation capability, and ability to resist air leakage, and accords ratings ranging from –50 to +15. The higher the ER, the better the window's performance.

Choosing windows

Wood-framed windows are the traditional choice and offer many benefits. They can be painted or stained. And quite apart from the insulating properties of the glass, the wood frame itself has good insulating properties.

Aluminum-frame windows are less expensive than wood, generally, and they need less upkeep. But they may be less attractive, particularly in older homes with more traditional architecture. And they are not as thermally efficient as wood frames. To avoid heat

loss, aluminum frames should have a thermal barrier on the inside.

A third choice is wood windows with vinyl and metal cladding on the exterior. These combine good insulating properties with low maintenance and moderate prices. Many have sashes

HOW TO MAKE WINDOWS GLEAM

A squeegee and sponge are the best tools to use for washing windows. Professionals say the secret to clean windows is to use very little detergent and not too much water (squeeze out the sponge before you apply the washing solution). Squeegee the glass immediately to prevent streaking. Wash when the sun is not shining directly on the window.

designed for easy removal during cleaning (left). Cladding is not paintable. Your color choice in exterior frames is limited to white and neutrals.

Washing windows

Use either window-washing fluid or a home brew combining a capful of liquid dishwashing soap per gallon of water. Wash the window from top to bottom so that the solution doesn't drip onto previously washed surfaces. Wash with vertical strokes outside and horizontal strokes inside; this will make it easier to find streaks and remove them.

Rubbing alcohol sprayed from a bottle also makes an excellent window cleaner. It removes greasy smudges, evaporates quickly, does not freeze in cold weather, and leaves no residue.

Removing window film

During the 1980s, ultraviolet window film was applied with heat to the room-side glass surface of many windows to make them more energy efficient. When such film becomes discolored, it needs to be removed. The task may

HOW TO REPLACE A BROKEN PANE

1. Use duct tape to make a large "X" on the broken pane. Wearing gloves and safety goggles, break the rest of the pane by tapping it with a hammer. Remove glass pieces from the frame with needle-nose pliers. Heat the hardened glazing compound with a hair dryer until it is pliable enough to remove from the sash channel with a chisel (left). Also scrape away loose paint. Sand and prime any raw wood.

2. Take a piece of the broken glass, along with measurements, to the hardware store so that you get the right thickness and size. Have the pane cut ⅛ inch shorter than the opening in both directions. Buy points with push tabs and glazing compound. Back home, apply a bead of glazing compound in the rabbeted channel where the glass will go. It can be dispensed from a caulking gun (below left) or rolled by hand into a ½-inch "rope." With gloves on, set the glass into place, and secure it with glazier's points pushed into the sash with the edge of a putty knife (left).

3. Finally, apply another thick bead of compound over the glazier's points. Hold the caulk gun at an angle to achieve a bevel (left) or roll another rope of compound and apply it to the juncture. Smooth the compound to a 45-degree angle with a putty knife, using long, smooth strokes to ensure an even edge. Allow the compound to cure for a few days before painting the sash. Paint over the glazing compound by ¹⁄₁₆ inch to seal out moisture in the joint.

seem daunting, but it is much easier if you mist the window first with soapy water. Allow it to soak in, and then scrape off the film with a paint scraper.

STORM WINDOWS

Storm windows are the old-fashioned way to reduce heat loss in winter. There are two basic types. Add-on storm windows fill the entire outside of the window and must be hung in place seasonally on hardware affixed to the exterior window frame. Combination storms (see page 54) remain in the window frame all year round, along with a half-sized screen panel. Because storm windows must be changed seasonally, must take heavy weather, and are often rather flimsily made, they need periodic maintenance.

Maintaining add-on storms

Plan to inspect and clean your add-on storm windows each fall before you hang them. It will be well worth the effort involved. Wear gloves; handle the storms carefully to avoid cracking the glass or twisting the sash, which could loosen the glass. If the storm has an aluminum frame, the gasket running all around the frame that holds the glass in place—the spline—may be loose in spots. Push it back into place with a screwdriver or putty knife. Aluminum frames also become spotted with oxidation deposits, a powdery-silver material similar to rust. Remove the oxidation with fine steel wool.

On a wooden unit, pry out loose and crumbling glazing compound and redo it (left). Tighten hanger hardware and

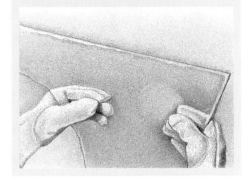

corner joints, if necessary, and unclog weep holes at the bottom of the sash. Last, wash the window glass both inside and out.

Maintaining wooden storms

Old wooden storms may look a bit clunky and are sometimes a hassle to take down and put back up because of their greater weight. But they have definite advantages over standard aluminum storms. Not only does wood insulate against cold transmission better, but wooden units are usually sturdier, and they can be repaired more easily than aluminum sashes.

Most wooden storms have slotted hangers attached by screws, left and right, at the top. The hangers slip onto a pair of hooks that are fixed to the window frame. In addition, the storms may have an eye hook or two at the bottom, allowing you to lock the unit securely to the sill from the inside.

Some have ventilation adjusters— pivot rods, for example—that make it possible to open the bottom of the storm outward a few inches, a nice feature when the windows cloud up or the weather turns warm briefly. Some have a rubber gasket that runs around the edge where the storm meets the house, to improve insulation even further. (If not, consider adding one yourself.)

Paint carefully

Wooden storms need to be covered well with paint so they won't rot or swell. But each coat of paint adds a bit of thickness, so a storm may not fit as well after it is painted. Before you paint, check the fit. You may need to sand or plane away old paint before applying new.

Reinforce loose corner joints

If the corner joints wobble, correct the problem before the storm falls apart. Use small mending plates on the inside corners, where they will barely show. To avoid splitting the wood with the screws, drill pilot holes first.

SCREENS

Screen frames can become loosened, as can the screening material itself. Before putting window screens up in spring, do the same kinds of annual checks you did on the storms. In aluminum screens you may need to reseat the gaskets that hold the screen material taut; use a screwdriver or putty knife. Wooden screens tend to work loose at joints and around the screen bead—that narrow piece of quarter-round trim that runs around the edge between the screen and the frame. If you need to resecure the bead with new nails, use very small brads to prevent cracking the molding. Cover nail heads, and paint exposed wood and nails to match the rest of the screen. Fix loose corners with metal corner braces.

Repairing screening

Inspect the screen material itself for tears or holes. These days, screens may be made of metal, fiberglass, or plastic, each requiring different repair materials and techniques. To repair gnat-sized holes in metal screens, use tweezers to straighten the rigid strands of broken wire, and dab a bit of clear silicone adhesive, clear fingernail polish, or quick-drying adhesive on the spot until a thin film forms. For larger holes, cut away any damaged wire that remains in the hole. Patch with a compatible metal screen patch (available at hardware stores), or make a patch from a leftover screen. Select a rectangular piece about 2 inches larger than the hole in all directions. Pull away the outside wires on the edges of the patch to make a ½-inch fringe of wire on each side. Bend the fringe wires on each side over a block of wood to make sharp right angles around the patch. Position the patch over the hole (below),

screen patch

threading the wire through the screen mesh until the patch lies flat on the screen. Working from the other side of the screen, use tweezers to fold the fringes over to hold the patch in place. Secure the edges with adhesive or clear nail polish.

Repair a small tear in a plastic or fiberglass screen with a No. 18 tapestry sewing needle and very fine nylon fishing line. Use a zigzag sewing stitch

THE BEST WAY TO PAINT SCREENS

Apply rust-inhibiting **paint** to a discolored or rusted metal screen with two paint pads. Load the first pad lightly with paint, and dab it on the screen. Then blot the area with a second dry pad from the other side to get just the right amount to stay on. Using a paintbrush causes drips and will clog the openings. Spraying paint works, but it wastes paint.

to avoid puckering. Seal the stitches with clear silicone adhesive, clear nail polish, or quick-drying glue.

If you have a large hole or tear, take the screen to your local full-service hardware store to have the screening replaced. Or you can do it yourself. Here are the steps involved:

◆ **Lay the window screen flat** and, using a screwdriver, pry up the flexible spline (or gasket) that holds the screen material in the grooved frame. Discard the old spline and the torn screening.

◆ **Take the old screening to a hardware store** and purchase a piece of the same material of the same outside dimensions. Also equip yourself with an inexpensive tool called a spline roller and splining rope.

◆ **Center the screening** on the frame. Take diagonal snips off the corners of the material and, using the spline roller, proceed to push the screening into the groove that runs down one side of the frame. Cut a length of

spline to fit, and force it all the way into the groove, tightening the hold on the screen underneath.

◆ **Repeat the steps** on the other three sides, keeping the screening as taut in the frame as possible. Cut off excess material outside the spline when done.

Cleaning screens
Old screens need cleaning once a year. Lean the screen against the base of the house, and apply water with a hose to the entire surface. Be careful not to use so much pressure that you risk stretching the screening out of shape. Let it dry, and check to see that none of the openings in the mesh remains blocked. If necessary, scrub the screen with a brush, dabbing gently so that bristles poke through to clean the mesh.

COMBINATION STORM/SCREENS
Some windows combine three functions in one; that is, they perform as ordinary glazed windows, but they also have permanent storm and screen sections

that can be slid into place in season. Typically framed in aluminum, combination windows have three channels running along each side of the frame to hold two glass sashes and one screen sash. The three channels are staggered to make three openings of slightly different sizes; each of the three sashes thus fits in one and only one of the channels.

Removing a sash

When working on any part of a combination window, it is generally most convenient to remove it from the frame. To remove a sash, examine the mechanism carefully. There are usually tabs located along the channels or on the horizontal sashes that can be pulled out to release the sashes from the slides that hold them. If they prove difficult to release, squirt window cleaner around the tabs and scrub with a toothbrush to loosen and remove grit. Pry tabs gently with a screwdriver if needed, but don't bang on the frame, because old aluminum can be brittle.

Once the tabs are free, raise the sash a few inches and pull the bottom of the sash toward you. Carefully twist the window until one of the guides at the top of the sash is disengaged from its channel. Now lift the sash out of the window to work on it.

Making repairs

Aluminum storm windows are often poorly constructed. Cheap plastic parts, including slide tabs and guides, may break easily; the narrow frames may warp; and the glass may be so thin as

to break easily, particularly in larger windows. Gaskets that seal the sashes against the frame's channels are prone to wear, and the gaskets holding the glass in place often do not work well.

In addition, the low prices that many installers of aluminum combination windows charge puts a premium on getting the job done very quickly; this can sometimes lead to workmanship that is less than careful, sometimes even shoddy. As a result, it is not uncommon to find one or more of these storms working and fitting poorly. If your aluminum storm windows have problems galore, consider buying new units from a reputable dealer. If the current windows are several years old, you may well recoup your investment in better insulation in just a few years.

Replacing broken parts

If a channel guide or slide tab is broken, you may or may not be able to get replacement parts, depending on the manufacturer. If you know the installer, start your search there. If the manufacturer's name appears on the unit, call hardware stores or storm window installers and ask if they have parts and can install them. Otherwise, take the broken part to the store to see if they have a match. They should be able to install the parts at minimal cost or else show you how to put them in yourself.

Hardware fixes

Operating hardware, such as extension arms, operating handles, latches, and in some cases hinges, needs to be

QUICK FIX

UNCLOG THE WEEP HOLES

Along the bottom of your storm-window unit, you may find two or more small grooves that make for small openings, called weep holes, when the storm is closed. If they are painted over, open them up with the end of a screwdriver.

If you are painting, don't seal them; they serve a good purpose. Condensation can cause moisture to build up between the window and the storm window. Weep holes allow the moisture to escape. Because they are small, they don't allow in a significant amount of cold air.

cleaned and lubricated periodically. Brush the parts with an old toothbrush to remove loose dust. Apply a few drops of a light household oil or silicone spray to the cleaned assembly, and work back and forth a few times to move the lubricant around and to check your work. Tighten any loose screws that you find.

Frames and faulty fits

Look at the top of your storm and screen unit, where a sash meets the window frame. Do you see anything that suggests a bad fit? Is the top of the sash not parallel to the top of the frame, for example? Can you feel any air movement on one side, even with the window closed? These are indications that the unit was put in out-of-square and will never effectively keep out the cold. Call the installer to correct the

55

problem, if possible, or hire someone else to reinstall the unit correctly.

Slide the sashes up and down, and examine where they meet the channels of the frame. There should be a gasket—often made of a fuzzy material—that seals the sash against the frame. If the gasket is worn or cracked, install stick-on weather-stripping or a new gasket. A poor seal wastes energy.

DOOR BASICS

Doors come in three basic types: solid-wood, solid-core, and hollow-core. Substantially older houses typically have solid doors hung in frames constructed on site. Doors in newer houses and replacement-door units are more likely to be of the solid-core prehung variety, meaning that they probably were constructed of veneer over an insulating core of some sort and were factory made as a matched set.

You may have several different types of doors in your house, each of which may require different types of maintenance and repair. Other than in decorative details—paneled or plain,

flush door

panel door

for example—doors differ in whether they are made for exterior or interior use, and whether they have provisions for retarding the spread of fire.

All exterior doors must be constructed of materials and adhesives that can withstand weather. They also must be strong and thick enough (1¾ inches) that they provide a good measure of security when they are equipped with an exterior-grade lock. Many have specific features built into them that also ensure good insulation. These days, they are just as likely to be made of steel or fiberglass as of wood. Interior doors are more likely to be 1⅜ inches thick and be made of wood. When replacing any door, be sure you take the location of the door into consideration along with the other factors.

A flush door (left) has a smooth veneer on each side over a solid core (wood or particleboard) or a hollow core (cardboard reinforcing), making it the less expensive option typically. A panel door (above) is made of interlocking panels, often solid pine or oak. Hollow-core doors are the least sturdy,

for obvious reasons, and can be easily punctured or damaged by moisture. But even well-made doors can become deformed, damaged, or misaligned in their frames over time, just through heavy use or possibly a defect in their initial installation. A hardware problem can also lead to a badly operating door.

How a door works

If a door sticks, doesn't close all the way, or doesn't latch properly, the problem could come from a variety of sources: the door itself, a hinge, the jamb, the stop, the strike plate, or the latch.

Even if you do not plan on repairing it yourself, with a few simple tests (see "Diagnosing Door Problems" on the facing page) you can determine the

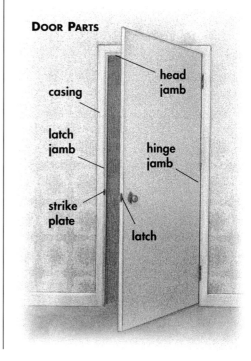

DOOR PARTS

casing
head jamb
latch jamb
hinge jamb
strike plate
latch

DIAGNOSING DOOR PROBLEMS

Door problems may come from the door itself or from the hinges, latch, or jambs. Since hinges are the easiest to fix and the most likely to develop quirks, check there first. Here are a number of diagnostic clues and corrective measures.

Problem	Diagnosis	Solution
Loose hinges	Hinges shift slightly from side to side as the door swings.	See "Tightening Hinge Screws" on page 58.
	When you grasp the door on the latch side and lift up, one of the hinges is loose.	See "Tightening Hinge Screws" on page 58.
	A loose hinge may signal a greater problem. Hinge screws loosen because the hinge is under stress, the result of the door chronically rubbing against the hinge jamb, the stop, the jamb, or the flooring.	Locate the rub point and correct it by filing down or planing the door at that location. Check the fit frequently to prevent taking off too much wood. Or move the stop.
Door springs open	Check to see that the hinge is not set too deeply into the door or the jamb. The hinge should be flush with the surrounding wood, not indented into the jamb or door.	Remove one or both of the hinges and shim out with pieces of pasteboard (see page 58).
Door always rubs against the jamb	If the hinges are tight, close the door just up to the point where it begins to stick. Examine the sticking point, then slide a credit card or a piece of paper between the door's edges and the jamb to find where the rubbing occurs.	Shim out the offending hinge, or scribe a line and sand or plane down the door's edge where it sticks (see pages 58–59).
Door rubs against the jamb in humid weather	Conduct the test for rubbing described above when conditions are the worst—most probably, when the air is most humid.	Shim out a hinge (see page 58). If that does not solve the problem, scribe a line and sand or plane down the door's edge where it sticks (see page 59).
Door rubs against the floor	New flooring—especially carpeting—has been installed and the floor's height is raised.	Take the door off its hinges (see page 59) and plane the bottom of the door to let it swing freely.
Latch doesn't work	If the door doesn't stay closed even though the latch's bolt moves in and out freely, the bolt probably isn't entering the hole in the strike plate.	Look closely at the latch bolt as you close the door to see if the strike plate needs to be moved up or down, or if it needs to be shimmed outward (see page 58).
	The latch rattles after the door has been closed.	Either the strike plate or the stop on the latch jamb needs to be moved so that the door will be tight against the stop when the latch's bolt engages it.
Door won't stay partially open	If a door will not remain half open, but persists in opening or closing, use a level to check the hinge jamb to see if it is plumb (straight up and down) in both directions. If it is out of plumb, then the house has settled.	Move one or both of the hinges. Or purchase an adjustable self-closing hinge, and adjust it so that the door acts as if its jamb were plumb.

cause of the problem, which will help you get a fair price for repairs. Some repairs can be handled easily without taking off the door, making it even simpler for a first-time do-it-yourselfer.

To deal with door problems, it also helps to know the standard terms used with doors and door openings:

◆ **Door jamb:** Three pieces that frame the door's rough opening.

◆ **Stop:** Three narrow pieces of wood that are nailed to the face of the jamb; they stop the door from closing too far.

◆ **Casing:** Decorative molding applied to the face of the wall, bridging the space between the wall and the jamb.

◆ **Lockset:** A set of hardware combining a doorknob or a handle, a lock or a latch, a strike plate, and its associated decorative elements.

◆ **Strike plate:** The metal piece on the door frame into which the door latch fits to secure the door when closed.

◆ **Threshold:** A raised strip of wood, often oak, that fills the space between the bottom of the door and the floor — essential in exterior door installations, optional with interior doors.

Repairing doors

This can be a thankless task, because some door problems take a good deal of time to fix even if they do not seem major. If the door itself is twisted or warped, or if the door is structurally unsound, the best solution usually is to install a new one, and often a new prehung door frame as well. This often requires advanced carpentry skills

TIGHTENING HINGE SCREWS

If a hinge is loose, its screws need tightening. You can do this without removing the hinge. Take out one or two screws at a time, and plug their holes with wood. You can use a golf tee, toothpicks, wooden matchsticks, cut pieces of shim—anything that will fit. Tap the wood in with a hammer until it is flush. Drive the screws back into place. If a screw isn't tight, take it out and add more wood to the hole.

for which you may choose to hire an expert. However, there are some minor door repairs that most homeowners can do themselves.

Moving a stop or strike plate

If the door latch is not catching, it may be because the stop is set wrong by a fraction of an inch. Try placing a block of wood against the stop and tapping with a hammer to move it in the right direction. If the latch bolt fails to engage the strike plate solidly, mark the jamb with a pencil to show the

needed adjustment (it will probably be very slight). Scribe the line with a knife, and chisel out enough of the jamb to raise or lower the

cardboard shim

shallow pocket into which the strike plate will be set. You may need to enlarge the latch-bolt hole in the jamb as well. Seat the strike plate, drill pilot holes for screws, and reinstall the strike plate in the new location. If the gap between the door and jamb is too large, shim the strike plate with a piece of cardboard cut to fit.

Shimming out a hinge

If the door is warped at the top or bottom, or if the hinge is set too deeply in the frame so as to cause the door to bind, you can shim the hinge. First, support the door by pushing some pieces of wood, books, or other objects under the bottom edge at two points so it will not

move once the hinge is disengaged. Remove the frame side of the hinge. Cut one or more pieces of cardboard to fit in the mortise (the cavity into which the hinge half is seated). When the hinge is perfectly flush with the door, reattach the hinge.

You may need to make several attempts before you get the hinge positioned just right. Once you shim the hinge out, you will have moved the door in the direction of the latch jamb, so you might need to sand or plane the other side of the door to achieve a proper fit.

Removing and reinstalling a door

Many hinges have removable pins around which they pivot. To remove a door, you simply slip the pin out. Support the door at the bottom. Place the tip of a screwdriver under the hinge pin, and tap upward. Remove the pin. If there is also a bottom pin, tap it out. With a helper, lift off the door.

On an old door, it may be difficult to tap out the hinge pins, and it might be easier to remove the screws on one side of the hinge. When putting the door back on, you must align the two

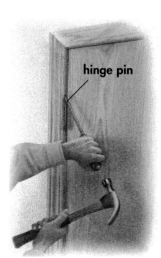

hinge pin

hinge parts perfectly before the pin can be reinserted. Have a helper hold the door while you guide the pin into place.

Sanding or planing a door

Sometimes you may need to sand or plane down a door if the door is too tight in its frame or if it rubs against newly installed carpeting. Reducing the surface of a door is not difficult, but it can be an awkward task. If possible, work with the door while it's still on its hinges. However, if you need to get at the hinge side or bottom of the door, you will have to remove it. Before removing the door, scribe a line indicating what portion of the door needs to be removed.

To do this, close the door until it just begins to shut—do not force it in, or your line will be inaccurate. Hold a pencil against the jamb or the floor, and run it along the length of the door, taking care to hold it in the same position the whole way so that you get a line that duplicates the line of the jamb or the floor.

Whether the door is still on its hinges or has been removed, support it so that it will not move as you work. A bar clamp attached to one corner of the door works well (above right). Use a plane or surface-forming tool to remove as much of the material as needed. Work in long strokes for a smooth line. Finish off the planing with a sanding block. Repaint or refinish the edge.

Loosening a sticky door lock

A stubborn or sticky lock can often be eased by rubbing the edges of its key

plane or forming tool

bar clamp

with a soft-lead pencil, thus transferring graphite onto the key. Work the key gently into the lock, moving it in and out to loosen the graphite into the works. Or squeeze powdered graphite (available in a tube at hardware stores and home centers) into the keyhole. Do not use lubricating oil, which over time can make a dirty lock even dirtier and more difficult to operate.

powdered graphite

2

Heating
Cooling
Lighting

FIREPLACE AND WOODSTOVE MAINTENANCE

*A fireplace or a woodstove conjures up the cozy charms of
a bygone era. Without proper design and care, however, either one can rob
your house of heat, pollute the environment, or cause a fire.*

To truly enjoy a fireplace or a woodstove, you need to know how it works and to commit yourself to regular inspections and maintenance that will make it more efficient and safer.

Don't assume that your existing fireplace or stove meets current building codes. An old woodstove, for example, may need a catalytic converter. A traditional fireplace may benefit from an insert (facing page) that is designed to burn wood more cleanly and to cut the creosote buildup in the chimney. To check the safety and legal compliance of an existing unit, contact your building department.

UNDERSTANDING YOUR FIREPLACE

Starting in the 1970s, concern for clean air and fuel conservation made communities more aware of the inefficiencies of many traditional fireplaces. New codes were written and manufacturers of fireplaces developed new designs.

Masonry fireplaces

A traditional fireplace, built by a mason, starts below the frost line with a concrete foundation and ends with a tile-lined flue that runs from the firebox (where you lay the logs) to well above the roof through a masonry chimney. A damper closes the flue when the fireplace is not in use and an ash door on the floor of the firebox lets you sweep ashes into a chute that you can empty

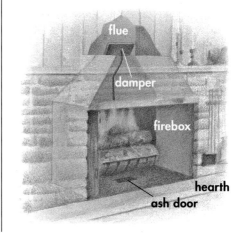

flue
damper
firebox
hearth
ash door

PRUDENT FIREPLACE PRACTICES

◆ **Check the flue** regularly for creosote buildup; have the chimney checked and cleaned at least once a year.

◆ **Open the damper** and look up the flue before lighting a fire; if you can't see all the way, there may be an obstruction. Never close the damper until the fire is completely out.

◆ **Never use flammable liquids** to start or rekindle a fire.

◆ **Burn only aged wood** in the fireplace. Treated wood, plastic, charcoal, leaves, trash, or pine branches either contain harmful chemicals or flare up too fast.

◆ **Use artificial logs** (p.64) one at a time; they can explode if stacked on one another or if they are put into a natural wood fire.

◆ **Keep a fire extinguisher** within reach of the fireplace, and install smoke and carbon monoxide detectors in the house.

◆ **Keep flammable items** (furniture, rugs, pillows, or curtains) at least 4 feet away from the fireplace and dispose of fireplace ashes in a metal container.

from the basement or into an opening outside. A masonry fireplace is a desirable architectural asset to a house. In use, however, they can rob your house of furnace-warmed air and pollute the environment with unburned toxic gases, while producing flammable creosote in the chimney and creating a fire hazard.

If the damper doesn't have a tight seal, a traditional fireplace can draw warm air up the flue even when it is not in use. (A quick fix is to place a large sheet of clear acrylic over the fireplace opening when it is not in use. If the surround is smooth, suction will hold the plate tightly in position.)

You can make inexpensive improvements to older fireplaces. Adding glass doors reduces heat loss as a fire dies down. A tubular grate with a blower may increase a room's heat during an occasional fire. A fireplace insert, although more costly, is a sound investment if you use a fireplace frequently.

◆ **Glass doors** can be mounted without much trouble in the fireplace opening. Better models will have vents above and below, and will seal tightly to the fireplace. The glass radiates heat into the room and cuts the loss of heated room air up the flue. Most glass door assemblies also include metal mesh screens that pull across the fireplace opening for spark control when the glass doors are open. Glass doors are not difficult to install in square or rectangular openings. Manufacturer's instructions vary, but typically you

need to drill holes in the masonry, set masonry anchors, and fasten the unit in place with screws. Many fireplace stores and home centers will install glass door assemblies for you for a modest fee. Units to fit arched fireplace openings can be special ordered.

◆ **A tubular grate** with extension tubes and a blower may help to circulate some fire heat. A fan draws cool air at floor level into the tubes, where it is heated, and then blown back into the room. If your fireplace is a standard size, you can install a grate yourself, plugging it into a receptacle near the fireplace. (Use electrical cord insulated to withstand the heat.) Be aware that an improperly installed grate can blow smoke back into a room.

◆ **A fireplace insert** is in effect a small wood-burning stove that fits into the firebox. The best models include catalytic converters and secondary combustion chambers to create higher fire temperatures and burn off pollutants, and a fan to circulate the heat into the room.

Factory-made fireplaces

A newer generation of manufactured wood-burning fireplaces uses "clean burn" technology to reduce emissions and improve heating output. Featuring an air intake, glass doors, and circulating fans, these fireplaces are much more practical and economical than their predecessors.

Because their chimneys don't require a masonry casing and can accommodate turns on the way to the roof, these fireplaces come in many designs and can be located almost anywhere in the house. You may find them used as room dividers, for example, with glass doors on either side.

Buy a fireplace insert from a fireplace or wood-burning stove dealer and have it professionally installed.

Gas-log fireplace inserts

To gain the warmth and beauty of a fire without the bother, use a gas-log insert, available through fireplace stores. These units, which can be amazingly realistic looking, burn natural or bottled gas. Some can even be turned on and off and the flame adjusted by electronic remote controls.

Have a gas-log insert installed by a professional; it needs to be properly vented through a flue and hooked up to the house gas lines. The greater the percentage of ceramic in the log, the longer it will last and the more heat it will absorb and radiate.

TAKING CARE OF A FIREPLACE

If you haven't used your fireplace for more than a year, or if you don't know

USING ARTIFICIAL LOGS

The paper-wrapped logs you buy at the grocery or hardware store are a great boon to people without a woodpile or the time to lay a proper fire. Made of dried recycled wood particles, kiln, wax and glue, artificial logs come in several sizes and can burn for as long as four hours. Simply light the paper wrapping with a match, and the log will shortly make a cheerful flame. Higher-quality artificial logs produce less creosote and smoke than natural firewood. Artificial logs are intended for fireplace use only; never use them in a woodstove.

the condition of a fireplace in a newly purchased home, hire a chimney professional (some still call themselves chimney sweeps) to make a thorough inspection before you test the fireplace yourself. Some fireplaces are simply decorative. If a fireplace flue has been sealed, you'll want to know if it can be opened and how much that would cost.

Have the chimney inspected and the flue cleaned at least once a year. If you use the fireplace every day in winter, it will need more frequent attention. If an inspection reveals problems in the flue lining or the chimney masonry, have these repairs attended to before you use the fireplace again.

Freeing a stuck damper

If a recently working damper suddenly won't budge, you may be able to unstick it yourself. Wear goggles for eye protection; dampers are dirty, and unlodging one will cause soot to fall. Look up from inside the firebox, and tap on the damper's handle with a short piece of wood, such as the handle of a hammer. If the damper won't move, spray the hinges with penetrating oil. Wait a few minutes, and then try again. For added leverage, slide a piece of pipe over the damper's handle, then try to push or pull it free.

Cleaning glass doors

The glass doors on a fireplace can be more difficult to clean than other glass. You can buy a product especially made for this tough job at a hardware store or fireplace dealer. Make sure the fire is out and the glass is cool before you start. Follow the manufacturer's instructions for cleaning. Scrub stubborn spots with a nonabrasive pad.

MAINTAINING A CHIMNEY

The upper part of a chimney that soars above the roof takes a beating from wind and the weather. Don't make it more vulnerable by attaching a TV antenna or satellite dish to it. Have the chimney inspected yearly for damage.

◆ **The facade.** The mortar around the bricks or stones that face your chimney may loosen and need repair (a process called tuckpointing), or the bricks or stones may crack. These are jobs for a mason and should be done promptly.

◆ **The flashing.** The joint between the chimney and the roof is protected by a series of overlapping pieces of metal called flashing. If flashing is damaged or worn, water may seep into the chimney. A roofer can replace the flashing; any damage to the masonry will require a mason.

◆ **The flue.** The inside of a chimney is subject to enormous temperature extremes and to buildups of creosote

flue cap

and toxic gases. It is not surprising that linings deteriorate over time and need replacing. Chimneys can be relined with flue tiles, poured concrete, or metal. The choice depends on the size of the chimney, local weather conditions, and the type of fireplace served. Consult a professional and have a professional complete the job.

SAFE OPERATION OF A WOODSTOVE

Like fireplaces, woodstoves have come a long way in efficiency and clean burning since the 1970s. Updated models use less wood to burn hotter and longer with less pollution. Make sure that your woodstove meets code requirements, is properly installed on a fireproof surface, and has the clearances from the walls and ceiling that are specified by the manufacturer.

A woodstove will burn more efficiently and will be safer if you keep it in top-notch condition. Here is how.

◆ **Clean out the ashes regularly.** Wear fireproof gloves and use a long-handled scoop. Place the cool ashes in a fireproof container with a tight lid.

◆ **Inspect the catalytic converter** regularly. If it appears worn or damaged, replace it. (Many newer models burn efficiently enough so they do not need a catalytic converter.)

◆ **Keep the stove's surface clean.** Touch up and restore its shine with stove polish or stove paint. Use only products intended for woodstoves.

◆ **Replace worn gaskets.** Most woodstoves have gaskets around the doors

and other moving parts. As the gaskets wear, they reduce the efficiency of the stove. A woodstove dealer can order replacement gaskets.

gasket

◆ **Inspect the stovepipe and flue.** Have a chimney professional examine and clean the flue—and disassemble, inspect, and clean the stovepipe—at least once a year; more frequently, if you use the stove every day in winter. You can learn to inspect and clean the stovepipe yourself.

Cover your floor and furniture with plastic, because this will get messy. Remove all the screws and set them aside. Put on heavy gloves, and pull the pieces of pipe apart. Keep the pieces in order. Clean the insides of the pipe with a pipe brush made for your pipe size.

If you need to replace any pipe pieces, use stovepipe recommended by the manufacturer of your woodstove. Assemble new pipe by sliding the creased end of one piece into the uncreased end of another. Secure each junction by drilling pilot holes and driving in sheet-metal screws.

MAKING A GOOD FIRE

Whether you are building a fire in a fireplace or a woodstove, it is important to start with the right kind of wood. Seasoned wood, logs that have been cut and allowed to dry out for six months or more, will burn cleaner and give off more heat than green wood, which still has a high water content. Two pieces of dry, seasoned wood will make a ringing tone when struck together; green logs will thud.

Softwood, such as pine or spruce, ignites quickly and is good for getting a fire started. Hardwood, such as maple, oak, ash, or birch, burns more slowly and keeps a fire going.

Building a fireplace fire

Always lay a fireplace fire on a grate or over a pair of andirons to allow air to circulate and feed the fire. To get more air at the fire, slide the grate forward (toward the room) slightly, but not so much that smoke enters the room. You can also improve circulation by setting the legs of the grate on fire bricks. Crumple newspaper into balls and set the balls under the grate or between the andirons. Pile kindling (small pieces of dry wood, preferably softwood) on the grate first, then add several light

DEALING WITH A CHIMNEY FIRE

Chimney fires can burn quietly for a while and then cause havoc. If you suspect a chimney fire, close the damper to the fireplace and the damper and all air outlets to the stove, if you can safely reach the handles. Get everyone out of the house and then call the fire department from a neighbor's. Wet down the roof with a hose. Deprived of oxygen, most chimney fires will die out quickly. But if flames break through a crack in the flue, or if burning ashes fall on the roof, the whole house could go up in smoke.

logs (3 inches or less in diameter) or pieces of split wood. Top this layer with two or more full-sized logs. Lay the logs with enough space between them for air to circulate, but close enough together that they can ignite each other.

When you are ready to start the fire, open the damper wide and put a match to the newspaper. Once the fire is established, close the damper down a bit, taking care that smoke does not enter the room. You can now add more logs, adjusting their spacing with a poker or fire tongs.

Building a woodstove fire

Place a pile of dry kindling over balls of crumpled newspaper and top with a mix of split wood—softwood for quick ignition and hardwood for long burning. Open the damper and air

inlet, light the paper, and shut the stove door. After a few minutes, when the fire is burning well, add enough larger hardwood logs to almost fill the combustion chamber. As soon as the larger pieces of wood have caught fire, close the air inlet two-thirds of the way or more (you will have to experiment with how far) to slow the burn rate and keep the fire going longer.

The outside temperature and the degree of wind chill will affect how fast the fire burns, and you will have to use trial and error in adjusting the air inlet and damper. If your stove has a thermostatically controlled regulator, these adjustments will be made automatically.

STORING FIREWOOD

Keep firewood outside for seasoning or just for storage. Stack it off the ground on a frame, which you can improvise from concrete blocks and boards or metal pipes, so that air can circulate around the logs to dry them out and to prevent them from rotting.

To protect the wood from rain, cover the top of the pile with a plastic or canvas tarpaulin tied to four posts, or make a lean-to type of roof that water will roll off. Keep the sides of the wood pile open to the air.

Firewood can be home to many insects, so bring in only enough logs to burn for a single day at any one time. Don't store firewood in the basement or garage. It is not only a potential source of insect infestation, but it also releases unwanted moisture into already damp air and poses a potential fire hazard.

HEATING SYSTEMS

A warm house in winter is easy to take for granted, but neglecting the machinery that keeps the house toasty can be expensive and even dangerous. Here's how to take care of your heating system.

Modern heating systems are efficient and effective, but they still require regular attention. A system that isn't maintained won't work as well or last as long as one that is cared for properly. You can handle many of the routine tasks yourself, but it's always best to have any heating system checked and serviced every year by a heating contractor.

Most homes have central heating, typically consisting of a forced-air furnace that produces heat and a system that distributes that heat throughout the house. The most common heating systems are described in detail on the following page.

TYPES OF HEATING FUELS

A heating system can be fueled by oil or natural gas. Electricity is another source of energy for heating. Wood, coal, and solar energy are less commonly used. By today's standards, coal and wood furnaces are dirty and labor intensive; replacing them may make your life easier.

An active solar heating system, which involves roof heat-collecting panels and pumps or fans, can be an effective supplement to your main heat-ing system. You can also take advantage of passive solar heating if your house has south-facing windows. Consult a solar designer or an experienced builder about the elements you will need to add for such a system.

Shutting off the fuel supply

Any fuel is a potential danger in a fire or a natural disaster, such as a tornado or flood. Always make sure that you and the other adults in your house know how to turn off your home's fuel supply in an emergency. But never attempt this unless you have plenty of time to do so safely. Never touch the main electrical shutoff if the floor is damp or the wiring is wet. Get your local electrical utility company to turn off the power.

If you smell gas, get out of your house right away, and call your gas company from a neighbor's house. If time permits, use a wrench to turn the gas shutoff valve on the meter intake pipe to a horizontal position (so that the bar on the valve is at a right angle to the pipe).

Fuel oil is stored in an outdoor or basement tank. Look for the shutoff near the tank bottom where the fuel line exits, or ask your supplier. For

WHAT TYPE OF HEATING SYSTEM DO YOU HAVE?

Hot-water

A boiler heats water and a pump circulates it through pipes to radiators or convectors and back to the boiler. Radiators on older systems look like steam radiators with two pipes. Newer upright or baseboard convectors are sleeker. Under the cover, you'll find a straight copper pipe surrounded by copper fins. Hot-water systems are sometimes zoned—different areas of the house are heated separately and each has its own thermostat. In this closed system, trapped air needs to be vented at least once a year. An expansion tank provides an air cushion that lets the hot water expand safely.

Steam

A boiler heats water until it vaporizes and rises through pipes into radiators. After the steam hits the metal walls of the radiators, it condenses and runs back to the boiler. In a two-pipe system, there is a separate pipe through which the condensed water travels downward. In a one-pipe system, the steam and water travel through the same pipe in opposite directions. A steam boiler builds up a tremendous amount of pressure, so it has a safety valve to let off steam if necessary. A steam system is not closed (like a hot-water system), so water needs to be added to the boiler from time to time.

Forced-air

A furnace heats air, which is blown through large sheet-metal supply ducts into individual rooms through warm-air registers. At cold-air registers, return ducts draw cool air from the rooms and carry it back to the furnace. There, the air passes through a filter before getting heated and blown back into the rooms. Besides supply and return ducts, the furnace also has an exhaust flue, to carry combustion gases out of the house. By far the most popular type of heating system, a forced-air system is also often used to circulate cool air from a central air-conditioning unit.

Basic care	**Improvements**	**Basic care**	**Improvements**	**Basic care**	**Improvements**
Clean and bleed radiators or convectors; lubricate the pump. Drain the expansion tank or the entire system if necessary.	Insulate pipes running through unheated areas; replace radiators with convectors; divide the system into heating zones.	Check the water and pressure levels in the boiler regularly; flush the boiler monthly; clean the radiators.	Install adjustable vents on radiators; tip radiators up to stop knocking; replace the boiler safety valve.	Clean or replace the filter monthly; clean the blower yearly; check the fan belt and lubricate the motor on older systems.	Insulate and repair leaks in ductwork; balance the heat distribution. Add a humidifier or central air conditioner to the system.

Radiant

The idea is very simple. Hot water pipes, electric cables, or sheets of electric film are embedded in the floors, walls, or ceilings of a house and radiate heat to people and colder objects. Older systems used copper or even galvanized pipe, which can corrode; newer systems use plastic tubing. The pipes are usually embedded in concrete floors or in walls. Electric cables, film panels, or metal foil strips are embedded in ceilings. Radiant heat is quiet and evenly distributed, but it is difficult to repair because access is difficult.

Heat pump

Efficient only in areas with mild winters, this system is basically a central air conditioner that also heats. As long as temperatures are not too low, the unit can extract heat from outside air and bring it indoors. The system saves money and space because it performs both heating and cooling duties. Most heat pumps are split systems, with an outdoor and an indoor coil. The outdoor coil absorbs heat, and a refrigerant carries it to an indoor coil. A blower picks up the warmth and sends it throughout the house through ducts, like those in a forced-air system.

Space heaters

In a centrally heated house, you can save money by setting the thermostat at 60°F or less and running space heaters in the rooms you are occupying at the moment. Portable electric units can be stowed away when not in use. But they are efficient only if electricity is cheap in your area. You can choose between convective (with a fan) and radiative (usually liquid-filled) types. Properly vented wall-mounted gas units are convenient and less expensive to run. A kerosene space heater can also be properly vented. But, in many localities, kerosene heaters are banned because they are fire hazards.

Basic care	Improvements	Basic care	Improvements	Basic care	Improvements
In a hot-water system, flush the pipes and replace the antifreeze. There is little to do for an electric system.	Replace older electric units with surface-mounted radiant heating panels or metal foil.	Vacuum the indoor coil; change the blower filter; wash the outdoor coil with a hose. Have it checked yearly.	If a pump does not adequately heat during cold spells, install supplementary heat sources, such as gas or electric space heaters.	For gas units, clean and check connections yearly. Electric heaters also require regular cleaning and safety checks.	Research energy costs and choose the type that is most efficient. A gas heater vented through the wall is most efficient.

GET FREE ADVICE FIRST

If your heating system is acting up and you suspect a minor problem, contact a heating contractor or the manufacturer.

◆ **Toll-free number.** Look for the company's 800 number on the furnace or boiler (or call toll-free information at 1-800-555-1212). Ask for someone who can give you technical advice.

◆ **Web page.** More and more manufacturers have a Web page, which is likely to include technical information or an E-mail address for technical support.

bottled gas, the control valve is on top of the tank. Turn the knob or lever clockwise to stop the flow.

THERMOSTATS

A thermostat automatically turns the furnace (or air conditioning) on or off at the temperature that you set. It also has switches for choosing between heating, cooling, fan only, and off settings. A programmable (setback) model has a built-in clock and timer that lets you set the times when you want the heat to come on and go off—both for convenience and economy.

Troubleshooting a thermostat

Most problems with thermostats stem from improper location or use. Don't place a lamp, television, or other heat source under a thermostat. A draft can cause a thermostat to register a temperature that is lower than the average temperature in the house, and send the wrong message to the furnace.

An electronic thermostat (with a digital readout and keypad) rarely causes trouble. Just be sure to replace the backup batteries with new alkaline ones when the low-battery light goes on. If an older mechanical thermostat (with levers for setting temperature and switching functions) behaves erratically, it may need to be cleaned. Gently pull off the cover and clear away the dust inside with a soft brush. Then clean the contacts on the levers: Slip a piece of coarse paper (such as bond typing paper) under each contact; then slide the paper around and move the lever back and forth. Never use sandpaper for this; it's too abrasive.

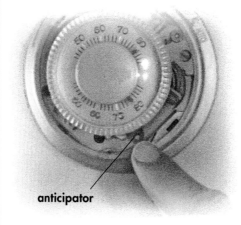

anticipator

If your furnace cycles on and off too often or too seldom and you have a mechanical thermostat, try adjusting the anticipator (above), a device that prompts the thermostat to cut the furnace off a bit early to allow for residual heat already in the system. The anticipator is usually a flat metal pointer on a scale. If the furnace cycles on and off too often, move the pointer a bit toward a longer setting (there's an indicator on the scale). If the furnace cycles too seldom, move it the opposite way.

FORCED-AIR SYSTEMS

The most effective step you can take to make a forced-air system more efficient overall is to stop leaks in the shell of the house and the heating system ducts. Weatherstrip windows and doors (pp.49–50), have cracks in the exterior siding caulked, and tape the seams between duct sections (p.71).

Minimize blockages in the circulation of heated air. Keep supply and return registers clean. Don't place furniture or curtains directly against or over them. Leave the door open to any room that has a supply register but no return register (a supply register feels warm when the heat is on). Or have the door to the room trimmed so that there's an inch gap at the bottom.

Within the system, the chief cause of poor airflow is usually a dirty filter. Change the furnace filter regularly when the system is in use. Also have the furnace and blower checked yearly by a heating contractor.

Changing the furnace filter

The filter collects dust from the air returning to the furnace for reheating. A clogged filter makes the blower work harder and reduces the system's efficiency. Start each heating season with a clean filter, then replace or clean it every month after that.

Disposable cardboard-framed fiberglass filters are by far the most common type. Some furnaces have a metal or

furnace

cold-air
return duct

filter

plastic element filter that you can clean and reuse. Clean this type of filter using a hose with a high-pressure nozzle. Let it dry fully before reinstalling it.

Most filters slide into a slot on the return duct next to the furnace. To change a filter, simply turn off the furnace at the thermostat, then slide out the old filter and slip in a new one (above). Some filters go inside the return duct and are reached by opening an access panel. Other filters fit inside the furnace next to or wrapping around the blower. To reach one of these, open the blower access panel on the furnace. Flip off the power switch for the furnace before opening the access panel.

Upgrading the filter for cleaner air

Most filters catch only large dust particles to keep them from getting into the blower motor. To capture more dust, mold, pollen, animal dander, and other fine airborne particles that cause allergy sufferers so much grief, have a heating contractor install an electrostatic filter unit. It has a reusable filter, which you wash monthly in a detergent solution. You can also have a unit installed that takes disposable pleated fabric filters, but they get dirty quickly and need to be changed often.

Cleaning the blower

If you have your furnace serviced once a year, a thorough cleaning of the blower should be part of the job. To do it yourself, turn off the power switch that controls the furnace and open the blower compartment. Vacuum the fan blades and the blower housing to remove as much dust as you can. If a vacuum attachment won't reach all the blades, use a bottle brush or rag-wrapped stick to clean them.

Lubricating the blower motor

The blower motor on an older furnace usually needs to be lubricated every year—another task that an annual servicing should take care of. Most of these motors have small oil ports covered with caps or rubber plugs on the visible part of the motor. Lift the cap or plug and add several drops of oil into each hole. Don't overfill. The blower motors on newer furnaces have permanently lubricated bearings that don't require oiling.

Stopping a squealing blower

The blowers on many older furnaces have a belt that connects the blower cage to the motor. If you hear a squealing sound or if the airflow seems weak, the belt may be loose or worn. To check it, turn off the power switch that controls the furnace and open the blower access panel. With a flashlight, inspect the belt. If it's cracked, frayed, or worn shiny, take it off and buy an exact replacement at a heating supplier. You can usually remove and reinstall a belt by pushing it over the lip of the motor pulley while turning the pulley.

Also check the belt's tension. Press down on it in the middle of its span. It should yield about ½ inch. Many units have an adjustment bolt on the base of the motor that moves the motor in or out to tighten or loosen the belt tension; on others, you loosen the motor mounting bolts and move the motor slightly.

Blower noise or weak airflow can also be caused by a motor that's not tightly bolted in place or by belt pulleys that don't line up. If the pulleys on the motor and blower don't align, loosen the set screw on the motor pulley and move the pulley.

Sealing leaks in the ductwork

Leaks in ducts can significantly reduce the efficiency of a forced-air system. Examine the joints between the duct sections wherever they are visible, especially in attics and basements. To reattach a loose flange, drill small pilot holes and drive in sheet-metal screws. Make sure the seams are sealed with tape. If the tape is worn, remove and replace it. To seal the seams, be sure to use professional-quality duct tape. Wipe the area clean and press the tape smooth to avoid air bubbles. Ductwork that runs through unheated areas should be insulated. If your ducts aren't insulated, have a heating contractor cover them with batts of fiberglass insulation. Or wrap them yourself with batts specially designed to fit ducts; the batts come with complete instructions for installation.

Balancing the system

Uneven heating from room to room can often be adjusted by opening or closing registers, but a better method is to adjust the dampers inside the ductwork. Usually located near where the ducts branch, dampers are flat panels that pivot inside the duct to control the airflow. They are adjusted by a handle on the outside of the duct (below).

Balancing a forced-air system is a trial-and-error process that may take a day or two. One way to do it is to get a few inexpensive identical thermometers and put one in the center of each room at table height. Then open all the registers and dampers. Set the thermo-

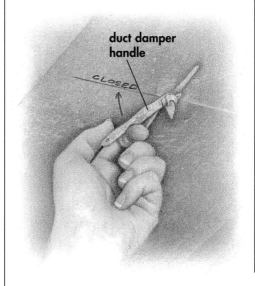

duct damper handle

CLOSED

stat to 68°F and start the furnace. After a half-hour, partly close the dampers for the warmest rooms. Continue to readjust the dampers until each room is at the desired temperature. When you finish, mark each damper handle's position. If the system also cools, balance it separately for the cooling season. A sunny room may need more airflow to cool down in summer than it needs to warm up in winter.

HOT-WATER SYSTEMS

A hot-water system rarely requires a lot of maintenance beyond annual servicing by a heating contractor. Air trapped in the radiators or convectors is the most common problem. It is vented by a process called bleeding (facing page). On an older system, the boiler's expansion tank may become waterlogged and need draining (p.74).

Caring for radiators and convectors

A hot-water system has either a radiator or convector in nearly every room. Accumulated dirt on a radiator or convector reduces its heating capacity. Vacuum radiators and exposed pipes regularly, using a crevice attachment for hard-to-reach spots. Remove caked-on dirt with a damp rag. Remove a convector's cover and vacuum its fins at least once a year.

Adjusting a radiator's heat output

To reduce the heat output of a hot-water radiator or convector, turn the inlet valve clockwise. To increase the heat, turn it counterclockwise. Hot-water units heat slowly; it may take a few days to find the best setting.

Replacing a broken valve handle

To replace a cracked handle, just remove the screw in the top and lift it off. Take it to a plumbing-supply store or home center for a replacement. If the stem is damaged (sometimes the screw hole gets stripped) or if you cannot find an exact replacement, buy a retrofit handle designed to clamp onto any stem.

Boosting a radiator's heat output

If a radiator or convector isn't heating well, make sure that the valve is open all the way. Also check that air can flow freely into the bottom and out the top. Window coverings and furniture placed too close to the unit are often a problem. On a convector, blocking air intake at the bottom in particular will

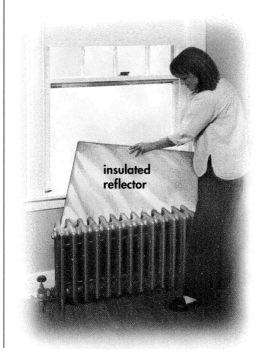

insulated reflector

dramatically cut its heat output, as will bent fins, which can be straightened with a putty knife. A unit that doesn't get as hot as others may have trapped air that needs bleeding (right).

To increase a radiator's efficiency, insert an insulated reflector between the radiator and the wall (below left). To make your own reflector, cover rigid insulation or poster board with aluminum foil.

Stopping radiator leaks

If a leak develops around the packing nut, located just below the handle, close the valve and gently tighten the nut clockwise with an adjustable wrench. Open the valve. If the leak persists, have a plumber replace the packing or the valve. The plumber may have to shut down and drain the system.

Before calling a plumber to fix a leak around the joint in the pipe that enters the radiator, try tightening the nuts using two pipe wrenches (below).

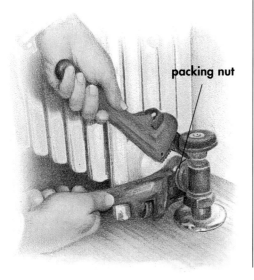

packing nut

Bleeding a radiator or convector

If a hot-water radiator or convector isn't heating properly even with its valve fully open, the problem may be air trapped inside. The solution is to vent, or bleed, the air out.

To bleed a unit, the boiler must be operating; turn up the thermostat if necessary. The bleeder valve on a radiator is opposite the inlet valve and near the top. On a convector, it is on a return pipe under the cover. Using a screwdriver, open the valve carefully and slowly. Let the hot water flow into a cup until it stops sputtering. Then close the valve. Some bleeder valves require a key, sold in hardware stores.

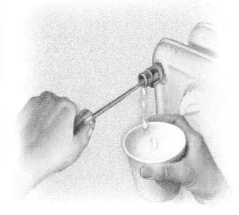

As a general rule, hot-water radiators or convectors should be bled once a year. The unit farthest from the boiler tends to collect the most air and may require more frequent attention. Bleed the whole system at the start of the heating season or whenever it has been off for a long time. To do this, start on the top floor, at the radiator farthest from the boiler, and work down, finish-

EASY PIPE INSULATION

To prevent the pipes that carry hot water to your radiators or convectors from losing heat en route through a cold crawl space or basement, you can quickly and easily insulate them yourself. Buy slitted foam pipe insulation that is ready to slip over pipes on straight runs. For corners, buy rolled fiberglass pipe insulation and secure it with a seal wrap.

ing with the one nearest the boiler.

Instead of a bleeder valve, some convectors have an automatic vent valve that slowly releases air as the system fills with water. Keep an automatic valve clean. If it drips, replace it.

Replacing radiators with convectors

You can exchange bulky radiators for trim baseboard convectors. Both units provide the same amount of heat. Though convectors take up less room, remember that you should not block them with furniture. A heating contractor can give you a cost estimate.

Zoned heating

To save energy, some hot-water systems are separated into zones, each with its own thermostat. This lets you lower the heat in the bedrooms during the day, for example. If there is no chart near the boiler, figure out which rooms are in which zone by turning up one thermostat at a time.

Quieting a squeaky pump

If the circulator pump and its motor (next to the boiler) have oil ports, open the caps and fill them with several drops of oil twice a year. A newer model may be permanently lubricated.

Draining a hot-water expansion tank

On an older hot-water system, the boiler usually has a large cylindrical expansion tank, which provides an air cushion that lets the hot water in the system safely expand. If water is dripping from the boiler's safety relief valve and the expansion tank feels hot all over, the tank is waterlogged and needs to be drained. Turn off the system and let it cool. Close the shutoff valve between the boiler and the tank. Connect a garden hose to the combination drain valve on the bottom of the tank, run the hose to a drain, and open the valve (below). After the tank has drained, close the combination valve

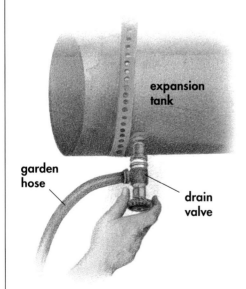

garden hose

expansion tank

drain valve

and reopen the shutoff valve. Bleed the radiators or convectors (p.73).

If the smaller diaphragm-type expansion tank on a newer hot-water system becomes waterlogged, have it recharged (refilled with air) or replaced by your heating contractor.

Draining a hot-water system

Over time, a boiler can become clogged with rust and other sediment. To check the boiler, turn off the burner and the water supply to the boiler and let the system cool. Then open the drain valve and let water run into a bucket. If you find sludge, your entire system needs to be drained. For best results, have a heating contractor power-flush the system using chemicals and hot water.

To drain it yourself, turn off the burner and the water supply, and let the system cool. Open the air vents on the radiators or convectors at the highest point of the system. Then connect a garden hose to the drain valve and run it to a drain. Open the valve and let the system drain. When it has emptied, close the air vents and turn on the water supply. Let fresh water flush the system until it runs clean, then close the drain valve and refill the system.

To prevent sediment buildup, add a rust-inhibiting compound (sold by heating supply stores) to the boiler. Unscrew and take off the pressure gauge on top of the boiler and pour the compound in through the hole.

STEAM HEAT SYSTEMS

Steam radiators get very hot, so be careful of what you put on them and how you touch them. Most steam heat systems have one-pipe radiators. Steam enters a radiator, condenses to water as it gives off heat, then drains out the same pipe. The less-common two-pipe radiators have both inlet and return pipes like hot-water radiators.

Quieting knocking radiators

On a one-pipe radiator, knocking occurs when a buildup of returning water blocks incoming steam. To prevent knocking, make sure the inlet valve is completely open (or closed). Also make sure the radiator is level or, if necessary, tilted toward the inlet valve. Place a carpenter's level on top of the radiator. If there are height-adjusting bolts under the radiator's legs, use a wrench to screw them out. Or put shims (wedges of wood) under the legs opposite the inlet valve (below).

level

shim

Adjusting heat from radiators

For a one-pipe radiator to work properly, the inlet valve must be all the way on or off. The only way to adjust heat on an individual radiator is to install an adjustable air-vent valve (right). On a two-pipe radiator, opening or closing the inlet valve controls its heat.

Checking the boiler water level
If the water level in a boiler sinks too low, the boiler can burn out. Unless your boiler has an automatic water feed, check the glass gauge that shows the boiler's water level every 10 days during heating season; more often in bitter weather. If the level is low, open the fill valve until the level is correct.

glass gauge

low-water cutoff valve

Flushing sediment from a boiler
About once a month during the heating season, you need to flush the boiler—that is, drain off a small amount of water from the low-water cutoff valve to keep the sediment from building up.

To do this, turn down the thermostat so that the burners are off. Put a bucket under the cutoff valve, then open the valve and let the water run until it's clear. Be careful; the water is hot. Close the valve, and open the supply valve to refill the boiler until the glass gauge is one-half to two-thirds full.

Checking the pressure
To operate safely with the pressure that builds up, a steam boiler has a pressure control. Check the pressure gauge just after the boiler switches off. If it is far above the pressure setting, have the control replaced immediately.

Boilers also have a pressure safety valve designed to open before an unsafe pressure level is reached. To see that it is working, check it while the boiler is running. Pull its lever very briefly, then let go. A little steam should escape while the lever is up and should stop completely when you let go. If the valve sticks or doesn't emit steam, have it replaced.

RADIANT HEAT SYSTEMS
With no moving parts and no visible heat outlets, a radiant system usually has few problems and requires little maintenance. Like a conventional hot-water system, however, a hot-water

radiant system has a boiler that you should have serviced each year. Never drill or poke holes in a floor, wall, or ceiling that contains electric cables or water lines. If a section stops producing heat, call for repair. If a water line leaks, shut off the water where it exits the boiler, and call for repair. If an electrical radiant system fails, check your main service panel for a tripped circuit breaker (p.93).

HEAT PUMPS
A heat pump looks and works much like a central air conditioner. It has a

TROUBLE SHOOTER

TROUBLESHOOTING A HEAT PUMP

Most of the problems you are likely to encounter with a heat pump are the same as the ones you would have with a central air conditioner (pp.82–83). Here are some to look out for.

◆ **If a thick, persistent frost forms** on the outdoor coil, clean the coil and remove any obstructions, such as leaves. Change the filter indoors.

◆ **If ice forms on the coil** and the unit doesn't automatically defrost it, switch the thermostat to cooling mode for ten minutes before calling for service.

◆ **If your heat turns on and off** too frequently, check and clean the thermostat (p.70). Also check for a clogged filter and outdoor obstructions.

◆ **If you smell an odor,** check for a clogged drip pan on the indoor unit. Make sure it can drain freely.

refrigeration system with an outdoor coil and compressor that are connected to a coil indoors. In winter, the outdoor unit extracts heat from air and delivers it to the indoor coil, where it is carried throughout the house by a forced-air system (p.68). In summer, the process is reversed, and the heat pump cools, just like a central air conditioner.

As a heating unit, a heat pump is effective only when the outdoor temperature is moderately cold. When it gets too cold for a unit to work efficiently, it automatically switches to a supplementary heating source—usually a costly electric heating element. As

a rule, don't turn down the thermostat at night; the system will only have to switch to more expensive supplemental heating to warm the house in the morning. If your system seems inefficient or expensive to run, consider adding space heaters (p.78) or even installing a different heating system.

GAS FURNACES AND BOILERS

Although gas furnaces and boilers are relatively trouble free, always have one checked and serviced once a year along with the system that delivers its heat.

Relighting a pilot light

Some newer gas furnaces have an electronic igniter that lights the pilot light or the burners directly; if it fails, have it serviced. Many units have a pilot light which stays on all the time. If it goes out, the burners cannot be lit. Controls vary from model to model, and instructions for relighting the pilot light nearly always appear on a label near the control valve. Follow them carefully. Most furnaces have a combination control valve with a gas knob and a reset button (or a single knob that does both functions). First turn off the electric switch that controls the furnace and turn down the thermostat. Then turn the gas knob to *Off.* Wait 5 minutes for the gas to dissipate (if the smell of gas persists, stop and call for service). Then turn the gas knob to *Pilot.* Depress and hold the reset button (or gas knob) and light the pilot (above right)—you might need a long match to reach it. Wait a minute before releasing the button. If the pilot goes out, try relighting it, and

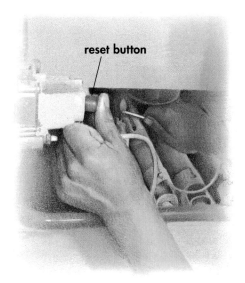

reset button

holding the button in longer, before calling for service. If the pilot stays lit, turn the gas knob to *On.* Turn on the power and raise the thermostat.

Changing a thermocouple

If a pilot won't light or won't stay lit, chances are you need to replace the thermocouple (below). This is a very common repair; a hardware store or

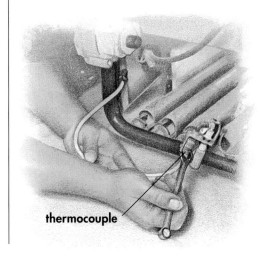

thermocouple

home center will have the part you need. Servicemen will usually charge plenty to do it, but you can install one yourself for a few dollars if you're willing to get a little dirty and perhaps twist yourself into awkward positions. Turn off the gas knob and shut off electrical power to the burner, and wait ten minutes for any gas to dissipate. Use a flashlight to locate the thermocouple. It's a copper tube with fittings at each end. Using pliers or a small wrench, unscrew one end from the control valve, and unscrew the nut that holds the other end to a bracket (this part gets heated by the pilot flame). Carefully note where the new thermocouple will need to go. Take the old thermocouple with you to buy a replacement of the same size. Bend the tube carefully as you position it, and tighten the nuts on each end. Relight the pilot.

Cleaning the pilot opening

If your pilot light goes out and won't light, the opening may be clogged. Close the gas shutoff valve, and shut off electrical power to the burner. Remove the access panel. To reach the pilot, you may need to remove the bracket holding it and pull it out a bit. Use a toothpick to clean

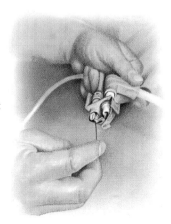

out the opening (below left). Work carefully, so you don't break the toothpick in the opening. Use a soft brush or a cotton swab to clean the area around the opening.

Cleaning the burners

To operate efficiently, the small holes in the burner must be clear of dirt. Clean them at the beginning of every heating season. Remove the panel or panels to get to the burners. Vacuum around each burner (below). Use a brush to loosen dirt as you vacuum.

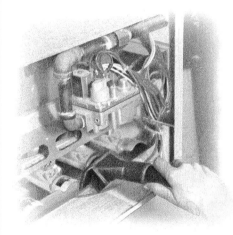

Adjusting the burner flame

To burn efficiently, gas burners require a properly balanced mix of gas and air. You can adjust the air intake by moving a plate or sleeve over an opening on the front end of each burner. To tell if this air shutter needs adjusting, look at the flame. A weak blue inner flame with a yellowish tip indicates too little air; a harsh blue inner flame, too much. A well-balanced flame has a distinct blue-green inner flame and an orange

outer flame. The color may differ with bottled gas. Ask your technician to show you what a good flame looks like. To adjust the air intake, loosen the screw on the air shutter (below) and gradually move the sleeve (or plate) to allow less or more air to enter. Newer burners with fixed shutters rarely need adjustment; if they do, hire a pro.

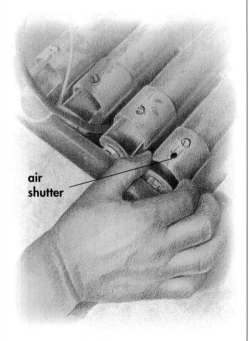

air shutter

OIL BURNERS

Have an oil burner serviced at the beginning of every heating season by your heating contractor or oil supplier. A thorough annual checkup conducted by a professional should include changing the oil filter, cleaning the fan, replacing the burner nozzle, inspecting the igniter assembly, and inspecting vent connections.

CLEAN AIR INDOORS

The oil crisis of the 1970s led to a major effort to make houses more energy efficient. Homes were insulated and weatherstripped to save on fuel. But they lost the fresh air that used to seep through cracks in the siding and loose joints around windows. If you have a new house, it probably has a built-in air ventilation system. If you live in a tight old house, here are things you can do to fight stale air.

◆ **Open windows** at opposite ends of the house to get a cross breeze.

◆ **Use an exhaust fan** to take out kitchen odor and bathroom moisture.

◆ **Consider an electrostatic air cleaner** to filter large pollution particles out of the air and collect smaller particles like a magnet. It can be installed in the ducts of a forced-air heating system or an air-conditioning system, or a free-standing unit can service a room.

SPACE HEATERS

Space heaters can be used to supplement a central system. It often helps to have a ceiling or box fan to circulate the air heated by a space heater. Be sure to choose space heaters that are economical to operate, not just inexpensive to buy.

Gas space heaters

A gas heater is expensive to install but may save money in the long run. A gas space heater must be vented; an unvented unit emits dangerous combustion fumes and violates the housing code in nearly all areas.

On a properly vented unit, harmful fumes are exhausted outdoors through a direct vent in the wall or through a flexible flue. If you have any doubts about the safety of a gas space heater, don't hesitate to have it checked. You can also install a carbon monoxide detector (p.345) in case the vent becomes blocked.

Clean a gas space heater regularly. With the gas off, remove the cover and vacuum out any dust, using a brush attachment and a crevice tool. If the unit has a pilot light, adjust the flame so that it burns smoothly without sputtering. If the burner had an air shutter, adjust the air-gas mixture so that it has a well-balanced flame as on a gas furnace (p.77).

Electric space heaters

There are two types of electric space heaters—radiative and convective. Radiative electric heaters are either filled with liquid or have a shiny metal reflector that radiates heat into the room. Convective heaters have a fan that blows out heat. As a general rule, radiative heaters work best in large rooms; convective units in smaller, clearly defined areas.

Always unplug an electric heater before maintaining or repairing it. If it is wired directly, remove the fuse or flip off the circuit breaker that controls it. Clean an electric heater regularly. Vacuum it and wipe it with a damp rag, especially if you have not used it for a while. Heated dust can cause a nasty odor and may even be a fire hazard.

If an electric heater doesn't heat or cuts on and off sporadically, unplug it and carefully examine the plug and the power cord. If the cord's insulation is burned, cracked, or worn—even if it just has a small nick—replace it. No heat or erratic heating may also signal a faulty on-off switch or thermostat. If the control panel is easily opened, you can replace either of these parts or the power cord, as on any other small appliance (pp.94–95).

The switch is usually held by a slide clip that you pry off with a screwdriver or by spring clips that you squeeze together to push the switch through the panel. The thermostat is usually held by a nut that you unscrew after pulling off the knob.

To order a replacement part, call the manufacturer's toll-free 800 number. Look for your heater's model number on a metal plate on the heater before you call so you're sure to get a matching part. Otherwise, take the heater to a service center recommended by the manufacturer.

Kerosene heaters

It's best to avoid kerosene heaters, which are doubly dangerous because of the harmful combustion fumes they emit and the flammability of the fuel. Unvented and portable units are especially hazardous. If you must use a kerosene space heater, make sure it's a fixed unit that has both fresh-air and exhaust vents. Take extra care when storing the kerosene.

AIR CONDITIONERS, HUMIDIFIERS, AND DEHUMIDIFIERS

Staying comfortable when the weather is hot is a luxury for some and a necessity for others. The most sensible path to comfort often involves lowering the humidity level in summer—or raising it in winter.

In many regions, summertime comfort can be achieved only with air conditioning. But if you expect to use the air conditioner for only a month or two out of every year, consider less-expensive alternatives. A whole-house air-exchange ventilator or an evaporator cooler may serve just as well to make summers more tolerable. However, if you do choose air conditioning, finding the right type for your situation will ensure you save money in the long run.

TYPES OF AIR CONDITIONERS

Window (or room) air conditioners are fairly easy to service and install, provided you have an adequate electrical connection. You can choose from units designed to cool a small bedroom to large models suitable for cooling two or more rooms. The bulk of a window unit—condenser coil and compressor—projects out the window while the fan and evaporator coil are on the inside,

just behind the front grill. The evaporator coil absorbs heat from the air that passes over it. Refrigerant carries the heat to the compressor and condenser coil where it is released.

A central air conditioner works the same way as a window air conditioner. A condenser coil and fan in an outdoor unit are connected by tubes to an evaporator coil and blower indoors in a forced-air duct system. The compressor can be located indoors or outdoors. Central air conditioning must be professionally installed.

CALCULATING COOLING NEEDS

The size of the area to be cooled is only one factor in determining the size of air conditioner needed. The amount of insulation in the house, how much shade the house receives, and the size, number, and orientation of the windows are also important. Rooms on the higher floors usually need more cooling than first-floor rooms. Also

MONEY SAVERS

FINDING AN ENERGY-EFFICIENT AIR CONDITIONER

Like most electrical appliances, air conditioners have become much more energy efficient in recent years. Air conditioner manufacturers are required to meet minimum standards for energy efficiency, but some models still can be significantly more energy efficient than others.

◆ **Check the black and white EnerGuide sticker** on each model. Window air conditioners are given an Energy Efficiency Rating (EER). The higher the rating, the lower the energy consumption.

◆ **Central air conditioners** are rated with a Seasonal Energy Efficiency Rating (SEER). The higher the SEER, the better the energy efficiency.

consider how much the room is used during the day.

It is worth your while to calculate accurately. If you choose an air-conditioning unit that is too small for the room, it will be overtaxed and never adequately cool your home. A unit that is too large may cool too quickly and not run long enough to remove humidity satisfactorily.

Calculating Btus

The cooling capacity of an air conditioner is measured in British thermal units (Btus). One Btu is the amount of energy required to heat 1 pound of water by 1°F. Have your dealer calculate your needs, or take out your tape measure and calculator and make the following calculations.

◆ **Multiply the room's length** by its width by its height to calculate the

total volume of the space that needs to be cooled.

◆ **Allow for the heat of the sun** by multiplying the total volume by 16 for a north-facing room, 17 for an east-facing room; 18 for a south-facing room, or 20 if the room faces west.

◆ **Factor for insulation** by dividing the result by 4 if your house has poor insulation, 5 if the insulation is good, or 6 if the house is super insulated. (See page 86 for how to assess this.)

The resulting number will tell you how many Btus of air conditioning that room needs. For example, if a room measures 12 feet by 14 feet with an 8-foot ceiling, it has 1,344 cubic feet. If the room faces east, multiply by 17 to get 22,848. If the house has good insulation, divide by 5 to get 4,569. In this case, a 5,000-Btu air-conditioning unit would be a good choice.

INSTALLING A WINDOW AIR CONDITIONER

casing

expandable curtain

sash

casing

1. Installing a window unit is not complicated, but the air conditioner will be heavy. The unit should come with complete instructions and installation hardware, and your retailer can offer additional suggestions. Begin by assembling the casing.

2. Place the casing in the window mount. Add the exterior bracing if it is required. Attach the window-mounting kit to the window frame. Be sure the unit will tilt down and away from the window on the outside. Screw down the pieces firmly.

3. Carefully slide the air conditioner into the casing. Pull the top window sash down, and slide the expandable curtains outward to seal the opening. You may need to use foam weatherstripping or removable caulk to completely seal the opening inside.

Assessing electrical capacity

Window air conditioners up to about 12,000 Btus can usually run on a 120-volt electrical connection. That means that you can plug a unit into a standard household outlet. Do not, however, plug an air conditioner into a circuit that already supplies power to other household appliances.

Also, be careful not to use an outlet that is controlled by a wall switch. Any air-conditioning unit that is larger than 12,000 Btus may require a 240-volt line, which should be installed by a licensed electrician.

WINDOW AIR CONDITIONERS

For best results, install a window air conditioner as close as possible to the area where it will do the most good. If you must choose one room to cool, your best choice might be a bedroom. That way, you can count on comfortable sleeping as well as a cool spot for reading and watching TV.

Most window air conditioners are designed to be installed in standard double-hung windows (those with sashes that slide up and down). But you can also find models that will fit in casement windows (those with sashes on hinges).

Installing in a wall

If no window is available where you want the air conditioner installed, look for a unit that can be installed in a wall. The installation is considerably more complex, because a carpenter must cut through the wall and frame a suitable opening for the air conditioner. This

may be only a day's work on a frame house. But a wall installation will be much more involved and expensive on a masonry house. However, it offers several advantages. It gives you the opportunity to put the air conditioner on a less conspicuous side of the house, and it won't cut down on window views.

Cleaning the filter and coils

Clean the filter at least once a month during the cooling season. It will help the air-conditioning unit run more efficiently. To reach the filter, turn off the unit and remove the unit's front grill (above), usually held in place by spring clips or hidden tabs along its top edge. Wash a foam or metal filter in soapy water, and let it dry. Replace a disposable filter with the same type. While the filter is removed, vacuum the evaporator coil and fins located just behind the filter.

At the beginning of each cooling season, unplug the air-conditioning unit. With a helper, carefully slide the air conditioner out of its casing onto a strong support such as a table. Vacu-

um the inside of the unit, paying special attention to the condenser coil at the rear. You may have to remove smaller units from the window before you can remove the casing.

Getting the most from your unit

If your air conditioner runs continuously and you're still not comfortable, it may be too small for the room, or it has lived out its useful life.

Before replacing it, make sure that nothing is blocking the front of the unit. Check that the louvers are open and properly directed. Seal any gaps around the air conditioner. Clean or replace the filter; clean the coils. Don't use an extension cord longer than recommended, and make sure it is a heavy-duty three-wire cord, not a lightweight household cord. Block out any direct sunlight and, if necessary, better insulate the walls.

After the air conditioner has been running for 10 minutes, take off the grill and feel the evaporator coil. Most of the surface should feel cold. If much of the upper evaporator coil is less cold than the bottom part, you may be able to get it back to full cooling output by adding additional refrigerant. Call a certified air conditioning service specialist to see if this can be done for your model. If the air-conditioning unit is only a few years old and has lost a significant amount of refrigerant, then it probably has a leak and should be repaired or replaced.

If the unit won't turn on, first check to see if the circuit breaker is tripped or the fuse is blown (p.93). Make sure the cord is plugged in. Unplug, and inspect the cord and plug for damage. If it still won't turn on, call for service.

CENTRAL AIR CONDITIONING

Central air conditioners work best when the area around the outdoor unit is kept free of debris. Trim bushes periodically so that they are at least 2 feet away. If you have any trees nearby, you will have to keep the grills cleared of leaves in the fall. Consider removing tree branches that cause problems. When mowing, bag the clippings when you are near the unit or direct them away from the unit. Cover the unit during snowy weather (p.83).

Wash the panels on the outdoor unit with water, then rinse with a hose. To prevent rust from spreading, lightly sand any scratches with metal-grade sandpaper and touch them up with any kind of outdoor enamel paint.

Changing the filter

Change or clear the filter on the indoor unit at least once a month during the cooling season. Shut off the power to the blower and the outside unit first. In most homes, this is exactly the same as changing the filter on a forced-air heating system (p.71).

Cleaning the condenser coils

Clean the condenser coil and fins on the outdoor unit once a year, at the beginning of the cooling season—more often if they get particularly dirty. Shut off the power to the unit, and turn up the thermostat. Remove the metal grill and, if necessary, the housing from the

Protect working parts with plastic.

unit. The grill is often held by bolts with cap nuts; the housing by screws. Cover the fan motor, and other electrical parts with plastic bags and seal them with string or tape. Gently brush away any visible dirt from the coil, then use a garden hose to wash it from the inside (above). Let the unit dry before removing the plastic bags protecting the electrical systems.

Cleaning the evaporator drain

The evaporator coils on most central air conditioners are sealed and inaccessible within the inside unit, so if the coils are clogged, you will need to call in a licensed service technician. But you can deal with the drain that carries away condensed moisture from the evaporator coils. If you find water puddles beneath the coils, the drainpipe from the evaporator is probably clogged with algae and bacteria. Disconnect the drainpipe near the evaporator and flush the trap with a hose. Pour in 1 tablespoon of chlorine bleach and reattach the drainpipe.

Checking the refrigerant

Refrigerant lines connect both indoor and outdoor coils with the compressor unit. The pressurized refrigerant circulates through the two units. Have the refrigerant level checked every other year by a certified service person. Low refrigerant levels cause poor cooling or make the condenser run continuously. If you find oily spots on or near the refrigerant lines, or hear a hissing sound, refrigerant may be leaking. Call for repair immediately.

Minor troubleshooting

If an outdoor unit makes a clanking noise while running, shut off the power to the unit and turn up the thermostat. Remove the grill and check for any obstructions that may be hitting the fan blades. Check to see if the fan is loose; it should spin freely and without

REALITY CHECK

AIR CONDITIONING IN THE WINTER?

The owner's manual for your car might suggest that you turn on the air conditioner several times during the winter months to keep the moving parts lubricated. It's good advice that can save you from an expensive repair job down the line. But house air conditioners are built to function when the ambient temperature requires cooling to be comfortable. To avoid damaging the compressor, never operate an air conditioner when the outside temperature is below 60°F.

wobbling. To tighten, use an adjustable wrench or a hex wrench. If your fan motor has oil ports (usually plugged with rubber or metal caps), add a high-grade machine oil; no more than 10 drops per port (or check your owner's manual). Tighten any loose screws in the housing. If the noise continues, call for repairs. If the unit won't turn on, check to see if the circuit breaker is tripped or the fuse is blown (p.93). Make sure the unit is switched on, and that the thermostat is on the Cool or Auto setting, with the temperature set below the room temperature. If it still won't run, call for repair.

Winter storage for air conditioners

Central air conditioners should be covered in winter, and window units can be covered while still in the window. Use breathable material for the covers. Plastic tarps keep moisture out, but they can also trap it inside, causing rust and premature failure of the unit. For central air conditioners, insulated covers are essential to prevent ice forming inside the unit. Your manufacturer may sell a suitable cover to fit your unit.

WHOLE-HOUSE AIR-EXCHANGE VENTILATORS

In Canada, innovations in household air-sealing and ventilation have led to the development of whole-house air-exchange ventilators. Most of these ventilators consist of units with two fan motors: one brings fresh air to the living areas around the house, while the other removes stale air from the bathroom, kitchen, laundry, and hobby

area. When properly installed, the ventilators create a balanced air flow, providing equal amounts of incoming and outgoing air. The fresh air is introduced near the ceiling where it is warmed by the heat rising in the room.

The best models also have efficient filters that improve the quality of incoming air by removing pollutants such as pollen. You can choose from two types of air-exchange ventilators. Heat Recovery Ventilators (HRV) remove moisture from a humid house; Energy Recovery Ventilators (ERV), which retain some moisture, are designed for houses that might become too dry with winter ventilation.

EVAPORATIVE COOLERS

Evaporative coolers offer economical comfort in areas where the summers are hot and dry. As the cost of air conditioning continues to rise, these cheaper alternatives are becoming more popular. The principle behind an evaporative cooler

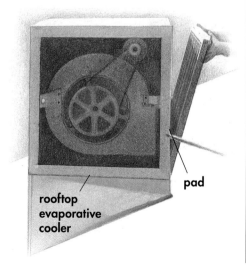

rooftop evaporative cooler

pad

is simple: Air is blown through netting panels soaked with water, bringing a moist breeze into the house. Most models are roof-mounted, but window units are also available. It is important to keep at least one window open when running an evaporative cooler. Otherwise, the house will start to feel like a swamp (in fact, these units are nicknamed "swamp coolers"). If you also have an air conditioner, don't run both cooling systems at the same time. Clean or change the pads (below left) every month. Check the pan to make sure water is recirculating freely. Drain the water in the winter, and cover the unit, to keep cold air from coming into the house.

HUMIDIFYING THE AIR

When it comes to comfort, air temperature and relative humidity are closely related. Most people are comfortable when the temperature is between 65° and 75°F and the relative humidity is between 30 and 65 percent. This is why it often makes sense to use humidifiers in the summer in warm dry climates, and during cold periods in areas with dry winters. In either case, you gain significant comfort for a small price.

If you have forced-air heating, a humidifier can be attached to the system and will add moisture to your home as it heats. A power humidifier, which sprays mist into the air stream, works better than a passive-type unit. If you don't have forced-air heating but don't like the idea of carrying buckets of water every day, consider installing an automatic unit, which is fed by tubes connected to your plumbing.

Evaporative   Ultrasonic   Warm-mist

How Humidifiers Work

All humidifiers increase the relative humidity in the house. But they differ significantly in appearance, operation, cost, and maintenance requirements. You can choose portable units, or have one central unit installed in the ductwork of a forced-air heating and cooling system. **Evaporative** humidifiers are least expensive. They rely on a rotating drum or belt to deliver moisture that is dispersed by a fan. **Ultrasonic** humidifiers contain a nebulizer that produces mist with high-frequency vibration. **Warm-mist** humidifiers, which are the safest, boil water in a chamber, then cool the steam by mixing it with air.

Adding water to a humidifier

You must add water to a humidifier to keep it operating properly. How much water you need and how often you need to add it depend on the unit and how often it is used. Humidifiers are equipped with a switch that turns the unit off when it runs out of water. Even if the unit is running, though, it may not humidify properly if the water level is too low. Always turn the humidifier off before removing the tank for refilling. If you get your water from a well or live in an area with hard water, you will get less mineral buildup if you use bottled distilled water in the humidifier rather than tap water.

Cleaning the humidifier

Every humidifier has its own cleaning and maintenance needs. Don't use a humidifier unless you've read the owner's manual and are prepared to keep the unit clean. If not kept clean, evaporative and ultrasonic humidifiers can spew bacteria, fungi, mold, and mineral dust, which can lead to harmful allergy problems or illness. Warm-mist humidifiers are generally safe because they boil the water they use, which distills out minerals and kills bacteria, mold, and fungi.

Mineral buildup inside a humidifier is a problem for most users, especially in areas with hard water. To remove calcium or lime buildup, use a solution of 1 part white vinegar to 3 parts water. For really difficult cases, use equal amounts of vinegar and water. Scrape off any leftover buildup with a putty knife. Wash the tank and filters with an antibacterial cleaner. On humidifiers with disposable foam filters, drums, or belts, buy and install replacements as directed in the owner's manual. If any parts appear corroded, have them replaced.

Checking the filter

The filter in a humidifier reduces mineral deposits and discourages the growth and spread of bacteria, mold, and fungi. Sometimes evaporative humidifiers contain disposable floating filters that wick water toward the fan. Ultrasonic humidifiers may contain replaceable mineral filters housed in a cartridge. Clean or replace any filter as often as the manufacturer suggests. Replace moisture pads in furnace-mounted humidifiers every year.

Getting rid of odors

Odors most often indicate the presence of bacteria in the water reservoir or filtering system. To kill the bacteria, clean the unit with a solution of 1 tablespoon of chlorine bleach per pint of water (or use an antibacterial cleaner recommended by the manufacturer). Rinse thoroughly with plain water.

Lubricating a humidifier

A squeaking or slow-turning fan can often be cured with a few drops of oil. Lubricate the bearings on the fan motor with a few drops of high-grade machine oil at least once a year. Some units require additional lubrication to ensure quiet and efficient functioning. Check the owner's manual for your unit's lubrication schedule and recommended lubricants.

Stopping leaks in a humidifier

Some humidifiers contain a float valve to maintain the proper water level. If the valve gets stuck because of mineral deposits, clean with a vinegar-water solution (p.84) and scrape away any buildup. If it can't be cleaned or appears worn, replace the float valve. Adjust the valve for the proper level.

DEHUMIDIFIERS

Like a humidifier, a dehumidifier may provide comfort for a small price. If you live in an area where you often hear, "It's not the heat—it's the humidity," taking the water out of the air can make summers more bearable.

Plug a dehumidifier into a grounded outlet (p.92). Position it so there is at least 12 inches of air space on all sides to allow adequate air circulation. To avoid having to empty the dehumidifier collection tank frequently, attach a garden hose to the drain hose connector. (Sometimes the connector is hidden behind a small cover that can be pried off with a screwdriver.) Run the hose to a floor drain.

Every month, clean the tank with a sponge and mild detergent. Pop off the grill and wash or replace the filter.

Every 6 to 12 months, vacuum the coils behind the filter as you would on an air conditioner (p.81). If the fan motor has oil ports, add two drops of high-grade machine oil to each port every year.

Running a dehumidifier when the room temperature is below 65°F may cause frost to form on the coils. Frosting can also occur if the coils need cleaning or if the airflow is obstructed. Improve the air flow by moving the unit farther from the wall. If frost persists, have the unit serviced. The most common source of a dehumidifier leak is an overflowing water collector. Empty the collector more often. Trace the path taken by water as it drips off the coils and into the collector; if the drain hole above the collector is clogged, it will cause a leak. Check for signs of corrosion as well.

CLEANING A DEHUMIDIFIER

1. Most people using a dehumidifier for the first time are surprised at how quickly the water collector tank fills. Check the water level several times a day at first. Don't be surprised if you have to empty it at least once a day.

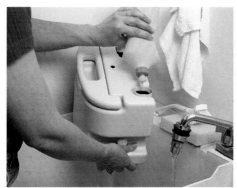

2. Wash the water collector tank every month with water and a mild detergent, then let it dry completely. Clean or replace the air filter, located under a grill at the back of the unit, at least monthly, as directed in the owner's manual.

3. Once or twice a year (depending on how much the dehumidifier is used), vacuum the coils. Use a toothbrush and mild detergent to clean the coils, taking care not to bend them. Rinse clean by spraying with water.

CUTTING UTILITY BILLS

*Using less electricity, heating fuel, and water is good for the planet
as well as for your budget. Here are some ideas
that are easy to adapt to your home.*

Not all energy-saving projects are equally cost effective. Some are expensive and take years to recoup the savings. You can make your utility dollars go the furthest by evaluating all your options before committing to any major expenditures.

CHECKING OUT YOUR HOUSE

There are many improvements that can make a house more energy efficient. But if you're wondering where to start, consider asking for an energy efficiency audit, provided jointly by Natural Resources Canada and local private contractors. For a fee of $100 to $300, an evaluator will diagnose your house's energy needs and prescribe cost-effective fixes, such as the addition of a new furnace or new windows. The evaluator's report will also estimate your long-term savings. To get the name of your local evaluator, call 1-800-387-2000.

Measuring drafts

Unless you are particularly sensitive to drafts, you may not realize how much extra fuel your heating system consumes to warm the cold air seeping into your house through nonthermal panes, loose window and door frames, shriveled caulking, and uninsulated walls.

To check how drafty your house is, use an indoor-outdoor thermometer. On a cold day, set the thermometer on the floor of an oft-used room to check the temperature at floor level. Then check the temperature on the ceiling in the same room. A difference of less than 10 degrees between the two readings indicates that the room is fairly tight. But if you find the difference is much higher—15 to 20 degrees, for example—you probably have cold-air infiltration. Check other rooms in the house the same way. When you find the sources of drafts in problem areas and begin to seal them, you should notice an improvement in your comfort as well as your fuel bill.

Budgeting an energy improvement

Replacing old windows provides a good example of how to evaluate the true cost savings of an energy-wise home improvement. New energy-efficient windows are expensive, but can significantly reduce heating and cooling expenses. When building a new house, it pays to install the most efficient windows that you can afford. On an older home, however, the long-term savings from replacing windows is less

Payback Worksheet

Energy-Saving Improvement	Initial Expense	Annual Savings in Fuel Consumption	Payback
Caulking and weatherstripping	$100	$100	Less than 1 year
Insulating attic	$1000	$200	2 to 3 years
Replacing doors and windows	$3500	$175	15 years
Installing new heating system	$5000	$200	15 to 25 years

"Payback" is a term used by home-energy professionals to measure how long it takes to recoup the cost of a home improvement. If you spend $500 to insulate the attic, and you estimate it will save $100 a year in fuel costs, the payback will be five years, an annual return on your investment of 20 percent. If you spend $2,500 to replace old windows and save the same $100 a year in fuel costs, your payback will be 25 years and your annual return on investment only 4 percent. The attic insulation gives a far better return, or payback, than the new windows.

clear-cut. With the cost of labor and materials, the payback period can easily reach 15 to 20 years. You may wish to consider other improvements first. Adding storm windows (p.51), weatherstripping (p.89), and low-emissivity (low-E) coating (p.91) can cut drafts for much less money. Repairing rotted window sills and loose panes also can improve energy efficiency for much less than the cost of replacing the window. See the table above to compare the cost versus savings of other improvements.

INSULATION

Insulation helps keep heat inside in winter and outside in summer. Because hot air rises, it is essential to insulate your attic. If it is accessible and doesn't have a floor, installing insulation—or adding more—is an easy job (pp.318–319). Installing insulation in walls is also easy if you are remodeling and replacing the interior wallboard or exterior siding. But if you want to insulate intact walls, have an insulation contractor blow loose-fill insulation into the wall cavities through small holes bored in the house's exterior; the holes are patched when the job is completed.

If your house has an enclosed crawl space, an insulation contractor may recommend that you insulate the interior foundation walls, which is often easier to do and more effective than putting insulation between the floor joists. In an open crawl space or unheated basement, it's necessary to put insulation between the joists.

Are your walls insulated?

The walls in older homes may not be insulated. To find out, start in the attic. If it isn't insulated, your walls probably aren't insulated either. Check the walls by removing the cover plate on an electrical receptacle on each exterior wall and inspect around the edges for signs

of insulation. If necessary, remove a piece of trim around a window or door to get a better look inside the wall. If the walls have been retroactively filled with blown-in insulation, you should be able to see traces of the plugs used to fill the holes near the top of the exterior siding. If you find insulation in one wall, that doesn't necessarily mean that all of the walls are insulated. A previous owner may have insulated only the north-facing walls, or never completed an insulation project. During your inspection, be sure to check for insulation in the basement. If there is none, insulating this part of the house can create a more livable area in winter.

Choosing insulation

Several types of insulation (above) are available at home centers for do-it-yourselfers. Professional insulation contractors offer more options, but some need specialized equipment to install.

The most popular type of insulation is blankets or batts of fiberglass or rock wool, which fit between wall studs and ceiling joists. The glass fibers used in traditional fiberglass batts are straight and can be uncomfortable to work with. Newly available fiberglass batts use a fiber that is formed with a random twist. The result is a cotton-like insulation that for most people causes no itch or irritation. Another common type is loose-fill insulation, which can be easily poured between ceiling joists. It also is the kind of insulation blown into wall cavities by a contractor when you have an older home's finished walls retroactively insulated. Cellulose is a popular form of loose-fill insulation. Made from recycled newspaper and wood fibers and treated with a flame retardant, it is recommended for insulating hard-to-reach areas. Loose-fill fiberglass and rock wool are also effective. A less common type of insulation is rigid panels of plastic foam, which are used on basement walls and under exterior siding during home construction or re-siding.

Insulation is rated by a system of R-values, which are rating numbers that indicate an insulating material's resistance to heat flow. The higher the R-value, the greater protection it offers. The amount of insulation required for a finished house depends on many factors, such as local fuel costs and climatic conditions. The box (below, left) gives Natural Resources Canada's minimum R-values for various parts of the house in four different zones of the country. The zones are defined by climatic data on the length and coldness of the heating season.

CAULKING

Caulk is a flexible gap filler that maintains a seal between building materials despite seasonal contractions. Every house needs it to seal cracks around windows and doors, between trim and siding, where wood and masonry meet, and around plumbing, venting, and electrical entry points. It's important to inspect your house's caulk lines every few years and re-caulk problem areas.

Caulk is sold in tubes, in clear and colored formulations. Use the right caulk for the right job. One hundred-percent silicone caulk provides good service and lasts more than 20 years. But it is expensive, not paintable, and tricky to apply. New so-called siliconized acrylic and latex caulks have many of the same positive properties as pure silicone, but are less expensive, paintable, and easier to apply.

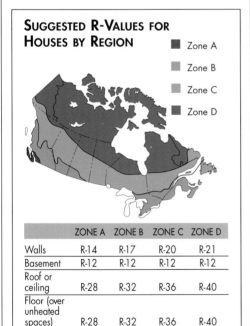

SUGGESTED R-VALUES FOR HOUSES BY REGION

- ■ Zone A
- ■ Zone B
- ■ Zone C
- ■ Zone D

	ZONE A	ZONE B	ZONE C	ZONE D
Walls	R-14	R-17	R-20	R-21
Basement	R-12	R-12	R-12	R-12
Roof or ceiling	R-28	R-32	R-36	R-40
Floor (over unheated spaces)	R-28	R-32	R-36	R-40

SEALING WITH SPRAY FOAM

Insulation is not effective if air is blowing through it. Make sure that your walls and attic are sealed against air infiltration before you add insulation. A handy product for sealing air gaps is polyurethane spray foam, available in aerosol cans at home centers. It requires no special tools or skills to use, but follow the instructions carefully. Don't touch the foam with your fingers while it is wet. The foam comes in expandable and less expandable forms. Expandable foams fill cavities too thick for caulk. However, they can exert enough pressure to cause jambs and siding to bulge, if not used sparingly. Less expandable foams are a safer choice to use around plumbing and wiring entry points and windows and doors.

Caulking is easy to do, although it takes practice. First scrape away any loose caulk and debris. Have a rag on hand, dampened with water (for latex, latex-silicone, or polyurethane caulk) or mineral spirits (for silicone and thermal plastic).

To place the tube in a caulking gun, pull the plunger all the way back and slip in the tube. Cut the tip of the tube at an angle. Puncture the tube's inner seal by pushing a long wire into the spout. Squeeze the trigger of the gun to start the caulk flowing.

To apply caulk, place the tip of the tube against the seam and move it smoothly along the seam as you gently squeeze the trigger, producing an even bead (above). For a smooth finish, wipe the bead with a caulk-smoothing tool, a plastic spoon, or an ice-cream or frozen-pop stick. Don't smooth the caulk with your finger. Some caulks contain harmful chemicals and some are hard to remove from your skin.

WEATHERSTRIPPING

One of the simplest and least expensive ways to cut heating bills—and make drafty rooms more comfortable—is to seal gaps around doors and windows, reducing the infiltration of cold air inside and the migration of heat outside.

Types of weatherstripping

No one type of weatherstripping is best for all uses. You may, in fact, want to use a combination of materials. Here are the most common types.

◆ **Aluminum with vinyl gasket** is good for doors and often comes in a kit with three pieces for the top and two sides of the door.

◆ **Felt stripping and tubular rubber or vinyl gaskets** can be stapled or tacked around door or window frames. The gaskets butt against the edge of the window or door. Attach them to the outside of a window so they won't be seen inside and are hidden outside by screens or storms.

◆ **Removable rope caulk** (p.49) is a temporary solution for weatherstripping around windows. It looks and feels like long strands of modeling clay and comes in coils. It presses into place around the window.

◆ **Self-adhesive rubber and foam tapes** are suitable for use at the top and bottom of window sashes and along door jambs. They are not very durable but are inexpensive and easy to install.

◆ **V-strips and spring-metal strips** press against the sides of windows and doors to form a seal. V-strips are available in plastic, which may be self-sticking, or in longer-lasting metal, which must be nailed into place.

Sealing a door

One of the most effective ways to seal a door is with a weatherstripping kit that comes with three pieces of aluminum with a vinyl gasket for the top and two sides. To install, close the door and mark a piece to fit one side. Cut with a hacksaw or tin snips. Press the

QUICK FIX

ADDING A DOOR SWEEP

Installing a door sweep is an easy way to close the gap at the bottom of a door.

1. If necessary, cut the sweep to fit with a hacksaw or tin snips.

2. Position the sweep so that it seals the gap but still clears the floor when the door opens. Mark the screw hole positions.

3. Pre-drill holes for the screws and attach the sweep.

piece lightly against the doorstop and drive in nails or screws. Do the same for the top and other side.

HOME APPLIANCES

A good time to make energy-saving moves is when you are buying home appliances. Investing in energy-efficient models can result in significant cost savings. Look for the black and white EnerGuide stickers affixed to an appliance. Because the sticker shows an appliance's annual electrical consumption, you can compare its energy performance with other similar appliances.

Replacing home appliances

In general, new appliances offer more energy-efficient features, run more quietly, and use less electricity or gas than older models. Most manufacturers tout their energy savings, making it relatively easy to compare makes and models.

◆ **A new refrigerator** with a top-freezer is likely to be more affordable and energy efficient than a side-by-side model. Also, a large top-freezer model uses only slightly more power than a smaller one—and if it cuts trips to the supermarket, it may be more cost-effective in the long run.

◆ **Many dishwashers today** (p.124) come with water-miser and no-heat dry features, which can significantly pare water and energy costs over time if you use the dishwasher more than once a day. You also will save money by running only full loads.

◆ **New gas ranges and ovens** (pp.133–134) come with electronic ignitions instead of old-fashioned pilot lights, which can tote up big cost savings since a pilot light eats up nearly half the fuel needed to run a gas stove.

◆ **The more you spend on new washers and dryers** the more energy features you'll find. By allowing you to set the water level and wash times to fit each load, you save on water and electricity. Front-loading washers also save more water than top loaders (pp.221–222). Humidity sensors on some dryers automatically shut off the dryer when the load is dry. As with a dishwasher, always run your washer and dryer with full loads.

PLUMBING, HEATING, AND COOLING IMPROVEMENTS

The systems that convey your water and conditioned air are prime targets for cost savings. Consider these options for making them more efficient.

Water heater savings

There are two simple ways to save energy on your water heater: wrap it in an insulating blanket (if it is an old uninsulated model) and turn down the temperature to 120°F. Also try wrapping the hot-water pipes to prevent heat loss in the plumbing itself.

You can save more energy by buying a new superinsulated water heater or installing point-of-use water heaters in key locations in the house. (Point-of-use water heaters heat water as it is being used, as opposed to maintaining a reservoir tank of hot water. Common abroad, point-of use heaters have recently been introduced in Canada.)

Replacing the heating system

Replacing an old furnace with a new energy-efficient model almost certainly will cut your energy consumption, especially if your existing furnace is in poor condition, consumes a lot of fuel, and requires frequent repairs. But if your furnace still functions reasonably well, your savings in fuel bills could be negated by the expense of the replacement. Before replacing your old furnace with a new unit, have it checked by a service technician. If the firebox is sound and in good operating order, you may want to consider simply having the furnace serviced and any problems repaired.

Programmable thermostat

You can definitely save on energy costs by heating or cooling your house less than you normally do. But using your thermostat (p.70) judiciously can also help. A programmable thermostat (below) can help you trim your utility bills by adjusting your home's temperature to your exact needs throughout the day. For example, you can have the heat increase just before you wake, cut back while you're out during the day, increase again just before you return home, then cut back at bed time. Most thermostats can be programmed for up to seven days. Electronic models with digital readouts are generally more efficient and versatile than mechanical ones. Make sure the unit is compatible with your heating and cooling system.

Use fans to cool
Don't underestimate the cooling power of fans, especially on warm, dry days when the house is stuffy. Even several fans running at once use only a fraction of the power consumed by a central air conditioning system.

Use inexpensive box fans to circulate air through your house. For best

results, note the direction of the prevailing winds, and position the fans in windows—one blowing in and one blowing out—to assist the wind. Similarly, a ceiling fan placed over your bed can also keep you comfortable at night by continuously circulating air. A whole-house air-exchange system (p.83) will help to keep a house cool during the summer months.

Add window film
Energy-efficient windows have a low-emissivity coating that blocks and reflects heat. But if the cost of replacing your windows is prohibitive, you can still benefit from some of the advantages of this modern window coating by installing low-E film on the interior of your existing windows. Most low-E films today require professional installation. Early do-it-yourself versions of film proved prone to discoloration, bubbling, and peeling. (For how to remove such film, see pages 51-52.) Installers clean the windows well and apply the film with a soapy solution. The moisture is squeezed out with a squeegee and the film is allowed to cure. Most low-E films last five years, but are relatively easy to replace.

Save on water usage
Water is a precious resource in many parts of the country, worth treating with care. In many regions, it is also increasingly expensive. These measures can cut your water consumption.

◆ **Check your faucets** periodically for drips—a single leaking faucet can waste thousands of gallons of water a year. (See pages 159–163 for how to repair leaks.)

◆**Taking showers rather than baths** is the simplest way to conserve water and energy: A 3-minute shower uses one fourth the water of a bath. A low-flow showerhead can achieve even greater savings. Older showerheads spray out 5 gallons or more every minute. Newer models can cut that usage to 2.5 gallons per minute or less, which can save even a two-person household more than 10,000 gallons a year. Installing a new showerhead is a simple do-it-yourself job (p.158).

◆**A showerhead with an on-off lever** lets you turn the water off temporarily without changing the temperature setting. You don't need the water running while you soap yourself up or wash your hair.

◆**Low-flow toilets**, which are now required in some new construction, use 1.6 gallons per flush versus 3.5 gallons for older models. By placing a plastic soda bottle full of water in the tank of an older toilet you can cut the amount of water per flush without the trouble and expense of replacing the toilet.

◆**Landscape with native plants** or plants from similar climates (see xeriscaping on page 275), cluster thirsty plants, and use soaker hoses, micro-sprinklers, and timers to reduce water consumption.

◆**Turn off the water while you shave or brush your teeth.** Don't leave the tap running when you don't need it.

◆**When you handwash dishes**, rinse in a basin of clear water, not under a running tap.

SIMPLE ELECTRICAL FIXES

Many electrical repairs and upgrades are surprisingly easy and can be safely handled by anyone who understands how to do the job correctly and safely.

Whether it's replacing a broken switch or installing a new light fixture, many simple electrical jobs can be easily done by the average homeowner—saving both money and the inconvenience of waiting to get the job done. But to do it safely, it's important for you to know what precautions to take and how to do the job properly. It's also important to understand the basics of how electricity works in your home and when it's prudent to turn to a licensed professional.

UNDERSTANDING YOUR SYSTEM

Electricity enters your home through an electric meter. From there it goes to a main service panel, which has circuit breakers or fuses and distributes the power to the house's various circuits. A circuit typically covers one part of the house and contains a number of outlets, such as receptacles and light fixtures.

Each circuit is a closed loop. Current leaves the service panel on the hot (usually black) wire and returns through the neutral (white) wire. When you flip a switch, the circuit is interrupted, cutting the flow of electricity to the fixture. Electrical systems also have a ground (bare or green) wire to carry excess current harmlessly to the ground in case of a short circuit.

Volts, amps, and watts

Electricity flows through wires much like water flows through pipes. The electrical pressure that causes current to flow is measured in *volts*. This pressure is set by your electrical utility company and is 120 volts for most circuits. (Some large appliances, such as electric ranges and dryers, require 240 volts.) The rate at which the electricity flows is measured in *amps* (amperes). The amount of power a lamp or appliance actually draws is measured in *watts*—a measure that takes both volts and amps into account. For example, a light bulb that draws ½ amp through a 120-volt circuit uses 60 watts (½ x 120).

Grounding for safety

Grounding provides a safety net for your house's electrical system. Ground wires normally don't carry current, but in an emergency, they provide a safe path of least resistance to the ground for an abnormal current flow. This helps to protect both you and your electrical gear.

The electrical code now requires that all new and upgraded wiring be fully grounded. But in older homes, the receptacles and lighting fixtures are often not grounded. Ungrounded receptacles have only two slots while grounded ones have a third round hole. This allows them to accept the three-prong plugs found on many heavy-duty appliances that need to be grounded to be used safely. Your receptacles may have that third round hole without really being grounded, however. People often replace ungrounded receptacles with grounded ones, and leave the grounding unconnected. This is dan-

gerous because it encourages you to use the receptacles for equipment that should be grounded.

To tell if a receptacle is grounded, use an inexpensive receptacle analyzer (p.94). Of course, it's safe to use older ungrounded receptacles for fixtures like lights that don't demand a lot of power. But if you suspect that your entire electrical system is not properly grounded, have it inspected by an electrician.

Fuses and circuit breakers

The size of a fuse or breaker in your service panel is determined by the expected load on a circuit and the size of the wires in the circuit. Fuses and breakers are designed to blow or trip when the demand for electricity is excessive, before wiring gets dangerously hot. *Never replace a fuse with one of larger*

amperage. Doing so creates a fire hazard.

If electrical use exceeds the capacity of a fuse or breaker, the breaker will trip or the fuse will blow, stopping the flow of electricity in the circuit. When that happens, try to figure out what caused the overload before resetting the breaker or replacing the fuse. Most likely, you have too many appliances drawing current on the same circuit; try plugging some of them into receptacles on another circuit. If that doesn't work, one of the appliances on the circuit may need repair.

Is your service adequate?

If you have circuit breakers in your service panel, chances are you have at least a 100-amp service. Older fuse boxes are usually rated at 60 or 100 amps. The amp rating is typically

UNDERSTANDING YOUR SERVICE PANEL

The main service panel is the box holding the circuit breakers or fuses. Circuit breakers or fuses shut off the electricity to individual circuits; electrical power to the entire house can be controlled by a separate device. In a circuit breaker panel, the main shutoff breaker is usually marked and located at the top of the panel. By turning the switch on the breaker to the "off" position, you can work safely on the wiring throughout the house (but always test individual circuits before touching any wires, just to be safe). Fuse panels are equipped either with a pullout box containing cartridge fuses, or a lever switch on the side marked for "off" and "on." A service panel should have a numbered list showing what each circuit controls. If yours doesn't, ask an electrician to prepare one. Never touch the main power wires.

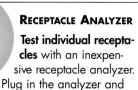

RECEPTACLE ANALYZER
Test individual receptacles with an inexpensive receptacle analyzer. Plug in the analyzer and compare the resulting light pattern with the code provided. It will show if the circuit is wired correctly or, if it is not, what the problem is. If a problem is spotted, turn off the power, remove the cover plate, pull out the receptacle, and change the connections according to directions. Or call in an electrician.

marked somewhere on the panel; it indicates the maximum amount of electrical service that the house can be wired for. Today, new houses are most often provided with 200 amps, but 100 amps will do for most people. Many people are living just fine with their 60-amp service.

Old wiring can be a hazard. If your wiring has frayed or brittle insulation, you may want to consider having your house rewired.

MAKING SIMPLE REPAIRS

Work on your electrical system only when you are absolutely sure that it is safe. Even experienced electricians err on the side of caution when verifying that power has been shut off on a circuit needing repair. The repairs in this section are ones that a motivated homeowner can do, but don't hesitate to call an electrician if you feel uncomfortable about taking on a particular job.

First, turn off the power

The basic rule when working with electricity is simple but very important: *Always turn off the power to a fixture or an outlet that needs repair* by flipping off the circuit breaker or removing the fuse that controls it at the main service panel. Then test the wires to confirm that the power is shut off.

An inexpensive neon tester, sold in hardware stores, can tell you whether a receptacle or a switch is powered or not. Make sure you buy a tester that's rated for 120/240-volt household current—not a 12-volt automobile unit.

To test a receptacle or switch, first turn off the power to the outlet at the service panel. Remove the cover plate, and then take out the screws holding the switch or receptacle to the box (step 1, facing page). Pull the switch out from the box, being careful not to

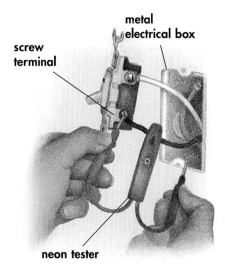

metal electrical box

screw terminal

neon tester

touch the wires. Touch one prong of the tester to the electrical box if the box is metal, or to the bare metal of the ground wire if the box is plastic; touch the other prong to one screw terminal, then to the other screw terminal. Then touch the prongs to the two screw terminals at the same time. If the tester doesn't light up at any point, there's no power. It's safe to continue the repair.

Replacing a switch or receptacle

If a switch stops working or if a receptacle is damaged or burned out, the solution is nearly always to replace it. The steps for replacing a receptacle are shown on the facing page. A switch is replaced the same way. Here are some points to keep in mind.

◆ **Replace a switch or receptacle** with one that has exactly the same rating. Replace a 15-amp unit with a 15-amp one and a 20-amp unit with one rated 20 amps.

◆ **Replace an older unpolarized receptacle** with a polarized one. An unpolarized receptacle has two equal sized slots; a polarized one has a long slot and a shorter one.

◆ **Don't replace a two-slot receptacle** with a grounded three-slot one unless the box is grounded or your wiring has a ground wire.

◆ **If you are replacing a receptacle** in a kitchen, bathroom, basement, or other water-exposed area, install a ground-fault circuit interrupter (GFCI) receptacle (p.96). A GFCI receptacle provides maximum safety and will work even in an ungrounded box.

REPLACING A RECEPTACLE

1. Turn off the power to the box at the main service panel. Unscrew the cover plate. Remove the screws holding the receptacle and carefully pull it out, making sure not to touch the wires. Then use a tester (facing page) to check that the power is off.

2. Unscrew and remove one wire at a time from the old unit and fasten it to the matching terminal on the replacement unit before removing the next wire. That way you won't lose track of which wire goes where. Hook the wire clockwise around the screw.

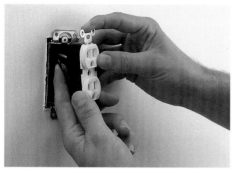

3. When all the screws have been tightened over the wires, gently push the unit back into the box. Fold the wires toward the back as you go. Screw the unit to the box, then replace the cover plate. Restore power at the service panel and test new receptacle.

◆ **The most common type of wall switch**—and the kind you will be replacing most often—is a single-pole switch. It has two brass-colored terminal screws and often another green one for a ground wire. It controls a light or receptacle from one location.

◆ **To replace a switch** that controls a light from two different locations, such as the top and bottom of stairs, you need a special three-way switch. It has terminal screws for three wires and often one for a ground wire. Less common is a four-way switch, which controls a light from three locations.

◆ **The number of wires** in a box for a switch or receptacle varies depending on whether the box is at the end of circuit (only one cable enters it) or whether it is in the middle of a circuit (two cables enter it). However, you should have no problem determining which wire to attach to which screw as long as you move the wires one at a time from the old unit to the matching screw on the replacement unit.

◆ **The black (hot) wire** on a receptacle goes to the brass-colored screw; the white (neutral) wire goes to the silver-colored screw. The green or bare ground wire goes to the green screw.

◆ **Many switches and receptacles** can be wired using holes in the back of the unit into which a wire can be pushed. Avoid this method—the wires may loosen as you push the unit in the box.

◆ **If your house has aluminum wiring,** use only replacement receptacles or switches that are stamped CO/ALR. You can tell if you have aluminum wiring by looking at the color (dull silver rather than copper) of the wires in the box or by checking for exposed cables in the attic or in the basement that are marked with AL or the word aluminum.

Stripping wire
Electrical wires are covered with protective insulation. The wires conduct electricity only if the insulation on the end of the wire is removed to expose the metal. Knowing how to strip insulation off a wire end is sometimes necessary when making electrical repairs. In a pinch, you can strip a wire with a pocket knife. Set the wire on a hard surface, then shave the insulation off of one side of the wire. Take care not to cut the wire itself. Peel the insulation back and cut off the excess with the knife. A wire stripper (p.96) is quicker and less likely to damage the wire. One type, called a combination tool, has dif-

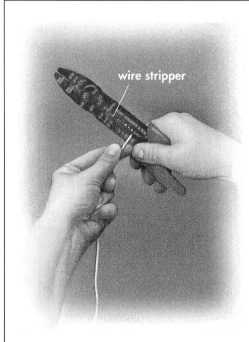

wire stripper

ferent slots for stripping different gauges of wire. Set the wire in the proper slot, squeeze the handles, then twist and pull the wire away from the wire stripper. Expose only enough of the wire to make a good connection—usually ½ to ¾ inch.

Joining wires

Instead of terminal screws, many light fixtures and specialty switches like dimmers have wires that you have to join to your household wiring. To join two wires together, strip ¾ inch from each wire end if necessary. Hold the bare ends of the wires parallel to each other. Using pliers, twist the wires together in a clockwise direction. Then twist on a plastic wire connector (also known by the trade name Wire Nut). Or you can skip twisting with pliers and use the wire connector to fasten the wires

together. Just make sure that both wires have been grabbed by the wire connector.

Understanding a GFCI

A ground-fault circuit interrupter (GFCI) is a safety device that can save your life. It protects you from an abnormal electrical current flow due to a short. When an electrical current is operating correctly, an equal amount of power is flowing to and from the intended target on two wires. If that current becomes disrupted, part of the current is taking another path. A GFCI senses the change in the current flow and immediately shuts off the power to the target.

The electrical code requires GFCI outlets in bathrooms and outdoors for new homes. In most cases, you can replace standard receptacles with GFCI receptacles. You can also have GFCI circuit breakers installed in your service panel. Plug-in GFCI adapters and GFCI extension cords are also available.

Troubleshooting a GFCI

If a GFCI trips constantly or fails to reset when you push the button, first check the wiring. Turn off the power to the receptacle at the service panel and verify that no power is reaching the box (p.94). Remove the cover plate and then the screws holding the GFCI in place. Carefully pull out the GFCI and inspect the wires; the connections should be tight, and wires should not be making contact with anything except the terminal screw. As a precau-

REPLACING A BROKEN LIGHT BULB

When a light bulb breaks while still in its socket, tend to the repair right away. Pull the plug or shut off power at the service panel. If the glass is completely shattered, you may have difficulty getting enough of a grip on the bulb socket to remove it. Use needle-nose pliers to twist the bulb socket. If you can't get a grip, push a soap bar or a potato over the remaining glass shards and turn. Replace the bulb and restore the power.

tion against shorts, wrap the terminal screws with tape (below). (If your newly installed GFCI doesn't operate correctly, make sure the wires have been connected correctly; check the instructions.) Push the GFCI into the

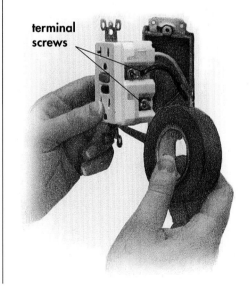

terminal screws

INSTALLING LIGHT FIXTURES

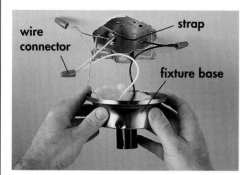

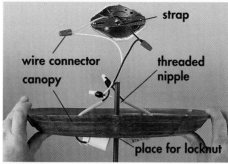

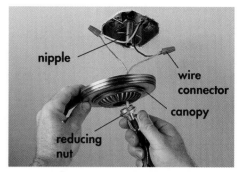

Flush-mounted fixture: Shut off the power and verify that it is off (p.94); disconnect the wires and remove the fixture. Use wire connectors to attach the new wires, black to black, white to white, ground to ground. Tuck the wires into the box and screw the fixture base into the strap.

Canopy fixture: With the power off, remove the old fixture. Attach the wires like color to like color, ground to ground, using wire connectors. Twist the threaded nipple of the fixture into the strap until the canopy is firm against the ceiling. Affix the canopy from beneath with a locknut.

Hanging fixture: Shut off the power and remove the old fixture. If the nipple is rusty, replace it to ease assembly. Thread the fixture wires through the reducing nut and canopy. Attach them to those in the junction box. Screw the canopy onto the reducing nut and fasten the nut to the nipple.

box, attach the screws and cover plate, restore power, and test. If the problem persists, you should replace the GFCI. If necessary, have an electrician check the circuit.

Installing a dimmer switch

Whether you choose a round dimmer switch or one that looks more like a standard switch with a lever on the side, the installation procedure is the same. Turn off power to the switch at the service panel. Remove the cover plate and the screws holding the switch to the box. Carefully pull the switch out of the box. Use a neon-bulb voltage tester to verify that no power is reaching the switch (p.94). Unscrew the wires from the old switch. Straighten the exposed wire ends and trim if necessary so that no bare wire will stick

out of the wire connectors. The wires from the dimmer can attach to either wire in the box. With pliers, twist the ends of the two pairs of wires together. Slip a wire connector over each pair

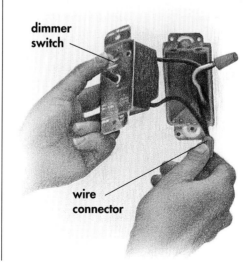

QUICK FIX

INSTALLING AN ILLUMINATED SWITCH

An illuminated switch has a light inside the toggle that glows when it is off. That makes it easier to find the switch in the dark. Consider putting one in a bedroom, for instance.

1. Turn off the power to the switch; remove the cover plate and the screws holding the switch to the box.

2. Carefully pull the switch out of the box.

3. Use a tester to verify that no power is reaching the switch.

4. Transfer the wiring from the old switch to the new one. Push the switch back in the box, attach the screws, replace the cover plate, and restore power.

of wires and twist clockwise, making sure that it fits securely. Join the ground wires the same way. Push the dimmer into the box, screw the dimmer to the box, screw on the cover plate, and slip the knob into place. Restore power and test.

Replacing fluorescent tubes

Buy a new tube with the same wattage rating as the old one. Standard fluorescent bulbs are labeled "cool white." Those labeled "daylight" or "color corrected" will cost more, but will also render colors better.

To replace a tube, grasp the old tube on both ends and twist to free the pins, then slide it out of the sockets. Reverse the process with the new tube, making sure that the pins are fully inserted into the sockets. When disposing of a fluorescent tube, don't break it; it contains mercury and will explode slightly when broken. Dispose of it whole, or contact your garbage service for recommendations.

Repairing a fluorescent fixture

If a fluorescent light won't light, flickers on and off, or is weak, first check the tube. Make sure it is inserted properly in its sockets. Look to see if it is discolored; change the tube if necessary. On an older unit, the ballast may be bad. The ballast is a rectangular black object that is fairly heavy; you can find it by removing the cover plate behind the tubes. Before replacing a ballast, however, compare its cost to the cost of a new fixture. The difference is often so small that it makes more sense to buy a

new fixture. Newer units have electronic ballasts, which are not replaceable.

On an older fluorescent fixture, the starter may be the problem. The starter is a small metal cylinder located near one of the sockets. To remove the starter, push it in, then twist it counterclockwise. Take it with you to a hardware store and get an exact match.

Rewiring a lamp

If a lamp cord is damaged, the only safe solution is to buy a replacement cord (with plug) at a hardware store and install it. Here is how to rewire the lamp:

◆ **Unplug the lamp and remove the bulb.** Unscrew the finial, if any, and lift the shade off the metal harp that holds it. Slide up the harp sleeves, exposing the clips at the end of the harp holder; squeeze the harp arms to release the harp.

◆ **Depress the outer shell of the socket** where it is marked "Press." Pull off the socket shell and insulating sleeve to expose the socket.

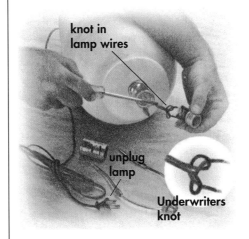
knot in lamp wires
unplug lamp
Underwriters knot

MONEY SAVERS

REPLACING INCANDESCENT LIGHTS WITH FLUORESCENTS

Compared with incandescent lights, fluorescent lights use considerably less electricity to produce the same amount of illumination. That is largely because incandescents (that is, the standard type of light bulbs we have all used for years) produce a lot of heat, which is wasted energy. A new generation of compact fluorescent lights is now available that can save you money. Typical compact fluorescent lights use about one-quarter of the energy used by typical incandescent lights, and may last ten times longer. They cost more initially, but compact fluorescents can be a money-saving choice in the long run. Full-spectrum fluorescent bulbs produce light that more closely resembles natural sunlight.

◆ **Free the old cord from the socket** by loosening the terminal screws. Untie the underwriters knot and unscrew the socket cap.

◆ **Remove the felt from the base of the lamp.** Cut the plug off the old cord and untie any knots in the cord. Splice the nonplug end of the new cord to the old one by hooking the ends of the wires over each other and securing the splice with tape. Pull the old cord up the lamp tube until the tape appears.

◆ **Remove the old cord.** Split the top 3 inches of the new cord; strip 1½ inches of insulation from the ends. Replace the harp holder and socket cap; then tie an underwriters knot (inset).

◆ **Connect the cord's ridged (neutral) wire** to the silver terminal; connect the smooth (hot) wire to the brass terminal. Reassemble the rest of the lamp.

Troubleshooting a doorbell

If a doorbell or chime stops sounding, begin by checking the service panel to see if the circuit breaker has tripped or the fuse has blown. (If this is the case, other lights and receptacles on the same circuit will also be dead.) If the doorbell is getting power, inspect and test the button. Remove the screws holding the button to the wall. Pull the button out carefully (see below) and inspect the connections in the back. The two wires should be secured to the terminal screws, with no exposed wires touching each other.

If the bell still won't ring, remove the wires from the screws. Hold one wire in each hand by the insulation, then touch the bare ends of the wires together. If the bell rings, buy and install a replacement button. If the problem persists, clean the chime or bell unit and check it for loose connections (below).

If the bell still won't function, the transformer may be the culprit. This component reduces the electrical current from 120 volts to 12 to 24 volts. Follow the wires from the bell or chime to find the transformer; it will be attached to a junction box and may be located in the basement, attic, or a closet. Turn the power off at the service panel, and check the transformer for loose wires. Turn the power back on, and holding the insulated handle of a screwdriver, touch both terminals briefly with the point and shaft; if you get a weak spark, the transformer is functioning. Or turn off the power again, unmount the trans-

former from the junction box and take it to an electrical supply store to have it checked. If the transformer is not the problem, the wiring is the most likely culprit. It's impractical to try and rewire the doorbell yourself unless you are an experienced do-it-yourselfer. Consider replacing the old doorbell with a wireless doorbell instead. Wireless systems are inexpensive and easy to install.

If you can reuse the old wiring, replacing a wired doorbell or chime is easy. Replacing the transformer is a more complex job. It is connected to a 120-volt current. Shut off the power to the transformer. Remove the cover from the box and unscrew the wire connectors. Loosen the locknut holding the transformer, then pull it from the box. Mount the new transformer—an exact duplicate—and attach the wires with wire connectors, matching the wire colors.

FIXING A DOORBELL

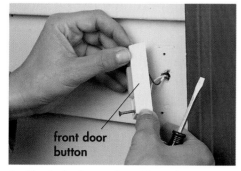

front door button

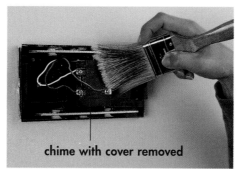

chime with cover removed

1. Check the button first. Clean the contacts and make sure the connections are tight. If it still doesn't work but the bell sounds when you touch the wires, replace the button.

2. Remove the cover from the bell or chime. Gently brush away dust or cobwebs with a soft, clean paint brush. Clean parts with a cotton swab dampened with contact cleaner.

3. Look for any loose connections in the chime and tighten those that you find. Make sure that no bare wires are touching each other (clip off excess wire).

B

Kitchens

Cookware

Appliances

KITCHEN ORGANIZATION AND CLEANING

Guests gravitate toward it, family members congregate in it, cooks create in it. Despite changing lifestyles, the kitchen remains the heart of the home. Here's how to keep it working smoothly.

Not just the place where meals are made and sometimes eaten, the kitchen often does multiple duty as home office, family center, and hobby room. No matter how many square feet it measures, a kitchen seldom seems big enough. The challenge is to put the space you have to its best use. Smart organization of your kitchen equipment and supplies is the quickest way to make the room seem more spacious and efficient.

KITCHEN ORGANIZATION

There's no avoiding some reaching and bending in a kitchen. To make it easier on yourself, however, try to store items that you use every day no lower than knee level and no higher than 10 inches above your head. Reserve the higher and lower shelves for things you don't need to use very often. You should put lightweight items, such as the stemware that you save for parties, on the highest shelves. Then you won't have to hold heavy things over your head as you remove them from the cupboard. Put awkward and hefty equipment, such as infrequently-used small appliances and large Dutch ovens, on the cupboard's lowest shelves.

Try to store cooking tools and utensils near the area where you normally use them. Keep pots and pans, spatulas, wooden spoons, and hot pads, for example, by the stovetop. In the same spirit, put knives, cutting boards, measuring cups and spoons, and mixing bowls near the food-preparation counter.

Not everything has to go into a drawer or a cupboard. You may find it even more convenient to take the tool that you need off a hook on pegboard or a wire rack that's mounted on a wall; off a magnetic bar designed to hold steel utensils that's fastened on the side of a cupboard; or out of a handsome wide-mouthed pottery jar or pewter mug that sits on the counter.

Pots and pans

Identify the pots and pans that you use most often, then find a place to store them where they'll be easy to pull out. Store heavy pots and pans that you use frequently no more than a foot above or a foot below waist level, making certain that they have sturdy support and can be removed and replaced without upsetting other cookware.

If the storage space in your cabinets is full and there's no room on the walls, consider suspending a metal rack from the ceiling to hang your cookware. (Be sure it is installed properly in a joist, so that it can carry the weight of the pots and pans.) Save your most frequently used—and most attractive—pieces for hanging on the rack. If you can position the rack directly over the cooktop, you can take a pan from storage to service in one quick motion.

Small appliances

Toasters, coffee makers, food processors, and other small appliances that you use almost daily need their own space on a kitchen counter with a nearby receptacle. Many of these appliances now can be mounted under a cabinet to allow you more working counter space. Consider an under-the-cabinet model next time you need to replace an appliance. Appliances that you use only occasionally, such as a standing mixer or slow-cooker, can be kept in cupboards. If you only use an appliance—the waffle iron, for example—once or twice a year, you can store it in the back of a cupboard or shelf in order to free up more usable space in the kitchen.

GOOD SOLUTIONS

STRETCHING CABINET SPACE

◆ **Cookie sheets,** carving boards and serving trays take up less space and are easier to get at if they're stored upright. To convert a conventional cabinet to store such items, begin by removing the shelves. Use wood screws to fasten scrap lumber supports to the top and bottom of the cabinet, positioning them ¼-inch apart. Cut dividers to fit from ¼-inch plywood and slide them in place.

◆ **In-cabinet wheeled bins** let you pull out the whole unit to easily get at cleaning supplies, pans, or canned goods in the back without taking out all the items up front. Measure your cabinet's depth, height, and width before picking out a unit to be sure it will fit. You will need no more than a measuring tape, drill, and screwdriver to install such a bin, following the manufacturer's instructions.

◆ **Installing racks** on the inside of cabinet doors consolidates storage of small items, such as spices and condiments, and makes them easy to find. Plastic-coated wire racks are available in many sizes and configurations. If the unit has hooks, hang measuring cups and spoons. Be careful positioning any holders so that the items on the door don't bump into the cabinet shelves and prevent the door from closing.

Linens

Store sets of place mats or everyday tablecloths with a piece of cardboard between them. Then, the ones that are on top of the pile won't get disheveled when you pull out the ones that you want below. You can make the dividers out of suit boxes or posterboard. For unwrinkled storage of your good tablecloths, see page 251.

Pantries

Group pantry supplies so that it is easy to do a quick inventory of what you have and what you need. Cereals, pasta, canned soups, cooking oils, condiments, and beverages like coffee and tea should each have a designated space. Store small cans, jars, and boxes in front of larger items so they're as easy to see as they are to reach.

Stepped plastic cupboard insets (above) also help in keeping supplies visible.

Special needs

To avoid misplacing the jewelry that you slip off while doing dishes, install a cup hook near—but not over—the sink in a protected spot. Hang rings, watches, and bracelets there while your hands are in the water.

If you have trouble opening jars and cans, put up a V-shaped gripper next to an electric can opener near the cook top.

Clutter control

Once a year, you should go through each drawer and shelf in the kitchen, checking for unnecessary duplications and items that you don't use. Do you really need more than one melon baller? Have you ever tried the gadget for making radish roses?

Discard any canned goods and jars that have passed their expiration dates or are more than a year old. Box up the non-food items you don't need and put them in a neighborhood garage sale, or give them to a friend who's just setting up housekeeping.

Storage you can buy

There are many attractive and inexpensive storage containers at home stores. Don't limit yourself; you can also find great-looking organizers at basket stores, craft shops, and flea markets. Here are some ideas.

◆ **Plastic bins** for fruits and vegetables come in many colors and can be stacked on a counter or the floor.

◆ **A plastic-covered wire roll-around cart** can hold anything from dish towels to cookbooks and can be moved from one work area to another—or out of sight into a closet.

◆ **A wooden or wire rack** installed in a deep cupboard or under a counter suspends stemware by its bottom and saves shelf space.

◆ **A freestanding cabinet** with a butcher-block top and a cupboard underneath gives you more counter space as well as more storage.

◆ **A folding bookcase** can fit in the extra foot of space at one end of a kitchen counter or island and hold a good selection of cookbooks.

KITCHEN CLEANING

Because cooking can be a messy process, all areas of the kitchen need frequent cleaning to keep them fresh, grease-free, and sanitary. Scrubbing and cleaning kitchen surfaces is as much a function of health and hygiene as it is good housekeeping.

The new rules

Disease-causing bacteria, frequently found in raw poultry and meat, have

GOOD SOLUTIONS

CABINET REFACING

This remodeling technique can freshen the look of a kitchen for a fraction of the cost of new cabinets. In refacing, new cabinet doors and drawer fronts are installed on the old cabinet frames, and all the visible parts of the frames are faced with matching wood or laminate veneers. The cabinet configuration isn't changed, but if your old cabinets were badly worn or simply not your taste, the change will be a happy one. Refacing should be done by a professional. Ask neighbors and friends for the names of reliable contractors from whom you can get an estimate and a catalog of refacing materials. The steps to refacing are shown below.

1. Take off old cabinet doors by removing the screws from the hinges.

2. Clean and sand the frame. Wipe with a tack cloth.

3. Cover the cabinet frame with peel-and-stick wood veneer or vinyl laminate.

4. Drill new holes for the new hinges, if necessary, and attach new doors.

PAINTING CABINETS

Step 1: Remove cabinet doors, drawers, and hardware. Drop the hardware in a box or can so that nothing gets lost; you can clean and polish it while the cabinets are drying. Place the doors and drawers in a dust-free area where they can stay several days while they're drying. Wash all surfaces with a strong detergent.

Step 2: Sand cabinet surfaces lightly with 100-grit sandpaper to dull the gloss and aid paint adhesion. Vacuum and wipe with a clean tack cloth (available at paint stores) to eliminate dust. Choose a water-based stain-resistant paint formulated for kitchens. It should be scrubbable and contain a mildew-cide against the high humidity of a kitchen.

Step 3: As a first coat, use a primer recommended for the type of paint you are using. Buy good-quality brushes to avoid streaks and errant bristles. When the primer is dry, lightly sand and wipe the cabinet surfaces again. Apply the first coat of finish paint, let it dry, sand lightly, and wipe again. A second finish coat should complete the job.

become a serious menace in recent years. The effects of salmonella and some strains of *E. coli*, for example, can be painful for everyone and deadly for susceptible people. Health Canada monitors the incidence of food poisoning, and the reported cases number up to a million annually. The following steps will cut down harmful bacteria in the kitchen.

◆ **Wash your hands** with hot, soapy water before handling food and after using the bathroom, changing diapers, or handling pets. Also do the same, scrubbing for a full minute, after handling raw meat, poultry, or seafood.

◆ **Wash cutting boards,** dishes, utensils, and counters with hot, soapy water after preparing each food item and before you go on to the next food.

◆ **Wash dishrags,** dishtowels, and sponges in the washing machine with hot water. Sponges can also be cleaned in the upper rack of the dishwasher (right) while plastic cutting boards can go on the lower racks.

◆ **Separate raw meat,** poultry, and seafood from each other and from other foods in the shopping cart at the grocery and in the refrigerator at home.

◆ **Never put cooked food** on an unwashed platter that previously held raw meat, poultry, or seafood.

◆ **Refrigerate or freeze perishables,** prepared foods, and leftovers within two hours of a meal.

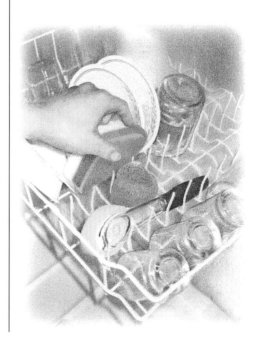

◆ **Defrost frozen foods** in the refrigerator or under cold running water, not on the counter.

Taking care of counters

Different counter materials require slightly different maintenance regimens, but there are general practices that apply to all. Many counters are not entirely heatproof, for example, so be careful about setting down hot pans or casseroles without a trivet or a pad.

Most counters will chip or dent if they are hit with a heavy object, so try not to bang heavy pots or equipment on them. Don't try to scrape off dried-on stains with a metal spatula. Use a plastic spatula (below) to prevent scratches or gouging.

Do your chopping and dicing on a wooden or plastic chopping board, not the bare counter. Chopping boards prevent scratches and dents in the counter surface, which are unsightly and can harbor dangerous bacteria.

plastic
spatula

dried-on
food

Identify your counter material (facing page) and follow these guidelines.

◆ **Butcher block.** Not to be confused with butcher-block cutting boards, butcher-block countertops are sealed for protection against water. Clean butcher block with a sponge dipped in a mild solution of dish detergent and water. It's important to condition the wood regularly by sealing it with beeswax. Or, apply a thin coat of mineral oil when the wood begins to look dull. (Vegetable oil will become rancid.) Let the oil soak into the surface for an hour or more, then wipe up any excess.

◆ **Ceramic.** The grout in a ceramic countertop becomes stained if it isn't sealed properly (pp.151–152). Clean stains with a solution of ½ cup liquid chlorine bleach to 1 quart of water.

◆ **Granite.** For everyday cleaning, wipe down granite with a damp cloth. Sealed granite is resistant to most stains, but unsealed granite is not. To remove stains, make a paste of whiting (calcium carbonate, found where silver polish is sold) mixed with a little hydrogen peroxide and ammonia, then let it work for an hour or two. (Test on an inconspicuous area first.) Once the paste has had a chance to do its job, simply wipe it away.

◆ **Laminate.** Wipe laminate countertops with a mild cleaner, such as liquid dish detergent and water. Avoid using abrasive cleaners or those that contain agents that could discolor the laminate. (If you're uncertain, test a small, unseen area.) Stains such as wine, beet

juice, or marker may require more elbow grease. Cover the stain with a thick paste made of lemon juice and baking soda. After letting the paste dry thoroughly, rub vigorously with a damp cloth or sponge. You can remove the ink from grocery price tags by using a soft cloth and a little rubbing alcohol.

◆ **Solid surface.** These countertops are synthetics that emulate marble or natural stone but are easier to clean. After each use, simply wipe down a solid surface countertop with a sponge and a weak solution of dishwashing liquid in water. Scrub stubborn stains with scouring powder and a damp sponge. Smooth out blemishes, minor burns, and scratches with a piece of 200- to 300-grit sandpaper. Then, smooth the previously scarred surface with very fine 800-grit sandpaper, and finish by polishing the area with a paste-type car wax.

CLEANING THE SINK AREA

Try to clean the sink quickly once a day with dishwashing detergent or a gentle scouring liquid or powder cleanser. For tough stains, follow the appropriate treatment below for your type of sink.

◆ **Porcelain sinks.** Fill the sink with lukewarm water. Add ½ cup of liquid chlorine bleach, and allow the solution to stand for an hour or two. If the stains are stubborn, line the sink with paper towels that have been saturated with bleach and leave overnight. Once the bleach has done its work, rinse the sink thoroughly.

POPULAR COUNTERTOP SURFACES

Butcher Block:

Made of hardwood, usually maple, butcher block is very warm and attractive.

Pros: Butcher block is easy to install, and if it gets badly nicked or scratched, it can be repaired easily by sanding and resealing.

Cons: Butcher block burns, scratches, and dents easily. It needs to be treated regularly with mineral oil or wax, or to be sealed with a polyurethane sealer. The joint between countertop and backsplash must be caulked to prevent seepage. Butcher block is moderately expensive.

Ceramic Tile:

A designer's delight, ceramic tiles come in every color and many designs.

Pros: Glazed tiles will not stain or scratch, nor will grout that is sealed with an acrylic sealer. Easy to install, even for a do-it-yourselfer. Repairs are easy and inexpensive.

Cons: Ceramic breaks easily if something heavy is dropped on it, and grout provides gutters for dirt. Grout will stain if not sealed and maintained. Ceramic tile ranges from inexpensive to moderately expensive, depending on the price of the tiles.

Granite:

This is the most popular natural stone used for kitchen and bathroom counters.

Pros: It is very strong and durable, resisting scratches and nicks. Granite that has been sealed resists stains and cleans easily.

Cons: Granite is heavy and requires a strong base. It must be custom installed, and a protective, penetrating sealer must be applied periodically for stain protection. Granite is expensive.

Laminate:

Known by trade names such as Formica and Wilsonart, it comes in dozens of colors and patterns.

Pros: The least expensive of all countertop materials, it can be installed by an experienced do-it-yourselfer.

Cons: Nicks and scratches are readily apparent. Will burn and scorch. Has visible seams, which can allow water and grime to get under the surface. Caustic cleaners or drain openers can discolor the surface.

Solid Surface:

Sold under brand names such as Dupont Corian and Wilsonart Gibraltar, it comes in dozens of colors and patterns. It is made of polyester or acrylic resins combined with mineral fillers.

Pros: Scratches and nicks can be easily buffed out with an abrasive pad. It can be installed without seams and can include sinks and backsplash for a continuous expanse.

Cons: Solid surface is easily scratched, can be discolored by heat, and requires a trained installer. Solid surface is moderately expensive.

Don't use bleach on a cracked or porous porcelain sink. It can penetrate to the iron base and cause further discoloration by rusting. Clean it with a combination of scouring powder and water. Repeat if necessary.

◆ **Stainless steel sinks.** Remove surface scratches with a piece of very fine steel wool, then buff the area to a sheen with a soft cloth.

Shining up faucets

Commercial glass cleaners, such as Windex or Glass Plus, will shine up most faucets and fixtures. If your water is heavy with minerals, however, an acidic cleaner like white vinegar will do a better job. In severe cases, a commercial product, such as Lime-A-Way or CLR, may be necessary. Use these products as directed. If you have brass fixtures, be sure any cleaner you use is safe for that metal.

To remove small spots of rust on chrome, scrub with aluminum foil. Ball up a small piece of foil with the shiny side out. Rub the rust until it disappears, then polish the chrome.

CLEANING UNDER APPLIANCES

◆ **The best cleaning tool** for tight spaces under and behind large appliances may be in the car; the long-handled brush you use to sweep snow from the windshield is just the right size and shape to go under the refrigerator or behind the stove.

◆ **For wider crevices,** try an old paint roller on an extension stick.

Maintaining a garbage disposer

To eliminate odors in the garbage disposer, grind cut-up citrus rinds while flushing the unit with cold water.

If food gets caught in the disposer, turn off the power and use a broom handle to move the flywheel back and forth by pushing against the hammer, a notched metal piece on the flywheel. Once it moves, you should be able to remove the problem-causing object with a pair of kitchen tongs. Never put your hand in a disposer to free a jam.

To prevent jamming, don't pack the disposer tightly. Never grind clam shells, glass shards, or bottle caps. Keep the cold water running fully while the disposer is on and for a minute after it has finished to clear the drain line. Never use chemical drain cleaner in a disposer; it can damage the machine's internal parts.

Cleaning large appliances

You can clean the exterior of most ranges and refrigerators with an all-purpose glass and surface cleaner, such as Fantastik or Mr. Clean, or a homemade solution of one tablespoon of dishwashing detergent in a gallon of warm water. (If you make the solution any stronger, it will leave a residue that's hard to rinse away.)

Wipe down cooktops regularly. Many ceramic cooktops are sold with a cleaning cream made especially for this purpose. You can also use a non-abrasive cleaner or a paste of baking soda and water. Do not use abrasive

---

RUN BONES THROUGH THE GARBAGE DISPOSER

They'll make a racket while being ground up, but small bones and fruit pits can do wonders to clean the inside of the grind chamber. Grind them with a strong flow of cold water. To further clean and freshen the disposer, use baking soda or a foaming cleaner.

---

cleaners or scouring pads, however; they can scratch the surface.

Stove hoods have a grease filter that should be removed and cleaned periodically. Put the filter in the bottom rack of the dishwasher or soak it in a sink of hot water and liquid dish detergent and rinse under a stream of very hot water. Wash the interior of the stove hood with a small amount of liquid dish detergent in a gallon of hot water. Hoods that don't vent to the outside have a disposable charcoal filter that must be replaced according to the manufacturer's directions.

Controlling insect pests

With food scraps, grease, and water lines to attract insects, the kitchen is the starting place for keeping such pests at bay.

◆ **Ants** can be held in check with baited traps or residual sprays that you can buy at the supermarket or hardware store. Apply the spray or set several traps around windowsills, exterior doorways, baseboards, and sinks.

◆ **Cockroaches** can be discouraged by a dusting of boric acid powder along baseboards and under the sink. If you see roaches in the kitchen, apply a residual spray of commercial roach killer. If it's not effective, try one with a different active ingredient. For severe infestations, you'll need to call in an exterminator.

◆ **House flies** can only reproduce outside, so good screens are your first line of defense. Indoors, you can wield a fly swatter or hang strips of flypaper to keep their numbers down.

◆ **Fruit flies** swarm around ripe fruit, sweet foods, and even vinegar, especially in late summer. Store fruit in the refrigerator, and other attractive foods in airtight containers.

◆ **Food moths and grain beetles** proliferate in flour, cereal, pasta, and other grain products. If they're a problem, discard the infected food, vacuum the area thoroughly, and scrub with liquid dish detergent and water. Store any new grain-based products in airtight containers, such as screw-top jars or plastic containers with locking lids.

Garbage can care

Wash out garbage cans regularly with a solution of ½ cup ammonia and 1 gallon of water. Sprinkle borax in each clean, dry container to keep it fresh.

You can discourage animals (dogs, raccoons, and crows are top contenders in the suburbs) from getting into the garbage by any one of the following suggestions.

◆ **Use heavy-duty cans** with tight-fitting lids that can't be chewed through.

◆ **Stretch a bungee cord** across the lid of the can and through the top handle, and hook the ends to the side handles.

◆ **Fasten garbage cans** to a sturdy post with rope or bungee cords, so that they can't be tipped over.

◆ **Keep garbage cans in a wooden bin** with a lid that can be fastened down.

REFITTING A SINK SPRAYER

If your sink sprayer is leaking beneath the sink, you may be able to fix it by simply tightening the hose connections with a basin wrench (see Step 1 below). To replace a cracked or leaking hose, buy a replacement hose at a hardware store or home center. Braided, reinforced hose will provide longer service.

Before beginning the repair, turn off the water at the sink. A leaking spray head can usually be repaired by replacing the washer or washers. Turn off the water at the sink (see page 153) and remove the spray head. There are washers at both ends; a hardware store will have replacements.

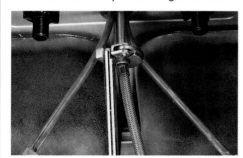

Step 1: Use a basin wrench (available at the hardware store) to loosen the nut connecting the hose to the faucet. You'll have to get under the sink to do this. Pad the area with a drop cloth (you'll be in an uncomfortable position) and have a flashlight handy.

Step 2: Remove spray head, and pull out damaged hose. Feed replacement sprayer into sprayer hole in sink. Wrap Teflon tape clockwise on faucet threads so tape won't come off as you attach the hose. Screw on the hose and tighten with the basin wrench.

Step 3: Attach the hose to the spray head. Clear the spray head of any mineral deposits by soaking it in vinegar and water and punching out any blockages with a straightened paper clip. Turn the water back on and use the sprayer to check for leaks.

COOKWARE, DISHWARE, AND KITCHEN TOOLS

Many stylish pots and pans, dishes, and tableware today use state-of-the-art materials. Others, your grandmother would recognize. Both, with proper care, can grace your kitchen and table for many years.

COOKWARE

Good cookware lasts a lifetime and can make cooking a pleasure rather than a chore. You don't need a full set of any one kind of cookware to stock a kitchen. Instead, choose the cookware material that best suit your needs and invest in a few good pieces that suit the kind of cooking that you do. Add new ones as you need them or can afford them.

Aluminum

Second only to copper as a heat conductor, aluminum alloy (right) is an excellent choice for both stovetop cooking and baking. Aluminum, however, can react adversely with acidic foods such as artichokes, asparagus, and tomatoes, giving the foods an off taste and darkening the pan. Good aluminum cookware will be thick and still lightweight. Anodized aluminum cookware has a fused charcoal-gray coating that makes it less reactive to acids and more resistant to scratches and sticking than aluminum alloys. Cleaning aluminum pots and pans is fairly routine.

◆ **Use a mild dish detergent** and a nonabrasive scouring pad, rinse, and dry. Don't leave food standing in an aluminum pan, or soak the pan for cleaning. Chemicals in water can pit the pot's surface, and alkaline dishwasher detergents can stain or streak it.

◆ **To brighten discolored** aluminum cookware, fill it with a solution of 1 tablespoon vinegar per quart of water, or 2 tablespoons cream of tartar per quart of water. Heat and simmer until stains disappear. Either formula will also remove filmy residue from the inside of an aluminum coffee pot.

Cast iron

Durable and reasonably priced, cast iron (below) heats slowly but evenly, and retains heat. It is a good choice for frying, baking, and slow cooking. Plain cast iron presents some problems, however; it is slightly porous and can absorb flavors, it reacts with some acidic ingredients, and it rusts. It also must be seasoned before it is first used and periodically thereafter. New cast-iron pans often are preseasoned or are coated with a silicone finish, a process that smooths and protects the

surface so food won't stick, rust can't form, and no flavors are absorbed. Caring for cast iron is not difficult.

◆ **To season** an untreated cast iron pan, apply a light coating of vegetable oil and heat the pan in a moderate (350°F) oven for two hours, then wipe it. If you use sufficient oil when you cook, cast iron will become more seasoned over time.

◆ **Don't put cast iron** pots and pans in the dishwasher. After use, scrub out with warm water and a sponge. (Detergent will wash away the seasoning.) After cleaning, dry immediately and apply a light coat of vegetable oil.

◆ **Remove rust** on a cast iron pan with fine steel wool. Reseason the pan before using again.

Clad metals

To make cookware that has the highest heat conductivity, the easiest cleaning, and the

greatest durability, manufacturers have started fusing several metals—copper, aluminum, and steel, for example—in a single pot. The resulting cookware (above) is impressive in its performance but expensive. Clean these pots and pans as you would other cookware made of the same exterior metal.

Copper

Copper cookware (below) is very expensive, very handsome, and very good at conducting heat. Professional chefs like using it because it heats and cools rapidly and evenly.

Because copper reacts with the minerals in certain foods, it is traditionally lined with tin, nickel, or stainless steel. Well-used copper pots with tin linings must be periodically retinned. The best copper pieces are heavy gauge (1/16- to 1/8-inch thick) and will feel well balanced when hefted.

Copper cookware is not hard to care for, but it does need frequent polishing to keep it looking good.

◆ **Never put copper pots** or pans in the dishwasher. Instead, wash them in soapy water using a soft bristle brush or sponge.

◆ **Don't use abrasive cleaners** on copper exteriors or tin linings; they can scratch the copper and wear away the tin. Clean the outside of copper pots with a nonabrasive commercial copper cleaner or a paste made of vinegar and salt, rinse, and polish with a soft cloth.

Enameled metal

Available in an array of bright colors, enameled cast iron and steel pots can do double duty as cookware and serving pieces. The enamel also makes the cookware nonreactive and nonabsorptive, so you can cook any kind of

food in enameled cookware.

Enameled cast iron cookware (above) has the advantages of cast iron without the drawbacks. It is, however, very heavy and slow to heat. Enameled steel cookware is lightweight and less expensive, but conducts heat less evenly. Good-quality enameled steel has thick steel, at least three coats of enamel, and a stainless steel rim to resist chipping.

All enameled cookware chips fairly easily, so it should be handled with reasonable care. Therefore, it is a good idea to check the manufacturer's recommendations before washing it in the

DOUBLE-DUTY COOKWARE

Simplify the inventory of pots and pans in your kitchen. Many pieces of cookware can do more than one job. You can make a perfectly serviceable double boiler, for example, by putting a shallow heatproof mixing bowl over a pan of water. A roasting pan with a lid or an oval Dutch oven with the rack from a broiler can become a makeshift fish poacher. You can bake a casserole in a soufflé dish, using aluminum foil for a top, if you need one.

dishwasher. In general, use non-abrasive cleaners that will not scratch the pan's surface. If light-colored enamel has become stained, you can soak the pot in warm water with a small amount of liquid chlorine bleach added.

Rolled steel and stainless steel

An excellent conductor of heat, rolled steel is a good material for cookware that is used over high heat, such as woks and crepe pans. Like cast iron, however, it rusts and food sticks to it easily. Season and clean rolled steel as you do untreated cast iron (see page 111). Stainless steel is a better choice for all-purpose

use. It is durable, corrosion resistant, and nonreactive. Because it is not an effective conductor of heat, however, stainless steel is usually combined with at least one other metal—such as aluminum or copper—with better heating properties to make cookware. Stainless steel pots are dishwasher safe and can also be cleaned with dish detergent. If overheated, they develop dark spots, which usually can be removed with commercial stainless-steel cleansers.

Nonstick coating cookware

Nonstick cookware is usually sold under the brand name of the interior coating. The best known is Teflon and its recent variants, Teflon2, Silverstone, and Silverstone SUPRA. These coatings are popular because they allow foods to be cooked with very little oil or fat. Methods for applying these coatings are improving all the time. Coated aluminum cookware, which is very affordable, is not only nonstick but also nonreactive. Coated stainless-steel cookware is sandwiched with aluminum to boost heat conductivity. More costly than aluminum, these pans gain durability in the bonding process and will last many years without denting, scratching, chipping, or loosing their nonstick qualities.

To season older nonstick cookware, wash it in hot soapy water and dry. Place one tablespoon of oil on a warm pan and rub it in with a paper towel or brush. Heat for 10 minutes in a 350°F. oven and wipe clean. If the pan has a wooden handle, season it on the cooktop rather than in the oven, taking care

that the oil does not begin to smoke. For new pans, read the manufacturer's instructions.

Wash nonstick cookware in dish detergent, rinse, and dry. To remove stains, bring a solution of two tablespoons baking soda and one cup water to boil in the pan. Season the pan before using it again.

Earthenware, stoneware, and clay

Used principally for baking dishes, these materials are poor conductors of heat, but they retain it well. All can crack if subjected to any rapid changes in temperature, so they are not recommended for stovetop cooking. Clay bakers should be soaked in water for about 30 minutes before use. Glazed cookware can be

cleaned with a dish detergent. Avoid abrasive cleaners. For unglazed baking dishes, do not use soap—it can soak in and permanently flavor the cookware.

Glass, ceramic, and porcelain

Oven-proof versions of these materials are traditionally used for baking dishes

A PANOPLY OF PANS

Sauté pan

A wide pan with straight sides that are about 2½ to 4½-inches high, the sauté pan usually has a capacity of 2½ to 3 quarts.

The high sides let you fry foods in fat. A cover allows you to braise or poach foods in liquid, or simmer stews.

Skillet

The skillet is shallower than a sauté pan with rounded or angled sides. Made of plain or enameled cast iron, aluminum, steel,

or copper, with and without nonstick finishes, skillets range in diameter from 5 to 12 inches.

Omelet pan

Usually 8 to 10 inches in diameter with gently sloping, curved sides, the omelet pan can be made of cast aluminum, steel, nonstick aluminum, or tinned copper. The shape of the pan allows the cook to fold the omelet

over and slide it onto a serving plate easily. Rolled steel or aluminum pans often are seasoned and used only for cooking omelets. These are not washed, but wiped clean or scoured with salt and a paper towel.

Dutch oven

A large, deep, covered pot that is round or oval, the Dutch oven is usually enameled cast iron or plain cast iron. It varies in size from 2 to 13 quarts. A Dutch oven is used for slow–cooking dishes, such as beef stew or

pot roast, over a burner. The name "Dutch oven" is appropriate: The sides of the pot heat evenly, keeping hot air circulating around the food, much as it does in a conventional oven.

Saucepan

Essential kitchen tools, saucepans range in size from 1 to 5 quarts. Used for cooking foods with liquid, saucepans need tight-fitting lids to hold down evaporation. A well-

designed saucepan—made of stainless steel, aluminum, anodized aluminum, copper, or enameled cast iron—is twice as wide as it is tall. Kitchens need several of varying sizes.

Saucepot

A large, deep pot—from 5 to 15 quarts— that has handles on both sides, the saucepot is usually made of aluminum alloy, stainless steel, or enameled steel. It's the preferred cooking pot for simmering long-cooking

foods, such as soups and stews, and for cooking pasta. Heavy models, which take a longer time to heat up, are excellent for slow-cooking spaghetti sauces. Inserts are available for steaming vegetables or shellfish.

Stockpot

Taller than its cousin, the saucepot, and usually as wide as it is tall, the stockpot is made of the same materials. Sizes range from 4 quarts all the way to 20 or more. For standard home use, 6 to 10 quarts is adequate.

Excellent for cooking large amounts of pasta or chili or for steaming lobsters, the stockpot is best for making party-sized batches of soup or fresh soup stocks that you can keep in the freezer for making other dishes.

AN OVERVIEW OF OVENWARE

Baking dish

Usually made of stoneware, porcelain, earthenware, or glass, and sometimes enameled cast iron, baking dishes range in size from individual gratin dishes to lasagna pans.

They are relatively shallow and open, although cooks often cover contents with aluminum foil. Used for baking large main course dishes or desserts such as cobblers.

Broiler pan

A two-part cooking pan, a broiler pan is designed to cook meat quickly on a rack under direct heat while its juices and fat collect in a pan underneath. Most ovens are

equipped with a large broiler pan. Smaller versions are preferred by most cooks because they are handier and fit more easily into a sink or a dishwasher.

Roasting pan

Made of aluminum, stainless steel, enameled metal, or even ceramic, roasting pans come in a wide range of sizes to suit different sized roasts. The depth of an open roaster ranges between 2 and 4 inches. A French roaster has a cover and may be 6 inches

deep or more. Most roasters have a rack to hold the meat or bird above the fat while it cooks. A roaster should fit the roast. An 18-pound turkey, for example, will require a larger roaster than a 5-pound chicken, so you may need more than one roasting pan.

Casserole

A casserole is made of heat-resistant, tempered glass or a ceramic that looks like porcelain and may be round, oval, or square with a tight-fitting lid. Many casseroles are handsome enough to go from the oven

straight to the table. Sizes range from 1½ to 7 quarts, with 3- to 5-quart sizes being the most popular. High-tech models can go directly from the freezer into the oven and later into the dishwasher.

Cake pan

Basic for baking, these pans come in sizes to match the amounts of batter or dough in standard recipes. Made of aluminum, glass, or steel, many have a nonstick finish inside.

Round cake pans are usually 8 or 9 inches in diameter. Square and rectangular pans are used for bar cookies and quick breads as well as cakes.

Springform pan

Used for making cakes that can't easily pop out of a regular cake pan, springform pans have a clasp that releases the sides from the base. They are usually made of tinned steel

and come in many sizes. A classic cheesecake, for example, requires a springform pan. The cake often stays safely on the base even when it is moved to a serving platter.

Baking sheet

Baking sheets come in several formats. Those with no sides are for baking cookies; those with short sides hold jelly roll cakes and other pastries. Flat cookie sheets some-times have a special layer underneath designed to keep the bottoms of cookies from burning. Some baking sheets have non-stick coating inside.

Soufflé dish

Soufflé dishes are round with deep sides to allow whipped batters to expand and set quickly during baking. Made of porcelain, heat-proof glass, or stoneware, these distinc-tive baking dishes come in many sizes, from individual soufflés to 3-quart family dishes. The smaller-sized soufflé dishes can double as custard cups.

Terrine

Usually made of enameled cast iron, earth-enware, or porcelain, and measuring about 12 x 4 x 4 inches, this baking dish is used to make a paté-like loaf of layered ground meats, vegetables, or seafood called a terrine. The 1- to 2-quart sizes are most common. Terrines can also be used to make patés and small, elegant meat loafs. Some terrine pans are handsome enough to be used as serving dishes.

Muffin pan

With indentations for anywhere from 6 to 24 muffins, these specialized baking pans are available in three muffin sizes—mini, regular, and large. The best muffin pans are made of heavy tinned steel or heavy alu-minum. A nonstick coating inside is a plus, insuring quick muffin removal and easy pan cleaning. If a pan doesn't have a non-stick coating, you can grease the indentations or use individual muffin papers.

Bundt cake pan

A circular cake pan with a hole in the middle, the bundt pan has fluted side walls that are traditional to the German bundt cake. These distinctive pans are available in aluminum or tinned steel. A nonstick coat-ing inside is useful because the crevices of the fluting can cause the cake to stick and cleanup to be tricky.

Pie pan

Made of aluminum or ovenproof glass, an 8- or 9-inch pie pan is essential for pie making. The 9-inch size is most often called for in recipes, so that should be your first purchase. The design of the pie pan—flat and shallow with short slanted sides—allows pie fillings to heat and set quickly. Tart and quiche pans have straight sides.

from pie pans to casseroles, soufflé dishes to gratin pans. Most are also microwave safe (check  the label). The newest ceramics, now used for a variety of baking dishes, can go straight from the freezer to the oven without damage.

All of these materials are easy to clean with dish detergent, or they can be put in the dishwasher.

Special cleaning problems

Be sure that any cookware you put in the dishwasher is rated dishwasher safe. Pans with wooden handles, for example, are not. Also, let cookware cool before you wash it to prevent warping. Then, in most cases, a scrubbing with dish detergent and a plastic scrubber will clean the cookware.

Even the best cooks burn their cookware occasionally. Here's how to attack the problem.

◆ **Use a nylon scraper** or a plastic spatula to scrape away any residue. Wet the burned area with water, then sprinkle it with salt and let it stand for ten minutes. Scrub the pan vigorously.

◆ **Sprinkle the burned area** liberally with baking soda, and add just enough water to moisten it. Scrub gently, then let it stand for several hours. If the burn still doesn't simply lift out, scrub the area vigorously.

◆ **Soak a non-aluminum pan** for 24 hours with two tablespoons of dishwasher detergent sudsed up in 2 or 3 cups of water.

GLASSWARE

All glassware—not just fine crystal—needs care to avoid breakage, scratches, and staining. With proper cleaning and handling, even everyday glasses will serve you for many years.

Cleaning Glassware

A late-model dishwasher can handle most glassware, including fine crystal, on the upper rack. There are, however, some pieces that require caution. Family heirloom glasses, plates, and bowls, or large pieces with an awkward shape, such as decanters or vases, should be hand-washed. Glued or repaired pieces, cut or etched glass, and hand-decorated glass, as well as any pieces that are rimmed with gold or silver, should all be hand-washed.

◆ **To wash crystal by hand,** use dish detergent and a small amount of ammonia. Place a rubber mat or dishtowel at the bottom of the sink, or use a soft plastic wash pan to guard against chipping or scratching the glass. Be extra gentle when washing glasses with gold or silver trim, which can wear away. Rinse the crystal in clear water; add a small amount of white vinegar to the final rinse to prevent streaking. Dry with a lint-free towel.

◆ **A quick washing method** for party glasses is borrowed from bartenders. You need a basin of hot sudsy water for washing and a basin of hot clear water for rinsing. Holding the base of the glass, pump it up and down in the sudsy water, then quickly pump it in the clear water (below). To dry, set the clean glassware upside down on a cotton dishtowel that is placed over a wire cooling rack.

Glasses used to serve milk or milk-based drinks will need more than pumping in sudsy water; wipe them out with a sudsy dishrag or sponge.

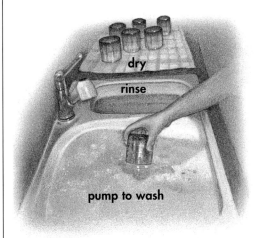

◆ **To remove glassware stains,** fill the receptacle—decanter, vase, or glass—with water and a teaspoonful of ammonia, and let it stand overnight. Another method is to gently scour a stubborn spot with a little baking soda. Avoid abrasive cleansers or scouring pads, which might scratch the glass.

◆ **Remove hard-water stains** or lime deposits with white vinegar and a nylon scrubber. Dip the scrubber in the vinegar and rub your glassware briskly but gently, taking extra care not to scratch or chip it.

Separating stuck-together glasses

In a stack, glasses sometimes become wedged, or a vacuum forms when one is placed inside another. Here's a trick to help separate them. Fill the top glass with cold water. Dip the bottom glass in hot water (below). The cold water will make the top glass contract while the hot water makes the bottom one expand. Give the differing water temperatures a minute to work, then gently pull the glasses apart.

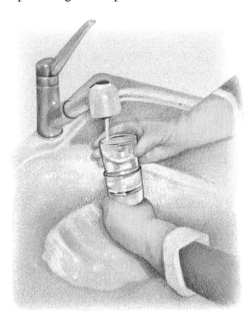

Repairing damaged glassware

If you have a scratch on the surface, or a small chip in the rim of everyday glassware, you may be able to grind it out. Take antique or valuable pieces to a restoration professional. When you do make repairs yourself, wear sturdy gloves. If a glass should break in the process, you could get a serious cut.

◆ **For fine scratches in glass,** mix jeweler's rouge (from a crafts store) with denatured alcohol to make a paste. Dip a small piece of soft cotton cloth into the paste and rub out the scratch with a circular motion. Rinse the glass with cold water, dry, and then polish it to a shine using a soft, lint-free cloth.

◆ **To grind down a chip** in the rim, wrap a wet emery cloth (available at hardware stores) around a small dowel. Holding the glass steady against a counter with one hand, rub the dowel back and forth across the chip until the rim becomes smooth. Then wash and dry the glass.

◆ **To repair a break** in a glass plate or serving bowl, use a slow-setting two-part epoxy glue and follow instructions for mending china on page 118.

Cleaning up broken glass

When a glass breaks, put on gloves and carefully pick up the large shards and discard them in the garbage. To safely clean up the remaining slivers and tiny pieces, use a moist paper towel. Bits of glass will cling to the surface of a damp towel when you pat it gently around the area where the glass broke. Follow up with a thorough vacuuming.

DISHWARE

The plates, bowls, cups, and saucers that serve your daily meals shouldn't just be utilitarian. From the most modest earthenware breakfast set to the finest porcelain saved for special occasions, the variety of colors and patterns in today's dishware can spruce up any table and suit any taste.

GOOD TOOLS

CLEANING ETCHED GLASSWARE

A well-lathered shaving brush can help you put the sparkle back into etched glassware. Deep crevices in the glass harbor stubborn dirt that only the stiff bristles of a shaving brush can dislodge. After scrubbing, rinse the glass in clear water and dry with a soft, lint-free cloth.

Types of dishware

The term china includes all pottery made by firing clay in a kiln, from the rarest porcelains to the most primitive earthenware. The differences among types of pottery depend upon the kinds of clays that are used, the firing temperatures used in production, and the qualities of glaze, decoration, and design. The basic types of china you will find in stores are listed below.

◆ **Porcelain** is a nonporous, translucent china prized for its rich patterns and strength. It is the most expensive pottery used in dinnerware. Some modern porcelain is safe for dishwashers and microwaves.

LEAD ALERT

◆ **Never use handmade pottery** to store and serve acidic foods such as vinaigrettes, fruit juice, tomatoes, or lemonade. Craft potters are not subject to the same quality controls as commercial ceramic producers, and acid may leech out lead in the glaze or decorations.

◆ **Never store wine in a lead crystal** decanter; the acid in the wine will, over time, leech out the lead. Drinking wine out of lead crystal glasses is safe.

◆ **Bone china** is a nonporous, translucent pottery made with bone ash, which gives it a brilliant white color. Not as expensive as porcelain, it is still costly. Some modern bone china is also safe for dishwashers and microwaves.

◆ **Stoneware** is a nonporous, opaque, heavy pottery that holds heat well, making it good for casseroles and dinnerware. Stoneware dishes, which are available in a variety of patterns, are dishwasher- and microwave-safe. Not as pricey as porcelain or bone china, stoneware is popular for everyday use.

◆ **Ironstone** is another nonporous, heavy pottery that is a favorite for everyday dishes. It's moderately priced and dishwasher- and microwave-safe.

◆ **Earthenware** is a porous, lightweight material, opaque, and not as expensive as other types of pottery. Its

lower firing temperature allows more brilliant glazes, making a wide variety of striking and colorful patterns possible. It is more likely to chip in everyday use than other types of pottery.

Washing the dishes

If your dinnerware can't go into the dishwasher, you can easily wash it by hand in the sink.

◆ **Place a terry towel** along the bottom of the sink to prevent scratches or chips. Use warm water, a mild dish detergent, and a sponge. Rinse the dishes in warm water and dry with a lint-free towel. Be particularly gentle with gold or silver trim.

◆ **Dried egg** can cement itself to patterned china. To remove it, rub the spot with a slice of lemon, and then wash.

Caring for fine china

You may want to display selected pieces of your fine china in a cupboard in the dining room because it makes a lovely accent. The rest of the set will have to go on cupboard shelves. Here's how to avoid damage when storing.

◆ **When you stack** plates and bowls, use fabric liners between them to avoid the top one scratching the one beneath it. Fabric liners made for this purpose are available, but a less expensive option is to use paper plates or doilies.

◆ **Use quilted, zippered cases** to keep the china that you don't use very often protected and clean. You certainly don't want to have to wash it *before* a party when you have so many other things to do. These fabric containers guard

against moisture, chipping, and dust. They come in a variety of sizes and shapes to accommodate everything from cups and saucers to platters.

Mending china and porcelain

The key to successful repair of dinnerware is to match the edges of the break precisely, and to hold the pieces together tightly while the glue sets. Use a clear, slow-drying epoxy glue which allows you time to adjust the pieces to an exact fit.

Work in a well-ventilated area to dissipate the glue fumes. Start by cleaning and drying the broken surfaces thoroughly, then fit the pieces together dry to determine the best order of assembly. Glue and join the pieces, one by one, then wipe off any excess glue with a cotton swab that's been dipped in an appropriate solvent. Finally, clamp and support the glued pieces, using one of the following methods.

◆ **For a plate that's broken in two,** anchor the larger piece in a large bowl that's filled with sand (below), balancing it so that the piece you attach will stand without support. Then position

sand

the smaller piece in place using two pinch-type clothespins.

◆ **For a plate broken into several pieces,** make a mold to hold the pieces while being glued. To do so, pack modeling clay around the bottom of an unbroken plate. Peel off the clay, lay it flat, and fit the pieces into the mold.

◆ **For a cup handle,** fit the pieces together, then wrap vertical and horizontal strips of masking tape around the cup and handle to hold the seam tight. Let the repair set before removing the tape.

◆ **Use masking tape** to hold awkward knobs or ornaments while the adhesive is setting.

FLATWARE

A beautiful table that's set for a festive occasion begins with sparkling silver or stainless steel flatware. Keeping your flatware ready for such an occasion isn't difficult, although silver certainly takes more attention than stainless, which simply needs buffing to get a nice glow. Here's how to keep both looking their best.

Caring for silverware

Don't reserve your fine silver for special occasions; get in the habit of using it as often as possible. Your table will look wonderful, and the patina of the silver will be improved. After each use, wash silver flatware immediately in hot sudsy water and rinse it in clear hot water; this will minimize the need for polishing. Prompt cleaning is especially important for pieces that have been in

---

MENDING CRACKED CROCKERY

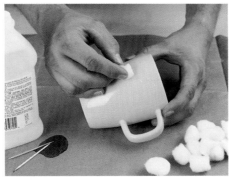

1. Cleaning a crack. Using a cotton swab dipped in soapy water, clean the area around the crack, then place the mug in a 125°F. oven for 30 minutes to make sure the crack has dried completely.

2. Adding epoxy. Mix a slow-drying epoxy glue, forcing the glue into the crack with a toothpick so that the crack absorbs as much of the glue as possible. Remove any excess glue with a cotton ball that's been dipped in acetone. Allow to set for at least 24 hours before using.

---

contact with tarnish-producing foods, such as salt, eggs, olives, mustard, vinegar, fruit juices, or cooked vegetables. Don't allow silver to air-dry. Hand-dry each piece with a clean, lint-free towel to prevent spotting. There are several ways to polish silver items, each with its special uses. Wear rubber gloves to protect your hands.

◆ **Dip polish** is quick and easy to use. You can lower a piece of silver into a jar of dip and, like magic, the tarnish is gone. For bigger pieces, you can apply the dip with a cloth for the same immediate effect. The only drawback is that dips don't help protect the silver from further tarnishing.

◆ **Paste or cream polish** takes longer to apply, but it gives your silver a deep

shine and also produces a protective coating, which means that you'll have to polish it less often. The technique for using paste or cream polish is to apply a small amount of polish to a soft, dry cloth. Then gently rub the piece of silver lengthwise.

Clean crevices between fork tines or in the silver pattern with a cotton swab, piece of string, or natural-bristle brush, dipped in the polish. When you have removed all the tarnish, wash the silver pieces in hot soapy water, rinse thoroughly, and dry with lint-free towels. Finally, buff each piece with a soft cloth. A pair of old cotton socks makes a good silver-polishing duo; use one to apply the polish, then use the other to buff.

TARNISH PREVENTION

◆ **Wrap silverware** in tarnish-inhibiting fabric or in tarnish-proof tissue paper, available from hardware stores and some supermarkets. Silver is easily tarnished by sulfur compounds in the air. The protective wrapping will slow down—or stop altogether—the process of tarnishing.

◆ **Rubber bands and plastic food wrap** can harm silver, causing stains and corrosion—even through tarnish-proof cloth or tissue. Never use either to wrap silver.

◆ **To remove heavy tarnish** from several pieces of silver flatware, cover the bottom of a pie pan or casserole dish with a piece of aluminum foil, making sure the shiny side is up. Place the tarnished pieces on the foil, add one heaping tablespoon of baking soda, and pour enough boiling water (below) to

baking soda

foil-lined container

cover the items. The tarnish will collect on the foil. Rinse the pieces thoroughly and polish with a soft cloth.

Caring for silver plate

Although silver and silver plate look alike, they require different care. The outer layer of silver plate is soft and thin; rubbing it too hard with a paste or cream polish and buffing it too often can wear the silver away. Instead, use a dip polish to remove tarnish without any rubbing, and give your silver plate a longer life. Use your silver plate often and keep it clean with soap and water to minimize the need for polishing.

Caring for stainless steel

When you are buying stainless steel flatware, look for the numbers 18/8 or 18/10 etched into the metal on the back, indicating an alloy of 18 parts chrome to 8 or 10 parts nickel. Flatware of this quality is strong and resistant to dents, scratches, and discoloring. Such stainless steel is dishwasher safe, but it will have fewer water spots and look nicer if you dry it by hand.

METAL SERVERS

Every household has a complement of serving pieces—from candle sticks to flower vases and fruit bowls—that are made of a variety of metals. You can take care of silver, silver plate, or stainless steel serving pieces the same way you take care of flatware made of the same metal (see left). For other metals, the care is somewhat different. Always

wear protective gloves when using polishes and solvents and work in a well-ventilated area. Here's how to keep metals shining bright.

Brass

Wash brass pieces in hot soapy water, and dry before polishing. You can use a commercial polish on brass or try half a lemon dipped in salt. If the brass piece isn't used in cooking, you can slow the tarnishing process by applying a thin coat of paste wax. (This is particularly good for outdoor brass hardware such as doorknockers or locks.) Rub delicate brass items with a thin coat of lemon oil to slow tarnishing.

Copper

Small copper items can be cleaned by boiling for an hour or more in a pot containing a mixture of one cup vinegar and one tablespoon salt per quart of water. Wash with soap and water, rinse, and dry with a lint-free towel. Use commercial copper polish on larger items. Just be sure to thoroughly wash the items afterward with soap and water to completely remove all the polish residue. Otherwise, it will leave a green stain.

Lacquered finish

Brass candlesticks, copper vases, and other metal objects are often coated with a clear lacquer to prevent air from tarnishing the metal.

For pieces that are not used for cooking or regularly filled with water, this coating can keep the metal looking shiny for a long time. Simply dust these items using a soft cloth and count your-

QUICK FIX

REPAIRING A SPOON

To smooth out a dented spoon, place the spoon bowl over a curved, oval surface that is hard enough to take hammering. A darning egg will do nicely. Gently hammer the spoon bowl back into shape with a rubber mallet. When the shape is back, assess the finish on the piece, and, if necessary, polish it.

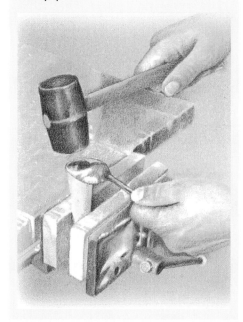

self lucky. Once the lacquer starts to wear off, however, you will have to remove it all to keep a uniform finish on the metal. Use acetone to take off the lacquer, clean the piece with the appropriate polish, and wash it in soapy water, rinse, and dry. Lacquer is available as a spray or in liquid form from hardware stores or home centers, but it is difficult to reapply evenly. You might want to have particularly fine pieces relacquered by a professional.

Pewter

Wash pewter dishes with hot soapy water, rinse, and dry with a soft cloth. Avoid abrasive cleansers or metal scourers, which can scratch pewter. Remove acidic foods—egg, salad dressing, oil, salt, fruit—immediately, so they don't get a chance to damage the metal. Polish with a commercial pewter polish. Pewter is soft, so handle it with care; it is easily dented.

CUTLERY

Chef James Beard once said that next to his hands, knives were the most important tools in the kitchen. Cooks differ in their preferences for particular knives, but most agree that a good knife feels balanced and comfortable in your hands. It must also be very sharp. A dull knife will cut badly and may cause accidents because you have to press harder.

Knives are made in one of two ways. Forged knives are hammered into shape out of a thick piece of steel; stamped knives are cut out of a sheet of steel. Forging is a time-consuming process requiring craftsmanship, which means that forged knives tend to be expensive. Stamping is automated, so the knives are less costly. You can see the difference: a forged knife has a thicker bolster (the area right in front of the handle) than tip, while a stamped blade is even throughout. When it comes to performance, many cooks can't tell the difference between high-quality knives of either kind.

There are two types of knife edges. A flat-ground edge has a strict V shape when viewed in profile. A hollow-ground edge has a slight curve on both sides of the blade, like the prow of an ocean liner. There is less steel in a hollow ground blade; as a result, it will wear faster. However, a hollow-ground edge is usually sharper, and its shape forces food to fall away from the knife as it cuts.

The type of steel used to make a knife can make a difference in its performance. Nearly all first-rate knives today are made of steel mixed with chromium, carbon, nickel, and other metals to make them strong, durable, and sharp. The goal is to find a knife that's hard enough to last, but soft enough that it can be honed to a razor edge. Most new knives are made of one of the following steel alloys.

◆ **High-carbon steel** knives have a durable edge and can be sharpened easily. They won't rust or discolor as older knives used to do. While they come with a moderate to high price tag, you can count on them to last a lifetime. They are sturdy, hardworking kitchen tools.

◆ **Stainless steel** is used for less expensive knives. It's easy to clean, but the blade can't really be sharpened once it looses its edge.

FINDING THE RIGHT KNIFE

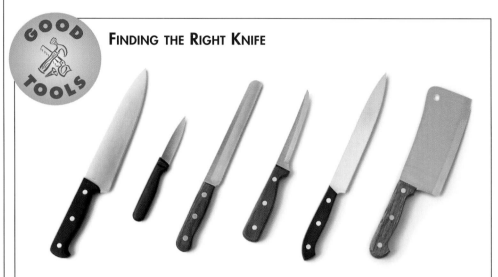

Cutlery for cooks, shown left to right, include a chef's knife for chopping, paring knife, serrated bread knife, boning knife, carving knife, and cleaver. The first three are basics for any kitchen; add the other knives only as you need them.

Caring for cutlery

Properly taken care of, good cutlery can be handed from generation to generation. Store your knives in a wooden knife block, on a magnetic rack, or in a partitioned drawer (p.123) to keep the blades from getting nicked. Never use a kitchen knife for anything but cutting food. If you stir hot foods with a knife instead of a spoon, the heat may damage the blade. Using a knife to open a box or pry off a jar lid will dull the knife and possibly cause an accident.

◆ **Wash good knives** by hand immediately after use (unless the manufacturer specifies that your brand is dishwasher safe). Avoid soaking knives in water, which will loosen wooden handles. Always dry knives thoroughly.

◆ **Sharpening knives.** Hand sharpening (right) requires the user to hold the knife at a precise angle to the sharpening stone to get the best edge. Sharpeners that work when the blade is drawn back through the sharpener are easier to use. New electric sharpeners make the job easier. Magnets hold the blade at the correct angle on either side of a grinding mechanism. The best models have settings for major resharpening, periodic tune-ups, and everyday maintenance.

◆ **Sharpening serrated knives.** Don't try to sharpen a serrated knife with a conventional knife sharpener. This knife depends on its notches for its cutting ability, and sharpening it requires a special skill or a special sharpening tool. Replace an inexpensive serrated knife that gets dull. With a good knife, invest in a sharpener or take the knife to a professional.

CUTTING SURFACES

Good knives should be used only on wooden or plastic cutting boards. Polyethylene is the favorite of many cooks. It's a thermoplastic that's heated, molded, cooled, and cut into a chopping block. Usually there is a rough surface on one side to help hold food in place while you cut it. While it's a matter of debate whether polyethylene is more hygienic than wood, it is easier to sanitize—just put it in the dishwasher.

Other cooks still prefer wood. Most wood cutting blocks are made of maple, cherry, or oak. Be sure to get one that is at least 1½ inches deep for a heavy and secure chopping surface. A hardwood cutting board should be periodically rubbed with mineral oil to help seal it against impurities. Using fine steel wool, rub the oil in and wipe off any excess. Season a new board about once a week for the first month. After you use the board, scour it with a brush and soapy water to remove food particles. Rinse and wipe with a clean cloth dampened with a bleach solution to help sanitize the board. If possible, store it upright with space for it to breathe front and back.

OTHER KITCHEN TOOLS

To fill out your supply of basic cooking equipment, you will also need a number of standard, simple kitchen utensils. Buy sturdy versions of these tools that are dishwasher safe. Pick heat-proof plastic or metal tools that can be used with hot or cold dishes.

For stirring and mixing, you need

stainless steel or wooden spoons; for lifting, tongs and a plastic or metal spatula; for lifting solids from liquid, a large solid spoon and slotted spoon; for serving, a ladle and pie or cake server. For handling hot dishes, you need hot pads or mitts. Use a colander for washing or draining foods. Kitchen scissors can be faster than knives for many chores, such as cutting up chicken or mincing herbs.

Measuring tools

For dry ingredients, you need a set of individual measuring cups—¼-, ⅓-, ½-, and 1-cup capacities—that you can level off at the top. For liquids, use a 4-cup heat-proof glass measurer, marked in ounces along the side. A set of measuring spoons—¼-, ⅓-, ½-, and 1-teaspoon and 1-tablespoon capacities— mete out seasonings.

QUICK FIX

KNIFE ORGANIZER

An inexpensive drawer insert, designed just for cutlery, keeps knives in individual slots where they are easy to find. Their sharpened blades are protected from harm by other kitchen tools in the same drawer. Buy one at a home center or kitchen store.

Baking tools

To mix batter or dough, you need bowls of various sizes in either stainless steel or pottery. Other tools include wooden spoons, rubber scrapers, an electric mixer, flour sifter, rolling pin, wire whip, grater, and pastry brush. If you like cake decorating, you will want a pastry tube and tips for applying icing.

Roasting tools

If you roast a lot of meat and fowl, you'll need a meat thermometer and a metal baster, as well as the appropriate roasting pans (p.114).

SHARPENING DULL CUTLERY

Hold blade at 20° angle.

Pull back of blade toward you.

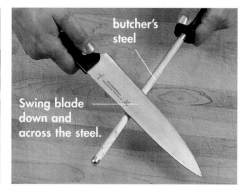

butcher's steel

Swing blade down and across the steel.

1. Using the medium-grit side of a combination stone, hold the knife blade at a 20 degree angle so that the tiny bevel at the cutting edge will be properly ground.

2. Pull the blade along the stone, using a pivoting motion to turn it toward you. Repeat on the other side of the blade, this time pushing away as you pivot.

3. A butcher's steel removes the burr left by sharpening. Place the knife edge near the tip of the steel. With a swinging motion of the wrist and forearm, bring the knife down and across the steel. Repeat on other side.

LARGE APPLIANCES

Major appliances are significant household investments. Here's how to shop for them wisely and how to keep them running smoothly and efficiently for years.

Routine and attentive cleaning—as well as proper use and care—is the best service you can give the large appliances in your home. Most should work well and without problems for years if you keep their filters, drains, and operating parts free of dirt, dust, and scum.

DISHWASHERS

Few labor-saving machines are as appreciated as dishwashers. They are relatively expensive, but the final cost depends on how many special features you want. In general, the more tricks the machine can do, the pricier it will be to buy.

Buying a dishwasher

When you choose a dishwasher, look for a machine that operates quietly, has a load capacity large enough for your family's needs, and offers a convenient and flexible rack configuration. You'll also want to check the appliance's EnerGuide for estimated annual operating costs to calculate how much payback you will receive from choosing an energy-efficient model.

Dishwashers today include a number of other new features that make them more efficient and easier to use. These may include:

◆ **Adjustable racks** with flexible loading options

◆ **Delay start** to begin wash operation at a different time

◆ **Electronic control** for cycle readout

◆ **Electronic diagnostics** to help solve problems

◆ **Flush control panels**

◆ **Hot-water temperature booster** so you can keep your water heater temperature at 120°F and avoid scalding hot water in the rest of the house

◆ **Child lock** for safety

◆ **No-heat drying option** to save on electricity

◆ **Special cycles** for pots and pans, light wash, or rinse-and-hold

Before you make a final choice, be sure that your home can handle the required voltage and water capacity of the machine you like.

Loading the dishwasher

If you have a pot-and-pan setting on your machine, you don't usually need to rinse dishes before loading them into the dishwasher. The jet sprays of the water system will pulverize and flush away food particles. Make sure, though, that you put the cookware in the lower rack, facing the spray arm. Secure pot handles to prevent them from blocking the spray arm.

Place platters and cookie sheets in the back or along the sides of the bottom rack. If they're placed in the front

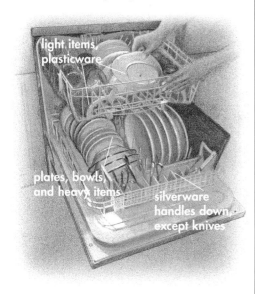

light items, plasticware

plates, bowls, and heavy items

silverware handles down, except knives

of the dishwasher, they'll prevent the water from reaching the detergent dispenser and the silverware basket.

Using the top rack

The top rack of the dishwasher should be reserved for smaller and lighter items, including dishwasher-safe plastics, children's cups, and baby bottles

and nipples. Empty all glasses and cups before placing them on the rack. (Glasses and other fragile items should never be washed on the bottom rack of the dishwasher where water pressure is more intense and may break them.)

To keep plastic cups from flipping over during the wash cycle, put them in the corners of the top rack where the water spray tends to be the weakest. Alternatively, you can anchor them between heavier objects or fit them snugly over two prongs.

Handling small items

To prevent small items like baby-bottle nipples and jar caps from flying around in the dishwasher while it's running, put them in a small mesh bag. Secure the top of the mesh bag with a rubber band, then loop the rubber band over a prong on the top rack. The small items will get clean while staying contained in the bag.

Silverware

To get silverware clean, place it in the basket with the handles pointing downward. The exception to the rule—for safety's sake—is knives; point them with their sharp ends down.

Take care not to let any thin utensil stick through the bottom of the silverware basket. It could stop the spray arm from moving and thereby interrupt the wash and rinse cycles.

It is best to hand wash small utensils, such as appetizer forks, chopsticks, and shish kebab skewers, for they can easily fall to the bottom of the machine and cause trouble.

MONEY SAVERS

RUN YOUR DISHWASHER EFFICIENTLY

A dishwasher uses the same amount of hot water and energy whether it's half full or fully loaded, so when you don't have a full load of dirty dishes, you should use one of the most underutilized functions on your dishwasher—the rinse-and-hold cycle. This partial cycle cleans heavily soiled items that shouldn't sit unwashed for any length of time, without using the energy of a full cycle on just a few items.

Filling the dispensers

It's best not to fill the detergent dispenser until just before you're ready to run a load. Dry detergent that sits in the dispenser may absorb moisture, cake, and lose its cleaning power, while liquid detergent may drip out of the detergent cup.

In hard-water areas, you may need to add a rinsing agent to avoid spots on glassware. There is a dispenser for that on most newer dishwasher models.

Black marks

As a rule, black marks that appear on china are the result of metal items rubbing against the dishware during the washing process.

When loading your dishwasher, you can avoid the problem by separating metal items from pieces of china and securing lightweight aluminum objects between heavier objects so they don't bounce around.

Dishwasher stains and deposits

Yellow or brown stains on the inside of your dishwasher—as well as on your dishes—are probably an indication of heavy iron concentrations in your water. To remove these stains, add a half cup of citric acid crystals to the water as the machine begins the wash cycle. (You also can use a compound that appliance dealers sell to remove rust from a water softener's resin beads; follow the manufacturer's directions.) A permanent solution would require installing an iron filter on your incoming water supply.

If you've discovered chalky deposits in your dishwasher, start the machine without dishes or a detergent, using the rinse-and-hold cycle. While the machine begins to fill, add one cup of white vinegar and let the cycle finish. Then add detergent (just as you would for a regular load) and run the empty machine through a full wash-and-dry cycle to complete the cleaning.

Odor removal

If you don't use your dishwasher daily, keep it from smelling dank with a handful of baking soda tossed into the bottom between washes. The baking soda will absorb any residual odors and keep your appliance smelling sweet.

Unsticking the dish rack

If your dish rack tends to stick, the rollers may be jammed. Turn the rollers by hand to loosen them. If they are worn or no longer round, replace them. Some rollers can be removed by taking out screws while others pull right off.

If, on the other hand, a rack is sticking because it's bent, you'll need to replace it. On many machines, you can lift out a rack just by pulling and tilting it. On others, however, you'll first have to take out the pins that hold the rack to the sides of the dishwasher. The rack should then remove easily.

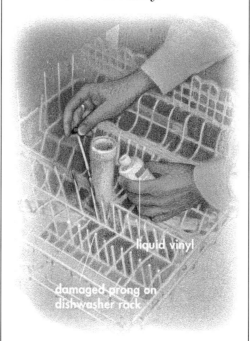

liquid vinyl

damaged prong on dishwasher rack

Repairing chipped prongs

Over time, the prongs on a dishwasher rack can erode and chip. Check with a local appliance store for a jar of liquid vinyl. It comes with a brush applicator for coating the damaged ends (above). Use steel wool to remove any rust before applying the vinyl. Or replace the rack with a new one—your local retailer or service person will need the make and model number of your dishwasher to order one for you.

REFRIGERATORS

When you are shopping for a refrigerator, remember that the bigger the capacity, the more expensive the appliance is to buy and to run. As a rule, two people typically need a minimum of 8 cubic feet of food storage, not counting freezer space. For every additional household member, add another cubic foot. Thus, for a family of five the refrigerator should be no less than 11 cubic feet.

Stocking a refrigerator efficiently

The refrigerator compartment operates most efficiently when there is room for air to circulate. Make sure that none of the circulation vents is blocked by items in the refrigerator.

◆ **Condiments:** Group like things together as much as possible, putting the smaller condiment items, such as a jar of pre-minced garlic, mustard, salsa, and so on, on the tray in the door or on a small lazy Susan on a shelf. They will be easier to find that way.

◆ **Leftovers:** Store leftovers in clear containers at the front of the shelves so they won't be forgotten. Too often leftovers go bad before they are used. If you find that you frequently have to throw away leftovers, it may be better not to store them at all. They take up valuable room on the shelf.

◆ **Moisture control:** Line the fruit and vegetable bins with paper towels. They help absorb moisture and can be used to wipe out the bins when it is time to clean them.

DISHWASHER REPAIRS

Before you pick up the phone to call a repairperson, here's how to do a little troubleshooting of your own. There are many simple problems that you can easily take care of yourself in just a matter of minutes.

Problem	Possible cause	Possible solution
Dishwasher won't run	No power to unit	Check for blown fuse or tripped circuit breaker; check that portable unit is plugged in
	Door not latched	Make sure door is latched
	Jammed or stiff door latch is not engaging door switch	Try opening and closing door a few times; apply penetrating oil spray
	Cycle-selecting button not depressed	Push button all the way
Dishwasher doesn't fill	Water inlet valve closed	Open the valve to the dishwasher located under the sink
	Float switch stuck in up position	Clear obstructions under the float switch
Dishwasher doesn't drain	Clogged filter screen	Clean filter screen
Dishes aren't completely clean	Water not hot enough	Test water temperature and reset water heater's thermostat
	Clogged spray arm or filter screen	Clean spray arm and filter screen
	Detergent dispenser not dumping	Move any dish or pan obstructing dispenser operation. Open front panel of door (see owner's manual) and check dispenser mechanism for a broken or corroded spring or lever
Dishes don't dry	Water not hot enough	Test water temperature and reset water heater's thermostat
	Water not draining	Check for a clogged filter screen
Dishwasher leaks	Improperly loaded dishes deflecting water through vent	Reload dishes following instructions in owner's manual
Dishwasher leaks from bottom of door	Oversudsing	Don't use non-dishwasher detergent or pre-rinse dishes in liquid soap
	Door gasket is worn or cracked	Replace gasket—some pop in, others are held by screws or clips
Dishwasher is noisy	Spray arm hitting dishes	Reload so that spray arm can rotate freely; check loading guidelines in owner's manual
	Low water pressure prevents machine from filling completely	Don't use water in other areas of the house while dishwasher is filling
	Silverware or broken dishware in bottom of tub	Remove piece. Let heating element cool completely before reaching into tub
	Dishes bouncing around	When loading, make sure lightweight items are held firmly in place

Beverages: Before refrigerating any liquid, put it in a tightly sealed container. Any moisture that evaporates inside a refrigerator just makes the unit work harder.

Refrigerating foods

Here are some guidelines for keeping refrigerated foods from spoiling.

Cottage cheese: The average shelf life of cottage cheese is five days, but there's a simple trick to keep it fresh longer: Refrigerate it upside down in the container. The creamy liquid will move from the original bottom to the original top, keeping the entire contents that much fresher.

Eggs: Cleaning dried egg from a refrigerator shelf is not an easy job. Because an egg can leak through even a tiny crack in its shell, it's a good idea to always store eggs in their protective carton, not in the door of the refrigerator. In addition, because eggs are porous, they will absorb odors if refrigerated out of their containers.

Fish: Place well-wrapped fish in the coldest part of the refrigerator for less than one day. To keep it any longer, you should freeze it.

Meat and poultry: Place well-wrapped meat or poultry in the meat drawer, if your refrigerator has one, or in the coldest part of the refrigerator.

Spices: Keep ground ginger, chili powder, paprika, and other spices that are red or orange in color in the refrigerator. Once opened, these spices lose their flavor quickly.

Vegetables: To keep beets, carrots, turnips, and other root vegetables flavorful and nutritious, cut off their leafy green tops before refrigerating. The tops will extract nutrients from the roots during storage. Wash leafy greens like spinach and kale and dry them thoroughly. Store them loosely wrapped in a paper, plastic, or cloth bag.

Vegetable oils: If you use vegetable oils infrequently, be sure to refrigerate the container once it's been opened. That way, there's less likelihood that the oil will turn rancid. The shelf life of refrigerated oil is about three months.

MAINTAINING AND CLEANING A REFRIGERATOR

A little maintenance and cleaning will help a refrigerator run smoothly and store its contents as it should. Here are some easy jobs to do.

Keeping the seal

Gaskets, the rubber lining that surrounds the doors and keeps the cold air inside, can become worn. From time to time, check the gaskets for tightness; they should fit snugly. To check the door seal, close the door on a dollar bill in several places. Look for slight resistance as you pull it out. If the gasket seems loose, follow the instructions for replacing a gasket on page 131.

The condenser coils and drain pan

A buildup of dirt and lint on the compressor coils causes a refrigerator to work too hard. To extend the life of your appliance and to help it run more efficiently, remove buildup regularly.

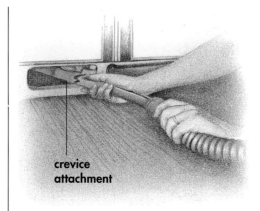

crevice attachment

The coils are usually located behind the bottom front grille; on older models and cycle-defrost ones (with freezers that need to be defrosted) the coils are located at the back. Before you begin, unplug the refrigerator. To get access to the coils, remove the grille by grasping it near both ends and gently pulling. Use a vacuum cleaner with a crevice attachment (above) and push the tool as far under the unit as you can. Try not to bend the condenser tubing or the coil fins. While you have the grille off,

baking soda

remove grille

you can take a moment and wash the drain pan. Use soapy water and, to keep the pan smelling fresh, sprinkle it with baking soda (below left).

Manual defrosting

Defrost a cycle-defrost freezer when the frost is ¼ inch thick. Never use a sharp utensil to scrape the frost as it can cause serious damage. Use a dull plastic scraper instead, and don't scrape against metal parts. If the frost is thick, you can boil a pot of water and place it inside the freezer. The heat will speed up the job.

Interior cleaning

When it's time to clean the interior of your refrigerator, remove all food and place the items that must stay cool to keep from spoiling (milk and meat, for example) in a cold ice chest. Unplug the unit before starting a thorough, top-to-bottom cleaning.

Wash all removable shelves and drawers in warm soapy water. Wipe down the walls of the refrigerator with an all-purpose cleaner or a solution of water and baking soda. Then rinse and dry the shelves and drawers and put them back in place.

Once the refrigerator is clean, plug it back in. Wait approximately an hour before replacing the food so that the refrigerator has a chance to lower the temperature efficiently first.

Eliminating odors

Keep an open box of baking soda in the refrigerator and change it on the first day of summer, fall, winter, and

REFRIGERATOR STORAGE: TIME AND TEMPERATURE

In order to prevent spoilage, foods should always be refrigerated at 34° to 37°F. Some foods may last longer than storage times listed below, but they will lose their texture, flavor, and nutritional value. To test the temperature in a refrigerator, set a glass of water in the center of the main compartment for 24 hours, then measure the temperature with a refrigerator thermometer. Check several times for fluctuations of more than five degrees, which could indicate a problem.

Food	Storage time
Dairy Products	
Butter, margarine	1–2 weeks
Cottage cheese	5 days
Hard cheese (Cheddar, Edam, Swiss)	3–4 months
Soft cheese (Brie, blue, Camembert)	2 weeks
Milk, hard-boiled eggs	1 week
Yogurt	7–10 days
Fish	
Lean fish fillets and steaks (cod, flounder, halibut, sole)	1 day
Oily fish fillets and steaks (mackerel, salmon)	1 day
Poultry and Meats	
Bacon	5–7 days
Beef roasts, steaks	2–4 days
Chicken or turkey, whole or pieces	1–2 days
Cooked meats	2–4 days
Ground beef, veal, and lamb	1–2 days
Ground pork	1 day
Lamb, veal roasts	2–4 days
Pork roasts, chops, sausage	2–4 days
Fruit	
Apples, citrus fruit, cranberries	1–2 weeks
Apricots, ripe bananas (skin will darken), berries, cherries	2–3 days
Avocados, melons, nectarines, peaches, pears, plums	3–5 days
Vegetables	
Artichokes, broccoli, cauliflower, green beans, eggplant, peas, peppers, radishes, spinach	3–5 days
Asparagus, cooked vegetables	2–3 days
Beets, green and red cabbage, carrots, turnips, squash	1 week
Corn	1 day
Lettuce, tomatoes, celery	1 week

spring. Control refrigerator odors by making sure all foods are wrapped, covered, or bagged in plastic or foil. Spoiled food in the refrigerator can leave lingering sour odors.

To rid the interior of offensive aromas, dampen a handful of cotton with vanilla extract and place the doused cotton in a small bowl. Place the bowl on the middle shelf of the refrigerator and leave it until the odors disappear.

Exterior cleaning

An all-purpose cleaner will take care of the usual fingerprints and smudges that refrigerator doors attract. To clean greasy areas, such as the top of the refrigerator, you will need to use a heavy-duty all-purpose cleaner, or a solution made up of one part ammonia to 10 parts water. Let the solution stand a while to break down the grease, then wipe off with rags or paper towels.

REFRIGERATOR REPAIRS

Occasionally a refrigerator needs minor adjustments and repairs. Before you call in a professional, do a little troubleshooting yourself. Many small refrigerator repairs can be done in a few minutes. All you need is the know-how and the right tools.

Leveling a refrigerator

A refrigerator that is not level is likely to have a door that sags or rattles. To determine if your appliance is level, place a carpenter's level on top of the unit. Check it first from side to side and then front to back. Look at the legs or casters. If one is not touching the floor,

TOUCHING UP SCRATCHES

1. Buy a small container of appliance paint at the hardware or appliance store. If there is a deep scratch, also pick up some fine grit wet-and-dry sandpaper. Sand the sides of the scratch carefully.

2. Apply the paint as directed on the label. Be sure that the room is well ventilated. The small applicator brush makes it easy to apply just the right amount of paint.

or if the unit is not level, adjust them.

First, remove the bottom grille. For threaded legs, adjust their height by turning the legs themselves with an adjustable wrench (below). For casters, use a screwdriver to turn the leveling

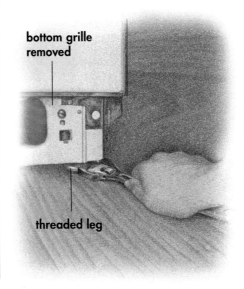

bottom grille removed

threaded leg

screw (a clockwise turn raises the unit). To work on the legs, you need to tilt the unit and rest it on a piece of lumber. When you've finished, retest the unit with your carpenter's level as before.

Fixing the light

If the bulb will not light when you open the door, make sure that the unit is plugged in and that the bulb is not loose. Then buy a 40-watt appliance light bulb. (Do not use a standard light bulb.) Unplug the unit and replace the bulb, removing any protective covering first. Plug the unit back in. If the light still does not work, the problem may be the door switch or the wiring.

To replace the switch, unplug the unit and pry the switch loose with a putty knife. Remove the wires from the terminals. Take the switch with you to an appliance store and buy a replacement. Connect the wires to the new switch, slide the switch back into place, and plug the unit back in. If the problem persists, you may have a more sophisticated electrical problem that requires professional help.

Replacing the door gasket

Refrigerators usually run for many years before needing replacement parts. The gasket, however, does become worn relatively quickly. You can buy a replacement gasket at an appliance store. Before you go shopping, make a note of the exact model number and size of your unit. It should be listed on a label on the door. The gasket is held

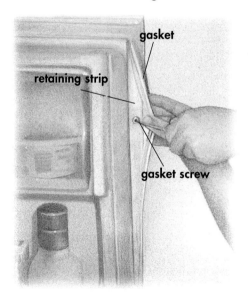

gasket

retaining strip

gasket screw

in place by a retaining strip. Lift the old gasket to see how it is attached. Remove the screws and the old gasket (above). Clean the mounting surface. Start at a top corner and install the new gasket, working toward the opposite corner. Don't overtighten the screws.

Changing door-swing direction

If you have a unit that has the hinges of the door (or doors) on the wrong side for easy access, you may be able to reverse the hinges and handles so that the door opens from the other side. Typically, the holes are factory-drilled and capped for this purpose. Switching the doors will also let you move the refrigerator to a better spot in the kitchen or keep the door from blocking traffic when it is open.

Check your owner's manual for specific instructions; on some refrigerators this can be a fairly challenging job. A service person can do it quickly if you don't have the manual.

Fixing an ice maker

Water is usually supplied to an ice maker through a ¼-inch line that runs from a nearby pipe—often beneath the sink or in the basement—to the back of the refrigerator. If your ice maker isn't producing ice, check that the stop arm controlling the on/off switch is in the down position and the valve supplying water is open.

If the ice cubes the unit is making have hollow centers, chances are that they are not getting enough water. If there is water standing in the bin, they are getting too much water. Adjust the water supply screw to change the water flow. Each half-turn of the supply screw changes the water flow by about 9 cubic centimeters (⅓ ounce); don't make more than 1½ turns in either direction. If these adjustments don't solve the problem, you should call a professional.

FREEZERS

Making the most of your freezer can make a real difference in your family's food budget. By freezing leftovers, soup stock, fruits and vegetables from your garden, and stocking up when frozen foods are on sale, you feed your family well for less. Here's how to prepare and monitor frozen items.

Stocking a freezer

To retain the best quality and prevent spoilage, frozen foods need to be kept at 0°F. Some foods may keep longer than the storage times listed on the chart on the page 132, but they'll gradually lose their flavor and food value. When stocking a freezer for the first time, use this formula: Add 3 pounds or less of food per cubic foot each day until the freezer is full. The gradual process makes it easier to maintain the necessary 0°F temperature, plus it will retard the growth of bacteria, helping your food last longer.

Wrapping food for freezing

If you're planning to freeze food for a short time, plastic bags or containers are perfectly adequate. To decrease the chance of freezer burn, which happens whenever air meets frozen food, be sure to wrap food tightly. Technically, freezer burn is not harmful, but it does spoil both the texture and the color of the food. Foods to be frozen for longer periods of time should be wrapped with heavy-duty aluminum foil, special freezer bags, or freezer wrap. Whatever you use, though, make sure that the package is secure, airtight, and

FREEZER STORAGE: TIME AND TEMPERATURE

Frozen foods keep best at an average temperature of 0°F. To test the temperature in a freezer, place a refrigerator thermometer between packages of frozen food and leave for 24 hours. Then measure the temperature. Check again a few hours later. Fluctuations of more than five degrees could indicate a problem.

Food	Storage time (in months)
Dairy Products	
Butter, margarine	6–8
Cottage cheese, yogurt, hard-boiled eggs	Do not freeze
Hard cheese (Cheddar, Edam, Swiss)	6
Soft cheese (Brie, blue, Camembert)	4
Milk	1
Fish	
Lean fish fillets and steaks (cod, flounder, halibut, sole)	6
Oily fish fillets and steaks (mackerel, salmon)	3
Poultry and Meats	
Bacon	1
Beef roasts, steaks	6–12
Chicken or turkey, whole or pieces	6–7
Cooked meats	2–3
Ground beef, veal, and lamb	3–4
Ground pork	1–3
Lamb, veal roasts	6–9
Pork roasts, chops	3–6
Sausage	2
Pies and Cakes	
Unbaked fruit pie, unfrosted cakes	6–8
Baked fruit pie	2–4
Frosted cakes	2–4
Fruit	
Apples, citrus fruit, cranberries, apricots, ripe bananas (skin will darken), berries, cherries, avocados, melons, nectarines, peaches, pears, plums	Commercially frozen: 12 Home frozen: 8–12
Vegetables	
Artichokes, broccoli, cauliflower, green beans, eggplant, peas, peppers, radishes, spinach	Commercially frozen: 8 Home frozen: 8–12
Asparagus, cooked vegetables	Do not freeze
Beets, green and red cabbage, carrots, turnips, squash, corn	Commercially frozen: 8 Home frozen: 8–12
Lettuce, tomatoes, celery	Do not freeze

clearly labeled with the contents and the date that it was frozen.

Cooling food quickly

To cool foods quickly before freezing—a casserole, for instance—set the warm pan in ice water for a few minutes (be sure you use freezer-to-oven bakeware that can withstand drastic changes in temperature). Then wrap the food as usual and freeze immediately. Not only does this save time, it reduces energy costs, too; the freezer won't have to work so hard to bring down the temperature of the food.

Take inventory

To make the most efficient use of frozen foods, keep an up-to-date list of your freezer's contents. Place the newest packages near the back or at the bottom of your freezer, moving older ones to the top or front so they're next in line for use. Then color code the different foods, posting a list of the items (including dates) near the freezer and checking them off as they are used. You'll be surprised how you'll cut the time spent searching for items.

Freezing food

To keep frozen foods at their best, it is important to understand how to package and handle them.

◆ **Meats:** When rewrapping prepackaged meat for freezing, cut the label from the original wrapping and tape it to the new package. You will have a record of the cut of meat, its weight, and the date of purchase. To prepare raw hamburger patties for freezing,

separate them with small plastic coffee-can tops, stack them in a pile, place them in a plastic bag, and seal. Freeze raw or cooked meatballs on a cookie sheet, then transfer them to a container, seal, and freeze. They will stay separate and you can use as many as you want when you need them.

◆ **Bread:** Bread will dry out quickly in the refrigerator, but it freezes well for up to six months if wrapped in plastic, then foil. When putting the bread in the freezer, don't crush the loaf. To crisp up the crust, remove the bread from its wrapping, thaw, and then put in a 350°F oven for 10 minutes.

◆ **Fresh berries:** To prevent fresh berries from turning to mush in the freezer, wash the fruit thoroughly, pat it dry, and place on a cookie sheet. Place the cookie sheet in the freezer until the berries are frozen, then pack the berries in airtight containers. By freezing pieces of fruit individually, you can take out only what you need for recipes and return the rest to the freezer.

◆ **Herbs:** You can freeze some fresh herbs, such as parsley, chives, and basil. Wash the herb, shake, then pat dry with paper towels. Mince it and freeze in a plastic container. In addition, fresh ginger root keeps well frozen. Put the ginger in a plastic bag and put in the freezer, grate it as needed.

◆ **Pies:** To freeze a freshly baked pie, cool to room temperature. Wrap in plastic and foil and label with a piece of tape, noting the type of filling and the date. If a pie has a sticky filling that is hard to wrap, freeze the pie first and then wrap it.

◆ **Ice cream:** To keep ice cream fresh and tasty after the first serving, press plastic wrap onto the surface of the remaining ice cream to prevent ice crystals from forming. Then replace the carton top and return the ice cream to the freezer. Don't let an open container of ice cream sit in the freezer too long; it is best eaten soon after it is purchased.

CHOOSING STOVES, COOKTOPS, AND OVENS

There are many types of cooking appliances today. A traditional freestanding stove combines the cooktop and oven into one unit. Standard models are 30 inches wide, although you can find them ranging from 20 to 40 inches wide. A freestanding stove is usually the most economical choice; built-in ones are more expensive. Dual-oven stoves offer a second oven (sometimes it is a microwave oven) mounted above the cooktop.

Choosing a separate cooktop and wall oven offers the greatest versatility. Most cooktops have four burners and are 30 inches wide. They can be installed on any countertop, even an island countertop in the middle of the room. The wall oven is mounted elsewhere in the kitchen. With the growing popularity of two-cook kitchens, it makes sense to consider installing a stove as well as a modular cooktop or wall oven.

Gas or electric?

It used to be that gas cooktops were much easier to control than electric ones; a twist of the control knob and the flame instantly changed. Electric burners were slow to heat or cool. Electric ovens, however, were roomier and had more even heating than gas ovens. In the last decade these differences have narrowed.

Electric cooktops have improved significantly. Newer types of elements promise quicker control than traditional coils, including automatically

COOKTOPS AND BURNERS

Gas Cooktops

Conventional Burner—An aluminum ring or cylinder is set into a large opening in the cooktop. A rack for heating rests on top.

Sealed Burner—A solid, porcelain-coated cap and burner element stem are sealed to the surface of the cooktop and then covered by a heating rack. Spills cannot run below the surface.

Electric Cooktops

Conventional Coil Burner—A flat, spiral burner uses electric resistance to become hot and then transfers that heat to the pot and the air around the pot. Spills go through the coils and are caught in drip pans below, which then must be cleaned.

Solid Element Burner—A cast-iron disc containing electric wires is sealed into the cooktop. Spills fall onto the cooktop surface and are easier to clean. A cast-iron element is slow to heat up and cool down.

Radiant Heat Burner—Wires, shielded by a smooth black glass-ceramic surface material, are heated through electric resistance, much like a conventional coil. The coil heats very quickly and the glass-ceramic surface is easy to clean.

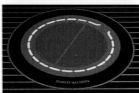

Quartz-Halogen Burner—Halogen-filled quartz lamp tubes, surrounded by radiant electric resistance wires, create an almost instantaneous heating element that glows red under a glass-ceramic surface material.

adjusting temperatures. Gas ovens, on the other hand, are now comparable to electric models both in oven size and heating performance.

If you do not have a natural gas line into your home, you can only have an electric model. If you can choose, compare the costs of purchasing and operating the two.

Self-cleaning or not?

Self-cleaning ovens add at least $100 to the price of an oven. However, the ease of cleaning may well justify the added cost. Self-cleaning stoves use a high-temperature cycle that reduces spills to ash, which can then be wiped away with a sponge.

THE STOVE HOOD

Stove hoods are venting devices designed to remove cooking odors, moisture, grease, and smoke from the kitchen area. Most stove hoods have a light and a fan that sucks up air and carries it out of the house through a duct. Non-circulating stove hoods (often used in apartment buildings) filter out odors and moisture but don't vent used air outdoors. Both hoods function as important fire breaks between the stove and cabinets above the stove. (Not only is the hood a physical barrier but, even more importantly, an operating fan constantly dilutes heat produced by the stove and can slow the progress of even a grease fire.) Ducted hoods remove cooking odors—especially important in newer, well-sealed, energy-efficient homes.

As a rule, stove hoods should be large enough to cover the whole cooktop, and, especially with commercial stoves, extend 3 inches beyond both sides. They are usually installed about 2 feet above the cooktop, but the exact height depends on the model. Manufacturers specify the recommended size for the ductwork that the hood vents into. While you may be able to use larger ducts than recommended, you should never use smaller ones.

Choosing a stove hood

Stove hoods are rated according to the noise they make and the amount of air they move. The greater the heat produced by an appliance, the greater the air movement required. Blower noise is measured in sones. One sone is approximately the amount of noise made by a typical refrigerator. Most conventional stove hood fans generate 5 to 8 sones when run at maximum speed. Air movement is rated in cubic feet per minute (cfm). The amount of heat an appliance produces is stated in British thermal units (Btus).

A conventional stove (producing about 36,000 Btus) needs a blower with a cfm rating of 160 to 200. A commercial stove or an indoor grill requires higher cfm ratings than a standard stove hood. For example, with a commercial stove (producing about 60,000 Btus), a blower rated at 500 to 600 cfm would be needed, producing 6 to 12 sones. Because a grill produces heat directly into the air unabsorbed by a pan, even a small grill of 14,000 Btus will need a hood rated at 460 cfm.

Hood blowers can be built into the stove hood or installed separately nearer the point where air is exhausted outdoors. Moving the blower 10 feet away from the hood will reduce the noise level by about 25 percent.

An alternative to a stove hood is a down-draft vent, which is useful for a stove that is part of a kitchen island or peninsula. Down-draft vents with intakes elevated above the appliance are more efficient than units flush with the burners.

Cleaning the stove hood vent filter

Most models have a mesh filter in the hood, which keeps grease from getting into the ductwork. Inspect the filter once a month, and clean it as often as necessary. Remove the filter and soak it in hot sudsy dishwater, using a grease-dissolving cleaner. Let the filter dry thoroughly before replacing it in the vent housing. If the filter is damaged, take it with you to a hardware or appliance store to be sure the replacement is the right size.

Some manufacturers have eliminated the filter because it reduces the pulling power of the fan. These models have detachable housings that must be cleaned periodically. Check the owner's manual for instructions.

CLEANING STOVES, COOKTOPS, AND OVENS

Keeping a cooktop and stove clean are important to their maintenance. Spilled grease or food can prevent a gas burner from working properly. Baked food in the oven can give the kitchen

and other nearby rooms an unpleasant smell. Let spills on electric coil elements burn off—you may damage the element if you soak it in water. If the gasket on the oven door is dirty, clean it with a sponge and soapy water. If you avoid food spills and clean small ones as soon as they occur, it will be a breeze to keep your oven clean, especially if yours is self-cleaning.

Replacing the drip pans

Drip pans under the coil element on an electric cooktop keep spills from dripping below the cooktop; they also reflect and contain heat from the coils. Drip pans that are dirty or have holes in them rob some of the heat from the pan. Keep the drip pans clean. If they are old, buy replacements at a hardware or appliance store. To access the drip pan, lift the coil and pull the terminals free. Remove the pan and take it with you when you shop for a replacement. Chrome-plated drip pans are inexpensive, although porcelain models are easier to clean.

Cleaning a gas stove burner

If the flame of a gas burner is weak or uneven, it may be clogged with spilled food. Gas burners vary from model to model, so it is important to check your owner's manual before cleaning.

To service most burners, you must first lift the stove top and prop it open. If the cap of the burner is removable, soak it in hot water and dishwashing liquid. Use a toothpick or thin wire to clean out the holes and crevices. Rinse well and allow to dry thoroughly before

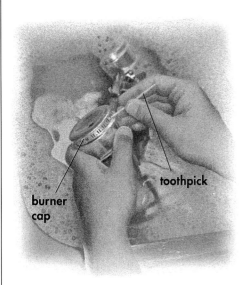

burner
cap

toothpick

replacing. If the cap cannot be removed, lift out the burner assembly following the manufacturer's instructions (you may need to remove screws first) and clean the assembly (above). If cleaning does not improve the flame, call for repairs.

Cleaning stove and oven knobs

Cleaning the knobs on electric and gas stoves is easy. They can be pulled off and soaked in warm water and dishwashing liquid. Scrub them clean, taking care not to rub off any markings. While they are soaking, clean the area that's usually hidden by the knobs. Let the knobs dry thoroughly before replacing them.

If any knobs are broken, or if their markings are hard to read, you can find new ones at an appliance store. Take the old knobs with you so you can find identical replacements. The openings must fit the knob stems exactly and can only be mounted in one position.

Cleaning oven surfaces

The most effective tool for cleaning an oven is also the most damaging. Strong abrasive cleaners and scrubbing pads can quickly scratch the surface. A safer alternative is a nylon scouring pad, available at most grocery and hardware stores. These often are recommended for use on nonstick cookware, and they are much more effective on hard-to-remove oven dirt than a sponge. Used with a suitable cleanser, the pads will remove baked-on grease without marring the oven walls.

About oven cleaners

Commercial oven cleaners that contain lye are effective, but they are also dangerous. The warning labels on such products are quite long and detailed, and they should be followed closely—lye causes serious burns and pollutes the air with toxic fumes. Oven cleaners can also damage the porcelain finish on self-cleaning ovens, which is why they are generally not recommended by oven manufacturers. You should check your owner's manual carefully before using oven cleaner. If you do not have an owner's manual, contact the manufacturer for advice. When you use lye-based cleaners, and any other undiluted heavy-duty cleaner, wear rubber gloves, safety goggles, and a long-sleeved shirt. Keep windows open for ventilation.

Caring for a continuous-cleaning oven

Ovens that are "continuous-cleaning" models have a textured surface that is supposed to remove light spills at nor-

SAFETY SMART

IF YOU SMELL GAS

◆ **The shutoff valve** on a gas stove or oven is near the point where the gas line enters—usually under the cooktop. If yours isn't there, consult your owner's manual or your appliance dealer. All adults in the house should know where it is.

◆ **If you smell a heavy gas odor,** immediately turn off any flames, open windows and doors, and get everyone out of the house. If your stove's shut-off valve isn't within easy reach, turn off your home's main gas shut-off valve at the meter or the bottled gas tank. Do not touch a light switch, pick up a telephone, or make any electrical connection that could create a spark. If you need light, use a flashlight. Report the leak to your gas company or supplier from a neighbor's telephone.

◆ **If you notice a faint gas odor,** check for a burner flame or a pilot light that has blown out. Check the oven also. If you're not cooking, probably a pilot light has gone out. Turn off any flames and air out the room. Relight the burner or pilot only after all gas odor is gone. If any odor persists after you've aired out the room, turn off the gas at your home's main shut-off valve and call the gas company.

◆ **When ventilating a room,** keep in mind that natural gas is lighter than air and collects in the upper reaches of the room; bottled gas sinks to the floor.

mal cooking temperatures. The surface causes spills to spread out, then slowly burn away. But larger spills must still be wiped up immediately.

REPAIRING STOVES, COOKTOPS, AND OVENS

Repairing and maintaining your stove can seem intimidating, especially if you have a gas model. But with a little care, you can handle some simple repairs and adjustments.

Adjusting a gas pilot light

Older gas stoves have burners that are ignited by a pilot light, a small flame that burns continuously. (Many newer gas stoves offer safe, energy-saving electronic, or "pilotless," ignition. An igniter produces a spark or enough heat to ignite the burner flame—instead of a pilot light.) If the pilot light is weak, the burners may take longer than necessary to ignite. If the flame is too strong, you are wasting gas. The flame in the pilot should be about ¼ to ⅜ inches high, with a sharp blue cone.

Most cooktop burners are controlled by a single pilot light under the stove top. First, find the pilot light, and then look along the tube that supplies it

pilot light

adjusting screw

with gas for an adjusting screw. With a screwdriver, move the screw in small increments until the flame is properly sized (below left). To raise the flame height turn the screw counterclockwise. To adjust the pilot light for the oven burner, remove the bottom cover from the oven. Turn the adjusting screw located on the safety valve or under the thermostat knob to correct the flame size. If you can't find an adjusting screw, check the owner's manual or call for service on the unit.

A gas stove that won't light

The cooktop burners and the oven are ignited by separate pilot lights. If either pilot light is out, relight it. If both pilot lights are out and will not light, the gas supply is probably cut off. Check that the valve of the gas line is open; it may be located in back of the stove or under the cooktop. A gas valve is open when the handle is pointing in the same direction as the pipe. If you have propane, the tank may be empty or the tank valve may be closed. Call your supplier for assistance.

If you had some work done recently on gas lines or appliances, it is possible that the main valve was shut off. Call your gas company to turn the gas back on and check all pilot lights. If the stove seems to be getting gas, but still will not work, call for service.

A pilot light that keeps going out

If the pilot flame ignites, but quickly goes out, try increasing the gas flow to the pilot by turning the adjusting screw. If the flame is the right height, change

the gas/air mixture. If the problem persists, look for drafts in the house that may be blowing the flame out. Open windows nearby or slamming doors (especially in a tightly weatherproofed house) may be the problem.

Adjusting the gas flame

The flame in a gas burner is produced by a careful blend of gas and air. If the mixture is not correct, the flame will not burn hot enough. Look for a uniform circle of flames that are 1-inch high. Each flame should be steady and mostly blue, tapering to a small, but distinct orange tip. Air shutters on burner tubes regulate the gas-air mixture and can be adjusted on each burner (below). Begin by lifting or removing the stove top and locating the air shutter. Turn the burner on High and open the shutter until the flame is noisy and unsteady. Then close the shutter slowly to produce the desired blue flames. There should be a safe distance between flame and

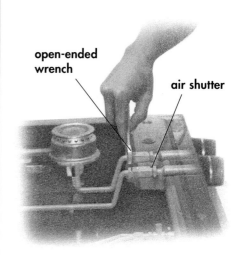

open-ended wrench

air shutter

shutter, but *be careful working around open flames.* When you have a good flame, tighten the retaining screw.

A pilotless gas stove that won't light

The igniter on a pilotless stove requires electricity to work. If your stove won't light, make sure that it is plugged in and that the circuit breaker isn't tripped or the fuse blown. Turn on a burner and hold a lit match over it. If it won't ignite, gas is probably not reaching the stove. Check to make sure that all gas valves are open. If the burner can be lit with a match, an igniter may be at fault. There are two igniters, each controlling two burners. Lift or remove the stove top and then turn on the burners. You should hear a click in the igniter or see sparks. If you don't, the igniter should be cleaned or replaced. Call for service.

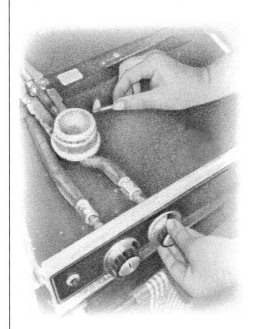

Replacing an oven light

If the oven light won't turn on, first make sure that the stove is plugged in and that the circuit breaker isn't tripped or the fuse blown. The oven should be off and cooled to room temperature. Most ovens need a 40-watt appliance bulb (not a standard light bulb). These are available at home centers and can be removed and installed like any light bulb. You may have to remove the protective cover in order to access the dead bulb.

If the light still won't work, the door switch may need replacement. Unplug the oven and pry the switch from the door frame with a putty knife or screwdriver covered with tape to avoid scratching the surface. Disconnect the wires, take the switch to an appliance store and buy a replacement. Install the new switch (p.130). If the problem persists, call for service.

Replacing elements

If a coil element in an electric cooktop is not working, remove it and insert another element of the same size from the cooktop. If the replacement works, you need to buy a new element. If it doesn't work, call for service. To avoid problems in the future, keep elements and burner drip pans clean and use flat-bottom cookware. There's no need to line drip pans with foil, however; today's chrome or porcelain drip pans are easy to clean.

Bake and broil elements in the oven heat poorly if they are bent or pitted. In either case, the best solution is to replace the element. Unplug the stove.

CONVECTION OVENS

A convection oven looks like a conventional electric oven, but differs in having a fan that blows the heated air throughout the compartment. The uniform heat produced by the fan makes the oven cook faster and more evenly than a conventional oven. Although they cost more to buy, a convection oven ultimately uses less energy than a conventional oven. Countertop convection ovens are also available, sometimes combined with toaster oven or rotisserie features.

Remove the cover, if necessary, and take out the screws holding the element to the wall of the oven. Remove any brackets and pull out the element. Take the element to an appliance store and ask them to check the continuity to verify that the element is bad. If it is, you'll need to install a replacement element.

Changing the stove hood light bulb

Stove hoods may contain one or more lights. Some models may use fluorescent lights, others will use incandescent. When changing the light, be sure to check the owner's manual for recommended wattage. If an incandescent bulb burns out frequently, install an appliance bulb. If the light won't work after you've changed the bulbs, make sure that the circuit breaker hasn't been tripped or the fuse is not blown. If the electricity is on and the light still won't work, call for service.

SMALL KITCHEN APPLIANCES

*They mix, they chop, they brew—and they cut down on cooking time.
Small appliances make life easier. Regular cleaning and basic
maintenance keep them running smoothly.*

Blenders, coffee makers, and microwave ovens are just a few of the small appliances that have become as important to meal preparation as ranges and refrigerators. It's not difficult to keep these devices in good operating order. They should be used only according to the instructions, maintained properly, and cleaned regularly. Though it's possible to make minor repairs on many appliances, not all of them should be repaired by the owner. Some are so inexpensive that a new one may cost less than a repair. Others must be worked on by a professional. Always read the owner's manual before attempting any repair, and check the base or access panel of an appliance for a warning against owner servicing. Owner servicing may void a warranty.

BLENDERS

Blenders are convenient appliances for mixing light foods, especially liquids. Heavy-duty grinding and chopping can be accomplished better and faster with a food processor. If a blender is used for these jobs, it can malfunction.

The blades of a blender sit in the bottom of a glass or plastic jar that rests on a motor base. The blades connect to the motor by either a metal drive stud or a coupling. To keep your blender in good working order, keep it clean. Bear in mind that blenders are designed for speed, not power, so they can easily become overloaded. Don't make your blender work too hard.

Cleaning a blender

Clean the blender right after use; the longer you wait, the more caked-on the food becomes. Fill the jar halfway with warm water, add a drop of liquid detergent, and cover. Blend at low speed for a few seconds. Run with clear water to rinse thoroughly. Clean the base with a damp sponge. Never immerse it in water or rinse it under running water.

Freeing jammed blades

If you turn on the appliance and you hear the motor humming but the blades aren't turning, turn the blender off immediately. First try reducing the load by cutting large chunks into smaller pieces or adding some liquid. Then try

running the blender at a higher speed. If the blades don't start turning right away, turn off the blender immediately to avoid damaging the motor. Unplug the blender and remove the blade assembly (below) by unscrewing the jar base. Check for any buildup of food

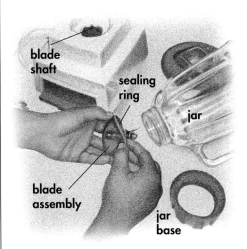

blade shaft

sealing ring

jar

blade assembly

jar base

material around the blades. Wash the blade assembly with dishwashing detergent. Rinse it thoroughly.

Fixing a leak

The most common source of a blender leak is a poor seal between the base and the jar. Remove the blade assembly (below) and check the jar and base for chips and the sealing ring for cracks. Replace any part that is damaged. If none of these parts is broken, then the blade shaft or its bearing may be worn out. Replace the entire blade assembly.

Disassembling a blender

If the blender operates erratically, and the previous suggestions haven't fixed the problem, disassemble the entire unit and examine the wiring. Unplug the blender and set the jar aside. Remove screws or bolts from the bottom of the base. Carefully slide the base away from the housing. Look inside at all of the wires; many are attached with slip-on connectors. If you find a loose wire, plug it back onto its contact. Reassemble the base and housing, plug in the blender, and test it.

COFFEE MAKERS

There are a variety of coffee makers available today; which one you choose will depend somewhat on how you like your coffee. Many people prefer coffee made from an automatic-drip coffee maker over that made in a traditional percolator. The heated water passes through the coffee grounds only once in a drip maker, while in a percolator the water washes through the grounds

automatic-drip

espresso maker

French press

over and over, possibly allowing it to become a little bitter and losing some flavor in the process.

Home espresso machines are popular with those who like the taste of strong coffee. Espresso is made by forcing hot water under high pressure through finely ground coffee. Models with pumps generally do the best job but are costly. Models that operate by steam pressure perform well and are moderate in price.

French press (or plunger) coffee pots have grown in popularity with the boom in specialty coffees. Many expert coffee tasters think the French press method produces the best cup of coffee. It requires virtually no maintenance or special washing procedure. Stove-top espresso makers are equally simple to use and maintain.

Maintaining an Automatic Coffee Maker

Cleaning the coffee maker after each use can reduce the buildup of scaly mineral deposits in the brew basket and the pot.

The tank and tubing of automatic-drip and espresso machines should also be cleaned from time to time, especially if you have hard water. The deposits can affect the performance of the machine as well as the taste of the coffee. Commercial cleaning solutions are available and may be recommended by the manufacturer, but you can clean just as effectively by using a solution of equal amounts of white vinegar and water.

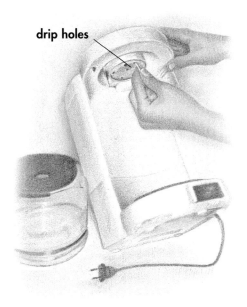

drip holes

In an automatic-drip coffee maker, pour the cleaning solution into the water reservoir, then turn on the machine until about half of the solution has run into the pot. Turn off the coffee maker for about an hour, then turn it back on and let the rest of the solution run out. Repeat the brewing cycle once or twice with clean water, making sure you rinse out all cleaning solution.

Cleaning the drip holes

The drip (or spreader) holes in the top plate of an automatic-drip coffee maker force the water to drip evenly over the grounds. When they become clogged, the result is weak coffee. After cleaning the machine with a cleaning solution or vinegar and water, empty any water still in the reservoir and turn the machine upside down. Clean the holes with a toothpick (left). If the holes can't be cleaned, you may have to replace the plate. Call the manufacturer for the nearest service store.

Maintaining an Espresso Maker

Scaly buildup can be removed from an espresso maker in the same manner as an automatic-drip coffee maker. See the owner's manual for specific instructions. To help maintain the pressure needed to force water through coffee grounds, the filter basket must form a tight seal with the gasket in the brew

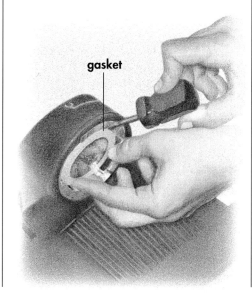

gasket

head. The gasket and screen are attached with one or more screws on most models. Once a month, clean the gasket and screen. Unplug the machine and allow it to cool before you begin disassembly. Be sure to replace the parts in the reverse order. If the gasket is worn, remove and replace it (below left).

Cleaning a steam wand

Clean the steam wand immediately after use; when milk froth is allowed to dry on it, cleaning can become a chore. Here's how to make the job easier.

◆ **To remove built-up residue** on the tip of the steam wand, set a glass of water under it and let it soak overnight.

◆ **Clear a clogged steam wand** by poking through the residue with a needle or a toothpick.

Dealing with vapor lock

Vapor lock is a common occurrence in pump-driven espresso makers. It happens when the boiler tank is low on water. The boiler fills up with steam, and the pump cannot push water into it. If you can hear the pump working, but water is not reaching the filter basket, let the machine cool down to room temperature. Fill the reservoir with water, and place one cup under the brew head and another under the steam wand. Turn on the power button and immediately turn on the pump. Water should start flowing through the brew head in a minute or two. When the cup under the brew head is half full, turn on the steam knob and let water fill the cup under it. Then turn off the steam wand and let the water fill the rest of the cup under the brew head. Finally, turn off the pump and proceed to make espresso.

You can reduce the chances of vapor lock occurring by priming the pump regularly (below).

Priming the pump

To keep a pump-driven espresso machine working properly, it is important that you prime the pump the first time it is used, any time it hasn't been used for more than a day, and after steaming milk. It is a simple procedure, and you may want to get in the habit of doing it before each use.

To prime the pump, fill the water reservoir and turn on the machine. When the ready light comes on, set a cup under the brew head (with the filter basket removed) and another under the steam wand. Turn on the brew switch and open the steam knob. Let an ounce or two of water pass through the steam wand, then close the knob. Allow an ounce or two of water to flow out of the brew head, then turn off the brew switch. The machine is now ready to use.

FOOD PROCESSORS

Food processors have removable blades that slice, shred, and mix foods. There are two kinds of processors: belt-driven and direct-driven. In a direct-driven food processor, the mixing bowl sits on top of the gear assembly; the spindle is connected directly to the motor. In a belt-driven model, the bowl sits to one side of the motor, and a rubber belt connects the drive shaft to the blade shaft, spinning the blades.

Safety catch

Because the blades are extremely sharp and can cause injury, all food processors have a safety switch that won't allow the motor to operate unless the cover is securely in place. If the unit doesn't run, first check that the bowl cover is locked in place.

Cleaning a food processor

To run smoothly, food processors must be cleaned after each use. Always unplug the unit for cleaning. Wipe all the parts, especially the spindle and blades. Caked food in the shaft of the blade or on the spindle can cause the blades to shimmy, damaging them or the gear assembly. If the blades vibrate and don't cut properly, shut off the machine immediately and unplug it. Remove any food caught under the blades, inside the blade shaft, or on the spindle. Use a nylon scrub pad (above) to scrub off hardened debris.

Food processor repair

On some models, the spindle or drive shaft is part of the gear assembly and can't be replaced separately. On other models, the spindle is secured by a locknut or special washer and can be replaced. On still other models, the spindle is covered with a plastic sheath. If you have one of these models and the sheath has become cracked, you can replace it. To remove the sheath, gently pry it and the attached spring-washer up with a screwdriver. Clean the spindle underneath with a nylon scouring pad. Then install the new sheath.

MICROWAVE OVENS

A microwave oven has a transformer, which boosts normal household current, and a magnetron that converts that current into electromagnetic waves. The waves cause food molecules to vibrate fast enough to generate friction, which creates the heat that cooks the food internally.

Microwave ovens that sit on the countertop have a capacity of between 0.6 and 1.6 cubic feet and generate between 600 and 1,000 watts. They can cook a lot of food quickly, but they also take up a lot of space. Smaller models that can be mounted under cabinets are usually less powerful and hold less food. Other features to consider when you buy a microwave are moisture sensors, quick-setting touchpads, a rotating carousel, and a child-proofing feature.

Cleaning a microwave

Unplug the oven, then clean the inside with warm water or a solution of dish

detergent and water. Use a damp sponge to clean up spills as soon as possible. Do not use abrasive cleaners or oven cleaners on a microwave oven.

Microwave repairs

Aside from the minor fixes discussed below, always go to a professional for service on a microwave.

◆ **Unstop the vents** with a toothpick if the oven suddenly runs inconsistently or shuts itself off. This sometimes happens if grease splatters clog the air vents. Unplug the oven first.

◆ **To replace a microwave oven light,** first unplug the oven. Remove the lamp compartment cover by removing the screw holding it in place. Remove the bulb and replace it (right). Microwave ovens typically require a 20-watt appliance bulb. Replace the lamp cover and plug in the oven.

MIXERS

Food mixers, both stand and portable, are basically a motor in a metal or plastic casing. The motor runs a set of gears that turn two shafts. Beaters snap into the shafts and rotate when the mixer is turned on. Most models have variable speeds for different functions. Portable mixers have enough power to whip cream, beat eggs, and mix simple batters. Stand mixers provide more torque for things like kneading heavy dough or mashing potatoes.

Mixer care

Forcing a mixer to work too heavy a load can cause overheating. If a mixer sounds strained, the beaters slow down, or the housing becomes warm, stop. Remove some of what you are mixing and try the process again.

Beater sockets can become clogged with hardened food, causing the beaters to grind together or shimmy. With the mixer unplugged, clean out the sockets with a toothpick. Never bang the beaters against a hard surface to clean them. If they're bent out of shape, they may grind together and strip the mixer's gears. To care for beaters, wipe off food with a rubber spatula and wash them in warm, soapy water.

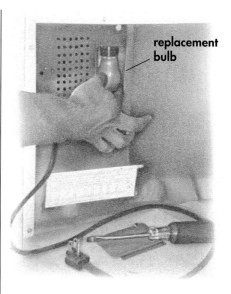

replacement bulb

TOASTER OVENS

A toaster oven can bake and broil food as well as toast bread, using one of two sets of heating elements. Most models have two upper elements for broiling and two lower elements for baking. The baking temperature is maintained by a thermostat, while toasting is usually controlled by a timer.

Toaster oven care

Most modern toaster ovens have "continuous clean" interiors, which means splatters are essentially burned off as you use the oven. To clean the inside of a toaster oven, unplug it and let it cool. Remove the racks and trays (including the crumb tray) and wash in warm soapy water. Sponge off the interior with a nonabrasive cleaner.

If one or more of the heating elements stops working, you should be able to get replacements. Call the manufacturer for the nearest service store.

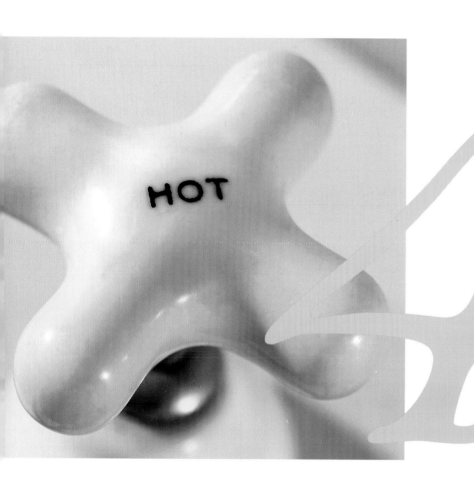

Bathrooms

Plumbing

ORGANIZING AND CLEANING THE BATH

The bathroom is as much a refuge as it is a necessity of life.
Making it a room that is both pleasing and functional is easy to do.

Like the kitchen, the bathroom calls for well-organized storage compartments and shelves to accommodate things both large and small. And while you could store such items as cleaning tools and supplies, the hairdryer, and extra bars of soap in another spot, it is handy to have everything you need in the bathroom at your fingertips. (Never store electrical appliances, such as a hair dryer or shaver, near the sink, bathtub, or shower.) Bear in mind, however, that the humidity and moisture in a bathroom limit what you can safely keep there. It may not be the place to put extra or guest towels, for example, unless you are expecting company.

GETTING ORGANIZED

Nearly every bath has a medicine cabinet over the sink. This shallow compartment is misnamed, for it is the last place you should store medications; the humidity can harm the contents. A better spot for medicines is high in the linen closet—a dark, dry, cool place that is out of reach of children. The medicine cabinet is traditionally a place where out-of-date sundries such as cough medicine and eyedrops are kept. Make it a policy to inventory these shelves every month or so, and throw out old bottles and jars. You will find the extra space you have created is very useful for the new sundries that you have collected.

Adding storage space

If you are like most householders, your bathroom is small and has little, if any, storage space. Happily, home centers and specialty closet stores are filled with shelving units and cabinets designed specifically for the bath. Before you venture into a store or order from a catalog, you need to calculate the space you have. Look for likely storage room under the sink, over the toilet, and in any unused nook or corner. Decide if you want your bath items visible or hidden—or both. Now measure your spaces, and you are ready to start looking at storage units.

Choosing a storage style

For a country-style feeling, you can hang wicker baskets on the wall and add an inexpensive wicker chest of drawers. Or for a more contemporary look, you can choose a covered-wire shelf system. The covering makes these wire shelves suitable for wet areas. In the shower, a covered wire rack can hang on the shower head or stick to a corner of the stall with suction cups. A covered-wire tray can span the tub and hold shampoo, rinse, and a bookrack.

In a children's bath, you can use a mesh bag (below) to hold toys while they drip after a bath and keep other bathtime needs on bright-colored plastic shelves.

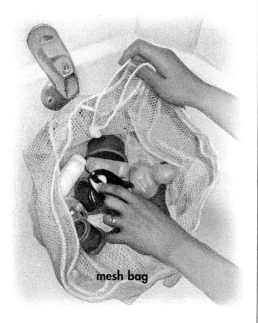

mesh bag

Creating a vanity

If your sink doesn't sit in a cabinet, making it part of a vanity, you can get the same effect by adding a skirt to the sink. A handsome pleated skirt around the sink can hide all kinds of cleansers and sponges in a plain and inexpensive utility bucket.

An easy way to make a sink skirt is to measure fabric to go around the sink—three times to make pleats or twice for gathers. Cut the fabric to height, adding a 2-inch hem allowance to both the top and bottom. Hem the skirt and make the pleats or gathers on the sewing machine. Machine-sew a length of loop tape (one side of a length of hook and loop tape) to the wrong side of the top hem of the skirt. Fasten the other (hook) side of the tape to the sink with a hot-glue gun. With the tape fastener system, you can easily remove the skirt, put it in the laundry while you wash the bathroom floor, and then reattach the clean skirt when it is dry.

If your sink is set inside a cabinet, the cabinet is not likely to have shelves or other storage compartments of its own. You'll find that there are many different add-on shelving units that you can easily install. Some are attached to the cabinet door; others are set on rollers and can be pulled out for easy access to the contents, even if it sits in the back of the cabinet.

VENTILATION AND MILDEW PREVENTION

Mold and mildew can cause problems in the bathroom. Excess moisture is the culprit, so it is important to be able to direct moist air out of the room quickly. An open window is often an efficient way to circulate air in the bathroom. If there is no window, or if a bathroom has a lot of bath and shower activity, an exhaust fan is needed to help clear the air. A bathroom heater, built into the ceiling, can also reduce moisture.

Don't use a space heater (p.69) for this.

There are other ways to control mildew. Clean your bathroom regularly with disinfectant. After showering, pull the shower curtain across, so it can dry thoroughly. For the same reason, close double sliding shower doors after use. If your bath has a closet, install vents in the doors or replace solid doors with louvered ones.

Maintaining an exhaust fan

An exhaust fan motor may sound like it is working, but it will not be doing its job if the grille covering it is clogged with dirt. Remove the grille by unfastening the screws or wires that hold it. Wash the grille in a mild dishwashing detergent and water. While the grille is soaking, clean any built-up dust and grime inside the fan's housing by vacuuming

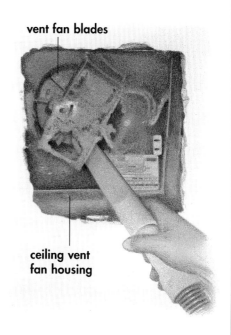

vent fan blades

ceiling vent fan housing

it with a crevice attachment (preceding page). Check that the fan's blades can turn freely, and that the housing is free of obstructions. Replace the grille and test. If the fan doesn't seem to work properly, call for service. You may have a problem in the ductwork that leads to the outside.

Defogging a bathroom mirror

After a shower, the bathroom mirror is always fogged over. Instead of smearing it with a towel or waiting for it to clear, try this simple trick: Turn a hand-held blow dryer directly on the mirror, using a low setting. The warm air will quickly clear the fog from the mirror without leaving streaks.

Start with the mirror ...

move on to the sink, tub, and toilet ...

and finish with the floor.

BASIC CLEANING

When a bath is the central location for a family's morning rituals, the surfaces quickly become dirty, and the moist air invites bacteria to grow. Daily, if possible, sponge down the tub, shower, and sink. That will save time when the weekly deep cleaning rolls around. The best time to clean a bathroom is right after taking a shower or bath, when the steam has loosened the dirt. Work from the cleanest surface (the mirror) to the dirtiest (the floor), cleaning the sink, tub, and toilet as you go (below left).

Using the right cleaner

There can be many types of surfaces in a bathroom—glass, porcelain, fiberglass, brass, and chrome—but all you need are four basic products: an all-purpose liquid disinfectant cleaner; a tub, tile, and sink cleaner; a toilet-bowl cleaner; and a glass cleaner.

You will also need a long-handled toilet brush, a scrubber sponge, and plenty of paper towels or rags. For hard-to-clean areas, such as the soap dish and shower door frame, you will find that a small brush such as an old, but clean, toothbrush or nail brush is handy to have in your cleaning bucket. Unless you have a large floor area which might call for a mop, you can get good results by just spraying the floor with an all-purpose cleaner such as Fantastik, or one of the special-purpose bathroom cleaners, and then wiping it clean with a sponge or rags.

Some areas in the bathroom, such as the toilet bowl and the shower and tub, are prone to troublesome stains. Tackle

MAKING A BATHROOM SAFE

◆ **Installing a grab bar** is an easy way to make a bathroom safer—for all ages, not just children, the handicapped, and seniors. To ensure that the bar will support the weight of a person, both ends should be attached to a stud (wood structural support). Grab bars are handy near the tub and in the shower, and in some cases near the toilet. Never use a towel rack as a substitute for a grab bar; it is not designed to bear that kind of load.

◆ **Avoid using electrical appliances,** such as space heaters, hair dryers, or radios near a wet tub or shower. Getting an appliance wet can cause a serious—even fatal—shock. All bathroom outlets should be equipped with GFCI's (ground-fault circuit interrupters) to prevent that possibility. Even so, you should not mix electrical appliances with water.

◆ **Prevent bathroom falls** by laying scatter rugs with nonskid backings and providing tubs and showers with adhesive decals or suction-backed rubber mats.

these surfaces by spraying the cleaner on the stains and letting it penetrate while you clean other surfaces in the room. When you return to the spot after a few minutes, chances are you will be able to wipe it clean.

Controlling odors

Bathrooms should smell as fresh and sanitary as they look. Use an air freshener if you like its scent, but keep in

mind that it doesn't actually get rid of odors. It just covers them up. To kill odor-causing bacteria, use disinfectants and cleaners containing pine oil. Baking soda, vinegar, and borax are good odor-removers as well.

Removing mildew

The easiest way to attack mildew is to don rubber gloves and spray on a commercial mildewcide such as Scrub Free Mildew Remover or Tilex Mildew Remover, wait a couple of minutes, then scrub the mildew away with a soft brush. Once you've gone over the entire area, rinse off the cleaner and wipe the tile dry. Or wet the surface with water, then spray it with a solution made

of one cup of bleach per quart of water. Work in a well ventilated room and keep towels and other fabrics out of the way.

For stubborn mildew stains, use a stronger mixture of bleach to water. Let stand, then scrub and rinse off.

CLEANING THE VANITY AREA

Faucets collect hard-water spots and soap scum. For a chrome faucet, use a soft cloth moistened with vinegar, window cleaner, or rubbing alcohol to clean away trouble spots. Then dry and polish with a soft, lint-free cloth. If there is a white, chalky buildup of lime, use a lime remover.

A lacquered brass faucet should be cleaned with a mild detergent. To protect the shiny layer of lacquer on the brass fixture, gently buff the surface dry. If the lacquer coating is scratched or coming off, you can prevent the edge from tarnishing by dabbing it with clear fingernail polish, letting it dry, and buffing it lightly. Use cream brass polish only on unlacquered brass.

Scum can collect at the spot where the faucet meets the sink. Clean this area regularly using bathroom cleaner and the toothbrush from your cleaning bucket. (For more on cleaning sinks and faucets, see pages 106 and 108.)

Removing stains from marble and other stone surfaces

Cleaning and maintaining natural stone can be tricky, because each type of stone has its own characteristics. The chemicals in some cleaners can react with the minerals in a particular stone

and cause discoloration. Use only cleaners, polishes, and sealers recommended by the stone dealer.

To remove light stains in marble or cultured marble (the most common stone material for vanity sinks), put on rubber gloves and mix a small amount of soap flakes with hydrogen peroxide. Rub the solution on the stain in the direction of the grain. Rinse with water and buff dry.

THE SHOWER

If you continually find puddles of water left on the bathroom floor after the morning rush of showers, you may want to consider replacing your shower curtain with a shower door. Here are some pros and cons of doing so.

◆ **Water spots** and soap scum can build up on both shower doors and shower curtains, but doors are easier to clean and less likely to harbor mildew.

◆ **A shower door frame** has a narrow track which is a haven for dirt and is hard to clean. You'll need to scrub it periodically with a small brush.

◆ **A shower curtain** can be easily changed if it becomes hard to clean or if you want another look; doors are more permanent.

Cleaning glass shower doors

To keep your shower doors spotless, wipe with a solution of ½ cup vinegar mixed with one quart water, or use glass cleaner. A laundry prewash or a tub and tile cleaner are other options. For heavy scum, leave the cleaner on for a few minutes, then wipe. Rinse and towel dry. Clean the track regularly, using a brush or cotton swabs if necessary.

Cleaning plastic shower curtains

To remove built-up soap film on plastic shower curtains or liners, machine-wash using warm water and one cup of a nonprecipitating water softener (check the label) to dissolve the soap residue. If the curtain is mildewed, add ¾ cup of liquid chlorine bleach to the wash cycle.

After washing the curtain for five minutes on the gentle cycle, hang it back on its rod to drip-dry, making sure that the bottom edge is inside the tub or shower stall and the curtain is spread out as if hung on a clothesline.

If your shower curtain is saturated with mildew, soak it right in the tub, adding bleach and powdered water softener. After about an hour, rinse the curtain—it will look as good as new.

Cleaning shower stalls

To clean a shower stall with an acrylic or fiberglass finish, use a damp sponge with a tub and tile cleaner, a mild non-abrasive cleaner, or baking soda. Gently scour, then allow the cleanser to work for a few minutes. Rinse thoroughly, and dry.

BATHTUBS

Enameled steel or cast iron tubs are tough and resistant to most chemicals. (Enameled steel is less resistant to chips than enameled cast iron.) They can tolerate occasional scrubbing with a mildly abrasive cleanser. But don't use

abrasive cleaners too often; they will wear away the finish, and scum will begin to cling to this rougher surface, making cleaning even harder. Before using a rust remover, read the manufacturer's label. Those containing hydrofluoric acid will harm any enameled finish and shouldn't be used.

Tubs with an acrylic or fiberglass finish need a gentle touch. Use no abrasive cleaners, and be careful of chemical cleansers. Some fiberglass manufacturers recommend the use of new-formula scouring cleansers. Products containing EDTA (ethylene diamine tetraacetate) are fine for fiberglass.

Rings in the tub

Bathtub rings are a greasy combination of body oils, soap, dirt, and sometimes minerals, if the water in your area is hard. Try wiping with undiluted ammonia (using rubber gloves), or sprinkle a damp sponge generously with baking soda, and wipe the ring vigorously. For stubborn stains, rub with a paste of water and automatic dishwashing detergent. Rinse clean and wipe dry.

Soap scum and mineral deposits

Hard water and soap team up to create a phenomenon known as soap curd—a hard gray film that can blanket tubs, sinks, and shower enclosures. A regular wipe-down with a damp sponge or a paper towel soaked in lemon juice will keep soap curd at bay. To attack a buildup of scum, don rubber gloves and apply a paste of cream of tartar and hydrogen peroxide. Scrub the paste lightly into the stain, and allow

to dry. Rinse thoroughly and buff dry. Or clean soap film and mineral buildup with commercial products such as Tilex Soap Scum Remover or Lime-A-Way.

Removing nonskid tape

If the pieces of nonskid tape in your tub are dirty-looking, you can remove them cleanly. First scrape them off (below) with a straight-edged razor blade that has been dipped in soapy water. (For safety's sake, mount the blade in a protective holder.) Remove any adhesive residue with a paper towel dipped in acetone or acetone-based nail-polish remover. Rinse the area thoroughly.

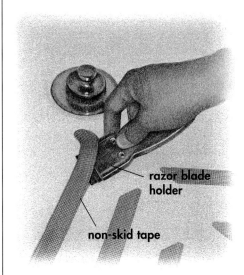

razor blade holder

non-skid tape

TOILETS

Toilet-bowl cleaners that sit in the toilet help to disinfect a toilet and may ease the task of cleaning, but they don't eliminate the need for regular scrubbing. Be sure to clean the outside of the bowl, as well as the seat and cover, with a disinfectant cleaner. Many toilet-bowl cleaners will get the job done. Undiluted chlorine bleach can work just as well. Pour about ½ cup of liquid chlorine bleach into the water in the bowl. After 10 minutes or so, swab the bowl and flush. (However, never combine chlorine bleach with any other cleaning product.)

Cleaning techniques

You can use a toilet brush with synthetic bristles mounted on a bent-wire head, or one with a spongy ball of cotton at the end. The wire-head brush is a more effective scrubber, but it can also scratch the bowl. Replace it as it becomes worn.

Scrub the whole bowl vigorously. Don't forget the area under the rim, where stains and fecal matter can hide. Allow the cleaner to stand in the bowl before you flush it clean.

After you have completely flushed away the bowl cleaner, spray a disinfectant cleaner, such as Lysol Basin, Tub, and Tile Cleaner, all around the outside of the toilet, including the seat, lid, and handles. Spray behind the toilet and at the bottom where it meets the floor, the front of the bowl, and the hinges. Let stand for a few minutes and wipe away with a rough cloth.

Toilet bowl ring

If your water is hard, you may find a ring developing inside the bowl at the water line. If the ring is not severe, a toilet bowl cleaner and a stiff brush or a nylon scrub pad may clean it away. If the problem is severe and your toilet

is made of vitreous china, you can use a pumice stone to scrub the deposit away. However, if your toilet is enameled or colored, you'll just have to keep scrubbing with a brush.

rim
holes

Unclog the holes

If a toilet has been neglected for a while, some of the rim holes located just under the lip of the rim may become clogged. If so, the toilet may develop a "lazy flush," not powerful enough to wash away all the waste. Poke the holes carefully with the bent end of a coat hanger (above). Once unclogged, water will rush out freely.

BATHROOM TILE, CAULK, AND GROUT

Grout and caulk in a bathroom, especially around a tub, are both essential elements and must be maintained, for

they are the barrier that keeps water from seeping into the walls. The smallest gaps allow water to sneak behind the tiles and do real damage to the bathroom wall and floor, and even to the ceiling of the room below.

Maintaining tiles

If some of your tiles have begun to dislodge from the wall, unfortunately, most of the damage is unseen. The wall behind the tile needs repair. Call a plumber and a professional tiler as soon as possible, because waiting will only make the problem worse.

If you have a few chipped tiles, you can avoid retiling by touching up the spots with paint. This won't look as good as new tile, but it's an inexpensive repair. Using an artist's brush, apply alcohol-based primer so the paint will adhere well. Allow the primer to dry, then use a matching appliance or automobile touch-up paint or blend paints to get the color you need.

HOW TO SEAL GROUT

Seal the surface of freshly cleaned or new grout to make maintenance easier. When grout is properly sealed, it will be less porous and less susceptible to stains.

1. Use a sponge to apply a commercial grout sealer.

2. Let the sealer dry. Do not use the tub or shower until it is completely dry.

REPLACING MISSING GROUT

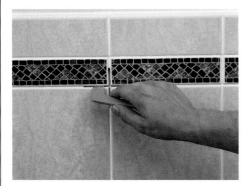

Step 1: Scrape away the old grout with a grout saw (an inexpensive tool available at tile dealers and home centers). Grout is hard, so expect the job to take some time. When all the grout is removed, vacuum the area thoroughly. Wash the surrounding surface with a solution of water and vinegar.

Step 2: When the washed area is dry, mix new grout as directed on the label. Spread grout with a rubber float, as shown above. Pack the grout firmly into the joints, not minding the mess, which you can take care of later.

Step 3: Remove excess grout with a wet sponge. After 30 minutes, use a kitchen knife to shape the grout joints to match the existing grout. Let the grout dry an hour. Use a soft cloth to remove any remaining haze. After the grout has set—24 hours or more—apply a grout joint sealer (see page 151).

Maintaining grout

Clean grimy grout with a regular bathroom tile cleaner, full-strength vinegar, or a solution of ¼ cup liquid chlorine bleach per quart of water, which requires gloves to protect your hands and a cloth or sponge to prevent spattering clothes or nearby fabrics.

Fill small gaps in your grout with new grout. Apply it with your finger and wipe away the excess. If you have a lot of gaps, replace the grout (above).

Maintaining and applying caulk

Don rubber gloves to clean grout with a commercial cleaner, rubbing alcohol, or a mixture of ¼ cup of liquid chlorine bleach per gallon of water.

Caulk seals the joints between tubs and walls. When caulk starts pulling away from the surface, or if it shows signs of mildew, it should be removed and replaced. Use a putty knife or small screwdriver to take out the old caulk. Clean the area with a solution of vinegar and water, then let it dry. Be forewarned, however, that preparing the seam—removing old caulk and cleaning the area—will probably take longer than applying the new caulk.

Use mildew-resistant caulk made specifically for tubs and tile. For small jobs, buy it in a ready-to-use tube that doesn't require a caulking gun. With a scissors or sharp knife, trim the tip of the tube to the size needed to fill the gap. (Start by leaving a hole about ⅛-inch in diameter—too big a hole will make for a sloppy job.) Point the tip into the gap and squeeze. Holding the tube at a 45-degree angle to the joint (below), draw it along in a smooth line, squeezing the tube with steady pressure as you go.

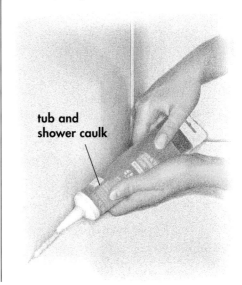

tub and shower caulk

MINOR PLUMBING REPAIRS

*Becoming familiar with the plumbing system
and having the proper tools is all it takes to tackle minor repairs
such as fixing a leaky faucet and clearing a blocked drain.*

Preventive maintenance can save you money and inconvenience. Periodically clean out the hair and soap scum from the bathroom sink and tub drains. Never pour food, coffee grounds, or liquid fat down the kitchen sink. Don't flush anything down the toilet except bathroom tissue and human waste. And fix leaky faucets quickly before minor problems lead to serious damage.

With the proper tools and a little know-how, fixing many minor problems in your plumbing system is fairly easy. You must, however take with you any parts that need replacing to the hardware store or home center to make sure that you get the correct piece. Some replacement parts come in kits.

SHUTTING OFF THE WATER

All adults should know how to shut off the water to the house, in case of a plumbing emergency. And whenever there is a leak or other plumbing repair (other than clearing a clogged drain), you must shut off the water supply to that area before doing the work.

In most houses there is a main shutoff valve, usually located on a pipe close to the water meter. It may be where the water first enters the basement (right). Or, the shutoff valve may be located in a box in the ground, usually between the house and the

main shutoff valve

street. Some boxes have valves that can be turned by hand; others need a long-handled "key." If you are not sure where this is, contact your local water department. The valve controlling a house's hot-water supply is usually found on the outlet pipe at the top of the water heater.

It is more convenient to shut off the water at the plumbing fixture that you will be working on. A stop valve (right) for each plumbing

stop valve

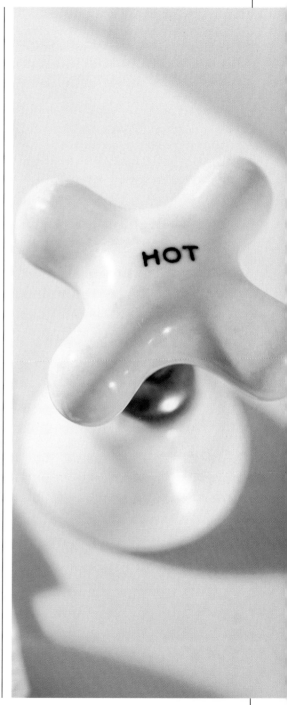

HOT

fixture and water-using appliance are normally on the wall behind the fixture or appliance or directly below it in the basement. If a leak is in the feeder line, you will need to shut off a more distant water valve.

TOILETS

Most household toilets work by using gravity to force a tankful of clean water into the bowl to push waste down a soil pipe and into the sewer system.

Removing a clog

To unclog a toilet, you'll need a plunger with a flanged cup, like the one shown below. The flange fits the opening more snugly than a regular plunger, and the larger air pocket inside the plunger increases its effectiveness.

Bail out excess water, leaving just enough to cover the plunger cup. Place the plunger into the drain opening, with the flange covering the opening. Stand directly over the plunger, and work it up and down. Move the handle of the plunger only; the cup should remain over the drain opening. After plunging vigorously 10 or 12 times, yank the plunger out. Repeat if necessary.

If using a plunger does not clear the clog, use a closet auger, or toilet snake, and push

flanged cup

TROUBLE SHOOTER

WHEN WATER RUNS CONSTANTLY

First, make sure the lift chain, if any, isn't twisted or tangled. Check the overflow tube (below). If water is overflowing the top of the tube, adjust the tank water level as shown below. It should be about 1 inch below the top of the overflow tube. (Too little water can cause inadequate flushes.) On an old toilet with a metal float rod and ball, bend the rod in the middle so that the ball is lowered.

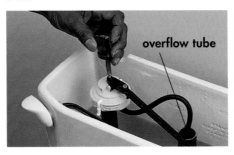

overflow tube

◆ **For a floatless ballcock,** change the water level by turning an adjustment screw, at the top here, counterclockwise to lower water level, clockwise to raise it.

◆ **On a floating cup ballcock,** pinch the clip on the side and slide it down a little to lower the water level. Make small adjustments and test by flushing the toilet.

the cable through the drain. Crank the auger handle to get the cable down the drain pipe. When the auger end reaches the clog, move the auger back and forth to push the obstruction through or pull it out.

Diagnosing leaks

If water is leaking around the bottom of the toilet bowl (at the floor) after a flush, tighten the nuts that hold the bowl to the floor. (You'll have to pry off the decorative caps first.) If tightening the nuts does not solve the problem, have a plumber replace the wax ring.

If water leaks from the bottom of the tank, tighten the nut securing the water supply tube to the underside of the tank. Also, check the nut on the

other end of the tube (that is, at the shutoff valve). If water pools on the floor under the toilet, check for a crack in either the bowl or the tank. If you find one, turn off the water to the toilet to stop the leaking, and have a plumber install a new bowl or tank.

Reducing condensation

Condensation forms on a toilet tank when cold water in the tank meets the warm air in the bathroom. To minimize condensation, you can install an insulation liner, sold as a kit at home stores. Drain the tank, and wipe it dry. Trim the insulation to fit the sides of the tank, then attach it with the adhesive supplied in the kit. Take care not to block the flush-valve assembly.

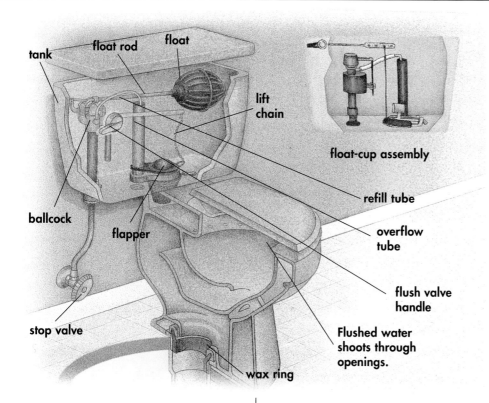

tank
float rod
float
lift chain
float-cup assembly
refill tube
overflow tube
flush valve handle
ballcock
flapper
Flushed water shoots through openings.
stop valve
wax ring

Fixing the handle

A toilet handle is attached with a locknut inside the tank. If the handle is loose, tighten the locknut by turning it counterclockwise. If the handle is broken, remove the nut by turning it clockwise, and disconnect the chain from the end of the trip lever. Slide the nut off the trip lever, then pull the handle and trip lever off the tank. Install a new handle, tighten the locknut, and reattach the chain.

Adjusting the lift chain

If you have to hold the handle down to flush the toilet, the lift chain may be too long. If the chain keeps the flapper from closing tightly, it may be too short. Adjust the chain by hooking it in a different hole or by attaching a different link to the clip.

Fixing a faulty ballcock valve

A brass or plastic ballcock controls the flow of water into the tank; it has a valve that is turned on and off by a float arm and float ball, or by a float cup, which slides up and down just below the ballcock. When the washers inside the ballcock become worn, the valve won't close completely and water will run continuously. If replacing the washers does not solve the problem, replace the entire unit (p.156).

Replacing a toilet seat

Close the seat cover and open the tabs covering the bolts that hold the seat to the toilet. To remove a bolt, steady it with a screwdriver as you undo the nut below with a wrench. If the bolts are corroded, apply penetrating spray and allow them to sit overnight. If the nuts still can't be removed, you can carefully cut through the bolts with a small hacksaw. First, protect the bowl with duct tape. Lift out the old seat, clean the mounting holes, and

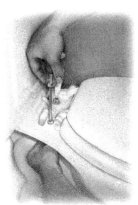

install a new seat of the same size. Set the new seat in place, and hand-tighten the nuts from below. Then tighten a half-turn with a wrench. Always measure a toilet seat's dimensions and the distance between the mounting bolts before you shop for a new seat. There are several sizes available.

SINKS

Some sink repairs are simple to do and require a minimum of tools. Working under the sink means squeezing into a tight spot so have all your tools within easy reach, and use rags and towels to make things as comfortable as possible.

Unclogging a sink with a plunger

If water has backed up into the sink, bail out most of it, leaving just enough

REPLACING THE BALLCOCK ASSEMBLY

ballcock assembly

replacement assembly

washer

1. To remove the old ballcock, shut off the water supply, flush the toilet, and sponge out any remaining water. Unscrew the supply-line nut and the ballcock locknut under the tank with a wrench (use locking pliers inside the tank to keep the ballcock from turning as you work).

2. Remove the old ballcock, and place the rubber washer on the new ballcock as directed by the manufacturer. Set the ballcock in place, attach the locknut and supply line, and attach the refill tube to the overflow tube. Turn on the water supply, check for leaks, and adjust the water level.

to cover the plunger cup. Stuff wet rags into the overflow drain. In a kitchen drain that's connected to a dishwasher, clamp off the dishwasher hose. Set the plunger cup directly over the drain. Pump vigorously straight up and down for at least a minute. If plunging doesn't work, try an auger, or snake. If both of these methods fail, you may have to disassemble the trap (below left).

Using drain cleaners

Never use a chemical drain cleaner if your sink is completely stopped—only if you have a sluggish drain. Never use a plunger after pouring it in: Splashed chemicals can injure your skin.

For a low-cost drain cleaner, pour a half cup of baking soda and a cup of white vinegar down the drain, followed by a gallon of boiling water.

Opening a trap to clear a clog

Place a bucket or can under the trap (left). To avoid scratching the chrome, wrap masking tape around the nuts on both ends of the trap. Loosen the nuts with pliers or a wrench, and remove the trap by pulling the pieces apart. Pour water from the trap into the bucket. Use coat-hanger wire to clear the blockage, or just pull the gunk out. Scrub out scum with a bottle brush and detergent. Reassemble the trap.

Stopping a leak from a trap

If a leak develops around the trap, you may be able to quickly fix it by tightening the coupling nuts above the trap. Place masking tape around the nut first to protect the finish. If the leak persists, remove the trap and take off the old washers. If the pipe threads are corroded, clean them with a wire brush and coat them with joint compound or Teflon tape. Put in new washers, and reassemble the trap.

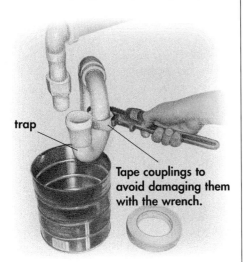

trap

Tape couplings to avoid damaging them with the wrench.

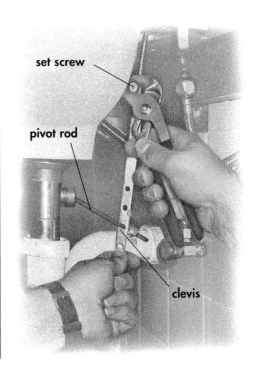

set screw

pivot rod

clevis

DIAGNOSING TOILET PROBLEMS

Many toilet problems are simple to identify and easy to handle yourself. The mechanism in the tank isn't complicated and replacement parts are available at any plumbing or home store. Replacing a wax ring or a toilet tank or bowl is heavy work that takes some experience. Call a plumber for those jobs.

Problem	Possible Cause	Possible Solution
Toilet won't flush at all.	Water supply is turned off.	Turn on water supply.
	Handle is loose.	Tighten handle by turning the locknut inside the tank.
	Lift chain is broken or disconnected.	Reattach the chain or replace it.
	Ballcock valve is broken.	Replace the ballcock assembly (see page 156).
Toilet won't flush.	Water level is too low.	Adjust the water level higher (see page 154). Lift chain is too long. Shorten the lift chain (see page 155).
Toilet overflows.	Clog in the toilet.	Unclog toilet (see page 154).
Toilet empties slowly.	Water level in tank is too low.	Adjust the water level (see page 154). Flush holes or siphon hole is clogged. Unblock holes by inserting a short piece of coat-hanger wire carefully (to protect porcelain). Turn wire to loosen mineral deposits or waste buildup.
Water won't stop running.	Handle is stuck.	Loosen the handle.
	Lift chain is tangled.	Adjust the lift chain.
	Float ball leaks.	Replace the float ball.
	Ballcock is broken.	Replace the ballcock assembly (see page 156).
Tank or bowl leaks.	Tank nuts are loose or water-connections are loose.	Tighten nuts on bolts connecting tank to bowl supply and on water-supply line.
	Tank or bowl is cracked.	Have replacement parts installed.
	Water is leaking around the bottom of the bowl.	Replace the wax ring (see page 154).
Water drops are on tank.	Condensation.	Insulate the tank.
Handle sticks or is loose.	Lift chain is twisted.	Adjust the lift chain.
	Locknut holding handle to bowl is loose.	Tighten the locknut.
	Handle needs cleaning.	Remove the handle assembly and clean it.
Toilet is noisy.	Flush valve leaks.	Clean mineral deposits and sediment with fine steel wool on a brass valve, or a plastic scouring pad on a plastic valve.
	Ballcock is broken.	Replace the ballcock assembly (see page 156).
	Refill tube is misaligned.	Adjust tube so that it empties into the overflow tube.

UNCLOGGING A SHOWERHEAD

Mineral deposits in hard water can clog showerheads over time, cutting down on the flow of water.

1. Remove the showerhead from the shower arm. Use an adjustable wrench or a small pipe wrench, wrapped with electrical or masking tape to protect the showerhead's finish.

2. Some showerheads are one-piece units; others can be disassembled. Remove any screws on the showerhead, then take apart as many parts as you can, making a drawing of the order they go in. Soak all of the parts in a solution of vinegar and water for several hours. Use a toothpick or pin to clean out the holes. Run water backwards through the head. Reassemble. Wrap a couple of layers of plumber's Teflon tape around the threads on the shower arm, then screw the cleaned showerhead back on. Tighten the joint carefully.

Adjusting a pop-up stopper

Most bathroom sinks have a pop-up stopper. If your sink won't hold water, or if the stopper will not lift up high enough, you need to adjust it. A horizontal pivot rod is attached to a vertical flat rod with holes, called a clevis, which is attached to a vertical lift rod by a set screw. Adjust the stopper by loosening the set screw and sliding the clevis up (to lower the stopper) or down (to raise it). When you have found the right position, tighten the set screw. If the stopper doesn't seem to travel up and down far enough, reposition the pivot rod on the clevis.

TUBS AND SHOWERS

Some tub and shower repairs are quite simple. Unclogging a tub drain, for example, is similar to unclogging a toilet or sink, and replacing a showerhead is essentially a matter of unscrewing the old and screwing on the new.

Unclogging a tub with an auger

If the tub is clogged, first try a plunger on the drain. If that doesn't work, remove the cover plate on the overflow hole and pull out the stopper assembly. Feed an auger through the overflow opening. After the clog is removed, let water run down the drain for several minutes. Replace the stopper assembly and cover plate. If the clog persists, call for professional routing of the pipes.

Replacing a showerhead

A new showerhead may provide you with a better shower while reducing hot-water consumption. The newer showerheads are designed to use less water, and some have a built-in shutoff valve that can help cut hot-water bills even further. Look for models with adjustable pulsating features and anti-scalding capacity, assuring that you won't get burned in the shower. If unscrewing the old showerhead is difficult, apply penetrating spray and let it sit for several hours. Use a tape-covered wrench or pliers to protect the finish, and install the new showerhead following the manufacturer's directions.

CHOOSING FAUCETS

Home centers and plumbing suppliers carry many different faucets. Here are two shopping tips:

◆ **Brass is better.** The color and finish on the outside may vary, but the best faucets have solid brass on the inside. Solid brass is especially durable and corrosion-resistant. The finish is decorative only. Most faucets have a chrome surface. Chrome plating is an inexpensive process that produces a shiny and durable finish. But chrome can be applied over plastic as well as over solid brass. Read the product literature carefully so you know what you are buying.

◆ **Choose a well-respected brand.** Older faucets are compression valve types, with rubber washers that must be replaced from time to time. Faucets with cartridge, ball, and ceramic-disk valves are called washerless but still have parts that periodically need to be repaired or replaced. If they are made by a well-known manufacturer, you will be able to find repair parts easily.

REPAIRING A FAUCET

Most faucet valves can be repaired by a householder armed with the right tools.

Getting the right parts

There are essentially four types of faucets, each with many variations, resulting in literally dozens of slightly different parts, such as washers and rings, for each model.

The only way to be sure that you have the correct replacement part is to take apart the faucet, remove the worn or broken item, and take it to the hardware or plumbing-supply store to make a match. Sometimes you'll need to use special tools to disassemble the faucet (see page 163).

Tub and shower faucets

The operating parts of a tub faucet are similar to those in a sink faucet, and the repairs are the same. Shower and tub faucet valves look different from sink valves because they are horizontal and often larger. You may have to shut off the water to the whole house before working on a shower or tub valve, because there will probably be no nearby stop valve. In some tub faucets, the working parts are recessed behind the tile; to repair the faucet, you may have to break the tile to reach them. You may want a professional to do this job.

On an older, compression-type shower valve, the problem is often with the seat—the ringlike metal piece that the stem's washer pushes up against. If washers wear out quickly, the seat probably needs to be replaced. Use a seat wrench (a standard tool that can be found at most hardware stores and home centers) to remove it. Take the seat with you to buy a replacement.

Keeping the aerator clean

If water pressure from a faucet is low, or if water squirts out erratically, first check the aerator, the cylindrical piece at the end of the spout. Wrap tape around it and unscrew it with pliers. Take the small pieces apart and clean them, especially the screen. Or you can replace the aerator with a new one.

Working gently with old parts

When taking apart a faucet, always wrap the ends of pliers and wrenches with tape to avoid scratching the faucet's finish. Due to mineral deposits or corrosion, some parts may be difficult to remove. Don't force anything. Instead, apply penetrating spray and allow it to sit for a couple of hours before trying again to remove the parts.

Beginning a faucet repair

Before you begin a repair job, turn off the water supply to the fixture by closing the shutoff valves. Open the faucets to drain the line. Close the drain stopper to prevent small parts like screws or washers from falling down the drain, and line the sink with a towel or rag to protect it from scratches.

As you disassemble the faucet, lay the parts down on a flat surface in the order in which you removed them. Examine each part carefully, replacing those that show signs of wear. Clean all the parts before reassembling.

How a compression faucet works

Regardless of the design, all types of compression faucets work basically the same way. When the handle is turned to shut off the water, the stem moves into the valve seat. A seat washer or diaphragm keeps the water from flowing. Turning the faucet on loosens the valve-seat seal, allowing water to flow. On the handle end, the stem is sealed with an O-ring or packing to prevent water from seeping out at the handle.

If the spout drips, it is probably because the seat washer is worn out or the valve seat is damaged. If water leaks out of the handle, the O-ring (or the packing) needs to be replaced.

Repairing washerless faucets

All washerless faucets work in a similar way. When you move the handle, a ball, a ceramic disc, or a cartridge moves, opening a channel through which the water flows. Moving the handle back closes the channel, stopping the flow of water. Washerless does not mean that the faucet will not drip or leak; O-rings, valve seats, and other parts can wear out just like washers. When you have disassembled the faucet, take the worn parts to the hardware store to get an exact duplicate.

REPAIRING PIPES

Supply pipes, which carry water to the fixtures, may be made of copper, galvanized steel (silver in color), or plastic. Drain pipes are thicker and are made of galvanized steel, plastic, or, in older homes, cast iron. Steel pipes usually cause the most problems.

Recognizing pipe leaks

Water dripping onto a ceiling under a bathroom may only mean you need to caulk around the tub and keep water off the bathroom floor. If the leak persists, however, you may need a plumber.

When a basement water pipe drips along the length, the moisture is probably due to condensation rather than a leak. Wrap it with foam insulation.

A drip in one place usually indicates a tiny hole or crack in a pipe. Fix any leak as soon as you find it, because it will only get bigger with time. Shut off water to the pipe. Tighten a pipe repair clamp and rubber sleeve over the hole (right). This is only a temporary solution. Have a plumber replace the pipe. With steel pipes, a leak can mean that

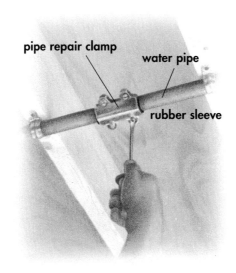

pipe repair clamp

water pipe

rubber sleeve

the pipes are badly rusted and more leaks are inevitable. Let a plumber evaluate the pipes.

To temporarily repair a leak at a pipe joint, use plumber's epoxy. Wear rubber gloves to mix the two epoxy components together and apply the mixture to the joint.

Frozen pipes

Prevent pipes from freezing in winter by cutting off water to outside spigots and leaving the taps open. Wrap exposed pipes in a crawl space or unheated basement with foam insulation or electric pipe tape.

If a pipe freezes, turn off water to the affected area and open the nearest faucet. Use a hair dryer to thaw it out, working from the open end of the pipe back to the frozen part. Keep the hair dryer moving and never let the pipe get warmer than your hand can touch.

REPAIRING A COMPRESSION FAUCET

To begin a repair, turn off the water to the faucet, open the spout to drain, and close the drain. Remove the handles. This is usually done by prying off a cap to get to a screw or fastener. Use a screwdriver or pocket knife to pry off the cap. Some compression faucets have a diaphragm rather than a seat washer; it is replaced the same way as the washer.

screwdriver

adjustable wrench

seat washer

1. With the cap off, use a screwdriver (typically a Phillips-head) to remove the screw that holds the handle to the stem's top. Lift off the handle.

2. Remove the locknut with an adjustable wrench by turning it counterclockwise. Pull up stem assembly by hand (you may need to turn it counterclockwise).

3. Remove worn seat washer by unscrewing the screw that holds it. Install new washer. Reassemble stem, put it back into valve seat, and tighten locknut. Replace handle.

REPAIRING A CERAMIC-DISK FAUCET

Before starting a repair, turn off the water to the faucet, open the spout to drain, and close the drain. Most leaks in a ceramic faucet can be repaired by cleaning the bottom of the disk cylinder and replacing three flexible washers, called inlet seals. If the faucet continues to leak after these repairs, replace the disk cylinder.

1. To begin, pry off the decorative cap at the base of the lever, using a pocket knife or screwdriver, to gently lift it all around its base. Take care not to scrape the finish as you work.

2. Remove the screw that holds the handle in place with a screwdriver. Once the screw is removed, pull straight up on the handle.

cowling

3. Twisting counterclockwise to loosen it, remove the cowling from the faucet base. If the cowling is stubborn, use taped pliers to get the turn started.

nylon retaining ring

4. Remove the nylon retaining ring with tongue-and-groove pliers, turning it counterclockwise. Note the position of the switchlike tab that protrudes from the cartridge.

washer

5. Gently pull the cartridge up and out. Take this piece to the store to buy replacement washers. If the bottom of the cartridge is encrusted with mineral deposits, scrub it clean with a synthetic scouring pad.

tab

6. Replace the cartridge, aligning it with the tab in its original position. (If the position is not correct, the lever will go on backwards.) Reverse the steps to reassemble.

REPAIRING A ROTATING-BALL FAUCET

Before starting a repair, turn off water to the faucet, open the spout to drain, and close the drain. To stop drips from the spout, replace the inlet seals and springs in the valve seat with duplicates. To stop drips from the base, replace the O-rings at the top and base of the faucet body or replace the whole ball assembly.

1. Pry out the decorative piece at the handle base. Use a hex wrench to remove the nut that holds the handle in place. (Most faucets came with the proper size wrench.)

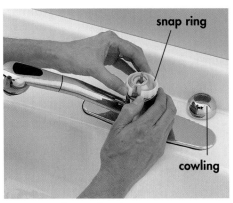

2. Remove the cowling by twisting it counterclockwise by hand. Remove the nylon snap ring by parting its opening and lifting it off the faucet base.

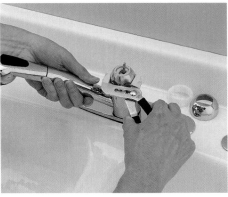

3. Use groove-joint pliers to carefully remove the cam that holds the ball in place. Turn the cam counterclockwise.

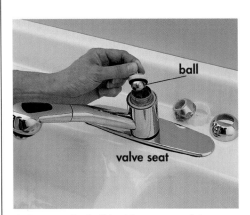

4. Remove the ball by lifting it out of the valve seat. As you do so, look for a positioning groove in the ball. To replace the ball, this groove must fit on a tab protruding from the valve seat housing.

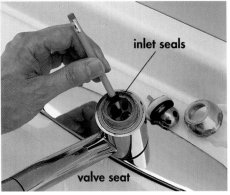

5. Remove the inlet seal (black flexible washers). Push a blunt pencil into a seal to grasp it, or use a needlenose pliers to pull it out. Take inlet seals to a home store to buy replacements. Install them in valve seat.

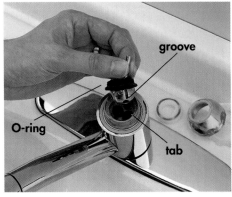

6. To reinstall the ball, line up the groove with the tab in the valve seat housing. If the O-ring at the top of the faucet body is worn, replace it. Reverse the other steps to complete reassembly of the faucet.

REPAIRING A CARTRIDGE FAUCET

Before starting a repair, turn off water to faucet, open the spout to drain, and close the drain. Most drips in a cartridge faucet are caused by a worn cartridge. In the faucet shown below, a special tool is needed to remove the cartridge. Some cartridges can be lifted out with pliers. Take the old cartridge with you to buy a duplicate. To stop leaks at the faucet base, replace the O-rings at the top and bottom of the cartridge housing.

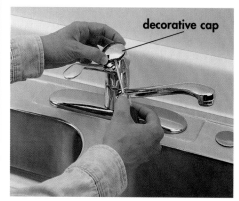

1. Pry off the decorative cap with a screwdriver or pocket knife. You may also have to remove a plastic piece that indicates the direction for rotating the lever to get hot or cold water.

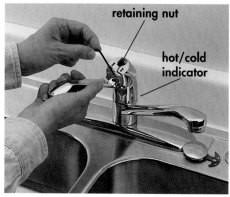

2. Use a hex wrench to remove the retaining nut that holds the handle in place. As you remove the handle, note the position of the clip beneath.

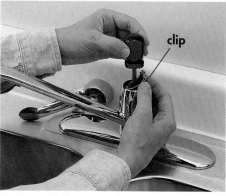

3. Use a Phillips screwdriver to remove the screw that holds the handle clip to the top of the cartridge. Pull out the clip.

4. Holding the faucet spout, remove the cowling from the faucet body by twisting it off counterclockwise.

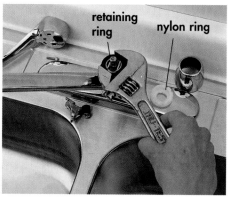

5. Remove the nylon ring beneath the cowling. With a large adjustable wrench, remove the retaining ring.

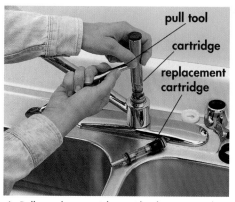

6. Pull out the cartridge with pliers or, in this case, with a special pull tool provided by the manufacturer. Drop in the new cartridge and reassemble faucet.

5

Home
Furnishings

Furniture

AREA RUGS

*A beautiful area rug placed just inside the front door will say "Welcome"
to guests as they enter. To keep their cozy manners and good looks,
area rugs need some care and attention.*

Area rugs can set a room's design style, define a conversation area, organize the flow of traffic, and much more. Their varied designs and colors give them almost limitless decorating possibilities. And, because they are movable, area rugs are easy to maintain. Some area rugs are even reversible for longer wear.

CHOOSING A RUG

Area rugs once were those less than 9 x 12 feet; anything larger was considered carpeting, whether or not it was tacked down. Definitions have softened so that area rugs now can be any size from a fireplace mat to a hall runner or a full room rug.

You can buy area rugs at department and home stores, home improvement centers, specialty and antique shops, at auction houses, and even through mail-order catalogs. Craft fairs often feature designers who weave, paint, knit, hook, crochet, braid, or needlepoint hand- and custom-made area rugs. And, if you know any of these crafts, you can make your own.

Rug considerations

Decisions in buying area rugs revolve around what you need, what you like, and what you can afford. Often the deciding factor, outside of price, is the design, not the type of rug or its upkeep. Be a little bit practical when choosing a rug. If the area rug is to be used in front of the kitchen sink, easy cleaning and cushioning comfort are key features to look for. A machine-washable rug, such as a cotton rag or nylon braid, would be ideal for this location. Save the "must have" silk rug for a low-traffic, low-upkeep area, like beside the bed or in the guest room.

While most of the fiber and construction choices available in carpeting (see page 16) are also available in rugs, rugs offer other options as well. Silk, for example, is usually reserved for hand-knotted Oriental rugs, and hand-painted canvas floor cloths are only available as area rugs.

The types of rugs

Most often it is the construction of an area rug that establishes its formality or informality. Rag, hooked, and braided rugs are considered informal and casual, perfect for country settings. On the opposite end, Aubusson and Oriental rugs generally appear in formal rooms with period furniture.

Needlepoint, Dhurrie, and Khilim rugs span the middle. There are always exceptions to rules. If you have a good eye for design and color—or an interior designer to help you—you can use area rugs in an eclectic manner, gracefully mixing rug and furniture styles to create a comfortable ambiance.

Here are some of the most popular types of area rugs.

◆ **Aubusson:** A flat tapestry pile made from a fine yarn, the original French style is characterized by a central medallion in the field with a wide border repeating some center details.

◆ **Braided:** Three fabric strips, with cut edges folded in by hand or machine, are braided; then the braids are stitched together in rounds, ovals, or straight rows to make these casual reversible rugs.

◆ **Dhurrie:** Hand-woven in India of colorful wool or cotton yarns that cover the cotton warp in a tapestry weave, these reversible rugs have soft colors and varied designs.

◆ **Hooked:** This rug is made with heavy yarn or a strip of fabric pulled through a mesh by a hook or needle to form a looped pile. Hooked rugs can be hand- or machine-made.

◆ **Khilim:** A style of Oriental rug, Khilims are hand-woven in Turkey, Iran, Turkestan, and some Balkan states with heavy, twisted wool yarn in a split tapestry weave that is reversible.

◆ **Oriental:** Any handmade or hand-knotted rug made in Turkey, Central Asia, India, or China is an Oriental rug.

The many styles are named for their regions or their makers. Machine-made reproductions at popular prices are available in many styles.

◆ **Needlepoint:** Tiny diagonal stitches are handmade across the threads of an even-weave canvas with wool yarn. An 18th-century art form, needlepoint rugs are often made in floral or geometric patterns.

◆ **Rag:** Torn strips of fabric with the edges visible or concealed are either woven, crocheted, or knitted to make rag rugs. Colors usually run randomly throughout this type of rug, and it is reversible.

Judging size and arrangement

In its friendliest, most congenial presentation, an area rug fits under the front and back legs of the furniture in its focal area. At the very least, the rug should fit under the front legs of all the pieces in the area. If you have no choice but to use a small area rug within a large space, then lay it at an angle to some furniture pieces to make it appear larger and more important.

When an area rug is placed only under one piece of furniture, it gives power to that piece. This can be helpful when you want to call attention to an heirloom table in a hallway, but not very gracious if you want equality within a conversation area.

The area rug in a dining room should extend well beyond the table on all sides, so that chairs remain on the rug when they are pulled out for seating. You don't want people half on and half off the rug during dinner.

REALITY CHECK

DON'T BEAT YOUR RUGS

People used to clean rugs by hanging them on a line and beating them—they even had special rug-beating tools. The great clouds of dust produced gave the impression that a lot of cleaning was going on. In fact, beating a rug can tear it apart. Braided rugs are particularly vulnerable. At most, give a lightweight rug a good shaking to start the cleaning process. The best way to clean is to vacuum and shampoo.

Rug pads and liners

Walking across an area rug laid against bare flooring will abrade or break yarns on the back of the rug. To protect your rugs, always use padding or a liner between the rug and the floor. Cut the material 1 to 2 inches smaller than the area rug to make sure the rug will conceal the edge of any underlayment.

Padding protects the rug by giving cushioning underfoot. Made of felted natural or synthetic fibers, it comes in thicknesses from $\frac{1}{4}$ to $\frac{3}{8}$ inch.

◆ **Jute and hair padding,** natural or synthetic, is used for large area rugs when furniture is arranged on top.

◆ **Rubberized jute and hair padding,** natural or synthetic, has a backing on each side and is used for area rugs about 6 x 9 feet or smaller. The rubberized finish with a waffle texture on both sides adds a non-skid feature.

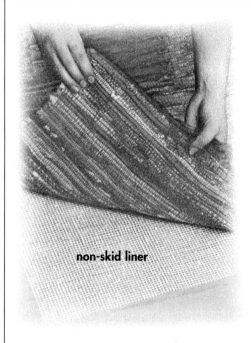

non-skid liner

Liners protect and add a non-skid quality. They are about ⅛-inch thick except for the paper-thin double-stick variety. Thick liners can add a bit of cushioning comfort.

◆ **Rubber open-mesh liners** are used under small- to medium-size rugs and runners. This type of liner is especially good with reversible rugs.

◆ **Thin double-stick plastic liners** are used to secure small- and medium-sized area rugs to bare floors or wall-to-wall carpeting. A peel-away plastic film protects each sticky surface until you adhere one side to the back of the rug and the other to the floor or carpet. The adhesive doesn't harm fibers as household tapes would. Once the tape is down, the rug will be well stuck so there will be no need to lift or move the rug during regular vacuuming.

REGULAR MAINTENANCE OF AREA RUGS

Since all rugs, including carpets, wear out from the bottom, regular maintenance is important. Grit and sand settle at the base of loop and pile constructions (see page 15) or lodge between the yarns of flat tapestry weaves, cutting fibers and wearing out the rug. So, to improve the life of your rugs, vacuum often.

The type of regular maintenance and the equipment you use is governed primarily by the rug's construction. Some maintenance and repairs for area rugs are the same as for carpets (pp.31–33). All hand-made rugs, whether antique or new, deserve and need tender care. While most can be vacuumed, rag rugs and bathroom throw rugs can be washed by machine.

When you buy a new rug, be sure to save any tags with care instructions and receipts with guarantees. Discuss both at the store. If you receive a quality rug as a gift and it has no care tag, consult a professional before proceeding beyond vacuuming. Antique rug dealers, dry cleaners, and specialty stores can be helpful resources.

Vacuuming area rugs

It takes time to vacuum well (pp.21, 23). A quick once-over only removes surface dirt and dust, so move the vacuum slowly, and revacuum each area.

◆ **The tank/canister type of vacuum cleaner** may be the best choice for most area rugs. Small, or lightweight rugs may not respond well to the agitator or beater action of an upright vacuum; its suction can be too strong, causing eventual distortion in the weave.

◆ **Area rugs** made from or in the same construction as wall-to-wall carpeting are best cleaned using an upright vacuum cleaner.

◆ **Vacuum fringes** with a hand-held dust or upholstery attachment on an upright, or use a canister or other hand-held vacuum cleaner (below).

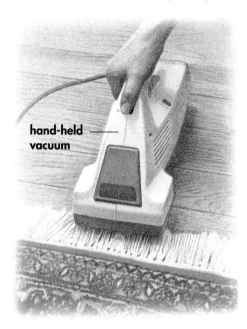

hand-held vacuum

Vacuuming hand-knotted rugs

Orientals and other hand-knotted rugs should be vacuumed only in one direction, "following the nap," so the yarns always lie flat. This technique puts less stress on hand-tied knots.

Shampooing, washing, and drying

As a general rule, shampooing is not recommended unless the area rug has the same construction as wall-to-wall carpet. Washable area rugs include hand-woven, braided, and rag rugs in cotton, cotton blends, or synthetic yarns and fabrics, as well as factory-made rugs designed for kitchen and bath use. If, however, a "washable" rug is also a valuable antique, professional dry cleaning by hand or machine is easier on the rug.

When a rug can be safely washed at home, you have two choices for drying it. One option is to machine dry it on a cool to warm setting. Remove the rug from the dryer before it is completely dry, block it by hand into its original shape, and lay it flat to finish drying. This will prevent the rug from curling at the corners or buckling. The alternative is to air-dry the rug flat on a drop cloth or clean beach towels. If you air-dry outdoors, be sure to do so in the shade. Except for commercial terry-type rugs, avoid the clothesline; the weight of the wet rug can cause creases and distortions of the weave.

Caring for sisal and similar rugs

Sisal, sisal hemp, and grass fiber rugs are popular both indoors and outdoors. They are often used on the front stoop because they are not damaged by water. Only two versions should not be washed, those finished with a non-skid backing, which can shrink, and those bound with a fabric tape, which also can draw up.

Dirt and dust are easily vacuumed away. If washing is required, do it outside with a brush dipped in soapy water. Rinse thoroughly with a hose.

Pin the rug to a clothesline for drying. Dry completely before putting the rug back in place.

Caring for floor cloths

Hand-painted canvas floor cloths are easy to care for. Newly made ones will most likely be painted with acrylic or latex paints and finished with several coats of polyurethane. A damp mop or sponge will quickly clean the surface. If you own an antique floor cloth, however, avoid water and clean with a dry dust mop or the dust attachment on a vacuum cleaner (the finish is likely a varnish incompatible with water).

Periodic maintenance and repair

At least twice a year, and more often for rugs in heavy traffic areas, vacuum the padding or liner and the bare floor underneath an area rug. This will remove any grit and sand which has worked its way through the back of the rug. One exception is the double-stick liner. While it and the rug can be removed and repositioned on the floor or carpet, the liner should be replaced when its tacking power is too diminished to hold.

Other regular maintenance should include the following.

◆ **Rotate and reverse rugs.** Area rugs, especially those larger than 3 x 5 feet, can experience wear within traffic paths. Periodically rotating and/or reversing rugs can prolong their life by dispersing the wear. With your semi-annual cleaning of the floor and padding under the rug, rotate the rug 180 degrees, if the design allows. Occa-

sionally, a one-way design such as a basket of flowers, cannot be rotated attractively. If a rug is reversible, flip it.

◆ **Area rugs in high-traffic areas** should be professionally cleaned about once a year. Send out those in low-traffic areas every two to three years.

◆ **If the fringe on a rug becomes untied or loose,** retie it with a slip knot. When fringe reduces in length to an inch or less, have it restored.

Storing area rugs

Before storing any area rug, make sure it is clean. Roll the rug up (pile or loop side out), following the direction of the nap. Wrap a clean cotton sheet or washed muslin around the rolled rug. Plastic wraps keep fibers from "breathing" and cause mildew and mold. Use cord to tie the rug in several places. Store the rug in a moderately cool, dry place, about 40° to 60°F. If you are having the rug stored by professionals, see that they follow these guidelines.

BLINDS, SHADES, CURTAINS, AND DRAPERIES

*Dress your windows to complement the style of your home
and to allow for the sunlight and privacy you need.
Then learn to keep them clean and operating smoothly.*

indow treatments can be a calm backdrop for colorful furnishings or a bold design statement behind simple furniture. Look through home magazines and books and visit designer showcase houses, museums, and store showrooms to get ideas before you shop.

Many department and home specialty stores offer "shop-at-home" services that send a professional with samples to your place. It's a good idea first to visit the store to make sure its inventory fits your taste and budget. Ask whether there is a charge for the service if you don't end up buying anything and whether you can cancel your order if you change your mind. If you are handy with a sewing machine, a drill, and a screwdriver, consider making your own window treatments.

MEASURING WINDOW TREATMENTS

If you are custom-ordering window treatments, the company will also do the measuring. If you plan to install and/or make window treatments yourself, then you will take the measurements. Different types and styles call for measuring different parts of the window. For commercial blinds and

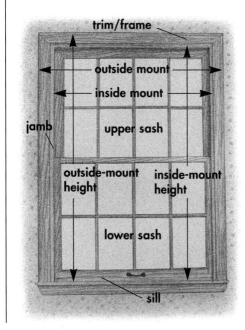

trim/frame

outside mount

inside mount

jamb

upper sash

outside-mount height

inside-mount height

lower sash

sill

shades that you will install, take your window measurements to the store and have them select the needed sizes.

For fabric window treatments you'll make yourself, install the rods first and then take measurements. If you are using a coordinating blind or shade that has an outside mount, install the blind or shade before you measure.

BLINDS

Blinds are commercially made window coverings that can have either vertical or horizontal slats, have an accordion or honeycomb construction, or are woven from natural or synthetic reeds. In one style, slats are sandwiched between two sheer fabric layers that diffuse light when the slats are open; in yet another style, slats are laminated vertically to a single fabric layer for a curtain effect.

The mechanisms for opening and closing blinds range from simple cords and easy-to-operate continuous chains to remote-controlled electronic devices.

Measuring and installing blinds

For an "inside mount," measure the width inside the frame from jamb to jamb; measure the length from the top of the upper sash to the bottom of the lower sash. For an "outside mount," include the left and right frame sides in the width, and the frame top to sill for the length. Usually installation will be within the window's frame unless the window style does not allow it or unless enough darkness cannot be achieved.

Installation is ideally a four-handed job; one person holds the raised blind, the other uses a level to arrange the blind straight and then marks the holes. For an inside mount, mark the brackets inside the window frame; for an outside mount, on top. Separate the blind from the brackets. Pre-drill small holes for the screws and then screw the brackets in place. Slide the blind into the brackets. Hold a continuous pull-chain bracket downward until tight; mark the holes and then screw it to the jamb.

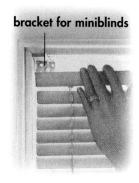

bracket for miniblinds

Washing blinds

Subject to dust and often rain, blinds need thorough cleaning once a year.

◆ **Aluminum and vinyl blinds** of a manageable size can be taken down and washed in the bathtub. Mix a mild

---

OPTIONS FOR BLINDS

Blinds are available in a wide variety of stock sizes and colors, plus unlimited custom sizes and styles. These allow you to control the direction and amount of natural light while providing some small degree of insulation. Some blind styles will adjust to allow a breeze to flow from the window into the room by tilting or raising the slats.

Horizontal blinds. Venetian blinds have 2-inch-wide wood, aluminum, or vinyl horizontal slats; miniblinds are 1 inch wide. Visible cloth tape or cord on the left and right sides, plus strings running through the blinds, are of a matching or customized color.

Vertical blinds. These vertical slats of vinyl, aluminum, wood, non-woven fabric, or laminated (also custom) fabric measure 3 to 4 inches wide. They draw completely to one side and are a good choice for sliding glass doors and large plate-glass windows.

Accordion or honeycomb blinds. Accordion blinds are connected to horizontal slats 1 inch wide or more; the honeycomb style has two or more such layers connected. Both are available in non-woven fabrics in various colors and thicknesses.

Roll-up blinds. Natural-fiber reeds from grasses or bamboo, or synthetics like vinyl, are laid horizontally and woven together to produce a semitransparent blind that rolls up from the bottom. They are inexpensive sunblockers on a porch or in a sunroom.

detergent with water, and scrub blinds with a sponge. Once clean, rinse them with water. Let them dry thoroughly, partially drawn up and flat in the tub, before reinstalling. You can speed up the drying time with a hair dryer. If you prefer, you can do the whole job outdoors on a plastic drop cloth, turning the blinds as needed. Rinse with a hose and hang on a clothesline to dry.

◆ **Wood blinds** will warp if they are exposed to too much water. They can, however, be washed while hanging in place at the window. Dampen a blind

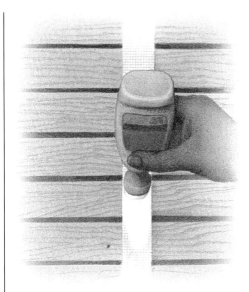

duster, a pair of absorbent gloves, or a lint-free rag with a mild detergent or an oil-based soap solution and carefully wash each side of each slat. Rinse using the same tool soaked in clear water. For each of these steps you will need to rinse out the tool often. Finish by drying the slats with a dry, lint-free cloth.

◆ **Accordion and honeycomb blinds** made of non-woven fabrics are easy to wash using the same method described for aluminum and vinyl blinds (p.171). Allow them to air-dry.

◆ **Laminated blinds** should first be vacuumed with a dusting attachment. For deeper cleaning, try an upholstery cleaner. Test the cleaner on an inconspicuous part of the blind first.

Repairing blinds

Given the variety of styles and manufacturers, your best guide to making a repair is to study a similar blind. For example, by comparing it to another blind, you can see how to retie a loose venetian blind cord that holds a slat. Shorten a venetian blind by following the manufacturer's directions.

◆ **Controls:** There is such a variety of pulley mechanisms for blinds that it may be safer to rely on a professional to repair a nonfunctioning one, especially if electronics are involved. Your warranty may cover the problem; contact the store where you bought the blind.

◆ **Dirty tapes:** To touch up small smudges or spots on white venetian blind tapes, lower the blind completely and apply a small amount of liquid white shoe polish—just enough to

touch up the spot (above). Allow the polish to dry before raising the blind.

◆ **Unbalanced blinds:** Occasionally a blind becomes skewed, causing it to lower or raise at an angle. To correct this, lower or raise the blind completely and then raise or lower it into position again. Repeat if needed.

SHADES

The unassuming roller shade can range widely in price depending on the materials used. Paper, vinyl, and sized (stiffened) or laminated fabric are just a few of the choices. Some shades have perforated surfaces, which allow in some light but block out harmful ultraviolet sun rays. Others have a laminated "black-out" backing, great for curbing the early morning sunrise for people who need to sleep in the daytime.

If you plan to use any shade as the single window treatment, consider one

VENETIAN BLIND– DUSTING BRUSH

◆ **The quickest way** to clean venetian blinds is to use a tool made especially for the job. The wooly cleaning portion of the brush is especially slotted to accommodate cleaning the top and bottom of the slat simultaneously. Lower the blind, open the slats, spray the brush with a dusting spray (if appropriate for the blind material), and slide the brush across the slat sections.

◆ **Use absorbent cotton gloves** and your fingers to substitute for the slotted tool.

with a matching valance that covers the top roll. Or, select a reverse-roll model, where the roll faces back.

Measuring and installing shades

Roller shades are easy to measure and install yourself, just like blinds (see page 171). If these jobs come with the purchase price of the shades, however, have the professional do it to secure your warranty. The Roman shade is measured the same way as other shades but installed quite differently. The top fabric edge is stapled onto a 1 x 2-inch board cut ½ inch narrower than the shade's width. Elbow brackets screw into the bottom of the board and to the window jamb or to the top face of the window frame for an outside mount.

Cleaning shades

Consult the recommendations of the manufacturer for cleaning roller and fabricated shades.

◆ **Sewn fabric shades:** When the face and lining fabrics are both washable, you can unmount the shade from the mounting board, wash and iron it according to the fabric's requirements, and re-install the shade.

◆ **Laminated shades:** Most laminated fabric roller shades are not washable. Clean them by vacuuming with the dusting attachment.

◆ **Non-washable shades:** Try removing small spots with an art-gum eraser or kneadable wallpaper cleaner.

◆ **Vinyl shades:** Vinyl roller shades are easy to wash. After removing a shade from the brackets, unroll it on a flat

OPTIONS FOR SHADES

Today's shades come in a wide variety of options, ranging from no-nonsense roller models to romantic balloon shades. All shades provide varying degrees of privacy and light control; pleated shades are the most energy-efficient. Bottom-up shades allow you to adjust for privacy while still letting the sun shine in.

Roller shade. Offered in many colors, textures, and materials, roller shades have several roll-up options.

Roman shade. Usually made in a decorator fabric and lined, a Roman shade draws up into neat overlapping folds.

Bottom-up shade. Offered in flat roller or accordion-pleated models, this shade pulls or rolls up from the bottom.

Balloon shade. Made of decorator fabrics, sheers, and solids, a balloon shade pulls up into scalloped poufs.

surface covered with a plastic drop cloth. Weight the ends to keep it flat, if necessary. Using a sponge with a mild detergent solution, start at the top and wash in rows down to the bottom. Turn over the shade and wash the reverse side. Then rinse each side with a sponge dampened in clean water. Towel off the drop cloth between each step to keep the work surface clean.

Weighting a roller shade

Occasionally the bottom hem of a roller shade with a lightweight wood slat inside will curl. To correct this, add a strip or two of bead drapery weights inside the hem. Bead weights are sold by the yard at sewing centers.

Adjusting tension

A weak spring can cause a shade to roll too slowly, or a too-tight spring can make it snap up at the slightest provocation—problems that are easily fixed.

◆ **To tighten tension,** partially unroll the shade and remove from brackets. Roll it up by hand, then reinstall it.

◆ **To reduce tension,** roll the shade up completely and remove from the brackets. Unroll it halfway, then replace the shade in its brackets.

Do-it-yourself shades

Home decorating and sewing centers sell kits with everything you need but the fabric to make a custom window shade. Select a lightweight fabric, such as cotton, cotton blend, or linen, that can take a hot iron setting, which you will need for bonding the fabric to the shade. Follow manufacturer's directions

to laminate your fabric to the non-woven base. Some shade-resurfacing kits use spray adhesive to bond the fabric to the base (above).

CURTAINS AND DRAPERIES

Decorators use a special vocabulary to talk about window treatments. Curtains are "unlined vertical elements," draperies are "lined vertical elements," valances are "soft horizontal top elements," and cornices are "rigid horizontal top elements upholstered on a board." A complete window treatment includes one, two, or three of

INSTALLING A ROLLER SHADE

This is an easy job that you can do yourself, but it goes more quickly—and accurately—with two people to position and install the brackets.

1. Slip the brackets onto the raised shade. Hold all the pieces temporarily where you want them mounted—inside or outside the window. While one person holds the shade in place, a second person uses a level to position it straight and marks the location of the screw or nail holes in the brackets on the window jamb (or frame).

2. Take down the shade. Remove the brackets. Hold each bracket over its marked holes on the window jamb or frame and install it with the nails provided. (If the installation surface is metal, use screws instead. If it is drywall, use screws with screw anchors, even if they were not provided with the shade.)

3. Insert the roller shade into the installed brackets, and test it for proper tension. Pull it up and down a few times to make sure it works properly. Adjust the tension as needed (see page 173).

these elements plus a blind or a shade.

If you have standard-sized windows, you can buy all of the elements of a window treatment ready-made in simple, usually solid-color fabrics. If you want more pizzazz or to coordinate your draperies with some of your upholstery, you will need custom-made service from a department or speciality store.

If you have a sewing machine, you can easily make tab and café curtains or soft valances yourself, either with your own design or using one of the many patterns available. A pattern will give you complete instructions. Pleating tape is also available; this works with special hardware to make pleated drapes with a minimum of sewing.

CURTAIN, DRAPERY, AND SOFT VALANCE STYLES

Curtains diffuse light and give privacy. Draperies dress up windows or offer privacy, darkness, and insulation. Traditional lengths for both are to the top of the window sill, to the bottom of the apron, or to the floor. Both can be stationary or can be designed to open and close on a traverse rod. The styles are varied (see below). Soft valances can stand alone as a simple window dressing or add a finishing touch to curtains and draperies. Some valances have a board mount; others are casually draped over the curtain rod.

Café curtain
Each of two tiers hangs from its own café rod by rings or a casing formed in the top of the panels. The bottom tier covers the lower sash. The top tier is about ⅓ the height of the upper sash.

Priscilla curtains
Ruffles are the characteristic feature of this curtain. Usually ruffles appear on top, hem, and center edges but can also be on outside edges. A ruffled tie-back completes this curtain style.

Knotted, tied, or pouffed valance
Fabric sewn like a long rectangular scarf—in one or two layers— is draped as desired over the window, then knotted, tied, or pouffed at the corners before draping downward.

Swag and jabot
This treatment has three parts: A swag across the top of the window and a jabot (the ornamental folds) at each side. The contrasting lining emphasizes the angled jabot hemline.

Tab curtains
These panels hang from decorative rods by fabric or ribbon loops or two ties joined to form loops with bows or knots at the top. Muslin is a traditional fabric favorite for this window fashion.

Pinch-pleated draperies
Pleats formed at regular intervals across the tops of the panels form the fullness. The pleats can be of many styles. The draperies can hang from visible or concealed rods.

Side panels with a valance
A valance, often similar to the top tier of a café curtain, remains fixed. Side panels can be lined or not, fixed at the sides, or constructed to draw across the window for privacy.

Selecting fabrics and linings

Most of the fabrics used for window treatments (below) are 54 inches wide. Sheers and laces, however, come in much greater widths that range up to 180 inches, making full, seamless curtains possible.

The selection of fabrics is enormous, from humble muslins to opulent lamés. Light- to medium-weight fabrics are generally used for unlined curtains and soft valances. They hang gracefully and will fold well for valance treatments. Although you can use any weight for draperies, lighter-weight fabrics may need an inner lining for body or insulation. But never select heavy upholstery-weight fabric (or one with a laminated back) for a window treatment unless it is for a cornice. It will be too stiff to fall nicely. Make sure that any velvets, cut velvets, or velveteens you use are soft enough to drape the way you want.

Curtains or draperies look best when they are full and generous. When you are buying panels that you want to close, be sure that they are wide enough to overlap each other in the middle of the window. If there is a question, always go for the wider cut. If you are making your own pleated curtains or draperies, buy enough material to cover the window width one and a half times. Buy enough sheer fabric to cover the window width three times.

Installing curtain rods

If you are having window treatments made for you, the supplier will measure the windows, determine the rods you need, and install both rods and window treatments as part of the package.

To do it yourself, first decide on the style and length of window treatment elements you want. You can install the rod just above and outside the width of the window frame to give the window the illusion of being larger or to maximize available light after the draperies

---

CHOOSING CURTAIN, DRAPERY, AND VALANCE FABRICS

When choosing a window treatment fabric, you must consider whether it needs to insulate and/or block out light, be washable, or have other features besides being decorative. If the fabric you fall in love with is lighter than you need for heat or sun control, you can interline it with cotton flannel, woven 54 inches wide to fit decorative fabric widths. Handle the decorative fabric and interlining layers as one, if you are making your own. Typically, lining fabric is white or off-white cotton sateen or muslin, available with a laminated black-out surface that also adds insulation. Valance linings can also be decorative fabrics when they are designed to show.

Sheers
Solids—such as voile—laces, burn-outs (opaque motifs on a sheer ground), open-weave casement, and leno (linen) are a few of the sheer fabric choices.

Cottons
Gingham, broadcloth, chintz (a shiny glazed finish), sateen, and plissé are all popular fabric choices that are available in easy-care cotton fibers.

Brocades
These rich-looking woven fabrics come in many weights and a variety of fibers, from cotton to wool. The raised design motifs are interwoven into the fabric.

Velveteens and velvets
Velveteens are cotton napped fabrics in plain, ribbed, or sculptured cuts. Velvets are woven from shiny fibers such as rayon and nylon and can be plain or fancy.

Muslins and linings
Use only pre-shrunk muslin, in white or natural color for facings or linings. Sateens for lining are white or off-white; higher-quality sateens, in colors, are for any use.

or curtains are hung. Or you can install the rods just at the edges of the window frame to keep a trim appearance. If windows are near the ceiling, try installing the rods just below the ceiling to give the window—and the room—more height. Spring-tension rods and wooden rods with inside brackets attach to the inside of the window jambs. Follow the instructions supplied with the rods to perform the actual installation.

Do-it-yourself measuring

The finished length of a curtain or drapery depends on its style and the rod's style. Here are two examples:

◆ **Finished lengths for side panels** on a plain curtain rod: You can allow ½ to 3 inches above the rod for a heading (an optional ruffle above the rod) if you like; then add (or start with) the depth of the rod plus ½ inch of ease; add the distance from the bottom of the rod to the sill or to the bottom of the apron or to the floor minus ½ inch, so fabric will not drag on the floor.

◆ **Finished lengths for side panels** on a decorative traverse rod with rings: Measure from the bottom of the rod to one of the three length positions described above.

Cleaning curtains and draperies

If a window treatment is made of decorator fabrics and has a lining and intricate swags or folds, have it dry cleaned. Some dry cleaners will provide a take-down and reinstallation service for an additional fee. This may be worth it when your window treatment design

CURTAIN ROD OPTIONS

Plain rods Buy these rods in the size range that includes your window's width; they adjust lengthwise. A single rod holds one curtain with a casing or rod pocket at the top; a double rod holds two curtains or a curtain plus valance.

Spring-tension rods Also purchased in size ranges, in several diameters, these adjust with a spring lengthwise for a snug fit between the side window jambs. Pick a rod diameter small enough to go into the curtain's rod pocket.

Traverse rods Conventional traverse rods open pleated draperies from the center to each side; one-way-draw rods let you pull them to one side of the window. Double traverse rods let you hang and operate two pairs of curtains.

Decorative traverse rods These look like café curtain rods but operate like traverse rods. They have eyelets or rings on a track for hanging the draperies. Choose drapery pins or hooks that allow you to still see the rod.

Café curtain rods Used with rings to suspend café curtains, this rod allows you to open and close the curtains manually. You can also use this rod instead of a plain rod for curtains that have a rod pocket.

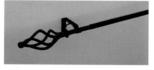

Wrought-iron rods These are decorative rods, typically mounted with brackets just above the window frame. They are ideal for softly draped toppers or tab curtains. Matching wrought-iron rings can be added.

Wooden rods With ornate or simple end pieces, wooden rods, available in various diameters, are usually mounted just above the window frame. You can open and close the curtains manually.

has special mounts or costly fabrics.

Few decorator fabrics are washable; but if your curtains are made out of gingham, broadcloth, or muslin, they should be able to go through the washing machine. Damp dry, then iron them. When you make your own cur-

tains of these fabrics, pre-wash the fabric before cutting them out. Prewash ribbons and other washable trims, too. Whenever you clean draperies, clean the rod and its hardware at the same time. Usually, a simple dusting will get the job done.

CARING FOR WOOD FURNITURE, AND FRAMES

Nothing can match the beauty of wood furniture, and as centuries-old antiques prove, it can last for generations if properly cared for. The same goes for the wood framing on your mirrors and art.

ater, rough handling, and negligence are wood's worst enemies. This is true for any piece of furniture or accessory that is completely or partially constructed of wood. With a few precautions and proper care, however, you can make good wood furnishings—ornate or plain, new or old—endure for generations to come.

SHOPPING FOR WOOD FURNISHINGS

When shopping for new wood furniture or furnishings, be sure to read the descriptive labels. Determine the type of construction and the kinds of wood included—solid, plywood, veneer, or inlay. Also determine the finish—paint, gilt, varnish, shellac, or oil—and any other details which will help you care for the piece properly.

Shopping for used furniture can be quite a different matter, since informative tags are not attached. Your source—antique dealer, auction house, estate sale, or second-hand shop— should be able to correctly identify a piece of furniture's wood and the features that make it special, especially if a sizable sum is being asked.

Identifying woods

Any single kind of wood, such as mahogany or oak, can come in many varieties of color or grain. To make a wood's identity even more difficult, many less expensive woods are often stained and finished to look like costlier ones. A good test is to pull out a drawer and look at the unfinished back side of the front panel to see the wood's true color and grain pattern.

Veneers, inlays, and laminates

Thin slices of decorative grained wood, paper, or other materials are often glued to a solid wood or plywood base to achieve a desired design. The characteristics of these processes are easy to recognize.

WHAT KIND OF WOOD IS IT?

Much of a wood's beauty lies in its natural color and distinctive grain pattern. While the color of wood can be altered with stains to disguise it as another wood, the grain of the wood will always enable you to identify the truth. Many varieties of a wood type may exist, but their grains will have similar characteristics. The photographs show samples of wood in their unfinished state to show off their natural color and grain patterns and again with a colorless sealing finish, such as polyurethane or oil.

Ash: Hard, strong, flexible; creamy color with brownish or grey markings (except for black-hearted ash). Like, but rarer than oak. Uses: frames, curved elements.

Beech: Soft, fine grain; blonde color with silver flecking to light reddish-brown markings. Easily disguised with stains. Uses: lacquered, gilded, unfinished pieces.

Birch: Hard, heavy, close-grained; light color with pale brownish markings. Easily disguised with stains. Uses: frames, unfinished pieces, moldings, plywood.

Cherry: Hard, strong, close grained; auburn color with soft tonal markings. Uses: simple to elegant cabinet work, inlay, exposed furniture frames, accessories.

Hickory: Hard, very heavy wood, close-grained; blonde color with tonal markings. Uses: chairs, stools, chests, cupboards, decorative accessories.

Mahogany: Hard, light-weight, easily carved, neither shrinks nor warps; timber types vary from blonde to coppery-red colors with fine pore markings. Uses: exposed and interior furniture frames, inlay, veneer, chairs, chests, tables.

Maple: Very hard, strong; pale cream or biscuit color to yellowish brown with fine, tonal markings still light in color. Uses: bird's-eye variety popular for veneers; chests, beds, tables, often teamed with darker woods.

Oak: Hard, heavy, strong; more than 300 varieties, yellow to golden brown with prominent flecks, rings, and pores. Uses: frame work, cabinets, chairs, chests, tables, beds, veneers, often disguised as other, more costly, timbers.

Pine: Very soft, medium-weight, with and without knots; white to light yellow, with wide dark markings. Uses: chests, beds, tables, chairs, plywood; usually for informal pieces, but knotless type can be stained to look more formal.

Walnut: Hard, strong, fine-grained, easily carved; dark golden brown with prominent tonal markings. Uses: exposed furniture frames, interior frames, inlay, veneer, chairs, chests, tables, beds, decorative accessories.

COMMERCIAL POLISHING CLOTHS

Homemade cotton rags are great for dusting, but a commercial polishing cloth will put an extra shine on your fine wood furniture. Usually yellow, polishing cloths are soft and have a fine flannel-like nap that helps them get into corners and crevices.

◆ **Veneer** is a thin layer of decorative grained wood glued to a sizable surface, such as a table's top and drawer fronts. The effect is a solid wood look.

◆ **Inlay** can employ one or many decorative grained woods (as well as metals, ivory, shells, and stones) inserted into a base wood that has been carved out to receive the inlay motif. The contrasting materials create decorative floral and geometric designs. Chests, tables, and boxes are most often inlaid.

◆ **Laminates** of specially finished paper or plastic are commonly applied to plywood. In this process, all visible surfaces are covered with a laminate that's made to appear like wood, stone, or paint. Laminated items like shelving and kitchen countertops can be scratch- and heat-resistant, impervious to water and dry conditions, and need only a soap and water clean-up.

PRESERVING VALUABLE ANTIQUES

The term "antique" is given to most items when they are at least 100 years old. The most valuable ones, "period antiques," were made in the time the design originated either by the original or another cabinetmaker. Your valuable antique may be a family table and chairs you've just inherited and want to preserve for future generations of the family to also enjoy. Custom-made furniture of any era, antique or not, carries a high value. This includes furniture made by large manufacturers that worked with non-mass production methods. These pieces will become the next generation's valuable antiques.

All wood furnishings need care, but antiques require special considerations to preserve their value and original integrity. The patina—the collected dirt and discolorment—that develops on old furniture over time and with use is a treasured asset, along with the original finish. So use restraint in dealing with antiques. Dust, wax, and polish, add some soap or beeswax to drawer slides to improve their movement, but don't do anything more without consulting a professional. Find someone knowledgeable about the type and vintage of furniture you own.

Routine care

When dusting your antiques, use a clean, soft cotton rag, such as flannel; it will collect the dust without needing spray or liquid additives. In carved wood details or gilded areas, dust gently with a large sable brush (a soft artist's brush). Protect and polish the wood with beeswax (paste wax) or a softer mixture of beeswax plus carnauba wax, using a flannel cloth. You can purchase these wax polishes in hardware stores.

Protecting tabletops

You can give further protection to tables and other wood surfaces by adding a ¼-inch thick glass top with polished edges, custom-cut to size and shape. Placing nickel-sized clear or brown pads under the corners of the glass will keep it slightly elevated above the table, so air can circulate.

KEEPING FURNITURE CLEAN

To keep the wood items in your home clean and protected, develop a regular schedule of dusting and polishing. Use products and techniques that work best for your furniture and its finish.

Dusting the right way

Dust does not harm wood furniture, but dusting the wrong way can. Cotton diapers, old table napkins, and terry towels make ideal cleaning rags that will not create static electricity.

Dust regularly. While the moisture in a dusting spray helps to pick up dust, other ingredients could dull a hardwood finish over time, and dusting sprays with silicone or oil can create a film that actually attracts dust. Dusting sprays are excellent for laminated and polyurethane finishes. You should add dusting spray to the cloth, rather than directly on the furniture—the spray can mistakenly hit upholstery and other places where it doesn't belong.

The right polish for your finish

When you polish, you are polishing the finish, not the wood itself. Select a polish appropriate for your finish; the label will tell you the types of surfaces that the polish is designed to clean. If you use a liquid or formulated polish, use the same type each time you polish, since one brand may cloud or dull if applied over another.

◆ **Oil finish.** An oil finish penetrates the wood and should be protected only with an oil-based polish. If you are unsure your furniture has an oil finish, apply a few drops of boiled linseed oil (available at home centers) to the wood and rub gently. If it is absorbed, the wood has an oil finish; if droplets form, the wood has a hard finish such as varnish, shellac, or polyurethane.

◆ **Hard finishes.** A hard finish creates a protective layer that sits on top of the wood. To determine your finish, dab a drop of acetone (found in some fingernail polish removers) on a hidden spot. Polyurethane will be unaffected, but lacquers, varnishes, and shellacs will dissolve. If the finish is shellac, it will be dulled or removed. Read the furniture polish label to find your finish or see if it's marked "multi-surface."

Removing built-up polish

Layers of polish can dull the finish of wood furniture. To remove the buildup, use a wood cleaner—not a stripper—to get back the original shine. Wood cleaners combine a mild solvent with oil to dissolve and lift built-up polish and dirt. Use a commercial one, or make your own by mixing two parts vegetable oil (olive or lemon oil) with one part vinegar or lemon juice. Apply it with a soft cloth and wipe clean.

Wiping up spills

Clean up any spill as soon as you can, especially acidic (soft drinks or fruit juice) or alcoholic ones. Wipe with a clean cloth that is dry or slightly damp. For sticky spots or dried-on residue, use a mild soap and water solution, but avoid overwetting the wood. Follow with a clean damp cloth and then a dry one, wiping with the grain of the wood.

Removing greasy buildup

Vegetable-oil-based cleaners will dissolve grease and accumulated grime on your wood without damaging its finish. Apply and wipe off with a clean cloth only. Repeat if necessary. When the wood is clean, rinse by wiping it off with a damp cloth, then wipe dry with a dry cloth.

Removing stains and marks

Chalky white stains can be minimized or eliminated. Apply toothpaste (not gel) with a clean cloth, and rub gently following the grain. Wipe with a clean damp cloth, followed by a dry one.

If toothpaste doesn't work, rub the spot gently with mineral spirits and #0000 steel wool, following the grain. Or, try coating the stain with a thick layer of petroleum jelly and leaving it there 48 hours. The jelly should soak into the stain and even out its color. Scratches and marks can be disguised in a number of ways.

◆ **Use a wax polish** containing a stain. This product is purchased by wood color, such a "light oak" or "dark oak."

Apply it with the usual two-step method. Since this is a thick liquid or soft paste, protect the floor or carpet with a drop cloth in case of a spill.

◆ **Wood filler** comes in a variety of colors as well. Apply it with your finger, then wipe away with a damp cloth.

◆ **Colored wax fillers**, those crayon-like sticks carpenters use to fill in the holes above recessed nails, will also fill in scratches on furniture. Match them to the wood's color.

◆ **A child's crayon**, selected in a matching color, will also fill scratches. Soften the crayon with a hair dryer, then rub it over the scratch. Wipe the excess away using a dry rag.

◆ **Fresh walnut or pecan meat** rubbed over a shallow scratch on light woods will disguise a small scratch.

REPAIRING AND PROTECTING WOOD FURNITURE

You can make simple furniture repairs yourself and perform several safeguards that will maintain and lengthen the life of your wood furnishings.

REPAIRING A WOODEN CHAIR

1. To firm up a wobbly chair, reglue the connecting elements, dowels, or spindles. First, sand off any old glue on the loosened area and in its socket. Any leftover glue will prevent the new glue from properly adhering.

2. Apply wood glue to both surfaces of the joint, in this case the end of the spindle and the socket. Refit the joint; a little glue should squeeze out around the edges of the joint. Wipe off excess with a clean, wet cloth.

3. Secure the joint after gluing with a clamp, such as the web or band clamp shown here. You may need more than one clamp. Allow the glue to set for at least a day before unclamping the chair.

Gluing pieces back together

Serious wood furniture repair is for professionals, but you can attempt minor fixes yourself, such as regluing a loose joint. Don't try to fix furniture with screws or nails; you could split the wood and cause a difficult repair.

Basic joint repair involves some disassembly of the piece, regluing with wood glue, and clamping the joints securely until the glue sets to prevent sharp edges from marring the table wood. Before you begin, decide ahead of time how you will clamp your reglued project while the glue sets and dries. Squeeze clamps or C-clamps are good for small jobs but sliding clamps or pipe clamps are best for big jobs. You can also improvise with rope, bungie cords or even rubber bands in no-stress areas. Next, take the pieces apart with care to avoid further damage and reglue them as shown above.

Preventing problems

Beside overlaying a table with glass (p.180), there are other preventive measures for wood furniture.

◆ **Cut felt or leather pads** to fit under decorative accessories and lamps. Glue the pieces to the base.

◆ **When dusting**, polishing, or just using a table, make it a habit to lift up the tabletop items, without sliding them, to prevent scratching the wood.

◆ **Use UV-grade shades** or blinds at windows to protect wood furnishings from strong sunlight and heat. You can also close curtains and draperies during the brightest hours of the day to prevent wood from fading and drying out.

◆ **Locate wood furniture** away from radiators and heat vents that can dry it and cause cracks.

◆ **Store unused furniture** in a location that is dry and slightly cool, away from humidity and heat. Attics and garages are poor storage places that can encourage mildew, mold, cracks, warping, and destroy inlays and veneers.

REFINISHING FURNITURE

Just because the finish on a piece of furniture is worn and weathered does not mean you should strip it. Don't do it if you think the furniture is custom-made or a potential antique.

When the varnish on a piece of furniture is just worn, you can revive it by simply sanding the old varnish down with fine steel wool in the direction of the grain, applying a thin coat of diluted stain, and then revarnishing.

If the paint or varnish on a piece of furniture is cracking, bubbling, or peeling you may need to strip away the old paint or finish and apply a new finish. Though stripping is a common do-it-yourself project, it can be very time-consuming, especially if your piece has an intricate design or lots of pieces.

Working with wood strippers

There are two types of wood strippers: solvent-based strippers and water-based strippers. Solvent-based strippers require a well-ventilated area, gloves, long-sleeved pants and shirts, and goggles for protection. They strip more quickly than water-based ones, but water-based strippers are less hazardous to work with. In either case, use paste strippers, as they adhere well to vertical surfaces.

All strippers need time to work, and the more layers of paint or finish you are removing, the more time it takes. Remove all drawers, doors, and hardware from the piece of furniture before starting, and work the surfaces one at a time. Brush on a thick coat of stripper and leave it in place for at least three minutes per layer of finish. Tough jobs take as long as 20 minutes; you may need to purchase special plastic wrap to keep the stripper wet while it works. Remove the dissolved paint or finish with a flexible putty knife; avoid stiff tools that might gouge the wood. On intricate carvings, use an old toothbrush to get into tight spots. Use No. 2 steel wool to remove any remaining stripper.

Finish stripping by cleaning off the residue. For chemical strippers, use turpentine or denatured alcohol; for water-based strippers, water. Let the wood dry, then lightly sand the surface before applying a new finish, according to the manufacturer's instructions.

MAINTAINING MIRRORS

It's easy to keep a mirror shining so it can reflect natural and artificial light. Remove fingerprints, dust, and grease from a mirror with a window cleaner added to a soft rag, not directly onto the mirror itself. This keeps your cleaner from running between the mirror and frame and damaging the silver surface on the back of the glass. Make sure your rag is free of any attachments, such as buttons and snaps, that could scratch the glass. For a homemade cleaner, use strong tea and buff with a soft dry cloth.

Remove slight scratches on a mirror with white toothpaste (not gel) that is made for brightening teeth. It contains small amounts of abrasive material that will gently rub out imperfections. Apply the toothpaste to a soft clean rag, and rub with a circular motion. Use a separate clean rag to remove residue and to polish.

MAINTAINING WOOD FRAMES

Frames—especially if they are richly carved—should be dusted as if they were valuable antiques (p.180), using flannel rags and a sable brush for fine details.

Repairing a loose frame

If your frame is starting to come apart at a corner, take care of the problem right away or the gap may widen and allow the glass to slip out and break. Take the frame off the wall and work on a firm but padded surface. Remove the glass. You may  be able to reinforce the corner joint by applying glue and clamping it for a day. Another solution is to use a metal frame-mending plate, available at a hardware store or home center. Lay the plate diagonally across the frame's back corner and mark its holes. Carefully drill tiny, short, pilot holes—don't go too far and pierce the face of the frame. Also make sure the screws are the right length before installing the plate, so they won't poke through the front.

Mounting pictures and mirrors

To hang a framed picture or mirror without cracking plaster, stick clear or painter's tape where the nail or picture hanger should go, hammer the nail through the tape, then remove the tape and hang the object. Large, heavy mirrors and pictures will hang more securely if you use two hooks placed at the same height, but several inches apart.

Frame it yourself

Metal frame sides are available in two-inch interval lengths at art stores. Putting them together is not difficult. Buy two of each length needed, and assemble them into a frame according to the manufacturer's instructions. You can then have mirrors or glass cut to fit the frame.

Making a wood frame from scratch is surprisingly difficult and custom framing can be expensive. Some frame shops rent "bench time," allowing you to use their tools (miter boxes and saws, for example) and offering advice on how to make frames from the moldings that you buy there.

UPHOLSTERED FURNITURE AND BEDS

Upholstered furniture can last for years with proper care. Mattresses will last longer, too, if maintained well. It's worth the time to develop habits that will keep your comfortable pieces looking and feeling good.

The upholstered furniture in your house, from sofas and chairs to the mattresses on your beds, are usually big-ticket household investments. For this reason, it pays to understand the basics of furniture fabrics and construction before you buy, and to take good care of your furniture once you take it home.

CHOOSING UPHOLSTERED FURNITURE

Upholstered furniture is composed of three elements: frame, support system, and fabric cover. Furniture prices generally vary, depending on the quality of these elements. Here are the options.

Frame

Furniture frames (also called the "carcass" or "bones") for top-of-the-line pieces are made of hardwoods, slowly dried in a kiln to prevent warping. Cheaper frames are made of softer wood and may be assembled in a less-than-durable construction.

Support system

Springs, webbing, and padding are the invisible but critical elements of upholstered furniture. Traditionally, expensive furniture has been constructed with hourglass-shaped, individually-tied coil springs. Many manufacturers now use "zigzag" or sinuous-wire springs, or rubberized webbing strips—less expensive but strong alternatives.

The soft innards of upholstered furniture come from stuffing placed over the springs and padding under the outside fabric. Separate cushions on high end pieces use either down feathers or a feathers "plus" combination, though foam, covered with a layer of fiberfill, is the most common cushion stuffing.

Fabric

Upholstery fabrics are tough as well as good-looking. Blends of natural and manufactured fibers, treated to block stains, make upholstery long-wearing and easy to clean. Here are some fibers and their common characteristics.

◆ **Cotton** is a versatile fiber, used for prints and wovens, and is comfortable to use in all climates. It, as well as any untreated natural fiber, is less stain-resistant than synthetic fibers.

WHAT'S INSIDE

A piece of upholstered furniture is a sandwich of several different components, including frame, springs, stuffing, and padding. These hidden elements are important to the long-term comfort and durability of a chair or sofa.

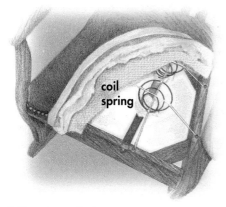

Coil-spring upholstery

This arrangement is the hallmark of a quality upholstered piece, and is best suited for heavy-use furniture such as sofas and easy chairs. Springs are tied to strips of jute webbing and knotted to each other with spring twine; eight-way hand-tied springs are optimum. Burlap covers the springs, followed by stuffing, sometimes muslin, then padding and the final decorative fabric cover.

Zigzag-spring upholstery

This arrangement mirrors coil-spring upholstery in every way except in the spring structure itself. Zigzag springs are a modern flexible support system. They run the width of the back and length of the seat. Their ends fasten directly to the frame using special clips that are nailed closed. Knots in spring twine link one zigzag spring to the next. No webbing is required underneath.

Slip- or drop-seat upholstery

With this simplest of upholstery arrangements, tacked strips of woven jute webbing are covered with a layer of burlap. Foam, felted natural, or synthetic hair stuffing is the layer above the burlap. A muslin liner is sometimes installed over this in high–end furniture. Padding—a layer of cotton batting or polyester fiberfill—will be next, just under the fashionable upholstery fabric.

◆ **Linen,** a high-end fiber, is prized for its crispness, strength, and durability.

◆ **Wool** is strong, durable, soft to the touch, and naturally resists water.

◆ **Rayon** is a smooth, soft, lustrous, and comfortable manufactured fiber. It wrinkles easily when used alone. Blended with other fibers, it adds silk-like luster to the finished fabric.

◆ **Nylon** is strong and abrasion-, rot-, and mildew-resistant. It has a low absorption for water and other liquids.

◆ **Acrylic,** a manufactured fiber, can offer many of the qualities of wool, a natural fiber. It is often used in plush or fleecy fabrics. Acrylic resists fading but is prone to pilling, the creation of small balls of fibers on the fabric's surface.

◆ **Olefin** is a strong, soil- and abrasion-resistant manufactured fiber that is used alone or blended with other fibers.

◆ **Polyester** is a strong, resilient, and abrasion-resistant fiber that adds luster when blended with other fibers.

◆ **Silk** is a strong, resilient, luxury fiber with a natural luster. Fiber size varies from fine to heavy, as in raw silk.

Protecting fabrics

Most fabrics designed for upholstery come from the manufacturer with a stain- and soil-repellent finish. When it is missing, the store should be able to add the treatment with a warranty when you buy a piece of upholstered furniture, or you can buy a spray-on form at a hardware store and apply it

COMMON TYPES OF SPOTS AND HOW TO REMOVE THEM

Before attempting to remove a liquid stain, blot out as much as possible. Pre-test, then treat the stain immediately. When necessary, follow up with a professional cleaning as soon as possible. Avoid stain removers on fabrics with soil-resistant finishes; they may create new stains.

Alcohol: Blot with a solution of one teaspoon liquid dish detergent in one cup water, then blot clean with a well wrung-out sponge dipped in clear water. If the stain persists, dab on a second solution of one part white vinegar to two parts water. Rinse with a wrung-out sponge and let dry.

Milk and ice cream: Blot with a solution of one teaspoon liquid dish detergent in one cup water, then blot clean with a well wrung-out sponge dipped in clear water. If the stain persists, dab on a solution of 1/2 cup water mixed with one teaspoon of ammonia. Rinse with a well wrung-out sponge and let dry.

Candle wax and chewing gum: Put an ice cube in a plastic sandwich bag and hold it against the wax or gum until it freezes hard. Scrape off as much as you can, and dab any remaining stain with dry-cleaner fluid or acetone.

Fruit juice, coffee, tea, and soda: Blot with a solution of one teaspoon of dishwashing liquid in one cup water. For stubborn stains, sponge with a solution of one part vinegar to four parts water. Rinse with a wrung-out sponge and let dry.

Grease spots (including wax and crayon): Rub with dry-cleaning fluid, and blot with a clean, dry cloth.

---

yourself. Fabric protection gives you time to pick up or blot away spills before they soak in. It cannot totally prevent damage to the fabric.

If you are considering buying a warrantied fabric-protection treatment, read your fiber and fabric information carefully. If a fabric was treated at the mill, a second treatment is unnecessary.

BASIC UPHOLSTERY CLEANING

Vacuum regularly with upholstery attachment tools—the broad throated one to dislodge dust from flat surfaces, including cushions, and the crevice tool to reach the inner corners.

Turn over loose seat and back cushions and throw pillows every few weeks to distribute the wear evenly. Unless you have a washable slipcover, never remove and wash cushion covers—the zippers are there solely to aid the "dressing" process as the piece is manufactured.

Cleaning codes

Many new sofas and chairs come with a care label indicating the type of cleaning required. The code classifications are "W," safe to clean with water or water-based cleaners; "S," dry clean or spot clean with dry-cleaning solvents; "W-S," safe for water or solvent; and "F," for foam cleaning.

If the spot or stain is small and the fabric has a "W" cleaning code and has no stain- or soil-resistant finish, then you may try removing the spot yourself. The chart, left, gives some tips for removing common spots, but always pre-test the solution first.

Pre-testing a cleaning solution

Working in a hidden area of the upholstery, such as the back side of a skirt or under a cushioned area, pre-test your dry-cleaning fluid or homemade cleaner. If the solution does not spot the fabric when you test it, you have a chance at success in removing the accidental spot. If the solution causes a problem on its own, do not proceed. Instead, blot out as much of the problem as possible and turn the job over to a professional, the sooner the better.

Professional furniture cleaning

In most cases, a professional's service will be needed to remove bad spots and stains, and deeply ingrained soil. If a friend cannot recommend someone, consult the Yellow Pages of the telephone book under "Furniture Cleaning." Typical methods offered will be steam-cleaning, dry-cleaning, and dry foam cleaning. Be aware that any cleaning procedure will destroy the original protective soil-resistant coating on your upholstery. You should apply a new stain-resistant finish; it won't be as effective as the factory-applied one.

Cleaning with homemade solutions

Read the instructions on the tag to see what type of care is recommended for your fabric. If you can't find that information, have a professional clean the upholstery. It's better to play it safe than to ruin the fabric and need to have the piece reupholstered.

For a homemade "W" class cleaner, mix one teaspoon of liquid dish or mild laundry detergent (with no bleach) in a cup of warm water. In another bowl,

UPHOLSTERED FURNITURE AND BEDS

mix a tablespoon of ammonia with ½ cup of water. Pre-test, then dab the solutions alternately on the spot. Blot with a clean damp sponge after each step. When clean, sponge with clear water and blot dry.

Pre-treating slipcover spots

The arms and backs of washable slipcovers will probably pick up the most soil. If necessary, try pre-treating these areas after removing the slipcover from the furniture but before washing.

With a hand mixer, mix ¼ cup liquid laundry detergent in one cup of water until it foams up to the consistency of whipped cream. Spread the suds over the soiled area and gently rub them into the fabric. When you see dirt lifting,

scrape off the dirty suds with a spatula (below left). Repeat if necessary.

Washing slipcovers

Slipcovers should always be professionally dry cleaned unless they are clearly marked "washable."

Give your slipcovers a good shake outdoors before you put them in the washer and check to see if pre-treating for stains is needed (see facing page). Always wash all the pieces at the same time (though it may take several machine loads) so the color stays even. Dry on medium to low heat; don't line dry, because the weight of the slipcover may distort the fabric. Slipcovers will fit best if you take them out of the dryer before they are completely dry. Put the slipcovers on the frame or cushions while they are still slightly damp. Smooth them into place, straightening seams and pinching pleats by hand or with a hand-steamer.

LEATHER OPTIONS

Leather furniture is available at surprisingly low prices today. However, skin and dye qualities can vary greatly. Aniline-dyed leather is superior to surface-dyed leather. The latter is sometimes called "painted" leather because the dye only coats the surface while the former penetrates the skin and is visible on the back. To check, open a zippered cushion and look at the back. The label will tell you the care needed; if not, seek professional advice. Here are some leather terms you should know.

◆ **Split leather.** When a cow's hide is doubled in size by slicing it in half

along its thickness, it results in two layers of equal thickness but not equal quality. The "split leather" is the bottom half of the hide, which has no grain, is stretchier, and has poor durability.

◆ **Top-grain.** The upper layer of a hide that has been split is the superior top-grain. To tell if leather is top-grain, examine it under a magnifying glass — the leather will show tiny natural pores.

◆ **Embossed.** Also known as "rectified" leather, this leather has had an artificial grain pattern heat-set into its surface to imitate a high-quality full-grain leather.

◆ **Full-grain.** This top-quality leather shows a natural (unaltered) grain.

Leather maintenance

Leather is treated with a protectant at the tannery, so generally cleaners are not recommended since they can harm the leather finish. Clean up spills immediately, but if a liquid does soak in, blot it with a weak solution of soap and water. Blot up greasy spots as much as possible, but do not use water. In times the oil will be absorbed into the leather and become part of the natural patina that develops over time.

Vacuum leather furniture regularly with the crevice upholstery attachment of your machine. An artist's brush is handy for lifting dust from tufted areas and pleats. Give the leather an occasional wipe with a soft, clean cloth dampened with warm water to retard the buildup of body oils on the surface.

CHOOSING A MATTRESS

When the side of the mattress where you sleep begins to sag and the box-spring seems uneven, it's time to replace your sleepset. Insert a piece of ½-inch plywood between the mattress and boxspring as a temporary solution while you shop. In the store, test a mattress by lying on it, using your normal sleep posture, for at least five minutes. Turn once or twice. If there are two of you, do the test together. Then consider the support system inside.

◆ **Foam** mattresses are filled with resilient polyurethane or latex foam instead of coil springs. For good support, the foam density should be at least two pounds per cubic foot. Some foam mattresses are filled with a special contour-conforming material. The best foam mattresses can rival innerspring mattresses in comfort, but inexpensive foam mattresses may sag fairly soon.

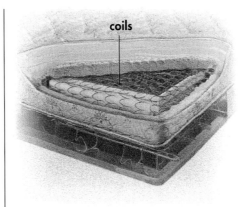

coils

◆ **Innerspring** mattresses (above) have coil springs that contour around your body. These mattresses come in a variety of configurations. More important to quality, however, is the number of coils and the number of directions in which they are tied—the more the better. A queen-sized mattress, for example, should have at least 300 springs, and some premium models have as many as 900 springs. The most luxurious innersprings are tied in eight directions and have extra padding to enhance comfort, but they do require extra-deep fitted sheets.

◆ **Waterbeds** (below) today have interior baffles or separate water-filled

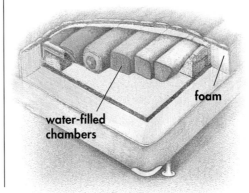

water-filled chambers

foam

chambers to minimize the wave action that gave earlier models a bad reputation. Waterbeds look like conventional innerspring mattresses outside but they require a special frame and heater. Standard sheets will fit them.

◆ **Air mattress** are built with air-filled chambers, padded with a layer of foam and ticking. They are lightweight and easy to move. Some allow you to regulate firmness separately on each side of the bed. An air mattress must be set on a box spring for full comfort.

Mattress sizes

Standard mattress sizes are:

- ◆ **Twin:** 39 by 75 inches.
- ◆ **Extra-long twin:** 39 by 80 inches.
- ◆ **Full:** 54 by 75 inches.
- ◆ **Queen:** 60 by 80 inches.
- ◆ **King:** 76 or 78 by 80 inches.
- ◆ **Western or California king:** 72 by 84 inches.

Mattress maintenance

Use a quilted mattress cover beneath your fitted sheet to protect the mattress from soil and light stains. Clean mattress stains as you would any fabric stains (p.233). About every three months, turn over the mattress, flipping it from head to foot one time and side to side the next. The side handles are an aid in turning and positioning the mattress, not in transporting. Vacuum the mattress and wash the cover regularly to remove dust and dust mites. To freshen it, sprinkle on baking soda, leave it for several hours, then vacuum.

CAMERAS, ELECTRONIC EQUIPMENT, AND TELEPHONES

Though these items are complex, there are things you can do to make your entertainment and office equipment last longer and perform better. You can even make some minor repairs yourself.

Most of the electronic gadgets available today are better made, less costly, and more efficient than their predecessors of only a few years ago. They are also more complex, with miniature microprocessors and other electronic components having replaced less-mysterious mechanical parts.

Now it is often less expensive (economically, if not environmentally) to buy a new model rather than repair an old one. However, many repairs don't require elaborate diagnostic equipment and training. And careful attention to maintenance and cleaning will reduce the frequency of breakdowns.

CHOOSING AND OPERATING A CAMERA

If you shoot only a few rolls of film a year, consider an inexpensive compact ("point-and-shoot") camera, or even a succession of single-use (disposable) cameras. Most compact cameras are fully automatic and have a built-in flash. You can choose from models offering medium- to long-range zoom lenses, which help produce better images of close-up and distant subjects.

If you want to pursue photography as a serious hobby, a single-lens reflex (SLR) 35mm camera with interchangeable lenses is the best choice. Available options include automatic focusing, built-in or accessory flashes, and the ability to control exposures automatically or manually. All of the major manufacturers produce cameras and lenses that will allow you to shoot quality photos, in either print or slide form. If you are willing to put up with fewer automatic features, hundreds of different models of affordable used 35mm cameras are available.

A new film and camera format called Advanced Photo System (APS) was introduced in 1996 as a means of making amateur photography as failsafe as possible. This system uses a 24mm film

189

CLEANING A LENS

A clean lens is often the difference between a good and a poor photograph. Excessive cleaning, however, can damage the lens coating; so clean only when necessary.

Step 1: Use a compressed-gas duster and brush (both available at camera stores), on a regular basis, to remove loose dust and dirt.

Step 2: If the lens still looks soiled or streaked, place a drop of liquid lens cleaner on a lens-cleaning tissue. Do not use regular glass cleaner or facial tissues, and do not pour the fluid directly on the lens. Wipe the lens using a circular motion. Work from the outside edges to the center. Finish cleaning with a dry tissue, using the same circular motion.

no-leader cartridge for ease of loading. Magnetic coding on the cartridge conveys to processors equipped to handle this film the exact conditions in which the film was exposed and can record on the back of the print the time and date the photograph was taken.

Even newer, digital cameras need no film but do require access to a computer to store images and view them in high resolution. However, images can be instantly viewed in low-resolution form and later modified before being printed on a color printer.

Learning photography techniques

The quality of the camera and lens is not as important as the photographer's attention to detail. Good photography does not take years of practice, but it does require some study. To learn how to compose a photograph, choose the appropriate film, and use natural and artificial lighting to their best effect, read the owner's manual, photography books, and photography magazines.

Protecting a camera in cold weather

Keep your camera away from cold temperatures as much as possible. If you want to take pictures outdoors on a cold day, don't just grab the camera and run outside. Rapid temperature changes cause condensation to form on the lens, making it difficult to capture a sharp image. Place the camera in a zip-lock plastic bag. Once outside, leave the camera in the bag long enough for it to adjust to the temperature. Condensation will form on the outside of the bag rather than on the

camera. Remove the camera from the bag to take photographs. Put the camera back in the bag before going back inside, and leave it there until the camera has warmed to room temperature.

Protecting the lens

The most fragile and expensive component in a camera system is the lens, which can be made of glass or plastic. Lenses can be scratched easily, and the protective coating can be damaged by improper cleaning. When the lens is not in use, always close the lens cover or replace the lens cap. Many professionals keep a filter on each lens at all times. Clear ultraviolet (UV) filters (below) are usually preferable because they reduce haze in outdoor photo-

UV filter

REALITY CHECK

CAMERA BAG TRAP

◆ **When you are traveling** a good camera bag seems an indispensable piece of photography equipment. It holds cameras lenses, film, flash, batteries, filters, and other accessories conveniently. A camera bag, unfortunately, also announces to all the world that it houses expensive equipment.

◆ **On the road,** then, carry a compact camera in a pocket or purse, taking it out only when you're taking pictures. If you need to carry more equipment, use a less obvious carrier, such as a large tote bag or small backpack, or carry your camera bag inside a larger and less conspicuous piece of luggage.

graphs while simultaneously protecting the lens. A UV filter will not affect indoor photographs at all. If the filter gets damaged, you can replace it for far less money than you can the lens.

Storing a camera

Keep your camera in a camera bag, or wrap it in a clean, soft cloth, and put it in a cool, clean, dry location. Avoid places where it will be subjected to temperature extremes or direct sunlight (such as the trunk of a car or near a window). If you don't use the camera regularly, remove the batteries after each use and keep them nearby so that you don't have to hunt for them. Don't put a camera on a shelf where it may get buried under heavy objects.

Replacing the battery

Batteries control many functions on a camera. Even an older camera with few automatic functions may need a battery to power the flash or trigger the shutter. Such batteries may last so long that users forget about them and assume the camera needs repair when it suddenly stops working. Newer cameras have so many electronically controlled functions that they require powerful—and often expensive—batteries.

Most batteries are easy to replace, but some cameras have batteries dedicated to memory functions that should be replaced at a service center. Check the owner's manual for directions on locating and changing the battery. To buy fresh batteries, check the expiration date. To prolong battery life, don't turn the camera on and off repeatedly. Remove the batteries whenever you plan to store the camera for more than a couple of weeks. Battery performance drops at temperatures below freezing. If you are outside in cold weather, keep the camera (and a spare battery) close to your body or in a pocket until use.

Cleaning battery contacts

The metal contacts that the battery touches must be clean in order for the battery to supply adequate power to the camera. Whenever you change batteries, inspect the contacts for corrosion or dust. Clean up small particles with a pencil eraser; be sure to remove any pieces of spent eraser from the camera. For tougher corrosion, scrape the contacts with the tip of a knife (above right) being careful not to cut any

wires. Wipe the contacts with a clean cloth. If a battery has leaked, have a service center replace the the contacts.

battery contact

If a camera gets wet

Most cameras are not water-resistant and should not be used in rain or snow. If you accidentally drop a camera in water, slow the process of oxidation by sealing the camera in a plastic bag with as much air removed as possible. Take the camera to an authorized service facility as soon as you can.

Take special care to protect a camera when using it at the beach or near salt water; clean it thoroughly with a dry cloth after use. If you want to take photographs in wet locations, or even under water, buy a waterproof camera enclosure or an underwater camera.

Improving flash performance

A camera with a built-in flash needs a strong battery to perform well. Change batteries if you have flash problems.

For a camera with a hot-shoe flash

191

connection, performance depends on battery strength plus a good connection. Change the flash unit's batteries when it starts taking longer to recycle between flashes, or when the flash's brightness fades. Clean the contacts on the hot shoe and on the flash with a cotton swab dipped in electrical-contact cleaner (available at camera shops) or denatured alcohol. When mounting the flash, insert it fully into the hot shoe and lock it.

CHOOSING A CAMCORDER

A camcorder combines a video camera and audio recorder in one compact unit. Full-sized VHS camcorders use the same cassettes as a VCR. They are heavy and rest on a shoulder when in use, making them steadier than hand-held models. Full-sized camcorders have largely been replaced by smaller formats. Compact VHS (also called VHS-C) camcorders use tape cassettes about the size of a deck of cards, which must be placed in an adapter to be viewed on a VCR. Even smaller are 8mm camcorders, which use cassettes about the size of an audio cassette. You can't replay the 8mm tape on a VCR; instead, the camcorder is connected directly to a TV for playback.

Extending camcorder battery life

Camcorders use rechargeable batteries. New models use less power than older units. Features such as zoom, LCD view screens, and picture stabilization reduce battery life. Remove the battery pack after each use, and recharge a low battery before you store it. Some models offer the option of a bigger battery.

Cleaning the contacts

If a camcorder won't work, and you are certain that the battery is charged, clean the contacts on the battery,

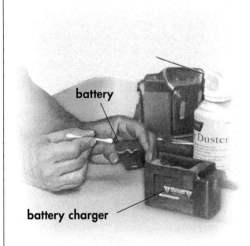

battery

battery charger

battery charger, and AC adapter. Dust as needed with an aerosol duster and clean the contacts with a cotton swab (above) dipped in electrical-contact cleaner or denatured alcohol. Remove minor corrosion with a pencil eraser, then use a clean cloth to wipe the area.

Replacing fuses

Some camcorders contain fuses that the user can easily replace. If a camcorder won't work, and the battery is charged and the contacts are clean, it may be that the fuse is blown. Disconnect the power source or remove the battery. Check the owner's manual for the location of the fuse or fuses. They may be under a marked cover on the bottom or rear of the unit. Or they could be inside the unit, requiring that you remove the housing to gain access. Pull gently with

needle-nose pliers to remove the fuse (below). If the fuse is soldered in place, take it to a camera shop.

Clean the contacts at each end of the fuse, put the fuse back in, and test. If the camera still doesn't work, take the fuse to a camera shop and have it tested; replace the fuse if it is faulty.

Replacing a belt

If your videotape cassette will not load or eject, or if tapes are being damaged when you operate the unit, try cleaning the unit with a cleaning cartridge (see "Cleaning the Heads" on the facing page). If that doesn't help, one or more of the internal belts may be damaged. A repair shop should be able to fix this for a small fee.

Improving camcorder performance

Treat your camcorder as you would a good camera: Keep the lens protected by keeping a lens cap on it whenever it is not in use; protect it from dust and

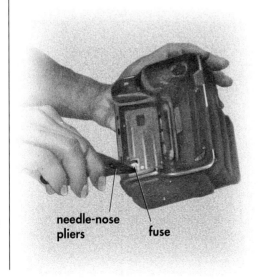

needle-nose pliers

fuse

wetness; and clean the lens periodically (see "Cleaning a Lens" on page 190). In addition, clean the heads regularly, as you would for a VCR (see below). You can also use a cleaning cartridge as an interim step. Put it in the camcorder as if it were a tape, then clean as directed by the manufacturer. Avoid pointing the camera directly at the sun. If you are moving the camcorder from a warm place to a cold place, or vice versa, wait an hour or two before using the camera. Drastic changes in temperature can lead to condensation, and if you use the camcorder while it is wet inside, damage could result.

CHOOSING A VCR

With the boom in video rentals and purchases and with the widespread use of camcorders, the videocassette recorder has become an indispensable part of any home entertainment center. VHS is the predominant VCR format. Super VHS (S-VHS) offers better picture quality and special effects. Digital VCR is too new and too expensive to have reached a wide audience, but it promises superior recording qualities and editing capabilities.

VCR options

Here are some features worth considering as you shop for a new VCR:

◆ **A four-head unit** will have hi-fi sound and will give a clearer picture when paused or in slow motion or fast-forwarding through commercials.

◆ **An auto channel set** quickly programs the channel selection, usually by skipping empty channels.

◆ **Hi-fi and MTS** convert hi-fi stereo soundtracks on videos and MTS stereo TV broadcasts into multichannel surround sound. You will need a compatible stereo receiver.

◆ **A unified remote** operates a VCR and TV made by the same manufacturer. Multibrand remotes can handle VCRs and TVs from different makers.

CLEANING THE HEADS BY HAND

When dirty, VCR heads will cause picture distortion; they require frequent cleaning for good clear pictures. Doing the job by hand gives better results than a cleaning tape. Don't touch internal parts with your hands, because body oils can damage them.

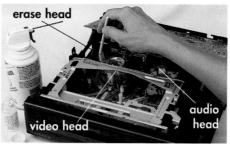

1. Using an absolutely lint-free chamois-tipped cleaning swab (available at electronic stores) is the most effective method to clean the heads. Unplug the VCR and remove the screws holding the housing (the top cover piece). Remove the housing by lifting or sliding it out. Locate the erase, audio, and video heads.

2. Remove dust from the unit by brushing gently with a clean paintbrush, or by spraying with canned air. Apply head cleaner or denatured alcohol to the swab. Hold the flat side of the swab against the head drum and slowly rotate the drum from above, without touching the sides of the drum with your finger. Do not rub the swab up and down.

3. Also clean other parts that the tape comes into contact with—the spindles, rollers, and capstans—using a swab dampened with cleaner. Let the unit dry for 15 minutes, then reassemble. If you don't want to disassemble the unit yourself, take the VCR to a service shop. A thorough VCR cleaning should not be expensive.

◆ **Commercial advance,** used during playbacks of taped TV programs, by-passes commercials by fast-forwarding to the next program segment.

◆ **VCR Plus** lets you enter a numeric code for a TV program you want to tape, and the VCR automatically sets itself for date, time, and channel.

◆ **Front panel audio/visual jacks** are very convenient for plugging in a camcorder or setting up video games.

◆ **Indexing** places electronic "bookmarks" on a tape when you start taping, making it easy to jump to that segment when you want to play it.

Improving the picture

If the whole image is poor, it may be a faulty tape; try another one. If the problem exists for all tapes, the VCR heads are probably dirty. (See "Cleaning the Heads" on page 193 for step-by-step instructions.)

If only part of the image is wiggly, bent, or scratchy, the problem is likely due to a tracking error. Locate the tracking control knob on your VCR, or the tracking buttons on your VCR remote control. (It may be behind a panel; check your owner's manual if you have trouble finding it.) Turn the knob slowly, or push one button, then the other until the image on the screen is good. When you change tapes, you may need to turn the tracking control knob back to its normal position.

Removing a stuck tape

If the tape won't come out when you push the eject button, don't try to force it out. Unplug the unit and remove the housing (the top covering). If there is a plate covering the top of the cassette, remove the screws holding it in place and lift the plate out. If you find that you cannot get at the cassette easily, take the VCR to a service center. Carefully pull the tape free of the head drum and rollers. Lift out the cassette. If the tape appears to be damaged, discard it. Otherwise, clean the parts (p.193), reassemble the machine, and test. If the problem persists, take the VCR to a service center.

CHOOSING A TELEVISION

Television sets are getting bigger and more loaded with accessories. The standard screen size has grown from 19–20 inches to 25–27 inches, with no significant change in price. And the picture quality on the larger sets is now much better. Large sets, with screens that measure 31 inches or more, can be the centerpiece of a full-blown home theater setup. Rear-projection sets offer even larger screens. Recommended features on new TVs include comb-filter circuitry, which enhances fine details and color and cleans up images; picture-in-picture, which allows you to watch another channel in a small picture superimposed on the screen; MTS stereo, which improves audio reception of stereo broadcasts; on-screen menus, which make it easy to adjust and program the TV using the remote control; and dark screens, which enhance contrast and so make the picture clearer.

Cleaning a TV

Clean the screen with a lint-free cloth dampened with a small amount of glass cleaner. Do not spray the cleaner directly onto the screen. TV sets have ventilation openings (slots or a series

---

FIXING A REMOTE CONTROL

1. If a remote control stops working, first replace the batteries. If the problem persists, open the housing: Remove screws along the edges or in the battery compartment. Pry the housing apart along the seams.

2. Clean inside of the unit with an aerosol duster. Clean the battery connections with a pencil eraser; use electrical-contact cleaner and a cotton swab to clean the circuit board. Let the disassembled unit dry for about 15 minutes before reassembling.

of small holes) in the cabinet that allow heat generated during operation to escape; if the vents become dirty or otherwise blocked, the TV can be damaged quickly. Wipe the area regularly with a dampened cloth.

Improving sound quality

The speakers on most TV sets are very small and provide poor audio output. Even if you don't have a stereo TV, you can boost the audio quality and volume of your set by connecting the TV audio output to your stereo receiver, which then directs the sound through the stereo speakers. Check your owner's manual for the exact connections you need. Typically, you will run cables from the "Audio Out" jacks on the TV to the "TV/LD

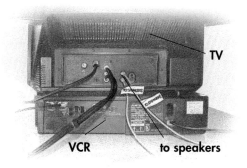

Audio In" jacks on the receiver (above). With the receiver set to TV mode, you can listen to TV shows and videotapes through stereo speakers.

Replacing rather than fixing TVs

Newer TVs use solid-state electronic components; old sets used vacuum tubes. Electronic components are diffi-

cult to replace; older tubes are usually impossible to find. And if a picture tube is shot, replacing it will cost more than buying a new TV. So if your TV is seriously damaged, it is almost always cheaper to replace it rather than trying to fix it.

What to do before you call for repairs

If your set is acting up, try some simple measures before buying a new set or calling for repairs. To make sure the problem is not with the cable provider, call your cable company and describe the problem. Or disconnect the cable wire and hook up an old-fashioned antenna; if you get at least a fuzzy picture, the cable company may be at fault. If your TV has a service switch in the rear, make sure it is set to "normal." Check all the cable and/or antenna connections to make sure they are secure.

Changing a fuse

Newer TV sets have one or more fuses that act as internal surge protectors. When a power surge hits the electrical connection, the fuse will blow and protect the set from damage. Some fuses are fairly easy to find and replace, while others require careful desoldering and disassembly of the set—jobs best left to a professional. Check your owner's manual for further instructions.

CHOOSING A STEREO RECEIVER

The receiver is the center of a home audio (and, increasingly, audio-visual) system. The receiver contains tuners for AM and FM radio, an amplifier, and controls for the audio sources.

The simplest and least expensive units are stereo-only receivers. They allow you to control a CD player, cassette player, turntable, and radio, and to direct sound to a pair of speakers.

Receivers with Dolby Pro Logic capability are required for a home theater. They can direct surround sound encoded on many movies and TV shows to five speakers. Dolby Digital Surround is a newer technology with even more channels, allowing home theater sound to resemble that of a good movie theater.

How many watts do you need?

Receiver power is measured in watts per channel. A typical stereo-only receiver might deliver around 100 watts to each of two channels. The center channels on Dolby Pro Logic receivers are rated separately, as are rear channels for surround sound.

Sales people may try to convince you that more power is better, but most

HOOKING UP A STEREO RECEIVER

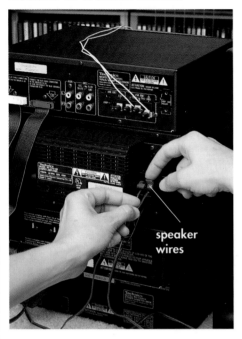

speaker wires

Attaching all those wires does not require technical knowledge since the back of your receiver will be clearly marked. But it is important to work systematically and carefully, or you'll end up with a tangle. Give yourself plenty of room to work, and run the wires where they will not be visible.

Use a wire stripper for the ends of speaker wires (see "Stripping Wire" on pages 95–96). To get the best sound out of speakers, wire them correctly. The higher your receiver's wattage and the farther the wires travel, the thicker the wires should be. Ask your dealer, or buy 14-gauge wire to be safe.

Make sure one wire travels from the red or positive (+) terminal on the speaker to the red or positive terminal on the receiver; the other wire should connect to the black or negative (–) terminal. If you are unsure, test your connections by reversing the connections at each end, and see which gives you the richest bass sound.

listeners will be perfectly satisfied with a low-wattage receiver, even a low-end model. Most of us just don't need to blast the music out. The type and size of room you intend to use for listening is an important consideration. If it has wood floors, wood furniture, and few if any rugs, it will require a less-powerful receiver than a room with thick carpeting, cushioned furniture, high ceilings, and heavy curtains. A larger room will benefit from more power.

Positioning stereo speakers
Proper speaker placement is essential if you want to maximize the quality of sound from your stereo system. Finding the best locations for the speakers requires some experimenting, and quite likely some compromises. Too often, people set speakers where it is convenient, without giving much thought to sound quality. And, in an effort to create a balanced appearance, they often place speakers equal distances from the receiver.

But it is you, not the receiver, that is listening to the sound. So first, establish your listening position (right). Then try to set the speakers so that they form an equilateral triangle with the listening position (that is, the speakers should be as far apart from each other as they are from you). In most rooms, speakers sound better if they are raised above the floor 3 to 6 feet.

From there, you can move the speakers a bit in search of the sound you want. Bear in mind that improving one aspect of sound may adversely affect another. You can improve bass response by moving speakers closer to the floor or walls. Midrange frequencies (singing voices, movie dialogue, and most musical instruments) are improved by moving speakers out into the room, away from walls and up off the floor.

Adding FM and AM antennas
You can spend hundreds for a stereo receiver, and still not get decent radio reception. (AM reception, in particular, is often actually better from a cheap portable radio.) Reception can be improved with an antenna.

Most new receivers come with moderately effective AM and FM antennas that can be attached to the marked slots in the back. An AM loop antenna sits on a shelf next to the receiver. Plug the wire ends into the AM slots on the receiver, then adjust the antenna for

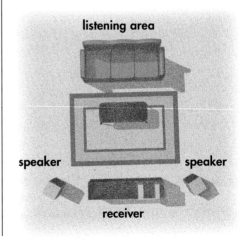

listening area

speaker   speaker

receiver

best reception. Indoor FM antennas are usually attached to the wall or ceiling to optimize reception. For the best FM reception, you may want to install an outdoor FM stereo antenna. You can buy a TV antenna with FM capacity, or a single-purpose FM model. An outdoor antenna should be attached to the roof or to the side of the house, with a wire running to the receiver. You may want to hire an electrician to run the wire.

Cleaning cassette players

The parts of a cassette player that touch the tape—rollers, capstans, and heads—collect oxide from tapes, as well as dust from the air, leading to muddy sound. Clean your tape player with a cleaning tape after every 20 hours of playing or recording time. This only takes a minute. For thorough cleaning, use a cotton swab wetted with head-cleaning compound from an electronics store. Turn the tape player on, and clean the heads, and the rollers and capstans as they turn.

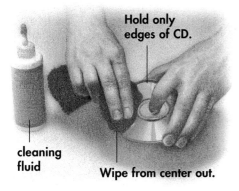

Hold only edges of CD.

cleaning fluid

Wipe from center out.

Cleaning compact discs

Compact discs are promoted as nearly problem-free, but they are almost as vulnerable as vinyl records. Smudges on the face of the disc can block the laser's ability to read information.

Always handle a compact disc by its edge, with a finger in the center hole for support. Do not touch the surface. Use CD-cleaning fluid and a lint-free cloth to clean individual discs (below). Wipe from the center out, not in a circular motion.

HOME OFFICE EQUIPMENT

More and more people are working at home, and more activities in the home are centering around the focal point of most home offices—the computer. The technology changes too rapidly to allow for a reasonable discussion of what sort of computer to buy, but basic organization and maintenance remain much the same. Considering the investment you have made in home office equipment, it just doesn't make sense to ignore cleaning and simple repairs.

Setting up a work area

A fully equipped computer setup may contain the computer unit, keyboard, monitor, printer, fax machine, scanner, and speakers. Each of these components takes up space, and the wires and cables connecting them all can create a maze of confusion. So plan where it all will go. Get measurements of the components you plan to buy, and match them with the available space. Plan a pathway for all those cables: They should not be visible yet should

USING A SIGNAL SPLITTER

Signal splitters are handy accessories for those who use an antenna. One type of splitter divides the signal from the antenna into UHF and VHF components. Another type allows you to connect a second TV to the same antenna connection. Other splitters allow easy switching between video games and TV reception. If you notice a deterioration in picture quality after installing a splitter, you may need to add an amplifier to boost the signal from the antenna.

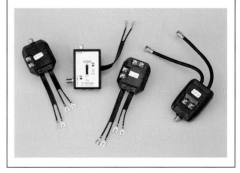

be easy to access. You may even want to label the cables using pieces of tape.

The components don't all have to be located together. The keyboard and monitor need to be close to each other, and the computer unit not too far away. But with long cables, you can place the printer, modem, fax, and scanner in another part of the room. Place speakers on a wall shelf. Consider buying a workstation designed to house all of your components (p.198). Its cost will probably be a small fraction of your equipment expenditures, and it may

197

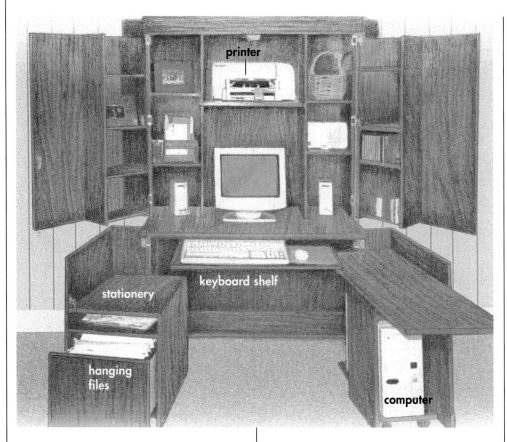

printer

keyboard shelf

stationery

hanging
files

computer

dramatically improve your work environment and increase productivity.

Choose single-function equipment

You may be tempted to buy a machine that combine functions, such as a fax machine that also prints, copies, and scans. A multi-function machine will keep your desk uncluttered and may save you a bit of money as compared with buying the individual, more specialized machines, but buying such a unit has drawbacks. Multi-function machines break down more often than single-function equipment. And if one function stops working, then all the other functions will be unavailable as well when you take the machine in for repair. Also, technology is changing rapidly, and you may someday wish to upgrade, say, your printer. If you choose to do so, it will be cheaper to replace a single-function printer than a multi-task machine.

FAX MACHINES

There are two types of basic, single-function fax machines. Thermal-paper machines are the simplest and least expensive. Images are transferred to heat-sensitive (thermal) paper, eliminating the need for ribbons, ink, or toner. Print quality on newer thermal machines is sharp, but the paper itself is thin and prone to curling. And thermal paper will discolor over time.

Plain-paper fax machines use regular paper. Ink-jet and laser faxes have better print quality than thermal faxes, and their output pages will store far longer without fading.

You can also send and receive faxes through a computer equipped with a fax-modem and the necessary software. This is a good choice if most of the faxes you send are generated by your computer. You can also use a fax-modem to send faxes of images reproduced on a scanner.

Cleaning a thermal fax machine

When print quality starts to decline, you probably need to clean your machine. Unplug the machine before working on it.

Clean the platen with a cloth dampened with denatured alcohol. Carefully turn the platen as you wipe it, and allow it to dry thoroughly before putting the machine back in service. If you notice black vertical lines on the paper when sending a fax or copying, it's probably because the scanner unit, which reads documents being sent, is dirty. Look for a long piece of clear glass in the front of the machine along the document path (facing page). Clean it with a lint-free cloth dampened with denatured alcohol or another solvent that the manufacturer suggests. Fax machines vary from model to model, so check the owner's manual for cleaning instructions for other parts.

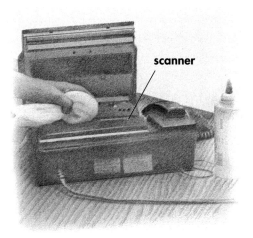

scanner

Solving sending and receiving problems

If you are having trouble sending faxes on a thermal machine, the exposure lamp (bulb) may need replacement. Unplug the machine and allow it to cool for a few minutes. Then turn the machine over and remove the bottom housing. Gently twist and pull the lamp from its sockets. When installing the new lamp, avoid touching the glass with your fingers, or you may get smudges on your faxes.

If received faxes won't print out, the paper may be loaded upside down. Thermal paper prints on only one side. Scratch the paper with a fingernail; the side that produces a black or gray line is the side that should be up.

Cleaning a plain-paper fax machine

If spots appear on faxes and copies, unplug the machine, open the front cover (see the user's manual that came with the unit) and clean the glass scanning window with a dry cotton swab.

In addition, clean the printer area to prevent the buildup of paper dust and ink. Use a clean, soft cloth to clean the platen area. (Never use a solvent such as paint thinner or benzene to clean the printer area.) Clean the paper feeder rollers with a small, soft brush.

COMPUTERS

Computers vary in operating systems, memory capacity, and software, but all share similar types of hardware and accessories. Here is how to keep them clean and in working order.

Making a mouse run smoothly

If the cursor on your computer screen suddenly stops moving smoothly, the mouse may need cleaning. Disconnect the mouse's cord from the keyboard. On the back of the mouse, remove the housing that covers the ball. This may involve unscrewing two small screws, rotating the housing, or pushing it forward. Remove the ball. Wipe it clean with a lint-free cloth dampened with denatured or isopropyl alcohol. Blow any dust and lint out of the ball socket. Clean the two rollers inside the mouse. You may need to use a toothpick to remove chunks of grease and hair. With a cotton swab dipped in denatured alcohol, wipe the rollers clean. Allow the parts to dry, then reassemble and reconnect the mouse.

Cleaning a keyboard

Clean and service the keyboard only when the computer is off. Every month or so, wipe the keys and the area around them with a dampened lint-free

cloth. If keys stick or you start getting characters on your screen that you did not type, clean the keyboard interior.

To do this, unplug the keyboard, remove the screws from the bottom, and carefully pry the housing apart. If it does not come apart easily, you may have missed a screw, or you may need to

canned air

press locking tabs. Then turn the unit upside down, and carefully shake out any debris. Use a container of canned air with a narrow extension tube to blow debris from beneath the keys. If there is sticky grime in the machine, use lots of cotton swabs soaked in water or alcohol to clean it away; this may take time. Reassemble the keyboard and turn the computer back on.

When a keyboard gets wet

If you spill liquid on the keyboard, unplug it immediately and set it upside

199

down on a towel to allow the liquid to drain out. Let the keyboard dry completely before attempting to use it again. If you spilled soda pop or some other liquid that gets sticky when it dries, you will probably need to clean the inside of the keyboard (p.199).

Cleaning the monitor

Use a soft, lint-free cloth and glass cleaner to clean the monitor screen. Spray a small amount of cleaner on the cloth, then wipe the screen. Do not spray cleaner directly onto the screen. Vacuum the ventilation slots on the monitor housing periodically.

Maintaining a hard drive

"Cleaning" a computer's hard drive involves running an operation on the computer to reorganize the data stored on the drive. On a Windows system, use two programs. ScanDisk checks the files and folders on the hard drive for data errors, and it also checks the condition of the surface of the disk. DeFrag is another helpful program. Over time, files break into fragments that are stored in different parts of the hard drive. The information is all there, but it takes longer for the computer to read a fragmented file. Defragmenting the drive will optimize performance.

Most Macintosh computers come with a utility program called Disk First Aid. Run it every two months or so, or whenever your computer is behaving sluggishly, to check the hard drive for errors. For Windows or Mac, follow directions in the Help index after running the appropriate program.

Cleaning floppy drives, backup units, and CD-ROM drives

Dirt and oxide buildup on a floppy disk drive or tape backup unit (TBU) can cause signal dropouts and scrambled or lost data. Dust and lint accumulated on a CD-ROM laser lens can hinder the retrieval of data. All of these drives should be cleaned periodically. There are inexpensive cleaning kits available for each type of device.

Moving a computer

A computer hard drive is most vulnerable to damage when the computer is on. Dropping or jarring the system can damage the hard drive at any time, but especially if the drive is reading or writing when the sudden movement occurs. So always turn the computer off before moving it—even if you are just sliding it from one side of the desk to the other.

When moving a computer to a more distant location, pack it in its original packing materials. If you no longer have them, don't risk damage by attempting to pack it yourself; contact the dealer or manufacturer to see if you can get replacement packing materials.

Connecting a computer

This is simply a matter of connecting a series of cables to their plugs; your manuals will show you where each goes. But it can become confusing because there are so many cables. In the future when something goes wrong with any part of your system, the first thing you will check will be the connections. So mark the cable ends now with pieces of tape that say "modem,"

"fax," "printer," and so on (below).

It is not unusual for an office area with computer equipment, lamps, and so on to need ten or more receptacles for plugs. Don't use household extension cords; buy a power strip that has five or more receptacles in it with surge protection (see "Surge Protectors" on the facing page).

Some cables just push in, while others have built-in screws or wire catches that hold them firmly in place. Always attach the cables as firmly as possible, because they can become loose when a machine gets shifted around.

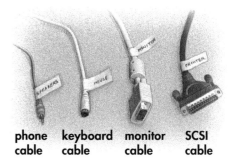

phone cable **keyboard cable** **monitor cable** **SCSI cable**

Connecting two machines to one port

You may end up with more machines (printer, modem, CD-ROM, or disk drive) than ports (receptacles) in your computer. If one of the machines has two ports, you may be able to plug another machine into it rather than directly into the computer. You might need to buy a "daisy chain" cable, designed to link two machines with different ports.

Another solution is to purchase a data transfer switch box. Plug two items into the switch box, and then plug the switch box into the computer port. You will need to turn the switch to the appropriate setting before using one machine or the other.

Backup units

A backup is simply a copy of a file, or a copy of the contents of an entire hard drive, that can be used in the event that the original is damaged or lost. In the early days of computers, people were content to back up their files onto floppy disks, which was often a very time-consuming process.

Today's computers, however, have hard drives that would require hundreds of floppy disks to back up. Tape backup devices are changing and improving as fast as computers themselves. Some units mount inside your computer, and others are portable, enabling you to transport the entire contents of your hard drive in your pocket. Zip and Jaz drives store mountains of data on small discs; recordable CDs do the same thing.

Cost, ease of use, amount of data to be stored, and methods of recovering the data all vary widely. Read current computer and consumer magazines and talk to computer vendors before deciding on a backup unit that's appropriate for your needs.

If you use your computer regularly, develop a regular backup schedule. Plan to do a full backup of the hard disk every week, and incremental backups of changed files every day. Keep a copy of your hard drive away from your house, preferably in an area secure from fire.

OPTIONS IN TELEPHONES

Cordless telephones are handy, and the quality of reception has improved. But a corded phone still offers the best assurance of good-quality sound. Have at least one corded phone in your house, because cordless phones require household electrical current to function, rendering them useless during a power outage. Corded phones use low-voltage power from the telephone line.

You can choose models that are compatible with caller ID, call waiting, and other services offered by phone companies. Memory features allow you to program the phone to dial phone numbers by pushing a single key. Speakerphones permit you to carry on a conversation without using the handset. Phones with built-in answering machines are available. Older cordless phones offered only two channels, which made them vulnerable to interference from phones nearby that were operating on the same channel. They also had a limited range. Newer models have as many as 100 channels and ranges of hundreds of feet.

Changing a cord

The phone is connected to the handset with a coiled cord. If the cord is soiled, wrap it around a wooden spoon handle and clean it with Formula 409 or Fantastik. Cords on new phones are usually too short to allow you to move around the room while talking on the phone. Longer cords are readily available and easy to install. (But if you have a phone that's not black, white,

GOOD TOOLS

SURGE PROTECTORS

A power surge is an increase in the voltage running through an electrical line. It is typically caused by the utility company switching sources of power, although a surge can also be generated within your own house. Lightning is also a common source of electrical surges. They are usually very brief—lasting perhaps only 120th of a second—but they can damage computer equipment. Computer hard drives are damaged by external forces every day, sometimes causing enormous losses for users.

◆ **Surge protectors** detect a dangerous surge and shut down the flow of electricity before it reaches sensitive equipment. A protector rated for 200 joules will offer basic protection; one rated for 400 joules is good protection; and a rating of 600 or more means exceptional protection. Higher joule ratings also mean higher prices.

◆ **An uninterruptible power supply** (UPS) is a more sophisticated form of protection. In addition to moderating the flow of electricity to a computer, it serves as a brief backup source of power in the event of a blackout. This additional power gives you time to safely close and back up your files before losing power.

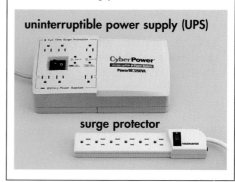

uninterruptible power supply (UPS)

surge protector

or off-white, you may have to contact the maker of the phone directly to get one that matches your phone.) To remove a phone cord, pinch the tab on each plug and pull it out. To insert, firmly push the plug in until you hear it click. If a cord becomes wound up on itself, disconnect one end and let it hang free until it straightens itself out.

Attaching a phone to a wall jack

A desk phone is connected to a cord which is in turn connected to a wall jack; pinch the tab to remove these connections, just as you would for a coiled cord. A desk phone can be moved around freely, while a wall phone is firmly attached to the wall.

Mounting a telephone on the wall can free up counter space; you may want to mount a cordless phone, or get a long-coiled cord, for freedom of movement. Many tabletop phones can be mounted on the wall. Typically you remove the base from the phone, attach the base to the wall jack, then snap the phone assembly back together. (Check the owner's manual for specific instructions.) If you don't have a wall jack, have the phone company install one.

Checking a jack

If the phone is not working, first check the four cord connections—two for the coiled cord connecting the handset to the phone base, and two for the cord connecting the base to the wall jack. If

they are firmly installed and the phone still doesn't work, try installing another phone that you know works. If the problem persists, check the wall jack.

Replacing a baseboard or wall jack

You can easily replace a baseboard jack if it's been damaged or become paint-encrusted or if you want a newer style.

Remove the screw on the cover and pull the cover off. Loosen the screws securing all the wires, and pull the wires free. Remove the screw or screws holding the jack's baseplate to the wall. Attach the new baseplate to the wall with a screw or two. Connect all the phone wires and jack wires to the terminals; be sure to connect green

---

CLEANING THE TELEPHONE TRANSMITTER AND RECEIVER

1. A dirty transmitter will make your voice sound muddy or crackly to listeners (ask yourself if your friends have complained). If the voice in your ear is unclear, the receiver may need cleaning. On some phones—usually older ones—you can unscrew the mouthpiece or earpiece. The transmitter is a separate piece that pops out; the receiver is attached by wires.

2. To clean the transmitter, first unplug the phone. Use a cotton swab moistened with electrical-contact cleaner or denatured or isopropyl alcohol to clean surface dirt as well as the metal contacts. With a small piece of emery cloth (or very fine sandpaper), also clean the metal contacts in the handset.

3. To clean the receiver, loosen the terminal screws and pull the wires free. Use a swab moistened with denatured alcohol to clean the wires and screws. Use a small piece of emery cloth to remove any corrosion. Reassemble, and test. If the problem persists, try plugging another phone in the jack, and test it. If you still have poor sound, contact the phone company.

CHECKING A PHONE JACK

1. Remove the screw on the cover, and pull off the cover. Set it to the side, taking care not to pull wires. Check for loose wires. Often, only two wires out of four are connected.

2. Make sure the wire and terminal colors match; terminals will be labeled "G" for green and "R" for red, for example. Use needlenose pliers or a screwdriver to make sure that each connection is secure.

3. A bare wire that touches the wrong terminal will cause problems. Snip away any excess wire, including any from wires that are not being used. Test the phone; if it still does not work, contact the phone company.

to green and red to red. Tighten the screws, and make sure that no bare wires can touch wrong terminals. Replace the cover, and test.

Improving battery performance for a cordless phone

The handset of a cordless phone is powered by a battery. The battery recharges when the handset is returned to the base, between phone calls. If the battery is low, the transmission quality will be poor.

Periodically clean the metal contacts on the handset and base with a pencil eraser. If the "battery low" indicator light comes on after only an hour or so of use, the battery probably needs to be replaced. Check the owner's manual for instructions. You can buy a new battery at an electronics store.

Improving cordless phone reception

If the sound on a cordless phone begins to fade or flutter, make sure that the antennas on the base and the handset are fully extended. If you notice interference on the phone line, it may be coming from other phones, a household appliance, television, a vacuum, or other electric sources.

Cordless phones can be switched between several channels. Some models will switch automatically when they detect interference, while others require you to switch channels manually. If you live in a highly populated area, you will likely appreciate a cordless phone with 25 or more channels. Keep trying different channels until you achieve the clearest sound.

Sometimes you can reduce the amount of interference by plugging the base into a different outlet. Moving the base upstairs in a two-story house may also help.

Connecting an answering machine

A typical answering machine has three connections. Unplug the phone cord from the telephone and insert that plug into the "Tel Line" connection on the answering machine. Run another cord from the "Telephone" connection on the answering machine to the telephone itself. Finally, plug the adapter into the round connector on the answering machine and into an electrical outlet.

Improving sound quality

If your answering machine uses one or two cassette tapes and you notice that messages suddenly sound poor, clean the tape path. Remove the cassette. Use a swab moistened with head-cleaning solution or denatured alcohol, and wipe the head, pinch roller, and capstan. Allow everything to dry for about 15 minutes before replacing the cassette and restoring service.

INDOOR FLOWERS AND PLANTS

Flowers and plants are an important asset to a home's decorating scheme. Fortunately, you don't have to be an expert to have healthy greenery and charmingly arranged flowers.

The beauty of cut flowers and indoor plants in your home is a joy that involves only a small investment of time and effort. Careful selection and regular care is all that's needed to keep them looking their best.

BUYING CUT FLOWERS

The fresher the flower, the longer it will last. The best, freshest flowers have firm leaves that show no trace of yellowing and that resist slightly when bent. Very fresh flowers usually will be only partly open (roses should still be buds), and their colors true, with no sign of browning. They should not shed any petals. If the flowers are in water, the water should look and smell clean, with no trace of decay. (Look at other flowers in the store. If they're tired and aging, chances are flowers you buy will soon look that way, too.) You can buy high-quality flowers just about anywhere. At a farmer's market, expect casual, common flowers sold loose or in unstructured bouquets. Florists, on the other hand, will carry more exotic flowers and certain flowers out of season.

Caring for cut flowers

Keep a beautiful arrangement fresher longer by taking a few simple steps.

◆ **Keep flowers out** of direct sunlight. At night, move the flowers to a cool spot, such as a basement or spare room. Don't put flowers in the refrigerator—it's too dry in there.

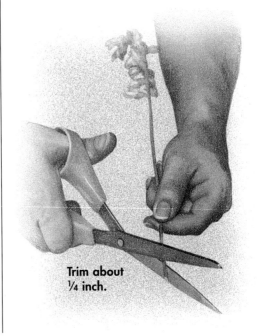

Trim about ¼ inch.

◆ **Change the water** in your flower arrangement frequently, replacing with tepid water to which you've added floral preservative. Available from greenhouses and florists, it makes flowers last much longer.

◆ **Every other day,** trim the ends of the flowers' stems by about ¼ inch (below left). You can trim one stem at a time or the whole bunch at once.

Cutting flowers from a garden

Fresh flowers from the garden last days longer if you cut and condition them properly. Harvest flowers early in the morning, just after the dew has dried, while they're at their brightest. Soak them up to their necks in a tall container filled with tepid water for several hours.

After conditioning, strip the lower parts of the stems to remove foliage. Bare stems look good in clear vases, and they will not foul the water as leaves would.

Recut the ends to improve the flowers' ability to take up water. (Cut rose stems under water.) If the flower gives off a milky sap, put the cut end of the flower in a candle flame for a second or two to sear it and prevent the sap from fouling the water. After arranging, fill with water containing a floral preservative.

Arranging tips

Anchor your flowers. For a bowl or a short vase, use green floral foam. Soak it in water and cut it with a knife to the size of the vase, allowing it to stand about 1 inch higher than the vase rim. Place flower stems into the

foam, inserting some horizontally for a fuller look. With taller vases, use a "frog" (a small bed-of-nails), or fill the bottom third of a glass vase with marbles, both will hold flower stems firmly in place.

When arranging, go for a mix of shapes. Use boldly shaped flowers, tall spikey flowers, and fluffy-looking filler flowers or foliage. If the arrangement will be viewed from one side only, place leaves in the background. Your florist will supply you with foliage, but don't be afraid to mix in foliage, such as hosta, from your own backyard. Herbs often look handsome in a flower arrangement.

BEAUTIFUL CUT FLOWERS

Some cut flowers look great when you buy them but wilt in a few days. Among those that will stay fresh a week or more are baby's breath (*Gypsophila*); bells of Ireland (*Molucella laevis*); campanula; coralbells (*Heuchera*); gaillardia; florist's carnations, or pinks (*Dianthus*); lisianthus; and yarrow (*Achillea*). Equally beautiful but shorter lived are delphiniums, purple coneflowers (*Echinacea*), and goldenrods (*Solidago*).

205

MONEY SAVERS

LIVING BOUQUETS

Some of the prettiest—and most economical—floral displays are those that you create yourself from inexpensive annuals purchased at a garden center.

◆ **Choose decorative pots** suitable for indoor use; be sure they have a drainage hole. Prevent moisture from the pots from harming your furniture by setting them on a nonporous drainage tray.

◆ **Plant your favorite annuals** in these pots. The annuals that work best are small, with a tidy growing habit and attractive foliage. Good candidates worth consideration include wax begonias, impatiens, geraniums, heliotrope 'Mini Marine', signet marigolds, pansies, and miniature roses.

◆ **Regularly rotate** each pot indoors to outdoors, leaving them indoors no more than a week at a time and giving them at least two weeks at a time when you put them outdoors.

pothos

spider plant

Boston fern

weeping fig

schefflera

snake plant

BEST-BET HOUSEPLANTS

Some houseplants are easier to care for than others. Look for plants that will do well in your settings; consult with the nursery about the proper amount of light, humidity, and temperature. Houseplants that are easy to care for include: spider plant (*Chlorophytum*); arrowhead plant (*Syngonium podophyllum*); Boston fern (*Nephrolepis exaltata bostoniensis*); English ivy (*Hedera helix*); jade plant (*Crassula argentea*); pothos (*Philodendron oxycardium*); schefflera (*Brassaia actinophylla*); snake plant (*Sansevieria*); Swedish ivy (*Plectranthus oertendahii*); umbrella plant (*Cyperus*); wandering Jew (*Tradescantia*); and weeping fig (*Ficus benjamina*).

Potting basics

You'll know that it's time to repot a houseplant when its roots have begun growing through the drainage hole or when it wilts between waterings.

To repot, knock the plant gently from its pot. Choose a pot no more than 2 inches wider than the original, and put a shard from a clay pot or a piece of fine wire over the drainage hole to prevent soil from washing out. Add a half-inch of pebbles or gravel in the bottom of the pot, topped with a little potting soil. (Use commercial potting soil, not soil from the yard.) Place the plant in the new pot, and gently tamp potting soil around the sides. Fill it 1 inch short of the pot edge to allow a space for water. Water well.

Indoor light basics

Proper lighting is one of the biggest challenges of indoor gardening. Too little, and you'll end up with yellowing, spindly plants plagued by disease. You can make sure your indoor plants are getting proper light by reading the plant label carefully or checking a good houseplant reference book.

The majority of houseplants do well next to an east-, west-, or north-facing window without drapes. Some plants, however, require more light and must be placed in the brightest spot possible: a south-facing window. If you are unsure of what your plant needs, experiment by placing it in several different places for two or three weeks at a time and noting the effect.

If you have more plants than light, consider an artificial source. This can be an architect's extension-arm lamp beaming down on a single large plant, or a shop light equipped with two fluorescent tubes, one warm-spectrum and one cool. (More expensive grow-lights are unnecessary if you use this combination.) High-intensity plant lights are bright enough to grow lettuces, herbs, and other sun-loving plants.

Watering basics

It's easy to kill a plant by overwatering. Most houseplants are happy with soil that is kept just barely moist. Water your plants with tepid (not cold) water whenever the soil feels dry; to test, stick your finger into the soil about an inch.

If your plant wilts or its leaves lose their sheen between waterings, you

FLOWERING HOUSEPLANTS

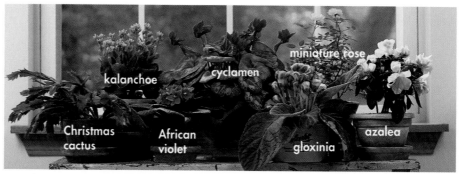

kalanchoe · cyclamen · miniature rose · Christmas cactus · African violet · gloxinia · azalea

Most flowering houseplants need more light than their greener counterparts. And they can be fussy in their demands for certain soils and fertilization. But if you have the interest—and a sunny window or two—you can add their beauty and fragrance to your home. Some of the easiest include: African violet, azalea, Christmas cactus, clivia, cyclamen, gloxinia, kalanchoe, and miniature rose.

know you're not giving enough water each time. Water leaking out of the bottom of the pot is usually a sign that you've watered enough. If the soil smells dank or the soil isn't dry, wait a few days and check again. Always water with an absorbent cloth on hand to mop up spills. Better yet, take your plants to the kitchen sink for an occasional deep soaking and a spray of water to rinse off dust and insects.

All houseplant pots should rest in moisture-proof drainage trays. Filling the trays with gravel or small pebbles, and setting the pots on these will give a water reservoir and add humidity.

Indoor trees

Whether you choose a weeping fig or a palm, a statuesque rubber tree or dramatic dracaena, indoor trees are usually easy to grow. They have the same requirements as their smaller houseplant cousins: adequate light and regular watering. Unlike outdoor trees, they need no pruning except for the occasional trimming of a dead or dying limb. All indoor trees should be in sturdy, moisture-proof pots. Ideally, each should also be in a tray or platform on coasters to make moving them—especially to check for spilled water—easy. Never set a clay pot directly on the floor. Unglazed clay wicks moisture and will ruin a wood floor or carpet. A daily misting with room-temperature water will keep them healthy.

Good choices for indoor trees, which can easily top 6 feet, include: palms, especially the majesty palm (*Ravenea rivularis*); one of the tall *Dracaena fragrans*, weeping fig (*Ficus benjamina*), kumquat (*Fortunella japonica*), spineless yucca (*Yucca elephantipes*), and false aralia (*Schefflera elegantissima*).

6

Clothing

Laundry

BASICS OF CLEANING CLOTHES

A well-planned laundry area can make wash day easier and more efficient. There are many timesaving options available to equip a new laundry room or to update an existing one.

Doing the laundry may not be your favorite pastime, but the whole process can be made more pleasant with a good laundry set-up. When you have room to sort and prepare (and even mend) the dirty clothes and a place to fold and press the clean ones, you'll find it easier to do the job right.

PLANNING A LAUNDRY AREA

While deciding what your home laundry area should include and where it should go, you also should consider the needs of your household. For example, a small-capacity washer and dryer would probably work fine for a one- or two-person household, particularly if dry cleaning and drop-off laundry services are used often.

A large household, on the other hand, probably could use a large-capacity washer and dryer with a fully equipped laundry area set up for high-volume washing.

Location

Families with small children should consider locating the laundry where it can also be used as a mud room, ideally situated between the backyard and the living area of the house. With this kind of arrangement, kids can strip off their dirty clothes and leave them there to be laundered before coming into the house.

A laundry located in, or right off of, the kitchen lets parents do several activities at the same time—for example, supervise the children's homework, prepare meals, and fold clothes. By the same token, a separate laundry area that includes enough space for a sewing machine and storage can easily become home to other pursuits, such as crafting or sewing.

Because laundry first accumulates near bedrooms or baths, a double hall-way closet is another logical laundry spot. If space is tight, a single closet can accommodate a stacked washer and dryer (p.222), as can the unused space under a stairway.

Basements have traditionally served as laundry areas, and can be combined with exercise equipment to make a laundry/workout area.

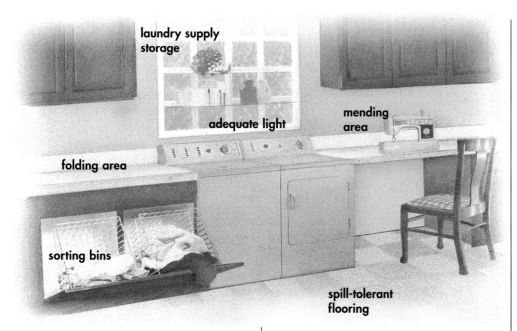

laundry supply storage

adequate light

mending area

folding area

sorting bins

spill-tolerant flooring

With a little imagination, a laundry room can go from good to great. For example, a shower stall with a clothes rod, a drain, and a faucet with a hose attachment will allow you to hang up drip-dry items or freshly ironed clothing, or to hose off muddy boots.

A pull-out table adds extra sorting and folding space. An ironing board can be installed either in a tall cabinet or in a drawer, where it can be pulled out when needed. Tall cabinets also can accommodate brooms, vacuum cleaners, and exercise equipment.

A rolling hamper can be stored in a cabinet, and a center island with recessed wheels provides movable folding space. Many space-saving storage centers are available for detergents, pretreat solutions, bleach, and dryer sheets. You can even create a recycling area by adding a few plastic bins put in a separate cabinet or simply placed under shelving.

Making the right connections

No matter where a home laundry area is located, it must be hooked up to the right utility connections. A washing machine needs a drain and plumbing lines for hot and cold water. Washers also need a 120-volt grounded outlet, as do gas dryers (for the motor).

Gas dryers also require connections to either natural or bottled gas. Electric dryers need a dedicated 240-volt circuit (see page 92).

All clothes dryers should be vented to the outside to prevent humidity and mildew problems in your laundry room or basement. Include extra electrical outlets for ironing, sewing, and task lighting, especially if the laundry area is home to other activities as well. Glare-free lighting makes clothing stains easier to see.

Planning for convenience

With the location and connections in place, it's time to start planning the space and features of your laundry area (above). Because a laundry room is home to water, detergents, and additives, the floor should be spill-tolerant resilient flooring, ceramic tile, brick, or stone (pp.13–15). Countertops should be surfaced with laminate or ceramic tile (pp.106–107). Countertops typically work best installed at 36- and 42-inch heights, or they can be installed at whatever height is most comfortable for you. Shelves located high on the wall can store bleach and detergents safely out of children's reach. A sink offers the perfect place for pretreating laundry or hand-washing delicate items. And a desk area can be turned into a sewing spot.

HOW A WASHER WORKS

A washer uses three kinds of energy to remove soil from clothing—mechanical, chemical, and thermal.

Mechanical energy comes from the washing action of the machine. In a top-loading washer, an agitator pulls the clothing through the water, and the spin cycle pulls the clothes outward. In a front-loading washer, the clothes are tumbled through a shallow pool of water.

Detergents, bleach, and other additives provide chemical energy. Thermal energy is supplied by warm or hot water. If you reduce any one of these elements, another must be increased. For example, if you lower the water temperature, you need to increase the wash time to compensate.

Loading clothes

Loading the clothes washer involves knowing two things—what to put in a load and how much. A washer works best when a load contains both large and small items. So if several sheets are headed for the laundry, try to split them into different loads and combine them with smaller items. For instance, a load might have a sheet, a few socks, some towels, shirts, and washcloths.

As for how much to put in the washer, make sure that all items are unfolded, loaded loosely, and can move easily throughout the wash process. In a top-loading washer, a full load comes to the top row of holes in the washtub. Clothes loaded in a front-loading washer can fill the entire tub; the washer's tumbling action dips them repeatedly in and out of the water.

Assuring appropriate water temperature

For hot-water loads, water heaters should deliver water that is 140°F and certainly no less than 120°F. To check the water temperature, put a candy thermometer in a glass and fill the glass with water that is running into the washer. If the water temperature is not appropriate, adjust the thermostat on your water heater.

Using the appropriate water temperature for each load of laundry helps assure optimum cleaning. In general,

hot water should be used for most whites and for colored items that are very dirty. Because a warm wash is safe for most other fabrics, it is the most frequent choice. And for clothes that have barely been soiled, a cold wash is adequate. Cold-water washes are also the surest way to keep brightly colored clothing from fading.

Choosing the best wash cycle

Every fabric is unique, and washers are designed to accommodate as many different types as possible. Check out the washer's back panel, where the cycle options usually include regular, permanent press, and knits/delicates. When a load includes cottons, linens, and other washables, set the washer for regular. Choose the permanent-press cycle for articles with a permanent-press finish or for garments made of man-made fibers, like polyester, nylon, or acrylic. Use the delicate cycle for clothes that are the most fragile. If there is any doubt that a garment can stand up to being agitated or tumbled, choose the delicate cycle. Lace- or embroidery-trimmed items, sheer lingerie, machine-washable woolens—even swimsuits or loosely knit sweaters—all may be washed on delicate. Also, if a care label reads "Hand Washable," be sure to choose the delicate cycle.

Avoiding residue

If a white residue or soap film is left on your clothes after laundering, putting them in the dryer should remove it. To avoid residue on clothing, use warmer water during the wash cycle. Detergent

needs water of at least 65°F to work properly, and it may not dissolve completely in cold water. Using liquid detergent rather than granular may help. Using less fabric softener or switching your fabric softener or detergent is another solution; a chemical reaction between the two can produce a residue. Also, try not to overload the washer. Residue is more likely to remain and not rinse away when there are too many items in the washer.

Avoiding tangling

Because a washer agitates or tumbles clothing while cleaning it, clothing sometimes comes out of the washer tangled. To avoid tangles, load the washer without twisting items around the agitator. Choose the right amount of water for the load; not enough water or too much water can cause tangling. A mesh bag to hold delicate items or items with straps also helps prevent tangling and snagging.

MACHINE-WASHING CLOTHES

Today's washers are sophisticated enough to handle almost any washing problem and will adjust to all but the most finicky fabrics. But you will maximize your machine's effectiveness by organizing your laundry, preparing it for washing, and using the right detergents and additives.

Sorting your laundry

Before you begin, always sort your clothes. Keep a few baskets or bins near the laundry area. Separate whites from colors, and light colors from

darks

lights

bright or dark colors, to prevent colors from bleeding into each other. Use a white basket for whites and colored baskets for colors (above) or sort by fabric type. White cotton, bed linens, and underwear benefit from warmer water and vigorous washing. Heavier fabrics and dark colors, on the other hand, require cooler water and a short wash time to prevent shrinking or fading. Permanent-press items of similar weights should be washed together, but in smaller loads to minimize wrinkling.

Sort also according to the sturdiness of your clothes to keep delicate items and jeans in separate loads. Soil can transfer from one garment to another, so wash dirty work and play clothes in one load, and lightly soiled clothes in another.

Preparing your laundry

As you sort your clothes, inspect each item carefully. Check pockets for non-washable items like crayons, lipsticks, or pens that can stain clothing permanently. Watch for sharp objects like nail files or pins, which can rip or tear clothes. Shake out loose dirt and brush off lint. Take out lapel pins as well as any ornaments or trim that might not wash well. Remove shoulder pads and loose belts where possible, and close any zippers or hook and eyes that might catch. Tie drawstrings together (below) to save you threading them through the casing later. Mend ripped seams, frayed edges, or pulled threads before washing. Pretreating stains helps avoid a second washing (see "Stain Removal" on page 234).

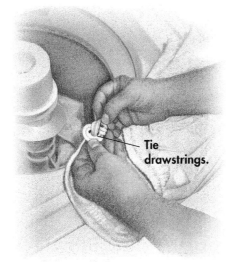

Tie drawstrings.

Avoiding pilling

Pilling is the accumulation of tiny fuzzy balls on loosely knit clothing or man-made fabrics such as polyester. Turn clothes inside out before washing and load washer loosely to cut down on fabrics rubbing against each other. Use fabric softener and a shorter wash time, and wash fabrics that pill easily separate from those that give off lint. To remove pills, use a razor, electric shaver, medium sandpaper, or a shaver-like tool designed for this purpose.

MONEY SAVERS

USING BLEACH

Bleach is a laundry additive used to get clothes cleaner and whiter. It also works as a disinfectant. (Blueing is another product that helps restore whiteness. It contains blue pigments, which counteract the yellowing that occurs with some fabrics.) Chlorine bleach is a liquid; non-chlorine bleach is available in either liquid or granular form. For convenience, some detergents include bleach.

◆ **Chlorine bleach** is safe for all fabrics except wool, spandex, mohair, and silk, but not for non-colorfast items; following label instructions is always the best policy. Chlorine bleach is fast-acting and strong; used improperly, it can severely weaken and damage fabrics.

◆ **To use bleach safely,** add it to the machine's bleach dispenser before loading. This avoids spilling undiluted bleach onto clothes. Should this happen, damage might not show up immediately, but clothes could eventually develop holes, rips, yellowing, or color loss. If the washer doesn't have a dispenser, dilute the bleach as recommended by the manufacturer, adding it to the wash after the load is completely wet.

◆ **Do not use bleach** if your water has a high iron content: It will spot your clothes. Never use bleach and ammonia at the same time: The combination can generate hazardous fumes. Non-chlorine, all-fabric, or oxygenated bleach is simply a milder form of bleach. Because it is milder, it doesn't remove stains or whiten as well, but it is safe for all fabrics. All bleach works faster in warmer water.

Avoiding lint

Lint is nothing more than small fibers of fabric that have broken off during normal wear or laundering. To keep lint to a minimum, sort fabrics before washing. Some fabrics, like terry cloth and chenille, give off lint easily, so wash them separately from fabrics like corduroy or polyester, which tend to pick up lint. Try not to overload the washer, which causes clothes to rub against each other. Use enough detergent, which helps suspend lint during the wash cycle. Fabric softener or a dryer sheet reduces static cling, decreasing the tendency of manufactured fibers to attract and hold lint.

Choosing laundry products

Today's laundry detergents were developed specifically for use in automatic washers—replacing soap, which was used when clothing was washed by hand. Soaps are mild and are still often recommended for baby clothes and delicate fabrics. In hard water, however, soap can leave a sticky residue.

Synthetic detergents contain surfactants that make water "wetter" and help suspend dirt until it is rinsed away. Some detergents also contain builders, which make the surfactants even more effective. These detergents are referred to as "heavy-duty" detergents.

Detergents come in two basic forms —liquid and granular—both of which remove soil, dissolve it, and suspend it in water. Detergents are designed to work with a washer's washing action, so it's important to choose your detergent based on the type of washer you

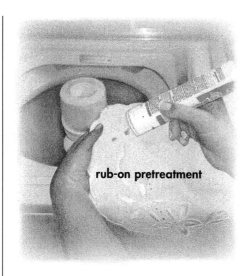

rub-on pretreatment

have. Regular detergents work in most top-loading washers, but a front-loading washer cleans better with detergents formulated to work with the tumbling action.

◆ **Granular detergents** are the most popular laundry product, possibly because they work best on clothing soiled with mud and clay, two common laundry problems. A granular detergent also works better than liquid detergent in hard water; it is more effective at minimizing rust stains.

◆ **Liquid detergents** have become popular in recent years for several reasons. They help save energy for one. Liquids dissolve easily in cold water, making them the best choice when you want to cut down on the number of energy-sapping hot and warm water washes. In addition, they clean oil and grease stains better than granular detergents, and they are easier to use for pretreating heavily soiled fabrics.

◆ **Allergy-sensitive detergents** are now being offered by manufacturers in both granular and liquid forms for the increasing number of people sensitive to certain chemicals, dyes, or perfumes in detergents. Look for label names that include the words "free" or "clear."

◆ **Pretreatment products,** available as aerosol sprays, pump sprays, and rub-on sticks (left), are laundry aids that can be used to pretreat heavily soiled clothing before washing. They are best for oil-based stains on clothes made of polyester materials.

◆ **Fabric softener,** a laundry additive, is designed to reduce static cling and minimize wrinkling. By providing a lubricating film, a fabric softener helps clothes feel softer, discourages lint, and adds a fresh scent.

Liquid fabric softener is added during the washer's rinse cycle or to the softener dispenser prior to running the machine. For washers without dispensers, add the softener to the rinse water as soon as the final agitation begins. Clothing absorbs rinse-added softeners, so avoid buildup by using only the appropriate amount of softener per load. Some detergents come with softener already added. You can also soften your laundry by adding a single, coated fabric-softener sheet to the dryer at the start of its cycle.

Undiluted fabric softener can leave an oily stain on clothing. Dryer-added fabric softener sheets can leave small streaks. If rewashing without softener doesn't take care of removing the stain, dampen the area and rub it with hand soap (below), then wash again. Fabric softener stains are easy to remove and seldom permanent.

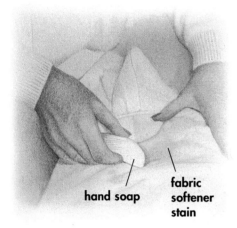

hand soap | fabric softener stain

Detergent action

More suds do not equal better cleaning, nor is more detergent necessarily the solution to a tough cleaning problem.

Detergents are specifically formulated to produce varying amounts of suds for different laundry situations. Normal sudsing detergents, for instance, produce visible suds. Low sudsers, on the other hand, are designed for use in soft water where too much sudsing can leave detergent on clothing even after rinsing.

Adding more detergent can solve some laundry problems, but it can be tricky estimating how much more to add, especially with the range of regular and concentrated detergents now on the market.

While manufacturers almost always include a scoop that's sized for one load, that load is based on an average—and very few loads are exactly average.

Rather than rely on the scoop, consider each load's size, how dirty the clothes are, and how much water will be used. Even the hardness of the water affects the amount of detergent you should use. As a rule of thumb, if the load is very dirty or very big, or if hard water is a problem in your area, add more detergent. Conversely, if the load is small or not very heavily soiled, or the water is softened, use less detergent. Also, put in the detergent before the clothes. It will dissolve more quickly, and clothes will come out cleaner.

Improving cold-water washing

Washing laundry in cold water saves energy, but clothes usually don't get as clean as with warm water. Detergents simply do not work well in water colder than 65°F.

There are ways to compensate, however. Because liquid detergents dissolve more quickly in cold water than granulars, they clean more effectively than granular detergents for cold-water laundering. You can also improve your cold-water results by using bleach judiciously, pre-soaking dirty clothing, and pretreating any stains.

Doing laundry in very cold weather can pose problems. Water in the pipes is often colder than it would be normally. (Wrapping pipes with insulation helps to reduce heat loss.) To offset the water's below-normal temperature, run some hot water in the washer first or use the warm setting. The mixture of very cold water on the warm water setting may average out to what would be considered a cold setting.

Determining water hardness

If you have hard water, you will need to use more detergent and higher water temperatures to get clothes really clean. Knowing how hard your water is makes it easier to make the correct adjustments. One way to determine water hardness is to buy a test kit at a hardware store. You can also call your local water utility for a reading, which is usually measured in grains per gallon (gpg). A reading of 0 to 4 gpg is considered soft, 4 to 9 gpg is soft to average, and 10 gpg and above is hard.

LAUNDERING UNUSUAL ITEMS

Dry cleaning is not the only choice for such items as large blankets or comforters, curtains or draperies, and down-filled items. Here's how you can wash many of these at home.

Blankets and comforters

Large, bulky items like blankets and comforters often have special instructions on the label. If so, follow them. If the item is washable, check to see if it fits in the washer. When dry, a blanket or comforter should not sit above the top row of holes in a top-loading washer. Wash a comforter by itself in warm water on the regular cycle, making sure it is submerged in the water. Most comforters will fit into a front-loading washer easily. If a blanket or comforter does not fit into a washer, take it to a commercial laundry. Both items can be dried in the dryer or dried on a clothesline or drying rack.

Curtains and draperies

Curtains and draperies are especially susceptible to the long-term effects of sunlight, which can weaken the fabric and expose it to tears or frays when washed. Consequently, it's best to wash in warm water on either the delicate or hand-wash cycle of the washer. If you have doubts, however, take window coverings to a dry cleaner. Always dry-clean lined drapes; the two fabrics may react differently when washed. Vinyl or plastic curtains can be cleaned simply by wiping with a damp cloth and a mild detergent or plain water.

Pillows and down-filled clothes

Some pillows contain filling that can become lumpy or stained when wet, so read the manufacturer's label for washing instructions. For instance, kapok pillows cannot be washed in a washing machine. (Kapok is a natural silky fiber, derived from the ceiba tree, that is used as a filler.)

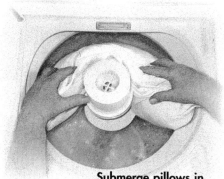

Submerge pillows in a half-filled washer.

If a pillow or down-filled vest is labeled washable, however, first fill the washer halfway with water, then submerge the pillow to get the air out of it (above). Let the washer fill, then wash the pillow or vest for 8 to 10 minutes on a regular or delicate cycle. Open the lid occasionally and press air from the items and balance the load as necessary. Because a front-loading washer tumbles its load, the action itself expels air from the items.

Diaper duty

Most families today use disposable diapers, but if you use cloth diapers—and opt to wash them yourself instead of using a diaper service—you will be faced with a three-step cleaning process. Diapers were designed to absorb some of the toughest stains, so they're also one of the hardest items to clean. First, rinse dirty diapers in cold water. The second step is a long soak—overnight, if possible—in a pail of diaper conditioner or borax solution. Once the diapers are pretreated, launder them in the washing machine on the regular cycle as the last step. Be careful not to overload your machine (most take three dozen diapers easily).

WASHING DELICATES

Today's gentler washing machine cycles have almost eliminated the need for hand-washing. Still, some delicate garments, particularly antique ones, need special treatment to retain their beauty, body, and shape.

Reading care labels

Care labels are the most reliable source of information on how to clean a given garment. In order to make the cleaning process as easy as possible, manufacturers use a set of universal symbols that identify the appropriate procedure (see page 220). Be sure to follow these instructions carefully.

Blocking a hand-washed sweater

Sweaters that have been hand-washed should be laid out carefully to dry so that they retain their original shape. Before washing, outline the shape of the sweater on a large piece of white wrapping paper. Place the pattern on a flat colorfast surface, such as a beach towel or waterproof counter. After washing the sweater, blot it gently

CHOOSING THE BEST LAUNDRY PROCEDURE

Once you've sorted your laundry (and checked the care labels when available) getting the best laundry results relies in part on choosing the right setting for each load on the washer and the dryer. Here are the settings for most loads of household laundry.

Type of Load	Wash Water Temperature	Rinse Water Temperature	Wash Cycle	Wash Time	Water Level	Laundry Products	Dryer Settings
Regular fabrics: Sturdy cottons and linens; everything washable except permanent press, delicates, woolens	Warm or cold for prewash or soak Hot (whites or heavily soiled) Cold (bright or dark colors or lightly soiled)	Cold or warm	Regular	7–15 minutes (depending on amount of soil)	Adjust to size of load	Any laundry detergent in hot or warm water Liquid or predissolved granular in cold water Chlorine or non-chlorine bleach Fabric softener	Regular cycle temperature
Permanent press, no-iron items: All permanent press and other no-iron fabrics	Hot (white or heavily soiled) Warm (colors or lightly soiled)	Cold	Permanent press	5–14 minutes (depending on amount of soil)	Adjust to size of load	Any laundry detergent Chlorine or non-chlorine bleach Fabric softener	Permanent-press cycle temperature
Delicates: Lingerie, loosely knit items, sheer fabrics, lace-trimmed or embroidered articles, hand-washable items	Warm or cold (bright colors)	Cold or warm	Knits/delicate or hand-washables	2-speed washers: 7–12 minutes All-fabric washers: 10 minutes	Adjust to size of load	Any detergent in warm water Liquid or predissolved granular in cold water Chlorine (but not if spandex) or non-chlorine bleach Fabric softener	Regular or knits/delicate cycle temperature
Wool: Machine-washable and hand-washable woolen items	Warm or cold	Warm or cold	Knits/delicate or hand-washables	2 minutes of agitation followed by soak	Adjust to size of load	Liquid or pre-dissolved granular detergent	Machine dryable: regular cycle temperature Others: block and allow to air-dry

with a white towel, then pin it to the outline of the pattern. Pins should be placed so that the edges of the sweater are not pulled out of shape or they will dry in scallops.

Being delicate with delicates

Delicate or antique items that have become stained should always be hand-washed. Pretreat any stain before washing. Today's gentler pretreat laundry products will probably suffice for most items, but a 10-minute soak in water with pre-dissolved detergent can also revive fragile garments.

Try not to rub or squeeze the garment. Instead, work water and suds gently through it, and change the water if it becomes dirty. The wash water should be lukewarm, as should the rinse water. Rinse repeatedly until no suds remain, then blot the garment with a dry towel and lay it flat to dry, away from direct sunlight.

When an item is aged and precious, such as an antique lace tablecloth, take special care even in hand washing it. Lace tablecloths may have been any shade of white, ivory, or ecru, so first determine what color you believe it to be (or want it to be). Then use diluted bleach accordingly. Lay the tablecloth on a flat surface and sponge it gently with diluted color-safe bleach, diluted detergent, or diluted hydrogen peroxide. If even the gentlest sponging appears to damage fibers, stop immediately and rinse gently and thoroughly. Lay the item flat to dry, making sure it is away from heat and light. If the process seems too potentially damag-

ing, take the tablecloth to a professional cleaner for advice. Some delicate cloths may simply be beyond repair.

Antique embroidery

Wash antique embroidery in warm, sudsy water and then dry flat. Test new embroidery for colorfastness before you wash it. To test, spread the piece (or sample pieces of the embroidery threads) on a white cloth, cover with a wet cloth; and press with a hot iron (below). If the white cloth is stained, the piece is not colorfast. You can clean it by dipping it in a solution of hot water and 1 tablespoon of borax.

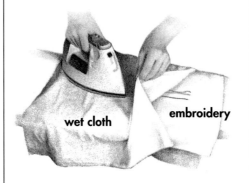

wet cloth   **embroidery**

Cashmere

Carefully hand-wash cashmere in cool, sudsy water, using a mild soap or detergent. Rinse well, but try not to lift the garment up when rinsing—it can stretch the wool out of shape. To dry on a clothesline, use two lines in the shade. Turn the garment inside out and pin it flat to a sheet, then drape the sheet over the two lines, making a kind of hammock (see page 228). You can also

dry cashmere by laying the garment flat on a drying rack that is made specifically for sweaters.

Lace

Lace can be deceptively delicate—even the weight of water could tear a favorite piece. If the lace is in good condition, wash it in a large jar with a lid. Add a mild detergent to warm water, close the lid, and shake. Add the lace and shake again for a minute. Rinse the lace in the same way, using clear water. Dry flat on a clean white towel. Another trick is to handsew fragile lace to an old sheet, then dip it into a basin of warm soapy water. Rinse twice in clear water. Let both lace and sheet dry before removing the lace.

Organdy

Organdy is made from muslin, so it can withstand washing. Use mild soap and hot water, dunking the garment gently and continuing until it comes clean. Rinse several times. Line-dry or air-dry on a hanger. To restore the stiff finish, press while still slightly damp on a low setting (check your iron for directions).

For extra-crisp fabric, take the garment off the line while it is still slightly damp, dip it in a bath of 4 cups warm water and 1 tablespoon borax, then hang it back up to dry. When it is almost dry, iron it. Or use spray starch to give organdy a crisp finish.

Satin

Dry cleaning is recommended for satin fabrics, but silk satin can be hand-washed in ice-cold water and mild soap. Satin made from acetate should be washed in warm water with liquid detergent or mild soap flakes. Dunk the garment in the water until the soil is gone. Rinse twice, then drip-dry. Crepe satin should be washed in warm water and liquid detergent or mild soap flakes, using the same dunking method. Rinse the garment twice; then drip-dry.

Silk

Wash silk in warm water and soap flakes, mild liquid detergent, or a hair shampoo containing protein. Slowly swish the garment in the suds; do not twist or wring. Then rinse three or four times and dry flat or hang to dry. Press silk while it is still damp.

Taffeta

Hand-wash acetate and rayon taffetas in as much water as possible so folds or pleats are suspended and aren't crushed. Dunk the item gently, drain the water, rinse, then hang to drip-dry. Hand-wash nylon taffeta in warm water and liquid detergent. Rinse twice; drip-dry.

Tulle

This delicate fabric, which is sheer, stiffened silk, rayon, or nylon, is used mostly for ballet costumes and bridal veils. Wash tulle according to instructions for fabric type (see chart on page 217). If washing gives the tulle ragged edges, trim it with scissors.

Velvet

If your velvet is made of silk, take it to a dry cleaner. Cotton and synthetic velvets, however, can be hand-washed. Test for colorfastness (darker, richer colors may run). If your garment is colorfast, wash it in cool, sudsy water with a liquid detergent. Swish the item around until it's clean. Rinse it three times, then allow it to drip-dry.

To set dark-colored velvet so it won't run, pre-soak the garment for 20 minutes in two quarts of cold water mixed with 1 tablespoon of Epsom salts. To restore velvet pile, smooth with a clothes brush after it is dry.

SPECIAL LAUNDRY PROBLEMS

In addition to taking extra care with fine fabrics, there are a number of tricks of the trade that can improve your laundry results.

◆ **To soften new blue jeans,** wash them several times or soak them for 12 hours in a small tub filled with cold water and fabric softener, then wash as usual. To prevent jeans from streaking, turn them inside out before washing.

◆ **To keep up the nap on corduroy,** turn clothing inside out before washing.

◆ **To wash nylons or tights,** place them in a mesh bag and wash with other delicate items without hooks, eyes, or other metal parts that could snag the stockings.

◆ **To get baby clothes their cleanest,** treat in a pre-soak product, then launder as usual. Soak items as soon after staining as possible and keep them wet until laundering.

◆ **To bring back the crispness to curtains,** launder and then dip in a solution of 2 gallons of warm water to 1 cup Epsom salts. Let drip dry outdoors or in the shower and touch up with iron.

◆ **To clean cloth-covered buttons** that still look dirty after laundering, brush with mild soap or detergent and a soft toothbrush.

◆ **To remove rings around shirt collars**, rub liquid laundry detergent into the stain or collect soap bits in a mesh bag and rub into the affected area. Wash as usual.

◆ **To whiten dingy handkerchiefs,** soak in a solution of cold water and 1 teaspoon cream of tarter before hand-washing with mild soap.

DRY CLEANING

Dry cleaning used to be called "French" cleaning, because it was the French who invented this chemical cleaning process. Dry cleaning is not really "dry" at all, however. Clothes are wetted with solvents and chemical agents, then they are treated and pressed with steam. Dry cleaning can include pre-spotting for stains, post-spotting for persistent stains, and hand-pressing to ensure perfect seams, pleats, and lapels.

Do not expect such thorough work from a one-hour cleaner, though. A true full-service dry cleaning operation will offer tailoring in addition to minor sewing repairs, mothproofing, sanitizing, and drapery or linen cleaning. Check with friends and neighbors to find out which dry cleaners in your area have a good reputation, and make sure your dry cleaner belongs to the provincial cleaners association, whose members follow a code of practices. Find out if the dry cleaner pre-tests

READING GARMENT LABELS

Care labels are the most reliable source of information on how to clean a given garment. Manufacturers use a set of universal symbols that identify the appropriate procedure. Often the care label is not located in the collar or on the waistband of the garment, but in a side seam. Here is how to interpret the care labels found on garments.

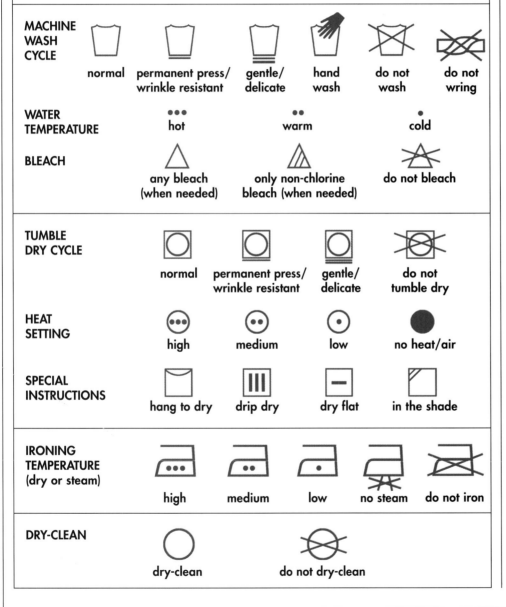

clothing, if they do all laundry on the premises (this usually is preferable), and if they try to remove stains more than once. The following situations always call for dry cleaning.

◆ **Tailored garments:** Always have professionally cleaned and pressed.

◆ **Delicate silk or any fabric of questionable washability:** Dry clean rather than risk harming the garment by washing it yourself.

◆ **Persistent stains:** If you've tried treating a stain with no success, take the item to the cleaners immediately. Some stains can be invisible until acted on by the dry-cleaning process.

To get the most from your dry cleaning, keep the following in mind. Always clean all parts of a matching suit at the same time; this way they will fade at the same rate. Point out stains or tears, and tell the dry cleaner what caused them if you know. Also let the dry cleaner know if a garment is delicate or has sentimental value. Note that repeated dry cleaning can cause white linens and cottons to gray or yellow, and may damage loose-woven woolens.

Save on dry-cleaning bills

To make fewer trips to the dry cleaner and still have clean clothes, do the following.

◆ **Remove lint and dirt** from wool coats and jackets with a garment brush.

◆ **Freshen garments** by hanging them on a line or hook outdoors.

◆ **Steam out wrinkles** (see page 230) in between dry cleanings.

CHOOSING AND MAINTAINING A WASHER AND DRYER

Washers and dryers last for years, so it pays to buy wisely when shopping for new machines and to keep the machines you currently own in top working condition.

Washers and dryers are the workhorses of the home-laundry area. Although most manufacturers turn out new models every year—with more cycle options, greater capacity, and greater energy efficiencies—the basic design of washers and dryers has not changed much over the years. Thus, the washer you've had for 10 years could probably keep pace with its newer cousins for another decade with proper care and maintenance. If you are looking for a new washer or dryer, however, assess your family's laundry needs before you buy. You don't want to purchase more appliance than you really need.

SELECTING THE RIGHT WASHER

Buying a washing machine is almost like buying a car: There are many makes and models, and you tend to get what you pay for. But many high-end models contain features you may never use, such as an extra-delicate cycle or special bleach and softener dispensers. If your household requires you to do laundry every day, a heavy-duty model with large capacity and three basic cycles may make more sense than a machine with lots of extra bells and whistles. As you are shopping, look for these basic features:

◆ **Convenient controls** that are legible, easy to operate, and logically arranged

◆ **Variable water levels** that allow you to adjust for small or large loads

◆ **Rustproof washtub**—stainless steel or plastic perform better than porcelain-coated steel

◆ **Easy installation and service access,** including self-leveling legs and minimal space requirements for water and drain hoses

Top loader or front loader

While the top-loading washing machine is the most popular model on the market, increasing numbers of consumers

REALITY CHECK

APARTMENT CROSSOVER

Stackable washer/dryer combinations, which were originally designed for apartments, take up half the floor space of a regular side-by-side washer and dryer while cleaning just as efficiently. Where space is at a premium, stacked units may be your only option. But stackable units can create new space in any home laundry for such options as a sink, a folding counter, an overhead clothes rack, or just more storage space.

are beginning to turn to more energy-efficient front-loading models. In a top-loader, the washtub spins on a vertical axis and laundry is loaded from the top.

In a front-loading washing machine, the washtub rotates on a horizontal axis and laundry is loaded from the front of the machine.

Top-loaders are easier than front-loaders for most people to use, and they can be opened in mid-cycle to add additional laundry. They also tend to hold bigger loads of clothes and wash them faster. Front-loaders, on the other hand, use less water (especially hot water) than top-loaders and less detergent. Front-loaders also are easier for people in wheelchairs to load, and they are built to handle unbalanced loads better.

Large, extra-large, or super size

Washing machines don't come in small, medium, or large sizes, but super or extra-large instead. The capacity of a washing machine is usually measured in terms of washtub size. "Super" machines are about 3 cubic feet, "extra large" total 2.5 cubic feet. When full, a "super" machine will hold 14 to 15 pounds of laundry and use 42 to 43 gallons of water per load, while an "extra large" model can handle 11 to 12 pounds of laundry and uses 39 to 42 gallons of water. The smallest washers, often marketed as "apartment-sized" or "compact," range from 1.5 to 2.5 cubic feet. If you routinely wash large loads, the "super" size is probably right for you. Don't buy a larger model than you need, however. Washers perform best when they are run at full capacity, so you would be wasting both energy and water if you regularly wash less-than-full loads.

Choosing the best controls

Most washing machines come with three basic wash cycles: regular, permanent press, and delicates. But an optional extra-rinse cycle might be useful if you are sensitive to detergent or regularly use extra detergent to wash especially dirty items. Temperature controls usually include hot wash–cold rinse (for whites or heavily soiled items), warm wash–cold rinse (for permanent press or normally soiled items), and cold wash–cold rinse (for delicate items). Some models allow you to fine-tune the temperature of the water used on each cycle, while others electronically regulate the water temperature in the washtub.

Single-lever laundry valve

Washing machine manufacturers often suggest that you turn off the water supply whenever the machine is not in use. That keeps water pressure out

WASHING MACHINE REPAIR

You can always call for service if any of the following goes wrong. But most of these problems are simple ones that even a novice can address. At the very least you can diagnose the problem.

Problem	Possible cause	Possible solution
Washer won't run	No power to unit	Check for blown fuse or tripped circuit breaker; make sure unit is securely plugged in.
	Lid not closed	Make sure lid is closed.
	Cycle-selection knob is in incorrect position	Make sure knob is in correct position and pulled out for operation.
	Overheated motor	Wait for motor to cool. Call for service if machine still won't start.
Machine fills with water but won't start	Faulty lid switch	Turn on washer; lid switch is located in small hole by the tub opening and is activated by small lever on the lid. Stick pencil in hole; if machine starts running, replace the lever. If it doesn't run, switch is faulty and needs to be replaced.
Washtub won't spin	Unbalanced load	Open lid and rearrange laundry in tub.
	Faulty transmission or loose drive belt	Replace or repair transmission or drive belt; call for service.
Washtub fills too slowly	Water valves may not be fully open	Open valves fully (on single-lever valve systems, make sure lever is in "on" position).
	Hoses may be kinked or blocked	Straighten any kinks. To unblock, shut off water to machine and unscrew hoses from back of machine. Remove obstructions, and clean and rinse any clogged filters.
	Low water pressure	Don't use water in other areas of house while washer is running.
Water temperature too hot or too cold	Water valves not open equally or are reversed	Open valves equally, and switch if reversed.
	Water heater temperature may be set too low	If water entering machine is less than 120 degrees (use a meat or candy thermometer to measure), raise thermostat slightly.
	Water may be cooling on way to washing machine	Insulate hot water pipe supplying washing machine.
Machine won't agitate	Clothing caught under agitator	Remove clothing from agitator.
	Blocked pump	Free obstruction to pump or replace pump.
	Faulty lid switch, timer, drive belt, solenoid, or transmission	Test and replace any faulty parts; call for service.

MONEY SAVERS

UNDERSTANDING ENERGUIDE LABELS

Because saving energy saves money on electricity bills, it pays to read the EnerGuide label affixed to major appliances, such as washers and dryers. Use the label to compare the energy consumption of different appliances in the same class. On the sample label shown below, notice:

◆ The appliance's estimated energy consumption in kilowatt-hours per year

◆ A bar scale with an arrow positions the appliance compared to the most energy-efficient and the least energy-efficient models in the same class

◆ The type and capacity of models that make up the same class

When buying new major electrical appliances, look for a model with the arrow on the bar scale that points farthest to the left on the scale. The farther left the arrow, the less it will cost to operate the appliance.

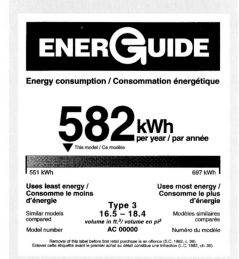

of the hoses and away from the washing machine, reducing the chances of a costly leak. This is a good idea if you are leaving the house for a long period. A single-lever laundry valve (p.222) makes it easy to open and close the water supply. If you don't have such a valve, have a plumber install one.

INSTALLING A WASHER

Most appliance dealers will install your machine for a fee. But you can install it yourself if the laundry area is already wired and plumbed for operation.

Water is supplied to a washing machine through two short hoses that run from hot and cold water valves or from a single-lever laundry valve to the back of the machine. Both ends of the hose must be screwed onto their connections. After you've attached the water-supply hoses, hook up the drain hose. Many laundry rooms are set up so that the drain hose empties into a washtub or basin, which then drains the wash water. Other laundry set-ups require the drain hose to be connected directly to a drainpipe. Before you connect the hose to a drainpipe, make sure the pipe is at least 1½ inches across to accommodate water draining from the machine.

To finish installation, adjust the locknuts on the feet of the washer to level it. (You won't need to do this if your model has self-leveling feet.) Then plug in the machine to a grounded 120-volt circuit. If possible, the 120-volt receptacle should be on a separate circuit to avoid unnecessary tripping of the circuit fuse or circuit breaker.

CHOOSING A DRYER

When looking for a dryer, you need to assess your needs first, then consider size, features, and power source (gas or electric). As with a washing machine, choose a dryer that has cycles and features that best fit your needs. Are you going to need more capacity than you have now? Is the size of your family (and the amount of laundry generated) going to change? Also measure the width, depth, and height of your available space. Finally, determine your price range.

As you're shopping, look for these basic dryer features:

◆ **Variable cycles** (including regular, permanent press, delicates, tumble-without-heat, damp-dry, and timed-dry)

◆ **End-of-cycle signal**

◆ **Reversible door**

◆ **Easy-to-empty lint filter**

◆ **Drum light**

◆ **Quiet operation**

Size does matter

Clothes dryer sizes are usually given in terms of capacity or drum size. Full-sized models have a drum capacity of 5 to 7 cubic feet and are 27 to 29 inches wide. Some manufacturers divide their full-sized models into "super plus" (7 cubic feet), "super" (6.5 cubic feet), and "extra large" (5 to 6 cubic feet). Other manufacturers offer the same-sized drum but distinguish their line of dryers with other features.

A larger drum will be able to dry bulkier items, such as quilts or bedspreads, and larger loads will be

CLOTHES DRYER REPAIRS

Like washing machines, dryers can be finicky, but understanding some of a dryer's problems can keep you from pushing the panic button.

Problem	Possible cause	Possible solution
Dryer won't start	No power to unit	Check for blown fuse or tripped circuit breaker; make sure unit is plugged in securely.
	Door not latched	Make sure door is latched.
	Selector knob is in incorrect position	Reposition knob in correct position.
	Overheated motor	Wait for motor to cool. Call for service if dryer still won't start.
Dryer runs but won't heat	Partial power to unit	Reset circuit breaker or replace any blown fuses.
	Gas-supply valve may be closed on gas models	Make sure valve is fully open. Call for service if necessary.
	Faulty heating coils on electric models	Replace coils or call for service.
Clothes take too long to dry	Exhaust duct may be blocked, too long, or too narrow in diameter	Wash or vacuum any lint buildup from inside duct, vent cap, or duct connection on dryer. Check owner's manual for correct duct length, diameter, and installation.
Dryer gets too hot	Clogged or incorrectly installed exhaust duct	Wash or vacuum any lint buildup from inside exhaust duct. Check owner's manual for correct duct installation.
	Faulty thermostat	Replace thermostat; call for service.
	Faulty burner or controls on gas models	Replace burner or controls; call for service.
	Faulty heating coils on electric models	Replace coils; call for service.

less wrinkled when they finish drying. Compact (also called "apartment-sized") dryers have a capacity of only 3.5 cubic feet and are about 24 inches wide.

A compact model can handle only small loads, but the machine can be stacked on top of a compact washer or placed in other tight spots. Some compact dryers can operate on regular 120-volt current; larger models must run on a dedicated, grounded 240-volt outlet.

Going gas or electric

Retailers and manufacturers usually feature electric dryers in their ads. But nearly every standard dryer is available as a gas model, as well. Electric dryers are cheaper than gas dryers, but gas dryers are considerably cheaper to operate. The amount you save in energy bills in the first year alone could make up the difference for the cost of the gas dryer. If you do not have natural gas or bottled gas, however, you will need to go electric. Electric dryers will require a dedicated, grounded 240-volt outlet.

Shopping for energy efficiency

Clothes dryers have become more energy-efficient in recent years. Older dryers had a thermostat to determine when the clothes were dry. The thermostat gauged the temperature of the air as it left the drum. As cool moisture was pulled out of the clothing, the temperature would rise, and the dryer would eventually stop running. Newer dryers have moisture sensors, metal strips inside the drum which determine the dryness of clothes through direct contact. Because moisture sensors are in direct contact with the clothes, they are likely to shut the dryer off sooner than a thermostat, making them more energy efficient than older models.

INSTALLING A DRYER

To install a dryer, you need to properly vent it and hook it up to a power source. Electric dryers require a dedicated 240-volt grounded circuit; gas models require a natural-gas or bottled gas hook-up and a 120-volt circuit to run the dryer motor. The installation of an electric dryer is relatively simple, but you must hire a professional to install a gas model if you are unfamiliar with handling gas hook-ups.

Before you make your connections, consider raising the dryer height by installing it on a wooden platform about 15 inches off the floor. It will make loading and unloading the machine physically easier plus provide extra space for storage below.

To avoid mildew problems inside the house and to curtail fire hazards caused by lint build-up, a dryer must be properly vented to the outside (unless it is a no-vent model, which has a heat exchanger that collects and contains the warm, moist air). Dryer-vent kits are sold at home centers and hardware stores. Install the vent through a hole cut in the outside wall behind the dryer. If it is not the outside wall, you will also need to cut a hole on the outside wall at the side and near the rear of the dryer.

MOVING A WASHER OR DRYER

If you need to move a washer or dryer, first disconnect the machine from any water, power, and vent hook-ups. Get a helper and some old carpeting, rugs, or pieces of cardboard. Tilt the machine onto its back legs while the other person slides the material under the front legs. Repeat the process for the back legs. Now you can slide the machine easily and without damaging the floor.

After you install the vent, connect the ducts from the dryer to the vent and then hook up the dryer to its power supply (electrical or gas).

Safely venting your dryer

A typical dryer vent consists of a vent cap that fits through a hole in the wall, a short duct that connects the dryer to the vent cap, and longer ductwork that connects the vent cap to an outside exhaust hood. The latter ductwork should be kept as short and straight as possible with no more than two 90-degree bends to avoid the chance of lint buildup. (Check the owner's manual

for recommendations on the maximum length of duct to use.) Make sure the exhaust hood on the outside of the house has a louver or swing-out damper to prevent backdrafts and to discourage animals from crawling in.

Choosing ducts

Dryer ducts should be no less than 4 inches wide. Flexible plastic or foil ducts are the least expensive option, but they are also the easiest to damage. The thin coatings on the ducts are easily torn, making them useless. They also tend to sag and kink, which allows lint to build up in the duct, posing a fire hazard. Better choices are flexible metal (thicker and stronger than the foil model) and rigid metal. In addition to choosing the best duct material, be sure the duct is the correct length. If it is too long or too narrow, it can slow down the removal of moist air from the dryer, thereby lengthening drying time.

Annual inspection

It is a good idea to do a thorough inspection of the dryer vent once a year to look for lint buildup or any other obstructions. Pull the dryer away from the wall, and disconnect the duct at both ends. Some ducts are held in place with clamps that can be unscrewed; others must be pinched with pliers to be removed. Wash or vacuum any lint from inside the duct, the vent cap, and the duct connection on the dryer. (This is less of a problem if you clean the dryer's lint screen after each use.) If there are signs of wear on the duct, replace it or patch it with duct tape.

DRYING AND IRONING CLOTHES

The variety of natural, synthetic, and blended fabrics in your wardrobe requires a new awareness of drying and ironing techniques.

Today's washers and dryers, along with modern easy-care fabrics, make it easier than ever to keep clothing wrinkle-free. However, you must dry your clothes correctly to begin with. And, for fabrics like cotton and linen that look best pressed, you may need a refresher in some time-honored ironing skills.

DRYING BASICS

The variety of requirements you'll find on the care labels of your garments demonstrates that different types of fabrics benefit from different drying methods. Some delicates should be drip-dried or line dried. Other fabrics are best handled in a dryer set on regular, permanent-press, or "fluff" or "air" dry cycles. Jeans, T-shirts, and towels are best dried on the regular cycle, then removed promptly to avoid wrinkles. Permanent-press, polyester, or garments made of other synthetics wrinkle less when dried on the permanent-press cycle, which has a longer cool-down time. Items that require minimal heat, such as throw rugs or pillows, are best dried on the "fluff" or "air" cycle, which circulates unheated air to remove

dampness. In all cases, your clothes will last longer if you keep drying time to a minimum and the temperature low. Do not allow your laundry to become overdry. In fact, elastic bands in gym shorts or thick socks should be slightly damp when removed from the dryer.

Banishing wrinkles

To avoid unnecessary ironing, remove clothes from the dryer and fold immediately when the cycle is finished. Items marked "no-iron" or "permanent press" will come out wrinkle-free if you remove them from the dryer quickly. If left in either the dryer or the laundry basket, the weight of the clothes and the remaining heat from the dryer combine to create wrinkles that can only be removed with ironing. Also, make sure your loads aren't too big. An overstuffed dryer almost guarantees wrinkles.

Saving energy when drying

To keep drying time to a minimum, be sure the dryer is vented properly (p.226). Don't overload the dryer and keep the lint screen clean (p.228) for maximum efficiency. If you can, dry one load

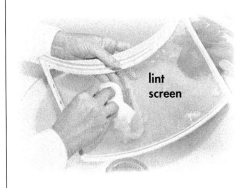

lint screen

right after another to use the heat that has already accumulated in the dryer to shorten your drying time.

Drip-drying and line-drying

Drip-drying is the gentlest way to dry a garment, and is the only way to dry certain fine fabrics. Button all buttons, close fasteners and zippers, and smooth seams before hanging to dry (use plastic hangers to avoid rust marks). Some garments may require a light pressing after drip-drying. For sweaters or other knits, lay the garment flat on a clean towel to preserve its shape. When line-drying, turn the garment inside out and

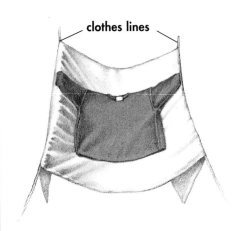

clothes lines

pin it to a sheet (or towel), then drape and clothespin the sheet over two clotheslines (below left), making a sort of hammock. Dry in a shaded area to prevent any fading.

Line-drying leaves clothes and linens crisp and fresh. White items are better suited to line drying than colored ones because the sun can fade colors; hang colored items in a shaded but breezy area. Items meant to feel soft and fluffy, such as towels, do better in the dryer. The dryer's tumbling action softens the fabric and increases its absorbency.

IRONING

Irons come in many sizes and weights, and with many features. Choose one with a contoured handle and built-in thumb rest that feels comfortable in your hand and isn't too heavy to lift or move. Look for an iron with both dry-heat and steam settings—the first for most garments, the second to dampen fabrics that are hard to iron or that wrinkle easily. Most irons feature no-stick surfaces, which makes for a smoother job of ironing. Also, look for such safety features as a setting that turns off if the iron is flat for too long, or one that turns the iron off if left unattended. A well-designed iron also is stable when sitting on its heel.

Tools to aid ironing

Next to a good iron, the most important ironing tool is an ironing board. Most models adjust to different heights, which can make ironing more comfortable. When purchasing the board, also buy a thick pad and a sturdy cover.

Another helpful tool is a pressing cloth. Available in sewing stores, pressing cloths have a chemical finish that protects fabric. (To make your own pressing cloth, see facing page.) In some cases, a pressing cloth can help refresh the fabric's finish. Sleeve boards (below) and tailor's hams are shaping tools you can use to help give clothes a more tailored look. These also are available in fabric shops.

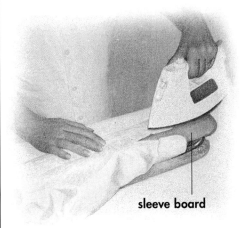

sleeve board

Ironing for best results

An iron is simply a tool to remove wrinkles. As with any tool, you get better results if you use it the right way. All fabrics are woven in a certain direction; this weave is called the grain. Always point the iron in the direction of the grain rather than against it. Use smooth, slow strokes to let the heat sink into the garment. Set the temperature to low and keep the iron moving to avoid scorching or overheating.

Pressing too hard can damage a fabric's finish. However pressing the iron's tip into the middle of a seam

helps to open and flatten it out. And because irons get hotter the longer you use them, iron lightweight items needing little heat first. You can iron heavier items with deeper wrinkles later. Practice makes for speed, so group similar garments together and let yourself get faster as you go. Sometimes it helps to start with clothes that require more complex ironing. That way, when the task becomes tiring, all that will be left are the easier items. Finally, take more care ironing the parts of a garment that need to look good longer, such as the collar and cuffs. For example, there's no need to lavish time on a shirttail, which wrinkles as you tuck it in.

Ironing vs. pressing

Ironing involves sliding the iron across the surface of a garment; pressing requires lifting the iron and setting it down gently on a garment without moving it over the surface. Ironing works best for tightly woven fabrics. Pressing works better on knits or fabrics that have a nap, such as corduroy or velvet: It helps keep the garment's shape without stretching it.

Avoiding ironing problems

You can sidestep most ironing damage by using low heat settings whenever possible, especially with synthetic fabrics, and ironing gently. When garments are pushed and pulled by a heated iron, their fit and finish will suffer, especially knitted fabrics, or those with a loose weave. Likewise, an iron can harm buttons and zippers, even melting those made of plastic. Never iron delicate trims like lace or sequins. Leather, vinyl, rubber, and elastic are not meant to be ironed, either. Finally, don't iron clothes when they are soiled. Heat from the iron can set stains permanently.

Testing fabrics first

The surface of many dark-colored garments can take on a shine after being ironed, particularly on seams or hems. To check how the garment will react, turn it inside out and press one of these thicker areas where it's not likely to be seen. If the iron feels like it is sticking to the fabric, or a shine is apparent, be careful in proceeding. You may have to use a very low heat setting and a very light touch to remove wrinkles. Also try pressing the garment from the inside to avoid leaving marks on the fabric.

Using moisture

Most synthetic fabrics iron best when dry, but natural fabrics, such as cotton or linen, which wrinkle more easily, often need some moisture. Either a steam-spray iron or a gentle misting of water from a spray bottle will work. Wools, tweeds, and corduroys, on the other hand, take nicely to a dampened pressing cloth, which adds moisture and protects the fabric finish. To avoid spraying or steaming altogether, set the dryer for a shorter drying time so garments come out slightly damp—the ideal condition for ironing.

Make your own pressing cloth

Prepackaged, chemically treated pressing cloths (below) are easy to find, but you can make your own. Choose a pressing cloth based on the type of fabric you are ironing—cotton for cottons, wool for woolens, for example. A piece of an old white sheet also will work fine. Make sure the pressing

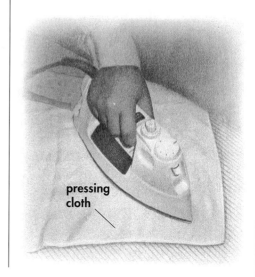

pressing cloth

DIFFERENT STROKES

For best ironing results, use specific ironing techniques for different fabrics and clothing items. Here are some of the best ways to remove wrinkles from typical fabrics and garments.

Item	Ironing technique
Corduroys	Place right side down on ironing board (add padding if board cover is thin) and steam-press with little pressure.
Cottons	Place right side up and steam- or dry-press. Turn dark cottons inside out to avoid fading.
Embroidery and laces	Place right side down on white towel or terrycloth; steam-press with little pressure.
Knits	Set iron on knit setting; press and lift iron (do not drag).
Metallics	Set iron on cool. Press lightly, using thin pressing cloth.
Nylons and polyesters	Steam-press on low setting for touch-ups only.
Shirring and smocking	Lay garment flat and move a steam iron slowly over raised areas, hovering slightly above the fabric.
Silks	Place right side down. Set iron to low and dry-press lightly using pressing cloth.
Velvet	Do not iron. Hang near steamy shower, then let air-dry.
Wools	Place right side down. Steam-press, using pressing cloth.

cloth is freshly laundered before using. When you are ready to use the cloth, dampen it first by running a wet sponge over it. Then lay the cloth on the fabric and briefly press the heated iron on it.

Pressing pleats

Pleats are one of the toughest pressing jobs to master, but taking time to pin pleats in place at top and bottom is a good way to start. Begin at the hem and work toward the top, removing pins as necessary without ironing over them. If pleats need to be very sharply creased, press each side separately.

Keeping your iron clean

You don't want to iron your clean clothes with a dirty iron, so make sure the soleplate is clean each time you use it. Most irons can be cleaned with a household spray cleaner, such as Fantastik, but check the manufacturer's instructions for recommended cleaning products.

You can also remove residue by rubbing the heated iron on a clean rag before using. If the iron has melted a synthetic fabric, heat the iron and then scrape off as much residue as possible with a wooden utensil before applying a cleaner.

Ways to minimize ironing

Buying permanent-press or loose clothing, which require no ironing compared to tailored garments, is one way to reduce your time behind a hot iron. Here are some others.

◆ **Hang clothing immediately** after wearing to avoid wrinkling.

◆ **When traveling, roll garments** softly instead of folding flat.

◆ **Hang a garment in the bathroom** while the shower is on; the steam will eliminate wrinkles.

◆ **Buy a clothing steamer** (right), available in department stores or luggage shops, to gently steam out wrinkles. It can also save on unnecessary trips to the dry cleaner.

STAIN REMOVAL AND SPECIAL CARE

Clothing stains are no cause for alarm if you follow a few simple rules for pre-treating them right away and cleaning them correctly later on.

The secrets of stain removal are promptness, patience, and persistence. Getting to a stain quickly, taking time to deal with it appropriately, and treating a spot more than once when necessary, are all steps that can help remove even the most tenacious stain.

Treating a spot immediately is the best way to make sure it doesn't become permanent. In fact, a spot doesn't really become a hard-to-remove stain until it has been absorbed fully into the fabric.

For example, if you have just spilled gravy on your suit jacket, excuse yourself and head for a restroom as soon as possible. (It could make the difference between saving the suit or discarding it.) First, lift off the spill as much as you can; then if the spot is still wet, try to absorb it by pressing a paper towel or cloth against it on both sides. If it has soaked in, soak the item in cool water, then blot it with a paper towel or clean cloth. Another way to treat such a stain is with a commercial product that absorbs soil and then is brushed off, such as K2R Spot Lifter.

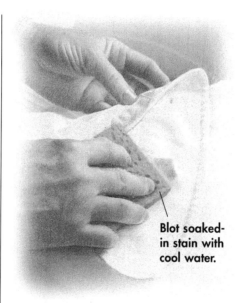

Blot soaked-in stain with cool water.

Rules of stain removal

Sometimes knowing what not to do is as important as knowing what to do. Here are a few basic rules for dealing with any stain (for procedures on removing a variety of stains, see chart on page 234).

◆ **Keep it cool.** Many stains, particularly those that are food-based, will set when heat is applied. Though you may need to wash the item in hot water eventually, pre-treating it right is vital.

◆ **Oil and water don't mix.** For oily stains, such as lipstick or grease, avoid treating with water, which can loosen color dyes or make a stain spread. Use a solvent to deal with this kind of stain.

◆ **Read care labels carefully** and follow directions. If a garment says "Do not dry clean," take the manufacturer at its word. Certain fabrics, particularly vinyl, leather, and synthetics, can be ruined with the use of solvents.

Tooling up for stain removal

Removing stains or applying cleaning products requires a few simple tools. Cotton swabs, squares, and balls have a variety of uses. A dull knife or an old toothbrush is handy for scraping dried-on stains. A generic spray bottle makes applying water easy, and an eyedropper can be used to apply cleaning solvent in small, precise areas. A clean sponge helps flush water through a stain while tissues, paper towels, old terrycloth towels, or any clean, colorless, absorbent fabric serves as a stain absorber. An artist's eraser can be used to clean marks on leather or suede. A suede brush and a clothes brush will round out your cleaning arsenal.

Stocking your stain-removal cabinet

You can readily find all of the products needed for stain removal at supermarkets, hardware, paint, and discount stores. Your cabinet should include laundry detergent, both granular and liquid; pre-soak products, such as 20-Mule Team Borax; pretreat products, such as Shout or Spray-n-Wash; rust remover; bleach (chlorine and non-

WHAT BRUSH TO USE

Clothes brushes can remove surface dirt and lint from clothing. Here are some options.

◆ **Natural-bristle brushes** are more expensive but more effective at removing dust and stains from clothing. Synthetic-bristle brushes are hard on clothing because the bristles are stiff.

◆ **Velvet-faced lint brushes** remove lint or pet hair from garments without harming napped fabrics.

◆ **Tape rollers** also remove lint and pet hair harmlessly, although you must replace the tape after each use.

◆ **Lint combs** remove lint as well as pills, or little fuzzy balls, on loosely knit clothing, such as sweaters.

bristle brush

velvet-faced brush

lint comb

tape roller

chlorine); cleaning solvents, such as acetone or denatured alcohol; rubbing alcohol; and white vinegar.

When storing cleaning products in the home, be sure to keep them in their own clearly-labeled containers and safely out of the reach of children.

When using cleaning products, particularly those that are flammable, work in a well-ventilated area. Wear protective gloves if necessary.

Testing for colorfastness

Before attempting to remove a stain, always test the fabric to see whether it is colorfast. Choose an inside seam or hem where the fabric is of double thickness and is out of sight. Apply the stain remover or pretreat product to the fabric, then hold it between two clean white cloths. Squeeze the fabric gently between them. If color transfers to either cloth, the fabric is not colorfast.

If the stain persists after you've used the pretreat product, try a different product or take the garment to a professional cleaner.

Using cleaning solvents safely

Cleaning solvents, such as acetone and denatured alcohol, and certain stain removers and household cleaners are flammable, so handle them carefully. Garments so treated should not be placed in the washer or dryer until all traces of solvent, including the smell, have been removed.

When using a solvent, place the item on an absorbent surface and work from the inside out. Dab—don't rub—the stain with a solvent-soaked cloth. When the stain is no longer visible, sponge with water to rinse, then let the garment dry overnight. Never mix solvents or stain removers, especially ammonia and chlorine bleach. Mixing the two can result in noxious fumes.

If you do not plan to launder a garment immediately after treating it, be aware that some solvents are strong enough to absorb color and even dissolve fabric if left on for more than a very short time. If the solvent makes a stain spread, rinse it out quickly and try another method.

Pretreating stains

Today's off-the-shelf pretreat products work well on most stains. If you need to use a stronger treatment, such as a stain-remover like Stain Wizard, the right application will make all the difference in getting rid of the stain. Make sure, for instance, not to sponge the stain farther into the fabric or spread it out farther than it has already gone. When swabbing a stain, avoid using too much remover, which can muddy the stain or create "chemical" rings. Work at a stain from the back side of the fabric, and gently pat it from the center toward the outside. Use a soft toothbrush to work in cleaning solvent on heavier fabrics.

Stopping a spreading stain

Most stains occur on the outside of a garment, and that's as far as they should get. To avoid letting the stain seep farther into the fabric, take the garment off as soon as possible, and turn it inside out. Lay it on an absorbent surface, such as an old white towel; then spray or gently sponge water on the stain from the inside. This will encourage the stain to exit on the same surface it entered, rather than doing any further damage. If taking off the garment is not possible, keep

sponging and blotting the surface area until the stain looks like it is gone.

Treating dried stains

Use the dull edge of a knife (below) or a spatula to lift off as much of a dried-on stain as possible without damaging the fabric. If it won't budge, soak it first with water or a small amount of solvent to help loosen the soil. If the process is slow, moisten two cloths with the solvent and position the stain between them. Patting the stain with a soft toothbrush also may loosen it.

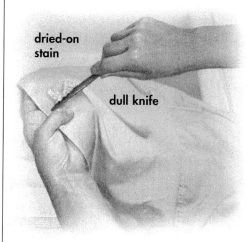

dried-on stain

dull knife

Air-dry to check a stain's removal

Sometimes it's hard to tell whether the stain is gone. To make sure a stain has been removed, let the item air-dry for a few hours and then re-examine the spot. Don't put the treated garment in the dryer before you have checked to see if the stain is gone. The heat of the dryer will set a stain if it is not thoroughly removed.

CARING FOR YOUR CLOTHES AND ACCESSORIES

Normal wear and tear will inevitably age your clothes. However, there are several simple ways to prolong the life of any fabric.

◆ **Buy well-made garments** or accessories. They may cost more upfront, but will pay you back in longer wear.

◆ **Always mend rips or snags** before laundering. If you wait to make repairs, the damage may worsen.

◆ **Use skin- and hair-care products cautiously**, making sure they do not touch your clothing. Try to keep makeup and lotions away from clothing, and point hair spray only in the direction it is needed.

◆ **Dilute bleach** and other products appropriately when doing laundry; some undiluted products can harm fabrics (see "Using Bleach" on page 213).

◆ **Keep clothing away from direct sunlight**, which can discolor it over time. Store your clothes with space between items so fabrics can breath: Items are less likely to discolor each other, and there is less chance of snagging zippers and buttons.

Laundering non-leather shoes

Wash shoes made from cloth or synthetic materials, such as tennis or running shoes, in the regular cycle of the washer if the manufacturer's label says to do so. Pretreat the shoes before you wash them to remove heavy stains. Put the shoes in with several towels to make the load go more smoothly.

TROUBLE SHOOTER

STAIN REMOVAL

Before treating any stain, read the manufacturer's care label. Always test any method on a hidden part of the fabric first. If the fabric can be bleached, add the appropriate bleach to the laundry.

Alcoholic Beverage—Sponge stain promptly with cold water for 30 minutes or longer. Rub detergent into any remaining stain while still wet. Launder. For wine, use the same treatment. Wait 15 minutes and rinse. Repeat if necessary.

Blood—Soak in cold water 30 minutes or longer. Rub detergent into any remaining stain. Rinse. If stain persists, put a few drops of ammonia on the stain and repeat detergent treatment. Rinse. Launder in hot water, using appropriate bleach.

Catsup—Scrape off excess with dull knife. Soak in cold water 30 minutes. Rub detergent into stain while still wet, then launder.

Chocolate—Soak in cold water. Rub detergent into stain while still wet. Rinse and dry. If a greasy stain remains, sponge with a cleaning fluid. Rinse. Launder. If stain remains, repeat treatment with cleaning fluid.

Coffee/Tea—Soak in cold water. Rub detergent into stain while still wet. Rinse and dry. If grease stain remains from cream, sponge with cleaning fluid. Launder.

Crayon—Rub soap flakes (such as Ivory Snow or Lux Flakes) into dampened stain, working until outline of the stain is removed. Launder as usual. Repeat if necessary. For stains throughout load of clothes, wash in hot water using laundry soap and 1 cup baking soda. If colored stain remains, launder with a detergent and appropriate bleach.

Felt-Tip Marker—Rub household cleaner such as Mr. Clean into stain. Rinse. Repeat as necessary. Launder. Some marks may be impossible to remove.

Fingernail Polish—Sponge white cotton fabric with nail-polish remover; other fabrics, with amyl acetate (banana oil). Launder. Repeat if necessary.

Fruit Juice—Soak in cold water. Launder in warm, sudsy water.

Grass—Rub detergent into dampened stain. Or soak in enzyme presoak. Launder. If stain remains, sponge with rubbing alcohol. Rinse thoroughly.

Gravy/Meat Juice—If dried, scrape off as much as possible with a dull knife. Soak in cold water. Rub in detergent while wet. Launder as usual.

Grease/Oil—Rub detergent into dampened stain. Launder, using plenty of detergent. If stain persists, sponge thoroughly with cleaning fluid. Rinse.

Ink (Ballpoint)—Sponge stain with rubbing alcohol or spray stain with hair spray until saturated. Rub detergent into stained area. Launder. Repeat if necessary.

Mayonnaise/Salad Dressing—Rub detergent into dampened stain. Rinse and let dry. If greasy stain remains, sponge with cleaning fluid. Rinse. Launder.

Mildew—Brush garment outdoors. Dampen stain and rub detergent into it. Launder in hot water using bleach. If stain remains, sponge with hydrogen peroxide. Rinse and launder again.

Milk—Soak in cold water. Launder in hot water using chlorine bleach. If grease stain remains, sponge with cleaning fluid. Rinse.

Mustard—Rub detergent into dampened stain. Rinse. Soak in hot water with detergent for several hours. If stain remains, launder in hot water using bleach.

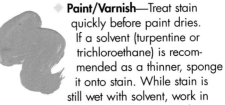

Paint/Varnish—Treat stain quickly before paint dries. If a solvent (turpentine or trichloroethane) is recommended as a thinner, sponge it onto stain. While stain is still wet with solvent, work in detergent and soak in hot water. Launder. Repeat if stain remains. Stain may be impossible to remove.

Perfume—Same treatment as for alcoholic beverage stains.

Perspiration—Rub detergent into dampened stain. Launder in warm, sudsy water. If fabric has discolored, try to restore it by treating old stains with vinegar. Rinse and launder. To remove odor, soak in presoak for 30 minutes or in 3 tablespoons salt and 1 quart water for 1 hour.

Scorch—For mild scorch stains, gently rub in detergent and launder. If severe scorching has damaged it, fabric cannot be restored.

Shoe Polish (Wax)—Scrape off as much as possible with a dull knife. Rub detergent into dampened stain. Launder. If stain persists, sponge with rubbing alcohol. Rinse and then launder.

Soft Drink—Sponge with cold water. Launder. Some drink stains are invisible after they dry but then turn yellow with age or heat. The yellow stain may be impossible to remove.

Tar/Asphalt—Act quickly before stain is dry. Gently scrape off as much as possible with a dull knife. Pour trichloroethane through cloth. Repeat. Rinse and launder. Stain may be impossible to remove.

Source: The Maytag Co.

PROTECTING YOUR CLOTHING INVESTMENT

Taking proper care of your clothing will keep your wardrobe looking its best while preserving your investment. To get the most life and wear out of your clothes, follow these tips for storing and preparing them for cleaning.

Use the right hanger

Wire hangers, such as those provided by dry cleaners, may be economical, but they are not practical for hanging clothes. They can stretch out delicate fabrics and knits. Rounded plastic hangers are far superior and they won't rust. Tailored clothing, like jackets and structured blouses, stores best on thick hangers, particularly padded ones. Pants and trousers retain their shape best when they are folded and hung over wooden or padded hangers.

Hanging is generally good for clothes if they are hung correctly. Center a garment on a hanger with the seams hanging straight and the

padded

rounded plastic

wooden

shoulder pads fitting properly. Hang with plenty of room between clothing items to avoid wrinkling.

Empty lapels and pockets

Even the smallest stress weighs heavily on garments over time. So before putting clothes away, take off lapel or other pins, and clear out all coins, pens, and other items from the pockets. Pins can rust or poke holes in fabric, and pens can leak. Coins put extra strain on pocket linings. Also remember to remove belts, which can stretch a garment out of shape.

Button all buttons and close zippers

An open zipper or a stray fastener can easily catch on other fabrics, creating rips and snags. So, when storing your clothes, as when you launder clothing, make sure to close all hooks-and-eyes, snaps, or Velcro, and zip up zippers. It's also important to button the buttons before hanging, whether it's a shirt, blouse, or jacket. Tailored garments that hang open can become wrinkled and lose their shape permanently.

Store knits flat

Because knits are loosely woven and tend to stretch, it's best to store them flat to help preserve their shape. Even the lightest knit item, such as a necktie, will stretch if it is hung over a hanger or a rod. After taking off knit garments, give them time to air, then fold and put away in drawers or other flat storage containers. Place heavier items on the bottom to avoid crushing lighter pieces of clothing on top.

acid-free paper

Preparing clothes for storage

Before putting clothes into storage, be sure that the closet or storage area has been dusted or vacuumed thoroughly, and that the clothes have been properly cleaned. Lining shelves with acid-free paper (available at art supply and framing stores) helps to preserve clothing, as does wrapping the clothing in folds of the paper (above). A supply of mothballs placed near the clothing, but not touching it, will discourage insects. Cedar, available in balls or blocks, also keeps insects at bay and smells much nicer. Wash your hands first, then wrap clothes in a clean, dust-free place. Antique clothing or fabrics and garments that have sentimental value should be stored flat, away from light and heat sources, wrapped in folds of acid-free paper (see page 253 for more details on clothing storage).

MONEY SAVERS

DAILY REGIMEN FOR WOOLS

Good routine care can often save a wool suit or coat a trip to the cleaners. Tweeds and other wool fabrics especially benefit from these simple steps.

◆ **Frequent brushing** keeps the fabric clean. Place the garment on a clean, non-slippery surface, such as a bed, or put it on a hanger and brush with one hand while holding the hanger with the other hand. Open up the lapels and collar. Run a finger along the surface of the fabric to determine the direction of the nap, and brush gently against the nap to extract dust or lint. Brush in one direction only, using long, sweeping strokes. Five minutes of brushing should do it.

◆ **Empty the pockets,** and remove dirt from pant or sleeve cuffs.

◆ **Always remove lint** from wool garments before putting them away. Use a damp clothes brush or tape roller (see box on page 232) or wrap masking or cellophane tape around your hand, adhesive side out. Move across the garment to pick up lint. A clean dry sponge also will remove lint from wool fabrics.

Storing special garments

Some items benefit from a little extra care before being put away. Here's how to prepare and store special garments.

◆ **Professional cold storage is best for fur;** but if stored at home, a fur should be hung on a well-padded hanger in a moisture-free garment bag.

◆ **Wash and iron linen** before storing. Roll rather than fold whenever possible to avoid creases.

◆ **Brush or clean wool clothing** (see box, left) and wrap the garments in acid-free paper. Use mothballs, cedar blocks, or cedar balls, or place in a cedar chest.

◆ **Store hats with feathers** in hatboxes with plenty of breathing room.

◆ **Hang wedding dresses or long gowns** on well-padded hangers in moisture-free garment bags. Long trains can be attached to the top of the hanger with stitched-on ribbon. Many dry cleaners will clean and preserve your dress, packing it in a special box for long-term storage.

◆ **Wrap beaded items** in acid-free paper and lay them flat.

◆ **Wrap silk** in acid-free paper, being sure to place extra paper in folds to protect the delicate fabric.

◆ **Store quilts** as flat as possible; wrap in acid-free paper, fold, and store. Refold often to avoid creases.

◆ **Wrap velvet** in acid-free paper and roll the garment loosely in the direction of the pile to avoid creases.

TAKING CARE OF LEATHER

Real leather requires some special care, but it is a sturdy material that can provide years of wear. Leather—smooth or suede—cannot be dry cleaned and may require special leather cleaning. There are some simple things you can do, however, to keep your leather goods looking clean and feeling supple without frequent professional care.

Leather is a natural material that needs to "breathe" to stay supple. Store your leather garments in a cool, well-ventilated closet. (Heat can make leather brittle, and excessive humidity will lead to mildew and fungus growth.) Never wrap leather garments in plastic; it can discolor the leather. Because leather is prone to stretching, place garments on padded hangers to help retain their shape.

Wear a scarf with a leather jacket to keep the collar area from soaking up body oils. Spot-clean leather and suede by carefully rubbing the soiled area with an artist's eraser. Faded leather can be touched up with a commercial leather stain; soften the leather with saddle soap, then apply the stain.

Cleaning leather garments

Proper brushing and wiping help keep leather and suede from deteriorating. A stain on leather that won't brush or wipe off should be taken to a leather cleaner as quickly as possible. Though you can try to clean it yourself with a leather-cleaning product, you may end up doing more harm than good. If grease is spilled directly onto a leather garment, a quick fix may be to sprinkle an absorbent material (such as flour or corn starch) on the stain, then immediately brush it off.

Suede, which should be treated only when dry, stays freshest when brushed gently with a clean dry sponge or soft towel after each wearing. Smooth leather can take wiping with a dry or slightly damp cloth, and both smooth leather and suede benefit from the protection against water and stains of silicone spray coatings that you can apply yourself.

Keeping leather bags looking good

Though it may be expensive initially, a good leather bag can last for years. In fact, a well-cared-for leather bag will take on its own special look and feel as it wears. To avoid stains and scratches, be careful where you set it down.

Practice preventive maintenance by giving the bag a periodic wipe with a damp cloth and a buffing with a leather conditioner. Keep scratches touched up with polish or leather conditioner. Use a chamois or other soft cloth to shine the bag. If clasps or straps on the bag need repair, fix them promptly to avoid unnecessary ripping or fraying.

Storing leather bags correctly helps keep them in their best condition. Keep bags from touching each other on the closet shelf. Wrapping the bags in tissue paper can accomplish this, as can simply allowing plenty of space between bags and other items being stored. As with other leather pieces in your wardrobe, be sure the storage area is cool and well-ventilated.

Caring for leather shoes

One of the simplest ways to keep leather shoes looking good is to buy the right size in the first place, which keeps the shoes from stretching. Another way to ensure long life for leather shoes is to have more than one pair and to change them regularly, giving them time to air out and regain their natural shape between wearings.

GOOD TOOLS

PACK UP YOUR POLISH IN YOUR OLD KIT BAG

Make your own shoe shine kit and keep it handy for cleaning and polishing all of your shoes. Here's what you'll need.

◆ **Polish and conditioners** Stock your kit with black, brown, and neutral polishes (liquid or cream), along with leather conditioners for smooth leather shoes, and saddlesoap for heavier shoes and boots. Include a small container of petroleum jelly for patent leather shoes.

◆ **Brushes** Your kit should contain a brush or sponge to remove stains, a small circular brush or toothbrush to apply polish, and a brush to buff the polish. You can store brushes in separate unsealed plastic bags.

◆ **Cloths and buffers** Every shoe shine kit needs plenty of soft cloths to shine polished shoes and to apply leather conditioner to boots and heavier shoes (recycle flannel shirts, nightgowns, or terry cloth towels for these). Also include a chamois cloth to buff shoes to a high shine.

If heels or soles wear down but the tops are still good, have the shoes resoled or reheeled. A good shoe repair shop can significantly extend the life of a pair of shoes. And finally, store leather shoes on shoe trees to help them maintain their shape.

Shining shoes

A good shoe shine not only keeps your shoes looking good, but it also protects and helps them last longer. First brush the shoes clean and free of dust and dirt. Do this on newspaper to keep your work surface clean. If your shoes are badly scuffed, stained by salt, or if the leather was recently soaked and is now dry and brittle, rub in a bit of conditioner before polishing.

To apply polish, hold the shoe by its inside, brushing polish gently onto all outside surfaces. Allow each shoe to absorb the polish, then use a chamois or clean cloth to buff them. Put shoe trees in newly polished footwear while it dries. Set shoes on newspaper, away from carpeting or draperies that could be stained by contact with drying polish.

SEWING AND MENDING

Don't let loose buttons or an unhitched hem mar the look of your clothes.
A few sewing basics can go a long way toward preserving your wardrobe.

Buttons, snaps, elbows, and seams are all stress points of clothing and frequently need mending, replacement, or repair. If you want to keep your wardrobe in top condition, being able to use a needle and thread not only will save you money, but will also make any quick fix, such as sewing on a button or restitching a hem, a stress-free venture.

SEWING SUPPLIES

Having the right supplies can make any mending job quicker and easier. Small, portable mending kits are available at any sewing or notions store and are ideal for carrying in a purse, briefcase, or suitcase when traveling. To put a home kit together, start with a small plastic container, a metal tin with a lid (an old cookie tin works well), or a waterproof zip-up packet. Inside, store various colored threads, needles of varying sizes, scissors, straight pins, a pincushion, marking chalk, patching material, a tape measure, and fusible webbing or double-faced mending tape.

When choosing mending supplies, all of which you will find at a fabric or sewing store, look at your wardrobe for color and thread type. Remember, for any mending job, you should always use thread a shade darker than the material you are repairing. If you have a lot of polyester clothing, choose polyester thread over cotton, and vice versa. For general purposes, always have a medium-weight cotton-wrapped polyester thread on hand.

Good needles for basic hand-sewing are called *sharps*. Get a package of assorted sizes so you can deal with light or heavy fabrics. For ease in threading, you may want to add a needle threader to your kit. Straight pins with round heads work best for most quick mending jobs; keep them in a small pincushion for easy access. A pair of sharp scissors is a must for clipping thread or cutting fabric neatly. Marking chalk, which washes off, is used for measuring hems. And while a flexible measuring tape works well for a travel kit, a yardstick works better for marking up hems and measuring accurately from the floor. For emergency hem fixes, fusible webbing or double-faced mending tape is a no-sew way to pick up a hem in a hurry (p.241).

THREADING A NEEDLE AND KNOTTING THE THREAD

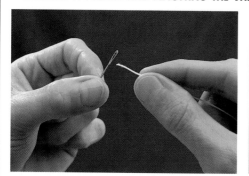

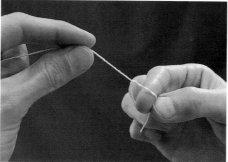

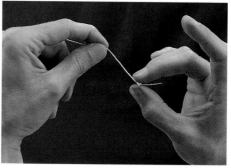

1. Cut the end of the thread coming off the spool diagonally. Hold the thread still, and move the needle over the end. If the raw end frays, cut it again and dampen it.

2. Cut the length of thread needed. To knot it, wrap the end of the thread around your index finger. Roll the twisted thread off your finger and onto your thumb.

3. Next, use your third finger to hold the thread in place. With the opposite hand, pull the thread loop taut, tightening up the knot in the thread.

NEEDLE AND THREAD BASICS

All you really need to know about hand sewing to handle most clothing repairs is how to thread a needle and knot the thread (above), how to make a few simple stitches, and how to make a knot to finish your work.

Tips for keeping thread unsnarled

To help keep thread free and clear of snags, start with a length of thread that is less than 2 feet long. While you may need to thread your needle more often, it is easier to sew using a shorter length and you will have fewer tangles. If static electricity causes your thread to snarl, spray thread very lightly with an anti-static spray like Cling-Free, or run the thread lightly along a bar of soap. If the thread becomes tangled as you are working, drop the needle and let the thread untwist itself. Then pick up the needle again and continue stitching.

Making a stitch knot

When you're done mending, you need to knot your work. Always place knots on the underside of the fabric. Take a small stitch, catching only a single thread of fabric. Pull the needle and thread through, leaving a small loop. Take another short stitch, but pass the needle and thread through the loop of the first stitch. Pull both stitches close to the fabric and cut the thread.

MENDING

Make emergency clothing repairs right the first time and you won't need professional help. Here's how to make the most common sewing repairs.

Resewing a button

Sewing on a button is a common but easy sewing repair (p.240). If you lose a button, look first to side seams, where manufacturers often sew in an extra button. If an extra button is not available for a shirt, borrow one from the bottom, which is usually tucked in and won't show. Then sew a similar button to the bottom. Coats, which often are made of thick fabrics, typically have shank buttons. To allow enough space for the buttonhole to fit under the button on bulky fabrics, you can create an extended shank by placing a toothpick between the fabric and the button. Sew on the button, remove the toothpick, then wrap extra thread around the stitching a few times before knotting it.

Sewing on snaps, and hooks-and-eyes

Snaps and hooks and eyes are meant to be invisible, so stitches holding them must be made on the inside of a garment. First sew on the upper part of the snap or hook, then chalk it and rub it on the fabric where the opposite part of the fastener will be placed. Sew only on the outside edges of the fasteners so that the snap or hook will close.

SEWING ON A BUTTON

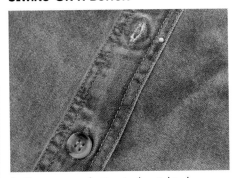

1. To sew on a button in the right place, first button all of the garment's buttons, then place a pin or chalk mark where the new button must be sewn on. Once the place is marked, unbutton the garment to make the sewing of the button easier.

2. Use a double thread. Hold the button in place and stitch through the holes—from underside to top of button and back—several times. Stitching over a straight pin helps keep the stitching even and not too taut. To end, make a stitch knot on the underside.

Mending worn elbows

Jackets made of loosely knit fabrics, such as wool tweed, first begin to show wear on elbows, where friction is highest during use. If the jacket is otherwise in good shape, buy a pair of suede elbow patches to cover the holes. Some elbow patches are iron-on while others must be hand-sewn in place. Pin the patches in place, try on the jacket to check the positioning, then stitch them in place. Use a thimble to push the needle through the punched holes around the outside edge of the patches.

Patching a hole

Children's play clothes and jeans that are worn at the knees or other stress points can be repaired with iron-on patches. Buy preshrunk patches which don't pucker when washed. Lay the garment flat, trim any stray threads,

insert cardboard inside the pants leg, and iron the patch on the hole, setting your iron on the temperature recommended by the manufacturer.

Sewing a ripped seam

Ripped seams are best repaired with a sewing machine. If you don't have access to a machine, you may want to hire a tailor or your dry cleaner to make the repair. However, a ripped seam can be repaired by hand, using a careful backstitch.

Start by anchoring the thread with a knot, then direct the needle through both layers of fabric and back out, making a small stitch. Insert the needle $\frac{1}{8}$ inch behind the emerging thread and take a $\frac{1}{4}$ inch stitch to come out $\frac{1}{8}$ inch ahead of where you began. Begin each following stitch at the front of the last stitch. On the underside of a row of

backstitching, the larger stitches overlap a bit, but the smaller stitches on top will look like machine sewing. Finish with a knot.

Fixing a snagged sweater

When a sweater is snagged, you need to resist the temptation to cut or pull on the yarn, which can trigger more unraveling. Instead, turn the garment inside out, then point a large sewing needle or crochet hook into the snag and gently wiggle the yarn toward the inside of the garment (below). Once you have determined the length of the snag, use the needle to push one half of the snag gently back into place under the adjacent stitch.

Repeat the procedure on the other half of the snag while holding the replaced portion in place. If the yarn is broken, use a needle threaded with closely matching yarn to close the hole carefully with small stitches from the

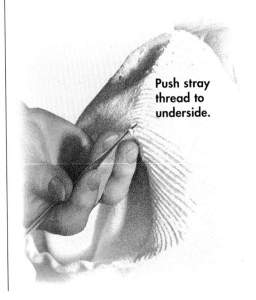

Push stray thread to underside.

underside of the sweater. Avoid using regular thread, as it can eventually cut into the yarn.

Repairing a hem

To mend an unraveling hem, use a simple slipstitch (below). Start by placing a knot on the hem a few inches back from where the hem thread has come loose. Direct the needle through the hem, then catch a single thread on the inside of the garment fabric. Repeat this stitch every ¼ inch across the opened area and a few inches beyond. Anchor it with a knot on the inside hem fabric. Press to hold the fabric and new stitching in place.

slipstitch

Hemming

To shorten a skirt or pair of pants, first measure the clothing item. Put on the garment with the shoes and belt you will wear with it. Have a helper mark the desired length with straight pins. Use a yardstick to measure accurately

from the floor. Turn up the hem and press it. If you are shortening the garment a great deal, cut away the extra fabric, leaving 1¼ inches for the hem. Press under the raw edge ¼ inch. Pin the hem flat, easing the excess throughout the width of the hem to avoid tucks. Hand-stitch with a slipstitch, following the instructions above.

WHEN TO CALL IN THE PROS

If your garment is expensive, the fabric hard to work with, or the repair complex, it is worth paying a professional to fix a garment. Ask your dry cleaner, or query friends, colleagues, or family to recommend a tailor or seamstress.

Repairing a frayed collar or cuffs

While a frayed collar or cuffs might indicate that a garment is beyond fixing, don't despair. Take the garment to a tailor, who may be able to turn a cuff under, reverse it, or make a new cuff from extra material. While the procedure may be expensive, it's often less expensive than replacing the garment, particularly if it is of good quality.

Mending moth damage

Unfortunately, the only real solution to heavy-duty moth damage is a professional reweaver. Reweavers use small bits of fabric from inside seams to piece the garment back together, and the results are often unnoticeable. A good reweaving job is expensive, but worth it to save a cherished piece of clothing.

Fixing zippers

To keep both metal- and plastic-toothed zippers sliding smoothly,

NO-SEW HEM REPAIR

For emergency hem mending, there are products available that are quick and involve no sewing. Double-faced mending tape will hold a hem in place until it's washed. Fabric glue dries in five minutes and is washable. Fusible web, below, applied with an iron, lasts longer; use a pressing cloth and follow manufacturer's directions for level of heat.

fusible web mending tape

periodically lubricate them by rubbing a dry cake of soap across the teeth. If the zipper becomes dirty, clean it with a toothbrush dipped in a solution of dishwashing detergent and water.

If the slider comes loose from the tracks of either type of zipper, pry off the bottom stop and rethread the track through the slider. If possible, reattach the stop and crimp it into place; but if the stop is damaged, use a needle and heavy thread to sew a new one. To replace a missing handle from a slider, attach a very small key to the slider.

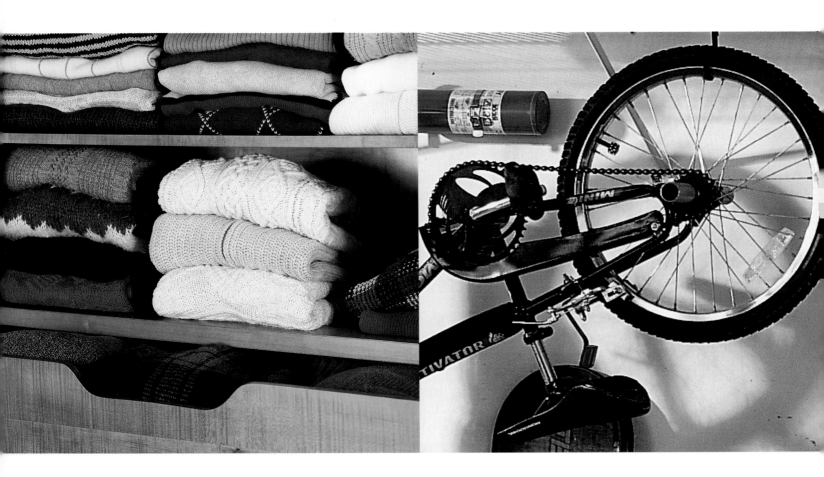

7

Organization

Storage

A PLACE FOR EVERYTHING

Storage space may be a rare commodity in your home; with a few tricks, you can maximize the available space and give your clothing, books, tools, and other paraphernalia suitable niches.

Finding the room you need to organize your things—whether it's in closets, the garage, or cabinetry designed for storage—can be a challenge, especially in homes where there is limited space. But proper storage will extend the life of many of your possessions—from wool sweaters to claw hammers—and give you peace of mind, because you'll know exactly where each item is whenever you need it.

TAKING INVENTORY

Most closets and cabinets can benefit from a more efficient design, but before you spend any money on new shelving, evaluate your possessions and decide what you really need to store. Only keep those items that:

◆ **Are being used currently** or have been used within the past year by you or your family,

◆ **Have strong sentimental value** for you or your family,

◆ **Will be needed in the near future** by you or your family.

As you plow through the clutter in each room of the house, make quick decisions about whether each item should be stored, repaired, given away, or thrown out.

Sort everything into appropriate bags or boxes, so that you can act on your decisions immediately. Put items you plan to keep near the storage area where you want them to go. Stack clothes that need repair in the mending basket by the sewing machine; set other items that need repair on the work bench. Label the charity box and put it in the garage or even into the car trunk, ready to be delivered. Seal the box or bag of tossables and put it with the garbage before you start having second thoughts about your decisions.

TRANSFORMING A CLOSET

The limited options for storage in most closets—clothes rod, shelf, and floor—almost inevitably contribute to a crowded clutter. If you want to really revamp a closet, first make a list of everything that needs to go into it, then decide whether you need an extra stack of drawers and a shoe rack or a brand-new organizational system. If you choose to buy a whole-closet system, take your list with you when you go shopping; it will help you to pick the best components for your needs.

Shopper's guide to closet components

Today's marketplace offers a variety of closet-storage inserts and accessories. In fact, whole stores are now devoted to selling closet components. To see what's available near you, browse through a home center or closet store. If you're not sure where to find one, look under "Closet Organizers and Accessories" and "Interior Designers" in the Yellow Pages of the telephone book. Some stores also have Internet sites, where you can see what's available and even order components without leaving the house.

For quick fixes, you can find wire baskets, tie racks, and clear stackable boxes in home centers or department stores that will help you reorganize the contents of your closet yourself.

To redo the whole closet, you can often get design help at a home or closet store—some offer it for free at the store or in your home. Once you have decided on all the components you need, you can put in the system yourself or hire a professional to install it.

Most shelves and accessories are made of epoxy- or vinyl-coated wire, also called ventilated shelving. Coated wire is a relatively inexpensive, lightweight, and practical material—this kind of shelving allows for plenty of air circulation. You'll find it in wide

GOOD SOLUTIONS

BEST CLOSET BETS

Shoes, socks, scarves, belts, and ties can be some of the trickier items to store efficiently. These closet components are handy helpers for keeping such items tidily tucked away.

◆ **Shoe shelves and racks** are available in many styles and in freestanding as well as wall-mounted and door-mounted designs. This hanging rack (top right) is ideal for closets with limited floor space. A new entry into the market is a narrow, floor-to-ceiling revolving shoe caddy that fits into the corner of a closet. Other shoe-storage options include tilted shelves in both laminate and wire that can be wall-mounted or positioned at foot level.

◆ **Drawer dividers** separate a drawer into smaller sections to help keep socks, scarfs and belts from getting jumbled or lost. Inserts can be found in many plastic or laminate shapes (middle right).

◆ **Tie and belt racks.** These come in a variety of clever forms, including pull-out bars with metal hooks. Tie racks can be attached to existing shelving or mounted on the closet wall. Put the rack in a place where ties can hang freely without wrinkling (bottom right).

mesh (great for towels and lightweight clothing) and sturdy narrow mesh—better for storing heavy items in the garage or pantry.

Plastic laminate (plastic-covered particle board, also called Melamine) components cost more than those made of coated wire. They are durable and attractive, and can be combined with wire storage units to create a flexi-

ble, functional closet. These components come in white, black, or wood finishes, such as maple or cherry.

Most closet systems include the components listed below.

◆ **Hooks** are available in metal and plastic. They can be screwed into walls or doors to hold robes, shirts, towels, and belts.

shoe rack **wire baskets** **fixed shelves** **double rods** **stacked drawers**

A well-organized bedroom closet

A thoughtfully ordered closet system (left) can simplify your dressing routine. It may eliminate the need for a separate dresser and it makes finding socks and belts a snap.

In the closet system at left, double rods accommodate shirts, jackets, skirts, and pants more efficiently than a single rod could, making the hanging areas less cramped. Shelves keep shirts, sweaters, purses and hats easily accessible. Shoes go in a rack and pantyhose, socks, scarves, and other accessories go in wire or laminate drawers.

Choices for a child's closet

The small size of a child's clothing makes it easy to maximize closet space. A well-planned closet (below) can also encourage children to dress themselves,

coated-wire shelving **accessible hanging space** **pull-out baskets**

◆ **Clothes rods** are a main component of laminate and wire closet systems, especially to separate hanging clothes of different lengths. They are often metal in laminate systems; in wire shelf systems the rods may be an extension of a shelf component.

◆ **Fixed shelves** are available in wire and laminate, and in a variety of sizes: narrow for shoes, sweaters, and pants; and wide for games, toys, bulky clothes, and boxes.

◆ **Gliding pull-out shelves** made of wire or laminate ease access to heavier items such as boots and jeans, or to high or low parts of the closet.

◆ **Wire baskets** come in a variety of sizes and shapes and can be useful in ventilated organizing systems. They are

often sold in stacking sets and are good for storing towels, laundry, jeans, sweaters, and toys. They can be built-in or freestanding.

◆ **Laminate cubbies** look attractive and keep shoes organized and purses and bags upright and neatly separated from each other.

◆ **Stacks of drawers,** available in laminate whole-closet systems, hold everything from hosiery to sweaters, keeping them dust-free and away from light. Some makers even offer special designs, such as jewelry drawers with velvet organizing inserts.

◆ **Casters** adapt various closet components, such as basket sets and shoe racks, into mobile units that can be shifted easily as your needs change.

hang up their clothes, and stow their dirty laundry. In this case, coated wire shelving adds more storage to a child's closet. Pull-out baskets, placed conveniently low, offer self-service bins for clothes and toys. A low rod offers accessible hanging space as well. If possible, find a spot for a hamper to keep dirty clothes picked up. Put shoes in a clear plastic box on the floor. Set up a box for socks, too. Low hooks are handy holders for in-season hats. Higher shelves and rods provide places for out-of-season clothing and the hand-me-downs waiting for the next growth spurt.

Keep in mind that children often play in their closets, so use blunt-edged hooks and make sure adjustable shelves can withstand some climbing. Look for a locking mechanism to prevent shelves from tipping.

A hardworking coat or hall closet

To make a traditional coat or hall closet more practical, try these suggestions:

◆ **Add a caddy** of pull-out baskets to hold gloves, scarves, and other accessories (coated wire won't rust, and the mesh design allows air to circulate and dry wet accessories faster).

◆ **A second shelf** overhead holds more hats or other items previously jammed onto one shelf.

◆ **A full-length mirror,** mounted on the inside of the door, gives you or your guests the chance for a last-minute look before leaving the house.

◆ **Put in a light**—either a battery-operated one that you put up yourself

---

WORKING OUT THE DIMENSIONS

When you design a closet for your own wardrobe, the measurements below will help you figure out how many feet of shelving your shoes will take, how deep the rod section for your slacks and blazers needs to be, and how wide a shelf your sweaters will take. Use graph paper to work out where the different elements will fit.

Item	Length	Thickness
Woman's dress	48–66"	1–2"
Woman's blouse	30–42"	1–2"
Woman's skirt	22–44"	1– 1½"
Woman's pants	46–50"	1–1½"
Man's suit jacket	38–42"	3" or more
Man's dress shirt	38–42"	½"
Man's slacks, folded	28–32"	½–¾"
Woman's shoes	10" long	7" wide
Man's shoes	12" long	9" wide
Folded sweater	14" deep	10" wide
Folded shirt	14" deep	8" wide

(it may be dim) or a permanent light, installed by an electrician. In a seldom-used closet, you may want to simply keep a large flashlight on the shelf.

MAKING A CLOSET SYSTEM WORK

If you have inherited a nice closet with shelves and drawers already installed, you must recognize that they reflect someone else's wardrobe, not yours. Don't be afraid to redesign the closet to suit your life style. Keep in mind three key elements of an efficient and hard-working closet.

◆ **Enough space** to store a season's wardrobe without compacting and wrinkling any of its pieces (see "Working Out the Dimensions" chart above for minimum space requirements).

◆ **Complete visibility** of all the elements in your wardrobe at once, so you can makes fast, good choices.

◆ **Easy access** to all the closet's contents from a pair of socks to a tuxedo.

Keep it together

Design your closet around a list of all the clothes you need to store. When allocating individual articles of clothing to spaces, put like items together so that you can see, for example, all of your blouse choices hanging in one place, all of your pants choices hanging in another. Keep all your sweaters together, folded and stacked on open shelves. If your belts go in a drawer, be sure that when you open the drawer, you will see them all. That way, you'll always find what you need quickly.

◆ **Arrange clothes by color** within groups (blouses or pants, for example). This organization—navy blues and blacks on the right and beiges and whites on the left with reds, greens, yellows and light blues in the middle—speeds up your picking an outfit.

◆ **Hanging items** should all face in the same direction to save space, prevent wrinkling, and keep the hangers from tangling with each other.

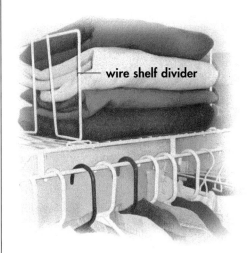

wire shelf divider

Going beyond the basics

You may find that some extras can help you fine-tune your closet system. You can impose greater order on open shelves, for example, with wire dividers (above). In closets with skylights, sun and dust can damage clothes. Use covered containers. Containers that have solid lids (to protect from sunlight) and clear sides (to make things easier to see) serve well.

Useful closet tools

Even a well-organized closet may still benefit from a few extras, such as the add-ons listed below.

◆ **Lighting**. You'll be able to match colors more accurately in a closet with a full-spectrum bulb in the light fixture. (For safety, a closet light should have a protective cover; poking around, you could easily hit it by mistake.)

◆ **Step stool**. Keep a small, sturdy folding step stool in one corner of your closet for the boost you need to reach upper-level shelves.

◆ **Retrieving pole.** To reach heights without stretching, use a pole with a hook on the end (to lift hangers) or an extendible pole with pincers. Either device is available in houseware stores.

MAINTAINING YOUR CLOSET

Keeping closets well-ordered takes some discipline, but you can make it easier on yourself by following a few sensible steps.

◆ **Set a schedule** for closet vacuuming and tidying up clutter. Work a different closet into your cleaning routine each week. Vacuum the floor and put away any unstored items, such as dirty laundry or shoes. Give children an incentive, such as a sticker or a special privilege, for tidying up their own closets.

◆ **Clean out your closet periodically.** Once or twice a year, look through your frequently-used closets for clothes that you no longer need or for seldom-used items that could be transferred to long-term storage elsewhere in the house. Get rid of shoes, bags, and clothing you don't wear (donate them to a homeless shelter or other charitable organization). If seasonal clothing takes up too much room, set up a separate storage area in another closet or in a dry basement.

◆ **Reevaluate.** Periodically, check to see if your closet organization really works. Are your shoes easy to get to? Are your sweaters getting wrinkled from the way they are stacked? If so, you may have to reorganize a bit. For example, if a closet clothes hamper takes up space that you need for shoe racks, get a hamper that hangs over the door or buy a handsome wicker one for the bedroom or bathroom.

When the closet won't hold it all

If your closet simply cannot contain all your clothes, consider the following.

◆ **Set up freestanding closets,** free-standing stackable baskets, or wire baskets on rollers in your bedroom, a spare room, or the basement.

◆ **Use sturdy under-bed boxes** made of plastic or laminate for blankets and extra bed linens.

◆ **Make a storage corner** in your bedroom or the guest room, then hide the stacked boxes with a decorative screen or curtain.

◆ **Stylish storage,** such as steamer trunks, vintage suitcases, or decorative boxes, do double duty. They add stylish storage space to a room, and can serve as tables or footrests, too.

STORING SEASONAL ITEMS AND KEEPSAKES

Out-of-season clothing, linens, books, and photographs all require special attention when you put them away.

Beyond everyday clothes and accessories, there are many other household items that need storage space. These include out-of-season clothing, special occasion and heirloom clothing made of delicate or valuable fabrics, table and bed linens, holiday decorations, books and papers, and photographs. In addition to needing a place of their own, some items, such as linens and photographs, require special handling to preserve them.

LONG-TERM STORAGE STRATEGIES

Haphazard storage of clothes and linens —whether you're stowing a raincoat or napkins—can lead to disastrous damage from mildew and insects. Because stored goods may sit unattended for months, you might not notice the damage until the pieces are unsalvageable. However, if you follow the basic rules for fabric storage, your clothes and linens will last for years.

◆ **Make sure clothing and linens** are clean when you put them away, and store them in a clean container or storage area. Perspiration, food, or dirt on stored clothes attracts insects.

◆ **Store clothing away from light,** which can promote the hatching of insect eggs.

◆ **Avoid unventilated areas** where temperatures and humidity are uncontrolled for storing off-season clothes; a damp basement, for example, promotes mildew growth.

◆ **Don't use plastic bags** or other air-tight containers, which tend to trap mold-feeding moisture.

◆ **Pack loosely** so that air can circulate around folded items in the storage area.

◆ **Forego starch, fabric finish, or sizing** (which keeps fabric crisp) on any clothes or linens before storing; the stiffeners can damage fabric over time.

◆ **Use a chemical desiccant** (to absorb moisture), such as silica gel or calcium chloride packets, but don't let it touch the fabrics or it may damage them.

◆ **Ventilate storage areas** when the weather is dry and cool.

STORING SEASONAL CLOTHING

Whether you are trying to give order to a pile of wet winter gloves, or stow your shorts and sandals for next

summer, how you store them will affect how long they last and how accessible they are when you need them.

Storing winter clothing in season

Coats, hats, scarves, and mittens can clutter your entryway, utility room, and kitchen table all winter long if you haven't allocated a convenient place for them. For coats and scarves, install hooks near the entry door that your family uses most often. Make sure some hooks are at a child-accessible height so your kids can put away their own outer wear. If you hang coats in a closet, allow enough space between them so they can dry, or hang them on the shower curtain rod to dry before storing them in the closet.

To keep mittens, gloves, and scarves in order, place bins on shelves in a pantry, utility room, or closet close to the main entry door. Choose bins with mesh sides (below) to allow airflow to dry damp gloves and hats. Label

winter gloves and hats

Allow space between coats.

a bin for each family member and make sure some are low enough for kids to reach easily.

Boot logic

To keep family members and friends from tracking snow and mud into the house, create a convenient area where they can remove their boots and shoes. Your family will cooperate more readily if this area is just inside the primary entry door. Include a bench or chair for boot and shoe removal. For storage, purchase a boot rack with a drainage reservoir or waterproof mats with raised edges so you don't have to contend with puddles.

Summer clothing basics

Shorts, bathing suits, and sandals take up less space than their winter counterparts, so you can enjoy having some breathing room in your closet and dressers. Keep in mind, though, that exposure to sun, sea water, and chlorine can affect warm-weather clothes. Be sure to rinse out bathing suits before drying and storing them to remove corrosive salt or chemicals from the fabric. Keep bathing suits, caps, goggles, and other swimming gear in wire baskets when they are not in use, so they dry thoroughly.

Hooks that support coats in winter can hold baseball caps and sun hats in summer; when visible, it is more likely they will be used. The boot rack with waterproof tray is useful in summer too; if sandals and sneakers are left by the door, your family won't track sand or garden soil throughout the house. Post an umbrella stand or wall rack

WORK SAVERS

RELEASE WRINKLES

Clothes kept in long-term storage often wind up badly wrinkled. When you take your clothes out of storage, get rid of wrinkles in a hurry by putting the items in the dryer for about 10 minutes on the air-only (no heat) cycle. Add a damp, clean towel to help eliminate stubborn wrinkles.

near the entry door to make it easy to grab umbrellas when a summer rainstorm threatens.

Packing away off-season clothes

Storing off-season clothes in transparent containers will make it a lot easier to find your favorite wool sweater or cotton T-shirt when the seasons change and you want it again. As a bonus, transparent and semitransparent plastic boxes are tidy and stackable, and will keep your clothes clean and dust-free in the off season. They're available in many sizes; look for those with hinged lids so you won't misplace mates.

If you don't want to invest in storage boxes, save the clear zippered bags that you get with the blankets and bedding you buy. To keep colorful clothes from fading, place transparent storage containers away from sunlight.

STORING DELICATE CLOTHING

When preparing old or favorite clothes for storage, pay particular attention to those made of beading, chiffon, rayon, silk, or taffeta. Here are some key points to remember about caring for these delicate fabrics.

◆ **Roll items** when possible to avoid the stretching and creasing that occur on hangers or in folded stacks.

◆ **When you fold delicate garments,** pad them with white, acid-free tissue paper (available in art supply stores). Refold them periodically to minimize creases.

◆ **Give breathing room** to clothes made of natural fibers, such as cotton, linen, silk, and wool. Store them in ventilated containers in a ventilated area.

◆ **Keep out dust and bright light** by covering stored clothes with washed muslin or old cotton sheets. Don't use new sheets; sizing in unwashed fabrics can have a corrosive effect.

STORING BED AND BATH LINENS

To keep bed linens and towels smelling fresh, start by storing them in a well-ventilated place. Coated wire shelves and louvered closet doors will keep air circulating around stored linens. Avoid overcrowding by getting rid of unused linens and making sure you have enough designated storage space.

A trick for keeping linens fresh: When you add clean towels, sheets, and pillowcases to the linen closet, put them at the bottom of the pile. As you use these items, take from the top so they'll rotate evenly in use and wear.

Space requirements for linens

If you have the space, you can easily customize a closet for proper storage of all your household linens. Here are standard space requirements for a linen closet.

◆ **Bath towels** need a shelf 16–24 inches deep and at least 14 inches high.

◆ **Sheets** need 6–24 inches of depth and an area 12 inches high.

Follow the frequency-of-use rules when organizing the linen closet: Put most-used linens within easy reach, seasonal items on the next level, and little-used linens on the highest shelves.

Finding space for blankets

Blankets, quilts, and other bed coverings can fill up precious storage space fast. Consider hanging them up instead of jamming bulky folded blankets into the linen closet. Buy a free-standing quilt rack to hang your blankets over and put it in an unobtrusive corner in a bedroom or in a spare corner of a closet.

Another solution is to build a closet-door blanket-hanging rack. (Doors should be solid, not hollow-core, to support the rack.) Cut holes for dowels (at least ¾ inch in diameter) in two 2 x 4s, cut to fit lengthwise on the inside of a closet door (about 4 feet). Insert the dowels and attach the unit to the door. You can hang up as many blankets as you have dowel room.

FROM CLOSET TO TABLE

Putting a little extra effort into caring for your table linens will pay off. They will last longer and look fresher for many years. Before storing table linens, wash them to remove any dirt or stains.

Repair any tears or holes, so they are ready to use when you pull them out of storage. Also remember the following:

◆ **Hard water can leave iron residue** in laundered items, which will rust and leave brown spots. If you have hard water, use a washing additive such as Iron Out to launder table linens.

◆ **Don't starch or size table linens** before storing them. Starch and sizing are corrosive and are best used on items that you use and wash frequently.

◆ **Potpourri, lavender,** and other sachets are fine for frequently used items, but don't place them directly on stored linens. The natural oils from dried flowers can cause fine fabrics to deteriorate.

Where to store table linens

If you store clean table linens properly, you won't have to spend much time ironing when you're ready to use them. Narrow cubbies and narrow, pull-out drawers (below) work well for napkins and placemats. You can also buy handy

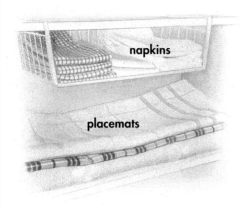

napkins

placemats

under-shelf wire trays (above) at most home centers.

For tablecloths, buy a doweled pull-out rack (below) that you can install in a large pantry cabinet. Tablecloths can be hung on the dowels and pushed in out of sight. As a last resort, hang clean tablecloths on padded hangers in a spare closet and cover them lightly with washed muslin or washed cotton sheets.

tablecloths

Although you might want to keep all your holiday decorations together, you can best care for holiday linens by storing them with your other linens in a well-ventilated place.

Storing in cedar
Cedar has long been the most popular agent to keep moths away from stored clothing. There are several ways to bring cedar into your storage areas.

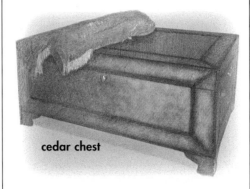

cedar chest

◆ **A cedar chest** (above) works well for folded clothes and linens and can double as a piece of furniture. If a cedar chest is out of your budget, you can buy clear plastic storage boxes with red cedar strips in the lids at home centers or discount stores.

◆ **A cedar-lined closet** protects hanging clothes. You can convert a regular closet with cedar panels and planks from a home center or hardware store.

◆ **Cedar hangers, drawer strips, balls, cubes, chips, and shavings** also repel moths (facing page), although they're not quite as effective as a cedar chest or closet. Put cedar chips or shav-

ings in a decorative bag (or a clean sock) and attach the bag to a hanger for closet moth protection.

Handling antique linens
Roll old quilts and fragile antique linens before storing to avoid permanent crease marks. You can fold and store them flat, but refold periodically to avoid creases. Wrap or cover them to keep out dust and bright light, which can cause deterioration, fading, and yellowing. Use washed muslin, old cotton sheets that no longer have sizing in them, acid-free boxes, or acid-free tissue paper (available in art supply stores). Store in a well-ventilated place.

PRESERVING KEEPSAKES
Porcelain and glass keepsakes and collectibles often need less storage space than they do display space. Fireplace mantels, corner cupboards or shelves, curio cabinets, and just plain open shelving are all places to hold Hummel figurines or a collection of glass animals. If you run out of display space, however, you will have to resort to putting some of your favorite things in storage.

Because most keepsakes and collectibles tend to be fragile, they should be packed carefully into boxes with padded packing material and acid-free paper, then stored in a low-traffic area where they are not likely to be disturbed. Label the boxes for easy retrieval later.

Consider displaying your keepsakes and collectibles on a seasonal or holiday theme basis. If so, collect your things

MANAGING A MOTH INFESTATION

If you discover holes and white larvae in stored clothing, you're most likely facing a moth infestation. Sort through the affected items and throw away anything you can't salvage. Take the rest to a dry-cleaner, letting the staff know about the infestation. Meanwhile, have your house exterminated for moths. Before returning cleaned clothing to the storage area, wipe off boxes, shoes, and other surfaces with a damp, clean cloth, then throw the cloth away.

Natural moth repellents

Cedar is nature's best-known moth repellent, but it's not the only one. Other natural moth repellents include lavender and dried orange peel. Don't allow them to come in contact with the fabrics that you store, however, because their oils can damage textiles over time. Instead, place them in open containers on closet shelves or suspend them from the ceiling in decorative, light fabric bags.

Mothballs and crystals

While cedar repels moths, mothballs and moth crystal products will repel and kill them when used in an enclosed space. Mothballs and crystals won't kill moth eggs that are already in your clothing when it's put into storage, however, so always clean clothing thoroughly before you put it away.

Mothballs and moth crystals are poisonous if eaten, so store them out of the reach of pets and children. It's best to suspend mothballs above cloth-

ing; the chemicals in these products emit a vapor that filters downward (it's heavier than air), making this method safe as well as effective. Place mothballs or crystals in a decorative bag or clean sock and hang them from the ceiling. To counteract mothball odor, add a pomander or an herbal potpourri to the storage area.

---

by season or holiday, and label storage boxes accordingly for easy access at the appropriate time.

STORING HOLIDAY DECORATIONS

If your household celebrates holidays with lots of decorative flair, carefully organizing your Christmas ornaments, Hanukkah menorahs, and other holiday items can save time, as well as wear and tear on treasured heirlooms.

You'll spend fewer hours looking for the decorations and more time enjoying the holidays.

Make holiday items easy to find

Pack and store Christmas ornaments and other holiday decorative paraphernalia in a way that will allow you to find them easily every year. Clear containers, for example, will let you see what's inside so you can quickly find

what you need. (This is particularly useful for Christmas lights and other decorations that go up first.)

If you use cardboard boxes, take time to label them, being as specific as possible. Don't use large boxes, or you'll have to sift through too many things next year to find that festive holiday centerpiece just before a party or to locate your tree stand the day you bring the tree home. Cover any unboxed items lightly with an old sheet to keep out dust and color-fading light.

Handle breakables with care

Pack fragile decorations with extra padding so they will last for years to come. Here's how.

◆ **Save the boxes** that come with purchased holiday decorations so you'll have a safe place for them.

◆ **If you don't have the original boxes,** buy decoration storage boxes designed with compartments to protect individual items. Wrap each piece carefully before storing. Empty egg cartons also offer safe compartments in which to store smaller breakables. Empty wine or liquor boxes also are compartmentalized, perfect for storing larger ornaments or holiday pieces. Be sure to wrap each piece in plenty of newspaper or tissue paper.

◆ **You can also pack breakables** in regular cartons, wrapping each one in several layers of white tissue paper. Place crumpled paper on the bottom of each box or container, and put large items in first. Use plenty of crumpled paper between layers and items.

◆ **Use small boxes** for fragile decorations. Wrap ornaments individually and place in small boxes. Put the small boxes inside larger ones, padding them thoroughly with crumpled paper.

◆ **Use bubble wrap** for extra protection in storing delicate, antique, or one-of-a-kind decorations.

Candle storage

To keep candles from warping, don't store them in a hot attic or near

KEEP LIGHTS TANGLE FREE

Keep Christmas lights tidy and tangle free in storage by wrapping them up on an H-shaped or reel-type holder. Available at home centers, these handy holders are designed to protect extension cords and Christmas lights. Holders make wrapping lights speedier and clips keep plugs safely in place. After winding them around the holder, wrap in paper and store in a cardboard box to protect bulbs from breakage.

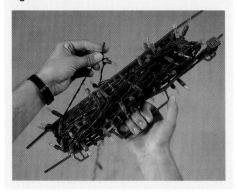

sources of heat, including ducts, pipes, or appliances that become warm from time to time.

In fact, keeping candles cool extends their life. If you chill candles for a few hours before lighting them, they will burn much longer. To prevent candles from fading, store them in closed containers.

ARCHIVING BOOKS AND PAPERS

All too quickly books, mail, and paperwork can pile up throughout your home, but with a good filing system, you can prevent the accumulation of unmanageable stacks that collect dust, make you anxious, and make it impossible to find the important piece of paper that you need.

To avoid this trap, think about how often you'll be referring to the various types of paper that come into your household and designate places for them. Incoming mail, school flyers, catalogs, and books you refer to frequently, such as telephone directories and address books, should be given a convenient location where they'll be easy to put away and retrieve (for example, in bins and boxes on your desk or in a large wicker basket by your bed to review before you go to sleep).

Other books and paperwork can go in a less-frequently used spot, such as a bookcase under a stairway, in a hallway, or on a stair landing. Because light can damage books and papers in long-term storage, find a place for them where exposure to sun is minimal.

Shelving books

Adjustable shelves—the kind that are held by clips that can be moved to different levels of the bookcase—are fine for paperbacks, but they may not be able to bear the weight of hardcover volumes, which are heavy. Make sure any bookcases for hardbacks have a tight-fitting back panel, cross bracing, and corner blocks. The most stable bookcases have stationary shelves locked into the side panels. This is particularly important for tall, floor-to-ceiling bookcases.

Caring for books

For the most part, books, like many household items, need regular dusting and good ventilation. When dusting older volumes, remove them from the shelves individually and use a wide, soft brush—such as an unused paintbrush or shaving brush—to whisk along the top edge, away from the bound end. Dust their spines and sides with a soft cloth. Once or twice a year, apply a leather preservative to books with leather bindings to clean and protect them. Take care of books in long-term storage the same way.

If your books develop a musty odor, put each book in a paper bag filled with crumpled newspapers for a few days. The paper should absorb the odor.

Preventing mold on books

To keep mildew from developing on books, take the following precautions.

◆ **Store books in areas** where temperature and moisture are controlled. If the only area you can store them is damp, run a dehumidifier in the room.

TAKE THE STARCH OUT OF MILDEW

If your books have gotten damp from excessive humidity or long-term storage, here is a quick way to save the pages from mildew damage. Sprinkle cornstarch throughout the book and brush it off several hours later after the moisture has been absorbed. If the pages are mildewed, take the book outside to brush off the cornstarch. This will prevent any mildew spores from being released inside your home.

◆ **If you have spilled water** on a book, try putting the book in a frost-free freezer to draw out the moisture before damaging mildew sets in.

◆ **Keep books off the floor,** especially at basement levels, where puddles—or worse, flooding—can damage them.

◆ **Don't pack books too tightly** on a shelf, but keep them upright to avoid damaging the binding.

◆ **Ensure proper airflow** by leaving a space of at least an inch between shelves and behind the bookcase, especially if it's against an outside wall.

◆ **Put a piece of charcoal** in a bookcase with glass doors to absorb any moisture inside.

◆ **For long-term storage,** don't use bookcases with glass doors—they are difficult to ventilate properly.

THE PAPER CHASE

Perhaps the most frustrating of household tasks is managing the mounds of paperwork that come in with the daily mail and every shopping trip. Don't let it overwhelm you. Instead, make it a priority to create an organizational system that gets your clippings, receipts, and valuable documents into their proper places, where you can find them.

Maintain a workable filing system

Filing household documents and records wisely will save hours of searching later. Here's how to keep files manageable.

◆ **Routinely set aside time** to sort through papers and household files. Throw away every item you can when you sort. Your first instinct of the value of something is probably right. If you're really not sure, put a note on the document about what you need to do to determine if it's worth keeping, and put that in your "to do" pile.

◆ **Use your computer to reduce** paper documentation. Computerize files of important information (copy them on disk, too), and explore online banking options. Most banks have Internet-based systems that may work with your current Web browser, or the bank will supply you with software to make the right connection.

◆ **To organize paperwork** that you must save, use file folders. It helps if you keep categories specific enough to make searching easy, but general enough to keep the number of files manageable. Always start file names with nouns. For example, "Letters, Personal," is better than "Personal Letters." Other headings you might use: Directions and Maps, Investments, Repairs, Medical Records, Insurance, Taxes, and Warranties.

◆ **For easy identification,** color code your files. You may wish to use colored folders: for example, green for investments or red for taxes. A cheaper, quicker method is to use colored labels, colored plastic tabs, or to write file names with colored markers.

◆ **To keep folders clean,** store them in alphabetical order within an enclosed container or drawer. Visit a home store or office supply store to find your options, including cabinets, stackable file drawers, plastic file boxes, and cardboard file cartons. Make an alphabetical list of your folders and tape it on the outside of the container or drawer.

◆ **Each time you consult a folder,** review all of its contents. Discard any items you no longer need.

Rotate and update your files

Once you have set up your filing system for household papers, be sure to rotate current files into long-term storage as required. For example, once you have filed your annual tax return, put copies of all relevant documents in a separate permanent tax file for easy retrieval (tax documents should be kept for a minimum of seven years). Then throw out all papers you don't need and start a new tax file for the current year. Update health insurance files with new policy provisions. Keep savings and investment files up to date with current balances and account numbers. Be sure to back up computer files on a separate disk.

TIME SAVERS

WHILE-YOU-WAIT TASK BASKET

Place a basket by your TV chair, by the telephone, in the kitchen, or in all these places. In the basket put quick-task items such as recipes or coupons for filing, non-essential mail, clipped articles, etc. This way you can keep occupied and be productive during a television commercial, while you are on hold, or while waiting for the pasta water to boil.

Safe-keeping for important papers

Some papers are more important than others, such as automobile titles, savings and investment documents, and anything related to the purchase of your home (such as your loan agreement and title insurance policy). Consider storing these papers in a fire-safe box (bolted to the floor, for the greatest security), or in a safe-deposit box at your bank. In addition, most home insurance companies advise making a personal property inventory (on paper, with snapshots, or in video form) and storing it in a safe-deposit box. In the event of a natural disaster, a record of your possessions will make filing an insurance claim easier.

Items of sentimental value should be stored conveniently and safely, too. Personal letters, newspaper clippings and programs kept in one place will be easy to move quickly in case of a flood or fire. A metal strongbox or footlocker works well for this purpose.

Hiding in plain sight

To store valuable documents, money, or jewelry, it is best to rent a safe-deposit box at a local bank. But if you prefer to keep some valuables at home, try foiling would-be thieves by hiding these treasures in ordinary places. For example, you can create good storage with an empty food can or within the pages of a book. Just remove the lid on a food can, empty the contents, and wash thoroughly before putting valuables inside. Secure the lid and place the can back on the kitchen shelf. Books can be good places to hide paper valuables.

You also can use a tissue box to camouflage your valuables. Carefully open a box, remove some of the tissues, wrap your valuables and place inside, layering tissues on top. Reseal the box and store with other tissue boxes.

Rounding up receipts and warranties

Keeping track of receipts and other paperwork for household purchases

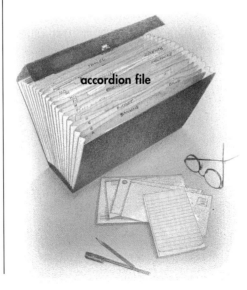

accordion file

can be a headache, but it's worth the effort if you need to return an item or to contact the manufacturer. Here are some filing ideas.

◆ **Check receipts** when you buy an expensive item; make sure the receipt clearly states what it is and when and where it was brought. Write on the receipt any information that is not clear, for future reference. Staple warranties and guarantees to the receipts.

◆ **Buy an accordion file** (bottom left) at an office supply store; they're available with tabs for alphabetical organization. Place the file in a convenient location, such as your desk or in the kitchen.

◆ **Annual sweep** At the end of each calendar year, look through the entire file and discard what you can.

◆ **Use ring binders** to make it easier to keep track of booklets and papers too useful to throw out but often difficult to find. Label the binders and keep them on a shelf in your home office or in another convenient place. As you pay bills and acquire owner's manuals, instructions, and store contracts, punch holes in those you need to save and slip them into the various labeled binders. Use tabbed dividers in different colors, available at office supply stores, to separate categories. The books' contents will be easy to retrieve and peruse.

◆ **Labeled freezer bags,** which are see-through and dust-proof, make ideal containers for miscellaneous items like disks, manuals, and warranties related to computers.

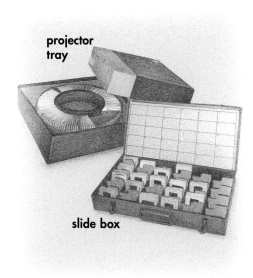

projector
tray

slide box

CARING FOR PHOTOGRAPHS

Today's cameras do almost everything but point the lens, making it easier to take more photographs than ever, but not easier to take care of them. Our forebears meticulously preserved their photographs in albums. Today's color photography actually requires more diligent care of snapshots than in years past. Photographs and negatives should be catalogued and stored on a regular basis. Color transparencies should be stored in boxed projector trays or inside slide boxes (above). Label the containers clearly on the outside.

Storing photographs

Because light can adversely affect the dyes used in prints and negatives, store both in dark places, such as boxes or albums. Look for metal boxes or buy special cardboard or plastic boxes intended for long-term storage of photographic materials. Avoid boxes not specifically designed for photos. Many containers made of standard plastic, cardboard, and wood include preservatives or volatile substances that can affect photographs and negatives over time.

When you buy a photo album, also be sure it is of archival quality. Magnetic albums, although common, are not a good choice. The cardboard covers can give off peroxides that stain the whites of prints, the plastic can give off gases that affect the images, and the adhesives can transfer to the backs of prints, causing the photos to tear when the prints are removed.

Where you store albums and boxes of family photos is important. Here are the major considerations:

◆ **Heat.** Temperatures over 75°F can permanently damage photos or negatives, so don't store them in an attic that's not temperature-controlled, and keep them away from radiators, warm-air registers, and sunny windows. If you place photo-storage items near a wall, make sure it's not a wall with a chimney or hot-air duct behind it.

◆ **Moisture.** Because high humidity can damage photographs and negatives, most basements are not suitable for storing photographs. Always store photographs and negatives at least 6 inches above the floor on any level of the house in case water from an overflowing sink, burst pipe, backed-up sewer, or leaky roof floods the room.

◆ **Fumes.** Chemicals found in household items such as mothballs, mildew inhibitors, wood preservatives, varnishes, and wood glues can give off fumes that damage photos and negatives stashed in cupboards or drawers.

Other chemical fumes that can harm photos include cleaners, foam-injected insulation, fabric treatments (such as permanent press and stain inhibitors), insecticides, and paints.

◆ **Insects.** Carpet beetles and other insects sometimes attack color negatives. Don't store negatives, cameras, or film in closets, cupboards, or drawers where you keep any fabric, which can attract egg-laying adult insects.

Preserve your negatives

If you display a favorite color print, it will deteriorate over time from light, heat, humidity, and chemical contaminants. Store its negative properly so you can make a new print later. Negative file sheets and binders (above) are available in art and photo supply stores. Label the contents carefully for easy retrieval when you need them.

ORGANIZING YOUR GARAGE, BASEMENT, AND WORKSHOP

Most of a household's tools for living, be they miter boxes or mountain bikes, need convenient storage spaces that are easily accessible.

Garages, basements, and workshops are, by their very nature, storage-intensive zones. Garages double as gardening sheds and bicycle racks. Basements acquire a household's overflow of everything from toys and tools to clothing and broken furniture. Workshops require safe, large-scale storage for tools, and small-scale storage for fasteners. With a good plan, you can make room for more than you might think in these three important storage areas.

A GARAGE FOR ALL SEASONS

The garage tends to become a catch-all space for extra stuff, but the time and thought you put into organizing it is an excellent investment. You walk through this space every day on your way to your car, so garage clutter is an inconvenience, and a possible source of danger. For starters, try the following.

◆ **Store bicycles** up and out of traffic zones. They can be suspended from walls with simple clips, available in hardware stores, or on sturdy racks (below) sold in bicycle shops and closet accessory stores. Some designs include shelves, or baskets for biking gear such as helmets, gloves, and water bottles. Fasten the racks into wall studs with screws.

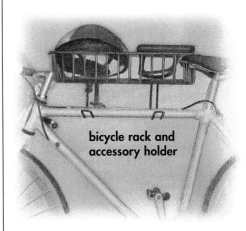

bicycle rack and accessory holder

◆ **Keep athletic gear in order.** Visit a home center or closet accessories shop and you'll find racks and shelves designed for all kinds of sports equip-

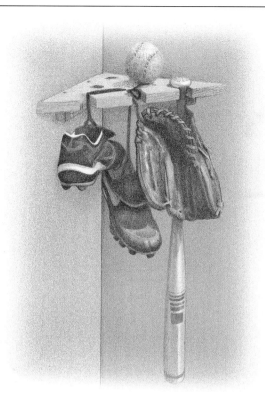

ment, including in-line skates, baseball bats, skis, soccer balls, basketballs, golf clubs, and tennis rackets. Or, use scrap lumber to create an inexpensive storage device for your family sports equipment, such as a rack for baseball gear (above). Cut a triangle from a scrap of 1 x 10 lumber. Bore 1¼-inch diameter holes for the balls and cut bat slots with a coping saw. Nail the platform to support blocks fastened to wall studs.

◆ **Store protective gear** close to bikes, skateboards, and rollerblades—on hooks and shelves near the garage door, for example.

◆ **Assign camping and sports gear** a place close to your car or van. Or, use a wheeled storage chest to keep this equipment, so that loading and unloading will be quick and convenient.

◆ **Install a fold-down table,** if space in your garage or basement is tight. It lays flush with the wall when not in use to keep traffic zones clear. When you need a surface for potting plants or making home repairs, it folds out into a locked horizontal position.

◆ **Stackable storage drawers** can be arranged to fit almost any space. They can hold workshop tools, garden supplies, or toys, for example. Clear plastic lets you see inside, while keeping the contents dust free.

◆ **Use inexpensive rain gutters** to create convenient storage (below) for molding, lightweight lumber, pipes, and other long, thin items. To install the vinyl or aluminum gutters, cut the lengths you want and use screws to fasten the mounting brackets to studs; snap the gutters into place. Use the

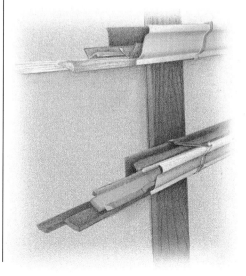

SIMPLIFYING CHORES

Workshop and garage chores will be quicker and easier to manage if you have these areas organized.

◆ **Create common storage spots** for tools and equipment that you use together. Keep hammers with nails close by, have garden tools and potting supplies in one particular niche (preferably near a door to the outside), and stow containers of ice-melting compound with snow shovels near the door to the driveway.

◆ **Keep frequently used power tools** close at hand. Mount a solid shelf over the workbench (below), cutting slots along the back for your circular and saber saws, and bore 1-inch holes along the front for your drill, power driver, and router.

◆ **If the household recycling center** is in the garage, make it as close as possible to the door into the house so that depositing bottles, cans, and cardboard is a simple matter. That way, you and your family won't be tempted to let recyclables stack up in the kitchen before you take them out to the garage. (The same tactic works for garbage and garbage cans.)

brackets alone as hooks for garden hoses, extension cords, and wire coils.

◆ **Put a bench in the garage** to provide a handy spot for your family to put on and remove sports gear. If you're buying a bench, check out home stores for a model designed with a storage shelf underneath to let wet boots and shoes drain dry. Or for the same effect, place a ridged plastic tray underneath the bench.

Between-stud shelves

Narrow 3½-inch-wide shelves installed between open studs will hold quart cans of paint, jars of fasteners, garden sprays, and other supplies (below). Using a 1 x 4, first make ¾-inch blocks to support the shelves. Attach the blocks to both sides of the stud with glue and 1½-inch screws. Cut the shelves to fit between the studs, then place them securely on the blocks.

To make wider shelves for the space between studs, use pre-manufactured angle-brackets (available in several

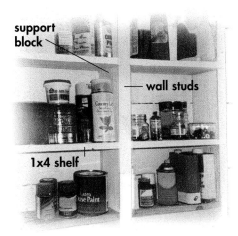

support block

wall studs

1x4 shelf

sizes). For a 10-inch-deep shelf, for example, you need 6-inch-long brackets. Cut the shelves from ¾-inch plywood. Using 1½-inch-long screws, mount a bracket on every other stud for a moderate load, or on every stud for heavier loads. Notch the shelves to fit around the studs, and attach them to the brackets with ½-inch drywall screws.

Up against the wall

Wall organizers, available in hardware and home stores, offer a variety of interchangeable hooks and snap-on pieces to hold garden hoses, clippers, shovels, rakes, hoes, and other tools. Wall-mounted mop and broom holders can help organize cleaning tools. They contain hooks and holes that fit broom handles, dust pans, and whisk brooms.

THE WELL-TEMPERED WORKSHOP

A workshop is most useful when your tools are easily accessible. To keep tools in order, try these inexpensive ideas.

◆ **Make a tool holder** out of scrap wire mesh (hardware cloth). Form the mesh into a handy U shape with flanges by bending it over the edge of a board. Attach the flanges to the wall with screws and washers. A mesh with ½-inch squares holds a variety of tools, such as screwdrivers or pliers.

◆ **Hold small tools** with an old leather or canvas belt. Tack it along the edge of a shelf, leaving small loops between nails. Slip tools into the loops.

◆ **Line up hand tools,** such as scissors, screwdrivers, and punches, where they

CORRAL CORDS

Use clip-style clothespins to keep power cords up and out of the way in your workshop. Screw or glue them to overhead joists or other out-of-the-action spots. You can also create a hanger that lets a cord move by slitting a short length of old garden hose diagonally (below). Open the slit to tack the hanger in place and to insert or remove the cord. Install a multi-outlet power strip under the front edge of your workbench to provide a handy place for plugging in power tools while keeping cords out of the way. Use a GFCI-protected power strip with a circuit breaker to prevent overloads, and make sure it's rated to handle the maximum amperage that you are likely to use on it.

are always at the ready by screwing a powerful magnetic strip to the side of a shelf over your workbench. The magnetic strips, designed to hold knives and available at kitchen stores, can hold all kinds of hardware items within convenient reach. They work equally well mounted on the side of the stand you use for your table saw and other large stationary tools.

To hold large tools, use hinged handles like those found on metal garbage cans. Mount them so the handle hangs away from the wall. You can slip a hammer or wrench into the handle for safe storage.

Versatile perf

Perforated hardboard (below) works not only on workshop and garage walls, but also inside cabinet doors and on the sides of your workbench. Lightweight ⅛-inch perf board is fine for hand tools, but you'll want to use ¼-inch perf board for heavier items. To keep perf-board hooks from coming loose, put a dab of hot glue on the end that hooks into the board. If you need to rearrange items and move the hook, a light tug will usually free it without much difficulty.

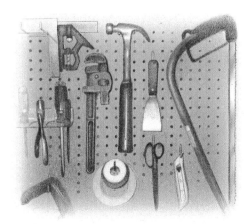

Control work-surface clutter

Try these ideas to organize other odds and ends that clutter up the workshop:

Create a string dispenser by cutting off the bottom half of a 2-liter plastic soda bottle. Nail the inside of the top half upside down on a wall; place the string inside with the end dangling through the bottle neck. Tie scissors to the dispenser with a length of string for handy cutting.

Round up rolls of tape by slipping them onto a toilet paper holder mounted on a wall or workbench.

Holders for bolts, nails, screws, picture hooks, and other small items can be made from small plastic containers. Use transparent tape to attach a sample item to the outside of each container so you can find items at a glance.

Make nail holders from gallon plastic bottles. Leave lids on and cut a section from the top of each one opposite the handle. When the bottles are stored on their sides and filled with nails, the weight of the nails keeps them from rolling. Off the shelves, the bottles can stand upright, and their handles make them easy to carry to any household job site.

ORGANIZE THE BASEMENT

Basements, like garages, are magnets for household overflow, especially if the space is unfinished and dry. A basement can be turned into a useful storage space with freestanding plastic or metal shelves, temporary wardrobes, and stackable storage boxes. Save the driest part of the basement for books, papers, and photographs. Organize the shelves by seasonal needs, if that makes sense, and label all the boxes clearly to help you find things quickly. Store everything off the floor, especially if the basement is unfinished, to avoid exposure to flooding.

Storage underfoot

One frequently neglected storage space in the basement is underneath the stairway. Built-in shelves (above) can hold pantry and paper goods, sports equipment, or toys. A second option is to build shelving units on casters to fit under the steps (below). It allows the shelves and their contents to be hidden away when not in use and easily rolled out when needed.

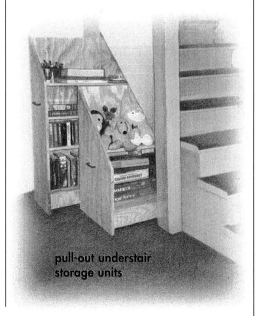

pull-out understair storage units

261

RECYCLING

*If you learn to reuse your discards or pass them on for others to use,
you will not only save storage space at home but also—and more importantly—
in your community's landfill.*

Almost every home has its junk; what you do with it can affect your budget and the efficiency of your home. Reusing discards in new ways saves you money and time because you're not out shopping and paying for new products. Recycling programs help get bottles, cans, and newspapers out of your house and into facilities that regenerate them into useful products. When done well, recycling can simplify your life.

RECYCLING WITHIN THE HOUSE

Effective recycling of household items requires a creative frame of mind. Before you pitch something, take a minute to ask yourself if there is any other use for it. A candle stub, for example, can be rubbed along the runners of a drawer and make the drawer move more smoothly. It can also be used for light in an emergency—or in a Halloween jack-o-lantern. So save it.

When you do save something, be sure to have a specific use for it and a place to keep it. Paper printed on only one side goes into a box in the study to be used as scrap paper for lists and telephone messages. Plastic produce boxes go right to the potting bench for starting seeds. Old T-shirts, towels, or linens get cut up and put in a basket designated for rags in the laundry room or basement.

Top candidates for home recycling are metal cans with plastic lids, plastic milk jugs, plastic bags, paper and plastic grocery sacks, newspapers, egg cartons, yogurt and other re-sealable rigid plastic containers, towels and other household linens, and boxes.

RECYCLING IN THE YARD

Your yard and garden present numerous opportunities for creative and pennywise recycling.

Reuse yard waste. Start a stick pile to use as kindling for your or your neighbor's fireplace. Use scrubbed rocks as paperweights. Fallen leaves or flower petals make quick table decorations, or when dried, mounted, and framed, simple but beautiful artwork.

Keep your compost working on yard and kitchen waste and shredded newspaper (p.291).

Turn household castaways into garden pluses. Scrap lumber, if it hasn't been pressure-treated, can be turned into stakes, window boxes, or planters. Pantyhose, cut into strips, make excellent plant ties. A leaky or cracked garbage can might be perfect for storing potting soil. An unsafe, weathered wooden ladder might make a charming trellis for a climbing rose.

Giveaway. If you can't use or reuse something, find it a new home. Greenhouses usually accept small plastic pots back, and will often buy larger ones. Send the food smoker you got as a gift, but never fired up, to a friend or thrift shop. Give the cultivator you don't really like—and used just once—to someone who would appreciate it.

RECYCLING IN THE COMMUNITY

Each day, every North American generates 4.3 pounds of waste, about 117,713 pounds (nearly 59 tons) in a lifetime. With recycling programs, about one-fourth of that waste—in the form of paper, plastic, metal, and glass—can be recovered and reused.

Recent years have seen advances in the accessibility to recycling programs in large and small cities across Canada. Paper is the largest component of residential waste, and paper recycling—the most widely available recycling program in the country—has grown impressively. In 1994, roughly 70 percent of households had access to curbside recycling or recycling depots, compared with 52 percent in 1991.

Accessibility to glass recycling programs has also increased from less than 50 percent in 1991 to more than 67 percent in 1994. Recycling programs for glass bottles, metal cans, plastics, and special disposal programs have also grown significantly.

To find out about your community's recycling program, and where the closest drop-off facility might be, call your local government or sanitation service. Also, look in the telephone book under "Recycling Services" or call for information from the reference desk at the local library.

Most curbside programs recycle only smaller items, such as metal cans and glass bottles. Your community may have drop-off facilities that will accept larger items, such as carpeting, furniture, and household appliances. Many communities also provide for the safe disposal of household hazardous waste, such as used motor oil or old oil paint.

Giving things away

Charitable groups, such as the Salvation Army and Neighbourhood Services accept many items—dishes, flatware, linens, clothing, toys, and furniture—as long as they're clean and in good condition. If you can't take your donations

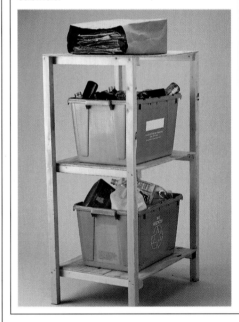

GOOD SOLUTIONS

RECYCLING BINS

One way to encourage recycling in your house is to make it easy to collect recyclable materials. Here are three options:

Create your own recycling center (below) by building a three-tier plywood shelf designed to hold laundry baskets designated for recyclable items.

Buy a home recycling system, such as those that hold three wastebaskets inside a plastic PVC pipe frame.

In remodeling a kitchen, plan for tip-out recycling bins, faced to match your cabinets.

to the organization, ask if it provides a pick-up service. To reach more directly into your community, contact local churches, synagogues, or shelters for the needy.

8

Yard
_____

Garden
_____

PLANNING AND MAINTAINING YOUR LANDSCAPE

Even if you are a plant novice, you can still have a great garden. All it takes is some basic know-how and a willingness to plunge into some outdoor work.

Looking at a beautiful garden from your window or door is a very rewarding experience. Such a garden can also yield fresh, delicious produce, dazzling flowers and provide a gracious setting for relaxing and dining with your family and friends.

To achieve a successful garden, you need to understand the soil, light, and moisture conditions in your garden and have a basic knowledge of local weather patterns.

KNOW YOUR WEATHER CONDITIONS

Selecting plants that thrive in your area is half the secret of gardening. A plant that is well suited to its surroundings will flourish with a minimum of help, while a plant growing in an inhospitable site will struggle no matter how much care you give it.

Your best tool for identifying suitable plants is the Plant Hardiness Zone Map, which appears on the fac-

ing page. Developed by Agriculture, AgriFoods Canada, this map divides the country into nine zones. Each zone is based in part on an average minimum temperature, which is an index of the local winter's severity. In most cases, and especially with trees and shrubs, this temperature is the crucial factor in determining whether a plant will survive in a given region.

Most plant descriptions—in catalogs or on plant labels, for example—indicate the zones in which a specific plant will thrive. For instance, the common flowering dogwood will be listed as hardy from zones 6 to 9. Or a plant may be described as "hardy to zone 6," which indicates that the plant will survive in zones 6 to 9, but not in colder zones.

Once you have identified the zone that you live in, buy only plants that are recommended for that zone or colder; then you can be reasonably confident that your new plants will survive. For example, the katsura tree

PLANT HARDINESS ZONE MAP

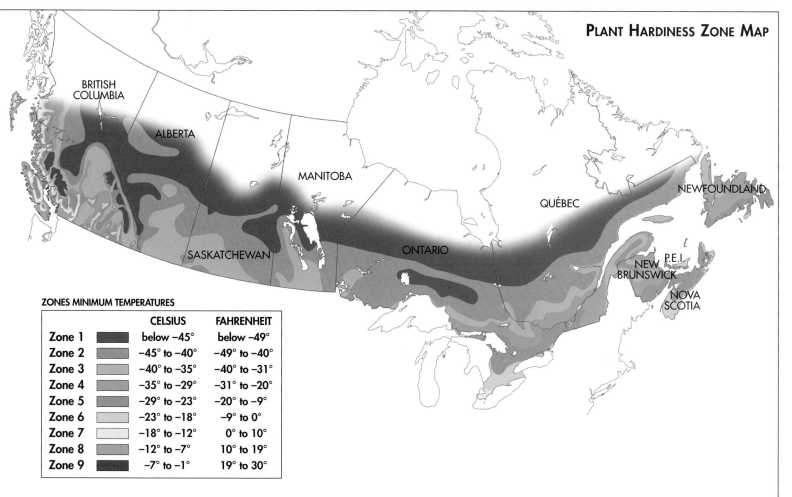

ZONES MINIMUM TEMPERATURES

		CELSIUS	FAHRENHEIT
Zone 1		below −45°	below −49°
Zone 2		−45° to −40°	−49° to −40°
Zone 3		−40° to −35°	−40° to −31°
Zone 4		−35° to −29°	−31° to −20°
Zone 5		−29° to −23°	−20° to −9°
Zone 6		−23° to −18°	−9° to 0°
Zone 7		−18° to −12°	0° to 10°
Zone 8		−12° to −7°	10° to 19°
Zone 9		−7° to −1°	19° to 30°

is hardy to zone 4. If you live in Winnipeg, located in zone 3, you will need to plant hardier species.

Microclimates

Plant hardiness can also be influenced by certain local conditions. A garden located at the top of a 1,000-foot mountain, for example, will usually have temperatures several degrees colder than a garden in the surrounding plains. And because water collects heat

from the sun, a garden that is located on the shores of a lake will be both warmer in winter and cooler in summer than a garden away from the lake. In summer, a garden near a lake may also benefit from the humidity contributed by the lake. Within any garden, there are certain spots that are colder and warmer, wetter and drier, or sunnier and shadier than others.

Local conditions may cause you to reconsider your hardiness zone. You

may find you can use microclimates to grow plants you would not expect to survive; but conversely, you may need to grow only plants rated a zone colder. Plant hardiness maps are only a guide. The zones shade from one side to another and there will be small areas that are warmer or colder within each zone.

Here are some specific strategies for using your garden's microclimates to best advantage:

◆ **Site plants that are only marginally cold-hardy** to the south of a building or hedge.

◆ **Save the most cold-hardy plants** for significantly low-lying areas, places where cold air and frost settle.

◆ **Fruit trees and other plants** likely to be damaged by a late spring frost should be planted on the north or east side of a slope or the house to slow warming and prevent premature blooming in early spring.

◆ **Place moisture-loving plants** near the bottom of downspouts or in low-lying areas where water collects.

◆ **Plants that like hot, dry conditions** thrive by sunny driveways and walks.

◆ **Plants described as shade-tolerant** usually prefer afternoon rather than morning shade.

◆ **Cut strong winds by** planting a windbreak on the north or west side of the house. It can reduce the speed of chill winds by almost half.

Soil basics

Few of us have a yard full of the black, crumbly loam that is ideal for most plants. Often the soil is thick with clay, which is rich in nutrients, but holds so much water that it drains poorly. Other soils are so sandy that they serve as a sieve to water, which rushes through them, taking the nutrients with it. Any soil can be improved over time. To determine the type you have, dig a spadeful and grasp a clump of soil in your hand. A clayey soil makes a sticky clod when damp; a sandy soil crumbles

in your hand even when wet; a loam soil forms a loose clump when damp but crumbles easily. If you find more than a few stones or pebbles in each handful of soil, your yields will probably be sparse. Discard the stones or replace the soil. Soil can be improved by working in plenty of compost several times a year. Break up clay soil by adding sand. To amend sandy soil, add sphagnum peat

clay

sandy

loam

moss. If even weeds have a hard time growing in your soil, or if it is full of debris, replace it. Excavate it to a depth of at least eight inches, and replace your old soil with fresh topsoil mixed with peat moss or compost.

Drainage

The phrase "well-drained soil" on a seed packet or plant description means that the plant will not do well if it soaks too long in water. Most plants will rot if they sit in water, so the soil must be able to efficiently drain water away from the roots. If water stays in a puddle for several hours after a rainfall, the

soil is not well drained. Depending on your soil type, you should add sand or an organic material such as compost.

PLANNING A LANDSCAPE

Do not make extensive changes to a new yard for a year or so—until you understand the landscape's peculiarities. Use a garden journal to record what you learn about the soil, drainage, shady areas, and any hot and cold spots. Use the first year to experiment. Plant a few annuals, perennials, some vegetables, and some plants in pots.

Make a list

The best way to design your landscape is to make a list of what you want and problems that need to be solved. You may want a vegetable or herb garden, a place for the trash cans, and a place to park bikes and store outdoor toys. And perhaps you would like an outdoor dining area and a shady retreat with privacy. Make a complete wish list, then trim it down to the most important items.

Decide on professional assistance

If you are unsure how to begin your landscaping project, or if you want some new ideas, consider bringing in a professional. An overall landscape plan not only gives you direction, but it also saves time and money in costly, back-breaking mistakes. A landscape professional will draw up plans for a lawn and garden that addresses your needs. You can then do the work yourself bit by bit, or you can sign a contract with a professional to do all or part

GOOD SOLUTIONS

DRAW ROUGH SKETCHES

Sketch your ideas out on paper, drawing rough thumbnails at first and then, if you want, detailed, to-scale plans later on. Realize, however, that even the best paper plan is just a starting point; expect your ideas to evolve. Take the time to photograph your landscape in each season of the year. Draw in what you'd like with a marker or grease pencil. Outline the garden beds that you are planning with a garden hose or by sprinkling flour on the grass and live with them for a day or two to test them out.

of the job. Professional help can be expensive: a landscape architect may charge more than a thousand dollars for a design. However, some nurseries have designers on staff who will create plans for free with the idea that you'll buy the plants there.

Hardscape

In planning your landscape, you need to look beyond the trees, shrubs, and garden beds. Great gardens have good "bones." The skeleton of a landscape is the hardscape: the paths, fences, steps, edging, patios, decks, and other "hard" elements.

When designing these elements, keep in mind that hardscape should serve a function. A path takes you from the garage to the back door. A fence blocks or backs a view. A deck gives you a high, dry surface on which to relax and entertain. An arbor supports vines and serves as an outdoor door-way, defining two areas of your yard. Two or more elements can combine to form an outdoor "room."

With a little know-how you can do some hardscaping yourself, such as laying a gravel path or installing brick edging along a perennial border. But unless you are an accomplished do-it-

yourselfer, it's best to leave the bigger projects to the pros. Hardscape is an enduring landscape element, it isn't cheap, and you want it done right.

Raised beds and large containers

Raised planting beds, large containers, and garden beds planted behind retaining walls add visual interest to a yard and make gardening easier. These features eliminate the need to bend down to the ground in order to weed and so reduce strain on your back.

To be sure that the plants are within easy reach, carefully plan the size and position of each raised bed and container. For instance, if you will be able to get at a raised bed from only one side, make it no more than three feet wide—the distance you can comfortably reach. If you can reach it from either side, it can be five or six feet wide. Position containers so they will not be awkward to get at.

raised planting bed

CREATE A GARDEN CENTER

Finding the right tools when you need them is the key to efficient gardening. Make your life easier by spending an hour or two organizing them—and make it easy to keep them organized.

◆ **Store all garden tools** in the same spot in the garage or other easily accessible spot. If you don't have a good place for storage, consider buying a weatherproof, free-standing garden tool cabinet or shed (below), and tuck it into a corner of the yard or behind a garage.

◆ **Hang large tools,** such as spades and rakes, on a wall so they won't tangle or take up floor space. Many of the smaller tools can be hung on pegboard. If you have space, you can store other small garden supplies on an all-purpose potting table. You can buy a ready-made table or you can make one out of scrap lumber and plywood fairly easily. Large bags of potting soil and other soil amendments are easier to handle if they are stored in large plastic wastebaskets or small garbage cans. Unused pots and seedling trays can sit on a wood shelf mounted on the wall.

◆ **A garden caddy is** an indispensable gardening accessory. Whether it's a rustic English wooden "trug" basket, a plastic bin with a handle, a small pail, or a cloth caddy that slips over a 5-gallon bucket, you'll save yourself innumerable steps. Stock it with a trowel, gloves, seed packets, sunscreen, hand sheers, insect repellent, tissues, and anything else you need in the garden.

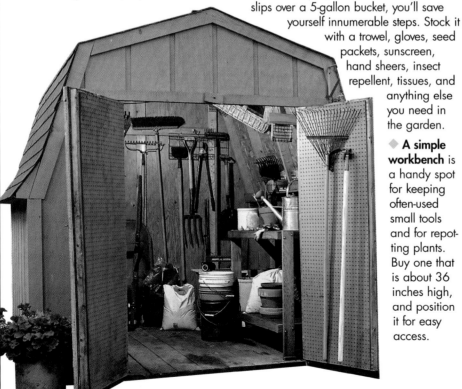

◆ **A simple workbench** is a handy spot for keeping often-used small tools and for repotting plants. Buy one that is about 36 inches high, and position it for easy access.

Creating privacy

All landscapes need what professionals call "a sense of enclosure." Whether it's a low hedge or a six-foot plank fence, a backyard needs a place where you can sit and relax and feel you're not being observed by neighbors or passersby.

A privacy fence is a ready-made solution and will last 10 to 20 years. However, building a fence that conforms to local zoning codes can cost several thousand dollars. In addition, such a fence may create an oppressive, prisonlike feel and make you appear unfriendly to neighbors. To create a fence that has lines that are less severe, you can incorporate openings or add latticework to the design. Climbing vines and other tall plants can also be planted in front of the fence to soften the straight lines.

Hedges are beautiful and less expensive to install, but can take years to mature and require maintenance. And if your yard is shady, you will find that they won't do well. If you choose to plant a hedge, consider planting an evergreen variety which will provide privacy year-round (see page 281 for planting details).

A trellis of vines is another solution that is decorative and doesn't seem as unfriendly as a fence. Perennial vines grow quicker than hedges. They soon provide the privacy you desire and the end result is likely to be very satisfying.

You may also be able to create a private space without building. You can carve a sitting area in that little nook created by the L-shape of the house, or reclaim the area on the side of the

MONEY SAVERS

SAVING MONEY ON YOUR LANDSCAPE

Landscaping doesn't have to cost thousands of dollars. Here are some ways to rein in a landscaping budget.

◆ **Do it yourself.** Whether it is digging and laying a mulch path, mowing the lawn or fertilizing it, you will save hundreds of dollars and learn more about gardening if you do it yourself.

◆ **Be patient.** Design your landscape, then break down the execution over several years. You will be able to spread out the costs and do more of the work yourself. Once you have it all "done," you will still spend years refining it.

◆ **Buy in bulk.** Gravel and topsoil purchased in little bags cost far more than having a landscaping company deliver them by truck. Potting soil is less expensive when you buy the largest size. Get together with a friend and buy mail-order plants and bulbs in large quantities.

◆ **Buy at off-peak prices.** Late summer and fall are great times to buy garden supplies in clearance sales. And in the early spring, garden centers often will mark down last year's merchandise to clear the shelves.

◆ **Look for bargains.** Discount-store bedding plants are usually fine—when they first come in. But do not buy them when they are wilted and possibly diseased.

◆ **Join a local garden club or horticultural society.** You'll learn by talking to others and most clubs have plant sales or exchanges where you can get new (and hardy) plants.

◆ **Propagate your own plants.** You can plant an entire hedge for free if you trim a neighbor's shrubs and then root the cuttings. And you can plant a perennial or annual bed for about $30 if you start the plants from seed. It takes practice to learn how to propagate plants, but you will save money—and have a lot of fun.

◆ **Be environmentally correct.** One of the great things about earth-friendly gardening is that it usually costs less: Non-chemical techniques cost less than buying garden chemicals. Composting yard waste is free; bagging waste may require stuffing large bags—and sometimes paying a fee to have them hauled away. Some municipalities collect and compost yard waste that they then make available, usually at a reasonable cost, to residents. Check with your local council.

---

garage as an outdoor space. (Think in terms of creating a ceilingless room.) All you may have to do is to spread some gravel, set up some outdoor furniture, and plant some tall ornamental grasses to block views.

CHOOSING THE PLANTS

Choose a variety of plants to form an ensemble, rather than buying piecemeal and hoping that they will look good together. Most successful gardens will have the following: foundation plants of trees and shrubs, as well as other trees and shrubs, a ground cover, some perennials, annuals, and vines.

Foundation plantings

Newly built houses often look naked because they have no foundation plant-ings—the small trees and shrubs planted around the perimeter of the house. Foundation plantings soften the straight lines of the building and ease the transition from the house to the flower bed and lawn.

Evergreens are a good choice in cold climates, because they keep their foliage and color all year round. Several yews in a row with a tall evergreen on the corner of the house is a time-honored arrangement, but explore your nursery for more creative combinations. Choose trees and shrubs that look good year-round and won't grow too large for the spot. Place them so they won't grow into the house, damage the foundation with their roots, or block entrances and windows when they are mature.

Trees

Trees may be evergreen or deciduous. Evergreens are great for spots that need some green year round; deciduous trees offer more variety, changing their look with each season, and offering beautiful leaves, flowers, and fruit.

Height can vary from one foot for a dainty alpine evergreen up to 100 feet for mature oaks. Spread varies too, up to 40 feet or more. Think about the characteristics you want—and don't want—in a tree. Consider height, width, form, bark texture and color, fruit or berries, flowers, when the tree drops its leaves and over what period of time, seasonal color and interest, disease problems, suitability to your climate, how much shade it will create when mature, pruning needs, as well as

PRAIRIES AND MEADOWS

If you have a large, open area and don't want to mow, consider planting it as a prairie or meadow. You'll need to kill all the existing vegetation first with a non-selective herbicide or with repeated tilling and hoeing. Then plant a wildflower seed mix purchased from a reputable dealer and formulated specifically for your region. Keep the soil moist until the plants have germinated.

◆ **To maintain your planting,** mow each fall. You may need to replant sections eventually as one flower or plant takes over too much, as desirable plants die out, or as a weed infestation occurs. Still, you'll find natural planting far more interesting than a lawn—and less work.

sun, soil, and water needs. A crabapple, for example, has gorgeous blossoms, but unless you choose a sterile variety, it will produce thousands of little fruits, which can litter walks and drives. Draw up a list of characteristics you would like and present it to a nursery.

Shrubs

Like trees, shrubs are classified as either evergreen or deciduous. They can fill a landscape with flowers, fragrance, greenery, color, and form in a way that belies their size.

Shrubs vary in height from just a few inches to 15 feet or more; in some cases they can be pruned to serve as a small tree. The spread varies as well. For example, a spreading juniper grows just two or three feet high but more than six feet across.

Entire gardens created with shrubs and shrub borders are low-maintenance alternatives to flower borders. When choosing a shrub, consider characteristics besides size—flower or berries; bloom time; leaf form and seasonal color; requirements for sun, soil, and water; and pruning needs. Draw up a list of the traits you want and a description of the planting site, and take it to a nursery. A good nursery will help you choose plants fitting your desired traits.

Ground covers

Ground covers require less maintenance than a lawn. Use these plants in areas that receive little traffic. Nearly any low-growing, spreading plant can be used for ground cover. The thicker and more vigorously a ground cover grows, the less you will need to weed the area and the less watering or other care it will need.

When selecting a ground cover, consider the following: height and spread; foliage color throughout the year; thickness of growth habit; disease resistance; soil, water, and sun needs. You will also need to find out how well the ground cover will coexist with other plants it might be near—some types of ground cover are so vigorous they choke out less aggressive plants. Top picks for ground cover include ajuga, hosta, ivy, lily of the valley, pachysandra, spreading juniper, and vinca.

Perennials and annuals

One of the easiest and best ways to add color to your garden is to include flowering perennials and annuals to your landscape design.

Perennials come back year after year. They are more expensive initially, but you will find that they save money over time. Flowering perennials bloom for two weeks, or even all season long, depending on the variety.

hosta

pachysandra

Annuals die after one year. They are less expensive than perennials initially, but must be replaced each spring. A few begin blooming in cooler weather, but most bloom in mid- to late spring and provide color for months.

Gardeners today have a nearly endless selection of these flowering plants. A good local nursery will feature those that are easiest to grow in your region. When choosing an annual, ask about its sun, soil, and water requirements; how long it blooms; what the flower looks like; and any diseases or pests that threaten it. When choosing a perennial, ask those same questions but also inquire if the plant dies back during cold weather and, if not, what the foliage looks like throughout the year.

Vines

Vines add greenery or color and take up little ground space, offering an effective way to create vertical interest in the landscape. Vines are also useful in creating privacy, hiding eyesores, and making the most of a small garden.

Whether you choose an annual or perennial vine, pay attention to how it will attach itself to its support. Some vines (such as bittersweet) twine; others (such as clematis and sweet peas) send out tendrils. Still others (such as Virginia creeper) cling to surfaces with "holdfasts" or tiny suction cups. The clinging types are somewhat permanent and are suitable only for brick, stone, and other surfaces that are virtually maintenance-free.

Some vines, such as large-flowered clematis, take two or three years to attain just six to ten feet. Others, such as wisteria, grow that much in a year, reaching 40 feet or more and toppling all but the sturdiest supports.

WATERING STRATEGIES

As the days grow hot and dry, you will find that watering is time-consuming and, in some regions, costly. Consider these options for watering. They can minimize the chore and make your watering more efficient.

brass fittings

⅝-inch hose

rubber or quality vinyl

PICKING THE BEST GARDEN HOSE

Although soakers, sprinkler systems, and drip irrigation have all but replaced hoses in many of the traditional watering chores around the garden, every household without a sprinkler system still needs a sturdy hose. And even if you have an automatic system, you still need a hose to wash the car and soak newly transplanted trees, shrubs, and flowers. Here's what to look for when you're buying a hose.

◆ **Buy a hose** long enough to reach the farthest points of a small garden. In large gardens, you may want to have two hoses since pressure drops in very long lengths.

◆ **Size** A ½-inch hose is light and works well for watering small beds and containers. A ¾-inch hose is bulky and can be awkward to move around, but delivers water faster to a portable sprinkler. If you have only one hose, a ⅝-inch hose is a good compromise.

◆ **Good construction** Three- or four-ply nylon, vinyl, or rubber, reinforced with mesh, makes the strongest hose.

◆ **Choose heavy-duty cast brass fittings,** which minimize leaks that often occur at the couplings. Plastic and other less-durable couplings can be easily crushed and may well crack in cold weather, but the quick-release fittings are very convenient.

Xeriscaping

Where water supplies are limited, gardeners can turn to xeriscaping, a water-wise way of gardening. Xeriscaping conserves water by using plants that are native to dry climates, groups plants according to water needs, and implements careful watering methods. Plants that require extra water should be clustered together. Drip irrigation systems and soaker hoses deliver water with little loss of moisture into the air. Other water-wise practices include limiting lawn size, mulching generously, and improving soil.

Milk-jug irrigation

Some plants, such as tomatoes, benefit from deep watering. You can save yourself hours at the end of a hose by rinsing out a plastic one-gallon jug and perforating its sides with a small nail. When you plant the tomato, bury the jug up to its neck a few inches away. To water the tomato, fill the jug. It will slowly drain for a day or so, delivering the slow, steady drink tomatoes love.

Getting the most from a garden hose

Store your hose coiled either on a hook mounted on the side of the house or in a free-standing caddy that makes it easy to reel the hose out or put it away. In late fall, when you have used the hose for the last time, unscrew it from the spigot and drain it. Turn off the water to the outside spigot from inside the house and leave the outside tap open to prevent frozen pipes. Store the hose in a garage or other sheltered spot.

GOOD TOOLS

WATER MEASURE

Install a rain gauge to find out how much rain your garden gets every week. As a rule of thumb, lawns, vegetable gardens, and other plantings need an inch of water a week. Sometimes rainfall will take care of that; otherwise, you'll have to water.

If a hose leaks at the spigot, replace the rubber washer in the "female" end of the hose and tighten the joint. For leaks in the hose itself, you can buy a hose repair kit at the hardware store. There are several designs, but all require cutting out the damaged section of hose and rejoining the ends. You will need a sharp knife and a screwdriver.

AUTOMATED WATERING SYSTEMS

If your garden gets parched because you do not have time to set up the sprinklers as often as you would like, consider automating at least part of your watering system.

Semi-automatic watering systems

There are some ingenious and inexpensive alternatives to a fully automated system on the market.

◆ **A soaker hose,** made of old automobile tires, is perforated with tiny holes. Lay it on the soil or under mulch along a hedge or through a flower bed, and attach it to a regular hose. Turn the spigot on and the soaker hose will slowly water an area up to several feet on either side of its length.

◆ **A manual-on, automatic-off valve** turns the sprinkler off at a pre-set time. Once you set up the sprinkler and turn on the water, you can go on about your business.

soaker hose

pop-up sprinkler head

◆ **A mechanical timer valve** is an inexpensive device for turning a sprinkler on and off automatically at pre-set times. Fitted between the spigot and the hose, the timer allows you to water when you are away or in the very early morning hours when water evaporation is least. It also prevents you from forgetting that the sprinkler is on and wasting water.

Improved sprinkler heads

Traditional sprinklers lose up to 50 percent of the water they spray through evaporation. New drip emitters and microsprinkler heads, connected by individual tubes to a main hose, solve that problem. The small sprinkler heads dribble or spray water a little at a time to large individual plants or small sections of flower beds.

Fully automated systems

An automatic irrigation system that is installed correctly will not only save you work, but will water more regularly and evenly, and yield a lush lawn and healthy plants. Such watering encourages deeper and healthier root systems, which in turn produce healthier plants.

A properly installed system is nearly invisible, and is tailor-made for your property, so that every inch of lawn and every garden plant will get just the right amount of water. The installation requires meticulous calculations and specialized techniques, so choose a contractor who is experienced in sprinkler systems.

A typical automatic system will have several zones, meaning that sprinklers will come on in different areas of your yard at different times.

micro sprinkler

A timer will control each zone. The system can then water not only large expanses of lawn, but also perennial and annual beds, as well as shrubs and trees. With careful planning, even vegetable gardens can be automatically watered. Drip emitters and microsprinklers make it possible to water your container plants automatically, too.

LAWNS, SHRUBS, AND TREES

*With careful selection and regular maintenance, the large elements
in your garden will be beautiful and long-lived assets
in your home's landscape.*

The fundamental structure of a garden is based on a selection of healthy, well-pruned shrubs, a few gracious trees, and, if space and water supplies allow, a lush rolling lawn.

CHOOSING GRASS

Depending on the conditions in your yard—the type of soil, the amount of water available and the degree of sun and shade—there are a number of different grass you can grow.

◆ **Kentucky bluegrass** is the most widely used grass for lawns in Canada. Even on the prairies it is in common use, providing additional water can be given. It is hard wearing and spreads by underground runners to give a dense turf that smothers weed seedlings. This type of grass grows best on open, fertile soils with at least six hours sunshine per day. Look for varieties such as 'Banff', 'Nugget', and 'Touchdown'. In a seed mix for sunny lawns, Kentucky bluegrass will generally make between 60 and 80 percent by weight.

◆ **Tall fescue** is becoming widely used for recreational areas because of its disease resistance and hard-working ability. This species should be allowed to grow taller than Kentucky bluegrass during the heat of summer. Set the lawn mower to cut at 3 inches. If you have young children, you might want to consider this grass. Look for 'Crossfire II', 'Mustang II', and 'Pixie'.

◆ **Creeping red fescue** is shade tolerant and does well on poor, dry soils and on acidic soils. It spreads by rhizomes and gives a fine turf, but is not very disease resistant where summers are hot and humid. It can survive on less nitrogen than most grass. 'Durlawn' and 'Pennlawn' are two good varieties.

◆ **Chewings fescue** is similar to creeping red fescue, but it doesn't spread by runners. Again, it is a fine-leaved grass that makes a good lawn in shade. Look for 'Jamestown II' and 'Victory'.

◆ **Perennial ryegrass** is not hardy in many parts of Canada, but is often included in a seed mix because it germinates quickly and acts as a nurse grass to protect slower germinating

COMMON LAWN PROBLEMS

Even the most carpetlike lawn can develop problems. If your lawn isn't healthy and you can't diagnose the trouble, dig up a patch of soil and take it to a reliable nursery for analysis. Here are some common situations you may encounter:

Problem	Solution
Grass won't grow under a tree	Replace with shade-tolerant ground cover such as hosta or vinca. If these don't survive due to root competition, use a mulch.
Grass won't grow on a slope	If the slope is hot and dry, more regular, deep watering might help. If you can't get grass established, try laying sod or having a professional "hydroseed"—plant seeds encapsulated in a special material to keep them from drying out.
Lawn is overrun with weeds	Apply herbicide in spring and fall. Do both because each application kills different weeds. If the problem is severe and doesn't respond in one or two years, you may have to kill the lawn with a non-selective herbicide and then replant.
Lawn has bare patches	Try reseeding these areas. In spring or early fall, scratch the bare patch with a ground rake and sprinkle with lawn seed. Mark off the area with stakes and strings, and water gently. Keep the area moist for the next few weeks, watering daily if necessary. If high traffic is the problem, consider creating a path or patio surface.
Lawn has brown spots or weblike threads	Fusarium patch makes 2- to 12-inch-wide brown spots or weblike threads in thatch and grass in early spring. Minimize shade and fertilization; improve drainage; apply fungicide in early fall.
Lawn is dotted with bleached or gray spots	Dollar spot causes numerous such spots to appear. Spots may merge to make larger, straw-colored areas, while cobweb-like growths may appear with morning dew. Fertilize; apply fungicide.
Lawn is dotted with small orange pustules on blades	Rust is the cause of these orange, smudgy spots. Fertilize grass and keep well watered. Mow frequently and remove clippings. Apply fungicide if condition persists.
Lawn has dead areas that spread slowly. Grass pulls out easily	Most common in spring or fall. This is the damage caused by white grubs, the larvae of several different insects. Skunks will dig them out, or you can water the lawn with chlorpyrifos.
Lawn has dead areas that spread quickly but grass does not pull out	Lay some white cloth on the lawn and water with hot water. If small brown insects appear on the underside of the cloth, this indicates the presence of chinch bugs. Apply Diazinon, sevin, or chlorpyrifos.

varieties. It is a good choice for an "instant" lawn in an area you may want to develop next year. 'Manhattan', 'Penn-fine', and 'Norlea' are good choices.

◆ **Other types of grasses,** apart from those described above, are available for special uses. Your local garden center will stock suitable mixtures for your area and advise you on special conditions that may apply.

LAWN-CARE BASICS

A beautiful lawn is usually not difficult to achieve, as long as you follow some basic rules of care:

◆ **Keep it mowed.** Letting lawn grass get too long often leads to thin turf.

◆ **Set mower blade according to the season.** In spring and fall, mow at 1½ to 2 inches high. During the heat of summer, longer grass is desirable because the blades are better able to shade weed seeds and prevent weeds from germinating. They also keep the soil cool and moist, reducing the need for watering. Increase the height of the cut to 2½ to 3 inches.

◆ **Water correctly.** Always water grass 1 inch deep or more. This develops deep, drought-resistant root systems. Once your lawn turns brown (has become dormant), allow it to stay that way until the weather becomes cooler. Don't water it; if you do, the lawn will come out of dormancy prematurely, which will put it under stress.

◆ **Choose the right type of turf for your climate.** Soft, carpetlike Kentucky bluegrass is a favorite of many homeowners, but it may not grow well

TIME SAVERS

LAWN SUBSTITUTES

Not all parts of your yard are well suited for grass. Areas under large trees, slopes, shady spots north of buildings, and baked areas next to sidewalks or drives would be more attractive if planted with a lawn substitute or landscaped with a decorative and useful hardscape feature.

◆ **Groundcover** is the most popular lawn substitute (see page 272). Established beds of groundcover are green year-round and take very little care.

◆ **Mulch** can attractively cover awkward areas under dense trees or near the street, where salt used to treat icy roads can sour the soil for flowers and shrubs. (See page 288 for mulch options.) Adding landscaping fabric (see page 287) before the mulch reduces weed growth.

◆ **Hardscape** is a practical choice. A deck or patio is a useful alternative for a large area where grass won't grow. Installing a surfaced walk in an area of high traffic will spare the grass and allow it to thrive on either side.

in your region, especially if you cannot give additional water in summer. Ask your local nursery or provincial Ministry of Agriculture about the best type of grass for your area.

◆ **Feed on schedule.** Turf grasses are nitrogen-hungry plants and need regular fertilization. Most grasses do well with a spring and fall application. Check with a reliable nursery for the best timing and methods for your area.

Fertilizing a lawn

As a rule, you should use a "complete" lawn fertilizer, one containing nitrogen, phosphorus, and potassium. Apply at a rate that provides 1 pound of nitrogen per 1,000 square feet of lawn in each application of fertilizer. Pay attention to how much fertilizer is being used, so the entire lawn will receive the same amount. Do not over-fertilize; it is not good for the lawn and can contaminate the local water through fertilizer runoff.

On smaller lawns, you can apply fertilizer with a hand-crank centrifugal feeder. Fertilize parallel sections, turning the crank at a smooth, consistent rate as you walk. To spray liquid fertilizer, fill a hose-end unit with fertilizer, and spray the lawn evenly. For larger lawns, use a hopper spreader. Fill the hopper and push the spreader up and down the lawn in long parallel strips. Take care that every spot

centrifugal feeder

hose-end sprayer

hopper spreader

receives fertilizer; even 2-inch-wide sections that are missed will clearly appear less lush as the lawn grows out.

Watering a lawn

Watering is critical for keeping a lawn looking good. The soil must be moist enough to support the growth of the roots, foster the development of new leaves, and replenish the chlorophyll; but it should not be too wet. Soggy soil keeps the roots from getting the air that they need. Most lawns need about 1 inch of water per week during the growing season. This can be applied with a sprinkler and hose or an automatic sprinkler system with pop-up sprinkler heads (see page 274).

Whatever method you choose, water early in the day—before sunrise is ideal—to minimize evaporation. A timer will make this easier and will prevent waste. To find out how much water you are delivering to your lawn, place small containers on several spots in the lawn, and measure the amount of water accumulated.

It can take several hours to water even a 30 x 30 foot lawn. Avoid wasting water by spraying hard surfaces, such as concrete or asphalt. It may be worth investing in several sprinklers so you can water only the places that need it (see page 278).

Aerating a lawn

Over time, the soil beneath a lawn becomes tightly compacted, making it difficult for roots to grow. The solution is to aerate the lawn—to poke it with a gridwork of small holes to loosen

HELPFUL LAWN ACCESSORIES

The right equipment will keep your lawn looking healthy and neat. In addition to a good mower, your basic lawn-care tool kit should include these items.

◆ **Grass shears.** Operating like a big pair of scissors, these shears are good for small jobs, such as trimming around posts and under fences. Short- and long-handled versions are available. The blades will last longer and be more useful if you have them sharpened annually.

◆ **String trimmer.** Spinning a nylon string fast enough to slice through weeds and grass, the string trimmer can cut grassy slopes and small lawns. Gas-powered models are heavy and loud. Electric models, lighter and quieter, have a cord to contend with. Keep these trimmers away from tree bark and shrubs, which they can damage.

◆ **Edger.** To create a crisp, neat edge between drives, sidewalks, or flower borders and the lawn, you need a long-handled edger. It cuts a distinct line, which you can fill with an edging material or simply let stand.

◆ **Portable sprinkler.** Driven by water pressure through a garden hose, inexpensive portable sprinklers come in many designs to suit the shape of any garden or lawn. Shown from left to right are a ring sprinkler, an oscillating sprinkler, two pulse sprinklers that are staked into the ground, and a revolving sprinkler.

up the soil. You can rent a spike-type aerator, which you pull either by hand or behind a tractor-mower, or a plug-type aerator, which actually pulls out little cylinders of turf and soil. You can also hire a landscape contractor to do this for you.

Using herbicides carefully

Weed killers do their job, but many homeowners, especially those with children and pets, are increasingly reluctant to use them. Consult a reliable nursery for information about the type and timing right for your yard.

Diligent weeding of your lawn, coupled with proper care—water, fertilizer, and mowing—may eliminate the need for herbicides. Once weed free, a well-mown and fertilized lawn should be dense enough to stop weed seeds getting established.

MOWING THE LAWN

Having the correct lawn mower for your yard can minimize the time and effort you put into mowing. A riding mower is needed only for the largest lawns. Because of the danger of tipping, it's not appropriate for any lawn with steep slopes.

A push-type power mower is suitable for most lawns. If you have a steep slope or a large lawn, or if you don't have much physical strength, buy a self-propelled model.

Mulching mowers shred the cut grass and deposit it back onto the lawn, where it mulches the grass, preventing weed germination, conserving moisture, and feeding the soil. It also saves you the trouble of raking or emptying grass from the mower's gathering bag—while reducing the burden on local landfills.

How to mow a lawn

Many people cut grass too short, "scalping" the lawn and inviting disease and weed problems. Others mow too seldom. Your grass may grow very quickly and need mowing twice a week. Or it may grow slowly and go two weeks without needing a mow.

Set the lawn mower to the correct height for the season (levers near the

CONSIDER A NON-POWER MOWER

After all but disappearing from the lawn-mowing scene in the 1950s, non-power reel mowers are becoming popular among homeowners who are concerned about emissions and noise from power mowers—and who like a good workout.

◆ **Reel mowers** are less hassle to haul out of the garage and present no starting problem. If sharp, the blades make a very clean cut on the grass, which is good for the lawn. And if you want to collect the clippings, attachable bags are available. Keep in mind, though, that reel mowers don't work well in thick, tall, or wet grass.

wheels allow you to do this), then cut often enough so that you never remove more than one-third of the grass blades. You can save time and effort by mowing your lawn in a spiral pattern instead of back and forth. Start from the outside and work inward. Don't

mow when a lawn is still damp from heavy dew or rain—it clogs the mower and takes longer to finish. Always wear substantial shoes to protect your feet from cuts when operating a power mower. Wear ear plugs to protect against long-term hearing loss.

Mower maintenance

Get the most out of your mower by following these simple maintenance steps.

◆ **Clean the mower.** With the gas tank empty, turn the mower on its side. Give it a good spray with a hose, especially the underside. Use a stick to scrape off any crusted-on grass. Scrub  with a soft brush and soapy water to remove any greasy matter, then rinse.

◆ **Keep the blade sharp.** It should be sharpened at least once a year, and ideally two or three times. Otherwise, the tips of the grass have a ragged cut edge and turn brown a day or two after mowing, giving the lawn a slight brown cast. To find a professional to sharpen the blade, look in the phone book under "Lawn Mowers—Sharpening and Repair."

◆ **Replace or clean the air filter** once or twice during the mowing season (above right). Replace paper filters when they get dirty. Plastic foam filters should be removed, washed in warm, soapy water, and then allowed to air-dry. Once dry, work 2 tablespoons of clean

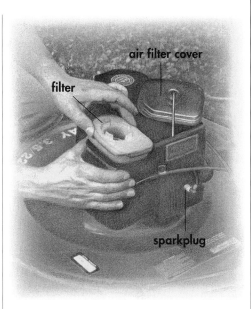

air filter cover

filter

sparkplug

mower oil evenly across and into the filter, just enough to lightly coat it. If the filter is made of paper and foam, remove the foam part and wash it in warm soapy water, let dry, then replace. Put in a new paper filter as necessary.

◆ **At the end of the mowing season,** empty the fuel tank by running the mower until it runs out of gas. If your mower has a separate tank for oil, empty it. Refill the oil tank with fresh oil but leave the gas tank empty.

◆ **Check your owner's manual** for any other suggested maintenance. If you don't have the manual, get the manufacturer's phone number from your dealer, and request one.

PLANTING TREES AND SHRUBS

Once you've selected the right tree or shrub for your yard (see "Choosing the Plants" on pages 271–272), identify the

exact location for planting. Bear in mind that trees, in particular, can damage the foundation of your home if they are planted too near it. Trees and shrubs set too close to your house can cause mildew and damage wood siding. Ask your local nursery for recommendations on planting tolerances. Always read plant labels and plant so that even when mature, the trees won't touch your house. Also plant shrubs so that they'll just brush the house when mature.

Digging the hole

Before you dig a deep planting hole for a tree or a shrub, contact your local utility service to find out if there are any underground utility lines at the site. You don't want to dig up or disturb gas, water, telephone, or power lines.

When you dig the hole, be sure that the root ball rests at the same depth as in its previous planting. Don't dig a hole that is too deep and then backfill it; the weight of the plant will sink the root ball below ground level. Dig a hole 2 to 4 feet wider than the root ball.

Preparing the hole

Add sphagnum moss to improve the excavated soil if it is sandy or clay-like, but don't overdo it. In addition, resist the urge to fertilize. Very rich soil in the planting hole doesn't help a plant. Recent research has shown that the roots tend to ignore the outlying soil, grow in circles in the richer soil, and actually stunt the plant's growth.

Planting out

If the root ball has a burlap cover, you can leave it on and just pull it back a little. Other root-ball covers are not biodegradable and should be removed altogether. Place the plant in the hole, and then stand back and look it over. Make sure the stem is straight up and down and that the prettiest, fullest side of the plant is most visible. Rotate the plant around in the hole and level it with a little soil under the root ball as necessary.

Fill the hole three-quarters full. Then tamp the soil with a wood plank or the back of a shovel and irrigate the hole with water. Let the water soak in, and finish filling the hole with soil. Add extra soil to build a shallow water-

protective collar

retaining "saucer" at ground level. Then water the plant thoroughly once again.

To make sure your new plantings get a good start, they need a little protection and support:

◆ **Add a protective collar around the base** of a young tree. Rabbits and mice and other critters often like to gnaw the bark of young trees. You can ward them off with sleeves made from flexible perforated plastic drainpipe. Cut 4-inch-diameter pipe into 24-inch lengths, slit each piece down one side, and gently slip one around the base of each sapling. The pipes protect the trees, and the perforations allow air to flow through to the covered bark.

PRUNING AND TRIMMING TOOLS

Pruning and trimming trees and shrubs keeps plants healthy and looking their best. Here are the basic tools you need for the job.

◆ **Hedge shears.** Resembling oversized scissors, these will snip many small branches at once. Buy shears that feel good in your hands and work easily.

◆ **Loppers.** For stems up to 1 to 2 inches thick, use loppers, or long-handled pruning shears. The scissor-type loppers make the cleanest, easiest cuts. They are preferable to the blade-and-anvil type, which require more strength to use and also crush as they cut, leaving a ragged wound.

◆ **Pruning shears.** Lop off fading flower blossoms with lightweight deadheading shears (far left). For trimming smaller woody branches, use heavy-duty pruning shears (left).

◆ **Pruning saws.** Use these for larger stems and branches. Look for a saw that cuts on both the push and the pull for fastest, easiest cutting. The bow type is the most common. A curved blade is easier to use than a straight one.

◆ **Stake a young tree loosely.** Letting the wind sway a newly planted tree helps strengthen the trunk. You'll be doing your transplants a favor if you keep the support stakes low and the support wires and ties loose—just tight enough to keep the tree from toppling over. Remove the stakes after the first year.

Planting a hedge

A hedge is a living fence, often made of privet or cedar. Most hedges will do best in full sunlight; shade can stunt their growth. If you plant parts of a hedge in sun and parts in shade, the hedge will eventually be different heights and have different densities, resulting in an unattractive hedgerow.

The best means of avoiding such a situation is to choose a shrub for partial shade, such as dogwood, witch hazel, or yews.

To create a hedge, stretch twine between two stakes. Plant the shrubs along one side of the string, spacing them 10 to 20 percent closer together than the mature spread of the plant.

PRUNING SHRUBS AND TREES

Many plants don't need severe pruning. Just remove dead or diseased wood, and cut off the spindly shoots and suckers from roots and lower branches. Shrubs that are getting too tall may need thinning and shaping to control their size.

Pruning deciduous shrubs

Most flowering shrubs should be pruned immediately after flowering. (Those that flower late should be pruned in spring.) If the shrub doesn't appear to be overgrown, you probably won't have to prune much. However, if the plant has a poor flower show, you can thin it to promote future flowering. Remove up to one-third of the shrub's branches, carefully selecting them so that you can be sure of retaining the shrub's natural shape.

Pruning deciduous trees

Take a gentle approach to pruning: Instead of severely pruning a specimen all at one time—called topping—prune over a 3- to 5-year period. Prune when it is dormant in late winter, not in spring when leaves are forming. Oaks and walnuts are exceptions to this rule—they should be pruned in early summer to ward off diseases. Trees with a strong sap flow—birch and maple, for example—are best pruned in late fall to give wounds time to dry. When pruning, cut away branches that rub against other branches, old stubs, broken limbs, dead wood, crowded branches, and thin shoots from the trunk or lower branches.

Pruning conifers

Firs, spruces, pines, or other needle-leaf conifers require specific pruning techniques. Just use your fingers to pinch off half of each "candle"—a new shoot with growth buds—before it turns green in spring. Take care not to remove the entire candle; doing so stops any further growth of the branch.

Cutting limbs

Trees may need to be "limbed up"—the lower branches removed to let in more light beneath. You can prune branches that are 6 inches in diameter or smaller, but hire a professional for larger jobs, since snapping limbs can cause significant damage. Large trees need pruning only once every several years.

To remove a limb safely, make three cuts, as shown at right: (1) Begin by making an undercut, about halfway

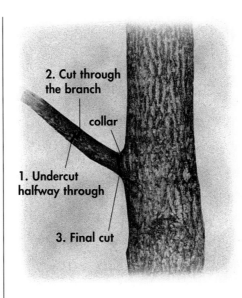

2. Cut through the branch

collar

1. Undercut halfway through

3. Final cut

through the limb. (2) Cut through the rest of the branch from the top. (3) Near the trunk, make a final cut through the branch at a slight angle. Retain the collar to aid healing. In general, aim for evenly spaced branches that create strong crotches where branches meet the trunk.

Pruning a hedge

Some hedge shrubs, such as boxwood, can be trimmed to just a couple of feet wide, while more sprawling shrubs, such as hibiscus, will need 8 feet or more. Because pruning stimulates new growth, prune evergreen and most deciduous hedges in spring. However, if your hedge produces spring flowers, wait until after they bloom to do any cutting.

Hedges do not have to be trimmed into neat, formal rectangles. Many hedges are loose and informal, incorporating a variety of plants. Pruning for any type of hedge starts with removing any dead wood and cutting back any broken or damaged branches.

To shape a formal hedge, use hedge shears. Make the hedge narrower on top than on the bottom, so that light can reach the bottom branches, keeping them green and preventing them from dying out.

If you have an informal hedge, use shears or loppers to thin it out, trimming old wood to the base of the plant. If you want to control the size of the hedge, selectively prune branches to retain their natural form. Don't cut off the ends of the branches; that will stimulate bushy growth that will shade the interior and create a dead center.

Renovating a hedge

If your hedge has suffered years of neglect, you may be able to revive it with radical pruning. Mature hedges that have gotten out of hand are often salvageable. Begin by removing any unwanted saplings or other stray plants that have infested the hedgerow. Then cut out any dead or damaged wood.

Finally, shape the remaining hedge. Some shrubs, such as yew or arborvitae, can be trimmed back severely without ill effect. But other plants, such as juniper, will not grow back attractively. If this is the case, trim lightly or consider replacing the hedge. With deciduous hedges, try thinning and lightly shaping the branches. Most deciduous hedges can withstand severe trimming. In fact, if they are severely overgrown or misshapen, you can cut them back to just a few feet and they will grow back within a year or two.

GARDENING BASICS

*Having the right tools, recognizing weeds and the first signs of disease,
and keeping the soil in top condition are the keys to a beautiful garden.*

The ABCs of good gardening
are pretty simple: Start with
the right plant in the right
spot, give it the soil it loves and water
its needs, and then keep watch for any
pests or diseases that might attack it, so
that you can nip them in the bud.

BUYING AND MAINTAINING TOOLS

Purchase good-quality tools and take
care of them. Cheap tools perform
poorly and will need replacing sooner.

◆ **Clean tools regularly.** Brush or
scrape off dirt and debris after each
use, and store them out of the weather.

◆ **Keep metal parts lubricated** by
rubbing or spraying them with household oil or penetrating oil. An easy way
to clean tools is to fill a bucket with
sand, and mix in some automotive or
lawn mower oil (leftover oil from your
car's last oil change is ideal). After
scraping off excess dirt, plunge a tool
into the bucket of sand several times. It
will emerge clean and well oiled.

◆ **Sharpen tools.** Take your tools to
a professional sharpener once a year,
or sharpen them yourself (see "Sharpening a Blade" on page 285).

◆ **Keep tools in good repair.** For
example, you should tighten the bolts
on wheelbarrows periodically and
check the air in the tires. Mend or
replace splintered wooden handles on
rakes and hoes. Patch leaking hoses.
If rust develops on metal parts of a
tool, remove it with a wire brush and
apply a coat of naval jelly.

HANDLING WEEDS

The easiest way to deal with weeds is
to prevent them in the first place. Take
a few minutes early on, and you can
save yourself hours of struggling with
mature weeds later.

◆ **Get them while they are small.** It is
easier to pull newly sprouted weeds out
of the garden. Mature, well-established
weeds can be hard to remove.

◆ **Follow good gardening basics** by
working plenty of organic amendments,
such as compost or peat moss, into the
soil. If you place appropriate plants in
appropriate sites, weeds will have a
tough time getting the upper hand.

◆ **Pull weeds after a moderate rain,**
or a few hours after watering with a
sprinkler. A good soaking makes the
soil moist so it is easy to remove the
weeds, but not so wet that the soil
leaves clumps on the tools. (Continued
on page 285.)

BASIC GARDENING TOOLS

While many clever gardening tools are available, all you really need are the tools below. They will enable you to do most gardening chores. (See also pages 278 and 281 for lawn-care and pruning tools.)

	Use	What to look for
	**Standard shovel and spade.** A shovel (front) is used for scooping loose materials, such as sand, while a spade (back) is made for digging; but many stores use the terms interchangeably.	D-shaped handles make it easier to lift what you have dug or scooped. Look for forged metal with a sharp digging edge. A slick metal surface allows material to slide off easily.
	(Left to right) **A trowel** is a mini-spade, for planting annuals and perennials. **A spading fork** is used for turning over soil and compost. **A square spade** is used for turning over existing beds, and planting large plants. **A drain spade** is an elongated shovel ideal for digging postholes.	Quality tools are forged rather than made of cast or welded metal. If the metal part wiggles even slightly, don't buy it.
	**Lawn rake** (near left) is a lightweight tool ideal for removing fall leaves, twigs, and other debris. **Ground rake** (far left) is used for smoothing new and existing beds.	Buy tools securely attached to the handles. None of the parts should wiggle. Metal will last longer and perform better than plastic or wood.
	**Broad hoe** (near left) moves soil, digs planting trenches, and weeds. **Shuffle or action hoe** (center) skims just under the surface, slicing weed stems. **Warren hoe** (far left) works in tight areas.	The metal part should be attached to the handle with solid-socket construction, so it will not come loose. Smooth wooden handles will resist splintering.
	**Watering can** is suited for watering jobs too small for a hose. **Garden hose** carries water longer distances. Attach two or more together to reach farther. **Adjustable nozzles** do everything from gently sprinkling new plants to delivering a hard stream for garden cleanup.	Watering cans should have at least a 2-gallon capacity but should be easy to carry when full. With other watering tools, brass parts and fittings are more durable than plastic. To choose a hose, see page 273.
	**Wheelbarrow** (near left) **or two-wheeled yard cart** (not shown) is for hauling leaves or soil, collecting weeds and debris, and many other uses. **Tool caddy** totes seeds and tools; made of canvas, it fits over a round 5-gallon bucket.	The sturdiest wheelbarrows are made of one piece of heavy steel with extra braces on the legs. They also have heavy wooden handles that are attached with countersunk bolts. For heavy loads, a yard cart is easier to maneuver than a wheelbarrow.

MONEY SAVERS

SHARPENING A BLADE

To sharpen a garden-tool blade, hold the tool in a vise. Use a coarse file or a second-cut (medium) file to re-establish the bevel along the cutting edge. To create a sharp digging edge, use a smooth (fine) file or a sharpening stone. Keep the file angle consistent and the pressure uniform; stroke in one direction only.

◆ **Weeds multiply rapidly after a good rain,** especially when the rain is followed by a warm spell. Be on the lookout for new weed sprouts.

◆ **Don't let a weed go to seed.** If a vegetable garden or an annual flower bed has become choked with weeds, it may be best to mow and rake the area in order to prevent the weeds from producing seed heads. Later, turn under what is left of the weeds.

◆ **Mulch repeatedly.** Mulch suffocates new and emerging seeds. Add a generous layer around shrubs and trees, in vegetable gardens, and in flower beds. See pages 286–288 for more on mulch.

◆ **Use chemicals as a last resort.** If the weeds have taken over, you may want to use an herbicide in your ornamental beds. Avoid using herbicides in vegetable gardens. Use a pre-emergent herbicide in spring before weeds appear. For problem areas, consider a non-selective herbicide, which kills everything it touches. Be sure to follow manufacturer's instructions carefully for use and disposal of the product.

HANDLING DISEASE AND PEST PROBLEMS

Disease or pest infestation can cause plants to look sickly even if they are fertilized and watered well. Prevent the problem from occurring, or nip it in the bud, by following these procedures:

◆ **Plant disease-resistant cultivars.** Look for plants bred to avoid diseases common to that plant.

◆ **Examine your plants often** for signs of disease and pest infestation. That way you can cure them before the damage becomes serious.

◆ **Give plants space.** Problems spread fast when pests can jump from plant to plant. Mix plants and avoid overcrowding them.

◆ **Keep the leaves and stems dry.** This will help prevent fungal diseases. When watering, soak the soil, not the plant. Try a soaker hose, which can be buried in the soil. Water early in the morning so water can evaporate by nightfall.

◆ **Put plants in the right place.** A plant that has too much or too little light, has the wrong soil, or is in an unsuitable climate is more susceptible to disease and pests than a plant with the right growing conditions.

◆ **Take care of your plants.** A plant with a weed-free environment, properly prepared soil, and enough water will be naturally resistant to pests and disease.

Insect or disease?

An insect is to blame if there are signs of chewing or burrowing or if a plant has been cleanly cut off. Webs also indicate insect infestation. If you are unsure, put a piece of white paper under or near the plant and gently shake or tap it. If specks of red, brown, or black appear on the paper, insects are the cause of the problem.

A disease is likely to be the problem if there are powdery residues, galls, mildew, funguses, rotting or shriveled areas, or mold. If the problem persists, ask an expert to help you diagnose and treat the problem. Here's where to find the best help:

◆ **Local nurseries.** Take in a part of the problem plant, and show it to a trained staff person.

◆ **Local garden clubs,** radio phone-in shows, Master Gardener hot lines are all good sources for identifying problems. If all else fails, look for a good garden near you and ask the owner for help.

◆ **The Internet.** You can search the Worldwide Web using the keyword "gardening" or go to this site:

COMMON LAWN AND GARDEN WEEDS

Weeds can be tricky to identify, but here are some of the more common ones you'll find in your yard and garden—and the means by which you can control these pesky plants.

Chickweed. An annual that spreads by seeds. Easy to pull, getting all the root system. Don't hoe, since bits of plant left in the soil can resprout.

Crabgrass. An annual that spreads by seeds. Pull, getting all the root system. Don't hoe, since bits of root and stem can resprout.

Creeping Charlie. Perennial that spreads by seeds and creeping stems. Very invasive. Easy to pull. If you hoe, rake up the pieces or they will resprout.

Knotweed. Annual that spreads by seeds. Pull small plants. For larger plants, hoe out the top of the plant, being sure to get all of the crown. It likes compacted soil, so hoe the area.

Plantain. Perennial. Dig out deep roots, or it will resprout. It likes compacted soil, so hoe the surrounding area.

Purslane. An annual that spreads by seeds. Pull. Don't hoe or otherwise cut out.

Spurge. An annual that spreads by seeds. Pull or hoe out. Keep the garden watered, since spurge likes dry soil.

Clover. Perennial that spreads by seeds and thrives in low-nitrogen soil. Pull or hoe out.

Dandelion. Perennial. Pull before it goes to seed, taking care to get all of the deep root.

http://www.gardening.com for access to many excellent Web sites.

USING MULCH

Mulching can make the difference between a healthy, easy-care garden and a scraggly, high-maintenance one. Mulch can be permanent or organic. Permanent mulches include landscape fabric, gravel, and stones. These are suitable only around permanent plantings, such as shrubs and trees. Organic mulches include grass clippings, shredded bark, wood chips, cocoa hulls, and pine needles. These break down over time and need to be replenished, but they nourish the soil as they decompose. They're ideal for vegetable and flower gardens where plants change each year. For a look at mulch options, see page 288.

Winter and summer mulching

During winter, mulch is used to protect perennials and permanent plantings from temperature extremes and heaving after the ground is frozen.

To mulch garden beds for the winter, wait until the ground has frozen, and then scatter a loose, airy mulch, such as chopped autumn leaves, straw, pine boughs or needles several inches thick. Don't use grass clippings or whole leaves—they can mat and suffocate plants. In spring, gently push or rake back mulch from perennial plants once they start to show signs of new growth.

During the growing season, mulch conserves moisture and suppresses weeds. To mulch during the growing season, wait until the soil has warmed, usually a couple of weeks after the last frost. In vegetable gardens and with annuals, wait until the plants are a few inches high, so they will not be covered

PLANT DISEASES AND PESTS

Blackspot. Small black spots followed by yellowing and leaves dropping off. Spray with a fungicidal soap or a fungicide containing mancozeb, or chlorothalonil.

Blight. Sudden withering and dying of leaves or stems. Trim and destroy the diseased plant portions; pull and destroy affected annuals; spray other plants with copper hydroxide.

Powdery mildew. Fine, gray residue on leaves. Spray 1 tbsp. baking soda, 1 gallon water, and ¼ tsp. insecticidal soap every two weeks; or spray with fungicide containing sulfur or triforine.

Rust. Crusty, orange spots; sometimes dark purple or dark brown, on leaves. Spray with sulfur, lime sulfur, mancozeb, chlorothalonil, or triforine during growing season.

Scab. Dark, scabby, cracked spots of various sizes, often enlarging. Remove diseased parts or fruits as is practical; spray with a fungicide containing mancozeb or chlorothalonil the following spring.

Aphids. Wilted, yellow flowers and leaves, sticky spots that can become infected with black sooty mold. Spray with a hard blast of water. In severe cases, spray horticultural oil, insecticidal soap, malathion, or rotenone.

Japanese beetle. Yellow patches of lawn where their grubs are feeding; large, chewed holes and skeletonized leaves. Release parasitic wasps or spray with Neem. For severe infestations, spray with carbaryl.

Mites. Can often see clusters in red, green, brown, or yellow. Spider mites make webs. Spray with hard blast of water every few days. For severe cases, spray with horticultural oil, insecticidal soap, or Neem.

Scale. Armored scales often have crusty, dull appearance. Soft scales have waxy covering. Prune infected plant parts; scrub off with toothbrush dipped in rubbing alcohol diluted with water; or spray with horticultural oil.

Slugs. Large, ragged holes in leaves, especially on low-growing plants. Spread sand, cinders, or diatomaceous earth around plants; put out a shallow pan buried to the rim and filled with beer for slugs to fall in and drown.

or shaded by the mulch. Spread the mulch 1 to 3 inches thick.

Landscape fabric

If you want to minimize weeding, consider using landscape fabric. This is a dark material that comes in rolls. Install it around trees, shrubs, and perennials.

Unlike landscape plastic, which is not porous, landscape fabric allows water and air to filter through.

To install landscape fabric, lay it on the ground, unroll as much as you need, and cut to fit around existing plants with scissors (p.289). Cut a hole in the fabric at each location where you want to place a plant. After planting, cover thoroughly with several inches of mulch, so none of the fabric shows through.

Landscape fabric is also good for use underneath non-permanent paths and patios, such as those made with wood chips or gravel.

MULCH OPTIONS

Mulches can be made of either organic materials, such as leaves or compost, or permanent materials, such as gravel. Organic mulches break down over time and must be replenished.

Grass clippings
Natural-looking and free, but break down quickly and can mat in weather. Don't use them from the first mowing after applying an herbicide.

Shredded bark or bark nuggets
Break down slowly and can be expensive. Use aged bark only; new bark robs nitrogen from the soil, so is unsuitable for use around annuals.

Wood chips
Break down slowly. Be sure to use aged chips only; new wood chips rob nitrogen from the soil.

Cocoa hulls
Break down slowly. Very attractive but can be expensive. They are lightweight, so they may blow away or erode.

Pine needles
Can last up to four years. During a drought, however, they can be a fire hazard. Tend to make soil more acidic.

Gravel
Dark-colored gravel absorbs sunlight and warms the ground; light-colored gravel reflects sunlight, making the ground cooler. Apply to a depth of 2 inches for weed control.

Straw
Inexpensive and good for winter mulch, but contains seeds that can turn into weeds. Not suitable for ornamental beds.

Compost
Excellent way to feed the soil. Inexpensive, if made at home or purchased by the truckload. Must be replenished two or more times during the growing season.

Autumn leaves
Free, but prone to blow away. Good for winter mulch if chopped. To collect chopped leaves quickly, mow over whole leaves with the gathering bag attached.

Sawdust
Inexpensive, but will deplete soil nitrogen if applied thickly (½ inch is enough). Buy carefully; some sawdust contains plastics.

landscape fabric

FERTILIZING

Fertilizer for plants can be liquid or powdered. Liquid fertilizer can be sprayed on leaves or poured onto the roots. Work powdered fertilizer into the soil or scatter it on top. Even easier to use are fertilizer stakes, which are inserted in the soil. Some fertilizers are formulated for particular plants, such as roses or lawn grass.

Most fertilizers contain three nutrients; numbers on their packages give the proportions of these nutrients. The first number is nitrogen, the second is phosphorous, and the third is potassium. A 15-30-15 fertilizer contains 15 percent nitrogen, 30 percent phosphorous, and 15 percent potassium.

An all-purpose fertilizer will probably serve your gardening needs. Use it according to the manufacturer's instructions. When in doubt, use too little rather than too much, since too much fertilizer can burn plant roots or contribute to unwanted plant growth.

Fertilizer is seldom needed for trees or shrubs (except roses). Use sparingly with perennials. Most annual flowers and vegetables benefit from regular, light fertilization. Plants in containers need more feeding because nutrients wash out during watering. If you work plenty of organic material, such as compost, well-rotted manure, and chopped leaves into the soil, you won't need to buy fertilizer.

COMPOSTING

Gardeners refer to compost as "black gold." This naturally created fertilizer releases the right amount of nutrients and improves drainage. It also attracts earthworms, which improve the soil by aerating it and leaving their own nutrient-rich castings. Because you make compost yourself, it is economical, too. And it will save you hours of bagging lawn waste that would otherwise go to the landfill.

Making compost

Starting a compost heap can be as simple as piling lawn waste, such as leaves and grass clippings, behind a garage in a bin made of stacked concrete blocks, or mesh wire tacked to wooden poles.

A more elaborate and more efficient system uses three bins. One bin has compost ready to use. The second has compost that is decomposing, while the third is being built up with current garden waste (see page 290).

Make sure you choose a level, well-drained location in a shady or semi-shady spot. It also helps to have it near a water source, because you need to sprinkle a compost pile with water to prevent it from drying out and to aid the decomposition process.

Put just about anything from your yard and kitchen into a compost heap, including eggshells, coffee grounds,

SAFETY SMART

GARDEN CHEMICAL DISPOSAL

Don't dump leftover garden chemicals in the garbage or down the sink. They can contaminate water supplies and otherwise harm the environment.

◆ **Use it all up.** Mix small amounts of chemicals, and use them completely so there are no leftovers. Share with friends or neighbors.

◆ **Disposal methods** for containers vary according to the product. Always read the label carefully and follow the disposal recommendations, if given. Don't rinse out the container unless the manufacturer specifies that you should.

◆ **When in doubt,** check with the experts. Your local government can tell you how to dispose of lawn and garden chemicals. Some cities have hazardous-waste disposal days. Others have designated sites for dropping off problem refuse.

◆ **Never reuse containers** that have been used to store chemicals.

vegetable peel, small twigs, and spoiled produce. Don't put in weeds, meat scraps or bones, bacon fat, cat litter, or dog feces; these attract other animals and can spread disease. Shredded or chopped materials decompose faster than bulky ones.

"Cold" composting is simply piling whatever materials you have onto the heap and letting them break down. It takes about a year before the resulting compost is usable.

Good Solutions

ORGANIC GARDENING

The definition of "organic gardening" is unclear. Some organic gardeners, for example, use liquid copper sulfate as a spray against fungal diseases. However, copper sulfate can be harmful to people and to fish. Here are some basic tenets of organic gardening that most people can agree on:

◆ **Stop using lawn chemicals.** Instead, take good care of your lawn so that healthy grass combats weeds and disease.

◆ **Feed the soil.** Great soil is the basis of a great garden. Improve the soil by using lots of compost or fish emulsion and by creating good drainage.

◆ **Keep up with your landscape chores.** Well-watered, weeded, and otherwise carefully tended plants seldom need the help of chemicals.

◆ **Attract wildlife.** Put up bird feeders, birdbaths, and birdhouses. Plant flowers and shrubs that attract butterflies and bees. You'll create a complex micro-environment in your garden with its own set of checks and balances, preventing pests and diseases from getting the upper hand.

◆ **Tolerate imperfection.** When you have to deal with a pest or disease, unless it threatens to spread, take it in stride. If the affected plant isn't likely to recover, tear it out and start over.

"Hot" composting works faster. Layer carbon-rich materials (dried leaves and plant parts, straw, sawdust, newspaper) with nitrogen-rich materials (grass clippings, manure, green leaves and plant parts, hay). Every few days, turn and water the pile to keep it moist. This creates compost in a few weeks, and the heat (caused by rapid microbial action) kills most weed seeds and disease pathogens, which cold composting may not.

Hot compost makes an excellent mulch. It's also good for mixing with vermiculite and sphagnum peat moss for an inexpensive potting soil.

Using compost

Properly made compost should smell like good soil. Even during the composting process you will only get any smell if you add to too much green material on its own, without adding brown compost or soil.

You can judge when your compost is ready by its look and feel. In a cold compost pile, the compost develops from the bottom of the pile upward.

Depending on the length of time it has been left, the top part may not be completely decomposed. If not, fork it off and add it to the current pile. Hot compost, because it has been turned several times, will be the same throughout although tough material, like orange rinds and small sticks, may not have broken down. Pick these out as you use the compost and add them to the composting bin.

Use either compost as a fertilizer and soil amendment by tossing a few spadefuls or trowelfuls into the bottom of a planting hole. In a new garden bed, spread them an inch thick and work it in as deeply as possible. You can also put a handful or two of compost into the bottom of indoor and outdoor container plantings.

If your soil tends to be clayey or sandy, when you turn over the soil in the spring, work in compost to a depth of 12 inches or so to create a more workable soil.

new waste

partially decomposed material

compost ready for spreading

GROWING FLOWERING PLANTS AND VEGETABLES

*Few things give more pleasure than the beauty of a flower bed
or the flavor of home-grown, sun-ripened vegetables.*

Start small with a flower garden or vegetable garden—just a few annuals in containers or a small plot for edibles. Soon you may want to expand your garden.

FLOWER POWER

Knowing a few basic methods can take the mystery out of flower gardening.

◆ **Prepare the flower bed carefully.** Time and money spent preparing the bed is well worth it. Whether your soil is sandy and drains too quickly, is clayey and drains poorly, or drains well, enrich it with compost (page 289). This improves drainage on clay soils and helps to retain moisture on quick-draining ones. To prepare a flower bed, turn the soil over to a full spade depth and add 2 to 4 inches of compost.

◆ **Start modestly.** At first, plant only those flowers whose growth and bloom habits you know well. Then add something new each year. When in doubt, plant annuals and add a few perennials each season.

◆ **Select and arrange plants** according to their flowering periods so you'll have blooms all season long. Keep a chronological list that tracks when the flowers in your area bloom. Follow plant labels exactly. Give plants correct light, soil, and water.

◆ **Keep it small.** Don't plant more than you can weed, water, and care for in your spare time each week. Even the best-designed flower bed looks wretched when neglected.

◆ **Add mulch.** Protect roots, suppress weeds, and retain moisture by covering the bed with 2 to 3 inches of an attractive mulch, such as wood chips. (See pages 286–288 on mulch.)

◆ **Deadhead daily.** Cut or pinch spent flowers every day. This keeps your flower garden looking neat and encourages more flowers to form.

Use flowers to solve problems

Flowers are a beautiful and inexpensive way to turn what could be problem areas into delightful points of interest.

PLANTING A FLOWER BED

1. Remove weeds and unwanted sod, including the roots, and dispose of them. Spread 2 to 4 inches of compost or well-rotted manure on first-time beds, and 1 inch on older beds. Use a spading fork to turn over and aerate the soil (above), and turn under the compost or manure. Then level the soil with a rake.

2. Try to plant on a cool or overcast day to prevent wilting. Arrange potted plants on the bed until you like the arrangement. Space plants per label recommendations or—for a more lush look—about 25 percent closer. Place perennials at least 3 feet from shrubs; annuals can be planted closer if you don't disturb established roots. To promote root development, pinch off any blooms.

3. Dig a hole so that the plant will sit in the soil at the same depth as in its pot. Make the hole several inches wider than the pot. Gently lift the plant out of the pot. Grasp the bottom of the soil-and-root ball, and tease the roots apart to encourage them to spread outward. Set the plant in the hole, fill in with soil, and firm around the plant with your fingers.

◆ **Use shade-loving flowers,** such as impatiens or begonias, wherever sun-hungry grass refuses to grow.

◆ **Use a fast-growing flowering vine** to disguise landscape eyesores, such as a garbage area or an unsightly garage. Create supports on smooth surfaces with garden nets attached to nails or screws. Popular flowering vines include clematis, with its gorgeous red, pink, or purple flowers, and hardy climbing honeysuckles (*Lonicera*) with large trumpet-shaped flowers that attract hummingbirds.

Annuals

Annuals—those flowers that live for one growing season and then die—

are terrific for beginning gardeners: They are easy to grow and bloom for months. Keep them deadheaded or they'll set seed and weaken. Use both warm- and cool-season annuals to keep your garden beautiful for most of the growing season.

snapdragons
California poppies
pansies

◆ **Reliable cool-season annuals.** Cool-season annuals (left) prefer cool, moist conditions. They bloom during mid- to late spring in cooler and northern climates, and will often give a second display in cool fall weather. Easy-to-grow cool-season annuals include: bachelor's-buttons (*Centaurea cyanus*); California poppy (*Eschscholzia californica*); calendula (*Calendula officinalis*); lobelia (*Lobelia erinus*); pansies (*Viola*); snapdragons (*Antirrhynum majus*); and sweet peas (*Lathyrus odoratus*).

◆ **Reliable warm-season annuals.** Warm-season annuals (p.293, top left) bloom later in the season, during the summer and into the fall. Warm-season annuals include: celosia (*Celosia*

marigolds
impatiens
petunias

cristata); geraniums (*Pelargonium*); impatiens (*Impatiens wallerana*); marigolds (*Tagetes*); petunias; salvia (*Salvia splendens* and *S. farinacea*); and zinnia (*Zinnia elegans*).

Perennials

Unlike annuals, perennials don't need to be replanted each year. However, the number of years that a perennial plant will live varies: Delphiniums last only a year or two; others, such as asters and coreopsis, last longer if they are dug up and divided every few years. Still other perennials, such as the peony, may outlast one's lifetime.

The bloom time of many perennials is often limited to a few weeks or less. (A few, such as coreopsis and some dianthus, bloom for months.) So a successful perennial bed must have a mix of flowers that bloom at different times.

Some perennials have leaves that are lovely in their own right. But the foliage of others, such as delphiniums and bearded irises, becomes unattractive after blooming. Consider planting warm-season annuals next to or among these plants. They'll grow tall and draw attention away from the ugly foliage.

Choose perennials that have proved reliable in your area. Some popular temperate-climate choices include: bee-balm (*Monarda didyma*); bellflower (*Campanula*); black-eyed Susan (*Rudbekia*); blanketflower (*Gaillardia*); coreopsis; daylily (*Hemerocallis*); dianthus; garden phlox; hardy asters and chrysanthemums; hostas; peonies; obedience (*Physostegia*); sedum; Shasta daisy (*Leucanthemum × superbum*); veronica; and yarrow (*Achillea*).

Bulbs for all seasons

Bulbs, tubers, and corms can provide color in your garden almost all year round (right). Snow-drops, aconites, and tiny irises appear in late winter, followed in early spring by cheerful daffodils and narcissi, crocus, hyacinths, and tulips in almost every color. In late spring, fritillaries, bluebells, lily-of-the-

irises
daffodils
hyacinths

valley, irises, and alliums come. Summer brings lilies, crocosmias, and gladiolus. In fall, come dahlias and nerines. Plant spring-bloomers in early fall, and summer-bloomers in spring. (See "Spring-Blooming Bulbs" chart on page 294).

◆ **Purchase bulbs** from a reputable dealer; bargain plants may fail to sprout

---

PLANTING BULBS

1. Loosen the soil with a spade. Use a gardening trowel, or a tool made for digging bulb holes. Set out the bulbs over the area before starting to plant. Space them apart about four times the diameter of the bulb, to give them room to multiply.

2. Add bulb fertilizer, such as bone meal, that contains phosphorus to the bottom of the hole. Plant bulbs, pointed side up, at the depth specified. Make sure that the bottom of the bulb is in firm contact with the soil. Fill the hole back in, and tamp it down lightly. Water thoroughly.

SPRING-BLOOMING BULBS

Bulb		Height	Bloom Time	Characteristics
Tulips (*Tulipa*)		3–30 inches	early to late spring	Wide variety of colors. Traditional tulips tend to die out in 2–3 years, but species and Darwin hybrids tend to last longer. Plant early-, mid-, and late-season varieties for longest season of bloom. Need full sun.
Hyacinths (*Hyacinthus*)		5–10 inches	early spring	Pink, white, blue, and even yellow hyacinths have outstanding fragrance, so plant them near a sitting area or sidewalk. They tend to die out after 2–3 years. Need excellent drainage and full sun to very light shade.
Crocuses (*Crocus*)		3–6 inches	very early spring	Purple, white, yellow, and striped. Among the first bulbs to bloom. Plant in groups of at least 10. Usually multiply. Like good drainage and full sun to very light shade. Snow crocus blooms earlier than giant crocus. Good for planting in lawns.
Snowdrops (*Galanthus*)		3–4 inches	very early spring	White. One of the first bulbs to bloom. Plant in groups of at least 10. Usually multiply. Like good drainage and full sun to very light shade. Good under trees. When overcrowded, lift and divide after flowering while the leaves are still green.
Squill (*Scilla*)		4–6 inches	very early spring	Delicate flowers in blue or white. Plant in groups of at least 10. Usually multiply and self-seed. Likes full sun to light shade. Grows well under deciduous shrubs and naturalizes well in grass.

or bloom. Good-quality bulbs are free of soft spots and other blemishes. Most undersized bulbs will not bloom well.

◆ **Plant small bulbs,** such as spring squill (*Scilla*) and grape hyacinths (*Muscari*), 3 inches deep. Mid-sized bulbs like lilies and gladioli go 6 inches down, while tulips and narcissus should be at least 8 to 10 inches deep.

◆ **Plant bulbs as soon as possible** after buying them so they will not dry out. Plant bulbs in groups for the best effect; never plant them in rows. Bulbs also need good drainage, so plant them on a slope, in sandy soil, or in well-drained raised beds (see page 269).

◆ **Do not cut down the foliage** after spring bulbs have finished blooming. Allow it to "ripen," since the browning foliage replenishes the bulb for the next year. Once the foliage pulls off with little resistance, you can remove it.

◆ **Dig up most summer-blooming bulbs** (except hardy lilies) after frost in all but the warmest areas of the country. First cut back the foliage to an inch or two. Then brush soil off the bulbs and roots, but don't wash them. Store the bulbs in a very cool (45° to 50°F), dry location in a paper bag or cardboard box full of vermiculite or slightly moist sphagnum peat moss. In the spring, replant them.

Roses

To thrive, a rose must like your climate. So you must choose a variety compatible with the climate of your area. You need to know how cold-hardy the rose is and how much summer heat it can withstand. Also consider whether your climate is arid or humid. Consult the Plant Hardiness Zone Map (p.267) and a reputable nursery in your area for guidance on choosing suitable roses.

◆ **When choosing a rose,** begin with modern shrub roses, which combine the winter hardiness of northern species with the lush, ever-blooming habits of southern species. Many have built-in resistance to the commonest disease. Ask your local nursery for roses in the Explorer and Parkland series.

◆ **Choose hybrid tea roses** only if a classic rose shape and excellent cut flowers are important. Hybrid teas, as a rule of thumb, tend to be more prone to disease and less cold-hardy. They also are leggier looking.

◆ **Check the bloom habits of the rose** you have in mind. Nearly all roses have a flush of bloom in early summer. Some then stop while others bloom again, some just once and others so often they seem constantly in flower.

◆ **For the best display of blooms,** fertilize roses at least every few weeks. There are special fertilizers for roses, but a general-purpose fertilizer will do. Using too much can result in lots of leafy growth but not many flowers.

◆ **Once a rose has bloomed** and the flower is fading, clip it off just above the first five-leaflet leaf. This deadheading will encourage more blooms.

◆ **Roses need at least six hours of sun** a day, and they like rich, well-drained soil that has been worked to a depth of at least 18 inches. They require 1 inch of water per week with as little as possible splashed on their leaves. A 1- to 3-inch layer of mulch around them conserves moisture and prevents soil-borne disease.

◆ **Stop fertilizing** two to three months before the first frost. Fertilizing after that point only encourages tender new growth that may be winter-damaged.

◆ **Make all cuts at a 45-degree angle,** slanting downward toward the center of the bush, and about ¼ inch above an outward-facing leaf bud. This encourages new growth outward.

◆ **How far you cut back rose canes** depends on the rose. Many climbing roses bloom only on old wood—the canes that grew last season and earlier. Cutting them back too far would prevent blooming. If a rose blooms on new wood, cut it back by about one-third.

◆ **Protect most roses with a 4-inch layer of mulch** where winters are mild. In colder areas, most roses need to be mounded: Mound soil over the base of the plant in late fall. Try to cover the bottom 10 to 12 inches of the stems. If possible, bring soil from elsewhere in the garden to avoid damaging rose roots close to the surface. In spring, once the soil has thawed, gradually remove the mound over a period of 3 to 4 weeks. This allows the tender, protected stems to acclimatize gradually. When buds start to grow, prune off any winter-kill.

Pruning flowering shrubs

The best time to prune most flowering shrubs, such as lilacs and rhododen-

FLOWERING SHRUBS

An easy option for busy flower lovers is planting flowering shrubs. Once they are established, most flowering shrubs need almost no care.

◆ **Flowering shrubs** bloom for just a few weeks, so choose shrubs with attractive foliage, and plant a variety of shrubs so you will have a succession of color.

◆ **Popular choices** include butterfly bush (*Buddleia davidii*); cotoneaster; dogwood (*Cornus*); flowering quince (*Chaenomeles*); forsythia; hydrangea; lilac (*Syringa*); magnolia; mock orange (*Philadelphus*); Nanking cherry (*Prunus*); potentilla; pussy willow (*Salix*); rhododendron and azalea; hibiscus; spirea; and sweet pepperbush (*Clethra alnifolia*).

drons, is right after the season of bloom. An earlier trimming removes buds that provide that year's show, while a late pruning may interfere with the production of buds necessary for the next year's blossoms.

VEGETABLE GARDENING

A successful vegetable garden that will supply your table with delicious produce should be located in a spot that gets at least six hours of full sun each day—the more sun, the better. Make sure the soil is well drained—water shouldn't pool after an average rainfall. A wire fence may be needed to keep out rabbits, deer, and other wildlife.

HARDY DECORATIVE PLANTS

Coreopsis. Semi-ever-green perennial. Yellow flowers bloom all summer if deadheaded regularly. May be low-growing, 6 inches tall, or bushy, up to 3 feet tall. Suitable for urban gardens, as it withstands pollution.

Daffodils (*Narcissus*). Bulb. 'King Alfred' is a favorite. Plant in sunny, well-drained soil. May have long, trumpet-shaped cups, or small flat cups. Aim for a nat-ural look, planting in irregular groups.

Daylilies (*Hemerocallis*). Evergreen or deciduous perennial. Dormant-foliage types do best in cool regions. Daylily flowers in shades of gold, yellow, pink, or red; may be striped.

Bearded iris (*Iris × ger-manica*). Rhizomatous (grows from underground stems). When planted in a sunny, well-drained spot, they last for many years and multiply rapidly.

Hosta. Herbaceous perennial. Likes cool, moist conditions and partial shade. Forms mounds or clumps of striking foliage that may be veined or striped. Small bell- or funnel-shaped flowers in sum-mer to fall.

Obedient plant (*Physo-stegia*). Herbaceous perennial. Spreads rap-idly in full sun to light shade. Spiky pink, white, or lavender flowers appear in late summer. So named because flowers stay put when pushed to one side or the other.

Ox-eye daisies (*Leucanthemum × super-bum*). Herbaceous peren-nial. These white daisies like full sun. After the first year, expect to find seedlings in your garden. They are easy to pull or hoe, however.

Peonies (*Paeonia*). Herbaceous perennial. Spectacular blooms appear in late spring to midsummer. They like full sun with adequate water. Tree peonies have woody stems and are more delicate than herbaceous peonies.

Rugosa roses (*Rosa rugosa*). Deciduous shrub. These roses are bothered by few pests or diseases, except in the warmest areas. They thrive in full sun without pruning or spraying. They bloom best with three or four feedings each season.

Yarrow (*Achillea*). Herbaceous or evergreen perennial. The more refined cousin of a com-mon weed, yarrow likes warm, dry conditions. Its flowers are excellent for cut arrangements and for drying. Yarrow reseeds and spreads.

As you select the plants for the garden, ask yourself the following questions:

◆ **Do I have the space?** Pumpkins are fun and sweet corn is delicious, but both take lots of room. Draw your garden planting plan on paper to make sure you don't crowd your plants.

◆ **Is the quality better?** Home-grown tomatoes outstrip anything in stores but other produce can be difficult to match in quality. Melons, for example, are dif-ficult to grow well.

◆ **Is it expensive** to buy in the store? Red bell peppers, fancy mesclun greens, and many other vegetables are costly at the supermarket. You can grow them at home for much less.

◆ **How productive is it?** It takes a wide, 5-foot-tall plant to produce artichokes. If your space and time are limited, grow only those crops, such as tomatoes, green beans, and lettuce, that allow you to harvest a lot of produce from a small area. A good selection could be one row of mixed lettuces, one row of spinach, one cherry tomato plant, one beefsteak tomato plant, three to four paste-type tomato plants for making sauce to freeze, four green pepper plants, one hot pepper plant, one row of carrots, one cucumber plant, one zucchini plant, one butternut or acorn squash plant, four eggplant plants, four broccoli plants, four cauliflower plants and one row of bushy green beans.

◆ **How much work?** For instance, tall-growing green peas need a special structure to support them. Modern bush varieties crop freely but only grow about 2 feet tall.

Preparing a vegetable garden

Once you've chosen a site for your vegetable garden, prepare the soil. Strip off any sod and remove any weeds. To do so, you can work the soil by repeat tilling. To till, use a spade or a spading fork for a small area. Rent a rototiller for a larger plot, or if you find the digging tough. Killing the sod with a herbicide and then digging it in will improve soil texture.

To make sure you have killed any unwanted plants, solarize the soil: Place clear plastic sheeting over bare soil for three to four weeks. This will kill most pests and weed seeds in the top few inches of soil. After removing the plastic, you can plant your new garden.

If possible, avoid using herbicides in a vegetable garden. If you must use a herbicide, make sure it contains glysophate as its only active ingredient. Glysophate quickly degrades into naturally occurring ingredients: nitrogen, phosphorus, and carbon dioxide. If you use such a product, follow the instructions on the label.

Vegetable gardens require soil that is loose enough so seedling roots can thrust their way through, but dense enough to support the roots. All soil intended for growing vegetables will benefit from digging in 1 to 3 inches of compost spread on top. If the soil is claylike (forms a dense ball when squeezed), also spread and dig in an inch of sand. If it's sandy soil (won't hold together when squeezed), spread and dig in an inch of peat moss.

◆ **Dig or till amendments** into the soil when the soil is slightly moist. If it's too wet, it will form large clods; if it's too dry, it will be too difficult to work. (Give it a soaking with a sprinkler if needed.) Till the soil to the maximum depth possible, usually about a foot. You can rent a tiller or hire someone with a tiller to do this for you.

To do an especially good job of preparing the soil, spade down another 6 to 12 inches, and loosen the layer of soil beneath the tilling. This assures better drainage and better-formed root crops, such as carrots.

◆ **Vegetables grow best** in soil that has a pH of 6 or 7 (pH is measured on a scale from 1 [very acid] to 14 [very alkaline]). If your soil is too acid, you can treat it with a dressing of finely ground limestone; treat very alkaline soil with peat moss.

To find out the pH—and the nutrient content of your soil—you can buy a kit that gives a reasonably accurate reading.

VEGETABLE GARDENING BASICS

As you plant, give your seedlings and sets (onions and potato eyes) enough space. Putting them too close makes them compete for water and nutrients and fosters fungal diseases. It also makes it harder to weed and harvest. Here are some tips for growing vegetables successfully:

◆ **Follow growing directions** on labels and seed packages exactly. Place plants with similar needs together, so it will be easy to remember which plants need more water or fertilizer, for instance. Thin seedlings after germination to half the spacing given on the packet. Later, take out and use every other plant.

◆ **Mulch.** Once your seedlings are established, spread organic mulch all around your garden, to retain soil moisture and to minimize weeds. (See pages 286–288 for mulch options and how to apply them.)

◆ **Keep it watered.** Vegetable gardens tend to be thirsty. As a rule, they need 1 inch of water per week.

◆ **Keep it weeded.** It's fairly easy to keep your vegetable garden weed-free

GROW LIGHTS

If you don't have a bank of south-facing windows, don't despair. Indoor grow lights let you start seeds or nurture beautiful plants. An inexpensive method is a shop light fixture with two fluorescent lights (below left), one cool spectrum, one warm. More expensive but more powerful are high-intensity lights. Halide lights (below right) are good all-round lights, useful for growing everything from seedlings to mature vegetables. Sodium lights are good for growing mature flowering or fruiting plants.

in early summer, but be especially diligent in July, August, and September, when weeds tend to take over.

◆ **Don't overfertilize.** Especially in new gardens, don't fret about fertilization. Too much fertilizer gives poor yield and tasteless crops.

◆ **Choose suitable varieties.** Good seed catalogues list the number of days needed from planting or sowing to maturity. Select varieties suitable for the length of your growing season.

◆ **Create paths** in the garden with straw, other organic mulches, or planks so you'll have easy access to areas of plants and not compact the soil.

◆ **Keep it harvested.** If you let produce age on plants, it attracts insects

and disease, and signals the plant to slow or halt production. Pick up produce that falls to the ground to avoid unwanted "volunteers" next season.

Starting from Seed

You not only extend the vegetable growing season by giving seeds an early start, you can also feed your family for pennies when you start vegetables from seed.

◆ **Use the proper soil.** It's worth the money to buy prepared soil mixes formulated especially for seed starting.

◆ **Maintain the proper temperature** for germinating seeds. Follow seed package directions exactly. A "cool spot" means between 55° and 65°F; a "warm spot" means 70° to 75°F.

◆ **Give new seedlings** lots of light. Put them in a south-facing window, or in a window supplemented with plant lights. Plant lights (left) should hang 3 or 4 inches above the plants.

◆ **Water carefully.** It takes a bit of a knack, but seedlings must be kept just barely moist. If you water them too much, they'll "damp off"—that is, get a fungal disease at the base of the stem and die. Water them too little, and they'll dry up. Check your seedlings once or twice a day to see that the soil has not dried out to a depth of more than a quarter inch or so.

HERB GARDENING

There are hundreds of herbs to choose from, but most people like to start with culinary herbs to use in cooking: basil, chives, cilantro, thyme, rosemary, parsley, sage, tarragon, mint, and oregano. Of these, tarragon, parsley, and mint are hardy in warmer zones. Here are some tips for growing herbs successfully.

◆ **Locate a small garden in a convenient location,** such as near the kitchen door. You can either scatter herbs in a nearby flower bed or pot them up in containers. Note that the various types

of mint will take over a garden or flower bed and therefore are best grown in containers.

◆ **Most herbs need full sun,** but they demand different types of soil. Basil, mint, cilantro, chives and parsley, for example, like rich, dark, moist soil, while lavender, tarragon, thyme, rosemary, sage, and oregano do better in thin soil with good drainage.

◆ **Pick herbs just before they're used,** preferably in the morning right after the dew has dried. Pluck off the leaves, and chop finely. Add fresh herbs to a soup, stew, or other cooked dish just a few minutes before serving.

CONTAINER GARDENING

Container gardening allows you to grow a variety of plants in a limited space. If the containers are movable, you can rotate them to show off your most attractive blooms. Clay pots, whiskey barrel halves, planter boxes, and window boxes are all attractive options. With plastic pots inside, you can use wicker baskets, bowls, wooden crates, or cans with interesting labels.

◆ **Containers need drainage holes** to ensure that plants do not sit in standing water. Drill holes in plastic using a regular drill bit. For ceramic pots, use a masonry bit; as you drill, hold the bit very steady to avoid cracking the pot.

◆ **Fill containers with potting soil.** It is lighter and richer than the soil from your garden—and it's weed-free.

◆ **Work a slow-release fertilizer** into the soil to make your container plants

very easy to care for. Or lightly fertilize container plantings every two to three weeks during planting season, because watering flushes nutrients from the soil.

Designing container gardens

Annuals, perennials, small shrubs, vines, vegetables, herbs, and small trees can be grown in containers as long as there's enough space and light, the soil is prepared properly, and the plants are fed and watered regularly.

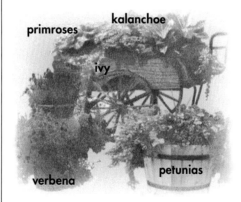

Beginners will have the best luck with annuals. These grow quickly and bloom for a long time. Look for plants labeled as ideal for containers or called "patio" varieties.

When mixing plants in a container, use contrasting flowers and foliage (above). Combine tall spiky plants, such as salvia, with draping plants, such as ivy or lobelia; add filler plants, such as shorter marigolds or ageratum.

Watering containers

The soil in containers, especially porous containers such as terra-cotta, dries out quickly. In very hot weather, containers

in a sunny spot might need to be watered as often as twice a day.

If you have many pots clustered together, you can buy a drip-emitter system to slowly water all the pots at once. Once this system is set up, all you need to do is turn on the spigot each time. Using a manual-on, automatic-off valve will make watering even easier (see page 274).

If all or most of your containers are watered from one spigot, consider using an easy-to-carry, lightweight hose to make watering easier. If you're going away for a day or two in hot weather, set your container plants in pans or buckets with a few inches of water in the bottom. The water will wick up, keeping the soil moist.

CUT DOWN ON WATERING

◆ **Reduce the need for watering** any plant by planting it in a plastic pot, then placing the plastic pot in a larger decorative container. Fill in the gap between the pots with soil. This will help keep the soil in the the plastic pot cool and moist.

◆ **Cut your container garden watering** in half: Add low-cost polymers to your potting soil. These tiny particles, which look like coarse salt, swell with water when wet and release it when plants need it most. Work the polymers below the first 2 or 3 inches of soil, to prevent them from wicking moisture away from the roots.

IN TUNE WITH NATURE

Wildlife brings its own rewards to the yard and garden: visual interest all year long as well as natural, nearly maintenance-free pest control. However, there are some issues that you have to deal with.

While some homeowners strive to rid their landscapes of insect and animal pests, others try to entice visitors from the animal kingdom to their gardens.

HOW TO ATTRACT WILDLIFE

Many outdoor creatures that accent a beautiful landscape are also helpful participants in the community. Bees pollinate fruits and flowers, keeping gardens productive. Toads and frogs are fascinating to watch and eat pesky insects at a ferocious rate. Dragonflies, ladybugs, and spiders also eat great numbers of unwelcome insects, such as aphids and mites. Here are tips for encouraging wildlife to come to your garden.

◆ **Diversify.** The more diverse the plants in your garden, the more wildlife you are likely to attract. Set up a complex mini-ecosystem in your backyard by choosing a variety of plants.

◆ **Don't be too tidy.** Humans appreciate neat gardens, but animals thrive in messier places. Removing faded flowers keeps the garden attractive and flowers bearing longer, but birds enjoy flowers that have gone to seed. Brush piles are an ideal place for butterflies and other creatures to overwinter.

◆ **Provide cover.** Most animals need a protected area. Shade trees provide protective cover for animals while fruit-bearing trees and shrubs provide food. Even a vine-covered wall can provide a potential nesting site for tiny birds.

◆ **Garden organically.** Chemicals throw off nature's balance and can kill helpful as well as harmful creatures. Many organic practices attract wildlife. Adding compost or other organic matter to the soil, for example, attracts earthworms. They, in turn, contribute to the health of the bed. Their constant burrowing tills and aerates the soil. They ingest organic wastes and deposit humus-rich castings in it. Earthworms also attract robins and other birds.

◆ **Go native.** Most native plants help feed or host local wildlife. They provide food for adult birds and good nectar for local butterflies, as well as shelter for birds and other creatures.

Attracting birds

If you feed birds in a protected area, and offer fresh water and a safe place to nest, birds will linger in your yard all year round.

◆ **Don't feed bread crumbs.** They are low in fat and are actually harmful for birds in winter, when they should consume high-energy foods, such as suet, fruits, nuts, and oily seeds.

◆ **Start feeding in the fall.** Most overwintering birds establish their food supply in the fall. So keep the feeder filled, even while on vacation.

◆ **Experiment with birdseed,** such as hulled sunflower seeds, thistle, safflower seed, black oil sunflower seed, and white millet, to see what birds you attract. Keep a platform feeder (a wood tray on a post, below) well supplied.

platform feeder

◆ **Make water available.** A birdbath is a sure way to attract birds. Make yours more appealing by setting a few stones in the water so they protrude half an inch or so. In autumn, when the temperature drops, install a birdbath heater to keep the water from freezing and to provide a constant water source.

◆ **Put up birdhouses.** Buy a birdhouse specifically designed for the birds you want to attract (a store-bought birdhouse should include this information). Then place at the correct height: 6 to 15 feet for chickadees, for example, or 20 feet or more for woodpeckers. Clean out the birdhouse in late winter each year to attract more birds.

◆ **Add landscape plants** that attract birds. Birds like a variety of plants, but berry-producing species are especially appealing. So are seed-producing plants, such as sunflower and purple coneflower, as long as you permit the fading flowers to go to seed.

Attracting butterflies

Like animated flowers, butterflies add color and motion to your garden. Here's how to make them feel welcome.

◆ **Plant flowers** that have the type of nectar butterflies love, such as butterfly bush, verbena, sedum, zinnias, Mexican sunflower, and lantana.

◆ **Butterflies are sun lovers.** (They can't fly when temperatures dip below 50°F.) They like to warm themselves on large flat stones that get morning sun.

◆ **Don't use pesticides.** Chemicals that kill harmful insects will also kill the insects you want to attract.

◆ **Keep the site sheltered.** High winds damage the gossamer wings of butterflies. Tall shrubs provide a windbreak and shelter for other wildlife as well.

butterfly house

◆ **A butterfly house** (above) makes a lovely accent. Be sure to place them in sunny spots near flower beds and sheltering shrubs or bushes.

UNWELCOME WILDLIFE

Gardeners wage an ongoing battle with animals that eat their plants. Using poisons is dangerous; they pose a dire threat to children and to pets. What's more, they are only marginally effective. Using a trap to capture or kill an animal is illegal in many areas. To find out about your local laws, check with the local provincial wildlife agency. There are some safe ways to control these animals, however. Here's what you can safely do to fight them off:

◆ **Rabbits.** Protect certain areas, such as a vegetable garden, with chicken-wire fencing. Bend the bottom three inches of the wire outward and bury it in the soil to prevent burrowing.

◆ **Deer.** Place eight-foot deer fencing around the entire area. Or try spraying shrubs with a mixture of one teaspoon dishwashing detergent, one egg, and one quart of water. The smell, repulsive to deer, is imperceptible to humans.

◆ **Squirrels and raccoons.** Rounded baffles (above) on bird-feeding posts will deter squirrels. Secure garbage can lids to keep out raccoons (p.109).

◆ **Mice and rats.** Never use rodent poison in homes with small children. You might be able to reduce a mouse population by eliminating their food supply or at least their access to it. Put pet food and bird seed in metal or glass containers with tight-fitting lids. Keep garbage in containers with tight-fitting lids. Don't feed birds in summer when birds have many other food

sources and the seed can attract rodents. Keep outdoor areas clean and free of gar-bage. Keep grassy or weedy areas mowed to minimize potential nesting sites.

◆ **Birds.** Drape mesh over fruit trees and strawberry patches just as fruit begins to form. Or build a chicken-wire fence—complete with a mesh roof—to keep birds out of a vegetable garden.

◆ **Snakes.** These reptiles help to control rodents. In Canada, there are only a few poisonous types, such as the massassauga, the prairie and timber rattlesnakes. However, if snakes are bothersome, eliminate habitats, such as wood or rock piles.

◆ **Moles, chipmunks, gophers,** and other burrowing animals. Burrowing animals improve soil texture in your garden; if they are not damaging plants, it may be best to live with them.

Keeping outdoor animals outdoors

The best way to get wild animals out of the house is to make sure they never gain access in the first place. Mice, birds, bats, squirrels, snakes, raccoons, and many other critters (and insects) can be kept out of the house by carefully sealing all possible entries.

Seal off any cracks around the foundation. Check under the siding where it overlaps the foundation. Also check around basement windows for possible points of entry.

In the attic, check vents, especially gable vents, to see whether animals can get through. They squeeze through amazingly small spaces. In both the

basement and attic, in cool weather, look for any spots where you feel cool air moving. Many animals follow air currents to gain entry into the house.

Seal cracks with caulk. Larger areas can be sealed with expanding foam insulation (p.88). Cover vents and other openings on the inside with ¼-inch hardware cloth (a type of wire mesh) nailed or stapled to the open area. Steel wool stuffed in crevices often keeps animals out. Use removable rope caulk around any basement and attic windows that you need to be able to open in an emergency.

The most effective and humane time to seal out animals is late summer when they are hunting for winter quarters. They will then be able to find a more natural home outdoors. If the animal is nocturnal, such as a bat, seal off openings at night after it has left the house.

When outdoor animals get inside

Rabies is becoming more prevalent, even in populated areas. Never try to handle an animal that is behaving strangely. Nor should you handle an injured animal. In such cases, contact your local animal control office or humane society for help.

If an animal gets into your house, stay calm. Most often, it will slow down after a few minutes of desperate running or flapping. If you shut the room's interior doors and open its windows and exterior doors, the animal may find its own way out. In the case of a small bird, carefully catch it in a bath towel and release it outside. Wear heavy leather gloves to avoid injury.

OUTDOOR LIVING AREAS

Decks and patios extend your living space. In these settings, entertaining can be gracious, informal, and lively.

When you begin to plan an outdoor space, you may not be sure what form it should finally take. Consider your options. How much room do you have? How much room do you need?

Decks, most of which are made of pressure-treated wood, are weather-resistant and can be raised to accommodate an uneven landscape. A deck, however, generally doesn't last as long as the more durable patio, which can be made of solid concrete, concrete pavers, bricks, or flagstones. But if your landscape is uneven, you may have to pay for extensive regrading in order to lay the patio.

PLANNING A DECK

If you would like to add a deck to your landscape, plan it carefully:

◆ **Walk around your property to find the best location.** Consider how much sun and shade you want to have on the deck and how private the spot will be. Wherever the location, it should be easy to access from the house, especially from the kitchen, if you plan to eat meals there.

◆ **Draw a detailed sketch.** Your drawing need not be artistic, but it should include as many details as possible. Consider what special features, such as built-in seating, planters, or a barbecue, you would like to have. Note any problems to be dealt with, such as sloping terrain or a nearby tree.

◆ **Have the plans approved.** Be sure they follow the zoning regulations in your community and are approved by the building department, which may require you to get a permit before you start construction.

MAINTAINING A DECK

A wooden deck is constantly exposed to the elements. The harsh ultraviolet rays of the sun cause discoloration, and moisture can lead to mildew or decay. Wood-eating insects and fungus also cause decay. Thus, it is important to treat all exterior wood surfaces—a deck, siding, a picnic table, or a fence—with a protective sealer.

Clear the deck

A well-swept deck will last longer. Piles of leaves or debris retain moisture

and speed the onset of rot. Watch especially for debris that is lodged between deck boards, at the point where the deck meets the house, or in other tight places. Use a putty knife or old screwdriver to clear it away. For the best results, call in a deck-maintenance professional (check the Yellow Pages or ask a knowledgeable neighbor), who will use a pressure washer to clean the deck and, if you wish, will also make repairs to the wood and seal it.

Inspecting for and treating rot

Give your deck a complete inspection every year. First check for rot. Use an old screwdriver to poke around for signs of decaying wood (above right). Wherever rainwater is likely to collect or you suspect rot, jab the wood with the screwdriver. If it feels soft, rot has begun. Pay special attention to stairways, places where decking meets a post, where the deck abuts the house, and the bottoms of posts.

Repair any rotted area right away, because it will only get worse. To make sure the rot will not return, determine why the spot attracts and retains moisture, and take steps to make sure it can dry out quickly. For instance, sweep away dirt or leaves in cracks. If the rot is far along, hire a carpenter to replace the boards.

Other deck problems

Cracks and splinters do not go away; they only grow more serious. You may be able to solve this problem by driving in another fastener or two. Remove and replace boards that are

rotted wood

dangerously cracked. If nails are popping up, driving them back is only a short-term solution. Instead, remove the nails and replace them with decking nails or screws.

If a cedar deck develops a few black stains, it may be a natural leaching of the wood. Clean them with a mild soap-and-water solution. If black stains persist in areas that are often moist, mildew is likely the culprit. Clean with a bleach solution, and take steps to ensure that the area can remain dry.

Sealing the deck

You need to reapply sealer every two to three years. Test how water-repellent the finish is by sprinkling water on it. If the water beads, the finish is intact. If it soaks in, it is time to add a new coat of sealer. Here are some options.

◆ **Plain, clear water repellents** effectively keep moisture from penetrating the wood. Water-repellent/preservatives contain a mildewcide or fungicide, in addition to a water repellent, for added protection.

◆ **Semi-transparent stains** contain a small amount of pigment, which adds a bit of color. These contain a UV (ultraviolet) blocker and will protect against the ultraviolet rays of the sun longer and better than clear sealers.

◆ **Solid-color stains and paints** are generally not recommended for decks. These finishes form a film on the surface and are easily worn away by foot traffic and must be reapplied often.

Keeping the color of a deck

Any wood will turn gray naturally as it weathers, even if it is regularly sealed with a water repellent. If you want to maintain the original color of the wood, use a semi-transparent stain or clear finish that contains UV blockers or UV-light absorbers. If your deck has already grayed and you would like to bring back the original color, look for a deck-renewing or deck-cleaning product at your hardware store, and use it as directed. Most products require you to spray or roll the solution onto the deck, then scrub with a stiff brush after the solution has been absorbed. Rinse thoroughly. Apply a finish as soon as the wood is dry.

Staining a pressure-treated deck

Pressure-treated wood makes it possible to build decks and other outdoor structures that are affordable and long-lasting. But most people are not fond of the greenish color. (If you are building a new deck, consider brown pressure-treated wood, which is already stained.)

To make a greenish pressure-treated deck resemble cedar or redwood, apply a semi-transparent stain made for use on pressure-treated wood. Check the color first on a piece of scrap wood. You may need two applications.

PLANNING A PATIO

The easiest patio to lay and maintain is one made with dry-laid bricks or pavers. Because these are laid in sand and are set without mortar, they go through freeze-and-thaw cycles without cracking. Flagstones laid directly into well-tamped soil or sand make an attractive, more natural-looking patio, for low-growing plants or moss eventually grow between the joints.

Planning a patio is similar to planning a deck (p.303). Some more tips:

◆ **How much space do you need?** Experts recommend a minimum of 25 square feet of patio per person and a minimum length of 16 feet. You need at least a 6 x 6-foot area out of any traffic path for a dining table and chairs.

◆ **How will you be using the patio?** Do you want space for a grill? Lounge chairs? Planters?

◆ **Use a garden hose to plan a curve** or an irregular shape. Lay the hose on the ground and adjust the shape.

MAINTAINING A PATIO

To prolong their life, seal paver bricks with water repellent. Flagstones set in a well-tamped foundation will endure beautifully; a rough site leads to cracks. To keep any unwanted weeds from growing between the pavers or bricks, line the site with landscape fabric (pp.287, 289) before paving; or pour boiling water on any new shoots.

Replacing a cracked brick or paver

If a cracked brick or paver is set in sand, use two putty knives to pry the damaged piece loose and remove it (below). Prepare the surface so that the new paver will rest evenly with the others. When buying a new brick, take the damaged one with you to find an exact match. Set the new piece in place to see if it is level. Then remove it and add or subtract sand to achieve the correct height (right); tamp it down well. Insert the brick, and sweep sand into the joint. Wet it with fine mist from a hose, then sweep in more sand.

If the brick is set in mortar, wear safety goggles and use a cold chisel and ball-peen hammer or mallet to break up the surrounding mortar. Remove any loose mortar from the cavity, then vacuum it clean.

putty knife

Buy a matching brick and a small bag of dry mortar mix. Mix the mortar with water and/or latex additive, following the manufacturer's instructions. Wet the new paver and the cavity. Spread mortar on all sides and the bottom of the cavity. Set the paver in place and smooth the joints. Wipe away

damp sand

excess mortar with a damp cloth. Let the area rest undisturbed for 24 hours.

OUTDOOR LIGHTING

Outdoor lights deter burglars, allow you to use decks and patios at night, illuminate foot paths, and highlight gardens and other features. Use fixtures appropriate for your needs. A pathway, for example, can be safely lighted with low-voltage lighting (p.306). For convenience, buy lights that can be set with a timer or photo-electric eye, so that they go on and off as needed. As a rule, use few fixtures and shine the lights toward the ground, away from people's eyes.

If you have a dimmer switch installed on your exterior spotlights or floodlights, you'll be able to produce diffused light at the touch of a dial, creating the ideal mood for a party in your patio. Be sure it is a heavy-duty dimmer, one designed for exterior use.

Adjusting a motion-detecting light

Mount a motion-detecting light no more than 12 feet above ground. Keep it away from reflective objects, other lights, or busy sidewalks, as any of these may make it behave erratically.

INSTALLING LOW-VOLTAGE OUTDOOR LIGHTS

Create a useful and attractive outdoor lighting scheme with an economical low-voltage system. Low-voltage lighting is safe, energy-efficient, and easy to install. A low-voltage kit includes a transformer (often with a built-in timer), lighting fixtures, and cable. If there is any chance that a cable will be damaged by a lawn mower, bury it 1 foot deep.

1. Mount the transformer near an electrical receptacle. An outdoor receptacle works best. Attach the cable to the transformer. Plug in the power cord on the transformer and adjust the timer.

2. Attach the cable to the contacts on the lighting fixture, then assemble the fixture. Follow the instructions in the kit carefully.

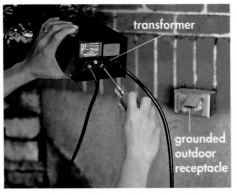

transformer

grounded outdoor receptacle

3. Dig a hole and insert the stake of the light fixture. Cover the cable with mulch, or bury it in a trench to prevent damage from garden tools.

Most models are adjustable (right). If the light comes on too often, or not often enough, adjust its range control. If the light stays on too long or not long enough, adjust the time setting. Often, pointing the sensor or the light in a slightly different direction will help.

OUTDOOR FURNITURE AND ACCESSORIES

Inexpensive plastic chairs and tables are a good choice for short-term use; but if you want to have patio furniture that lasts, you may want to invest in more durable pieces. Cast-iron or wrought-iron furniture will last for generations with minimal maintenance. Wicker requires more looking after, but

it makes up for this by giving a softer, more natural look to your porch, deck, or patio.

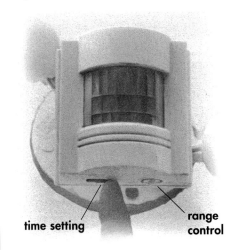

time setting   range control

Maintaining iron furniture

Rub new or newly painted wrought- or cast-iron furniture with a mixture of 1 part lanolin to 4 parts petroleum jelly, and let the coating air-dry. Inspect the furniture annually for flaking paint and rust spots; clean any spots with steel wool and naval jelly, available at hardware stores. Rinse with clear water. After the furniture is dry, retouch it with a rust-retardant primer, followed by two coats of exterior enamel.

All-weather fabrics

Cushions should be covered in all-weather fabric and stuffed with water-shedding polyester fiberfill: Acrylic

WORK SAVERS

LOOK FOR LOW-MAINTENANCE, ALL-WEATHER WICKER

If you like the look of wicker but are concerned about its exposure to the elements, consider all-weather wicker. This wicker is made either from natural wicker impregnated with a protective plastic sealant or from woven plastic that mimics the real thing. Unlike natural wicker, it can be used on open decks and patios and can be left outside year round.

fabric looks and feels very much like cotton, but it dries quickly and resists fading and mildew. To clean, scrub the surface with soapy water, rinse, and air-dry. Coated-fiber fabric has a more open weave than acrylic. Sponge its surface with soap and water.

Wicker maintenance

Like wood, natural wicker can be damaged by exposure to too much sun and moisture. To clean, use a soft toothbrush or stiff paintbrush to loosen dirt deep in the weave, then dust with a whisk broom or vacuum it with a brush attachment. Wipe the wicker every month or so with a cloth that has been dipped in clear water and wrung out well, and clean spills with mild soap and water. Never use abrasive cleaners or solvents, because they can harm the finish or damage the wicker itself.

If the weave of the wicker is becoming loose, give it a thorough soaking with the garden hose and let dry in the sun. As it dries, the wicker will shrink and tighten back into place.

Barbecues

Barbecuing can be done over charcoal briquettes on a grill, or on a gas-fired or electric grill. To start a charcoal fire, use an electric igniter or place wadded paper beneath the fuel in a metal starter can and light the paper. Avoid charcoal lighter fluid; never use gasoline or any other highly combustible liquid.

To clean the grill rack, scrape off burned-on food with a stiff wire brush made for the purpose. In the case of extensive food buildup, you can put ½ cup ammonia in a heavy-duty trash bag, insert the grill rack, and close tightly. Lay it flat and set out overnight. Rinse the grill thoroughly afterwards.

FENCES

If you would like a fence around your yard, design it to take advantage of standard lumber sizes. For example, two pickets for a 4-foot-tall fence can be made by cutting one 8-foot-long board in half. Pre-made fencing usually comes in 6- or 8-foot sections, so plan your fence's length in those multiples. And if you are shopping for fencing materials, consider polyvinyl. It looks almost like wood but doesn't fade, rot, crack, or peel. Installed with posts like wooden fencing, it costs a little more, but it may carry a lifetime guarantee.

Repairing a fence

Before you tackle any single repair, inspect the entire fence. If one post has a severe lean to it, give the others a firm shake to see if they are wobbly too. If one picket is rotten, probe others with an old screwdriver to see if they are spongy as well. If most of the framework seems solid, go ahead and perform the repairs. But if the framework is falling apart or if half the posts are rotten, consider building a new fence.

SWIMMING POOLS

If you are thinking about installing a swimming pool, you can find out from a reputable swimming-pool contractor and dealer about the required building permits you will need, property setback and fencing requirements. Also talk with your homeowner's insurance agent to see if you are covered for potential mishaps.

pool filters

POOL-CLEANING TOOLS

Keeping a pool clean not only makes it more attractive, it is essential to maintaining the pool. Invest in the right tools, and you will find that cleaning is more efficient and less of a bother.

◆ **A leaf skimmer** is a lightweight net that helps you remove large particles that enter your pool, such as leaves, bugs, and twigs. Use a succession of aluminum extension poles to reach as far as you need to.

◆ **A liner brush** wipes the walls of your pool. This will help prevent the buildup of algae and other slime. Different types are available for concrete and vinyl-lined pools. Use the same extension poles as for the skimmer.

◆ **A hand-operated vacuum** allows you to clean the bottom and sides of your pool. Choose one made for your type and size of pool—one that is too powerful will damage a vinyl lining.

◆ **An automatic pool cleaner** creeps around the pool, cleaning all the surfaces. It has its own debris bag. Because it makes pool vacuuming easier, it may be worth the cost. Buy a model that is designed for your type and size of pool.

Above-ground pools are a popular choice because they are relatively less expensive. They are sold in kits and can be easily disassembled if you move.

ROUTINE POOL MAINTENANCE

Trying to cut corners on pool maintenance will only cost you money in the long run. The owner's manual will help you prevent a multitude of problems.

You may decide that it's worth the cost to hire a professional pool service to maintain your pool. In addition to regular cleaning of the filter (see right and page 307), do the following regularly:

◆ **Test the water.** Use a reagent kit to test for pH, alkalinity, and chlorine level. Have a pool dealer analyze the water for calcium hardness once a year.

◆ **Adjust the chemistry.** After testing the water, add any chemicals necessary to stabilize it. Wait about 8 hours before retesting. At the beginning of the swimming season, check and adjust the water every day.

◆ **Trim or remove nearby bushes and trees** to reduce the amount of debris that falls into the pool. Remove the debris regularly with a leaf skimmer.

◆ **Shower before using the pool.** Sweat, skin oil, suntan lotion, and urine contaminate water and can clog a filter. Make it a house rule that all swimmers take showers first. Also encourage young children to use the toilet before going swimming.

◆ **Cover the swimming pool** when it is not in use. Pool covers are intended to keep debris out of the pool, retain heat, and slow down water evaporation. In summer, solar blankets are widely used. During the winter, you can install a cover of vinyl or woven polyethylene fiber. These covers cost a few hundred dollars. The loop-lock cover, made of polypropylene mesh, costs well over $1,000, but it is designed to provide greater safety.

Cleaning the filter

If the filter becomes clogged, it won't be able to keep dirt out of the swimming pool, and that can lead to a damaged pump. Check your filter pressure gauge several times a week; your owner's manual will tell you how much pressure the filter can stand before it needs to be replaced or cleaned.

Follow the pool manufacturer's directions for cleaning carefully.

Pool safety

You must guard against the tragedy of accidental drowning.

◆ **A fence around your pool** is probably your best defense against tragedy. Check with your building code department for requirements or recommendations regarding swimming pool fencing.

A well-designed fence will be high enough to keep kids from climbing over, and low enough to keep them from slipping under. The gate should have self-closing hinges to ensure that it isn't left open inadvertently. The fence should be built with material that allows good visibility into the pool so you can conveniently keep an eye on things. Chain link offers good security but is unattractive. A fence with closely spaced boards also does the job.

◆ **A pool cover** can prevent someone from falling into the water, but it should not be used as a substitute for a fence.

◆ **To reduce slipping** on the deck, use a nonskid material around the pool.

Winterizing an above-ground pool

Leave most of the water in the pool over winter. Ice expands upward, so frozen pool water exerts little pressure on the sides, and it helps to protect the pool from ground freezes, which can buckle the pool. However, any water seeping under the pool can cause disastrous frost heaves; so make permanent repairs to any liner leaks before you winterize the pool.

Clean all debris from the pool. Turn off the filter pump, scrub the sides with a liner brush, and vacuum the bottom with a pool vacuum. Lower the water level to slightly below the pool's built-in skimmer. Add winterizing chemicals as directed on the label of a winterizing kit, which you can buy at a pool store.

Remove the catch basket of the skimmer, and fill it with a Styrofoam® plug. Then remove the pump and its filter, and store them indoors. Drain the plumbing lines and blow them dry with an air compressor. Plug the pump inlet hole with a stopper, which is available at pool stores.

hot tub filters

HOT TUBS

A hot tub is heavy: the average tub holds 250 to 300 gallons of water and needs a sturdy foundation of crushed stone or concrete. To operate, a pump circulates water through a filter and then through a heater, which brings the water to about 100°F. (Sitting in very hot water for more than a few

minutes may adversely affect the young, the elderly, and people with medical conditions; if in doubt, consult a physician.)

Leaks in a wooden hot tub

Small leaks can occur if a gap opens between vertical wood staves. Dark spots near the gaps suggest a leak. Use a putty knife to pack the gaps with cotton string, which swells and reseals the seam. If water has started dripping through the tub, the problem is more severe. In this case, talk to the dealer immediately.

Cleaning a hot tub

Treat hot-tub water much as you would pool water, testing it and treating it with chemicals to maintain proper sanitation and the correct pH level. Keep leaves out of the water, and leave the cover on when not in use. Clean or replace filters every other week.

Whenever you detect slime on the sides or bottom, drain the tub and scrub the inside with a mild bleach solution. Then rinse the hot tub thoroughly before refilling.

Diagnosing a mechanical problem

If the pump won't work, make sure that the switch to the pump is on. See if the circuit breaker has tripped; if it has, and continues to do so after you reset it, call for service. If an electric heater is broken, check the circuit breaker; then try turning off the power and tightening any loose wires leading to the thermostat. If the water is heated by gas, make sure the gas shutoff valve is open and the pilot light is lit (p.76).

LIVING IN A RURAL AREA

Living in the country brings freedom—and some challenges: You need your own water supply, sewage treatment system, and refuse disposal. You also need to be able to handle a variety of tasks, both routine and emergency.

Living in the country means taking an active role in basic services. Knowing the fundamentals of these systems will make rural life more relaxing.

SEPTIC SYSTEMS

Homes that are not connected to a municipal sewage system have a septic system, a personal sewage treatment plant in the backyard. In a typical system, waste water runs into a septic tank, where microbes break it down into solid sludge and liquid effluent. The effluent flows out of the septic tank into a distribution box; from there, it is piped into a series of perforated or clay pipes that run through the drainage field. The sludge settles to the bottom of the tank and must be pumped out every two or three years.

Using a septic system

Bacteria is present in a tank from the first flush and will thrive thereafter except in very unusual circumstances. If you know what a septic can and cannot handle, you should have little trouble with your septic system.

◆ **Limit water use.** One simple measure that will help a septic system run smoothly is to reduce unnecessary flow into the tank and system. An overloaded septic tank will push solids out before they have a chance to break down completely. Eventually this will clog the septic field and hamper its capacity to diffuse effluent into the atmosphere. Be vigilant about drips and running water. A malfunctioning float valve in a toilet tank, for example, can leak one cup of water a minute, pouring an additional 90 gallons of water each day into the system.

◆ **Stagger baths and wash loads** to avoid overloading the system during any one period of the day.

◆ **Never use additives** that claim to eliminate tank cleaning. Such additives can actually be harmful, liquifying the sludge and clogging the drainage field.

◆ **Use only plain white toilet tissue.** Dyes are harmful to bacteria needed for decomposition. Many scented tissues have been treated in a way that inhibits deterioration; they are generally not good for a septic system. To test whether a brand is okay, place a few sheets in a jar filled about three-quarters full with water, screw the lid on tightly, and shake vigorously for about 15 seconds. If the paper is shredded, it will be fine for the septic system.

◆ **Don't put inorganic or bulky items,** such as feminine hygiene products or contraceptive devices down the toilet. They can clog the intake openings of the septic tank.

◆ **Keep garbage,** such as grease, fat, coffee grounds, paper towels, and facial tissues, out of the sink or toilet drains.

◆ **Avoid soil compaction.** Don't park on or drive over the the septic field. Keep heavy equipment away from it as well. The soil must stay loose so that the effluent can seep out freely.

◆ **Avoid drain cleaners and bleach.** These chemicals can kill the waste-eating microbes in the tank. Specifically avoid products containing lye.

◆ **Don't use** a garbage disposal.

◆ **Don't pour** paint thinner, pesticides, photography chemicals, motor oil, or other hazardous materials down sink or toilet drains.

◆ **Use liquid laundry detergent.** Liquid detergents are less likely to contain filler that is not good for the septic system. Some powdered detergents have an agent that is used to seal soils.

Locating the tank
If you don't know where your tank is, try poking around. Usually the tank will be close enough to the surface that a long metal rod jabbed into soft ground will sound as it strikes the concrete or metal of the tank. In winter, watch for a spot in your yard where snow melts quickly. A rectangular thawed patch will often reveal the tank's location.

Water-wise septic systems
In areas where water shortages are a concern, systems are available that recycle gray water, the water leftover from showers, baths, sinks, dishwashers, and sometimes laundry (as long as diapers or other items containing unhealthy substances aren't included). This recycled water is often fine for watering lawns and gardens.

Maintaining a septic tank
Given a modest amount of attention every few years, your septic system should run smoothly.

If you hear a gurgling sound when water drains from a tub or washer, or if it drains slowly when flushing a toilet, act immediately. These are warning signs that the intake pipe of the tanks may be blocked.

◆ **Check the sludge level.** Once a year, use a long pole to measure the sludge line. The level of semi-solid sludge in the bottom of the tank should be no more than half-way up from the bottom of the tank to the surface of the liquid that floats above it. Have the tank pumped if the build-up is near the half-way point.

◆ **Pump it away.** The only maintenance a well-installed septic tank needs is periodic pumping by a professional service.

As a general rule, a 1,000-gallon tank that serves four people in a home will need to be pumped every three years or so.

Don't delay pumping. You may save a little money in the short run, but you may ruin the system, which will be very expensive to repair.

WATER SUPPLY
Wells are the most common source of water in rural homes. Other sources include springs, streams, lakes, and stored seasonal runoff water.

Municipalities test water regularly, but in the country, individual homeowners are responsible for making sure their water is safe. In wells, the presence of nitrates, due to agricultural chemical run-off, is a growing concern in some regions. In addition, a parasite called *Giardia lamblia* often shows up in rural surface water sources. To make sure your water supply—whatever the source—is safe, have it tested regularly. Ask your local department of agriculture about water safety concerns in your area, as well as the best testing facilities to use. Once you have identified problems with your water, you can install appropriate water-treatment equipment.

Water is in short supply for some rural homeowners, especially in the West. Banks and lending institutions may require well or water system flow tests on wells before they will qualify a potential homeowner for financing. In most areas, five gallons per minute is the required minimum flow. Make sure your water supply is safe and adequate before you buy any property.

311

Water pumps and pressure tanks

Two types of water pumps are used: A submersible pump sits in the water source; a jet pump sucks water up from the surface. Both pumps send water into a pressure tank, which maintains an even water pressure for your home.

If a pump stops pumping, check for a blown fuse or circuit breaker (p.93) and check wiring connections. If the problem isn't solved, call for service.

If the pump is switching on and off too often, the pressure tank may have lost air pressure. Shut off power to the pump at the electrical service panel. Drain the pump by running the drain valve, then opening a faucet in the house. Close the faucet and the drain valve, and restore power to the pump. Call for repair service if that doesn't solve the problem.

Check the tank for leaks periodically by inspecting the outside of it. If a leak develops, it will appear as an oozy rusty blemish. Tank plugs are available, but plugging is only a temporary measure. Replace the tank as soon as possible.

Drilling a new well

Local codes will stipulate how deep your well should be drilled. It must be deep enough so that you will have water even during dry periods, and it must be far removed from any sources of groundwater pollution. Look for a driller who has a good reputation in your area. You will pay by the vertical foot, so the cost may be surprisingly high or surprisingly low, depending on how quickly the driller runs into drinkable water.

POWER SUPPLY AND SANITATION

After a storm in the country, homes may be a day or more without electricity. So, it is a good idea to have a generator, especially if your electrical lines are aboveground, where severe ice or wind can down them.

Few rural homeowners have natural gas piped to their houses. Instead, they rely on bottled gas stored in a large tank, which is refilled once or twice a year. If you are buying a home with a gas tank, have the gas company check to see that it is in working order. If you are building a home, you may have to buy a tank. However, many gas companies will rent you a tank for an annual fee.

Disposal of refuse

As with many other services that are conveniently provided in town, disposal of waste and garbage in the country may be the responsibility of the homeowner. Recycling and composting can reduce household waste by half. Some rural homeowners let their garbage collect for a few weeks at a time, keeping it covered in watertight containers. They then dump it in a landfill. In some areas, rural landowners are allowed to dispose of garbage in their own landfill or by burning. Check with your municipality for regulations governing your area.

Private landfills are convenient, but pose problems in the long run when people forget where garbage is buried. This adds a complicated twist to property sales. Such landfills should not be used for certain items, such as batteries, tires, petroleum products (including paints and oils), pharmaceutical supplies, asbestos, appliances, garden chemicals, and other hazardous wastes. These need to be taken to the local landfill where the operator can dispose of them properly. Otherwise, these materials will contaminate soil and leach into water supplies. More and more, rural communities are organizing hazardous waste pickups for items such as used tires and paints.

Burning waste

If burning is allowed in your area, it should be the disposal method of last resort. Burning pollutes the air with smoke and contaminants. It also creates ash, which contains concentrated contaminants. Newspaper and magazine ink, for example, often contains lead, which remains in the ash. Dispose of ash at the local landfill; never spread it on soil. Burn garbage in a large metal barrel (below). To keep any sparks from the fire from flying out, make a screen for

Bricks hold screen in place.

the top, using fine wire mesh. Use stones or firebricks to weight it down while burning, so it cannot blow away.

EMERGENCY SERVICES

Emergency services in the country are likely to be slow. Once help is called, it may take some time for the emergency crew to arrive. Some rural areas close to an urban area are served by private ambulance services that vary in speed and quality. However, it's not uncommon for an ambulance to take an hour or more to reach a rural home.

Because it can take so long, the St. John Ambulance advises rural residents to take an extensive first-aid course, designed especially for rural residents. It instructs people on what to do when emergency help is delayed.

Fire service also can be slow in rural areas. While some towns have fire departments that serve nearby rural areas, other communities rely on volunteer fire departments. Because of the slow response time for fires, homeowner's insurance for a rural home can be expensive.

TRANSPORTATION

In the country, stores, schools, and restaurants are miles away and there may be no local public transportation. Therefore, you need a reliable, well-maintained car or truck. Ideally, you should have two vehicles—just in case one breaks down. You want to consider buying a special vehicle suited to rougher terrain.

◆ **Pickup trucks** can do many jobs, from hauling an antique bed home

from an auction to stocking up on horse manure for the garden. Be aware of how heavy a load a truck you buy is designed to carry (half-ton or three-quarter-ton, for example), and never overload it. A sturdy truck is also good for navigating less-than-perfect country roads and off-road terrain.

◆ **Four-wheel-drive vehicles** are useful if you live on a dirt road, especially in wet weather. They are also helpful on roads that are not regularly plowed in winter.

SPECIAL EQUIPMENT

With so many chores to do around a country homestead, power equipment can save time and effort. This equipment isn't cheap, so if you expect to use it only occasionally, consider renting. When you operate these pieces of equipment, you should wear safety goggles and ear protectors. Always wear sturdy steel-toed work boots or shoes and avoid loose clothing that might catch in blades or other fast-moving parts.

◆ **Brush cutter.** Unlike a regular mower, this will travel over rough ground and cut through small saplings. Most feature a cutter bar with powerful, scissor-action teeth.

◆ **Logsplitter and chainsaw** are useful pieces of equipment if you plan on using a wood stove as a significant heat source or if you have a heavily wooded site that needs thinning.

◆ **Tiller.** A good investment if you'll be tending a very large vegetable garden or creating many flower beds. A variety

of sizes are available, ranging from "mini" tillers with just 2 horsepower capacity, to those with 11 horsepower or more. Since most gardens should be worked at least 12 inches deep, the deeper the tine tills, the better.

◆ **Lawn or mini tractor.** This can do more than just mow the lawn. Attach a cart to it and haul firewood and other loads. Or use it for plowing snow from your driveway or access road. In the spring, it can prepare a large garden. Tractors equipped with a power take-off feature make it possible to add useful attachment machines such as snow blowers and chipper/shredders. However, these tractors are expensive.

GOOD TOOLS

CHIPPER/SHREDDER

Underbrush and other unwanted foliage can grow very quickly; cutting it down with saws and loppers and carting it away can be a big job. A chipper/shredder will save you work and time. As a bonus, it reduces saplings and prunings into wood chips that are ideal for use as mulch around trees and shrubs and for creating rustic paths.

Attic

Roof

Basement

UPGRADING YOUR ATTIC

*Not just a storage space, the attic plays a key
role in the efficiency of your heating and cooling systems,
as well as the upkeep of your roof.*

Attic insulation is essential to the productive heating and cooling of your home. Air sealing, widely used for preventing warm, moist air from getting into cold attics, is also vitally important. Attic ventilation—the movement of fresh air through the attic to keep it dry and cool—is often overlooked by home-owners. Without ventilation, the attic isn't a safe place to store the furniture, papers, and other household items that so often end up there.

ATTIC INSULATION

In Canada, up to 15 percent of the heat in the average home escapes through the roof. During the winter, you need adequate insulation in your attic floor (p.88) to retain heat and, thereby, reduce your heating bills.

Installing attic insulation doesn't need special skills, but it's a messy job that involves crawling around in tight places and working with fiberglass, which takes some precautions (see box on page 318). You may want to hire a professional to insulate your attic.

Simple tests

If your heating bills are higher than those of neighbors with similar-sized homes, inadequate insulation and/or poor air sealing may be the culprits.

The next time there's a light snow, go outside the day afterwards and take a look at your roof and the other roofs on your street. If more snow has melted on your roof than on the other roofs with similar slopes, the chances are that more heat is escaping from your house into your attic to melt the snow—and you are paying for it with higher heat-ing bills. Any clear spot on your roof may indicate that, just below it, lies the site of a warm air leak, such as ceiling electrical box.

If you think you may need more insulation in your home, ask several companies to have a look and give you an estimate. Also, ask for details about their services, including air sealing.

AIR SEALING

Before adding insulation, check for any air leaking into the attic from the rest of the house. The purpose of air sealing is to stop warm, moist air on the lower floors from getting into the cold attic, where it may form ice. For example, air flowing through holes in a single electrical box fixture just below the attic may create as much as a 10-pound ice deposit on the rafters or the underside of the roof sheathing. (For tips about sealing air leaks, see page 318.)

Ice dams

A combination of air sealing, good insulation and good ventilation is important in preventing the formation of ice dams during the winter. An ice dam occurs when a roof's surface is warmed by attic heat so that snow melts, runs to the edge of the roof, and refreezes.

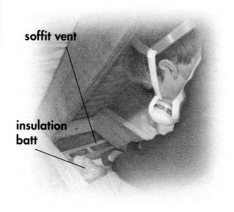

soffit vent

insulation batt

When more snow melts and trickles down, it is blocked by the dam of ice, and it flows up under shingles and often into the attic, causing permanent

damage to roofing and attic framing. To keep the snow from melting too quickly and forming ice dams, you need a cold attic, which you get with no warm-air leakage, adequate attic-floor insulation, and a flow of cold air going through the attic from the soffits to the roof vents.

Check the vents

Before you start an insulation job, check for vents in the soffit, gables, ridge, and other places in the roof (see box below). See that insulation sits 1 inch back from any vent openings (left). You may have to frame to install baffles to hold the batting back.

If you think your attic needs new ventilation, and you live in an area

VENTILATION DEVICES

In the heat of the summer, a well-ventilated attic in your home will allow the hot, humid air to escape upwards; during the winter months, good ventilation keeps the roof cold and, thereby, helps to minimize the formation of ice dams and icicles.

soffit vent

roof vent

gable vent

Soffit vents, spaced evenly along the soffit (under the eaves), permit the flow of outside air into the attic for proper ventilation.

Roof vents near the roof peak let warm, moist air flow out of the house. Air must move freely from soffit vents to roof vents.

Gable vents, like roof vents, allow the flow of air out of the attic. They are louvered and screened to keep out rain and bugs.

SAFETY SMART

PROTECT YOURSELF FROM INSULATION FIBERS

Because fiberglass is made of bits of spun glass, the fibers can irritate nasal passages and cause skin rashes. Always wear long-sleeved shirts and pants when working with fiberglass, and secure them at the cuffs and legs. Shield your eyes with protective goggles, and wear a face mask to prevent inhaling the tiny bits of glass. People with sensitive skin may develop a rash or have trouble breathing even after taking these precautions.

where snow accumulates heavily on the roof, consider installing roof vents that stand high on a collar that keeps them above the snow. Make sure all the gable vents are specially louvered to prevent penetration of blowing snow.

INSTALLING ATTIC INSULATION

Fiberglass roll-type or batt-type insulation is easy to install yourself. Roll it out and place it between the joists of the attic floor. You can rent equipment for blowing in loose-fill insulation, such as vermiculite.(It can also be poured

by hand.) But, for most homeowners, this job is best left to a professional.

Choosing insulation

For types of insulation and the thickness that are suitable for your attic, see pages 87–88. If you plan to make a floor in the attic, so that you can use the area for storage, make sure the insulation will not rise above the top of the joists. Joists are usually either 16 or 24 inches apart, so buy insulation of the correct width to fit snugly. If you wish to raise the attic floor, you can add a piece of 2 x 3 or 2 x 4 wood over the joists to increase the level of insulation.

Vapor retarders

A vapor retarder—polyethylene film, generally—keeps moisture from penetrating an insulated space. Place the retarder on the warm-in-winter side of the surface being insulated (the ceiling of the room below the attic floor, for example). Installing insulation between attic-floor joists of new houses presents problems. Increased use of roof trusses has reduced the space available for insulation. Placing a vapor retarder in the attic can be difficult once the ceiling is installed. In this case, you can create a vapor retarder by painting the ceiling below the attic with two coats of oil or a coat of a latex vapor barrier primer paint—and forget the plastic sheet.

Sealing air leaks

This will add to the effectiveness of insulation installation and is your best safeguard against moisture damage. Check under existing insulation and look at electrical boxes. Seal the electrical boxes with polyethylene. Replace

recessed light fixtures with airtight, fireproof fixtures. Seal around plumbing stacks, the attic hatch and the bathroom fan. Make sure the fan sends its steam outdoors, not into the attic.

Caution

If you step into the space between the joists on an attic floor, your foot may break through the ceiling of the room below, resulting in possible injury and a costly repair. Don't crawl around the attic with your knees on top of the joists. Set boards or pieces of plywood perpendicular to the joists to make a

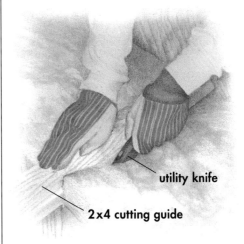

utility knife

2x4 cutting guide

working platform; move them around as you work. Make sure each board end is supported by a joist. Wear head protection to avoid bumping yourself on the roof joists or shingle nails.

Getting started

You will need a good flat work surface for cutting batts or rolls to length, a straight piece of 2 x 4 wood for a cutting guide, and a sharp utility knife.

For ceiling joists (that is, the floor of the attic), simply lay the insulation in place. Hang safety lights from the attic ceiling to see clearly while you work.

Laying the batts

Start at a corner where the floor meets the roof rafters, and roll toward the middle of the room. Don't cover any soffit vents (p.317). Take the time to cut your insulation precisely, since heat will be lost wherever there is a gap. Measure with a tape measure, and mark the insulation for cutting by giving it a quick, short slice with a utility knife. Position the insulation on a scrap of plywood a few inches longer than the batt is wide. Place a 2 x 4 across the insulation; press down to compress it; and slice through, using the edge of the 2 x 4 as a cutting guide (see left).

Don't forget the access hatch

A great deal of heat is lost through the access hatch into an attic. If there is an attic stairway, glue rigid insulation board to the back of the door and fill the area under the steps with loose-fill insulation. If there is a simple push-up access panel, glue rigid foam insulation to the back of it and add weather stripping and hooks to close it tightly.

An attic room

If you want to finish a part of the attic as a heated room, you will have to insulate the ceiling of that part of the attic instead of the floor. Wear a hard hat to protect yourself from protruding roofing nails. Work from the top down, and leave a 2-inch gap between the insula-tion and the roof sheathing. To get at least R-20 level insulation, add foam insulation boards horizontally directly over the fiberglass, and nail through to the rafters. Buy foam with wood or metal stropping built into the edges for attaching drywall.

MAKING AN ATTIC FLOOR

If your attic floor has exposed joists and visible insulation, you can't really use it for storage until you have made a safe floor. A box slipping between the joists, for example, could damage the ceiling of the room below.

Installing a rough floor in an attic is not difficult. First, measure your access hatch, and choose boards that will fit through it. One option that will fit most access openings is to have a home center cut sheets of ½-inch plywood into strips 8 feet long and 16 inches wide.

You may not need to cut the pieces to exact lengths, since a storage floor doesn't necessarily cover the entire attic. Board ends, however, need the support of a joist, which means that butted ends must share a joist. So if you will be laying two or more boards in a row, make sure they meet in the middle of a joist (see box). Attach boards to joists with screws, pounding in nails might damage the ceiling below.

Access options

If you have a simple hatch leading to the attic, you will have to haul a ladder inside every time you need to get something out of storage. If you use your attic often, consider having a hatch with a pull-down ladder installed. If your ceiling opening is at least 22 x 25 inches and the ceiling height 8 to 9 feet, a pull-down unit will fit.

INSTALLING AN ATTIC FLOOR

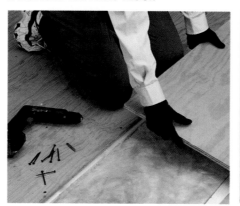

1. Slide the plywood boards into position, perpendicular to the joists, making sure that the ends have the support of a joist. Stagger the joints over the joists.

2. Two or three fasteners per board should be enough to secure the floor. If you use deck screws, make the job easier by drilling pilot holes first, using a ⅛-inch bit.

SEALING ROOFS AND GUTTERS

Homeowners usually don't think about their roofs or gutters until something goes wrong. But a yearly check and some preventive maintenance are a good investment.

Nothing strikes terror into a homeowner's heart quite like a leaky roof. That's because often you don't know you have a leak until you notice signs of moisture inside the house—peeling paint on a ceiling or stained wallpaper, for example. Look after any leak right away, because a little water can do a lot of damage to interior walls and ceilings. A yearly general inspection may help you find and fix potential leaks before they happen.

UNDERSTANDING YOUR ROOF

The life span of your roof depends on many factors—the roofing materials, climate conditions, and how well it was laid. If a roof starts to leak only a few years after installation, suspect damage from tree limbs, high winds, or poor workmanship. Always use a reputable and experienced roofing contractor who stands behind his work.

Flashing

Wherever there is a joint in a roof—between sections, around a chimney or vent, or where roof and siding meet—special care must be used to keep water out. Flashing is used to bridge the gap between the two surfaces, which may expand and contract at different rates or separate as the house settles. The most common materials for flashing are copper, galvanized steel, and aluminum. Neoprene collars are used for flashing around vents on the roof. Metal flashing comes in sheets, rolls, or preformed designs for drip edges, window and door drip caps; step flashing for chimneys; and valley flashing.

It is important that flashing is installed correctly to do its job; it is definitely a job for pros. Small holes or gaps can be temporarily fixed with roofing cement, but they are a sign that the metal is wearing out and needs replacing. Hire an experienced roofing contractor to inspect and repair or replace the flashing on your roof.

Signs of wear

Checking out a roof is a tricky job. If you have an unfinished attic, you can study the underside of your roof during the next rain. Use a flashlight to look for signs of water along the rafters and

ROOFING MATERIALS

Material	Description	Maintenance

Asphalt and asphalt-fiberglass shingles, the most common roofing material, are made of roofing felt or fiberglass, saturated with asphalt and surfaced with ceramic-coated mineral granules, which give the shingles a wide range of colors. They are moderately priced and last 15 to 30 years.

Repairs to damaged shingles are relatively easy to make. With proper framing, a second roof can be laid over the first one, saving you the expense of having the old roof torn off.

Wood shingles and shakes are usually made of cedar, which has a natural resistance to decay. Shingles are smooth on both sides; shakes are split on one side and have a rugged, hand-hewn look. Both are expensive and may raise your fire insurance rates. Shingles can last 20 years; shakes, up to 50 years.

Regular fungicide and oil treatments should be applied to prevent mildew, especially in humid regions, and to minimize curling and cracking.

Slate tiles are split and cut from natural stone. Because slate is heavy, it is most commonly installed on roofs with a steep pitch. Strong roof framing is needed. Good slate roofs can last from 50 to 200 years or more and are fireproof.

Falling debris can crack or dislodge slates, and slate nails can wear out, presenting a problem on old roofs. Replacing slates requires a professional, especially on a roof with a steep pitch.

Clay tiles are made of kiln-fired ceramic clay. They come in half-cylinders, flat shingles, and a variety of other styles. Some styles are interlocking, making it difficult to replace one tile. They are expensive but can last 50 to 100 years.

Hire a roofer with clay-tile experience for repairs. Sometimes, it is possible to slip a piece of metal under a tile to repair a leak.

Metal is an increasingly popular roofing choice. Metal roofs are usually aluminum; but stainless steel, copper, and galvanized steel are also used. While moderately expensive, they can last up to 35 years.

Small holes and tears can be temporarily sealed using fiberglass mesh and roofing cement, as for a flat roof (p.325). For larger problem areas, have a roofer replace whole sheets.

Roll roofing is similar in composition to asphalt shingles but is laid in wide, overlapping strips. Roll roofing is easy to install and economical, but ugly. It is normally used in places that are not visible from the ground.

Patch roll roofing as you would other flat roofing (p.325), or re-cover the area with new roofing.

Built-up roofing is used for flat or nearly flat roofs. Traditionally, built-up roofs were made with hot coal tar and gravel. The use of coal tar is now outlawed, but some hot tar roofs still exist. Today's "tar and gravel" roofing is made with modified bitumen, asphalt (rather than coal) derivatives, or various forms of rubber and PVC.

Because water can accumulate during heavy rains, a built-up roof must seal absolutely. When leaks develop, they are often at joint areas or at places where the roofing is punctured by vents or soil stacks. See page 325 for repairs to a flat roof.

ROOF WORK RULES

Anytime you're working on your roof or gutters, be sure that the ladder is securely footed on the ground at least a quarter of its length away from the house and that it extends at least 2 feet above the eaves for maximum stability. Always wear slip-resistant shoes. Never work on a wet or cold roof—it's dangerous for you and can harm the roof. Don't use an aluminum ladder near electrical wires; use a wooden or fiberglass ladder instead.

at least 2 ft. above eaves

¼ of ladder length from house

framing or in the insulation. Do an outside inspection of your roof on a sunny day. Look for the following signs of wear and tear:

◆ **Bare spots on asphalt surfaces.** The protective granular surface of shingles wears off and the asphalt begins to harden over time. Look for an accumulation of granules in the gutters.

◆ **Broken shingles.** Damage can be caused by extremely high winds, falling branches, or snow and ice buildup. A broken or torn shingle can be an entry point for moisture, and such a shingle should be replaced.

◆ **Buckling.** If your roof looks lumpy or wavy, the shingles are buckling, a sign of old age. A few buckling shingles should be replaced; many buckling shingles suggest that it is time to reroof.

◆ **Curling.** If asphalt shingles start to curl up at their ends, they will be easily ripped and torn by wind and ice. This curling can be a sign of poor attic ventilation and moisture buildup beneath the shingles (see pages 316 to 319).

◆ **Clawing.** The opposite of curling, clawing is a curling under at the bottom of a shingle, part of the normal aging process of an asphalt shingle. A roof with many clawed shingles will need to be replaced soon.

When to replace and when to patch

If a roof has been damaged by a falling branch, or if one small section is clearly in worse shape than the rest of the roof, patching may be a good solution. But if your roof is near the end of its life cycle (the roofer will tell you when you choose a roofing material what its life expectancy is), or if the symptoms listed above appear over all the roof, you are wise to have it replaced. Remember that a leaky roof can cause expensive damage to your home's interior; it doesn't pay to take chances and hope that a worn-out roof will last another year or two.

Get bids from at least two reputable roofing companies. Ask for recommendations from friends or neighbors who know the contractors' work. Lean toward local professionals who have been in business at least 10 years.

Does the old roof need to be torn off?

Asphalt shingle roofing is heavy; too many layers will cause undue stress on your roof's framing. (Remember that in cold climates, the roof must support both the weight of the shingles and the weight of snow during winter.)

Local building codes allow two, or perhaps three, layers of roofing, but no more—check with your local building code department to be sure. If your roof already has three layers of shingles, all will need to be taken off before a new roof can be installed.

To check how many shingle layers your roof has, look at the side edge of the roof—not the bottom edge, where an extra layer is sometimes applied. Lift up the shingles slightly and count the layers; don't count the roofing felt at the bottom.

A "tear-off job" costs more than a simple reroofing job—a good argument for choosing the best, longest-lasting shingles you can afford. The roofing company will need to place a dumpster very near your house so that they can shovel all the old roofing into it. Be sure that the contract for the reroofing spells out that the roofers will carefully clean up after themselves and will replace any landscaping or pavement that gets damaged in the process.

MAKING MINOR REPAIRS

An ambitious homeowner can repair asphalt and wood shingles; and some repairs to flat roofs are within the skills of an experienced do-it-yourselfer. You may also be able to use roofing cement to make a temporary repair on flashing. Repairs to slate and clay tile roofs, however, should be reserved for roofers who specialize in those materials. And, if you are uncomfortable getting up on a roof, have all your roofing work done by a professional.

Finding the source of a leak

Shingle roofs can leak anywhere that there are cracks, splits, worn-away shingles, fissures, or other spots where the material is compromised. The most likely points for leaks are in valleys and around flashings at soil stacks and vents, chimneys, and vertical wall joints. Check these areas carefully for signs of wear.

Roof leaks are frustrating to trace because the place where water shows up inside the house is rarely directly below the leak in the roof. Water travels along rafters and beams, and it usually surfaces some distance away from the spot where it enters the house. One effective way to locate a leak is to take a strong light up into the attic during a rainstorm. If the leak has been active for a while, you may see a discoloration in the roof sheathing or in a rafter. You may be able to trace the discoloration back to the leak source.

Once you have found the leak inside, you need to pinpoint it on the roof surface. Measure from the leak in two directions—up to the roof ridge (the area where the two sloping sides of the roof meet) as well as down to the eaves and over to the side of the roof. Use those measurements on the roof to find the damaged shingle. Although it may be tempting to poke a nail up into the leak spot through the roof, don't do it: You may damage a good shingle as well as the bad one.

Roof repair materials

Check your basement or garage for replacement shingles; often, roofers will leave the homeowner a partial bundle. If you can't find leftover shingles, take a broken shingle to a home center to find a match. Choose roofing nails that are long enough to poke well into the wood sheathing. The more layers of roofing you have to go through, the longer the nails must be.

REPLACING A WORN ASPHALT SHINGLE

1. If a shingle is worn away or has a hole in it, remove it without damaging the surrounding shingles. To do this, lift the shingles above it gently, and slide a pry bar in to remove any nails. (This works best when the shingles are warm and flexible, from 65° to 80°F, but not hot and easily damaged.)

2. Brush away any debris, and slide in a new shingle. You may need to pry surrounding tiles gently with the flat end of the pry bar. You may find that additional nails, fastening shingles above the repair area, need to be removed in order to slide the new shingle in.

3. Secure the new shingles with roofing nails above each slot in the shingle, being careful not to damage the shingle above. Use a putty knife or paint stir-stick to apply roofing cement under the new shingle and under the shingle above; be careful that no roofing cement will be visible.

REPLACING A WOOD SHINGLE OR SHAKE

1. To remove a badly worn wood shingle or shake, first split it along the grain using a hammer and chisel. Slide the pieces out by hand. You can hold upper shingles up with wedges of wood while you work.

2. Do not try to remove the nails that held the old shingle; doing this will only break the shingle above. Instead, use a hacksaw blade to cut the nails flush to the surface. Cut a new shingle so that there will be a ¼-inch gap on each side.

3. Apply roofing cement to the back of the new shingle and to the top of the underlying shingles as shown. Slide the shingle into place; you may need to tap it all the way in with a piece of scrap wood and a hammer at its base.

Use roofing cement to make temporary repairs to the joint between flashing and a wall, to glue down a curled shingle, to seal a crack in a flat roof, or to patch an area that will not be visible. Fibered cement (or roof patch) is usually a better choice than the liquid type because it will not run. "Wet and dry" roof cement will allow you to seal a spot while it is still wet, and you will actually see the hole getting sealed. For very small repairs, buy roofing cement in a caulking tube.

Repairing a cracked asphalt shingle

Properly maintained, an asphalt shingle roof will last 15 to 20 years. If a single shingle is torn but otherwise in good shape, you can fix it easily. Pick a warm but not hot day (65° to 80°F), when the shingle will be pliable. Lift up the pieces carefully. Be sure to lift up all the way back to the beginning of the tear. Use a putty knife to apply roofing cement under both sides of the tear, and press down firmly. Wipe away any excess cement using a rag soaked with mineral spirits.

Repairing wood shingles or shakes

If a wood shingle or shake has split or is curling up, you may be able to nail it back into place. Drill a pilot hole, then drive in roofing nails to make it sit flat. Cover the nail head with roofing cement. If a shingle has developed a hole—as sometimes happens when a knot works loose—slide a piece of metal flashing under the shingle so that it extends several inches above the hole.

Maintaining wood shingles

Wood shingles and shakes are susceptible to damage from fungus and moss growth, especially in humid areas. Moss, algae, and mildew can be scraped off or removed with a powerful spray from a garden hose. Prevent them from coming back by spraying on a coat of fungicide. After the roof has been cleaned with a solution of liquid chlorine bleach and water, have a roofer install zinc strips near the ridge of the roof. Zinc ions, washed down by rain, discourage the growth of fungi.

Repairing flat roofs

A topcoat of fiberglass (white) or aluminum (silver), which you can apply yourself with a squeegee or mop, protects a flat roof from damaging ultraviolet rays of the sun by reflecting them away. Heat bakes the oils out of unprotected tar roofs and makes them brittle.

Inspect a flat roof at least once a year for blisters, cracks, tears, and storm damage. Make repairs promptly. A hot-tar built-up roof will need more

attention than a modified bitumen roof. Wherever the roofing curves upwards at a vertical wall or chimney, make sure the top edge is tightly sealed against the surface. Apply a liberal amount of roofing cement, perhaps using a caulking tube, and smooth it so that water has no opportunity to puddle.

For small repairs, see "Repairing a Flat Roof" below. For large areas with lots of small cracks, the solution may be to apply silver or white topcoating. If there are numerous problem spots, or an area larger than 4 feet square is cracked or blistered, have the roof resurfaced by a roofing company.

Sealing flashing against walls

Some flashing has a bent upper edge that is inserted into a wall or chimney. Others are simply glued to the wall with roofing cement. Flashing that is pulling away can cause serious leaking problems. You may be able to put the flashing back into place temporarily using roofing cement. But you will need to call in a roofer to make more permanent repairs.

GUTTER MAINTENANCE AND REPAIR

Once or twice a year, in late spring and fall, clean and inspect the gutters. Begin by looking for blockages in the gutter channels and at the downspouts. Check for leaks, which occur most often at

REPAIRING A FLAT ROOF

Blisters, which indicate that roofing felt has separated from the underlying layers or from the wood sheathing, should be treated if they seem likely to break open. Repair tears and cracks using Steps 2 and 3. Buy fiberglass mesh that is especially made for roof repairs.

1. Sweep away dirt and loose gravel. Slice the blister open lengthwise with a utility knife. (If there is water under the blister, it may be coming from an open spot nearby.) Use a putty knife to smear roofing cement under both sides of the cut.

2. Press the layers of roofing material flat. Nail each side with roofing nails, spaced 3 inches apart. Cut a piece of fiberglass mesh 6 inches longer and 2 to 3 inches wider than the patch. Apply roofing cement to sealed blister and place the patch on the cement.

3. Gently press the mesh into the cement, smoothing out any wrinkles with a spreading tool at least 3 inches wide. Cover the patch with another coat of roofing cement, smoothing the surface so water cannot collect on it.

GUTTER RELIEF

Leaves clog gutters, necessitating your scooping them out (right). For a modest cost, you can install guards that will lessen, if not eliminate, the need for seasonal gutter cleaning. One design (below, top) is a metal mesh that comes in a roll and is friction-fitted into the gutter. Another design (bottom) is a series of perforated vinyl shields that clip onto the outside edge of the gutter and slip under the bottom course of shingles.

seams and rusted spots. A leaking gutter may cause water to seep into a basement and possibly even weaken your home's foundation. Water running down wood siding will ruin paint and will cause rot.

Cleaning gutters

Cleaning gutters is a dirty job but is not difficult. You should wear heavy-duty gloves because gutter edges and seams can be sharp and jagged.

Attach a mesh bag, such as the kind onions and potatoes are sold in, to the bottom end of the downspouts. Leaves, twigs, and other solid debris will collect in the bag as you clean and can then be disposed of quickly and easily.

Set up an extension ladder (p.322). Some gutters—especially those made of aluminum—are scratched easily; so wrap the parts of the ladder that will touch the gutters with rags or tape to protect the gutters. Some gutters cannot take the weight of a ladder and a person without bending. If that is the case with your gutters, you can buy a set of ladder stabilizers, which allow the ladder to rest against the house and not the gutters, while still giving you access to the gutters.

Scoop debris out of the gutters by hand or with a trowel. Or make an effective scoop from a piece of heavy cardboard. Start cleaning at the downspout end and move up. Mark any loose fittings or rusty areas with chalk for future repairs. Move the ladder frequently as you work. Finally flush the cleaned gutter with a garden hose, starting at the high end.

If you have standing water, check the slope

For water to flow freely, a gutter should slope downward to its downspout about ¼ inch for every 4 feet of length. Set a level on the gutter's front edge to check. Long runs may be raised in the middle to slant toward downspouts at each end. Most gutters need to be supported about every 2½ feet. If a gutter has standing water, it may be due to a sag; correct it by bending or reinstalling a hanger. If a whole section of gutter is not sloped correctly, call in a gutter installer to correct it.

Supporting droopy gutters

Make sure that all hangers are firmly anchored and attached to the gutter sections. For gutters with spike-and-sleeve supports, make sure the spikes are firmly nailed into the fascia board.

If the fascia board is rotted, have it replaced by a carpenter. Temporarily solve the problem by installing

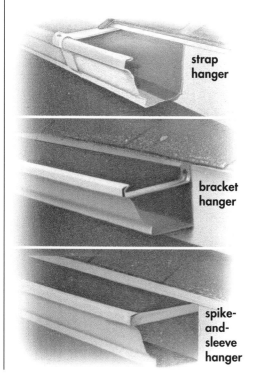

strap hanger

bracket hanger

spike-and-sleeve hanger

FIXING A LEAKING GUTTER

1. Remove any leaves or accumulated grit from the leaking gutter. Wipe the area of the leak dry. Scrape away peeling paint and rust, using a wire brush, scraper, and sandpaper.

2. Purchase a small roll of fiberglass plasterboard joint tape at a hardware store or home center. Cut a piece and position it to cover the crack or hole with an inch or two to spare at each end.

3. Using a paint stir-stick or putty knife, apply a coat of roofing cement. Smooth it carefully, completely covering the mesh. Smooth any excess roofing cement on the underside of the gutter.

a strap hanger. If a strap hanger has come loose, reset it by carefully lifting up the shingle and driving a roofing nail in. If you find that the wood underneath is rotted, call in a roofer or a carpenter for repairs.

Fixing gutter leaks

If a gutter is leaking at a seam, an endcap, or a corner joint, apply gutter caulk to the leaking area, and smooth it with a putty knife so that water can still flow easily. If the parts have started to come apart, disassemble them, apply gutter caulk, and reassemble (you may need to remove and reinstall screws).

If a gutter leaks at several points in in the middle, that may signal that rust has started to eat up the entire gutter system and that a total replacement will soon be necessary. If the problem seems localized, or if your gutters are made of a non-rusting material, it makes sense to patch (see "Fixing a Leaking Gutter," above).

Downspout cleaning

Downspouts—the vertical parts of a gutter system—can become clogged with leaves, twigs, and debris. Use a drain auger to break through any obstructions. Or flush with a garden hose. Install a leaf strainer at the top of each downspout to prevent clogs.

Choosing replacement gutters

If you have to replace gutters or downspouts, you will find a variety of types and styles from which to choose.

◆ **Steel.** Available with enamel or galvanized finishes, steel gutters require periodic painting to prevent rust.

◆ **Aluminum.** Though not as strong as steel, aluminum is easier to handle and is rust-proof. Seamless aluminum gutters, manufactured on the spot by professionals with special equipment, have no joints except at corners, giving them a clean look and eliminating many potential leak points.

◆ **Vinyl.** Very durable, vinyl gutters often carry a lifetime warranty. Though resistant to dents, vinyl gutters fade over time, giving them a worn appearance. They can be painted with high-quality 100% acrylic paint.

◆ **Copper.** Very expensive, copper gutters are used primarily in restoration projects. Copper joints are soldered and need periodic resoldering. Copper is corrosion-resistant, and it oxidizes to a pleasant soft green.

BASEMENT WATER SYSTEMS

Your basement is likely to be the location for appliances that heat and condition your water. Not only do these systems need regular maintenance, the basement itself needs to be defended from incoming moisture.

Water heaters, water softeners and filters, and sump pumps are all appliances that make a household run more comfortably. You can prolong their lives, saving yourself hassles and money, with regular maintenance and upkeep.

WATER HEATER

A water heater (often called a "hot-water heater") is basically an insulated bottle with a heater. One pipe carries cold water to the heater; another pipe carries hot water out. As hot water is drawn out of the tank, cold water enters. This lowers the temperature in the tank, causing a thermostat to activate and call for heat.

In a gas model, a burner beneath the tank kicks in and heats the water to the desired setting. Harmful by-products of combustion are drawn out via a flue that runs up the middle of the tank and out of the house.

In an electric model, heating elements inside the tank perform the same function. The tank is insulated on the inside to hold the water temperature

as steady as possible to limit the number of times the burners must turn on. Because they do not produce fumes, electric heaters require no venting.

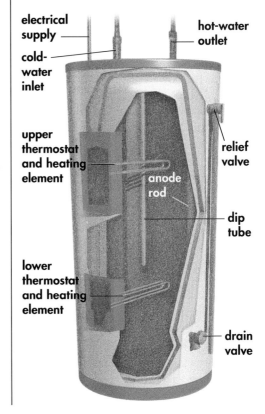

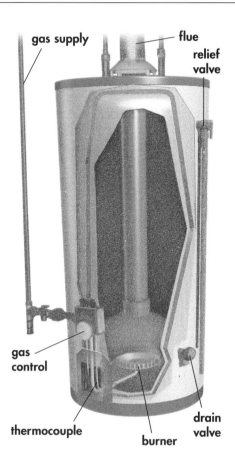

gas supply

flue

relief valve

gas control

thermocouple

burner

drain valve

Water heater problems and their solutions

If a tank's liner has corroded, causing the unit to leak onto the floor, the water heater must be replaced. But other smaller problems can be fixed:

◆ **Noisy tank.** A rumbling noise is a likely sign of overheating; the thermostat may not be telling the burners or heating elements to shut off. Immediately cut off the burner in a gas heater or the electricity to an electric heater. Check that the pressure relief value is operating. If the water is too hot, call

a plumber. If the water is barely hot, there may be sediment in the tank; open the drain valve and let out a few gallons of water.

◆ **No hot water.** On a gas unit, the pilot light may have gone out; you may have to clean the burner (p.77) or replace the thermocouple (p.76). On an electric model, the thermostat may be faulty; call a plumber to replace it.

◆ **Not enough hot water** (hot water runs out quickly). See that the thermostat is set high enough—above 120°F. Check for leaking bathroom or kitchen faucets that can drain away hot water. On a gas unit, the heat exchanger may be clogged with dirt; flush the tank (see below). On an electric model, the lower heating element may be faulty; have it replaced. If everyone in the house has always raced to be first to take a morning shower when the water is still hot, the water tank is simply not big enough; replace it with a larger one.

◆ **Water not hot enough.** Make sure that the thermostat is turned up high enough. On an electric model, the lower heating element, which does 90 percent of the work, may be worn out; have it replaced.

Regular maintenance

Water heaters actually require very little attention. There are just a few precautions you should take:

◆ Flush your water heater every year or so. Near the bottom is a small tap to which you can attach a garden hose. By flushing a few quarts of water, you remove scale, sediment, rust, and

CHECK THE FLUE FOR FUMES

If the flue on your gas water heater is not installed correctly, harmful carbon monoxide fumes will enter your house. A quick check to see if it is drawing properly: Light a match, blow it out, and hold it near the base of the flue (at the top of the water heater). If the smoke is quickly sucked up into the flue, it is drawing well. Check the pipe at all points, to make sure there are no large gaps where fumes can escape; make sure each joint is tight, and connected with three screws. To be completely sure, have your gas company send someone out to check for carbon monoxide. They should do this for free.

mineral deposits that settle on the bottom and reduce heat transfer. If you find a significant amount of sediment, repeat this every few months until the flushed water runs clear again.

◆ Check the anode rod, a sacrificial metal piece that diverts corrosion from the sides of the tank, every few years;

replacing one that is encrusted will extend the life of the water heater. Some newer water heaters don't have this rod.

Pressure relief

If pressure or temperature in a water heater gets dangerously high, a relief valve located either on top or on the side of the tank will activate automatically, spitting out the too-hot water. Test this valve twice a year by pulling on its handle; if water rushes out of the attached pipe, all is well; if nothing happens, have a plumber replace the valve.

Water heater blankets

An insulating blanket, made with an inch or two of fiberglass bonded to a vinyl cloth backing, can keep your hot water hot for longer, saving on the cost of reheating it. Available at home centers, they are designed to fit specific sizes of water heaters. They are available for both electric heaters and gas heaters. Blankets for electric heaters cover the entire unit. Gas heater blankets surround only the middle of the tank so that the material has no chance to block the flue or get near the open flame of the burner. Some gas heater manufacturers, in fact, prohibit the use of these blankets with their product.

Relighting a gas heater

When your gas water heater's pilot light goes out and you smell the odor that is placed in natural gas, call a service technician immediately and vent the room where the heater is located. If you don't smell gas, you can relight the pilot. Turn the gas cock to "pilot," light

a match, press the reset button, and light the pilot. Let it burn for about 30 seconds, then turn the cock to "on."

If the pilot refuses to stay lit, you may need to change the thermocouple (p.76). A furnace's thermocouple is the same as a water heater's.

Replacing heating elements and the thermostat on an electric heater

Electric water heaters have two thermostats, one for each heating element. If your water is not getting hot enough, the upper thermostat and element may need replacing. If water gets hot but only for a short while, the lower thermostat and element need to be replaced. A plumber will be able to handle the job for considerably less than the cost of a new water heater.

DEALING WITH HARD WATER

If your water has a high mineral content, it may be what is called "hard" water. Soap lathers poorly and leaves a sticky film in hard water, which also can leave gray, curd-like deposits in your washing machine that irritate sensitive skin. Hard water also allows corrosive scale to build up inside the plumbing system. Water heaters, dishwashers, and washing machines work less efficiently and wear out more quickly with hard water. Also, hard water often has an unpleasant taste.

Testing for hard water

A simple test for hard water is to fill a jar with tap water and add a small amount of liquid dishwashing detergent. Screw the cap on tightly and shake. The high mineral content in

hard water will inhibit the formation of soapy suds and cause the bubbles that do form to dissolve quickly.

Adding a water softener

The antidote to hard water is a water softener, a treatment device that is connected to your water-supply pipe. The softener captures excess minerals in a column of plastic resin beads. The beads are then bathed in a brine (salt water), which removes the minerals and flushes them away. With automatic softeners, the resin is rinsed with salt at regular intervals. You can buy or rent a water softener. In households where dietary salt is restricted, the water softener can be hooked up to only the hot-water supply. That way, water used for cooking and drinking won't be salty.

Softener upkeep

The salt in a water softener, which carries away the offending minerals, such as magnesium and calcium, must be replaced periodically. You can buy water softener salt at grocery and hardware stores, or from the company that installed your softener. Pour the additional salt into the storage container as directed by the manufacturer.

If the motor stops running, check the power cord, and make sure power is supplied to the receptacle (see page 94). If the motor still does not operate, call for service.

WATER FILTERS

A water softener will significantly reduce calcium, iron, and other minerals; but other water problems call for other types

UNCLOGGING A WATER SOFTENER

If water is not being softened even though the salt container is full and the motor is operating, you may have a clog. The two most likely spots are the brine line, and the injector and its screen. If your water has a high silt content, you may also need to clean the brine intake. Remove it from the brine well inside the brine tank, and clean it with a toothbrush and running water. Empty the brine tank and flush it with a hose before refilling it with salt.

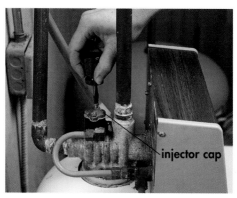

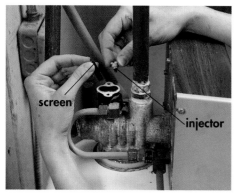

1. Check and flush the brine line. Unplug the water softener and switch it to "bypass." With a crescent wrench, loosen the fittings holding the line, and pull the line out. Squirt warm water into the line with a turkey baster to clear any clogs.

2. Remove the injector cap. (On some units, this is horizontal rather than vertical.) With the softener turned to "bypass," remove the screws holding the injector cap. You will need to replace the gasket underneath it; buy one at a plumbing-supply store.

3. Remove and clean the injector and screen. Gently lift out the screen, which will be conical or cylindrical, and the injector. Blow through the injector to clear any clogs. Wash both with soapy water and a small, soft brush, and reinstall them.

of treatment. Depending on the problem you have, you may want a device that treats all the water entering the house, or one that treats only drinking water at the kitchen sink.

Assessing your water problems

If you suspect that your water may be impure, contact your local department of health or your municipal water department. They will be able to tell you if there is danger from pesticides, microorganisms, or lead. It is the job of the municipal water department to eliminate all health dangers. If you have a well, have your water tested every two years. A test for bacteria will cost less than a test for all contaminants.

Many problems are nuisances rather than health hazards. Water may taste and smell bad due to sulphur content or heavy chlorinization by your water supplier. Iron and other minerals may cause water to produce stains. These problems can often be remedied with home filters such as the following:

◆ **Iron or oxidizing filter.** A water softener removes a good deal of iron, but if you have severe iron problems—indicated by rust stains on sinks and on washed clothes—you may need an additional iron or oxidizing filter. Have it installed by a plumber.

◆ **Activated-carbon filter.** Also known as an activated-charcoal filter, this removes the nasty taste from heavily chlorinated water and will also clear water of pesticides. If you have well water with a high sulfur content (which smells like rotten eggs), this filter, in conjunction with a water softener, will help. The carbon or charcoal in these filters must be replaced regularly. If you install one for the whole house's water supply, you may have to replace the filter material quite often.

◆ **Reverse-osmosis filter.** Expensive and bulky, with one or two holding tanks, this filter removes bacteria and

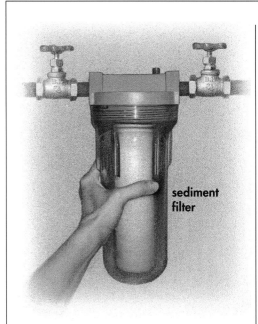

sediment filter

harmful chemicals that other filters can miss. Often installed under a kitchen sink, it requires a fair amount of space.

◆ **Sediment filter.** Essentially a fine screen, a sediment filter traps particles that can cloud your water and clog the aerators on your faucets. A sediment filter (above) is usually used with an activated-carbon filter.

Filters for fresh taste

If all you need is better-tasting water, you can buy an activated-carbon filter that you pour water over in a pitcher, or one that hooks directly onto your kitchen sink faucet. Both are effective if you replace the filter periodically.

To filter all the cold water at the kitchen faucet, buy a canister-type filter and install it on the cold-water line under the sink. A plumber can install it, or you can do it yourself. For the type

shown below, there is no need to shut off the water. A saddle T valve can be installed simply by clamping it onto the cold-water supply pipe, then turning a screw that pierces the pipe. Attach the filter canister to the wall or cabinet side, and hook up the flexible lines to the saddle T and the faucet. Other types require you to cut into the cold-water supply line and do slightly more serious plumbing work. Follow the manufacturer's directions for breaking in the filter. You may need to lubricate the canister, and the water may contain bits of charcoal at first.

SUMP PUMPS

During heavy rainstorms, and in the spring when the ground becomes saturated with snow melt, water can seep into a basement and actually flood it. To prevent this, many homes have a sump pump, which sucks water up and sends it out of the house.

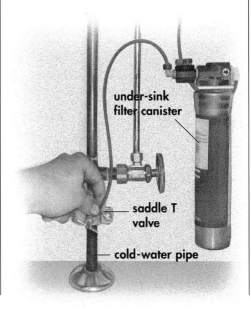

under-sink filter canister

saddle T valve

cold-water pipe

A sump pump sits in a tank, called a sump pit, that is installed at the lowest point of the basement floor and is made of concrete, clay, tile, or fiberglass. (Sump pits are sold at lumberyards.) Water that collects around the foundation of the house is funneled through clay tile and drainage rock channels into the sump pit. When water fills the pit to a certain level, the pump is activated. It draws water out of the basin and discharges it through a drain with a check valve to prevent backflow.

Types of pumps

There are two kinds of sump pumps for home use. Submersible pumps are concealed in a sump pit; pedestal pumps sit on a column that protrudes out of the pit, holding the motor above the water. Both operate on electricity; receptacles for sump pumps should be at least 4 feet above the basement floor and protected by a ground fault circuit interrupter. Do not use extension cords with sump pumps. Both kinds of pumps draw water in through a filtered trap and pump it out of the basement through a discharge pipe. Most pumps are automatic, triggered by a float-operated switch when the water rises, shutting off when the water subsides.

Buying a sump pump

Submersible pumps are recommended when the sump pit is near living areas, like a home office or rec room. Because they operate underground in the sump pit, they are quieter than the pedestal type. Submersible pumps are more expensive; and they are likely to wear out faster because they are under water most of the time. Pedestal pumps are noisier, but less expensive and easier to repair. A unit's cost depends on its pumping power in gallons per minute. The least powerful pumps are cheapest to buy, but cost more to operate because they run more often.

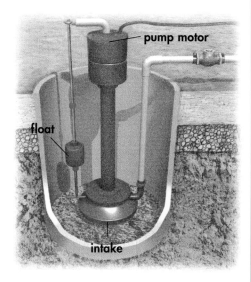

Pump maintenance

Submersible pumps last from 5 to 15 years, and pedestal pumps last up to 25 years. Clean and inspect the pump, the inlet screen, and the check valve yearly. If your sump pit routinely catches water from a dehumidifier or a washing machine, clean the filter more often and check that the float is not waterlogged or stuck. To test a pump, run water into the sump tank. The pump should run smoothly. If it sounds like it's working hard, or if it works slowly, unplug it, remove it, and clean the inlet screen.

SOLVING MOISTURE PROBLEMS IN BASEMENTS

Basement water—whether leakage during rainfall or general moisture—is not just a nuisance. Over the years, such moisture can weaken your home's foundation. If the problem is an occasional leak during a hard rain, and if the water all runs into a drain, you might choose to live with it. However, general moisture or persistent leaking should be dealt with. Begin by determining the source of the problem.

Is dampness due to seepage or humidity?

To determine whether moisture on a damp wall comes from inside or outside the house, tape a piece of heavy-gauge plastic, about 16 inches square, to the wall below ground level, and seal all the edges with tape. After several days, remove the plastic. Dampness underneath the plastic indicates that water is seeping into the basement from the outside and through the concrete. If the plastic-covered area is dry and the wall around it is damp, water is condensing from moist air inside the basement.

First, try redirecting rainwater

Most basement moisture problems can be alleviated or even solved by sending rainwater away from the house. Water collecting around the foundation of a home can exert as much as 500 pounds of pressure per square foot, which will force water through even tiny cracks.

So look to your gutters and downspouts first. If they are clean and work-

GOOD TOOLS

AUXILIARY PUMPS

You usually need a sump pump in times of bad or stormy weather, which is exactly when power is likely to be interrupted, meaning that the pump can't do its work. You can buy pumps with an auxiliary unit designed to operate when the primary cannot run. Auxiliary pumps operate on a rechargeable 12-volt battery. If your pump is protecting expensive flooring or a home office with computer wiring or important files at floor level, an auxiliary pump will be a comfort.

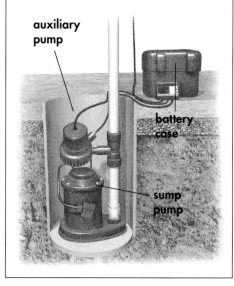

ing, try extending your downspouts out away from the house (see page 334). As an emergency measure, you can attach an extension, such as an extra piece of gutter, to the bottom of each downspout. You can buy splashblocks at any home center. Or buy curled flat plastic splash blocks that unroll only when water goes through them from the drainpipe. If none of these devices cuts down on seepage into the basement, consider having underground drainpipes installed by a landscaper. Be aware, however, that these drainpipes can freeze up in the cold weather.

If diverting rainwater away from your house doesn't keep the basement dry, check the grading around the house: It should slope away from the foundation. Examine your house's perimeter after a rainfall. If water collects in a kind of moat, or if there are puddles near the house, that means that water will seep down and exert

extension

splash block

pressure on your foundation. Fill puddles with well-tamped soil, bermed upward toward the foundation so that the water will run away from the house. If an area slopes toward the house rather than away from it, consult a landscaper to solve the problem.

Caulk the outside
Basement-level windows, outdoor masonry steps, door openings, or a patio may have cracks that will let water into your basement. Look all around the house, and seal any possible leaks carefully with a waterproof caulk (see page 89).

For slow seepage, apply a sealer
Slow seepage through basement walls may be thwarted with a coat of waterproofing basement paint. Better yet, purchase a cement-based sealer made for damp basements. Most of these

TROUBLE SHOOTER

ELIMINATING LEAKS AND MOISTURE PROBLEMS

Most problems of seepage and dampness in the basement can be solved either by directing rainwater away from the house or by installing a dehumidifier in the basement during the summer. Improving basement ventilation with fans and open windows can help dry up condensation.

Symptoms	Cause	Solutions
Leaks during rainfall. Water may slowly seep or even trickle or pour from one or more spots.	In a newer basement, the tie-rods may not have been sealed. In older basements, cracks caused by settling can lead to leaks. Water pressure due to improper drainage will make the problem worse.	First, improve drainage so that water runs away from the house. Second, plug leaks with hydraulic cement (facing page). If the leak persists, you may need to waterproof the foundation.
General dampness: moist pipes, damp walls, perhaps causing mildew, throughout much of the basement.	Moisture is being produced in your basement from a source such as a shower or a clothes dryer that is not properly vented.	Make sure the dryer is venting out; install and use an exhaust fan in a shower area. Or, install a dehumidifier (p.85).
Dampness in one or two areas of the basement, often at a point where a wall meets the floor.	Concrete is somewhat porous, and if a lot of water pressure is exerted against it, moisture will seep through.	Improve drainage so water runs away from the house. Brush on a basement wall sealer if the problem is minor. In severe cases, you may have to waterproof the foundation.
Moisture on the floor, perhaps only a slight dampness. Put a piece of plastic on the floor; if it becomes wet after two days, subterranean seepage is the culprit.	The water table in your area may be high, exerting water pressure up against your basement floor, especially during the rainy season.	This problem cannot be completely solved. Install a sump pump to get rid of some of the water. Improve drainage so that water runs away from the house.

have a dry and a liquid component that mix together. Wet the wall thoroughly, then apply the sealer with a stiff brush. Fill in any cracks as you go by working the sealer into them with the brush. Some products require a second coat.

Severe water problems

If none of the methods discussed above and at right stops water from coming into your basement, hire a waterproofing professional. If the house is new, it is possible that your wet basement problems may be the result of incorrectly poured concrete. Contact the builder and your new home warranty program to see if corrective measures are in order.

Otherwise, you must rely on the waterproofing professional, who may suggest that you need to seal your basement walls from the outside. This is an expensive and disruptive procedure, but it does work.

To seal basement walls from the outside, the first step is to excavate a narrow pit around the house, deep enough to expose the outside basement walls. Next, a trench is dug at the base of the wall and filled with drainage pipes and gravel to ensure good drainage. Then the wall must be cleaned of dirt, and a sealer applied, either with a paint roller or with a special machine that blows a sealant onto the wall. Sometimes a rubberized sheathing is used. Thick-gauged plastic sheeting should then be applied over the sealer.

Finally, the trench must be refilled again with soil, and the area around the foundation of the house is replanted.

STOPPING LEAKS FROM THE INSIDE

If you find one or more small spots on a solid concrete basement wall that leak during rainfall, you might be able to stem the seepage with hydraulic cement, which is designed to plug leaks in concrete walls.

1. Place a garden hose next to the house, turn on the water, and go inside. When the crack starts leaking, circle the spot with a wax crayon. Turn off the water. Open the crack with a mallet and cold chisel until it is an inch wide. "Key" the hole— angle the chisel so that the bottom of the hole will be wider than the top. This will help the patching cement grab hold and maintain its position.

2. Remove loose concrete with a wire brush. Turn the hose on again, just enough so the leak trickles. Pour some of the dry hydraulic cement into a small bucket, add some water, and mix until you get a putty-like consistency. Roll it between your hands to get a rope shape that is about the size of the hole.

3. With the water still trickling, push the cement into the hole. The leak should stop after a minute or so. If the leak does not stop, remove the cement and try again. Once the spot stays dry, turn off the hose.

If you can't stem leaks in a block foundation from the outside, drill holes at the bottom of the basement wall, just below the leaks. Let the water flow out, directing it to a drain along a vinyl channel sealed to the floor.

10

Home Safety

Poisonings

Emergencies

MAKING YOUR HOME SAFER

Ensure the health and safety of your family by learning a few basic strategies for maintaining your dwelling responsibly.

*H*ome safety issues can seem overwhelming. Hardly a month goes by without a breathless news bulletin on some new hazard in our lives. However, you can master the fine points of clean interior air, fire and disaster safety, and reasonable protection against break-ins and theft. Just take a little time to understand each household danger, what preventive measures to take, and what to do when an emergency does occur.

HAZARDOUS HOUSEHOLD PRODUCTS

Thousands of products containing hazardous chemicals are routinely used and stored in households. Most accidents with these involve flammable and combustible materials. In addition to the risk of fire, these products also may be ingested by children. To a lesser extent, there are dangers associated with absorption of some substances through skin contact. Such chemicals don't necessarily damage the skin, so the victim may not even be aware that they are being poisoned. Cancer, liver or kidney damage, birth defects, and central nervous system damage can

result from repeated, long-term exposure, though the effects may take years to be apparent. Act cautiously around potentially dangerous products, which fall under the following categories:

◆ **Flammable/combustible:** Can easily be set on fire. Examples: paint thinner, oil-based paints, some insect repellents, kerosene, hair sprays.

◆ **Explosive/reactive:** Can detonate or explode through exposure to heat, sudden shock, pressure, or incompatible substances. Examples: many aerosol spray cans, batteries, ammonia.

◆ **Corrosive:** Their chemical action can burn and destroy living tissues. Examples: heavy-duty cleaners, paint strippers, drain cleaners, muriatic acid, oven cleaner, toilet bowl cleaner.

◆ **Toxic:** Capable of causing injury or death through ingestion, inhalation, or skin absorption. Some toxic substances can cause cancer or fetal harm. Examples: flea sprays, certain medicines, weed killers. Warning labels may not tell you exactly what the danger is, but only that there is a danger. Check labels for warnings.

What you can do

The following precautions and habits will go a long way toward keeping your family and household visitors safe:

◆ **Buy responsibly.** If you need to buy a hazardous substance, purchase only what you can use soon, or give the leftover portion to a friend who will use it promptly. Choose the safest product available, or use a nonhazardous alternative. (See pages 106, 108, and 148–149 for examples.) Purchase hazardous liquids only in child-resistant containers to protect kids and pets in your home and neighborhood. Avoid aerosol containers if at all possible because they disperse their contents in tiny droplets that can be deeply inhaled into the lungs and quickly absorbed into the bloodstream. Also, aerosols ignite and explode easily.

◆ **Store safely.** Keep hazardous substances in their original containers and place in a locked cupboard. Never decant hazardous substances into food or beverage containers, where they might be mistaken for edible substances.

gasoline · motor oil · antifreeze · brake fluid · paint thinner · paint

Store flammable liquids, such as gasoline, in a well-ventilated garage or detached shed. Keep them away from any source of heat, sparks, or flame—including a furnace, fireplace, oven, space heater, electric switch, or motor.

◆ **Use wisely.** Wear protective gloves, goggles, and clothing. Read and follow label instructions. If they aren't readable and you are unsure about using a product, don't experiment. Never leave opened products unattended; if you need to leave a work site while using a hazardous substance, close the container and take it with you. Always let gasoline-powered equipment—lawnmowers, weed trimmers, garden tractors, or chain saws—cool off before refilling their tanks. Gasoline is the main cause of serious fires involving flammable liquids.

◆ **Dispose responsibly.** Don't pour leftover hazardous products of any kind down the drain or into the toilet; and don't dump them on the ground or into storm drains: You may end up dumping harmful chemicals into your community's land and water supply. Also, such practices are almost certainly against local safety codes and punishable by fines and other sanctions. Don't burn hazardous products, either, because the fumes thus created are dangerous. Most communities have depots where such materials can be taken for proper handling and disposal.

PREVENTING COMMON ACCIDENTS

Avoiding falls and shocks and a host of other home accidents is good for every-

one. However, some family members are more at risk than others. Children, either your own or visiting youngsters, often get into dangerous situations. There are a number of steps you can take to protect them.

Start by having a designated storage area where tempting, dangerous objects such as guns, darts, and archery gear can be kept under lock and key. And no matter how safe your home environment may seem, remember that there is no substitute for adequate adult supervision. Following are some areas that require particularly close safety inspection and prudent adult habits.

Kitchen

Do not leave young children alone in the kitchen. Equip cabinets that contain cleaning products with easy-to-install childproof latches (below). In addition, consider the following:

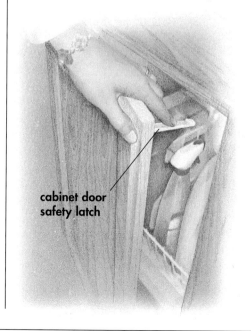

cabinet door safety latch

◆ **Keep small appliances** at the back of counters, and electric cords well out of reach. Unplug appliances when not in use so children can't operate them; this also avoids shocks in case a youngster pulls one into a water-filled sink.

◆ **Store plastic storage bags** out of children's reach. Tie knots in used plastic bags before you throw them away. This will keep youngsters from playing with them and possibly suffering accidental suffocation.

◆ **Place sharp knives** on the top rack of the dishwasher or in the silverware basket with blades down to reduce the risk of injury to a curious child.

◆ **Fill the detergent dispenser** cup of your automatic dishwasher only when you're ready to run it.

◆ **Keep pet food and water bowls** away from toddlers and infants.

◆ **Use a covered trash basket,** and install a safety latch on the cabinet where it is kept. This will prevent little ones and pets from foraging in trash that may contain broken glass, splintered bones, or poisonous substances.

◆ **Teach older kids** to use appliances safely and with supervision, including the microwave oven.

◆ **Place food and drinks** near the center of a table or at the back of a counter. Avoid using tablecloths except for special occasions: They are easily pulled off by toddlers and pets.

◆ **Exercise extreme caution** around the stove when children are present. Cook on back burners, with the pot

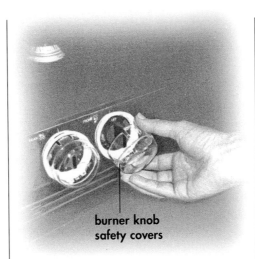

burner knob
safety covers

handles turned back out of small children's sight line and reach. Use safety covers (above) for stove knobs if they are within reach of a young child. Store cookies and other tempting foods away from the stove. And keep a step stool far away from the cooking area.

Living room and bedrooms

The following measures may be too drastic if your home is visited only infrequently by a child but are recommended if you have children or grandchildren around regularly.

◆ **Check furniture placement** to be sure everything is secure. The TV is a particular hazard when it is heavy and tippy, especially on a high shelf. Secure large wall mirrors and artwork.

◆ **Keep small decorative items** out of reach. They can present a choking danger. Put sharp objects away, too.

◆ **Some recliners** can cause serious injuries by closing on a child's fingers, arm, or head. Choose a recliner model

that doesn't snap shut hard, and keep children away from its scissors-like mechanisms when operating. Likewise, remove any chest or trunk that has a heavy, hinged lid, or fasten it closed.

◆ **Secure electrical cords,** especially in traffic zones. Insert plastic safety caps into all open electrical receptacles. Teach children to stay away from electrical cords and outlets.

◆ **Install screens and safety rails** by fireplaces and on radiators to prevent burns. Keep kids away from wood stoves and space heaters, or avoid using them while small children are present.

◆ **Keep toddler's toys** on reachable shelves, or else out of sight. Make sure a toy chest has a safety lid. Teach kids not to climb inside furnishings.

◆ **Use protectors** (below) to cover sharp corners on tables and other furniture that children might bump into.

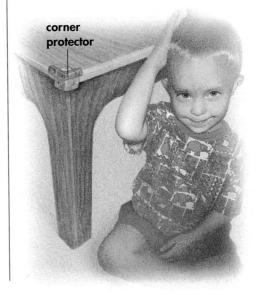

corner
protector

◆ **Falls are a leading cause of injuries** in children. Don't allow kids unsupervised access to balconies, porches, or windows. Pull climbable furniture away from windows.

◆ **A baby's crib** should meet safety regulations. Slats should be no more than 2⅜ inches apart so a newborn's head can't get wedged between, and the mattress should fit snugly. Stop using a crib when the child can climb over its rails.

◆ **Secure drapery cords** out of the reach of children. Don't place a crib or young child's bed within reach of these or within reach of electrical cords, outlets, lamps, wall mirrors, or pictures.

Stairs

Falls on stairs are a leading cause of injuries in children. A few precautions can reduce the dangers significantly.

◆ **Use safety gates** (below) to keep small children away from stairs. Use only gates that meet current safety standards; older accordion-style gates can trap a child's arms, legs, or head.

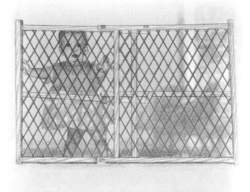

◆ **Balusters should be close together** to keep children and pets from falling through or getting their heads stuck. If balusters are more than 4 inches apart, install a barrier while your kids are young. Be sure the railing is sturdy, and discourage even supervised sliding down the banister, since a youngster is pretty sure to then try it on his or her own in your absence.

◆ **Wooden stairs and socks** or slippers make a slippery combination. Carpeted stairs are safer, especially if they have no raised metal edges for the child to trip over. Keep stairs and landings free of clutter.

Bathroom

Never leave a baby or young child alone in the tub. A toddler can drown in an inch of water. And don't leave water in an unattended tub. Use this checklist to cut down on other risks.

◆ **Purchase a soft cover** for the bathtub spout (right) to protect kids from painful collisions with the tub spout.

◆ **Keep hair dryers** and other electrical appliances unplugged, out of reach, and away from sinks and bathtubs to prevent burns and electrocution.

◆ **Use tub mats** to prevent slipping. Nonslip strips and appliques often are too widely spaced to protect children.

inflatable spout cover

◆ **Adjust water heater temperature** down to between 120° and 130°F— hot enough for an adult shower, but not so hot that it could scald a child. Make it a habit to turn faucets off tightly so they're not easy for children to turn on.

◆ **Keep cologne,** makeup, bubble bath, and other hazardous products in a closed cabinet, out of reach and sight.

SAFETY FOR OLDER FAMILY MEMBERS

Older folks have some heightened risks around the house, mostly from falls, which can have devastating effects on their brittle bones. Here are some basic prevention tips.

◆ **Brighten dark stairways** and hallways with better lighting and brighter bulbs, and install secure handrails on one or both sides of stairs.

◆ **Install non-skid bath mats** and grab bars in bathtubs and showers.

◆ **Put low-voltage night lights** in bedrooms, hallways, bathrooms and any other place traveled late at night.

◆ **Secure rugs firmly** with underlayment or self-adhesive gripper strips, and remove small throw rugs entirely.

◆ **Provide a one-step safety stool** for reaching out-of-the-way shelves and cabinets.

◆ **Clean and dry floor spills** and slippery surfaces in kitchen, bath, laundry, and garage before they are walked on.

◆ **Get into the habit of sitting for a moment** before getting out of bed; rising abruptly can cause dizziness. Avoid sitting in low chairs to reduce strains on aging joints and muscles.

EXTINGUISHER TYPES

Portable fire extinguishers are labeled for the type of fire they are intended to extinguish (see below). Class A extinguishers are filled with pressurized water and quench fires involving ordinary combustibles such as wood, cloth, paper, rubber, and many plastics. Class B extinguishers handle fires fueled by flammable liquids such as gasoline, oil, grease, oil-based paint, solvents, and flammable gas; they are filled with powdered sodium bicarbonate or wet foam to suffocate flames. Class C units are for fires involving energized electrical equipment, including wiring and appliances; they contain nonconductive dry chemicals or gas.

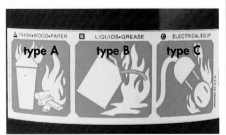

Many household fire extinguishers are multipurpose. ABC units can be used on any kind of fire, but either a B or BC extinguisher is recommended for kitchens. Fire extinguishers are also rated according to force. The higher the "ULC" number on an extinguisher, the more extinguishing agent it contains, the longer it can operate when discharged, and the larger the fire it can handle. Often there is a different rating for different types of fire. A rating of 1 for A fires and 10 for B and C fires will handle most minor fires. Large extinguishers are the safest choice, but only if you and other family members can wield the greater heft comfortably.

◆ **For better traction** on stairs and bare floors, wear supportive low-heeled rubber-soled shoes or slippers, rather than socks or slippers with fabric soles.

◆ **Attach electrical cords** to baseboards with ready-made plastic clips.

FIRE SAFETY

Just as important as a good homeowner's insurance policy are a sensible plan for dealing with fires should they occur, and having the right tools at hand for minimizing damage.

Fire extinguisher primer

Used properly, a portable fire extinguisher can save lives and property by putting out a small fire or containing it until the fire department arrives. Keep an extinguisher on every level of your house. Locate them in plain view, above the reach of children, near an escape route, and away from stoves and heating appliances, where fires are most likely to begin. Extinguishers come in several sizes and classes (see box, left). Be sure to have the appropriate class and size for each location, and know how to operate them.

Maintaining fire extinguishers

Every fire extinguisher ought to be checked monthly to make sure that it is under full pressure (the gauge will tell you), that the nozzle is open, and that the pin that keeps it from discharging inadvertently is in place. Disposable fire extinguishers must be replaced after use or if they lose their pressure due to age. Rechargeable models need to be serviced periodically, even without use. Read the maintenance manual, or ask your dealer for guidance.

SMOKE DETECTORS

Smoke detectors alert you to both smoldering and burning fires by sensing abnormal amounts of smoke or invisible combustion gases in the air. The majority of fire-associated deaths are due to suffocation rather than burns, so detectors are among the best forms of life protection you can buy.

Choosing a smoke detector

Smoke detectors use one of two proven technologies. A photoelectric detector sounds an alarm when its internal light beam is obscured by smoke, steam, or dust. An ionization detector senses invisible ions or charged particles created by fire, even in the absence of smoke. Both are excellent, though the ion detector is more selective.

Battery-operated smoke detectors are easy to install yourself, but AC-powered detectors are wired into your home's electrical system and should be installed by an electrician. Be sure they have battery backup so they will work during a blackout or an electrical fire that shuts off power in your house.

Purchase smoke detectors displaying a label from Underwriters Laboratories of Canada (ULC) and/or the Canadian Standards Association (CSA). Make sure the siren is loud enough to awaken the soundest sleeper in your home.

Where to install

Place at least one detector on every level of your home and outside each

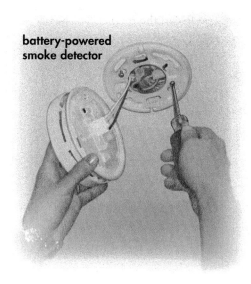

battery-powered
smoke detector

sleeping area. If fans or air conditioners might drown out the sound of a smoke detector, install them in bedrooms as well. Consider installing smoke detectors in the utility room and garage.

Install a ceiling-mounted detector (above) near the middle of a room or hallway. Place it at least 3 feet away from air-supply registers, which could pull smoke away from the detector. Also avoid corners, where air doesn't circulate well.

In the kitchen, install a smoke detector away from cooktops and ovens to prevent frequent false alarms. In basements, install a smoke detector close to the stairway but not at the top; there may be dead air space in front of the closed door, where smoke will rarely reach. Avoid placing a smoke detector close to the furnace exhaust as well.

Maintaining smoke detectors

Fire inspectors report that in a large number of residential fire deaths, a detector was in place but failed to operate, because either the battery was dead or the detector had been deliberately disconnected. Be sure you and your home don't fall into this tragic trap.

Most smoke detectors chirp periodically when batteries are low to remind owners that it's time to replace them. Following the manufacturer's instructions, check them once a month even if you hear no noise. For most, you only need to press a button (use a broom handle for ceiling units). Replace batteries at least once a year and always use fresh batteries. Develop a testing routine—for instance, check detectors on the first day of each month. Make it a tradition to replace your smoke detectors' batteries at the beginning of each calendar year, or perhaps when you turn back your clocks in fall at the end of Daylight Savings Time.

Use a vacuum cleaner to clear dust and cobwebs from the face and grillwork of smoke detectors once a month, when you check the condition of the batteries. Finally, it is prudent to replace smoke detector units that are more than 10 years old.

FIRE PREVENTION

Fires have many causes, including faulty wiring, careless use of electrical or gas appliances, children playing with matches and other unsafe materials, careless smoking and cooking habits, a defective furnace, appliances and supply lines, and improperly stored flammable substances. Most preventive measures require only a modest investment of time.

SAFETY SMART

PREVENTING ELECTRICAL FIRES

Here are steps you can take to decrease your chances of electrical fire:

◆ **Never overload** an electrical receptacle with extension cords or three-way adapters. If you need to plug a lot of things into a single receptacle, use a power strip.

◆ **Never run electrical cords** under carpets or rugs, over nails, in traffic areas, or where there is chance of wear.

◆ **Don't misuse extension cords.** Never use a standard household extension cord for a major appliance or a heat-producing appliance; instead use a heavy-duty appliance cord that can carry the load.

◆ **When purchasing** any electrical device, choose only one with the Underwriters Laboratories of Canada (ULC) or Canadian Standards Association (CSA) rating.

◆ **Don't pull on an electrical cord** to unplug it. Grasp the plug firmly and pull out straight so you don't bend the prongs.

◆ **Replace any cord or plug** that is cracked or discolored or feels hot to the touch when in use. If the original wire or plug is polarized (one prong is wider than the other), or if it has a third grounding prong, replace it with similar equipment.

◆ **Call an electrician** if your lights flicker and your appliances run sluggishly, or if you have a fuse that repeatedly blows or a circuit breaker that trips often. These are signs that the system is overloaded.

◆ **Don't use a bulb** with more wattage than a lamp or fixture is rated to accommodate, or the unit will overheat.

Fires and children

Buy child-resistant lighters, and keep matches and lighters where kids can't see them or reach them, preferably in a locked cabinet. Teach your children to avoid playing with fire and to give any matches they find to adults. Warn them against covering light bulbs with paper or cloth. Occasional supervised opportunities to light and extinguish candles can satisfy their curiosity in a safe way.

Fireplaces and supplemental heaters

Use fireplace screens to keep sparks from igniting carpets and furniture. Hire a qualified chimney sweep yearly to clean and check your flue for cracks, leaves, and birds' and wasps' nests.

Check building and fire codes before you purchase and install supplemental heating equipment such as a wood stove or a space heater. Purchase only ULC- or CSA-tested equipment, and use only the fuel recommended by the manufacturer. Make sure the unit you buy can't be tipped easily and will shut off automatically if it is tipped over. Locate the unit at least 3 feet away from a wall or anything else that can burn. Turn off all portable heaters while you're sleeping or away from home. See page 63 for more information on fireplace safety; see page 69 for more on space heaters.

Furnace safety

Have a professional clean and check your furnace at the beginning of each heating season. Inadequate servicing is the cause of most furnace fires. Change filters regularly to avoid overheating.

Flammable substances

Solvent-soaked rags, if stored in a warm place, can actually burst into flames by themselves. Dry out all rags that have been used with oil-based paints, turpentine and paint thinner, and other petroleum-based solvents, and either dispose of or store them in containers with tight-fitting lids.

Store burnable trash in metal cans with lids, away from heat sources such as water heaters, space heaters, stoves, and furnaces. Keep matches away from heat, preferably in closed containers.

"Safe" smoking habits

Careless smoking is a major cause of fires and fire-related deaths. Don't let anyone smoke when they're drowsy or when they're drinking alcohol alone or when they're in bed. Provide smokers with large, deep, non-tipping ashtrays that are placed on hard, flat surfaces rather than on upholstered furniture. Before emptying ashtrays, soak the butts with water. Empty them only into metal trash cans that don't contain any waste paper. Better yet, have a "No Smoking" policy in your home.

Holiday fire prevention

Holidays, especially Christmas and Hanukkah, bring an increased risk of residential fires. If you use lighted candles, keep them a safe distance from flammable materials, and warn children of their dangers. Place a Christmas tree well away from a fireplace or an exit. In decorating, use ULC- or CSA-rated lights, and check them annually for frayed wires. Keep wrappings and gifts

HOME FIRE SPRINKLERS

Automatic fire sprinklers used along with working smoke detectors greatly increase the chances of surviving a fire.

◆ **Sprinklers are relatively inexpensive** and they enhance property value while lowering insurance rates. Consider installing them if you are building, buying, or remodeling a house.

◆ **New technology** allows fire sprinklers to be connected to your standard home plumbing system. Individual sprinkler heads are activated only where fire strikes. Contact your local fire department or a vendor for more information.

away from tree lights. If using a real evergreen tree, keep it watered well. Always turn off holiday lights overnight and, on a Christmas tree, whenever it will be left unattended.

Kitchen fire prevention

The most dangerous room in the house in terms of fires is the kitchen, followed by the laundry room. Here are some ways to reduce risks in these locations.

◆ **Heat oil in pans slowly** and with care—hot grease can self-ignite. Clean grease-catching stove vents and wall fans regularly to avoid starting fires.

◆ **Keep pot holders,** dish towels, and other flammable items well away from cooktops. Don't let sleeves or clothing dangle near burners.

◆ **Don't leave the kitchen** when the range is turned on. It's too easy to get caught up in a conversation or in another project and forget about it. If the doorbell rings, remove pans from the cooktop before answering it. Set the oven timer when using the oven.

Dryer vent

Check the exterior vent of your clothes dryer periodically for lint buildup, and clean it out. If it is a recurring problem, have a professional check the venting. If your dryer is not working efficiently even after removing this lint, have the problem checked immediately: There may be hidden blockage, which is a fire hazard.

INDOOR AIR QUALITY

Modern homes are tightly sealed and well insulated for energy-efficiency. The one drawback is that any pollutants in the home will have a hard time escaping. The main sources of concern are carbon monoxide; tobacco smoke; biological pollutants, such as mold and dust mites; asbestos; radon; lead; and formaldehyde. It doesn't take much effort to check for these problems; the solutions are usually not very expensive. A resource book is *The Clean Air Guide, How to Identify and Correct Indoor Air Problems in Your Home,* published by Canada Mortgage and Housing Corporation. To order this CMHC guide, phone 1-800-668-2542.

Carbon monoxide

Carbon monoxide (CO) poisoning occurs when a person has inhaled this lethal gas. It may get into the house atmosphere from an improperly vented furnace or chimney, or a gas hot water heater with a corroded or improperly installed vent pipe. Other potential sources are a barbecue grill operated in an enclosed space, or a car left running in a closed garage. While CO is not explosive, it kills hundreds of North Americans yearly through asphyxiation and sends thousands more to hospital emergency rooms for treatment. It's important to recognize the symptoms of CO poisoning and learn to protect yourself and your family.

◆ **CO is colorless and odorless,** so you are not likely to notice its presence if there is a leak in your home or if auto exhaust penetrates from the garage. But depending on the concentration of carbon monoxide in the air, the exposure time, how susceptible you are, and how heavily you breathe while you're exposed, you'll experience some or all of the following symptoms: fatigue, nausea and vomiting, dizziness and weakness, headache, blurred vision, and loss of coordination.

◆ **If you suspect a leak** and you can identify the source, turn the source off immediately or call your gas company or a repair service for help. Meanwhile, open windows and doors to clear the air. If inspection indicates unacceptable levels of CO, its source should be identified and repairs made to the unit or its venting system.

◆ **Good heating system maintenance** reduces the chances of carbon monoxide poisoning. Follow recommended guidelines for regularly cleaning and inspecting any furnaces (pp.67–77), wood stoves (p.65), space heaters (pp.69, 78), chimneys (p.64), and other CO-producing equipment.

◆ **Install CO detectors** in the furnace room, near the fireplace, and close by the sleeping areas. Look for detectors approved by Underwriters Laboratories of Canada (ULC) or the Canadian Standards Association (CSA). The best detectors are capable of reading low levels of CO, so you'll know about a problem before it becomes serious.

Another good feature to look for is "peak-level memory," which records and saves high-level readings even after they decline; this is important where CO levels fluctuate depending upon the amount of use the faulty equipment gets. Like smoke detectors, CO detectors work only if installed properly and equipped with live batteries; so follow the recommendations given on page 343 for regular testing and replacement of smoke detectors.

Asbestos

Asbestos is a mineral fiber that was widely used in home construction before the late 1970s, when it was banned for most household purposes. When inhaled, microscopic asbestos fibers have been shown to be a health risk, capable of causing lung cancer, cancer of the abdominal linings, or chronic respiratory illness. The danger of such construction-material fibers becoming airborne and being inhaled, however, is considered very low so long as the materials are in good condition and are not disturbed.

Here are some common locations for asbestos in the home:

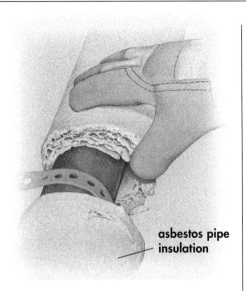

asbestos pipe insulation

◆ **If you have old pipes** or a furnace wrapped with a cloth-covered insulation material that looks like thick cardboard and is light in color (above), it probably is asbestos.

◆ **If you have textured paint** on your ceiling or walls and your house was built or painted before the late 1970s, it may contain asbestos fibers. Some older patching materials and joint compounds also contained asbestos.

◆ **Older asphalt or vinyl tiles,** as well as vinyl sheet flooring, probably contain asbestos.

◆ **Fire-retardant surfaces,** such as sheets used to protect walls from heat, and door gaskets for wood stoves, often contain asbestos.

◆ **Vintage acoustical ceiling tiles** often contain asbestos fibers.

Treating asbestos

If you see something in your home that looks as though it may be asbestos and it is loose or cracked, the simplest solution is to take steps to ensure that it remains undisturbed. Wrap asbestos pipe insulation. Cover wall and ceiling materials with new drywall, wallpaper, or two coats of paint.

If, however, you are determined to remove it, call in an asbestos inspector to examine it and other parts of your house. (To find the name of an inspector, check in the Yellow Pages of the phone book under "Asbestos Abatement and Removal," or contact your provincial or local health department.) An inspector may remove pieces for testing. If asbestos is found, you will need to hire a specialist to transport the asbestos waste to a landfill site where it will be disposed of in a special area reserved for dangerous products.

RADON

Radon is a colorless, tasteless, and odorless gas released into the atmosphere from the natural radioactive decay of radium, an element found in nearly all soils. Because it is a gas, it seeps upward from the ground and migrates into homes through cracks, joints and other openings in foundations, slabs, and crawl spaces. Once inside, it can accumulate to become a health hazard if the house is not properly ventilated. Breathing high levels of radon over a long period is believed to increase the human risk of some types of cancer, including lung cancer.

Dealing with radon

If high levels of radon are reported in your area, purchase a radon-testing kit

GOOD TOOLS

TESTING FOR RADON

To test a home for radon, purchase an inexpensive do-it-yourself radon test kit, or hire a professional company. The most common radon test uses a small charcoal canister. Leave it open for a few days in your home, then send it to a lab for evaluation. A written report usually takes a few weeks. If the initial test reveals excessive levels of radon, have the company perform another test over a longer term to better assess your situation.

(above). Use it as instructed, and submit the results for lab analysis. If this indicates that you have a problem, start by sealing radon entry points, which are the same places that water tends to seep in. Caulk around pipes; patch cracks in basement floors; install a tight-fitting cover for a sump pump; and cover leaky basement walls with waterproof sealer. The next step is to increase your home's ventilation so as to expel radon gas to the outside.

If these measures do not reduce the radon level, call a professional, who may recommend installing a complex mechanical ventilation system. For more information about radon, contact your provincial health department.

LEAD

Lead sometimes leaches into drinking water, and it may be in the fumes emitted by various substances as they burn or melt. It may also appear in old paint, where it can chip or flake off into fine dust, causing brain retardation in children, and brain damage and chronic liver and kidney diseases in all ages.

Even at low levels, lead poisoning in children has been traced to permanent disabilities and behavioral problems. Although your house may be lead-free, your children can be exposed through dirt on playgrounds or along city streets. For peace of mind, you can have your children checked for lead exposure with a simple blood test.

Lead in paint

Most homes built before the mid-1970s have heavily leaded paint. Lead paint, even in good condition, is a problem in locations such as windows where the painted surfaces rub against each other. But any lead paint is now considered hazardous to young children.

Lead can be detected in paint using any of several types of tests. Testing kits are available in hardware stores, but their accuracy is questionable. For testing recommendations, contact your health department or the provincial branch of the Canada Mortgage and Housing Corporation.

Renovations that involve removing and disposing of lead paint should be done by a specialist wearing a ventilator mask and protective clothing. Look in the Yellow Pages of the phone book under "Lead Abatement and Removal" or "Environmental Consultants" for a certified lead-paint-removal contractor.

Lead in water

In many homes, the original copper pipes supplying water were soldered with a material containing lead; and occasionally, the pipes themselves may be lead. You can identify a lead pipe by pressing it with a knife or screwdriver: If you can make an indentation easily, the pipe is lead and should be replaced.

Some older cities still have lead pipes as part of their underground public water system. To deal with this problem, these cities add small amounts of corrosion-inhibiting chemicals to their water supply. These chemicals reduce to safe levels the lead leaching into the water. If you suspect that there is lead in your water, contact your local water department on how to have your water tested. One method of minimizing the amount of lead in your water is to install an under-sink filter that removes not only lead but also other impurities.

HOME SECURITY

There is no way to guarantee a burglar-proof house, but there are reasonable steps you can take to make your house less appealing to a potential intruder and to discourage an entry attempt.

Reducing "burglar appeal"

Burglars most often enter a house through an unlocked door or window, so develop a habit of locking entry points. Basement windows are popular with intruders because often they are easy to open and crawl through. If your garage is attached to the house, make sure the garage door is secure. In addition, take these precautions:

◆ **Make the house look occupied** even when it isn't. Burglars prefer to work in empty houses, so always make your house look like someone is home. Use timers to turn lights on and off. Do the same with the radio and TV, but vary the pattern to simulate something like normal use. A burglar staking out a house will suspect timers are turning on the appliances and lights if they go on the same time every day.

◆ **Make discovery difficult** by hiding valuables in unlikely locations. Burglars like to work fast, and they are well aware of where most people store jewelry and other valuables. Because so many people choose the refrigerator, try to be more original, or get a sturdy home safe (page 349).

Exterior doors for security

The first consideration is the sturdiness of the door and the hardware by which it is hung. It makes no sense to install quality locks if the entry doors are insubstantial. Solid-wood doors, at least 1¾ inches thick, offer reasonably good security. Better yet are metal or metal-clad doors. Some are handsome enough to satisfy even the most discriminating tastes. Be forewarned, however: If a door has glass insets, or if there are side light windows on either side of the doorframe, security is somewhat compromised. This is so because the glass permits the burglar to see inside and also because he may be able to break

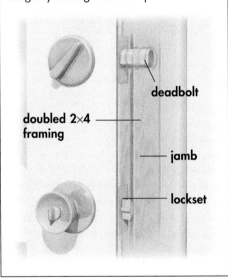

doubled 2×4 framing

deadbolt

jamb

lockset

DEADBOLT SECURITY

Deadbolt locks should be installed on all of your exterior doors. Deadbolts are typically placed above the lockset. If you choose to install one yourself and you have the tools, you'll find instructions and helpful templates to make it a fairly easy job. A good-quality deadbolt has a long, hardened-steel bolt that is especially difficult to cut through or pry loose. Heavy-duty 3-inch mounting screws on the jamb side of the door grip the framing, and a tough cylinder guard adds protection.

the glass and reach inside to unlock the door. So have the glass replaced with shatterproof plastic.

Locks

Four kinds of locks are commonly used on residential exterior doors: lockset, mortise lock, rim lock, and cylinder deadbolt lock. Often, they are used in combination for added security.

◆ **Standard locksets**—also called cylindrical or key-in-knob locks—are installed as a single unit in a single hole in the door. The least expensive choice, a standard lockset has the entire latching and security mechanism built into the doorknob. The outer knob has a key-operated cylinder, and the interior has either a pushbutton or a turn lever by which the latch and deadbolt are set and released. Unfortunately, this type of lock can be jimmied open with little effort. Or the entire outer knob can be sheared off with a heavy blow.

◆ **Mortise locks** are mounted inside a deep pocket cut into the door's edge. Pressing down a thumb lever on the exterior or turning the knob on either side actuates the spring-latch portion. The security lock portion consists of a separate deadbolt operated by a key from outside and a thumb lever inside. This makes for a sturdier combination, though it is in the nature of the mortise pocket that it creates a weak spot along the door's edge. So it's a good idea to protect the pocket area with a wraparound reinforcing plate made for this.

◆ **A rim lock** is often used as an auxiliary lock. It mounts on the inside of the door near the edge, usually about 6 inches below or above the doorknob, and it requires a second cross bore hole in the door. It consists of a surface-mounted hardened steel deadbolt assembly (a stile) on the inside of the door, a surface-mounted strike (also hardened steel) on the adjacent interior jamb, and an exterior cylinder key lock. The door is locked by turning the key

on the outside or the latch on the inside of the rimlock, an action that slides the vertical deadbolt through the eyes of the strike.

◆ **A cylindrical deadbolt lock** is installed in the same way as a cylindrical lockset. A double-keyed deadbolt requires the use of a key on the inside as well as on the outside. This prevents an intruder from breaking the window and reaching through to turn the knob. But a double-keyed lock can also slow the departure of residents if the key is not handy—which could lead to disaster during a fire. In many areas, fire codes prohibit the use of double-keyed deadbolts. It is best to use a single-keyed model, with a thumb turn on the inside.

◆ **Auxiliary locks** such as a crossbar and a brace offer extra security. The crossbar lock has several elements: a lock mounted on the inside center of the door, a pair of horizontal steel bars, and steel fittings to match on the adjacent door frames. The door locks by inserting a key from the outside or turning the knob on the inside, either action ratcheting the steel bars sideways to engage the fittings on the sides.

The brace lock, also known as a police lock, mounts on the inside of the door, above the conventional lockset. It consists of a lock unit, a heavy steel bar that runs downward at an angle from the lock, and a steel-lined pocket set in the floor. When in position, the police lock is particularly resistant to break-ins with pry bars. Generally unattractive to look at and presenting something of an obstacle to traffic in a small front hall, the bar portion can be removed and set aside during the day if a high level of security is not necessary.

Security storm doors

If you like to keep doors open in summer when you are at home but are concerned about the resulting breach of security, consider having heavy-duty security storm-screen doors installed. These are equipped with deadbolt locks and decorative wrought-iron grillwork that let you enjoy breezes while keeping intruders away.

Sliding-door security

A favored point of entry for burglars is the sliding glass door. Being glass, it is eminently breakable by the determined intruder. And the slider can be lifted out of its tracks and removed by someone with strong arms. While you can't prevent a break-in, you can foil door removal by inserting metal spacers or protruding screws in the top grooves of the moving door's tracks. Drive screws partway so they do not engage the top of the door but fill the space. To prevent the door from being forced sideways, lay a length of pipe or a cutoff broom handle to fit between the frame and the jamb, or buy a lock-and-pin set made just for sliders.

Basement security

Basements are the most vulnerable entry point in a house. Their windows usually are small, are of lesser quality, and are easy to break or force open. Metal security grates are available for basement windows, but you can block intruders by putting metal bars across the windows. Buy bars that are made of ¼-inch-thick steel. Purchase burglar-bar units that fit your windows—they are often adjustable to allow for a variety of sizes—or simply buy bars and space them out about 6 inches apart. Attach them with long screws driven into framing members, or with long masonry screws. If the bars mount on the outside, be sure that you use special security screws that are not easily removed.

Investigate the tightness of your basement door, and be sure it provides as good protection as your conventional doors do. Look around the perimeter of the house. If potential break-in areas are screened by trees and shrubs, you may be creating a staging area for a burglar to work unnoticed. Consider trimming back trees and shrubs.

Choosing a safe

For a modest price, you can own a small container that will keep valuable papers and photos secure from damage during a fire. For more money, you can make it very difficult for a thief to gain access to jewelry and other valuables.

◆ **A safe box** carries a minimum class-C fire rating, which means it will keep papers from harm during a fire that reaches 1,700°F—hotter than the average house fire—for an hour. For extra protection, choose a safe rated B or A.

◆ **A lightweight wall safe** can be built into your house's framing. Hire a safe company to do this. A safe rated TL is

Q U I C K   F I X

SECURING YOUR HOUSE DURING VACATION

Even without security devices, you can quickly secure your home. The main object here is to make it look as though you are still at home. Here are a few tips:

◆ **Use timers,** which you can buy at hardware stores and home centers, to turn lights on and off at normal intervals (see page 347). Plug-in timers, as the name implies, go between the lamp and the receptacle; security timers are wired into your electrical system and can turn overhead lights or appliances on and off up to 24 times a day.

◆ **Keep a car parked** in the driveway.

◆ **Arrange for the lawn** to be mowed regularly, as often as you normally do it.

◆ **Stop mail and newspaper** deliveries, or have a friend retrieve them daily.

◆ **Leave the regular recording** on your answering machine. It should never include vacation information.

◆ **Contact the police** to alert them of your absence. They may be willing to drive by your house from time to time.

resistant to the prybar and drilling tools that thieves use. For greater protection, get a safe rated TR (resistant to torches) or TX (resistant to explosives).

◆ **A combination safe** offers protection against burglary and fire. This safe, weighting up to 500 pounds, can be bolted to a basement or closet floor.

SAFETY SMART

SECURING WINDOWS

Most new windows are equipped with sturdy locks, but older windows may have less reliable ones. A variety of inexpensive window locks are available at home centers and hardware stores. Most are inexpensive and can be easily installed with a hand drill and a screwdriver.

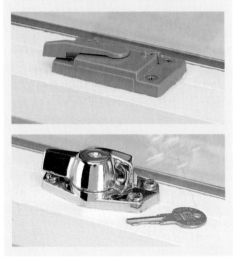

Security alarm systems

Simple home alarm systems have sensors around windows and doors that trigger an alarm when an intruder tries to enter the house. A keypad allows you to turn the system on and off. More sophisticated systems also employ pressure-sensitive pads that trip the alarm when someone walks on them, and volumetric sensors that detect the presence of an intruder by monitoring a room's atmosphere.

The alarm may be a light or siren or both, to scare off a potential burglar while alerting occupants and neighbors. Other systems send a phone alarm to police or to a private service that then alerts authorities. In a "hard-wired" system, the control panel uses regular household electrical current. Most systems that use a monitoring service are hard-wired and installed by professionals. In addition to the cost of installation, there is usually a monthly fee.

Security lighting

Well-designed exterior lighting helps deter prowlers and makes it safer for occupants to find their way home in the dark. Light the corners of the house and the surrounding shrubbery, showcasing the landscaping while making it hard for burglars to hide. Much of this can be done with energy-efficient low-voltage lighting (pp.305–306).

Motion-detector floodlights are a practical choice. They switch on when movement is detected at night but remain off otherwise. They should be installed out of reach of a potential intruder, with the bulbs directed straight down from the eaves or toward the house. See page 306 for instructions on adjusting these.

Photoelectric lights are another security light option. These are simple units that can be screwed into standard light sockets; they automatically turn on at dusk and off at dawn.

What to do after a burglary

If you come home to find that your house has been entered, leave immediately because the intruder could still be inside. Go to a nearby phone and call 911. Wait for police to arrive before going back inside. To help police capture the thief—and perhaps recover stolen property—don't touch anything in the house, including doorknobs or the phone. The culprit may have left fingerprints or used the phone. Insist that the police dust for fingerprints.

You'll be at an advantage if you have routinely updated an inventory of possessions, including the serial numbers of common theft items such as stereos and cameras. A detailed description of jewelry also helps. This will help in filing police reports and insurance claims.

GOOD SOLUTIONS

WIRELESS WONDER

A simple wireless alarm system uses independent sensors that adhere to window glass and that set off an alarm if a break-in is attempted. Others rely on radio transmitters to send a signal to the receiver, which sets off the alarm. Available at electronics stores and home centers, they can be easily installed by a homeowner.

POISONINGS AND ANIMAL BITES

Armed with accurate information about the best first-aid options,
you can act calmly and rationally when faced with an emergency.

Accidental poisonings and bites from animals are among the most common medical emergencies in the home. Make your family safer by knowing beforehand what to do.

POISONING

Readiness for an accidental poisoning comes down to three things: Post the phone number of the Poison Control Center on or by your phone, act quickly and calmly, and keep a supply of ipecac on hand.

Ipecac is a safe and effective over-the-counter drug in concentrated syrup form. A vomit-inducer, it is often used as a means of forcing ingested poisons out of the system before they are absorbed into the blood. So keep some on hand. However, there are instances where vomiting can actually worsen the problem. The Poison Control expert will ask you to identify the poison involved, if possible, before making a treatment recommendation.

You do not want to induce vomiting if the swallowed substance is a petroleum product (benzene, kerosene, gasoline, or turpentine), nor should you use ipecac if a caustic substance, such as cleaning fluid, liquid furniture polish, insect repellent, ammonia, bleach, lye, or drain cleaner is involved. Ipecac is also contraindicated if the person is having a convulsion.

Kids and poisons

Accidental poisoning occurs primarily in children under age five. They are curious and unaware of danger, and often use their sense of taste to investigate common but toxic household products. Here are some tips to prevent such a tragedy. Insist that every mature member of the family follow these practices, and teach youngsters from an early age to take seriously the dangers of accidental poisoning.

◆ **Purchase known poisons** only in containers with child-resistant lids. Keep them in locked cabinets, out of the sight and reach of children.

◆ **Assume that ordinary products** used in household cleaning, as well as cosmetics and beauty products, are toxic, too. Handle them with care, and any time you are not using them, put them well out of reach.

◆ **Never leave medicines or vitamins** on a bedside or kitchen table or in a purse. Don't take medicines while small children are watching, because they may try to imitate your action later.

◆ **Treat tobacco and alcohol** as dangerous. Do not leave them where young children can find them.

◆ **Ask overnight guests** to store their medications in a locked place, such as a chest in your guest bedroom.

◆ **Get rid of any poisonous plants.** Examples include oleander, caladium, dieffenbachia, elephant ears, monstera, philodendron, and English ivy. Keep nonpoisonous plants out of reach of small children and pets; they may contain irritants.

◆ **Lock the basement and garage** and keep them off-limits to young children. To be doubly safe, lock up toxic chemicals, including antifreeze and garden chemicals and pesticides.

Poisons and pets

Like small children, animals frequently taste what they find. Use the recommendations given above for children to safeguard the pets in your household. Also be aware of the following additional poisoning hazards:

◆ **If you treat your lawn** for weeds and other pests, leave one area untreated, and confine your dog to that spot until the treatment dissolves into the soil following rain or a watering.

◆ **Pesticides** for ants, roaches, and rodents are attractive to pets. If you must use them, make a controlled application where your pet won't be able to reach, spraying deep into crevices and along joints under cabinets. Avoid poisons in boxes, which pets may try to chew.

◆ **Use garden chemicals with care.** Read caution labels before you buy. Always store garden chemicals out of your dog's reach. Look for pyrethrum, rotenone, diatomaceous earth, and *Bacillus thuringiensis* (packaged as "organic garden spray" or "organic insect liquid killer").

◆ **Car antifreeze** tastes good to dogs and cats but usually is fatal. Store it in sturdy, closed containers. Wipe up any spills, and hose the area thoroughly.

◆ **Chemicals to remove snow** and ice from driveways and walkways often end up on your pet's paws. Read the labels, and purchase products that are safe for both vegetation and animals.

◆ **If your pet is vomiting,** having trouble breathing, shivering, convulsing, or bleeding for no apparent reason, it may have been poisoned. Call your vet.

ANIMAL BITES

Animal bites and scratches can lead to injury, infection, and even death. Here are some wise precautions:

◆ **Stay away from an unfamiliar dog** unless the owner is present. Enter a home where a dog lives only if someone who can control it is home. Be wary of dogs raised in homes where there are no children when introducing a child.

◆ **A dog is more likely to bite** when it is in pain, is hungry, is frightened, or is overexcited. Keep your dog or cat healthy with proper nutrition, regular veterinary checkups, and rabies shots. Teach children to avoid any dog or cat that's sick or frightened.

◆ **Never leave a baby or toddler alone** with a pet. Even a friendly animal may mistake a small human for a playmate and engage in rough play. Small children may unintentionally provoke a pet by pulling a tail or grabbing an ear.

◆ **Stay away from an animal** when it is eating or sleeping. Likewise, avoid a dog that is growling, baring its teeth, or holding its head and tail low.

◆ **Don't try to separate** animals that are fighting or mating. If you must interfere, use a long stick, or squirt with the full force of a garden hose.

◆ **Never attempt to feed** a wild animal by hand, however friendly and tame it may seem. If you see an animal behaving strangely—a nocturnal animal out in full daylight, or one that is wobbling strangely—suspect rabies and get away quickly. Report the sighting to the police or your local wildlife center.

◆ **If you are confronted** by a hostile animal, don't look it in the eye. Animals instinctively interpret this as a threatening gesture. Stand still, or back away slowly. Talk in a friendly, soothing voice. If you're holding food, toss it toward the animal immediately.

Treating an animal bite

If the wound is severe, go to a hospital emergency room or call 911 immediately. Even if the bite seems minor, it's generally a good idea to see a doctor promptly to avoid the chance of infection. If you are aiding another person, remain calm and reassuring while you check for bleeding. As in any situation where you are administering first aid for open wounds, protect yourself and others by wearing sterile gloves if you have them. If not, put several layers of dressings or a layer of plastic wrap between you and the wound. Always wash your hands thoroughly before and after you give first aid.

If the bite wound is not bleeding severely, wash it well for at least five minutes with mild soap and running water. Then apply a bandage. If the bite is actively bleeding, do not attempt to clean it. Elevate the wound so that it is higher than the victim's heart, to reduce pressure and to slow bleeding. If the wound is gaping, press the edges together; lay several layers of dressing, preferably sterile bandages, on the wound, then press firmly on the dressing with one hand.

If blood soaks through the dressing, do not remove it. Apply another layer on top and keep pressing. If bleeding continues, press harder, using both hands. Continue to apply direct pressure until you get medical help or until the bleeding stops.

The rabies risk

Rabies is a rare but fatal infection in humans. The virus is transmitted by the bite of some animals, especially unvaccinated dogs and cats, skunks, raccoons, foxes, and bats. There is no cure for rabies once symptoms develop, but if immunization is given within two days of a bite, rabies can almost always be prevented. If you live where rabies is rampant, your doctor may recommend regular preventive vaccinations.

If you are attacked by an animal and you can't immediately find out whether it has been vaccinated for rabies, contact the police or animal control authorities. When in doubt, the animal will be examined for rabies. If the animal is found to be diseased, the bite victim will be treated accordingly.

Spider bites

Nearly all spiders produce venom; but only a few are harmful to humans, and bites from these are rarely fatal. The principal villains are black widow and brown recluse species; they may strike indoors or out. The black widow spider is identified by a hourglass-shaped red marking on its back. If bitten by one, apply an ice pack and head for a hospital. The usual treatment is medication to ease pain and muscle cramps.

The bite of a brown recluse spider may not produce symptoms until days after the bite occurs—a blistering lesion, perhaps accompanied by a rash, fever, and nausea. If you have any of these symptoms, consult a doctor.

Fleas

Flea infestations are more an annoyance than a hazard. They occur most often where pets live, and they may become a "crisis" after a pet host leaves, when the fleas have no place to feed but on humans. Treat rugs, upholstered furniture, and drapes with a flea-killing insecticide, and vacuum thoroughly to remove flea eggs, discarding the vacuum bag in an outdoor garbage can. To prevent attacks, treat pets for fleas regularly. New products available from your veterinarian are very successful.

Snake bites

In Canada, snake bites are uncommon. The only poisonous Canadian snakes are pit vipers—the massasauga, prairie and timber rattlesnakes—that you should learn to recognize if you live near or travel to their habitats.

If someone is bitten, keep the victim calm and in a sitting or lying position. Raise the involved limb and immobilize it; pack it with ice, if possible, to reduce the spread of venom. Apply a sterile bandage to the wound and seek medical help, describing the snake, if you can. Modern treatments for snake bites, administered promptly, are very successful and long-term effects, rare.

Pet containment

One way to protect dogs from danger—and trouble—is by means of a pet-containment system, which you can install yourself. It consists of a wire that's buried in a shallow slit around the perimeter of the yard, a radio transmitter that plugs into a standard electric outlet, and a receiver collar. As the dog approaches the invisible boundary, a radio signal alerts it that it is reaching its limits. If it proceeds closer, the collar delivers a slight shock. With training, most dogs learn to stay within boundaries, and the chances of their running into traffic or menacing the neighbors are greatly reduced.

HOUSEHOLD EMERGENCIES AND DISASTERS

Prepare for nature's big punches by having the right tools on hand and by learning techniques that can save the house and its occupants.

You may never experience a house fire or a tornado; but preparing for them, as well as for routine power failures, does not take a lot of effort. And being ready brings peace of mind. As a minimum, have a basic disaster kit on hand and keep its contents up to date (p.358).

POWER FAILURES

If you have reason to anticipate a power outage, lay in adequate food supplies and fill your car's gas tank, since gas station pumps will not be able to dispense gasoline without power. If you own a home generator, check the motor's operation and supply of spare fuel. Do the same with a portable stove if you have one. Fill bathtubs with clean water, as water service may be interrupted. Get fresh batteries for the portable radio. Have at least one phone that is not cordless; a cordless phone depends on a radio transmitter that is powered by electricity and consequently is useless in an outage.

If you plan to use kerosene lamps or lanterns, add lamp oil and wicks to your list. Locate them strategically throughout the house. Do the same with candles, candle holders, and chimneys. Make sure candles are placed in the open, away from draperies, and on noncombustible surfaces.

Freeze jugs of water. Place one in the refrigerator; leave others in the freezer to extend refrigeration. Remove fresh food for today and something still frozen for tomorrow. Then leave the refrigerator and freezer closed. Sealed off, an unpowered freezer can keep food frozen up to 48 hours (p.133).

When the power goes off, unplug the refrigerator, air conditioners, computers, TVs, stereos, answering machines, and other electrical appliances. Otherwise, when electricity is restored, a sudden and simultaneous power demand by all this equipment could overload one or more circuit breakers or fuses and put you in the dark again.

A HOUSEHOLD FIRE ESCAPE PLAN

To increase your family's chances of surviving a fire, develop an escape plan.

◆ **Draw a floor plan** of your home, and mark all possible escape routes. Every room should have at least two exits (a window large enough for an adult to fit through is fine, but make sure windows are easy to open and that your kids know how to open them). If you live in an apartment building, don't count elevators as part of your escape route, because they won't operate in a fire; use stairs instead.

◆ **Decide where everyone will meet** outside the house in the event of a fire. That way, you'll know that everyone is safe.

◆ **Practice evacuating** your home blindfolded. During a fire, smoke may make it impossible to see. Practice staying low to the floor when escaping.

◆ **Learn to stop, drop to the ground, and roll** to put out clothing that catches fire.

◆ **Purchase approved escape ladders** for rooms on upper floors. Practice using them. Ladders may not be usable by elderly family members or those with handicaps. (A first-floor bedroom is a much better idea for them.)

GAS LEAKS

A gas leak from a kitchen stove, oven, wall heater unit, furnace, boiler, or another gas-operated unit can cause an explosion, start a sudden fire, or even cause asphyxiation. You must act quickly and prudently, as follows:

◆ **Get everyone out of the house** as calmly and safely as possible. Don't try to find the source of the gas odor or wait to see whether it gets worse.

◆ **Don't use the telephone,** turn on lights, or make other electrical connections inside the house: It could cause a deadly spark. Go to another location immediately, call the utility company, and report the possible emergency.

◆ **Turn off the main gas line** to the house from the outside only if you can do so quickly (see pages 67, 70).

HOUSEHOLD FIRES

Every household should have a fire-safety plan in place virtually from the moment the occupants move in. And members should review the plan periodically to be sure that everyone knows his or her role and that no part of the plan needs updating—due to a change in the mobility of a family member, for example. Formal fire drills, while they may seem excessive, are really a very good practice. Here are some basic ways of preparing everyone in your house for a fire emergency:

◆ **Plan an escape route** from every room in the house (see "A Household Fire Escape Plan" at left).

◆ **Make it a family routine** to keep halls and stairways free of obstacles so that escape routes are clear.

◆ **Sleep with bedroom doors closed.** In the event of fire, the door helps to retard smoke and heat. If the fire detector alarm or smoke detector should sound, feel the bottom of the door.

Do not open it if it is hot. Stuff towels, blankets, or rugs under the door, then open a window and make your escape.

◆ **If the door is not hot,** open it slowly, with your face turned away; leave the room; and close the door behind you to prevent backdraft. Tie a wet rag around your nose and mouth if you have a water source, and take short breaths. Because smoke and fire rise, stay low as you move toward an exit.

◆ **Teach youngsters** how to make an escape rather than hiding under a bed or in a closet, as their instinct tells them to do. Put an adult in charge of helping any elderly member or young child to escape.

◆ **Do not pause to dress** or gather precious belongings. Do not search for a hiding pet. Your goal must be to get out as quickly and safely as possible.

◆ **If you are trapped** on an upstairs level, stuff damp sheets or curtains in the heating and air ducts as well as under the door to block smoke. Use a phone to call for help, or use a flashlight or brightly colored cloth to signal out the window. And yell for help. If necessary, open a window slightly at the top to let smoke out or at the bottom to let fresh air in. Don't break the window—you may need to shut it if there's smoke outside or to prevent outside air from feeding the fire.

◆ **If you must jump,** climb out and try to get a grip on a windowsill first, lower yourself, and then let go. Bend your knees to make the landing easier on your body.

TROUBLE SHOOTER

HANDLING COMMON HOUSEHOLD FIRES

Be prepared to handle the small emergencies that can quickly escalate. Different types of fires require a different response. Know when to stop fighting the fire and get out of the house.

Type of Fire	What to Do
Grease	Turn off the burner. If the fire is in a pan, quickly slide a lid over the pan to smother flames. Or use a B-type extinguisher, designed to fight grease fires. Do not put water on a grease fire, because that will cause it to spatter and possibly spread. If a grease fire is small, you also can put it out with a liberal sprinkling of baking soda.
Wood, paper, plastic	If you have a fire extinguisher rated A, use it. If not, pour water on the fire. Take care to keep water away from any electrical receptacles or cords.
Chimney	If you suspect that there is a fire inside your chimney (p.66), close the damper if possible (it may be too hot to touch), evacuate the house, and call the fire department. Turn a hose on the roof near the chimney.
Christmas tree	Fir trees contain resins that are extremely flammable. You may be able to put out a small fire quickly with an ABC extinguisher. If not, evacuate the house and call the fire department.
Flammable liquid	If the flammable liquid was only the cause of a fire, use an ABC fire extinguisher. If there is danger that more flammable liquid will catch fire, evacuate the house and call the fire department.
Oven	Close the oven door to suffocate the flames. Turn off the oven.
Appliance, light, or cord	Pull out the plug or shut off the power at the switch or the electrical service panel (p.93). If the appliance continues to burn, use an electrical multipurpose ABC-type fire extinguisher, or a C-type extinguisher specific to electrical fires. If you don't have an extinguisher, smother the flames with a nonflammable rug or blanket. Don't use water. If the fire continues after two minutes, leave the house. Call the fire department from another house.
Dryer	Keep the dryer door closed, and shut the door to the room. Turn off the gas or electricity if possible. Call the fire department.

FIGHTING A SMALL FIRE

If the fire is confined to a small area and is not spreading, you may decide to stay and fight it with a portable fire extinguisher. Such devices can save lives and property by putting out a small fire or containing it until the fire department arrives. However, they are not designed to fight large, spreading fires. Even when used against small fires, they are useful only under limited conditions. Here's how to decide when to use a fire extinguisher and what to do:

◆ **Know the location** of every fire extinguisher, and which type of fire each is good for. There won't be time to read directions during an emergency, and using the wrong extinguisher can make the fire worse. Use the extinguisher only if it is within easy reach.

◆ **Have everyone else** leave the building immediately. Have someone call the fire department, even if the fire seems to be easily controllable.

◆ **Have an unobstructed escape route.** Keep your back to the exit, and if possible keep 6 to 8 feet from the flames.

◆ **Follow the four-step PASS procedure:** P = Pull the pin; A = Aim the extinguisher at the base of the flame; S = Squeeze the handle; and S = Sweep the nozzle rapidly from left to right to cover the base of the fire.

◆ **If the fire does not begin to subside** immediately, leave the area at once. The working life of most extinguishers is only about eight seconds.

Aim at base of flame.

◆ **If you do put out the fire,** have the fire department inspect the site, even if there appears to be no danger. Fire can lurk within the walls or reignite from hot embers that may not be visible or not producing heat that you can feel.

◆ **Clean up carefully.** Most household fire extinguishers leave you with a serious cleanup job after you have used them. Wipe away residues as soon as possible, because they may contain caustic substances that damage paint and electronic equipment.

TORNADOES

In an average year, some 60 tornadoes are reported in Canada. The most frequent and severe tornadoes occur in southern Ontario and Alberta. The season begins in May and lasts until September. The worst of them carry winds of 250 mph or more, and their path of destruction can be in excess of 50 miles long. Every family should be prepared.

Before a tornado

Choose an area in your home—a basement or storm cellar, or a windowless interior hall or bathroom on the lowest floor—as a designated shelter. Hold drills to practice going there quickly. Equip it with a disaster supply kit (p.358). Agree on a place to meet after the tornado in case you get separated.

When a tornado strikes

For reliable warnings, place a portable, battery-operated radio in a high-traffic area of the house. Environment Canada issues weather watches, advisories, and warnings, quickly broadcast on national, regional and local radio and TV, and on its own Weatheradio, which can be picked up by a special battery-operated receiver. (A weather watch means that conditions are favorable for a tornado, although one or more has not yet developed. A warning means that tornadoes have been observed or are forecast for a specific area.)

Also learn to recognize the visual signs of a tornado. A funnel cloud is the classic indicator, but an approaching cloud of dust and debris may announce a tornado. Other warnings: a dark, often greenish sky; large hail; or a loud roar similar to a freight train. Tornadoes may develop along the trailing edge of a thunderstorm or hurricane.

During a tornado

If a warning is issued and you are at home, go at once to the designated shelter. Avoid any windows, and crawl under a sturdy piece of furniture, such as a workbench or heavy table. Use your arms to protect head and neck.

At work or school, seek a solid part of the building. Try to avoid places with wide-span roofs, such as gyms, cafeterias, auditoriums, and shopping malls.

If you are outside or in a mobile home or car, seek shelter in a solid building. If none is available, lie down in a ditch or low-lying area a safe distance away from anything that might become flying debris. Cover your head.

After a tornado

Get out of any building where you smell gas or chemical fumes, or where there is substantial damage, because it

SAFETY SMART

EMERGENCY COMMUNICATION PLAN FOR NATURAL DISASTERS

Family members may be in different locations during a tornado, earthquake, or other disaster. So develop a plan for re-uniting after the disaster. It's often easier to call long-distance than locally after a disaster; so ask an out-of-province relative or friend to serve as the family contact. Make sure everyone in the family knows this person's name, address, and phone number.

may collapse in the aftermath. Use the phone only for emergency calls. Turn on a radio or TV to get the latest emergency information. Clean up any spilled medicines, bleaches, and flammable liquids immediately.

Watch pets closely. Stress may cause them to become aggressive. Confine dogs for several hours where they feel secure, such as in a kennel or crate.

LIGHTNING

You are at risk of a lightning strike whenever you hear thunder, even if a storm is not directly overhead and rain has not yet arrived. If your house is in an exposed location, consider installing rooftop lightning rods to carry the electrical charge safely to the ground.

Safety during a lightning storm

When the storm is approaching, seek safety inside a building or a metal vehicle. Once you're inside, stay away

DISASTER SUPPLY KIT

To prepare for the kind of calamitous events that can disrupt normal home life, keep the following emergency items stored in a waterproof box in your family's chosen shelter area.

◆ **For emergency lighting,** stock candles along with a waterproof butane lighter instead of matches, which can be damaged by water. Have several flashlights loaded with fresh batteries plus some spares. Check flashlights, batteries and bulbs for liveliness at least once a year.

◆ **Have enough canned food and bottled water** on hand. A rule of thumb is 1 gallon per family member daily for at least three days. Be sure to have a nonelectric can opener and other basic implements, including paper plates and cups. Replace the food supplies regularly.

◆ **To monitor weather and emergency broadcasts,** purchase a portable radio and extra batteries. Keep it where you plan to shelter or in a spot where you know you can find it. Check it at least every year. Consider buying a special receiver to pick up Environment Canada's Weatheradio.

◆ **A good first aid kit and manual** will prepare you to take immediate and appropriate action in case of injuries. Check the packages regularly, and throw away any medicine that has exceeded its expiration date. Better yet, have a family member take a first aid training course.

◆ **A supply of cash and one or more credit cards** will allow you to buy gas, food, temporary accommodations and other emergency purchases if you have to evacuate your house. You might also set aside a few spare bank cheques on the chance that your working cheque book is not accessible.

◆ **Sturdy shoes** will allow you to remove rubble and/or make emergency repairs. You might also store a pair of heavy socks and work gloves inside the shoes.

from doors and windows. Do not use the telephone. If you are wearing a headset, take it off. Turn off, unplug, and stay away from computers, TV sets, power tools, and small and large appliances. Should lightning strike exterior electric or phone lines, a shock can travel and destroy connected equipment. Likewise, avoid stoves, metal pipes, sinks, bathtubs, and other conductive materials. Don't handle flammable materials in open containers.

If you're outdoors and no structure is available, go to an open space and squat low, but do not lie on the ground. If you're in the woods, find an area protected by a low clump of trees. Never stand under a single large tree in the open. Avoid towers, fences, phone lines, and power lines. Stay away from lightning attractants, such as golf clubs, tractors, fishing rods, bicycles, camping gear, metal canopies, and tool sheds. Also stay away from rivers, lakes, and other bodies of water. Avoid proximity to other people, if possible—separate yourself by at least 15 feet.

After lightning strikes

If someone has been struck by lightning, call for emergency medical assistance immediately. While you wait for help to arrive, provide first aid. (There is no danger to you of getting shocked from them.) If the victim is burned, look for injuries where the lightning entered and exited. If the strike caused the victim's heart and breathing to stop, let a trained person give cardiopulmonary resuscitation (CPR) until medical professionals arrive and take over.

FLOODS AND FLASH FLOODS

In Canada, floods cause more property damage than any other kind of natural disaster. If you live in a flood-prone area, contact your municipal or provincial emergency measures organization. Learn your community's flood alert signals. Also, get a copy of the evacuation route recommended by the local emergency organization. This plan may include information on the safest routes to shelters. If you live in a flash flood area, you should have several alternative routes to choose from.

To ensure your speedy recovery from the effects of the flood, stockpile emergency building materials, including plywood, plastic sheeting, nails, hammer, saw, pry bar, shovels, and sand bags. It's also advisable to have check valves installed in sewer traps to prevent floodwaters from backing up.

If your house is located in a frequently flooded area, talk to your insurance agent about getting adequate coverage against flood damage.

Before a flood

Listen to a battery-powered radio for the latest storm information. Fill bathtubs, sinks, and jugs with clean water for drinking in case the water supply becomes contaminated. Check that your disaster supply kit (facing page) is fully supplied and up to date. Some other useful precautions include:

◆ **Bring in patio furniture,** grills, trash cans, and other outdoor belongings.

◆ **Move household valuables** and essential house and family records to the upper floors or take them with you to high ground.

◆ **Turn off electricity** at the service panel (see page 93), and close the main gas valve (see pages 67 and 70) if evacuation appears necessary.

◆ **Prepare your car** for evacuation. Fuel up and put the evacuation map and disaster supply kit on board.

During a flood

If you're advised to evacuate, do so immediately. Evacuation is simpler and safer before floodwaters become too deep for vehicles to drive through. Follow the recommended evacuation routes; shortcuts may be blocked. If, however, you come to a flooded area, turn around and go another way. If the car stalls, abandon it immediately and climb to higher ground. Many deaths have resulted from attempts to move stalled vehicles.

Should the waters start to rise inside your house before you have a chance to leave, do not try to walk or swim through the flooded area. As little as 6 inches of moving water can sweep you away. Go to the second floor, the attic, or if necessary, the roof and wait for rescue. Take along dry clothes, blankets, a flashlight, and a portable radio.

After a flood

Flood dangers do not end when the water begins to recede. Listen to a radio or TV, and don't return home until you're told that it is safe to do so.

◆ **Stay out of buildings** if floodwaters remain around them. When entering

SAFETY SMART

INSPECTING YOUR HOUSE AFTER A DISASTER

Following a tornado, flood, earthquake, or hurricane, first see to the safety and health of family and neighbors. Then inspect your house carefully.

◆ **Check for gas leaks.** If you smell gas or hear a blowing or hissing noise, open a window and quickly leave the building. Turn off the gas at the outside main valve if you can, and call the gas company from a neighbor's home.

◆ **Look for electrical system damage.** If you see sparks or broken or frayed wires, or if you smell hot insulation, turn off the electricity at the main fuse box or circuit breaker (see page 93). If you have to step in water to get to the fuse box or circuit breaker, call an electrician for advice.

◆ **Check for damage to sewer** and drain lines, and if you suspect damage, avoid using toilets and other plumbing fixtures, and call a plumber. If the water-supply pipe appears to be damaged, or if the water smells, contact the water company if that's your supplier, or a plumber if you have well water. Avoid using tap water.

◆ **Take plenty of pictures** of all the damage—to both the house and its contents—for insurance purposes.

buildings, do not turn power back on until an electrician has done a safety inspection. Wear sturdy shoes to protect against broken glass and nails, and watch out for slippery surfaces. Use battery-powered lanterns or flashlights, and do not light matches or use any open flames, since gas may be trapped inside. Examine walls, doors, and windows to see that the building is not in danger of collapsing.

◆ **Watch out for animals** that may have come in with the floodwaters. Use a stick to poke through debris.

◆ **Throw away food** that has come in contact with floodwaters. Floating sewage and chemicals may contaminate them. Always boil the drinking water until the local authorities declare the water safe.

◆ **Pump out flooded basements** gradually—about one-third of the water per day—to avoid structural damage.

◆ **Service damaged septic tanks,** cesspools, pits, and leaching systems as soon as possible. Damaged sewage systems are health hazards.

◆ **Call your insurance company** to file a flood claim. When you begin to rebuild your home, use flood-resistant materials and techniques to protect yourself and your property from future flooding damage.

EARTHQUAKES

In Canada, earthquakes can happen in any region of the country. More than 2,500 earthquakes—most are of small magnitude—are recorded each year across the country. However, it is advisable to know what to do if a major destructive earthquake occurs.

Preparing for an earthquake

You can't stop fault lines from forming, but you can reduce the chances of breakage and fire damage in your house. Fasten shelves securely to walls, and keep large or heavy objects on lower shelves. Store breakable items in low cabinets with secure latches.

◆ **Secure the water heater** to wall studs with metal earthquake straps and bolts. If you have a gas heater, be sure the connecter between the gas supply and the heater is the flexible kind, or have it replaced. Bolt other large appliances to the floor. Repair deep cracks in ceilings and foundations.

◆ **Identify places offering shelter** in each room: under sturdy furniture; against an inside wall; away from glass, including windows, mirrors, and pictures; and away from heavy bookcases or furniture that could fall over.

During an earthquake

If you're indoors, stay inside. Do not leave the building, because objects can fall on you. Take cover under furniture such as a table or desk (below), or

against an inside wall, and hold on.

If you happen to be outdoors when an earthquake occurs, move into an open area—away from buildings, street lights, and utility wires. Stay there until the shaking comes to an end. If you're in a moving vehicle, stop quickly and stay in the vehicle until the shaking has stopped.

After an earthquake

Be prepared for aftershocks, which can occur hours, days, weeks, or months after a quake. Although they're smaller than the main shock, aftershocks may bring down weakened structures.

Listen to a battery-operated radio or TV for emergency information. Stay out of damaged buildings; if you are not at home, return there only when authorities say it is safe.

If you're at home, clean up spilled medicines, bleaches, and gasoline or other flammable liquids immediately. Leave the area if you smell gas or fumes from other chemicals. Open closet and cupboard doors cautiously.

Closely examine the entire length of the chimney for damage before using a fireplace or heating system. Unnoticed damage can lead to a house fire.

HURRICANES

Hurricanes are violent tropical storms from the Caribbean that hit eastern Canada, usually between June and November. September is usually the peak month. In Canada, the torrential rain and flooding that accompany hurricanes are greater hazards than the strong winds. If you live in a hurricane-prone area, there are some basic ways to reduce your chances of personal injury and major property damage:

◆ **Stay tuned for weather bulletins.** Make sure you have emergency food supplies, containers of water, a radio, a flashlight, extra batteries, candles, and a first aid kit. Fuel your getaway car.

◆ **If conditions worsen,** bring in loose, heavy outdoor objects such as lawn furniture, toys, and garden tools.

◆ **Tape or board up windows** or close storm shutters. Protect furniture from flooding by moving it to a higher floor.

◆ **If you have to evacuate,** unplug the appliances and turn off the electricity, water, and gas. Load the car with emergency supplies and clothing, as well as sleeping bags and blankets to use in the shelter. Lock up before you leave. Drive inland or to higher ground.

◆ **After a hurricane,** return home only when the authorities advise that it is safe. Drive only if necessary, and avoid flooded roads and washed-out bridges. Avoid loose or dangling power lines; report them immediately to the power company, police, or fire department.

◆ **Enter your house with caution.** Open windows and doors to ventilate and dry your home. Use the telephone only for emergency calls. Check refrigerated foods for spoilage. Photograph the damage to the house and to its contents, for insurance claim damage.

WINTER STORMS
During the winter, home-heating systems are vulnerable to power failures. The damage to power lines and equipment caused by freezing rain and sleet storms can interrupt the electric power required to operate furnace, forced-air circulation and thermostat controls. If the power interruption lasts for a long time, the heat loss can result in a cold, damp house, harsh living conditions, and property damage.

Advance precautions
If you foresee staying at home during a prolonged winter power failure, first set up an emergency heating system.

◆ **If you have a fireplace,** make sure you have a good supply of wood or even old newspapers.

◆ **Install a standby stove or heater** that can operate without electricity. If necessary, have the stove or heater properly vented, possibly to an unused flue. Purchase fuel-burning heaters certified by the Canadian Standards Association or the Canadian Gas Association. If your standing heating unit will be using the house's oil or gas supply, get a competent technician from the fuel supplier to connect with the shut-off valves.

◆ **Check with your power authority** before installing emergency generators for furnaces, appliances, or lighting.

◆ **Stock up on ready-to-eat foods,** a nonelectric can opener, and some bottled water.

◆ **Keep flashlights, lanterns, candles,** lighters, and waterproof matches in a handy place.

◆ **Make sure you have a first aid kit** and any prescription medications that you may require.

◆ **Have extra blankets,** sleeping bags and warm clothing in case you have to go to a shelter.

During and after a winter storm
When the power goes out, stay indoors and keep warmly dressed. Use a battery-operated radio to listen for the local news.

Generally, it will take several hours before your home gets too cold. Before this happens, turn on the emergency heating. To prevent pipes from freezing, wrap them in insulation or layers of old newspapers. Letting the faucets trickle will also prevent freezing.

If you can't keep warm during a winter power failure, it is best to leave for a warmer location. Before you go, turn off the main electric switch. Also, turn off the water main where it enters the house; protect the valve, inlet pipe, and meter or pump with blankets or insulation. Drain the water from your plumbing system. Starting at the top of your house, open all taps and flush the toilets several times. Go to the basement and open the drain valve. Drain your hot-water tank by attaching a hose to the tank drain valve and running it to the basement floor drain.

After the power returns, turn on the main electric switch. Open the main water intake valve to the house. Close the drainage valves, starting with the lowest and let the air escape from the upper taps. Refill the water heater before turning its power back on. After a prolonged power failure, check food supplies in refrigerators and freezers for spoilage.

Basic Workshop Tools

You can do many maintenance and repair tasks yourself, if you buy a small arsenal of tools and equipment. You will save some money and have the satisfaction of not having to wait for someone else to do the job.

MEASURING TOOLS

Framing square. This specialized carpenter's square has tables and formulas for calculating area, volume, and slope length.

Retractable steel tape. This spring-loaded 25-foot tape that is 1 inch wide will handle almost any situation. The metal hook on the end catches on a workpiece, making long measurements a one-person job.

Chalk line. This case filled with chalk and 50 to 100 feet of line on a reel marks a long, straight line between two points. Pull the line from the case, hold it taut, and snap it to leave a chalk mark as a guide. This is useful in hanging wallcoverings and for cutting long lines.

Speed square. Use one to check a 90° angle and to mark angled cuts.

Level. Use a 2- or 4-foot level for testing shelves and leveling a refrigerator. Held vertically, it can also test for plumb.

Plumb bob. A line with a weight attached establishes a straight, vertical line (plumb), as needed for hanging wallcovering. Suspend the line from a height and drop the weight to the ground; wait for the weight to steady.

CUTTING TOOLS

Multipurpose tool. This is an all-in-one tool for working with wire: You can cut wire, strip casings from wire, and cut small pieces of thin metal with it.

Utility knife. This versatile knife has a variety of blades to cut wood, vinyl, and other materials. A good model will have a button that adjusts the length of the blade and retracts the blade into the handle for safety. Replacement blades are often stored in the handle.

Soft sharpening stone. Use this stone to sharpen dulled tools and blades. Lubricate the stone with oil as you sharpen.

SAWS

Miter box. This U-shaped box has slotted cut guides so you can make 45° miter cuts on small pieces of wood, such as molding and trim.

Keyhole saw. The point of the saw allows you to make plunge cuts in wall-board or drywall. The blade is 10 inches long with about 9 teeth per inch (tpi). It can also cut light metal and wood.

Backsaw. This fine-toothed handsaw has a reinforced upper edge for making straight cuts. It is typically used with a miter box (above).

Hacksaw. Use this handsaw to cut metal. It has extra-hard teeth, a sturdy frame with a pistol-grip handle, and a narrow blade from 8 to 16 inches long with 14 to 32 tpi.

Crosscut saw. This saw's knife-like teeth slice through wood fibers, cutting stock across the grain. The standard blade is 26 inches long with 7 to 12 tpi. Protect the blade by keeping it in its cardboard sheath.

SHAPING TOOLS

Butt chisel. This short-bladed chisel is easier to work with than other chisels. It is useful for trimming rough edges and making notches. Keep its beveled edge sharp at all times.

Cold chisel. This chisel has a steep bevel for rough work. It can be struck with a hammer to chop off rivets and bolts and remove tile.

Block plane. This small plane can be used with one hand or two and is useful for shaving wood to close tolerances. It also works well on end grain.

FASTENING AND UNFASTENING TOOLS

Curved-claw hammer. A 16-ounce model will suit most people and most jobs. It will drive common or finishing nails but not case-hardened cut nails or concrete nails.

Pry bar. A versatile tool for unfastening jobs, the tool has a nail-pulling blade at one end and a prying tool at the other, useful for removing molding and trim and separating other materials that are glued together.

Nail set. A punch-shaped tool countersinks nails in wooden cabinets, furniture, moldings, and trim. Position its point over the head of a finishing nail and strike the top with a hammer so that it sits below the surface of the wood. Fill the hole with wood putty and sand the surface smooth.

Screwdriver. A good multi-type screwdriver will have slots for Phillips and square-drive (Robertson) screw heads. Some models have a ratchet operation for fast work, as well as a switch for reversing the direction of the drive.

Quick-Grip bar clamp. This bar clamp has a movable jaw with a pistol-shaped handle. To slide the jaw, pull the trigger near the handle; squeeze the grip to apply jaw pressure. The jaws have removable protective rubber pads. This tool comes in a wide variety of styles.

Staple gun. This tool makes quick work of fastening screens or tacking fabric, plastic sheeting, tar paper, and carpet underlayment in place. Adapters can be added to enable a stapler to drive other fasteners.

C-clamp. Named for its C-shaped frame, it comes in large and small sizes and holds objects firmly in place as glue dries, or to make work easier. To tighten the screw against the work, turn the T-handle.

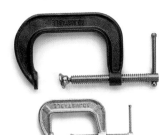

Hex (or Allen) wrenches. A six-sided key fits into a setscrew recessed flush with the surface. Either wrench end will fit inside the screw. By inserting the short end, you'll have greater torque; in limited space, use the long end in the screw.

Locking pliers. These pliers clamp firmly on objects. A knob in one handle controls the width of the jaws. Close the handles to lock the pliers; release a lever to open them.

Channel pliers. Adjustable from about ¼ inch to 3 or 4 inches, these pliers are handy for fastening nuts, bolts, and lag screws—even for light plumbing.

Slip-joint pliers. Serrated jaws and coarse contoured teeth grip objects of different shapes. The jaws can be set in two positions.

Adjustable (crescent) wrench. This versatile smooth-jaw wrench turns nuts, bolts, small pipe fittings, and chrome-faced pipe fittings. The movable jaw is adjusted using the worm gear, which is accessible on both sides of the head.

Needlenose pliers. The thin, tapered jaws are smooth and won't mar or scratch. They are ideal for working with jewelry and other soft metals.

DRILLS

Corded or cordless drill. A variable-speed reversible (VSR) drill is one of the handiest tools you can own, especially if you also buy a magnetic sleeve with a series of screwdriver bits. For boring holes, use a set of twist-type drill bits. For boring holes larger than 1/4 inch in diameter, spade bits are the most economical choice. A cordless drill enables you to work anywhere without an extension cord, but be sure to keep its battery fully charged between uses.

PLUMBING TOOLS

Pipe wrench. Use this tool to tighten and loosen metal pipe and tubing.

Drain auger. Use a 1/4-inch flexible-bulb auger to unclog a drain. It has a thin wire with coiled spring on the end. Crank the auger handle clockwise while pushing the wire back and forth in the drain until it breaks up the blockage.

Plunger. The rubber cup fits snugly over a sink drain or a toilet's outflow passage; pumping action creates a vacuum and sucks out an obstruction. Use this larger one for a toilet.

PAINTING AND SCRAPING TOOLS

Putty knife. A flexible blade spreads and smooths wood putty and filler, glazing and spackling compounds, patching plaster, and other similar materials. The type with a stiff blade, shown, scrapes away paint, glue, and wallcoverings.

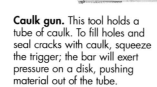

Caulk gun. This tool holds a tube of caulk. To fill holes and seal cracks with caulk, squeeze the trigger; the bar will exert pressure on a disk, pushing material out of the tube.

Paint pads. A wall pad is 6 to 10 inches wide; an edge pad is narrower and suitable for trim. Pads apply paint evenly and work faster than brushes but slower than rollers.

Drywall tools. With 6- and 8-inch taping blades, you can feather on subsequent layers of drywall compound for smooth patches on walls and ceilings.

Paint roller pan, sleeve, and frame. Choose a professional-quality roller sleeve. A medium nap is the best choice for most surfaces. The roller frame should spin smoothly.

Sanding block. A block holds abrasive sheets and makes sanding much easier than using a piece of sandpaper alone. Several types are available.

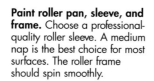

Paint roller extension pole. A threaded pole will allow you to paint ceilings and walls without a ladder.

Basic Workshop Tips

Prepare for each project and develop the skills needed to get it done safely and well.
Here is how to make your repair chores go smoothly.

Choosing and planning the work

A do-it-yourself project often takes longer than you think. Be sure you have enough free time to do the work, or you may find yourself living with an unsightly half-finished job. Don't assume that doing it yourself will always save you money. If you make a mistake in plumbing, for instance, it will cost more to have a professional come in after you.

Buying and renting the tools you need

Buying the basic hand tools shown on pp. 362–365 will enable a beginning do-it-yourselfer to tackle most minor projects. The only power tool essential for a homeowner's tool kit is the power drill, for it is both versatile and labor-saving. As time goes by, you'll need more specialized tools for specific jobs. A good rule of thumb: Don't buy a specialized tool before you need it, and don't hesitate to buy one when you do. Professional-quality tools are expensive because they are made for heavy use; bargain-priced tools may not hold up well. Often it is best to choose a mid-priced model that feels solid and comfortable in your hand and that is backed by a warranty. You can rent almost any power tool for a day or a weekend; but before you do so, be sure to enlist the help of someone who knows how to use it safely. In addition, most home centers will cut non-treated lumber or plywood, ceramic tile, and glass for you, usually for a fee.

Safety with tools

All tools are safer and more effective when well maintained. Keep blades sharp; keep moving parts clean and, if called for in the manual, lubricated. Read and follow the instruction manual for each tool carefully. Wear safety goggles, heavy-duty work gloves, and hearing protection as needed. Never work if you are tired, medicated, or upset. Keep a fire extinguisher and a first-aid kit within reach and in plain sight. Use power tools with extreme caution. Never work in damp conditions. Unplug the tool when not in use and when you are making an adjustment or changing a bit.

Tips for using tools

◆ **Driving nails.** If you are a beginner, you can move your hand halfway up the handle. This will give you less power but more control. To drive a nail, hold it upright and tap it gently with the hammer; then take your hand away. Hold the hammer at the end of the handle and lift the tool, swinging your forearm from the elbow. Let the weight of the hammer do the work. For rough work, drive nails flush with the surface; for finish work, countersink the nails (below).

◆ **Driving a small brad.** If a nail is too small to grab it with your fingers, or if you are afraid of smashing your fingers as you drive the brad, poke it through an index card. Hold the card to position the nail as you drive it with a hammer.

◆ **Prevent damage to walls when driving a nail.** Before driving a nail into a plaster wall, put a piece of masking tape over the area to prevent cracks from forming.

◆ **Countersinking and filling.** For a finished look, use a nail set to sink the head of the nail below the surface $\frac{1}{8}$ inch or so. Use your finger or a putty knife to fill the hole with wood filler, allow it to dry, and sand it smooth.

◆ **Measuring for a cut.** Measure twice, cut once. Finding a mistake after you have cut the material may mean having to start over again.

◆ **Drilling holes.** To make sure the drill bit will not wander when you begin drilling, use a nail set to make a small starter hole. If you need to drill to a certain depth and no farther, wrap a piece of tape around the bit to use as a depth guide. Don't push hard as you drill, and pull the bit out every once in a while to empty the hole of particles. Avoid overheating the bit; if you see or smell smoke, stop and let the bit cool.

◆ **Drill pilot holes before driving screws or nails.** It is a very good idea to drill a pilot hole before driving a screw, and before driving a nail close to the edge of a board. This prevents the board from splitting, and it actually causes the screw or nail to hold better. Use a drill bit that is slightly thinner than the fastener you will be driving.

◆ **Drilling in masonry and concrete.** Use a special masonry bit. Brick may be easy to drill into, but concrete is usually more difficult. As you work, spray the hole and the bit with window cleaner to keep the bit cool and to bring dust particles out of the hole.

◆ **Driving screws by hand.** Make sure the screwdriver tip fits snugly into the screw head; if the tip is too small, you may strip the screw head. Press and turn clockwise. If a screw is hard to drive, push down with the palm of one hand as you turn with the other. Rub candlewax on the threads of the screw to make it easier to drive.

◆ **Driving screws with a power drill.** A drill with a magnetic sleeve and the right-sized bit will make this easy. Place the screw on the bit first, then set the tip of the screw into the pilot hole. To keep the screw from wobbling, hold the screw head as you begin driving the screw. If a screw is loose in its hole, remove it, tap in a toothpick or other small piece of wood covered with glue, and drive the screw again.

◆ **Removing screws.** Make sure that the screwdriver tip fits snugly in the screw head. You may need to use a knife or ice pick to clean old paint out of the screw head. Turn counterclockwise. If the screw is stuck, press down on the handle with your palm and turn the shaft of the screwdriver with an adjustable wrench.

◆ **Removing nails.** A flat pry bar may do the least damage to surrounding surfaces; tap it under the nail head with a hammer. When the nail is out ⅛ inch or so, switch to the claws of your hammer. Place a scrap of wood under the hammer's head to add leverage and protect the surface. Often you can pull finishing nails (without heads) through from the back side of the board, eliminating all damage to the board. With a pair of clamping pliers, grasp the nail close to the wood surface, and use a rolling motion to pull the nail out.

MUST-HAVE MATERIALS

Here's a list of often-used materials that you'll want to keep in stock:

◆ small squirt can of all-purpose household oil

◆ aerosol can of penetrating oil

◆ tubes of latex/silicone caulk

◆ removable rope caulk

◆ aerosol can of foam insulation

◆ wood filler (in paste form)

◆ spackling or joint compound for patching walls.

◆ **Marking for a cut.** Use a pencil with a hard lead, and mark the cut using a 'V' rather than a straight line; the tip of the V will be the precise location. Place a speed square on the work, and draw a line through the 'V'. The saw blade will remove about ⅛ inch of material. To be sure you cut the correct side of the line, draw a large 'X' on the waste side.

◆ **Cutting with a handsaw.** Support the board so the waste can fall away. Place the heel of the saw blade (closest to the handle) on the cut line at a 60-degree angle if you are cutting across the grain and at a 45-degree angle if you are cutting with the grain. Gently press your thumbnail against the blade and pull the saw toward you several times to start the cut. Then push and pull the saw along the waste side of the cut line. To ensure a square cut, check that the saw is always perpendicular to the cut line. Don't push hard; let the saw teeth do the cutting. At the end of the cut, you may need to grab the waste portion so it will not splinter as it falls away.

◆ **Finding studs and joists.** When attaching a heavy object to a wall or ceiling, first find the wood framing piece, or stud, behind the wall surface (or joists above the ceiling). Studs are usually placed vertically 16 to 24 inches on-center. Purchase a stud sensor, or wrap a hammer in a cloth and tap lightly; listen for a solid rather than a hollow sound. Drive a finishing nail to make sure you have found the stud.

Buying, Selling, and Moving

You may buy or sell a home for several reasons:
Your job requires a transfer, you anticipate a growing family or an empty nest,
or you've found the home of your dreams. The process needn't be stressful.

If you are a first-time home buyer, you are taking a step into an exciting new arena. Because homeownership is a major investment, you need to be sure that your new home fits your needs and your budget.

BUYING THE BEST HOME YOU CAN AFFORD

The first step in house-hunting is to talk over your needs and wants with your family. Here are some topics to discuss.

◆ **Future family needs.** Visualize the plans you would like to put in place. For instance, you should have enough bedrooms and bathrooms to suit the next five years or so. If you have, or plan to have children, they will need good schools and access to recreation and friends.

◆ **Career.** Assess the current and future situation. Are you going to want to work at home? Retire soon? How long do you want your commute to be?

◆ **Lifestyle.** Do you prefer the quiet country life or a busy urban setting? Consider, too, how you like to entertain and relax. How important is having a formal dining room or a comfortable family room? Do you need a guest bedroom? How much space do you want for a yard and garden?

◆ **Old versus new.** Older homes generally offer a level of craftsmanship and architectural individuality that is hard to find in new homes. But if simple lines and maintenance-free living are more your style, look at newer properties.

Select the right professionals

Once you begin looking for a home, take the time to find a reputable real estate representative. Ask friends, associates, or the local board of the Canadian Real Estate Association for recommendations. When you interview real estate agents, make sure that you are clear about how they are compensated for a sale, and that you understand your obligations. In most provinces, the law requires brokers to tell you who they represent. You may want to look into the option of a buyer-broker, who represents the buyer exclusively.

Later on, you will need a lawyer (or notary in Quebec) to handle the legal work involved in a home sale. If you don't already have one, ask friends for recommendations and then interview lawyers over the telephone and face-to-face.

Determine your price range

How much of a mortgage can you take on? The three most important factors are your down payment, your gross household income, and the mortgage interest rate. Lenders also consider your monthly payments for credit-card purchases, car loans, and other long-term debts. Real estate agents can provide tables to assist buyers in assessing what they can afford. According to Canada Mortgage and Housing Corporation (CMHC), the most common formula states that your monthly housing expenses—including monthly mortgage principal and interest payments, taxes, and heating expenses—should be no more than 32 percent of your gross monthly income. (In the case of a condominium, these expenses should include half of the monthly condo fees.) This is your gross debt service (GDS) ratio.

In addition, the total of the housing expenses and all other long-term debt repayment expenses must not exceed 40 percent of gross household income. Lenders add up these debts to deter what percentage they are of your monthly income. This figure is your total debt service (TDS) ratio. Based on these ratios, lenders will advise you of the maximum house price they think you can afford. To get a clearer estimate of how much a lender will loan you, meet with one and ask for a prequalification. There's no obligation involved, and it helps you get a realistic picture of what you can afford before you start house-hunting. However, prequalification does not guarantee that you will get that loan when you bid on a house later on.

Preapproval is a surer bet. For preapproval, you must make a formal loan application to a lender, who will check and formally verify your information. If all goes well, you will end up with an approval for a loan (subject to a satisfactory property appraisal and title search). This is an advantage if you are competing with someone else for the same property.

In any event, don't forget to set aside money for closing costs—the taxes and fees you have to pay in cash when the property changes hands—as well as moving expenses.

Getting the best deal

Before you start your search for a house, it may be worthwhile to learn about the art of negotiation. Talk with people who work in fields where negotiations are common, and read up on real estate transactions. You'll be glad later, when decisions must be made quickly.

In order to calculate your initial bid, and to establish the fairness of the seller's asking price, look at similar homes in the area and compare asking prices. In addition, ask you real estate representative to give you a "comparative mortgage analysis"—a document that describes recent sales of similar homes nearby. These "comps" will show both asking and selling prices and will provide a brief outline of the features of each home. Look over several months' worth so you can get a feel for trends in the market.

WHAT TO LOOK FOR IN A HOME

If you find a home that looks and feels right, walk through it again with an eye on the floor plan. (Fixing an unsatisfactory floor plan is a lot harder than changing paint colors or carpets.) Ask these questions:

◆ **Does the home have an open, light-filled layout?** Not only is this a more pleasant setting for you and your family to enjoy, it also appeals to most people, making it easier for you to sell the house later on.

◆ **Is the kitchen large enough?** Is there enough counter space and cabinet space where needed? Are the stove, refrigerator, and sink arranged in a convenient work triangle?

◆ **Are there enough bathrooms?** Are they private?

◆ **Will it be easy to get groceries** from the car to the kitchen, or will you have to struggle up a flight of stairs?

◆ **Are sleeping areas far enough** from TV-watching areas and recreation areas?

◆ **Is there enough closet and storage space?** Don't count on attics and basements for storing clothes and books unless these spaces are climate-controlled and easy to reach.

Assessing the location

The neighborhood is considered the major factor in a home's worth and resale possibilities. Assess the neighborhood traffic at various times of the day. Cul-de-sacs and low-traffic streets are more desirable than busy streets. If you are house-hunting in a new development, call the developer's offices to find out how the completion of other roads will affect traffic in front of the house. Your quiet street could be slated to become a major artery someday. Be mindful of other nearby forms of transportation, too, even if they're not visible from the house. For example, a train might toot its whistle at 5:00 AM every day. In addition, assess these considerations:

◆ **Look closely at neighboring houses and yards** to see whether they are well maintained.

◆ **Research the schools in the area,** even if you do not have young children. This can affect resale value later on.

◆ **Contact the local municipal office about planning and zoning bylaws.** Future developments, such as a new highway or industrial park, can affect your property value and property tax.

◆ **Check on public transportation,** the nearest hospital, fire department, and other public services in the neighborhood.

Assessing a Home's Physical Condition

Take a closer look at the house to make a basic assessment of its condition and structure. The following checklist for buyers will give you a good starting place. (Sellers are well advised to take note of this list, too.)

◆ **A solid foundation.** There should be no holes or cracks. The ground should slope away from the house so that water is directed away, and there should be no sunken spots in the yard—an indication of a drainage problem.

◆ **A clean, neat exterior.** Brick and concrete surfaces should be free of missing mortar, flaking, and cracks. Siding should be painted (or new) and free of blistered, warped, or rotted spots. Window screens should be intact.

◆ **A roof in good repair.** No shingles should be missing.

◆ **A well-maintained interior.** All walls should be freshly painted and free of cracks.

◆ **A dry basement.** Musty odors or stains on the walls or floor are indicators of a problem. Buyers should ask questions if basement floors have been freshly painted.

◆ **Sturdy, level floors.** Wood floors and any carpets should be clean and in good condition.

◆ **Windows that open and close easily** and insulate against heat and cold.

◆ **Adequate water pressure.** Try running several faucets at once, or running a faucet and flushing the toilet simultaneously, to see how much water pressure you lose.

◆ **A hardworking kitchen** with up-to-date appliances and adequate working spaces.

◆ **Bathroom tiles** should have no mildew in the grout.

Bidding on the Home and Closing the Deal

If you still like what you see, it is now time to have your real estate agent or lawyer make a written offer to purchase. The more houses you've toured and the more comps you've studied, the more secure you'll be about knowing what to offer. You can assume that the sellers have built some room for negotiating into the price and that they'll likely propose a counteroffer to yours. How far apart the numbers are will depend on the market, how long this home has been for sale, and whether the price has already been reduced.

It helps to know about the sellers' situation. If they have already purchased another home, for example, you probably have a bit more leverage. Make concessions that will appeal to the sellers. If they are building a house that is not finished yet, they might like a chance to rent the house from you while you save a few dollars by staying in your apartment.

Your offer must be accompanied by a good-faith deposit. The money will actually be held by a third party, such as a lawyer or escrow company, until the sale is completed or cancelled. If the sale is completed, the money will be part of the cash down payment. The offer should include all terms and conditions of your purchase, including inspections.

Hire a home inspector

A home inspector is a professional who will examine the house and make a report about its condition, including structural soundness, and any necessary repairs. An inspector can also assess the presence of pests, such as termites, and environmental hazards, such as asbestos. It is always a good idea to have a home inspected. According to the CMHC, the fees range from about $150 to $350 for a house that costs $300,000 or less. Larger, more expensive homes cost more to inspect. A two-hour inspection carried out by an engineer who provides a written report will be in the high-fee range. Your inspector should have "errors and omissions" insurance, which means he will be held financially responsible for any costly repairs he fails to report. Municipalities can also give you inspection reports on the property for a fee.

In most provinces, inspectors are unregulated, so inquire about credentials and get references. Ask your friends, a real estate agent or the local professional association of home inspectors. If your inspector offers estimated costs for replacing or repairing defects in the home, be sure to ask if such estimates are included in the fee. Ask how the inspector will present results to you, too; it is usual to have a meeting face-to-face plus a written report of the findings.

An inspection contingency in your purchase offer may require the seller to make repairs within a certain amount of time, or allow you to cancel the deal if an inspector finds

BUYING, SELLING, AND MOVING

problems. Often, the two parties will collect estimates for repairs and work out concessions, such as cash credits.

When all terms and conditions of the purchase agreement have been met, you can proceed with the details of the closing. You may do a final walk-through inspection just before closing to make sure repairs have been made and that the house is in the same condition as before negotiations began.

SELLING A HOME

Try to see your house through the eyes of a potential buyer. Imagine that you're seeing it for the first time; you may spot problems that you have been overlooking. Refer to the checklist in "Assessing a Home's Physical Condition" on the facing page to find out which cleaning, repairing, and replacing tasks help a home sell quickly. Ask a real estate agent for advice: What needs to be done to make this home attractive to potential buyers? Where should you invest your time and money? For example, it will probably be worth your money to give the walls a fresh coat of paint throughout the house, or to replace an outdated, undersized water heater. Tackle the most pressing problems first. However, be wary of over-investing in upgrading your home. For example, it is very unlikely you will recoup the cost of new kitchen cabinets or a remodeled bathroom. However, such improvements may help your home sell faster, if not for more money.

Pack away personalized items such as doormats and plaques, so potential buyers can imagine themselves in your house. If walls need painting, use only neutral colors. Remove all knickknacks and personal collections (these are distracting to those walking through the rooms). First impressions should be positive. Repaint the front door and polish the knocker and lockset.

Consider having your home inspected; otherwise, you could face a lawsuit if you fail to fix or disclose a problem with your house, such as chronic basement flooding or a preexisting leaky roof. An inspection will give you peace of mind, and it may enable you to ask for a higher price.

Real Estate Agent or "For Sale By Owner"?

The thought of saving the commission—usually 5 to 7 percent of the sale price—inspires many people to sell their home without professional help. To make the best decision for yourself, consider the following:

◆ **The buyer may expect to share the spoils** with you in the form of a lower price if you sell your house without an agent.

◆ **If you would like to save money** but you want help with paperwork and details, consider hiring a discount broker. They usually charge either a flat fee or a commission of 3 to 4 percent of the selling price and will offer fewer services than a full-service agent. Services may include paperwork, negotiations, and following up on a buyer's mortgage application.

◆ **A real estate agent will subscribe to** the Multiple Listing Service, which describes all homes listed by agents in the area. A seasoned agent also can offer information about the market, assistance with negotiating, and connections with potential buyers (including out-of-towners).

Determine your price range

Pricing is difficult for sellers because they tend to overestimate the value of their homes; it is hard to be objective about your own home. If you overprice, you'll miss the opportunity to attract buyers during the first three or four weeks that the property is on the market, a high-traffic period of time, since buyers like to check out the new listings. Ask your real estate agent to give you a recommendation, as well as written comparables, or "comps" (see page 369).

You may also want an appraisal, an estimate of fair market value made by an unbiased professional real estate appraiser. He or she will use available market data, calculations of replacement cost, physical depreciation of systems, and other factors to determine the market value of your home.

For selling as well as buying, learning the art of negotiation is very helpful. Seek advice from your agent, or read a book on real estate and negotiations. Later, when things are moving quickly, you will be ready to respond to offers with decisiveness, and forge a win-win situation.

The economic environment determines how much money people will spend. When people are feeling secure in their jobs and interest rates are low, they are more likely to spend more money. When interest rates rise or the stability of the economy is uncertain, the opposite is the case.

Show your house successfully

Once your house is on the market, be ready to have it shown on a moment's notice. That means keeping the house basically spotless—it may pay to hire a cleaning service.

◆ **Vacate the premises, taking the dog or cat with you,** every time your home is shown. It's awkward for potential buyers to assess a home and difficult to imagine themselves living in it if you are there while they are looking.

◆ **Create an inviting atmosphere.** Before you leave, switch on lights and open all the curtains and shades so your home looks bright and inviting. Be sure that there is no pet odor or greasy cooking odor.

◆ **Add a subtle homey touch.** Place fresh flowers or bowls of fruit out on tables and counters.

◆ **Keep the home furnished.** A house empty of furniture, curtains, and wall decorations looks cold and uninviting—and it gives the impression that you're desperate to sell. If possible, don't set your moving date until the house is sold.

Field an offer and close

When you receive an offer, ask your real estate agent about the bidder: Is the potential buyer someone who has already sold a home? A couple with kids who need to be settled in before the school year starts? Someone who has been pre-approved for a loan? What you learn can help you decide how to respond. The process of making offers and counter-offers can continue through several rounds.

If you receive two offers, you may be able to play them off each other to lessen contingencies, demand a faster closing, or even get a higher price. However, consult with your agent and proceed cautiously, or you may lose both offers.

Once a price has been agreed upon, your agents and lawyers will arrange for a closing. If you haven't had a formal inspection done, the buyers will initiate one now, and the contract will include contingencies based on those findings. Be cautious, however, about agreeing to contingencies regarding the sale of the buyer's current property, which can take your house off the market and keep your sale in limbo. At this point, you will also have to handle other details, such as arranging to cut off utilities.

PACKING AND MOVING

Packing and moving your possessions is a major job, but it can be done with a minimum of stress. Take it step by step, and you will be pleased with the results.

Getting ready to move

To make the move as painless as possible, streamline your worldly goods and plan each step of the way.

◆ **Get rid of anything you no longer need.** Take an objective look at what can be sold and what can be given to charity. Everything else you don't need should be thrown away. Otherwise, you'll waste time, energy, and money packing it and having it carted to your new home.

◆ **Contact moving companies to get estimates.** As you find out about costs, also find out what they will do to make your move as smooth as possible. Those extras may make the whole process that much easier.

◆ **Start central files or folders** for documents related to the move and your new location. Collect all receipts, as you may be able to claim them as a tax deduction. Write or call for information on schools, parks and recreation, community calendars, and maps.

◆ **Lay out a floor plan for each room,** using the new space and your existing furniture as your guideline. That will lessen the number of decisions to make on the day you move into your new home.

◆ **As you begin to pack,** mark each box with the room where it is to go and a numbering system or code that tells you how important it is to open each box. Pack the seldom-used items first. Save the essential items for last, and mark these "Load last, Open first." List specific contents, too, so you can find what you need without too much searching. Indicate which boxes contain breakable items.

◆ **Notify the post office, friends and family,** the publishers of magazines to which you subscribe, and credit card companies of your new address well in advance of the move.

◆ **Contact the utilities** in your old and new locations so that you can stop service in the one and start service in the other on moving day.

◆ **Reserve a truck,** if needed, at least a month before your moving date—earlier if you're moving during the peak season of May to September. Be sure to ask about insurance and liability when you call the various companies. Check your own auto policy; some cover rental trucks or offer insurance riders that will insure your possessions while in transit. Before you start packing, make a list of what you're moving and how much it's worth; you'll need this list later if you need to submit an insurance claim.

◆ **As moving day approaches,** plan your grocery shopping so that you have as little as possible on hand.

◆ **Order packing supplies from the mover,** or if you are doing it yourself, reserve ropes, dollies, furniture ties, padded straps, blankets, and pads from the truck-rental company.

If you are doing all or part of it yourself

Packing and moving by yourself is doable, especially if you have not yet amassed many belongings. Plan your move carefully and take precautions against back strain or injury.

◆ **Collect small, sturdy boxes;** they'll be easy to carry and won't be too heavy when filled. Bulky but lightweight items, such as pillows and blankets, can go in larger boxes. Buy heavy-duty package-sealing tape and some marking pens.

◆ **When you pack, use newspaper,** but don't let newsprint touch your possessions, because it's likely to release ink. Use plain tissue paper for the first layer, then use newspaper as padding. Or use bubble wrap and packing peanuts instead.

◆ **Use convenient wardrobe boxes** from a moving company or truck-rental store to pack hanging clothes.

◆ **Pack fragile items carefully.** Moving and truck-rental stores sell special crates for mirrors and glass. Glassware wrapped carefully in tissue paper can be nested three or four at a time, but stemware must be wrapped individually. If you have collected some liquor or wine cartons with cardboard dividers, you can neatly pack the wrapped bundles inside.

◆ **Pack your truck tightly and carefully** to prevent damage. Load large pieces of furniture first, then fill in the spaces with boxes and smaller items. Strap large items to the truck walls.

◆ **A furniture dolly with straps** is essential for moving heavy appliances. To use a dolly, tilt the piece back to a helper, slide the dolly under it, and then set it back down. Tighten the strap firmly.

◆ **Lift with your legs,** not with your back. Repeated lifting of even moderately heavy pieces can produce serious strain.

◆ **To move a heavy piece down a flight of stairs,** lay it on a quilt or heavy blanket. Have a couple of strong people control the descent of the piece with their shoulders as they back down the steps, lifting the leading edge of the "skid" slightly with their hands as they go.

◆ **To move a couch with legs,** lay it on its back or side on a heavy blanket or a moving quilt and slide it along.

Moving day

When the big day arrives, go over the paperwork with the movers and take inventory as each piece is loaded onto the truck. If the move is over a long distance, verify with the movers when the truck will arrive, and plan to be there when it does. Roll up all bed linens from the beds and pack them in a "Load last, Open first" box. Finish packing the suitcases and loading the car. You can make life easier on this hectic day by doing some or all of the following:

◆ **Arrange to keep pets out of the way.** By placing your dog or cat in the home of a willing neighbor or in a kennel for a day or two, you will prevent your pet from possibly running away or becoming overly agitated.

◆ **If you are driving a rental moving truck,** have the telephone number of the rental company handy when you pull out of the driveway. That way, you will be able to call if you have problems along the way.

◆ **Monitor the unloading process carefully.** Appoint one person to check items off the inventory list as they are unloaded, and have somebody else direct the movers on where to place the items.

◆ **Plan to take your time unpacking.** Arranging and organizing your household should not happen all at once. Instead, take a week or two and do it right.

INDEX

X, Y, Z

Acknowledgments

The editors are especially grateful to the
following individuals and organizations
for their help in providing information
for this book.

Ace Hardware
American Heritage Fireplace, Inc.
American Society for Testing and
    Materials
Best-Vac
Brick Institute of America
Broan Manufacturing Co., Inc.,
    a Nortek Co.
Canada Mortgage
    and Housing Corporation
Canadian Carpet Institute
Canadian Standards Association
Century 21
Dayton Hudson Corp.
Easy Living Store
Emergency Preparedness Canada
Enbridge Consumers Gas
Environment Canada
First Alert
The Happy Sweeper
Hare Roofing
Home Depot
Home Hardware
Household Hazardous Waste Project
Hurricane Protection Industries, Inc.
In the Swim
Jo Ann Pullen
Maytag Corporation
Natural Resources Canada
Ontario Hydro
Quality Doors
Regional Municipality of
    Ottawa-Carleton
Safe Guard
Smith & Hawken
Top Side Roofing, Inc.
Underwriters' Laboratories of Canada
Wagner Plumbing & Piping, Inc.
White Flower Farm
Wisconsin Pharmacal Co.

Photo Credits

Front cover: Silverware drawer: William
    Abranowicz/A+C Anthology;
    Clothesline: Sadlon Photography;
    Bedside table, Chair with cushions:
    Colin Cooke; Closet: California
    Closet
Spine © PhotoDisc
Back cover, all: David Hautzig

pp.2,3,6; 12 Left, 17 Right, 24, 34,
    48 Left, 62 Left, 67, 79, 86, 92,
    102, 110, 124, 139, 146 Left,
    153 Right, 166, 170 Left, 178,
    184, 189, 210, 221, 227, 231,
    238, 244, 249, 258 Left, 262
    Left, 266, 275, 283, 291, 300,
    303, 310, 316, 320, 328 Left,
    338, 351, 354; all chapter open-
    ers: David Hautzig
p.104 Quality Doors
p.204 Left © PhotoDisc
p.222 Maytag Corporation
p.294 Crocus, Hyacinth (Hyacinthus),
    Scilla, Snowdrops (Galanthus),
    Tulip; p.296, Daffodil (Narcissus
    "Unsurpassable"), Daylillies (Heme-
    rocallis "Mallard"), German
    bearded iris (Iris "Champagne Ele-
    gance"), Hosta ("Francis Williams"),
    Obedient (Physostegia "Variegata"),
    Peonies (Paeonia "Kansas"), Rugosa
    roses (Rosa "Fru Dagmar Hastrup"),
    Yarrow: Whiteflower Farms, Route
    63, P.O. Box 50, Litchfield, Ct
    06759-0050; The Daffodil Mart,
    30 Irene St., Torrington, CT 06790-
    6668
p.296 Ox-eye daisies, Coreopsis:
    Karen Bussolini, Photography
p.316 Left © PhotoDisc
p.358 Canadian money, credit cards:
    Mike Haimes

CONVERSION FACTORS

To change:	Into:	Multiply by:
inches	millimetres	25.4
inches	centimetres	2.54
feet	metres	0.305
yards	metres	0.914
square inches	square centimetres	6.45
square feet	square metres	0.093
square yards	square metres	0.836
cubic inches	cubic centimetres	16.4
cubic feet	cubic metres	0.028
cubic yards	cubic metres	0.765
pints (imperial)	litres	0.568
quarts (imperial)	litres	1.136
gallons (imperial)	litres	4.546
gallons (U.S.)	litres	3.79
ounces	grams	28.35
pounds	kilograms	0.454

LUMBER WIDTHS AND THICKNESSES

Lumber is ordered by thickness, width, and length. When you order in imperial measurements (2 inches x 4 inches x 8 feet, for example), the thickness and width figures (in this instance 2 x 4) refer to nominal size—the dimensions of the piece as it left the saw. But what you get is the smaller, actual size remaining when the piece has been planed smooth; in actual fact, a piece $1\frac{1}{2}$ inches x $3\frac{1}{2}$ inches x 8 feet. (Length is not reduced by the processing.)

Metric measurements on the other hand always describe the actual dimensions of the processed piece.

Imperial (in.) nominal size (actual size)		Metric (mm) actual size
2 x 2	($1\frac{1}{2}$ x $1\frac{1}{2}$)	38 x 38
2 x 4	($1\frac{1}{2}$ x $3\frac{1}{2}$)	38 x 89
2 x 6	($1\frac{1}{2}$ x $5\frac{1}{2}$)	38 x 140
2 x 8	($1\frac{1}{2}$ x $7\frac{1}{4}$)	38 x 184
2 x 10	($1\frac{1}{2}$ x $9\frac{1}{4}$)	38 x 235
4 x 4	($3\frac{1}{2}$ x $3\frac{1}{2}$)	89 x 89
4 x 6	($3\frac{1}{2}$ x $5\frac{1}{2}$)	89 x 140

LIQUIDS

$\frac{1}{4}$ cup	60 ml
$\frac{1}{3}$ cup	80 ml
$\frac{1}{2}$ cup	125 ml
$\frac{2}{3}$ cup	160 ml
$\frac{3}{4}$ cup	180 ml
1 cup	250 ml
$1\frac{1}{2}$ cups	375 ml
2 cups	500 ml
3 cups	750 ml
4 cups	1 litre

SPOON MEASURES

$\frac{1}{4}$ tsp	1.25 ml
$\frac{1}{2}$ tsp	2.5 ml
1 tsp	5 ml
1 tbsp	15 ml
2 tbsp	30 ml

TEMPERATURES

To change from degrees Fahrenheit to degrees Celsius, subtract 32, then multiply by $\frac{5}{9}$.

FASTENERS

Nails are sold by penny size or penny weight (expressed by the letter d). Length is designated by the penny size. Some common lengths are:

2d (25 mm / 1 in.)	20d (102 mm / 4 in.)
6d (51 mm / 2 in.)	40d (127 mm / 5 in.)
10d (76 mm / 3 in.)	60d (152 mm / 6 in.)

Below are metric and imperial equivalents of some common bolts:

10 mm	$\frac{3}{8}$ in.	25 mm	1 in.
12 mm	$\frac{1}{2}$ in.	50 mm	2 in.
16 mm	$\frac{5}{8}$ in.	65 mm	$2\frac{1}{2}$ in.
20 mm	$\frac{3}{4}$ in.	70 mm	$2\frac{3}{4}$ in.